**Contributions to Economics**

The series *Contributions to Economics* provides an outlet for innovative research in all areas of economics. Books published in the series are primarily monographs and multiple author works that present new research results on a clearly defined topic, but contributed volumes and conference proceedings are also considered. All books are published in print and ebook and disseminated and promoted globally. The series and the volumes published in it are indexed by Scopus and ISI (selected volumes).

More information about this series at http://www.springer.com/series/1262

Jason García Portilla

# "Ye Shall Know Them by Their Fruits"

## A Mixed Methods Study on Corruption, Competitiveness, and Christianity in Europe and the Americas

Springer

Jason García Portilla
Swiss-Latin American Center (CLS-HSG)
University of St. Gallen
St. Gallen, Switzerland

ISSN 1431-1933 ISSN 2197-7178 (electronic)
Contributions to Economics
ISBN 978-3-030-78497-3 ISBN 978-3-030-78498-0 (eBook)
https://doi.org/10.1007/978-3-030-78498-0

Published with the support of the Swiss National Science Foundation (SNSF). Funding Data Identifier (formerly Fundref ID): 10.13039/501100001711. Contribution number: 10BP12_205749



This Springer imprint is published by the registered company Springer Nature Switzerland AG.
The registered company address is: Gewerbestrasse 11, 6330 Cham, Switzerland

*Beware of false prophets, which come to you in sheep's clothing, but inwardly they are ravening wolves.*
***Ye shall know them by their fruits.***
*Do men gather grapes of thorns, or figs of thistles? Even so every good tree bringeth forth good fruit; but a corrupt tree bringeth forth evil fruit. A good tree cannot bring forth evil fruit, neither can a corrupt tree bring forth good fruit. Every tree that bringeth not forth good fruit is hewn down and cast into the fire.*
***Wherefore by their fruits ye shall know them.***
*Not every one that saith unto me, Lord, Lord, shall enter into the kingdom of heaven; but he that doeth the will of my Father which is in heaven. Many will say to me in that day, Lord, Lord, have we not prophesied in thy name? and in thy name have cast out devils? and in thy name done many wonderful works? And then will I profess unto them, I never knew you: depart from me, ye that work iniquity.*
*(Matthew 7:15–23, King James Version)*

# Foreword

In 1905, Max Weber asked the provocative question, "why do Protestant lands seem to be more prosperous?" He was not wrong. Since the spread of the Reformation in the sixteenth century, the world's leading economy has been predominantly Protestant: first, the Dutch Republic after it won independence from Spain, then Britain took the lead in the eighteenth century, and the USA took its place in the twentieth century. Protestant success has also been apparent at the local level. In Weber's Prussia, where he gained the inspiration for his famous thesis, Protestant areas seemed to well out-pace Catholic ones. Is this just a coincidence? Or is there something about Protestantism that has enabled economic success? A century's worth of work following in the footsteps of Weber has attempted to answer this question. Jason García Portilla's *"Ye shall know them by their fruits": Corruption, Competitiveness, and Christianity in Europe and the Americas* is a worthy addition to this literature.

The question is not so much about the correlation Weber pointed to. There was a clear correlation in Weber's time, which still exists today (although it is much weaker) that places with more Protestants tend to be better off economically. The question is whether Weber had the right *causal* story. Weber claimed there was a certain "Protestant Ethic", stemming in part from the Calvinist doctrine of predestination, that encouraged Protestants to work harder, save more, and be thriftier. These are all characteristics that should lead to economic success if widely shared among a population. Recent research contests Weber's argument, however. García Portilla's book fits nicely with this research. He notes, correctly, that at best Weber's "Protestant Ethic" is one of many pathways connecting Protestantism to economic success. I think that is probably too generous to Weber!

For my money, the two most convincing mediating causes connecting Protestantism and economic outcomes are literacy and political economy. Recent work, especially that of economists Sascha Becker and Ludger Woessmann, has combined impressive data analysis with historical anecdote to understand the "Protestant edge" in literacy. The reason for this edge likely dates to Luther himself. Luther was adamant that his followers learn to read—although the main reason he desired this was so that they could read the bible. Luther practised what he (literally) preached. He wrote in German, which was nearly unheard of for a man of the church at the time. He translated the bible into the vernacular. From a very early period, Protestants set up schools for both boys and girls. In one study, Becker and Woessmann find that the *entire* Protestant economic edge in late-nineteenth century Prussia (home to Weber!) can be explained by literacy differences. Once these are accounted for, there is no "Protestant edge". This telling leaves little room for the Protestant ethic.

Another factor contributing to the Protestant edge is political economy. Specifically, where the Reformation spread in the sixteenth century, the Catholic Church was removed from power. The ramifications of this went well beyond the religious sphere. In the political sphere, the medieval church was a major player. Not only was it the largest landowner in Europe (by a large margin) but it also played a key role in legitimating political rule. In return, the Church tended to receive favourable policies, tax exemption, and help suppressing "heresies". This political economy "equilibrium" was undermined by the Reformation. The question is—and it is one I have spent much of my career trying to answer—where did Protestant European rulers turn when they could no longer count on the Church for legitimation? Of course, they still desired to stay in power. The Reformation undercut one of the sources of their power by removing the Church as an agent of legitimacy.

To whom did they turn? I have argued in many places (including my book *Rulers, Religion, and Riches: How the West Got Rich and the Middle East Did Not*) that parliaments were the natural group for rulers to turn to supplement their legitimacy. Parliaments already existed throughout Europe, bringing together landed elites, urban elites, and churchmen together in a forum in which they could bargain with the crown. They were the obvious group for power-starved rulers to turn. This ended up being a key turning point in European economic history. Those places that adopted the Reformation—especially England and the Dutch Republic—saw an immense rise in the power of their parliaments over the subsequent centuries. The economic elites in these parliaments were certainly self-interested. However, their self-interest tended to align with the types of things that portend broader economic success: property rights, investment in infrastructure, protection for shipping, and the like. Policies along these lines were key for the economic rise of these states. Protestants ended up getting these types of policies first. Other parts of Europe, and the rest of the world, would have to wait.

There are many other reasons that Protestantism has been associated with economic prosperity in the past. García Portilla nicely describes many of these in this book. Protestant missionaries were likely responsible for mitigating some of the worst aspects of colonialism. Legal systems associated with Protestant states have been shown to be more conducive to economic growth. Religious competition among various Protestant sects was a likely cause of lower corruption. And the list goes on. If anything, the Protestant economic advantage is now over-explained!

If the Protestant edge is indeed over-explained, this is simply a reflection of how important the broader question is. The modern economy emerged in a Protestant state (Great Britain). The greatest twentieth-century economic and military power (USA) was predominantly Protestant. The research on this issue is convincing that this was not simply a coincidence. Economists, sociologists, and political scientists have spent hundreds of thousands of pages trying to understand why this happened. They have used a multitude of methods, focused on various parts of the world, and have dug deep into history to help us better understand the role that religion can play in economic growth (and stagnation). Jason García Portilla has followed very nicely in this tradition. By bringing together multiple methods to shine light on one of the "big questions" in the social sciences, García Portilla brings new insight to a much-studied question. Here is hoping this is the beginning of much more to come from him.

Chapman University, Orange, CA, USA Jared Rubin

# Preface

Why are historical Catholic countries and regions generally more corrupt and less competitive than historical Protestant territories? How has the institutionalisation of religion influenced the prosperity of countries in Europe and the Americas?

*"Ye shall know them by their fruits"* addresses these critical questions by elucidating the hegemonic and emancipatory religious factors leading to these dissimilarities between countries. The book features up-to-date mixed methods interdisciplinary research contributing to existing studies in the sociology of religion field by demonstrating the effect of the mutually reinforcing configuration of multiple prosperity triggers (religion, politics, and environment) for the first time. It demonstrates the differences in the institutionalisation of Roman Catholicism and Protestantism by applying quantitative and qualitative methods and by performing a Qualitative Comparative Analysis (QCA) in 65 countries. This monograph provides a comprehensive survey and empirical research of different theories of development, focusing on the influence of religion.

High corruption and low competitiveness are common denominators in countries with pervasive Roman Catholic traditions. In contrast, historically Protestant countries, both in the Americas and in Europe, tend to have higher levels of transparency, education, social progress, and competitiveness. According to the Gospel of Matthew, Jesus Christ declared that *"Ye shall know them by their fruits"*. He was referring to the true and false prophets who would come on his behalf. This parable inspires this book, which examines the relationship between religious systems ("prophets") and social prosperity ("fruits"). Its main question is: *How does Protestantism influence competitiveness and transparency compared to Roman Catholicism in Europe and the Americas?*

In this book, a comprehensive methodological framework has been developed, consisting of different epistemological approaches (mixed methods). The correlational (quantitative) part established the interrelations between the investigated variables (i.e., corruption, competitiveness, environment, and institutional religion), while QCA further inferred causal relations for 65 countries in Europe and the Americas. The qualitative part used critical discourse analysis (CDA) to examine four case studies (Switzerland, Uruguay, Cuba, and Colombia).

Combining the following three main factors accounted for uneven socio-economic and institutional performance in Europe and the Americas: (1) *Religion*: (1.1) Historical Protestantism and its positive influence on law, institutions, and language (highest performance); (1.2) anti-clericalism (medium-high performance); (1.3) Roman Catholicism or Orthodoxy (medium-low performance); (1.4) Syncretism (low performance). (2) *Political non-religious influences*: (2.1) Communism (low performance). (3) *Geography and environment*, which modulate overall performance.

This book contributes to existing research in the sociology of religion and development studies fields by demonstrating the effect of the mutually reinforcing configuration of multiple prosperity triggers (religion–political–environment). Historical Protestantism largely influenced prosperity by promoting education, by secularising institutions, and by stabilising democracy. Protestantism has also proven highly influential in the successive historical law revolutions that gradually mitigated the power of pervasive feudal institutions and of papalist medieval canon law. In contrast, traditionally Roman Catholic countries have generally upheld a medieval model of extractivist institutions until anti-clerical (non-communist) movements were able to weaken this influence in some countries.

Reinach, Switzerland
March 2021

Jason García Portilla

# Acknowledgements

I express my deepest gratitude to all those who have made this book possible.

I wish to briefly acknowledge the generous support received from various institutions and individuals: the Swiss National Science Foundation (SNSF); the Swiss Federal State Secretariat for Education Research and Innovation (SERI); the Swiss-Latin American Centre (CLS-HSG); the Swiss School of Latin American Studies (SSLAS); and my professors, colleagues, and friends at the University of St. Gallen and beyond.

Given the transdisciplinary (mixed method) approach of this study, I have benefitted from numerous friends and scholars from different disciplines, who have generously contributed to its successful completion. Experts from various fields have been instrumental to crystallising my initial ideas and to improving earlier drafts and versions. I am profoundly indebted and grateful to all of them. The names of those individuals who have graciously helped me with different parts of this study are mentioned in the following pages.

I express my sincere thanks to my family (biological and spiritual) for their tireless support. Having understood the importance of this study, many have even sacrificed funds, their health, and even their marriages. My heartfelt gratitude to all of you!

The most important acknowledgement and dedication are reserved for he who inspired both this book and the following wisdom:

> And ye shall know the truth, and the truth shall make you free
> (John 8:32, King James Version).[1]


[1] *The Holy Bible, King James Version.* Cambridge Edition: 1769. Scripture quotations from The Authorized (King James) Version. Rights in the Authorized Version in the United Kingdom are vested in the Crown. Reproduced by permission of the Crown's patentee, Cambridge University Press.

This study would not have been possible without the commitment and support of numerous individuals at different stages. The following list, although not exhaustive, mentions various direct contributors. I am most grateful to all of them. The last 7 years have indeed been the best in my life, not least for making a long-awaited dream come true.

My heartfelt thanks to:

Prof. Dr Yvette Sánchez, who graciously accepted to supervise my research when I was still "fishing fishes" in the climate change "ocean". Her goodwill enabled me to benefit from an open window of opportunity, in the form of a Swiss Government Excellence Scholarship (ESKAS). This funds three years of research in Switzerland and part of my field trips. Hence, I am also grateful to Helen Obrist and the ESKAS team at the Swiss Embassy in Bogota, to the Swiss Federal Government in Bern, and to the University of St. Gallen (HSG).

In addition to patiently supporting my research, Prof. Sánchez, as co-head of the Swiss-Latin American Center *"Centro Latinoamericano Suizo"* (CLS-HSG) and the SSLAS (Swiss School of Latin American Studies), funded my field trips and my participation in several international conferences and national workshops to present preliminary versions of this study.

Prof. Dr. Christian Büschges, another co-head of the SSLAS, kindly accepted to co-supervise my research and generously offered important guidance from the outset. Prof. Dr. Karen Elliott, whom I also deeply esteem, provided expert guidance on (yet not limited to) the QCA part of this study.

The following paragraphs acknowledge various scholars whose expertise supported my research in particular areas:

*Quantitative part*

Karl Bailey generously helped me create the first database. Pavel Chlup and Maria Kralova provided invaluable help with the quantitative and QCA models. Luc Davie and Bianca van Dellen contributed to the quantitative model on corruption. Tina Freyburg, Carsten Trenkler, and Roland Fuess offered valuable comments that helped sharpen the correlational models and conclusions.

*QCA part*

Karen Elliott, Pavel Chlup, and Maria Kralova offered expert advice on QCA, as did Jorge Sion and Charles Ragin at an earlier stage of the project. I am grateful to Patrick Emmenegger for his detailed and timely comments.

*Qualitative and CDA parts*

Patrizia Hoyer provided substantial advice at an early stage. Thanks to her and Chris Steyaert, this study was extended to an enriching CDA approach. Paul Mihas graciously offered detailed feedback on and support with the qualitative design, coding, and identity memo. Tabea Bereuther's comments on a previous version of the coding and qualitative design were immensely helpful.

*Mixed Methods design and case studies*

The mixed methods and dialectical pluralism meta-paradigm in the research owe much to Burke Johnson's brilliant advice. Andrew Bennett provided ongoing invaluable support with optimal case selection and case studies configuration. Andrei Gomez provided helpful critical feedback.

*Critical readers of previous versions of the manuscript*

Mark Kyburz, Per Wikström, Rocío Robinson, Jens Koehrsen, Kathrin Neumüller, Mathias Urbatzka, Benjamin Hoffmann, Johannes Rueegg, Alfred Kieser, Vanessa Boanada, Esperanza Osorio, Yonatan Gez, Simon Grand, Florian Wettstein, Cecilia McGuire, Simon Richardson, and Johanna Higgs have all helped to considerably improve the document's accuracy, flow, and consistency.

*Other commentators*

I thank Jesse Zink, Nicholas Miller, Gerald Ströck, Elke Breitenfeldt, David Kirkpatrick, Emma Wild-Wood, Walter J. Veith, Malena Haenni, and Odile Schwarz-Herion for their helpful insights.

*Field trip collaborators*

In Colombia: Juan Carlos Prada, Disney Beltrán, Hebert Gamarra, Luisa Piedrahíta, William Beltrán, and Javier Sosa, for their help at the National University of Colombia and beyond. In Cuba: Yoendris Rodríguez, Sergio, Olivia, and Julio. Their support was essential, especially with contacting interviewees, as well as collecting and analysing the gathered information. I also thank all my interviewees for their generous time and patience.

*YES friends in Switzerland*

Dominik Mösching, Fabio Segura, and Roger Baud supported me before I embarked on my PhD journey in Switzerland, at a stage when this was still a dream.

*Other encouraging friends*

Björn Giger, Simon Knöpfel, Andy and Jane Sailer (and all their families), the FGZ, Becki Wikström, Gabi Lang, Alex Pinilla, and Annatina Aerne for their kind and charming support.

*The administrative staff at the University of St. Gallen (HSG)*

Anna Schlegel, Felix Keller, Andrea Guepfert, Beatrix Kobelt, and the GSERM team were always ready to patiently help answer my many queries.

*Last but not least: my family*

My wife Silvia, whom I met nearly halfway through my PhD journey, has funded my research since the end of the generous ESKAS scholarship. Moreover, she has been an excellent field research assistant, German and Swiss German translator-teacher, exceptional housewife, and loving partner. Paul and Mirjam Wright whom we love and consider our parents in Switzerland have supported this research in various ways. My parents-in-law: Peter, who passed away while I was writing this book in its early form as a dissertation, and Lotti, my mother-in-law, have supported the research process throughout. My Colombian relatives: My mother Eunice did her very best to help me become a successful professional (a challenging task for a middle-class family in Colombia). Her support goes far beyond that, though. Also, Granny Aura, uncle Omar, and Isabel have certainly contributed to each achievement in my career. My cousins Diana, Aurelian, and Richard and Martine "*les coquinos*", Gerlin and his family, Mauricio, Nicole, among others, listened to my concerns and encouraged me to develop and complete my book.

Finally, I am also most grateful to all those people not mentioned here for their invaluable support.

# About This Book

This book is divided into seven main parts, which are subdivided into 25 chapters:

**Part I: Introductory Considerations and Research Setting**

Part I introduces this book and is organised into two chapters. The introduction (Chap. 1) sets the historical context and describes this book's outcome, contributions, and limitations. Chapter 2 presents the research setting, including the research aims, research question and hypotheses, and the research model. The research model synthesises understanding and serves as a rationale for the entire book. The model exhibits the main exogenous theoretical determinants of corruption and prosperity, which are tested empirically. The following chapters (Chap. 3–12) develop the research model. Therefore, when numbers or capital letters appear *in italics* between parentheses in headings and subheadings, please refer to the research model components and relations (Fig. 2.1).

**Part II: Conceptual Framework**

Part II details the *outcome* and *conditions* of the research model (transparency/prosperity) in three chapters. Chapter 3 (the *outcome*) defines corruption and competitiveness from different perspectives, including moral and theological ones. Transparency and prosperity are linked as part of the same outcome, prosperity equals competitiveness, and competitiveness includes transparency.

Chapter 4 briefly surveys prosperity and transparency in Europe and the Americas and shows, roughly, that historically Protestant countries perform higher than Roman Catholic ones. Chapter 5 (*conditions*) touches on some influential theories that have sought to explain prosperity differences between countries from diverse disciplinary perspectives.

**Part III: Theoretical Foundations (Amplifying the Conditions of the Research Model)**

Part III explains and interconnects the relevant factors (or variables and conditions) used to determine corruption and prosperity in the research model. It consists of six chapters: Chapter 6 explores relevant empirical studies and provides possible explanations for the robust associations between corruption and religion. Chapter 7 discusses the prosperity–religion link and reviews some prominent empirical studies refuting and confirming Weber's thesis and balancing the evidence gathered. It also emphasises the importance of seriously considering the institutional (and hegemonic) influence of religion in addition to the cultural influence (of religious adherents). Chapter 8, the most comprehensive in Part III, characterises the relations between religion, institutions, and the transparency–prosperity nexus. It explains how economic prosperity, democracy, and transparency are part of a feedback loop that constitutes a single phenomenon. More importantly, this chapter deepens the institutional analysis by concentrating on the particular historical influence of religion on the different legal traditions in Europe and the Americas. It is the cornerstone of Part III and, as such, of the entire study.

Chapter 9 demonstrates the influential association of Protestantism and prosperity by explaining its historical focus on education and human capital building. On this basis, Chap. 10 characterises the relations between culture, religion, and corruption/prosperity. It advances the explanations of the prosperity–religion nexus from the perspective of cultural attributes (e.g., trust, individualism, and *familialism*) by comparing Roman Catholic and Protestant theologies. Chapter 11 briefly explores the influence of religion and hegemony on language by concentrating on English, German, and the Romance languages widely spoken in Europe and the Americas. Chapter 12 discusses the influence of the environment and geography on prosperity and corruption and reviews some leading empirical works.

**Part IV: Research Paradigms, Methodology, and Research Design**

Part IV has two chapters. The first (Chap. 13) discusses the research paradigms underpinning this study. Chapter 14 introduces the methodology and research design. It explains the mixed method approach of this study (quantitative, qualitative, and QCA). Each of the chapters in Part V (empirical results) includes methodological protocols.

**Part V: Empirical Results (Macro and Meso Components)**

This part is divided into two components: macro and meso. Chapter 15 corresponds to the macro-quantitative component. It discusses how competitiveness and corruption were modelled, how the methods were applied in the correlation analysis and which empirical results were achieved. Chapter 16 contains the meso component (Qualitative Comparative Analysis, QCA). It discusses the QCA research model, the QCA methodology, and the analysis of the QCA results.

**Part VI: Component 3 (Micro): Case Studies**

This part is organised into six chapters. Chapter 17 examines the criteria for selecting the cases analysed in this study. It explains the application of critical discourse analysis (CDA) as its principal empirical method. It discusses CDA methods and data treatment as well as the empirical analysis of CDA results. Finally, it compares and summarises the case selection criteria.

Chapters 18, 19, 20, and 21 offer in-depth discussions of the case studies (Switzerland, Uruguay, Cuba, and Colombia). Switzerland provides more information than the other cases: It is an extremely positive case in the world and the only European country discussed here. Chapter 22 presents a comparative overview of the four case studies (Switzerland, Uruguay, Cuba, and Colombia).

**Part VII: Discussion and Conclusions**

Part VII has three chapters. Chapter 23 presents general conclusions based on integrating the theory and the results obtained from all methods. It also offers seven specific conclusions for each of the prosperity determinants considered. Chapter 24 examines further considerations derived from the research, while Chap. 25 provides some brief concluding remarks.

**Empirical Expectations**

*Some sections along the document contain empirical expectations since they correspond to variables or conditions tested in the study. Further, sections treating Latin America appear throughout the study. Historically, this region has been an outlier in the Christian world (Europe and the Americas), with high corruption and low prosperity levels. It provides rich material for analysis and hence three of the four case studies deal explicitly with Latin America. Generally, each chapter starts with a brief outline or a short introduction. The various sections further structure the corresponding main chapters and parts.*

# Contents

# About the Author

**Jason García Portilla** earned his PhD in Organization Studies and Cultural Theory at the University of St. Gallen (Switzerland, September 2020), funded by the Swiss Government Excellence Scholarship ESKAS.

In addition to his work on the religion–development–environment nexus, Dr Garcia Portilla is an expert in climate change and sustainability, with 12 years of progressive experience in the field. He spent over 2 years working as an official negotiator of the United Nations Framework Convention on Climate Change (UNFCCC). During this assignment, he represented the Colombian government in seven rounds of negotiation and took part in several international initiatives, including the Global Platform for Disaster Risk Reduction. He has also worked with UN agencies and international NGOs on climate issues, environment policy, and development. He was appointed as a reviewer of the 5th Assessment Report of the Intergovernmental Panel on Climate Change (IPCC). He holds a degree in Ecology and two Master's degrees: an MA in Political Science from the University of Los Andes in Colombia and an MSc in Climate Change and Policy from the University of Sussex in the UK (funded by the British Chevening Scholarship). He has a strong track record of producing publications on the role of policy approaches in climate change and sustainability. He also has a broad range of teaching experience, from undergraduate courses in environmental issues and political science to extensive tutoring and mentoring both undergraduate and master's students.

# List of Abbreviations

| | |
|---|---|
| CDA | Critical discourse analysis |
| CPI | Corruption Perception Index |
| DP | Dialectical pluralism |
| ECLAC | Economic Commission for Latin America and the Caribbean |
| EPI | Environment Performance Index |
| GCI | Global Competitiveness Index |
| GDP | Gross domestic product |
| GLOBE | Global Leadership and Organizational Behaviour Effectiveness Research Programme |
| GT | Grounded theory |
| MM | Mixed methods |
| NT | New Testament |
| OT | Old Testament |
| PDI | Power Distance Index |
| PG | Prosperity Gospel |
| PRI | Proportional reduction in inconsistency |
| QCA | Qualitative Comparative Analysis |
| SPI | Social Progress Index |
| TI | Transparency International |
| UK | United Kingdom |
| USA | United States of America |
| VIF | Variance inflation factor |

# List of Figures

# List of Tables

# Part I
# Introductory Considerations and Research Setting

# Chapter 1
# Introduction

This book seeks to understand the prosperity differences between countries in Europe and the Americas by elucidating the hegemonic and emancipatory religious factors leading to these dissimilarities. One key question in this respect is why Roman Catholic societies are different from Protestant ones although both are considered Christian.

This introduction is divided into two sections. Section 1.1 sets the historical context and provides relevant background information. Section 1.2 outlines the intended outcome of this study, its contributions to the literature, and its limitations.

## 1.1 A Historical Challenge Inspiring this Study

About two thousand years ago, Jesus Christ described the true and false prophets coming on his behalf as follows: “Ye shall know them by their fruits” (King James Bible, 1769, Matthew 7:16). He also directly challenged the moral authority of the Jewish authorities, who were under Roman rule at that time. His teachings were perceived as a threat to the conflicted Jewish and Roman establishments. These convened to agree his crucifixion (one of the cruellest Roman death penalties) under a legal deal.

The Roman Empire, together with the Jewish authorities, not only executed Jesus and most of his disciples but also brutally persecuted their early followers (Bruce, 2007), who were considered a “sect” (e.g. King James Bible, 1769, Acts 24: 5). Although many suffered cruel deaths, the “Christian sect” attracted an increasing number of followers.

After combatting this “sect” for around four centuries, the Romans eventually embraced Christianity as their official religion under Emperor Constantine. This political move would, however, compromise Jesus’s original teachings, as preserved in the Holy Scriptures. The new Roman syncretic religion thus rejected and at the same time adopted biblical principles to purportedly uphold Christianity while in



J. García Portilla, *“Ye Shall Know Them by Their Fruits”*, Contributions to Economics, https://doi.org/10.1007/978-3-030-78498-0_1

fact perpetuating pagan Roman rituals and traditions (i.e. veneration of icons instead of the God from Israel; Sun-Day worshipping instead of the Sabbath) (Bacchiocchi, 1977). Yet Constantine soon witnessed the decline of the Roman Empire. Nevertheless, his "Christian universal religion-state" began to flourish, thus prolonging the political, legal, and cultural heritage of the Roman Empire (Agnew, 2010, p. 41; Hofstede, 2001, p. 109; Pirenne, 1936, p. 397). The Roman Church-State (Catholic) succeeded and extended the Roman Empire's heritage ironically speaking on behalf of Jesus, the same crucified under the Roman law.

History has shown that forgery became a widespread method through which the Roman imperial system accumulated considerable power to extend the supremacy of the popery beyond the duchy of Rome. These fabrications included the Donation of Pepin in 756 (Peter's supposedly gold letter written in heaven, which enabled him to claim that he was the first Pope); the false Donation of Constantine (for which the Roman Catholic Church inherited the lands of the Roman Empire); and other deceptive decretals (i.e. decrees) issued to grant canon law immunity against any secular institution (Heussi, 1991; Merryman & Pérez, 2007). Moreover, the Catholic Church imposed Roman traditions on Jesus' teachings, banned the Holy Scriptures and continued the cruel persecution of dissenters.

The Roman Church-State also enforced various forms of tyranny during the subsequent Dark Ages to perpetuate its institutional hegemony. These violent measures included crusades, inquisitions, and the maintenance of people's ignorance. Only translations of the Scriptures into Latin were permitted, thus preserving the monopoly of keeping and interpreting the Bible. Christian groups, like the Waldensians, which sought to keep alive Jesus' legacy were oppressed as "heretic sects" to maintain the Roman monopoly over faith. Consequently, the Inquisition murdered countless victims, making the Roman Church-State that institution that has caused most human suffering in history. The Church-State had legal control over monarchies and exerted political power across Europe and beyond.

In 1492, the Spanish Roman Catholic Monarchy "discovered" a new continent to expand its dominion: the Americas. Vast territories were brutally conquered and forced to adopt the Roman Catholic faith. Over time, a new syncretism—of Native American, African, and Roman beliefs—was enforced in Latin America while the medieval, extractive, and hierarchical model of society was perpetuated.

In Europe, various dissenters such as Jan Hus or William Tyndale dared to challenge the supremacy of the Roman Church-State. Like many others, they were convicted of heresy and cruelly executed. It was, however, not until the sixteenth century that Martin Luther succeeded in translating the Scriptures into the German vernacular from original Greek (Erasmus' *Textus Receptus*) and Hebrew texts (instead of Latin) (Burger, 2014). This advancement, along with Johannes Gutenberg's invention of the printing press made the Bible more accessible for ordinary German-speaking people. These and other favourable developments initiated the Protestant Reformation (after attempts to transform the Roman Church from within had failed). The movement was based on returning to the original teachings of Jesus Christ (under the *Sola Scriptura* principle). It gradually expanded its influence, first in Northern Europe and later in North America.

By keeping people ignorant of such and other historical facts, the Roman Catholic Church-State has managed to control Western civilisation for over a thousand years. Today, with more than a billion followers, the Roman Catholic Church-State is still the most extensive centralised global organisation ever seen in the world. However, popular belief now seems to accept the impression of a symbolic (that is, almost non-existent) Roman Catholic State. Just as modern secular society seems to embrace the idea of a weakened Roman Church, which seems to have renewed its discourse and continues to exercise an influence comparable to that of any other world religion.

Yet the discourse of Roman Catholicism shifted only recently. Over the past few decades, the Second Vatican Council (1962–1965) has promoted democracy and human rights (Anderson, 2007; Levine, 1981). However, descending from Aristotelian and Aquinian principles, the Roman Church-State had always considered democracy the least favourable social order. When having to decide between communist (i.e. atheist) and democratic ideologies in the mid-twentieth century, the Roman Church-State supported the latter as "the lesser of two evils" (Cook, 2012, pp. 24-25).

Currently, intransigent conservative ideologies still prevail (i.e. corporatism in Latin America) after the inertia of long-standing Roman Catholic hegemony (Beltrán, 2008; Figueroa, 2016). Also, Romanism still rejects personal interpretations of the Scriptures as only the clergy's reading and understanding are deemed legitimate.

The following chapters show that the effects of the Protestant Reformation in the political, education and legal institutions and systems of those countries in which it gained influence are far-reaching and well documented. Yet evidence exists that the shift in Roman Catholic discourse reflects its attempt to perpetuate its hegemony against Protestant "competition" (Anderson, 2007, p. 394; Cook, 2012; Gill, 1998, pp. 7, 48). Moreover, Roman Catholicism still exercises an important institutional dominion in countries under its influence, including most Latin American countries. The Iberian conquerors first imposed Roman Catholicism in Latin America while tradition and established institutions have since perpetuated its hegemony—to this day. Protestantism, on the other hand, has more often emerged from voluntary persuasion contrasting Roman Catholicism's seemingly global corporate strategy.

This study emerged in the context of the five-hundred-year anniversary of Martin Luther preparing and publishing his 95 theses in the German town of Wittenberg. The theses exposed the rampant corruption and tyranny of the Roman Catholic Church and initiated the Protestant Reformation.

Figure 1.1 summarises the historical rationale underlying this study.

## 1.2 Intended Outcome and Contributions

This subsection describes the relevance of this research. It explains the theoretical and methodological gaps that it seeks to close.

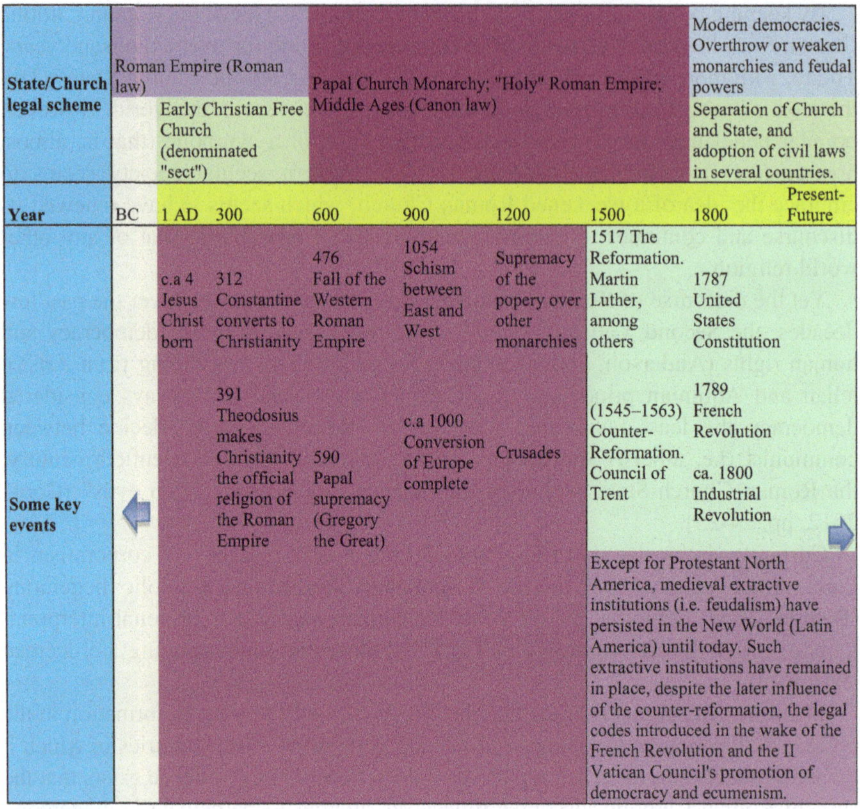


**Fig. 1.1** Historical timeline of religious-political trigger events in Christendom (Source: Author's collection). Based on the theoretical framework of this study. Among others, sources include Woodberry (2012), Miller (2012), Acemoglu et al. (2011), Snyder (2011), Bruce (2007), Berman (2003), Witte (2002), Heussi (1991), D'Aubigne (1862), and Eusebius of Caesarea (ca. 340 AD) (n.d.)

### *1.2.1 Theoretical Gaps: What Makes this Research Different?*

This study may be justified as follows: good theory emerges from personal engagement and contact with global problems rather than from literature gaps (Kilduff, 2006, p. 252). Beyond that, it addresses and seeks to close several theoretical and methodological gaps.

First, it identifies a lack of a systemic (and complex) prosperity theory across countries (Chap. 5). What becomes apparent is that even prominent authors explicitly neglect the influence of other factors and theories than those they have defined themselves (Acemoglu & Robinson, 2012; Diamond, 1997; Sachs, 2001).

However, several empirical studies have suggested that various factors common to different countries (i.e. institutions, religion, geography) should work together, in reality, to produce different possible prosperity outcomes (La Porta et al., 1999;

Paldam, 2001; Treisman, 2000). My model (Fig. 2.1) and research build upon these previous results and expand understanding in five ways: (1) by adopting a QCA causal approach; (2) by placing greater emphasis on the institutional influence of religion; (3) by considering other proxy variables (e.g. GCI as a prosperity proxy instead of GDP; concordats with the Roman See as a proxy of the institutional influence of Romanism in a given country); (4) by providing more theological, legal and historical information; and (5) by examining a comparative set of European and Latin American cases.

This study adopts multiple causality approaches, in order to test variables from different theoretical fields (e.g. culture, environment) instead of relying on monocausal explanations. It investigates these variables (or conditions, factors, and prosperity theories) from a systemic perspective and using different methods (i.e. quantitative and QCA).

This systemic approach comprises several components: (a) *Dialectic Pluralism* (DP) as a metaparadigm (Chap. 13); (b) a multi-theoretical perspective (i.e. considering divergent theories one at a time); (c) multi-lingual analysis (Spanish, English, French, and German) of the literature or primary data (i.e. interviews), which provides greater aggregated, comparative value than monolingual research; (d) a multi-cultural perspective when analysing and comparing different cultures and values in Europe and the Americas; (e) a transdisciplinary methodology, given the researcher's background and the different theories analysed (these stem from various disciplines, including environmental studies, geography, sociology, cultural studies, political science, law, economics, linguistics, and theology).

Therefore, this research rejects neither the mechanicist paradigm nor the systemic one. On the contrary, it brings these paradigms into dialogue under the "complexity paradigm" (Chap. 13).

The second theoretical and methodological gap that this study strives to close is the hegemony gap in the sociology of religion. Typically, a large gap exists between scientific knowledge and lived reality (Orlikowski, 2010). Moreover, an obvious hiatus is evident in the sociology of religion, in particular regarding *critical* approaches to religion, that is, the ones that take "issues of domination and inequality seriously" (Hjelm, 2014, p. 857). Much recent scholarship in the field "seems to descend almost exclusively from Durkheim and Weber" (Hjelm, 2014, p. 855). Consequently, existing approaches tend to confine themselves to the influence of specific religious denominations and their followers rather than investigating the institutional power of religion over society.

Max Weber (1905) made a significant contribution to understanding the work ethic and its role in building trust and prosperity in Protestant societies. Hjelm observes, however, that Weber's contribution lay not in discerning the hegemony and domination of a political-religious institution (such as the Roman Catholic Church-State). In moving beyond Weber's traditional, culture-only approach, this study aims to fill the various theoretical gaps left by his work. It therefore seeks to establish a historical understanding of the means and methods that were used to perpetuate the hegemony of the Roman Church-State for over a thousand years during the Dark Ages. This hegemony has been inherited and remains predominant in most Latin American countries to this day. Here, this study helps to understand not only the decline of this hegemony in Europe and the Americas but also the potential emancipatory influence of the Protestant Reformation.

The third theoretical and methodological gap that this study seeks to close concerns the institutional and cultural dimensions of religion. At least two dimensions of the influence of religion need to be taken seriously: institutional and cultural (adherents) (Manow, 2004, p. 9). However, most empirical works considering religion as a prosperity determinant pay little attention to the institutional effects of religion. Instead, they concentrate mainly on religious affiliation (by using the proportion of adherents as the only indicator of religion) (Acemoglu & Robinson, 2012; Hofstede, 2001; La Porta et al., 1999).

Such traditional research paradigms have focused on the *cultural* influence of religion (*à la* Weber) and have neglected the *institutional* impact of religion. Typically, cross-country empirical approaches have ignored the decisive power relations or the historical agreements (concordats) between individual countries and the Roman Catholic Church-State. More recently, however, Barro and McCleary (2005) and Barrett et al. (2001) have made essential contributions to establishing the relation between the population affiliated to a given religion and the adoption of a *state religion.* The association between state religion and the proportion of religious adherents gives rise to an inertia that may persist for decades if not centuries (Barro & McCleary, 2005).

Similarly, only very few studies in so-called new economic history have focused on the *institutional impact of religion* on prosperity. This is not surprising as interdisciplinary approaches in this field are relatively young (a couple of decades) (Michalopoulos & Papaioannou, 2017).

Insights from disciplines such as political science (Manow & van Kersbergen, 2009), international relations (Snyder, 2011) or law (Berman, 2003; Witte, 2002) have been crucial to understanding the institutional influence of religion on prosperity/institutional patterns. Yet these findings have often not been integrated into the array of explanations provided by empirical studies associating religion and prosperity. It is therefore necessary to build a comprehensive transdisciplinary theory based on the findings of different disciplines. This in turn will enhance their explanatory power.

This study pursues such "synthesised coherence" by connecting "together work that previously had been considered unrelated" (Golden-Biddle & Locke, 2007, p. 33). Thus, it considers cultural *and* institutional approaches to religion, both theoretically and empirically, and argues that both are necessary and complementary. It empirically investigates the relation between corruption/competitiveness and religious adherents (as a cultural proxy) in quantitative analysis. It subsequently adds complexity by studying associated institutional religious factors and further conditions in QCA.

### 1.2.2 Methodological Gaps

Most empirical studies lead from theory to data (Eisenhardt, 1989). This is particularly the case for the vast empirical information supporting the prosperity theories explained briefly in Chap. 5.

Eisenhardt encourages researchers to complete the research cycle (see Fig. 1.2) by conducting research via a less traditional route: from evidence to theory (Eisenhardt, 1989, p. 549). This study runs the entire research cycle from compiling information in a general model of prosperity theories to further triangulating empirical data and theorising (Chaps. 2 and 5; see also Part III).

The starting point of this study can be located anywhere on the cycle (Johnson, 2016). For instance, the prosperity theories in Chap. 5 lead to the hypothesis (Chap. 1). The data collection methods (mixed) (see Part IV and methodology sections in Part V) follow the hypothesis. Subsequently, data analysis leads to describing the patterns needed to continue the theory building cycle.

I have not found any studies that combine a Mixed Methods Approach (MM), Qualitative Comparative Analysis (QCA), Critical Discourse Analysis (CDA), and the sociology of religion. This study is the first of its type and possesses the inherent *strengths of typical mixed research*, among others: (a) generating and tested a grounded theory; (b) harnessing the strengths of additional methods to overcome the weaknesses of other methods by applying both; (c) providing stronger evidence for conclusions reached through converging and corroborating findings; (d) adding insights and understanding that might be missed when using only a single method;

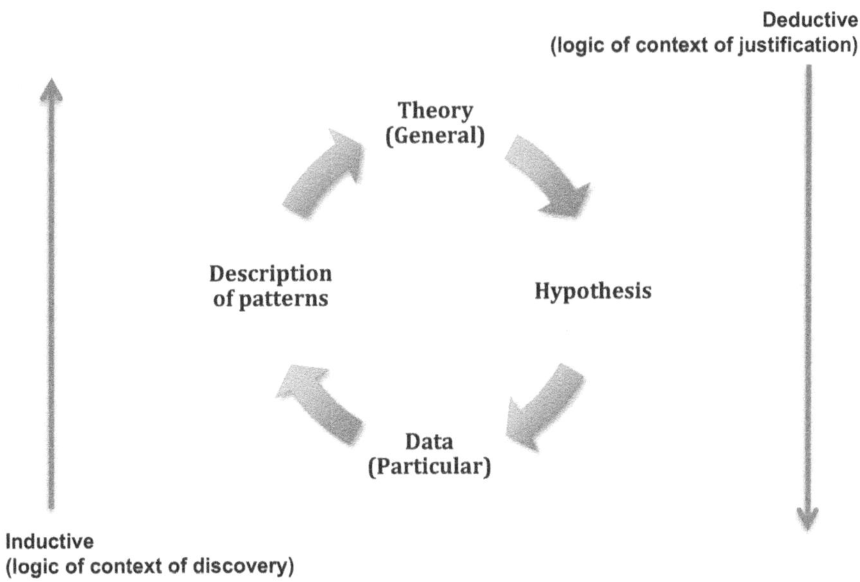


**Fig. 1.2** Theory generation cycle (adapted from Johnson, 2016)

(e) increasing the generalisability of the results; f) combining qualitative and quantitative research to generate more comprehensive knowledge, an important condition for informing theory and practice (Johnson & Onwuegbuzie, 2004, p. 21).

In sum, two arguments justify the theory building process in this study: (1) the lack of a comprehensive model capable of synthesising, testing, and explaining corruption and prosperity based on previously unrelated theories and (2) the need for a critical theory of the role of religion, institutions, and social domination in Europe and the Americas.

### 1.2.3 Limitations

On the theoretical level, I do not discuss each of its various topics in-depth. Vast amounts of information have already been produced, in what is in effect an immeasurable field of investigation: the origins of countries' prosperity. Instead, this study is systemic in that the relations and ramifications are more important than the depth of each topic and case. Although the sociology of religion is central to this research, the concepts and findings of other disciplines are also drawn upon. Consistent with its systemic approach, this book emphasises the relations between fields. Thus, it offers no detailed analysis of various influences—environment and geography, language and ethnicities—on prosperity. This study explores neither Western evangelical movements nor liberation theology or ecumenism in-depth even if these topics are addressed. Finally, this research considers neither the recent rise of Islam in Europe due to the migration crisis nor the Jewish influence in Europe and the Americas.

Methodologically, this study exhibits the typical and inherent *weaknesses of mixed research* (Johnson & Onwuegbuzie, 2004, p. 21). Among others, it is more time consuming, is a greater drain on resources, and is more challenging as it involves a single researcher learning about and carrying out both qualitative and quantitative research concurrently.

Last but far from least, the research topic is highly sensitive and apt to generate controversy. Its research design is ambitious, which required delicately balancing surface and depth when analysing the results and writing these up. This study favours comparing different sources and cases, which at times meant sacrificing analytical depth. The biases inherent in this research are explained in Chap. 13.

## References

Acemoglu, D., Cantoni, D., Johnson, S., & Robinson, J. A. (2011). The consequences of radical reform: The French revolution. *The American Economic Review, 101*(7), 3286–3307.

Acemoglu, D., & Robinson, J. (2012). *Why nations fail. The origins of power, prosperity and poverty*. New York: Crown Business.

Agnew, J. (2010). Deus Vult: The geopolitics of the Catholic Church. *Geopolitics, 15*(1), 39–61.

Anderson, J. (2007). Religion, politics and international relations. The Catholic contribution to democratization's 'third wave': Altruism, hegemony or self-interest? *Cambridge Review of International Affairs, 20*(3), 383–399.

Bacchiocchi, S. (1977). *From Sabbath to Sunday. A historical investigation of the rise of Sunday observance in early Christianity*. Rome: The Pontifical Gregorian University Press.

Barrett, D. B., Kurian, G. T., & Johnson, T. M. (2001). *World Christian encyclopedia* (2nd ed.). Oxford: Oxford University Press.

Barro, R. J., & McCleary, R. M. (2005). Which countries have state religions? *The Quarterly Journal of Economics, 120*(4), 1331–1370.

Beltrán, W. M. (2008). Aproximación histórico-interpretativa al proceso de diversificación religiosa en Colombia. In S. Y. Grupo Interdisciplinario de Estudios de Religión (Ed.), *Mirada pluridisciplinar al hecho religioso en Colombia: Avances de investigación*. Bogotá, DC: Universidad de San Buenaventura.

Berman, H. (2003). *Law and revolution II: The impact of the Protestant reformations on the Western legal tradition*. Cambridge: Harvard University Press, Belknap Press.

Bruce, F. F. (2007). *Außerbiblische Zeugnisse über Jesus und das frühe Christentum*. Giessen: Brunnen.

Burger, C. (2014). Luther's thought took shape in translation of scripture and hymns. In *The Oxford handbook of Martin Luther's theology*. Oxford: Oxford University Press.

Cook, E. (2012). *Roman Catholic hegemony and religious freedom: A seventh-day Adventist assessment of Dignitatis Humanae*. Texas: Graduate Faculty of Baylor University.

D'Aubigne, M. (1862). *Histoire de la Reformation au XVIie siecle*. Paris: Librairie de Ch. Meyrueis et Compagnie.

Diamond, J. (1997). *Guns, germs, and steel. The fates of human societies*. New York: W.W. Norton & Company.

Eisenhardt, K. M. (1989). Building theories from case study research. *Academy of Management Review, 14*(4), 532–550.

Eusebius of Caesarea (ca. 340 AD). (n.d.) *Historia Ecclesiastica (Church history). Kirchengeschichte. Aus dem Griechischen übersetzt von Phil. Häuser*. Retrieved from https://www.unifr.ch/bkv/bucha9.htm

Figueroa, H. (2016). *La persistance des idées traditionalistes en Colombie. Religion et politique (1886-1952)*. Paris: L'Harmattan.

Gill, A. (1998). *Rendering unto Caesar: The Catholic Church and the state in Latin America*. Chicago, IL: Chicago University Press.

Golden-Biddle, K., & Locke, K. (2007). *Composing qualitative research*. London: SAGE.

Heussi, K. (1991). *Kompendium der Kirchengeschichte*. Tübingen: Mohr Siebeck.

Hjelm, T. (2014). Religion, discourse and power: A contribution towards a critical sociology of religion. *Critical Sociology, 40*(6), 855–872.

Hofstede, G. (2001). *Culture's consequences. Comparing values, Behaviours, institutions and organizations across nations*. Thousand Oaks, CA: Sake Publications.

Johnson, R. B. (2016). *Mixed methods research design and analysis with validity: A primer. Version 4.2*. South Alabama: Department of Professional Studies, University of South Alabama.

Johnson, R. B., & Onwuegbuzie, A. J. (2004). Mixed methods research: A research paradigm whose time has come. *Educational Researcher, 33*(7), 14–26.

Kilduff, M. (2006). Editor's comments: Publishing theory. *Academy of Management Review, 31*(2), 252–255.

King James Bible. (1769). *The Holy Bible, King James Version*. Cambridge Edition: 1769. Scripture quotations from The Authorized (King James) Version. Rights in the authorized version in the United Kingdom are vested in the Crown. Reproduced by permission of the Crown's patentee, Cambridge University Press.

La Porta, R., Lopez-de-Silanes, F., & Vishny, A. S. (1999). The quality of government. *Journal of Law, Economics and Organization, 15*(1), 222–279.

Levine, D. (1981). *Religion and politics in Latin America: The Catholic Church in Venezuela & Colombia*. Princeton, NJ: Princeton Legacy Library.

Manow, P. (2004). *The good, the bad, and the ugly: Esping-Andersen's regime typology and the religious roots of the Western welfare state* (MPIfG Working Paper, No. 04/3). Cologne: Max Planck Institute for the Study of Societies. Retrieved from: http://www.mpifg.de/pu/workpap/wp04-3/wp04-3.html

Manow, P., & van Kersbergen, K. (2009). Religion and the Western Welfae state – the theoretical context. In P. Manow & K. van Kersbergen (Eds.), *Religion, class coalitions and welfare states* (p. 304). New York: Cambridge University Press.

Merryman, J., & Pérez, R. (2007). *The civil law tradition: An introduction to the legal Systems of Europe and Latin America* (3rd ed.). Stanford: Stanford University Press.

Michalopoulos, S., & Papaioannou, E. (2017). *The long economic and political shadow of history—Volume 3: Europe and the Americas*. London: CEPR Press Centre for Economic Policy Research.

Miller, N. (2012). *The religious roots of the first amendment*. New York: Oxford University Press.

Orlikowski, W. J. (2010). Practice in research: Phenomenon, perspective and philosophy. In L. R. D. Golsorkhi (Ed.), *Cambridge handbook of strategy as practice* (pp. 23–33). Cambridge: Cambridge University Press.

Paldam, M. (2001). Corruption and religion. Adding to the economic model. *Kyklos, 54*(2–3), 383–414.

Pirenne, H. (1936). *A history of Europe*. Read Books. ISBN 9781409724605.

Sachs, J. (2001). *Tropical underdevelopment* (Working Paper, 8119). National Bureau of Economic Research (NBER). pp. 1–37.

Snyder, J. (2011). *Religion and international relations theory*. New York: Columbia University Press.

Treisman, D. (2000). The causes of corruption: A cross-national study. *Journal of Public Economics, 76*(3), 399–457.

Weber, M. (1905). *Die protestantische Ethik und der Geist des Kapitalismus*. Zürich: Verlag Wirtschaft und Finanzen.

Witte, J. (2002). *Law and Protestantism: The legal teachings of the Lutheran reformation*. Cambridge: Cambridge University Press.

Woodberry, R. (2012). The missionary roots of liberal democracy. *American Political Science Review (APSR), 106*(2), 244–274.

# Chapter 2
# Research Setting

This chapter is divided into four sections. Section 2.1 details the research aims, and Section 2.2 presents the main research question. Section 2.3 formulates the general hypotheses. Section 2.4 presents the research model, which synthesises understanding and serves as a rationale for the entire book. The model exhibits the main exogenous theoretical determinants of corruption and prosperity, which are tested empirically. Exogenous long-term factors include culture, religion, and environment. Given the aim of this research, particular emphasis is placed on religion (Catholic and Protestant; institutional and adherents).

## 2.1 Research Aim and Focus

This study applies grounded theory to expand existing understanding of the relation between two of the world's main Christian religious systems—Roman Catholicism and Protestantism—and two key prosperity indicators (corruption and competitiveness). It also explores the intrinsic factors potentially enabling this relation to be established and perpetuated.

To achieve these aims, I adopt a hybrid (combined) approach involving Grounded Theory (GT) and four case studies from a mixed-methods (MM) perspective. In fact, "MM-GT works well in connecting theory generation with theory testing, linking theory and practice" (Johnson et al., 2010). The resultant theory pursues an "emancipatory 'knowledge interest'" (Fairclough, 2001, p. 230; Habermas, 1972) and thus challenges established approaches to prosperity problems (see prosperity theories, Chap. 5).



J. García Portilla, *"Ye Shall Know Them by Their Fruits"*, Contributions to Economics, https://doi.org/10.1007/978-3-030-78498-0_2

## 2.2 Research Question

A direct relation between political power and the power of the Roman Catholic Church-State has persisted throughout Latin America since the Conquest (Gill, 1998; Gill, 2013; Levine, 1981; Munevar, 2008). These institutional relations can be traced back the European colonisers (Acemoglu & Robinson, 2012; Engerman & Sokoloff, 2002; Woodberry, 2012).

Consequently, this study explores the influence of Protestantism and Roman Catholicism on corruption and competitiveness in present-day Europe and the Americas. Previous scholarship has already highlighted the relevance of this topic. For instance, Hjelm (2014) observed:

> If ever there was a time for a critical, engaged sociology of religion, this would be it. Yet, the paradigmatic discussions (as represented by textbook knowledge) still revolve around the question of disappearance versus resurgence of religion, with little or no attention paid to religions' role in reproducing and transforming inequality (Hjelm, 2014, p. 856).

Corruption and competitiveness are the so-called prosperity indicators. Reviewing these indicators in Europe and the Americas (Chap. 4 and Appendices 1–5) reveals that historically Protestant countries generally perform better than predominantly Roman Catholic ones. Based on this evidence, the main question of this study is: *How does Protestantism influence competitiveness and transparency compared to Roman Catholicism in Europe and the Americas?*

## 2.3 Hypotheses

This section presents the general hypotheses of this study. Specific configurational empirical expectations are introduced in Part III.

Christianity has been central to Western civilisation. Yet the diverse historical trajectories of the various Christian denominations have first established and subsequently determined different sets of societal norms and institutions. This book explores *the influence of Christianity on prosperity in present-day Europe and the Americas.*

It posits two main hypotheses:

**Hypothesis 1** *Roman Catholicism has negatively impacted prosperity (competitiveness and transparency) in Europe and the Americas.*

**Hypothesis 2** *The Protestant Reformation has positively impacted prosperity (competitiveness and transparency) in Europe and the Americas.*

The general assumption, however, is that religion might work in combination with other long-term persistence factors triggering prosperity, i.e. the desired outcome (see research model, Fig. 2.1). Other prominent theoretical triggers of prosperity are institutions and legal traditions, which are also implicitly linked to my hypotheses on religion (i.e. state religion, see Chap. 8). However, environmental factors are exogenous (i.e. not directly related to the first two hypotheses) and therefore require a separate hypothesis:

**Hypothesis 3** *Environmental performance positively impacts prosperity in Europe and the Americas (i.e. moderating or moderated by the impact of religion).*

This study investigates the influence of Christianity on prosperity within the framework of the sociology of religion. It therefore focuses mainly on the first two hypotheses.

## 2.4 Research Model[1]

The research model considers the variables and factors discussed in this study to be interdependent. I take the model entirely and not residually and attach theoretical and empirical importance to all the variables (theories). Generally, the same factors (theories) that are associated with prosperity as a whole (i.e. GCI) are also associated with corruption in the literature (see Chaps. 3, 6 and 7).

Parts II and III (conceptual and theoretical background) break down the research model (Fig. 2.1) and explain its components and relations in different chapters. These explain some of the complex relations theoretically and concentrate on my principal variables of interest: religion and prosperity/corruption (see the subsections concentrating on Latin America). Some relations are not covered since they are less relevant to the purposes of this study (e.g. environmental influences on culture and vice versa).

Figure 2.1 (see below) synthesises the logic underlying this study by interrelating the variables of interest (i.e. conditions in QCA). It is general and thus does not include all research variables. Some of the variables or conditions are embedded within others and vice versa (see Appendices 1–5 for details). The figure also represents the research model structuring this study:

[1]Originally published as "Research Model" in: Garcia Portilla, J. (2019). "Ye Shall Know Them by Their Fruits": Prosperity and Institutional Religion in Europe and the Americas. *Religions*, *10*(6), 362. MDPI AG. Retrieved from https://doi.org/10.3390/rel10060362

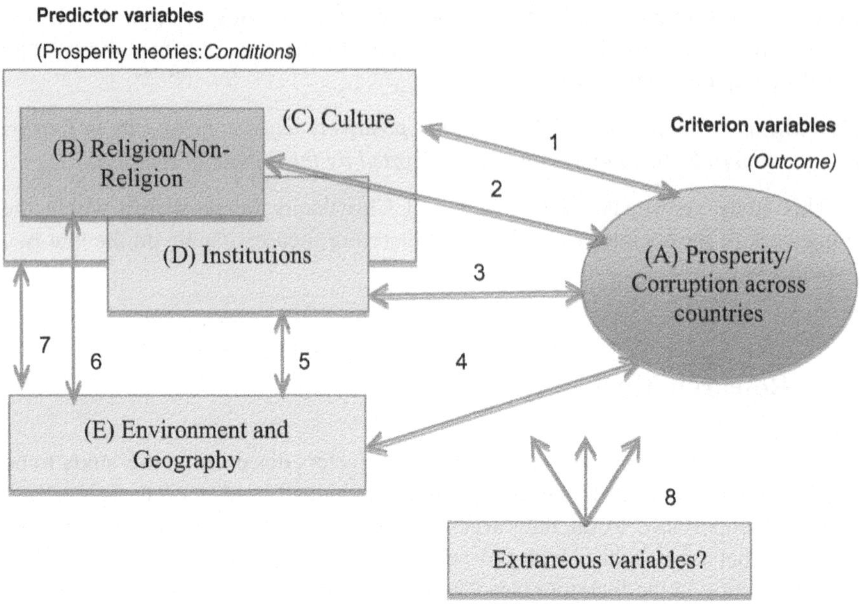


**Fig. 2.1** Research model (Source: Author's figure). Note: Arrows and numbers indicate potential causal relations, which are explored in the following chapters (see the corresponding capital letters and the numbers between parenthesis in the headings and subheadings referring to the relations in this figure)

## References


Acemoglu, D., & Robinson, J. (2012). *Why nations fail. The origins of power, prosperity and poverty*. New York: Crown Business.

Engerman, S., & Sokoloff, K. (2002). *Factor endowments, inequality, and paths of development among New World Economies* (NBER Working Paper No. 9259). Retrieved from https://www.nber.org/papers/w9259

Fairclough, N. (2001). The discourse of new labour: Critical discourse analysis. In S. T. M. Wetherell (Ed.), *Discourse as data – A guide for analysis*. London: SAGE.

Garcia Portilla, J. (2019). "Ye shall know them by their fruits": Prosperity and institutional religion in Europe and the Americas. *Religions, 10*(6), 362. MDPI AG. https://doi.org/10.3390/rel10060362.

Gill, A. (1998). *Rendering unto Caesar: The Catholic Church and the state in Latin America*. Chicago, IL: Chicago University Press.

Gill, A. (2013). Religious pluralism, political incentives, and the origins of religious liberty. Global challenges. In A. Hertzke (Ed.), *The future of religious freedom* (pp. 107–127). New York: Oxford University Press.

Habermas, J. (1972). *Knowledge and human interests*. Heinemann Educational Books.

Hjelm, T. (2014). Religion, discourse and power: A contribution towards a critical sociology of religion. *Critical Sociology, 40*(6), 855–872.

Johnson, R., McGowan, W., & M., & Turner, L. (2010). Grounded theory in practice: Is it inherently a mixed method? *The Research in the Schools. Mid-South Educational Research Association, 17*(2), 65–78.

Levine, D. (1981). *Religion and politics in Latin America: The Catholic Church in Venezuela & Colombia*. Princeton, NJ: Princeton Legacy Library.

Munevar, J. (2008). Transformación doctrinal y actitudinal de la participación política de las iglesias cristianas evangélicas en Colombia. In Grupo Interdisciplinario de Estudios de Religión, Sociedad y Política, & GIERSP (Eds.), *Mirada pluridisciplinar al hecho religioso en Colombia: Avances de investigación* (pp. 375–399). Colombia: Bogotá.

Woodberry, R. (2012). The missionary roots of liberal democracy. *American Political Science Review (APSR), 106*(2), 244–274.

# Part II
# Conceptual Framework

# Chapter 3
# The Outcome (Criterion Variables)

***(A)*: Corruption and Prosperity**
This chapter defines *corruption* and *prosperity* based on various underlying perspectives.

## 3.1 Definitions of Corruption *(A)*

Corruption is a widely used term. Dozens of definitions exist in the literature (Gingerich, 2013; Paldam, 2001; Rose-Ackerman, 2006; Treisman, 2000). However, one standard definition identifies corruption as illicit private benefit(s) (Paldam, 2001, p. 389). Another highlights the abuse of public authority or resources for the purpose of pursuing political goals or financial advantages at the expense of others (Gingerich, 2013, p. 10).

According to the Cambridge University Dictionary (2014), corruption is "illegal, bad, or dishonest behaviour, especially by people in positions of power". One common antonym is "transparency". In the world of business, this refers to activities performed openly, i.e. "without secrets, so that people can trust that they are fair and honest" (Cambridge University Dictionary, 2014).[1]

Moreover, corruption is a scourge associated with economic failure that nations have long tried to remove, albeit with little success (Chase, 2010). Corruption is symptomatic of state-society relations. It involves undermining the fairness and legitimacy of the state and leads to wasting and poorly targeting public funds (Rose-Ackerman, 2006, p. xvi). Corruption occurs when private wealth and public power overlap (Rose-Ackerman, 2006, p. xvii). Whereas corruption subverts human

[1]Definitions of '<corruption>' and '<transparency>' from Cambridge Dictionary, www.dictionary.cambridge.org, © Cambridge University Press. Used with permission. Reproduced with permission of the Licensor through PLSclear.



J. García Portilla, *"Ye Shall Know Them by Their Fruits"*, Contributions to Economics, https://doi.org/10.1007/978-3-030-78498-0_3

rights, high transparency levels are also associated with guaranteeing human rights (Gebeye, 2012; OHCHR, 2019).

Corruption may also be understood more broadly. As a moral category, it denotes rot and putrefaction (Rose-Ackerman, 2006, p. xiv). This is its common meaning since the Old Testament. Leviticus 22:25 (King James Bible, 1769) identifies corruption as a deficient inner state: "*Neither from a stranger's hand shall ye offer the bread of your God of any of these; because their corruption is in them [. . .]*". However, one of its most important uses in the Holy Scriptures is its reference to Jesus Christ as the Holy One, as the one who did not corrupt (King James Bible, 1769, Psalms 16: 10; Psalms 49: 9; Acts 2: 27–32; Acts 13: 34–37).

In the Gospel of Matthew, the word "corrupt" refers to the warning that Jesus gave about false prophets coming on his behalf (as the title of this study indicates). Jesus compares the false prophets with the corrupt fruits of corrupt trees (King James Bible, 1769, Matthew 7: 15–23). A similar reference occurs in Luke 6: 43–45 and in Matthew 12: 33 (King James Bible, 1769): "*Either make the tree good, and his fruit good; or else make the tree corrupt, and his fruit corrupt: for the tree is known by his fruit*".

Among Protestants, Matthew 7 (King James Bible, 1769) is perhaps the most common of several scriptural warnings as it provides a basis for demonising the Roman Catholic clergy (Johnstone, 2006, p. 47). Roman Catholic clerics were depicted as "deceitful workers [that] fashion themselves like unto the apostles of Christ" and as Satan's servants, who were instructed to use the scriptures in their deceits (Becon, 1844, p. 405 as cited in Johnstone, 2006, p. 47). Therefore, reformers like William Tyndale also employed the same scriptural reference ("false prophets") to denounce the Roman Catholic Church-State in the sixteenth-century (Tyndale, 1849, pp. 121–8; Johnstone, 2006, p. 47) (see also Sect. 10.4.2.1).

Yet, historical Protestants have broadly understood "corruption" as being a phenomenon associated with a demonic influence which, therefore, permeates all humankind, not just state churches or governments (see also Sect. 10.4.2.1). As Johnstone (2006) observes:

> Godly writings give evidence of an in-depth knowledge of the conventions of Protestant demonism, particularly the defining nature of man's corruption through the fall of Adam for his constant persecution by the Devil, and his reliance on God for protection. 'Sin and corruption conceived in the heart of man is the spawn of the devil'. . .(p. 109)

The term corruption is central to this book. It is discussed in detail in Sect. 4.1 and in Parts III and V. Those sections explore the different theoretical and empirical outcomes of corruption and prosperity in those two religious systems claiming to follow the teachings of Jesus Christ: Roman Catholicism and Protestantism. Applying Jesus' parable of "false prophets" (King James Bible, 1769, Matthew 7: 15–23; Luke 6: 43–45; Matthew 12: 33) extends beyond the clergy to *a corrupt religious-political system, one that uses the name of Jesus (like a false prophet's) and thus produces corruption and a lack of prosperity in the respective countries under its influence (corrupt fruits).*

### 3.1.1 The Corruption Perceptions Index (CPI) as an Outcome (or Criterion Variable)

Corruption is difficult to study empirically (Treisman, 2000). Actual corruption is hard to measure, and standardising perceptions may prove challenging. Thus, for instance, if a society has high ethical standards, its citizens may perceive small infractions as outright corrupt, whereas a society with different standards may be perceived as less corrupt even if objectively measured as more corrupt. Therefore, corruption is culture sensitive.

However, expertise and subjective perceptions are the only information on corruption levels widely available for cross-country empirical research (i.e. Corruption Perceptions Index (CPI); World Bank; see Lambsdorff, 2006, p. 3; Gingerich, 2013). The coverage of such aggregate indicators (i.e. CPI) makes them the most empirically researched corruption measures, provided one assumes that they correlate with real corruption levels (Lambsdorff, 1999, 2006; Mauro, 1995; Habib and Zurawicki as cited in Gingerich, 2013). The different cross-national corruption ratings established by diverse organisations using various techniques are highly correlated, both with each other and across time (Treisman, 2000, p. 400).

Some studies at the individual (i.e. national) micro-level employ more objective data (i.e. convictions for corruption) and higher conceptual precision than cross-country research using aggregate indicators (Gingerich, 2013). Nevertheless, such micro-level data is unavailable and not standardised across countries. Furthermore, it suffers from validity issues (Lambsdorff, 2006, p. 3).

The Corruption Perceptions Index (CPI) of Transparency International (TI) (2016) is a composite index. It draws on the corruption indices of 11 independent institutions (including the World Economic Forum, the European Intelligence Unit, and the World Bank). The index summarises perceptions of business people and country experts around the world, both residents and expatriates. CPI values range from 0 to 10. Lower values indicate a higher degree of corruption (i.e. a lesser degree of transparency).

The empirical part of this study focuses on 65 countries in the Americas and Europe. I selected the *CPI*-aggregated measure on account of its comprehensive coverage and ideal availability to perform a cross-country analysis and to compare the findings with previous studies.

## 3.2 The Global Competitiveness Index (GCI) as a Prosperity Proxy (Outcome or Criterion Variable) *(A')*[2]

I define prosperity in its broader sense—of being successful—rather than restricted to economic terms (i.e. GDP). On this basis, I link the concepts of "prosperity" and "competitiveness" (GCI), which both result from related identical conditions. The World Economic Forum developed the Global Competitiveness Index (GCI) as a comprehensive proxy of prosperity to track the performance of nearly 140 countries in terms of twelve categories: institutions, technological readiness, innovation, higher education and training, health and primary education, business sophistication, infrastructure, macro-economic environment, labour market efficiency, market size, financial market development, and goods market efficiency. Through empirical and theoretical research, the World Economic Forum identified such categories as determinants of productivity which in turn is the primary determinant of economic growth and prosperity (World Economic Forum, 2016).

Thus, the World Economic Forum defines competitiveness as "the set of institutions, policies and factors that determine a country's level of productivity, which in turn, sets the level of *prosperity* that the economy can achieve" (World Economic Forum, 2016, p.11). Accordingly, I often use prosperity and competitiveness (GCI) indiscriminately.

The GCI is a highly comprehensive measure and ranks countries on a prosperity scale. The existence of institutions, education, transparency, and other factors already included within the GCI (or prosperity) means a significant advantage for the purposes of this study. First, these variables are closely related, theoretically and empirically, and thus belong to the same "prosperity phenomenon" (GCI). Consequently, their causality need not be discussed, as they are not isolated but aggregated in the GCI. Second, such aggregated factors (GCI) allow focusing on other background (i.e. exogenous) causes determining the "competitiveness phenomenon". Therefore, I focus on potential (i.e. theoretically conceivable) exogenous variables not included in the GCI. These, for example, include religion and culture, legal origin and state religion (as background proxies for institutions), or environment and geography.

The GCI (and its drivers) also correlate with indicators of equality (i.e. Inclusive Growth Performance, Gini coefficient) and environmental sustainability, exhibiting win-win synergies (rather than trade-offs) between these factors (World Economic

[2]Originally published as "Outcome: Prosperity and the Global Competitiveness Index (GCI)" in: Garcia Portilla, J. (2019). "Ye Shall Know Them by Their Fruits": Prosperity and Institutional Religion in Europe and the Americas. *Religions*, *10*(6), 362. MDPI AG. Retrieved from https://doi.org/10.3390/rel10060362

Forum, 2012; World Economic Forum, 2019; World Economic Forum & European Investment Bank, 2017).

By way of illustration, throughout the Holy Scriptures, "prosperity" is often associated with following the moral commandments of the law (see Table 8.4). For instance, "Keep therefore the words of this covenant, and do them, that ye may *prosper* in all that ye do" (King James Bible, 1769, Deuteronomy 29:9). In turn, the Bible links short- or long-term misfortunes as both being consequences of rebellion:

> if thou wilt not hearken unto the voice of the Lord thy God, to observe to do all his commandments and his statutes which I command thee this day; that all these curses shall come upon thee, and overtake thee (King James Bible, 1769, Deuteronomy 28:15).

This principle refers exclusively to the free-will moral observance of the law in the Bible and is not to be confused with the blind obedience of hierarchical structures and dogmas. Obedience of hierarchies often enforces coercion instead of a rational internalisation of values, and has, in turn, a negative influence on prosperity (Guiso et al., 2006; Licht et al., 2007; Tabellini, 2005), (see Sects. 8.1.1 and 10.3). Protestant countries have applied the biblical moral principles of the Decalogue in their legal systems (Table 8.4). In contrast, Catholic countries have mostly based their legal systems on the hierarchical Roman and Canon law, which mostly derives from the Catholic Sacraments and Greek philosophy rather than from the biblical commandments (Table 8.3).

Chapter 4 and Appendices 4 and 5 indicate clear distribution patterns for competitiveness and corruption in the countries studied here: high competitiveness and low corruption in traditionally Protestant countries; lower competitiveness and higher corruption in traditional Roman Catholic or Orthodox countries.

## 3.3 Competitiveness and Transparency as Prosperity Proxies

The lack of competitiveness, corruption, income inequality, and policy distortions are strongly associated empirically (Rose-Ackerman, 2006); (Lambsdorff, 1999). However, deriving clear causality arguments from these features is problematic. While corruption, for instance, may cause the other variables, it is at the same time also likely to result from these (Lambsdorff, 1999). Thus, the causes and the consequences of prosperity (and corruption) are difficult to distinguish by considering these variables.

### *3.3.1 Economic Indicators and Corruption*

Gross domestic product (GDP) per capita is the most robust variable related to corruption across empirical studies as wealthier countries tend to exhibit less corruption (Paldam, 2001); (Treisman, 2000). Goldsmith's (1999) sample of 66 countries found a negative correlation between corruption and different indicators of economic freedom. Paldam's (2002) study of 77 countries reached similar results, including more explanatory variables.

No apparent doubt exists about a robust negative correlation between GDP per capita and corruption. However, similar agreement exists that no clear causality can be derived from that correlation (Lambsdorff, 2006, p. 24). Causation may run from low economic growth to corruption or from corruption to low growth or, and this is more likely, in both directions, thus creating virtuous or vicious loops. However, assuming economic growth as the primary cure for corruption amounts to simplistic and misleading "wishful thinking" (Rose-Ackerman, 2006, p. xvi).

Although various scholars have attempted to establish a causal link between corruption and prosperity (or vice versa) (e.g. Treisman, 2000, p. 430), causal associations suffer from pressing endogeneity issues (Lambsdorff, 2006). In practice, both variables should be interrelated in both directions (Lambsdorff, 1999); (Morris, 2003); (Uildriks, 2009). Therefore, I consider the two variables complimentarily (as a whole outcome), since their causal separation might be neither useful nor desirable for the specific purposes of this study (see Fig. 2.1).

In fact, the Global Competitiveness Index (GCI) as a prosperity proxy usefully includes the Corruption Perception Index (CPI) (World Economic Forum, 2016). Consequently, I subsume both competitiveness and corruption under the prosperity umbrella.

## References


Cambridge University. (2014). *The Cambridge university dictionary*. Cambridge University Press. Retrieved from https://dictionary.cambridge.org. https://doi.org/10.26226/morressier.60546d5e30a2e980041f1f70.

Chase, G. (2010). Religion's impact on corruption. *Journal of Business and Economics Perspectives, 5*(1), 102–112.

Garcia Portilla, J. (2019). "Ye shall know them by their fruits": Prosperity and institutional religion in Europe and the Americas. *Religions, 10*(6), 362. MDPI AG. https://doi.org/10.3390/rel10060362.

Gebeye, B. A. (2012). *Corruption and human rights: Exploring the relationships* (Working Paper No. 70). Retrieved from http://www.du.edu/korbel/hrhw/workingpapers/2012/70-gebeye-2012.pdf

Gingerich, D. (2013). *Political institutions and party-directed corruption in South America. Stealing for the team*. New York: Cambridge University Press.

Goldsmith, A. (1999). Slapping the grasping hand: Correlates of political corruption in emerging markets. *American Journal of Economics and Sociology, 58*(4), 866–883.

Guiso, L., Sapienza, P., & Zingales, L. (2006). Does culture affect economic outcomes? *Journal of Economic Perspectives, 20*(2), 23–48.

Johnstone, N. (2006). The synagogue of Satan: Anti-Catholicism, false doctrine and the construction of contrariety. In N. Johnstone (Ed.), *The devil and demonism in early modern England*. New York: Cambridge University Press.

King James Bible. (1769). *The Holy Bible, King James Version.* Cambridge Edition: 1769. Scripture quotations from The Authorized (King James) Version. Rights in the Authorized Version in the United Kingdom are vested in the Crown. Reproduced by permission of the Crown's patentee, Cambridge University Press.

Lambsdorff, J. G. (1999). Corruption in empirical research — A review. In *9th International anti-corruption conference, Durban, South Africa 10–15 December, 1999*, (pp. 1–18). Durban, South Africa.

Lambsdorff, J. G. (2006). Causes and consequences of corruption: What do we know from a cross-section of countries? In S. Rose-Ackerman (Ed.), *International handbook on the economics of corruption* (pp. 3–51). Cheltenham: Edward Elgar.

Licht, A. N., Goldschmidt, C., & Schwarz, S. H. (2007). Culture rules: The foundations of the rule of law and other norms of governance. *Journal of Comparative Economics, 35*(4), 659–688.

Mauro, P. (1995). Corruption and growth. *Quarterly Journal of Economics, 110*(3), 681–712.

Morris, S. (2003). Corruption and Mexican political culture. *Journal of the Southwest, 45*(4), 671–708.

OHCHR. (2019). *United Nations Human Rights Office of the High Commissioner.* Retrieved from https://www.ohchr.org/EN/Issues/CorruptionAndHR/Pages/CorruptionAndHRIndex.aspx

Paldam, M. (2001). Corruption and religion. Adding to the economic model. *Kyklos, 54*(2–3), 383–414.

Paldam, M. (2002). The cross-country pattern of corruption: Economics, culture and the seesaw dynamics. *European Journal of Political Economy, 18*(2), 215–240.

Rose-Ackerman, S. (2006). *International handbook on the economics of corruption.* Cheltenham: Edward Elgar Publishing.

Tabellini, G. (2005). *Culture and institutions: Economic development in the regions of Europe* (CESifo Working Paper No. 1492).

Transparency International. (2016). *Corruption perceptions index 2016.* Retrieved from https://www.transparency.org/news/feature/corruption_perceptions_index_201.

Treisman, D. (2000). The causes of corruption: A cross-national study. *Journal of Public Economics, 76*(3), 399–457. https://doi.org/10.1016/s0047-2727(99)00092-4.

Tyndale, W. (1849). An exposition upon the V. VI. VII. Chapters of Mathew (c. 1532). In H. Walter (Ed.), *Expositions and notes on sundry portions of the holy scripture.* Cambridge: Parker Society.

Uildriks, N. (2009). *Policing insecurity: Police reform, security, and human rights in Latin America.* Plymouth: Lexington Books.

World Economic Forum. (2012). *The global competitiveness report 2012–2013.* Geneva: World Economic Forum.

World Economic Forum. (2016). *The global competitiveness report 2014–2015.* Full Data Edition. Geneva: The World Economic Forum.

World Economic Forum. (2019). *The global competitiveness report 2019.* Geneva: World Economic Forum.

World Economic Forum, & European Investment Bank. (2017). *Beyond the equity-efficiency trade-off: Practical ideas for inclusive growth and competitiveness in Europe.* The Europe Inclusive Growth and Competitiveness Lab.

# Chapter 4
# Diagnosing Corruption and Prosperity in Europe and the Americas *(A)*

This chapter diagnoses prosperity in Europe and the Americas based on three indicators: Corruption (CPI), Social Progress (SPI), and Competitiveness (GCI). GCI and CPI have already been introduced and correspond to the outcome that is modelled empirically (Parts V and VI). SPI will be introduced in Sect. 4.2.

## 4.1 Corruption in Europe and the Americas (CPI)

Figure 4.1 displays a clear distinction between two trends. On the one hand, the USA, Canada, Australia, and Northern Europe tend to be perceived as the most transparent regions in the world. In contrast, with few exceptions, Latin America and the rest of the world are perceived as corrupt to highly corrupt.

Countries in Northern Europe, including the UK (which colonised North America), rank along the same values as the USA and Canada (see green circles in the map). In contrast, southern Europe (Greece, Italy and especially Spain and Portugal, the colonisers of Central and South America) exhibits higher corruption. Interestingly, Uruguay and Chile (the least traditionally Catholic countries in South America) have unusually lower CPI levels than the rest of Latin America. Parts V and VI further analyse this situation based on empirical observations and case studies.

Pervasive mistrust and corruption mar the social and public sphere in most Latin American countries (Uildriks, 2009, p. 6). Corruption and mistrust profoundly

Some parts of this chapter were originally published as "Diagnosis: Prosperity in Europe and the Americas" in: Garcia Portilla, J. (2019). "Ye Shall Know Them by Their Fruits": Prosperity and Institutional Religion in Europe and the Americas. *Religions*, *10*(6), 362. MDPI AG. Retrieved from https://doi.org/10.3390/rel10060362





J. García Portilla, *"Ye Shall Know Them by Their Fruits"*, Contributions to Economics, https://doi.org/10.1007/978-3-030-78498-0_4

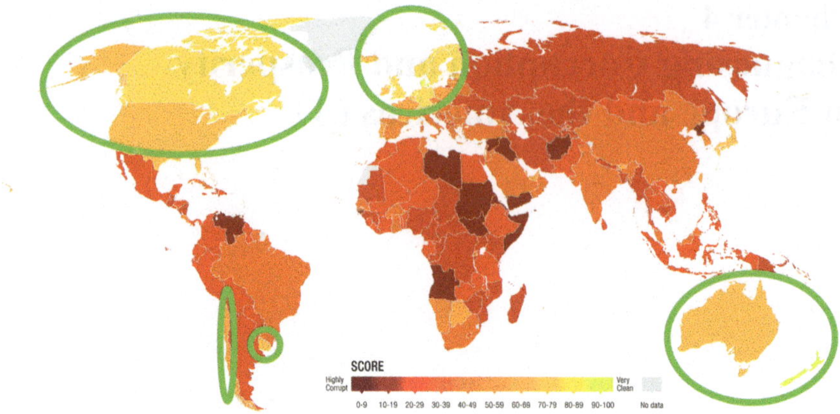


**Fig. 4.1** Corruption Perception Index (adapted from Transparency International [TI], 2016). Used with permission

hamper social prosperity in different regions (Fukuyama, 1995; North, 1998). Both factors seriously affect coexistence and contribute to social fragmentation (Mockus et al., 2012, p. 6).

Similarly, Luzzani (2002) observed that cultural acceptance of bribery in Latin America makes public administration work more smoothly in this region, combined with Latin America's generalised "inadequate laws, irreverence for the law even when it is adequate, and the impunity of those who are corrupt" (Luzzani, 2002, p. 168). His conclusions coincide with Mockus (2001), who found that openly illegal and frequently even morally reprehensible behaviour is culturally accepted or tolerated in specific contexts in Latin America (p. 3).

Thus, rather than being a problem solely of political institutions, corruption is deeply ingrained in the cultural background of societies. In Latin America, corruption is widespread not just within state agencies but also in broader society, and it is an inextricable part of how most things are achieved. Indeed, within the continent as a whole, most aspects of public life are notoriously corrupt (Uildriks, 2009, p. 8).

Equally, for Diament (1991) "corruption in Latin America is not merely a social deviation, it is a way of life" (p. 20).

Within Europe and the Americas, Latin America ranks highest on the Corruption Perception Index, followed by Southern Europe (Fig. 4.1). Historically, the Roman Catholic and Orthodox Church-States have dominated the institutions and culture of those areas of the world (Inglehart & Baker, 2000); (Gill, 1998). Is this a coincidence or not?

Exploring the moral, cultural, and legal roots of the Latin American ethos calls for reference to the continent's religious origins. Political power and the hegemony of the Roman Catholic Church have been directly related across Latin America since the Conquest (Munevar, 2008). The closely intertwined connections between religion and politics since the Conquest and before have been historically fundamental to the Latin American social and institutional ethos. Church and state have provided each other with legitimation and institutional, material, and ideological support (Levine, 1981, p. 3).

In Latin America, these institutional relations can be traced back to their European (i.e. Iberian) colonial roots (Acemoglu & Robinson, 2012; Engerman & Sokoloff, 2002). Ever since the Middle Ages, the Spanish and Portuguese conquerors implemented a hierarchical, elitist, and corporatist model of Christendom that was sanctioned by the Church (Beltrán, 2008; Figueroa, 2016; Levine, 1981).

Although far from monolithic, historically the Roman Catholic Church-State has gained a widespread controversial reputation, partly due to medieval institutions such as the Inquisition or the indulgences. Systematic examples such as the abuse perpetrated by the conquerors and legitimated by the Church in Latin America (Navarro, 2016), or the current children abuse scandals, are well-known worldwide. Although indulgences may no longer be valid as initially promulgated by Pope Leo X in 1517 in the *Taxa Camarae*, the Jesuit Jorge Bergoglio, also known as "Pope Francis", employed this concept in his papal Bull *Misericordiae Vultus* (2015): "A Jubilee also entails the granting of *indulgences*" (Bull of Indiction of the Extraordinary Jubilee of Mercy, n. 22). Bergoglio has also used the concept of indulgences to promote events like the Catholic World Youth Day in 2013 (Kington, 2013). Similarly, the Vatican has recently issued a "Decree of the Apostolic Penitentiary on the granting of special Indulgences to the faithful in the current pandemic, 20.03.2020" (COVID-19).

Religion is an essential underlying driver of corruption (or transparency) in the state and society (Lambsdorff, 2006; Rose-Ackerman, 2006). Exploring the influence of the Roman Catholic tradition on corruption and prosperity in Latin America "remains an urgent priority for future research" (Treisman, 2000, p. 442). This study follows this call by broadly comparing prosperity and corruption in Europe and the Americas.

## 4.2 Social Progress in Europe and the Americas (SPI)

The Social Progress Index (SPI) is a comprehensive framework for measuring social progress independently and complementarily to GDP. Economic performance alone (GDP) does not fully explain social progress (variables have a correlation of 0,78) (Porter et al., 2015). The SPI is a robust and holistic measurement framework for national social and environmental performance. Norway, Sweden, and Switzerland have the highest SPI scores in the world (around 88 each). Mediterranean countries score around 80. All Latin American countries rank in the middle range of world distribution (from Uruguay, 79, to Guyana, 60) (Porter et al., 2015).

Figure 4.2 shows the different SPI scores in the Americas. Following the historical trend, Canada and the USA have better prosperity conditions (i.e. SPI and GCI) than all Latin American countries. Uruguay has the highest SPI value in Latin America (and is therefore one of the cases studied in detail below).

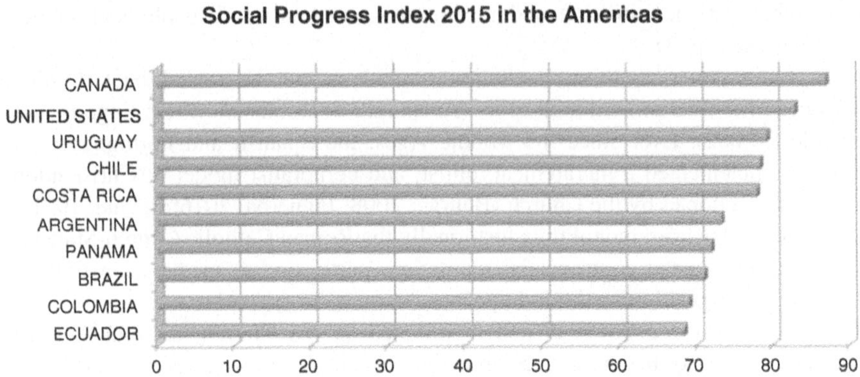


**Fig. 4.2** Social Progress Index in the Americas (2015) (adapted from Porter et al., 2015). Note: The SPI is not modelled empirically as it contains information about environmental performance that would allow inducing endogeneity in the models when including the EPI. Competitiveness (GCI) has a similar trend as SPI. GCI is modelled empirically as this index is comprehensive and does not directly include "environmental performance"

## 4.3 Competitiveness in Europe and the Americas (GCI)

Switzerland has the highest GCI score worldwide. The "advanced economies" (USA, Canada, Australia, New Zealand, Northern Europe) follow in the top 90–100% of the most competitive countries. The next group (70–80% of the most competitive countries) includes Italy, Spain, Portugal, Austria, and Ireland. Latin America and the Caribbean rank among the 40–80% most competitive regions (World Economic Forum, 2016).

Except for some countries (e.g. Uruguay and Chile), the CPI, GCI, and SPI confirm a long-established trend: Latin America is the only region in the world that is both "third-world" and "Christian" (Levine, 1981, p. 35; Grier, 1997). The next section briefly presents several approaches to explaining prosperity differences across countries.

## References

Acemoglu, D., & Robinson, J. (2012). *Why nations fail. The origins of power, prosperity and poverty*. New York: Crown Business.

Beltrán, W. M. (2008). Aproximación histórico-interpretativa al proceso de diversificación religiosa en Colombia. In S. y. Grupo Interdisciplinario de Estudios de Religión (Ed.), *Mirada pluridisciplinar al hecho religioso en Colombia: Avances de investigación*. Bogotá, DC: Universidad de San Buenaventura.

Diament, M. (1991). Corrupt to the Core. *Hemisphere, 3*(3) (Summer), 20–22.

Engerman, S., & Sokoloff, K. (2002). *Factor endowments, inequality, and paths of development among new world economies* (NBER Working Paper No. 9259). Retrieved from https://www.nber.org/papers/w9259

Figueroa, H. (2016). *La persistance des idées traditionalistes en Colombie. Religion et politique (1886–1952).* Paris: L'Harmattan.

Fukuyama, F. (1995). *Trust: The social virtues and the creation of prosperity.* New York: Free Press.

Garcia Portilla, J. (2019). "Ye shall know them by their fruits": Prosperity and institutional religion in Europe and the Americas. *Religions, 10*(6), 362. MDPI AG. https://doi.org/10.3390/rel10060362.

Gill, A. (1998). *Rendering unto Caesar: The Catholic Church and the state in Latin America.* Chicago, IL: Chicago University Press.

Grier, R. (1997). The effect of religion on economic development: A cross national study of 63 former colonies. *Kyklos, 50*(1), 47–62.

Inglehart, R., & Baker, W. (2000). Modernization, cultural change, and the persistence of traditional values. *American Sociological Review, 65*(1), 19–51.

Kington, T. (2013). *Vatican offers 'time off purgatory' to followers of Pope Francis tweets.* Retrieved from https://www.theguardian.com/world/2013/jul/16/vatican-indulgences-pope-francis-tweets

Lambsdorff, J. G. (2006). Causes and consequences of corruption: What do we know from a cross-section of countries? In S. Rose-Ackerman (Ed.), *International handbook on the economics of corruption* (pp. 3–51). Cheltenham: Edward Elgar.

Levine, D. (1981). *Religion and politics in Latin America: The Catholic Church in Venezuela & Colombia.* Princeton, NJ: Princeton Legacy Library.

Luzzani, T. (2002). *South America. Global corruption report 2001. Transparency.* Mexico, DF: Instituto Ciudadano de Estudios sobre la Inseguridad (ICESI).

Misericordiae Vultus – Bull of indiction of the Extraordinary Jubilee of Mercy. (2015). Retrieved from https://w2.vatican.va/content/francesco/en/apost_letters/documents/papa-francesco_bolla_20150411_misericordiae-vultus.html.

Mockus, A. (2001). *Cultura ciudadana, programa contra la violencia en Santa Fe de Bogotá, Colombia, 1995–1997.* Washington, DC: Banco Interamericano de Desarrollo.

Mockus, A., Murraín, H., & Villa, M. (2012). *Antípodas de la violencia: Desafíos de cultura ciudadana para la crisis de (in)seguridad en América Latina.* Washington, DC: Banco Interamericano de Desarrollo.

Munevar, J. (2008). Transformación doctrinal y actitudinal de la participación política de las iglesias cristianas evangélicas en Colombia. In Grupo Interdisciplinario de Estudios de Religión, Sociedad y Política & GIERSP (Eds.), *Mirada pluridisciplinar al hecho religioso en Colombia: Avances de investigación* (pp. 375–399). Colombia: Bogotá.

Navarro, J. (2016). Religions and law: Current challenges in Latin America. In S. Ferrari & R. Cristofori (Eds.), *Law and religion, an overview* (pp. 111–127). New York: Routledge.

North, D. (1998). *Instituciones, cambio institucional y desempeño económico.* México, DF: Fondo de Cultura Económica.

Porter, M., Stern, S., & Green, M. (2015). *Social progress index 2015.* Retrieved from https://www.socialprogress.org/?tab=2&code=NOR

Rose-Ackerman, S. (2006). *International handbook on the economics of corruption.* Cheltenham: Edward Elgar Publishing.

Transparency International. (2016). *Corruption perceptions index 2016.* Retrieved from https://www.transparency.org/news/feature/corruption_perceptions_index_201
Treisman, D. (2000). The causes of corruption: A cross-national study. *Journal of Public Economics, 76*(3), 399–457.
Uildriks, N. (2009). *Policing insecurity: Police reform, security, and human rights in Latin America.* Plymouth: Lexington Books.
World Economic Forum. (2016). *The global competitiveness report 2014–2015.* Full Data Edition. Geneva: The World Economic Forum.

# Chapter 5
# Conditions (Predictor Variables): Theories Explaining Prosperity Differences *(B)*, *(C)*, *(D)*, *(E)*

Numerous theories attempt to explain cross-country prosperity and corruption differences, which are empirically associated with a broad range of highly correlated factors (Acemoglu & Robinson, 2012; La Porta et al., 1999; Michalopoulos & Papaioannou, 2017; Rose-Ackerman, 2006). The main problem consists in isolating the underlying triggers of prosperity and corruption, as causes are often also consequences operating simultaneously in feedback loops (Lambsdorff, 2006). Essentially, potential prosperity factors can be clustered into three groups: (1) cultural and religious values; (2) institutions and economic growth; (3) environment and geography (Fig. 2.1, Sect. 5.7, and Appendices 1–3 explain the theories, categories, variables, and sources used here in greater detail). This chapter will be limited to defining the conceptual scope of each of these groups of theories for this study (i.e. predictor variables—see Fig. 2.1). Part III (Theoretical Foundations) will further explain the relationships (arrows—see Fig. 2.1) between these groups of theories (predictor variables or conditions) and prosperity (criterion variables or outcome).

Culture and institutions are comprehensive, interdependent concepts and religion interacts as a subset within them both (see Fig. 2.1 and Chap. 10). Institutions and culture have evolved and interacted with mutual feedback effects, thus determining the prosperity of nations. Empirical evidence supports the claim that causality exists in both directions. Culture may change in different ways depending on the type of institutions, while institutions may work differently depending on the cultural context (Alesina & Giuliano, 2015, p. 938).

## 5.1 Culture *(C)*

Abundant empirical research demonstrates that cultural variables determine several economic choices (Alesina & Giuliano, 2015; Guiso et al., 2006; Volonté, 2015). Cultural variables "play an important role in corporate governance practices around the world" (Volonté, 2015, p. 78) and "they even affect the speed of development



J. García Portilla, *"Ye Shall Know Them by Their Fruits"*, Contributions to Economics, https://doi.org/10.1007/978-3-030-78498-0_5

and the wealth of nations" (Alesina & Giuliano, 2015, p. 898). However, culture is a vague concept with no agreed-upon definition. Moreover, culture is a notoriously difficult term to quantify (Paldam, 2001, p. 383), and "difficult to operationalize" (Volonté, 2015, p. 80). Similarly, Alesina and Giuliano contend that defining "culture is an arduous task" since theoretical and empirical definitions of culture are often not easily related (p. 899).

Theoretically, culture has been characterised in a myriad of forms, frequently being defined in relation to rituals, practices, customs, and ways of life (Droogers, 2004, p. 217). The author also observes the empirical challenges of culture as a concept. Anthropologists have concentrated on culture as a fundamental capacity, viewing people as "meaning-makers" (Crick as cited in Droogers, 2004, p.17). For Droogers, the human capacity to create meaning defines culture. Yet, meaning occurs in an intangible, supernatural reality, which is non-empirically verifiable (p. 218).

Comparably, other definitions of culture exhibit similar empirical challenges. For instance, Geertz (1973) defines culture as "a historically transmitted pattern of meanings embodied in symbols" (p. 89), while Greif (1994) observes

> Cultural beliefs are the ideas and thoughts common to several people that govern interaction—between these people and among them, their gods, and other groups—and differ from knowledge in that they are not empirically discovered or analytically proved (Greif as cited in Alesina & Giuliano, 2015, p. 900).

In turn, Alesina and Giuliano refer to "culture as values and beliefs", but they argue that the theoretical literature on culture has also been ambiguous in this regard. On the empirical (quantitative) side that links culture to economic/institutional outcomes, the authors observe that

> ...most papers (if not all) follow the definition adopted by Guiso et al. (2006), where culture is defined as "those customary beliefs and values that ethnic, religious, and social groups transmit fairly unchanged from generation to generation." Empirical papers, therefore, combine values and beliefs in the same definition. (Alesina & Giuliano, 2015, p. 900).

Nevertheless, there is no agreement on the empirical constitutive elements/variables of culture. For instance, Alesina and Giuliano explain the following "cultural traits": *trust, family ties, individualism, generalised morality, work attitudes*, while Herskovits (1952, 1966) describes, among others, the following cultural elements: *technology, economic and social organisation, religion, magic, art, folklore, music, and language*. Meanwhile, the Global Leadership and Organizational Behavior Effectiveness Research Programme (GLOBE) further develops the proposal of Hofstede (2001), presenting the following "cultural dimensions": *power distance, uncertainty avoidance, human orientation, collectivism, assertiveness, gender egalitarianism, future orientation, performance orientation* (House et al., 2004). Yet, measurements of cultural variables (e.g. GLOBE (House et al., 2004); Hofstede, 2001) often overlap with institutions (Volonté, 2015, p. 79) and lack data in many countries in Europe and the Americas. Therefore, this study has excluded GLOBE and Hofstede datasets from the empirical (quantitative and QCA) settings.

For Volonté (2015), attempts to measure culture face two challenges: First, it is problematic to isolate analytically cultural-specific effects given their identification with other national formal institutional characteristics (e.g. law). Intra-country cultural heterogeneity is thus often ignored. Second, no clearly observable variables constituting culture exist.

However, several empirical studies have identified three proxies of culture as appropriate: *religion* (the most prominent in the literature) (Acemoglu et al., 2001; Alesina et al., 2003; Granato et al., 1996; Guiso et al., 2006; Mazar, 2008; Paldam, 2001; Stulz & Williamson, 2003; Volonté, 2015), *language* (Alesina et al., 2003; Mazar, 2008; Volonté, 2015), and *ethnic measures* (Alesina et al., 2003; Guiso et al., 2006). Of course, other extraneous elements can also be present, but these three are the most operational. In fact, the combination of these three cultural proxies is consistent with the historical "cultural project" promoted by the Roman Catholic Church (i.e. Hispanicism in Latin America). This "cultural weapon" has specifically consisted of the triad "religion, language, and race" (Figueroa, 2016); (see Chap. 21). Thus, the integration of these three predominant proxies can empirically (quantitatively) define *culture* in this study. This empirical definition of culture is practical for this research since it can be easily operationalised (e.g. data availability) and does not directly overlap with institutions. Furthermore, this narrow approach has the advantage of reducing the risks of reverse causality (thus focusing on the causal arrow where culture affects prosperity, rather than the contrary) (Guiso et al., 2006, p. 25). Therefore, two-thirds of the empirical setting (correlations and QCA) include the proportion of the population that belongs to the main ethnicities, languages, and religions in each country in Europe and the Americas. Qualitatively, however, culture may be referred to in a broader sense in this study, to include other elements such as values (Alesina & Giuliano, 2015) or power distance (Hofstede, 2001).

### *5.1.1 Cultural Determinism of Prosperity*

Despite the abundant empirical research demonstrating that cultural variables determine economic outcomes (Alesina & Giuliano, 2015; Guiso et al., 2006; Volonté, 2015; Hofstede, 2001; GLOBE (House et al., 2004)), culture has been heavily criticised as a theory that "does not work" as a determinant of prosperity (Acemoglu & Robinson, 2012; McSweeney, 2015).

Acemoglu and Robinson (2012) illustrate how cultural differences are not significant factors. For instance, while North Korea is one of the world's poorest countries, South Korea is one of the most prosperous despite both countries sharing the same language and cultural background (p. 43). Likewise, the authors exemplify the vast prosperity differences between Nogales's high quality of life (in Arizona, USA) and its poor southern neighbour (Nogales, Sonora, Mexico). The inhabitants of both Nogales—i.e. Arizona and Sonora—have the same cultural background. Yet, the Mexican Nogales face high crime rates, corruption, poor education and an inadequate health system (Acemoglu & Robinson, 2012, p. 13). Nevertheless, the authors accept that cultural theory can be helpful as social and cultural standards matter, are difficult to change, and may support institutional differences.

In his critique, McSweeney (2015) argued that cultural determinism makes it impossible to define a "national culture" and that the quantitative approaches in cultural theory underestimate the subnational levels. The author highlights several inconsistencies in the main assumptions that ground the theoretical contributions in cultural and management theory (GLOBE, Hofstede, Hall, among others). McSweeney mentions the difficulties of defining "culture" and "national culture" within a geographical domain. Another issue concerns the misleading acceptance of an invariant or stable "culture". Furthermore, citing numerous sources, McSweeney criticises the statistical or numerical approach of cultural studies.

Firstly, McSweeney discredits any notion claiming that culture permanently and predictably influences, affects, impacts, manifests, or has effects, consequences, or outcomes on the social behaviour of defined populations (McSweeney, 2015, p. 16). He maintains that such claims simply point to correlations, statistical associations, or relationships that provide no evidence for causality (p. 18). McSweeney's objection is very valid. Generally, it has been wrongly and widely accepted in science that correlations are necessarily associated with causality. Indeed, a statistical correlation might be spurious, while causal inferencing is a more complicated process. This study approaches this problem by adopting a mixed methods approach consisting of qualitative and QCA methods to establish causal inference (see Methodology, Chap. 14).

Secondly, McSweeney challenges the notion of geographical boundaries as being appropriate for defining countries and culture (he cites various examples, including India, Turkey, or the former Czechoslovakia). Although these examples are historically accurate, they do not serve to generalise a theory that accounts for reality. For example, if we accept that no boundaries exist, how could we explain the institutional and regulatory differences that exist in every country? Why do some countries require a visa for citizens from other countries? Why can some countries provide higher levels of freedom to their citizens than others? In this sense, institutional theory and history provide better answers to these questions (Acemoglu & Robinson, 2012).

Thirdly, McSweeney claims that the link that GLOBE, Hofstede, Hall, and others establish between culture and actions on a national level provides zero empirical evidence and that their conclusions are biased. This strongly discredits the empirical work undertaken by GLOBE, Hofstede, Hall, and others. Despite McSweeney's objections, Hofstede's and GLOBE's pioneering quantitative approaches have been helpful in a myriad of empirical (quantitative) studies (Staeheli, 2003; Stulz & Williamson, 2003; Volonté, 2015). No single theory or science can devise a perfectly rigorous empirical model, including all possible variables and all the desired representativeness. It is essential to have at least one point of departure, which explains why these works are considered here.

Fourthly, related to the previous criticism, the importance of subnational heterogeneity is also a valid point raised by McSweeney. However, in practical terms, it would be virtually impossible to collect empirical information on a microlevel from every single town and even community in the whole world in order to generate a satisfactory model in McSweeney's terms. Moreover, from an institutional point of view, (regulatory, political, and institutional) differences exist between countries as a whole (as discussed) and therefore produce different prosperity outcomes. This argument is discussed in the following sections and empirical findings of this study (see Sect. 8.3.2; Fig. 8.3 and Table 8.2; Parts V–VII; Appendix 4.2).

Finally, although McSweeney (2015) raises crucial issues and heavily criticises GLOBE, Hofstede, Hall, and other authors, he proposes neither a new model nor a better empirical approach. Citing Wagner (1975), he limits himself to asserting that speaking about national cultures is futile. However, it is better to have a point of departure than none. Science is about generating information and insights that allow us either to explain or to predict reality.

## 5.2 Institutions and Economic Growth *(D)*

Theoretically, institutions are "the rules of the game in a society" (North, 1990, p. 3). Institutions can be either formal, i.e. official and openly codified (e.g. constitutional laws), or informal, i.e. as an unwritten rule and socially shared values (Helmke & Levitsky, 2004). Informal institutions are frequently more persistent than formal ones (North, 1997) and pertain to how laws are enforced (Woodruff, 2006). Empirically, North (1990); Alesina and Giuliano (2015); and Volonté (2015) have defined *informal institutions* as a synonym of *culture* given the practical overlaps of these concepts. Consequently, isolating *institutions* empirically "would be possible only if one counts formal institutions (formal legal systems, formal regulation) as institutions" (Alesina & Giuliano, 2015, p. 902). In turn, Acemoglu et al. (2006) refer to political and economic institutions in their definition, considering institutions as mechanisms through which social choices are determined and implemented.

Institutional theory and other related approaches such as economic theory provide the most robust empirical and theoretical explanations of why some countries are more prosperous than others. For North, the radically different evolution of Anglo- and Latin America reflects the imposition of distinct metropolitan institutions on each colony (North, 1990). The main argument advanced by Acemoglu and Robinson (2012) is that institutions are decisive when explaining the differences and inequality among nations. For the authors, geographical or cultural theories can be influential, but they are useless in terms of clarifying why countries ultimately fail or thrive (Acemoglu & Robinson, 2012). Other economists such as Preston (2012) have also developed extensive theoretical approaches on this issue. Yet, different controversies remain regarding which, where, and how institutions matter for economic prosperity (Alesina & Giuliano, 2015; Glaeser et al., 2004; Woodruff, 2006), (for details, see Chap. 8).

### *5.2.1 Colonialism as an Overarching Explanation and as the Overlapping of Cultural Proxies*

The attributes of the colonising countries have greatly determined present-day institutions in the former colonies, both informally (i.e. culture) and formally (i.e. laws) (Acemoglu et al., 2001, p. 21; North, 1990; Volonté, 2015). Therefore, the colonial legacy of such countries is associated with various factors (e.g. religion, language, and legislation). Typically, Spanish and Portuguese-speaking countries are historically Catholic and apply French civil law, whereas English-speaking countries are historically Protestant and apply common law (Volonté, 2015); (Mazar, 2008) (see Chaps. 8, 9, and 10).

Furthermore, most countries in Europe and the Americas were colonies themselves. Most Latin American countries are former Spanish and Portuguese colonies, while the USA and Canada are former British colonies. At the same time, European colonisers (e.g. Great Britain, Spain, Portugal, France, Germany, or Holland) were colonies of the Roman Empire. This colonial (rather than the indigenous) heritage has substantially shaped institutions in most of the colonised countries. Colonisers often transferred or imposed their solid institutions and *status quo* to their colonies. Thus, when "the conquerors colonised much of the world, they brought with them their culture (laws and institutions); they settled and shaped the present public administration" (Mazar, 2008, p. 176). While many former colonies revised their legislation after independence, only few have shifted far away from the original code (Mazar, 2008; Merryman & Pérez, 2015; World Bank, International Finance Corporation & Oxford University Press, 2004).

The Protestant Reformation led to an institutional deviation of the medieval *status quo* in its countries of influence (see below). Such deviation was transposed to the colonies. In turn, Spanish and Portuguese colonialism upheld the medieval *status quo* by emphasising the authoritarian and feudal-hierarchical roles of the Roman Church and the states (Andreski as cited in Grier, 1997, p.47; Acemoglu et al., 2001).

Religion and the state were united for the majority of colonial history. The state enforced religion, meaning that it was mostly not a matter of individual choice. However, the modern sovereign state system emerged from the Thirty Year War waged by Protestants against the imposition of Roman Catholicism by Ferdinand II (leading to The Peace of Westphalia in 1648). The separation of church and state occurred first and foremost in Protestant territories since the Reformation (Snyder, 2011; Wilson, 2009; Witte, 2002). This separation established itself as a driving force of prosperity (Grier, 1997; Fanfani, 1936).

Nonetheless, colonialism has largely been treated separately from religion (or even as a competing explanation). This conceptual error has led scholars to empirically test endogenous variables. On the one hand, religion is typically reduced to its proportion of adherents (which can normally result from the effect of historical institutions and more recent trends, such as Pentecostalism or Agnosticism) (Sect. 10.4.3). On the other, colonial institutions include the historical and institutional influence of religion (which is more important than the number of adherents) (e.g. Protestant British colonies as against Roman Catholic Spanish/Portuguese colonies). Therefore, it is not surprising that empirical studies such as Grier (1997) find that Protestantism (adherents) does not significantly lessen the gap between the economic performance of former colonies notwithstanding an overwhelming correlation between Protestantism and economic growth (GDP). Thus, the weight of British colonial institutions (including Protestantism) in historically Protestant countries ought to be more decisive than the current Protestant (mostly Pentecostal) adherents within historically Catholic countries, for instance.

Furthermore, Woodberry's (2012) empirical findings also help better understand that religion and colonialism have been intervening and complementary mechanisms rather than competing explanations. Colonial institutions, including religion transported from Europe, were highly influential in the New World (Woodberry, 2012, p. 244). Thus, North America, for instance, inherited the same institutional outcomes that distinguished Great Britain from Spain or Portugal as far back as the Protestant Reformation (Sects. 8.2.2 and 8.3.4).

## 5.3 Religion (Cultural and Institutional Influences) *(B)*[1]

### *5.3.1 The Institutional Influence of Religion Has Been More Decisive to Prosperity than the Cultural Effect of Religious Affiliation (Adherents)*

At least two dimensions of the influence of religion need to be taken seriously: institutional and cultural (adherents) (Manow, 2004, p. 9). Yet, religion is mostly considered as an important expression of culture (Guiso et al., 2006; Mazar, 2008; Volonté, 2015). For Anderson (2007), "culture was historically shaped in large part by religion and because most religious traditions sat uneasily with democratic ideas and practices, it was hard to see democracy thriving outside the Anglo-Protestant world" (p.383).

Furthermore, religion is usually assumed to be central to economic development (Becker & Woessmann, 2009, p. 533). Thus, many empirical studies associating cultural variables with economic outcomes widely follow the Protestant ethics-based theory proposed by Max Weber. The work ethics Weberian theory is considered "…the most famous link between culture and economic development" (Acemoglu et al., 2006, p. 401).

[1]Originally published as "Introduction" in: Garcia Portilla, J. (2019). "Ye Shall Know Them by Their Fruits": Prosperity and Institutional Religion in Europe and the Americas. *Religions*, *10*(6), 362. MDPI AG. Retrieved from https://doi.org/10.3390/rel10060362 

Accordingly, most empirical studies linking religion and economics associate variables of religious adherence and economic performance. The dominant research paradigm has centred on the influence of *the proportion of believers* (so-called *market share* or *cultural influence of religion*) on prosperity/corruption, but has mostly disregarded the *institutional influence of religion*. Consequently, sociological explanations of the prosperity–religion nexus are often either solely Weberian (work ethic) or sheer hypothesis. This means that they have not further developed or been related to other disciplines and historical sources (see Sect. 7.1).

Studies such as La Porta et al. (1999) and Barro (1997) have effectively isolated the effects of religion adherence (yet, not of religiosity) on political, economic, and legal outcomes (McCleary & Barro, 2006). However, the Weberian cultural argument that the beliefs of individual Protestants led to higher productivity has failed to work in several other cases (e.g. Acemoglu et al., 2001, 2006; Cantoni, 2015; Delacroix & Nielsen, 2001). Quantitative studies analysing the influence of institutions (Acemoglu et al., 2001, 2006) or cultural determinants (Hofstede, 2001) on prosperity have also reduced religion to its adherents' influence on institutions, culture, or prosperity. For instance, Acemoglu and Robinson (2012) dedicate an entire chapter to criticising Weberian Protestant ethics as a theory that is unable to explain prosperity differences across countries. Likewise, Hofstede (2001) states that industrialisation is what brings people to believe in more "inclusive" religious systems such as Protestantism, rather than vice versa. Such assertions result from empirically analysing the proportion of believers while disregarding the historical and institutional influence of religion. Thus, considering religion only as a cultural factor (i.e. adherents) results in trivialised or misunderstood relations between religion, institutions, and prosperity/transparency. Moreover, the difficulty of separating the effect of religious adherents from other possible (and varying) causes of prosperity (e.g. institutions and geography) adds endogeneity to cross-country studies (Becker & Woessmann, 2009, p. 533).

Nevertheless, the relationship between religious institutions and the state is identified as being the most important explanatory variable in the theory of Religious Competition (based on Rational Choice Theory; see Sect. 7.2) (Chaves & Cann, 1992; Wilde et al., 2010). Yet, the effect of religious institutions has been largely ignored, favouring religious pluralism as a means to measure competition (Olson, 1993; Wilde et al., 2010).

Undoubtedly, robust statistical data exists for nominal religion adherents in cross-country studies. Hence, most of the literature on religion as a corruption/prosperity determinant has only considered the proportion of adherents, even if religion cannot be reduced to this sole indicator. The ample data available on religious adherents may partly explain why most empirical literature utilises this variable as a proxy of the cultural effects of religion on prosperity/corruption.

The objective of this section (and book) is not to critique the mostly studied *cultural influence of religion* but to concentrate on the *institutional path of religion*, which the author believes is more crucial to prosperity in the long term. Indeed, the historical effect of religious institutions (i.e. state–church, law, education) is more lasting and pervasive than current individual religious choices based on "freewill"

(Becker & Woessmann, 2009; Inglehart & Baker, 2000; Merryman & Pérez, 2007; Witte, 2002). Guiso et al. (2006) observed in this regard

> . . .people choose neither their parents nor the religion of their parents [. . .], parents have a natural tendency to teach their children what they have learned from their own parents, without a full reassessment of the current optimality of those beliefs. . . (p. 32, 25)

In fact, the individual's religious orientations are largely the resultant heritage of the historical institutional interactions of state and church. According to Vallier (1970), *this is not necessarily connected to the influence of individual's religious beliefs. Rather, it is related to the institutional repercussions that religious corporations have on the operation of civil power structures, social groups, and on the continuity of general ground rules that affect role processes and daily exchanges* (Vallier, 1970, pp. 157–58).

In the end, religion and politics were quite evidently integrated until the Protestant Reformation. Thus, institutional religion preceded and gave rise to the state (Snyder, 2011). Certainly, a key feature of various relevant studies (e.g. Becker et al., 2016; Becker & Woessmann, 2009; Gill, 1998; Woodberry, 2012) has been the identification of Protestantism as a destabilising element of institutional Roman Catholic hegemony. Such an element has proven more important than the effects of religious believers per se. The influence of institutional religion is pervasive to this day, both in Europe and in the Americas (Figs. 8.1, 8.2, and 8.3; Table 8.2).

Furthermore, the crucial element that determines the dominant religion in a country or region has been how the state has supported that religion. The fate of the Reformations was ultimately dictated by rulers' decisions on which religious denomination to follow, which causes to endorse, and how harshly to suppress the propagation of heterodox doctrines. These choices were so crucial that *no Protestant success has ever been achieved in Catholic-Protestant disputes without either state or foreign assistance.* The counter-reformation eventually regained territories with large Protestant communities that persisted under Catholic jurisdictions, such as Hungary, Bohemia, and parts of France (te Brake as cited in Nexon, 2011, p. 152).

However, it is not always easy to empirically differentiate between cultural and institutional influences of religion as they are well connected (Barro & McCleary, 2005). Barro and McCleary (2005) developed a close empirical approach to institutional religion in their classification of "*State religion*" (an independent indicator considered in the QCA analysis in Chap. 16). "*State religion*" is, however, mostly also related to population adherence and does not account, for instance, for the international agreements (concordats) between the Roman See and individual countries. My study brackets those indicators and thus lends theoretical and empirical weight both to the institutional (e.g. including concordats) and, to a lesser extent, the cultural (mainly operationalised as adherents) influences of religion.

Therefore, in this study, *religion* contains "institutional variables" (e.g. state religion, concordats) as a subset of institutions, and "cultural variables" (e.g. nominal religion adherents) as a subset of culture.

### 5.3.2 *Definitions of Protestantism and Roman Catholicism*

Engelhardt (2007) observes that Protestantism and Roman Catholicism have historically defined themselves as being set against each other in a "mutually defining dialectic" (p.28). The Protestants first defined themselves "in their protest against the heresies of Rome" (e.g. papal universal jurisdiction, purgatory, and indulgences) (p. 37) (see Sect. 10.4.1.3). The author continues, "[b]y default, Protestants thought themselves constrained to put the Bible in the place the church had traditionally held" (p. 37). In turn, the "Roman Church then defined itself against the Protestants in the Council of Trent (1545–1563) and through the Counter Reformation" (p. 29).

#### 5.3.2.1 Definition of Protestantism

Protestants are defined as being members or followers "of several church denominations denying the universal authority of the Pope and affirming the Reformation principles of justification by faith alone, the priesthood of all believers, and the primacy of the Bible as the only source of revealed truth" (Merriam-Webster, n.d.-a). Likewise, this study refers to Protestants as members of historical Protestant churches (e.g. Lutherans, Methodists, Baptists, Seventh-day Adventists, or Presbyterians) (Pew Research Center, 2014, p. 7). The Protestant Reformation is defined as a sixteenth century movement in Europe that rejected the Roman Church's abuses, initially attempted to modify and improve the Catholic Church, and ultimately established the historical Protestant and Reformed Churches (Merriam-Webster, n.d.-a; Cambridge University Dictionary, 2014; Oxford University Press, 2016).

For his part, Köhrsen (2017) distinguishes three streams of Protestantism: (1) Historical Protestantism; (2) Non-charismatic forms of evangelicalism; and (3) Charismatic forms of evangelicalism (Pentecostalism). For Köhrsen, many historical and non-charismatic Protestant communities have undergone a charismatic turn, thus moving them closer to the Pentecostal movement today (pp. 3–5).

Although this book refers to the Pentecostal movements, this research often emphasises the historical streams of Protestantism, given their accumulated institutional influence (see Sect. 8.3 and Chap. 9). Therefore, historically Protestant countries are so defined according to their traditional religious heritage (Inglehart & Baker, 2000), which does not necessarily reflect whether the majority of their current population are Protestant adherents.

#### 5.3.2.2 Definition of Roman Catholicism

The Roman Catholic Church-State (Roman Catholicism or Romanism) is defined since the Reformation as "a Christian church having a hierarchy of priests and bishops under the pope, a liturgy centered in the Mass, veneration of the Virgin Mary and saints, clerical celibacy, and a body of dogma including transubstantiation and papal infallibility" (Merriam-Webster, n.d.-b). Evidently, the Roman Church-State is not a monolithic entity, but differentiation exists within it (e.g. the Latin Rite and the Eastern Rites; or contrasting ideologies such as the extreme right (Opus Dei) and left (liberation theology) (Figueroa, 2016; Werz, 2008), (see Sect. 10.4.1.4). The Roman Church-State is a complex and diverse organisation (Gill, 1998). As Agnew (2010) observes

> The Roman Catholic Church is perhaps an extreme case of a faith tradition with a highly organised hierarchical structure that operates worldwide but must adjust itself to local and world-regional contexts that can challenge and subvert its central doctrines, operational principles, and political compromises with secular authorities (p. 43).

However, regardless of the internal differentiation, Canon Law has defined the papacy as the "Supreme Authority of the Church" since the Middle Ages (i.e. including post-Vatican II) (Canons 330–367; Molano, 1983). Molano observes that according to Canon Law, the "Supreme Authority of the Church" is the head of both individual Churches and their congregations, including the Universal Church, structured as a communion of Churches or "*Corpus Ecclesiarum*" (Molano, 1983, p. 20).

Furthermore, the "Vatican is a centralized bureaucracy that oversees the various aspects of the international Church related to people, theology, education, law, missions, and ecumenism" (O'Reilly & Chalmers, 2014, p. 196). Since the Vatican State was created through the Lateran Treaty with Mussolini's National Fascist Party, "the Church has, if anything expanded its presence as a unique 'church-state'" (Agnew, 2010, p. 46). For instance, the number of states entertaining diplomatic relations with the Roman See almost quadrupled after Vatican II (from 46 to 177) (Ragazzi, 2009; The Permanent Observer Mission of the Holy See to the United Nations, 2020).

Therefore, this study considers the Roman Catholic Church not merely as a religious organisation, but as the oldest state that "inherited the mantle of the Roman Empire and its imperial territoriality" (Agnew, 2010, p. 41). As the author explains, "...when the Roman Empire collapsed in Western Europe, only the Church represented institutionally in perpetuity what little was left of the *pax romana*" (Ibid).

Although this book highlights the existence of less intransigent sectors, the research often emphasises the most conservative and intolerant wing of Roman Catholicism (which has been historically dominant, institutionally) (Figueroa, 2016). Thus, by focusing primarily on an institutional level, there is a risk of labelling the Roman Church-State a "black box". However, as Gill (1998) argues, there are many compelling reasons to study the Roman Catholic Church as a single entity. Firstly, the Catholic Church's hierarchical structure tends to limit internal divisiveness. Although there may be continuing discussion within the Church over policy direction, there is a general loyalty to authority with regard to taking action. The author illustrates such Catholic deference to authority with some bishops who may disagree with keeping the priesthood celibate, but they rarely ordain married priests in their dioceses. Likewise, Catholic Church leaders have a deep desire to show and preserve a united front, especially regarding significant policy decisions. A fractured Church loses bargaining power as well as spiritual legitimacy. Crucial policy positions (such as openly rejecting a military regime) would almost certainly be disputed within the hierarchy, but bishops usually disregard any disagreement and defer to the final decision (pp. 9–10).

## 5.4 Dependency and World Systems Theories

According to dependency theory, local allies who control social, cultural, economic, and political institutions in developing countries implement policies and programmes designed by developed nations. Thus, in this view, the misery and inequality abounding in Latin America are, for instance, not fortuitous but a consequence of capitalist progress in the developed world (Levine, 1981). This dependency theory strand has been very influential in Latin America and corresponds to the Marxist version, one of whose leading advocates is Andre Gunder Frank (Drexler-Dreis, 2017, p. 275).

Such ideas inspired the Economic Commission for Latin America and the Caribbean (ECLAC) to explain Latin America's role in the global economy as being restricted to a primary product exporter (Prebisch, 1950). Later, the gradual failure of ECLAC reformism led to a revision of these views (Preston, 2012, p. 6). Indeed, traditional institutional approaches aiming to alleviate prosperity problems such as inequality, poverty, or corruption include the highly technically based and controversially discussed policy recipes of the ECLAC, the World Bank, or the International Monetary Fund (IMF). While aiming to guide governments in Latin America and the developing world, such policy recipes have often failed or even worsened the social situation in certain developing countries (Stiglitz, 2002). This observation suggests that the causes of structural prosperity have not been adequately addressed.

And yet, dependency theory is widely accepted a priori. Dependency theorists, liberation theologians, and leftist Latin American governments commonly accept US "imperialism" as a predominant cause of poverty in Latin America (Castañeda, 2006; Galeano, 1971; Gutiérrez, 1973). However, there is little empirical evidence to support this approach. For example, Venezuela and Bolivia are not wealthier since opposing the USA; in fact, the opposite is true. Likewise, Colombia and Costa Rica are not more impoverished for being US allies.

Dependency theories regard the core (prosperous) countries as so-called hegemons. Semi-peripheral and peripheral countries are usually former colonies. Such a division raises other crucial questions: Why does Spain, as the coloniser of Latin America, still face economic problems to this day? Why does the USA appear as a hegemon if it was once a British colony? Why did the USA achieve prosperity levels that other colonies could not? Dependency theory does not properly answer these questions and instead misleads analysis. For example, it mistakenly assumes that US "hegemonical exploitation" has caused the poverty problems of Latin America, thereby disregarding other real structural problems.

However, dependency theory might be helpful in order to trace the hegemony of colonial institutions and elites. Empirical and historical evidence shows that after the former Spanish/Portuguese colonies gained independence, hegemony was handed to local elites. Consequently, the relative socio-economic situation of Latin America did not change much; instead, the extractivist tendency persisted (Acemoglu et al., 2001; Acemoglu & Robinson, 2012). Yet, "dependency" analyses typically exclude or deny the historical ties and dependency on the Roman Church-State. Nonetheless, this study reveals a clear tendency: the greater the Roman Catholic influence in a country (e.g. the Church's substantial control over education), the worse the country's conditions (see Sect. 8.3.2; Fig. 8.3 and Table 8.2; Parts III, V–VII; Appendix 4.2).

### *5.4.1 World Systems Theory*

Dependency theory has led to further developments, including World Systems Theory, which divides the world into peripheral countries, semi-peripheral countries, and core countries.

This theory is only applicable on a global level (Papademetriou & Martin, 1991, p. 10). Therefore, world systems theory is criticised as:

> a grand historical generalisation, a by-product of a univocal, reductionist and sense-loaded interpretation of history in which all countries pass through similar processes, as if following a grand script or some rigid laws of historical development (Arango, 2000, p. 291).

This theory suggests the existence of a global economic behaviour centred on capitalist penetration from industrialised countries to peripheral areas. Furthermore, peripheral countries provide a permanent flow of resources and migrant labour that most prosperous countries require (Wallerstein, 2006). The global system's existence depends on international flows of capital, supply resources, markets, and labour.

## 5.5 Factor Endowments Theory (Institutions and Geography)

Factor endowments theory extends institutional theory as it also considers various political and institutional insights along with geographical factors. Among such theorists, Engerman and Sokoloff (2002) explain differences in growth rates of per capita income in the New World. They found that the initial differences between the degree of inequality in the Americas can be mainly attributed to endowment factors:

> ...that great equality or homogeneity among the population led [in the North], over time, to more democratic political institutions, to more investment in public goods and infrastructure, and to institutions that offered relatively broad access to economic opportunities. In contrast, where there was extreme inequality, as in most of the societies of the Americas, political institutions were less democratic, investments in public goods and infrastructure were more limited, and the institutions that evolved tended to provide highly unbalanced access to economic opportunities and thereby greatly advantaged the elite" (Engerman & Sokoloff, 2002, p. 4).[2]

Accordingly, initial inequality and soil and climatic conditions on the equator led to the production of large quantities of high-value crops, such as sugar cane or tobacco in Central and South America. Such crops were characterised by extensive scale economies associated with the use of slaves and a self-ennriching elite that perpetuated inequality over time. In contrast, the US and Canadian economies were developed based on a "free land" model, which provided plots suitable for family farms to all those who settled and worked the land for a specified period. This model led to an equal distribution of land and wealth (Engerman & Sokoloff, 2002).

Factor endowments theory is based on empirical research that correlates wealth inequality, human capital, and political power to account for divergent economic growth records. Consequently, this notion only partly explains countries' failure or success by solely concentrating on their economic growth. Furthermore, this theory provides no comprehensive explanation that would in turn lead to a holistic understanding of countries' prosperity, as the present study claims. It focuses exclusively on the macro-economic achievements of countries and fails to explain other related aspects such as corruption.

Like environmental and geographical theory, factor endowments theory does not consider the historical differences between the European colonisers of the Americas—i.e. the differing influence of the Iberian Peninsula and Great Britain on their respective colonies. European colonisers had different cultural backgrounds (e.g. Spanish or English). Thus, they did not merely "behave differently" in North America because it was not densely populated compared with South and Central America, where they found a densely concentrated population. This assumption would not explain the cases of Brazil or Argentina, which were not densely populated before European colonisation and currently display extractive institutions like the rest of Latin America.

Moreover, another related question is whether Canada and USA would be the countries they are today if the Spaniards and Portuguese had colonised North America. Huntington (2004) argues that they would most probably not; in turn, they would look like other Latin American countries, sharing similar vices, institutions, and cultural heritage. Great Britain built egalitarian societies in North America, whereas Spain and Portugal replicated their "extractive" and elitist models throughout Latin America (Acemoglu & Robinson, 2012). In sum, in tándem with

[2] 

environment and geography theories, factor endowments theory can be considered as another piece of the explanation puzzle.

## 5.6 Environment and Geography *(E)*: The Environmental Performance Index *(EPI)*

Vast empirical information supports a strong association between environment/geography and prosperity. The theoretical explanations also make sense (see Chap. 12).

The *Environmental Performance Index (EPI)* is expressed in percentages and aggregates more than 20 indicators reflecting national-level environmental data (Hsu et al., 2016, p. 27). It comprises nine categories: health impacts, air quality, water and sanitation, water resources, agriculture, forests, fisheries, biodiversity and habitat, and climate and energy. The EPI is a comprehensive index and results from the transformation of "raw datasets into comparable performance indicators, which requires standardizing raw values according to population, land area, gross domestic product, and other common units of measurement" (Hsu et al., 2016, p. 28).

Previous studies have already found robust correlations between environment (EPI) and competitiveness (GCI), suggesting that the most competitive countries also have the best environmental conditions and performance (dos Santos & Siqueira Brandi, 2014; Kasimovskaya & Didenko, 2014). Moreover,

> ...there is no necessary trade-off between being competitive and being sustainable. On the contrary, many countries at the top of the competitiveness rankings are also the best performers in many areas of sustainability (World Economic Forum, 2012).

In Part V, the EPI is incorporated into regression analysis and QCA models on account of its precise and comprehensive nature. Such incorporation reflects the abundant empirical literature linking countries' prosperity indicators to environmental and geographical variables (see Chap. 12).

## 5.7 Summary of Theories Explaining Differences in Prosperity and Insights from New Economic History

Table 5.1 summarises the leading prosperity theories, which are based on empirical (i.e. quantitative) research. The table shows postulates, issues, and authors in diverse fields approaching the difference of prosperity across countries.

Table 5.1 presents a non-exhaustive list of perspectives that shows why some countries are more prosperous than others. However, the listed theories do not address the prosperity phenomenon from a holistic perspective (i.e. in all its complexity). Likewise, this table mainly presents theories (and advocates) that base their empirical research on quantitative data and methods.

**Table 5.1** Prosperity theories in different fields (Author's figure)

| Leading determinist theories (based on quantitative empirical research) | Main postulates | | Critical issues not addressed explicitly by the theory in question | | | Main advocates | Data restrictions or issues to model (this research) |
|---|---|---|---|---|---|---|---|
| Dependence; world systems | Divides the world into core countries (hegemons), semi-peripheral countries, and peripheral countries (former colonies) | Hegemons are exploiters; the role of the former colonies in the world economy is restricted to being primary product exporters. | Why do the colonisers of Latin America (Spain and Portugal) face prosperity issues until today? Why could the USA achieve prosperity levels that the other colonies could not achieve? Why is a former British colony considered a hegemon? | | | (Wallerstein, 2006); (Prebisch, 1950); (ECLAC; Prebisch; Singer; Furtado; Pinto; Baran; Gunder); (Preston, 2012); Liberation theologians. | Only around one-fourth of the countries in the database provide data on colonial power (binomial) |
| Institutions[a] | Institutional feedback loops explain prosperity and inequality among nations. | Although geographical or cultural theories can be compelling, they are useless. | Who has the power to mould institutions? | Which ethical and moral principles are able to establish trustworthy institutions? | These theories often provide anecdotal explanations that illumine changes in different institutions/legal systems. | (North, 1990); (Acemoglu & Robinson, 2012) | Endogeneity. GCI index already includes institutional indicators. |
| Legal origin[b] | "The economic consequences of legal origins are pervasive". The differences between legal origins are profound enough for them to manifest themselves in different strategies for exercising social control over economic life, "even after centuries of legal and regulatory evolution". | | Who has the power to develop the legal codes? | Which ethical and moral principles are able to establish trustworthy legal codes? | | (La Porta et al., 2008) | No issues (full access to comprehensive databases for all countries). |

| | | | | | |
|---|---|---|---|---|---|
| Culture | Similarities and differences in norms, values, beliefs, and practices among societies may determine the prosperity of nations. | It is impossible to define a "national culture". Quantitative approaches to culture underestimate subnational levels. | Cultural theory fails to explain outliers (e.g. Nogales (US-Mexico) or North-South Korea). | (Hofstede, 2001); GLOBE (House et al., 2004) | Less than 20 countries in the database provide data for Europe and the Americas. Weak representativeness of the samples and categories utilised. |
| Religion and values[b] | The Protestant reformation ended the millennium-old hegemony of the Catholic Church in Western Europe and established the basis for prosperity, thus changing political and economic fortunes. | Failing the context of other theories (e.g. legal origin, environment), prosperity theory based on religion and values is unable to explain outliers. For example, why are Ireland or Austria, or subnationally (e.g. Bavaria in Germany, Lucerne in Switzerland) prosperous despite being predominantly Roman Catholic regions? | | (Weber, 1905); (Huntington, 2004); (Fukuyama, 1995); (Becker et al., 2016) | No issues (full access to comprehensive databases for all countries). |
| Environment and geography[a] | Geography directly impacts prosperity. Favourable environmental and climate factors enabled European states to develop and conquer other lands. | Neither geography nor the environment are able to explain historical "reversals of fortune" (e.g. prosperity on the American continent before and after European colonisation), or why cases such as Russia or Argentina are outliers in a large continental trend. Climate theory has been criticised since the nineteenth century. | | (Diamond, 1997); (Sachs, 2001); (Brown & Lall, 2006) | No issues (full access to comprehensive databases for all countries). |

[a]One model linking postulates of both theories is "Factor Endowments"(Engerman & Sokoloff, 2002)

[b]Legal origin might be considered part of institutional theory and as such is also related to institutional religion (Chap. 8). However, its data is not directly included in the GCI, and thus resolves the endogeneity problem of institutional indices. Religion and values can be part of cultural theory; however, the respective datasets differ (i.e. neither the GLOBE nor Hofstede's database contains such data)

In contrast to the above theories, I approach the prosperity/corruption phenomenon holistically. This means that rather than excluding theoretical approaches (cultural, institutional, environmental), I regard those approaches as intervening triggers (not as competing explanations) from diverse disciplines. Therefore, all the theories listed here are considered valid and complementary. The next sections complement the identified prosperity triggers and interrelations with empirical and theoretical evidence from different disciplines (see research model, Fig. 2.1).

### 5.7.1 Insights from New Economic History

*New Economic History* is an interdisciplinary approach dedicated to analysing the causes of prosperity through integrating historical and other social sciences with mathematical models and econometric techniques. Such integration reconciles previously exclusivist disciplinary approaches through combining factors, theories, and disciplines, rather than offering mono-causal explanations. In contrast, the neo-classic economic approach considered history, geography/ecology, and culture (including religion and social norms) as "residuals". The neo-classical approach left little room to explicitly model "residuals", which has long been the dominant approach in the literature (Michalopoulos & Papaioannou, 2017).

Moreover, separate mono-causal prosperity theories tend to refute advances made in other research fields. For instance, Sachs (2001, 2003) claimed that environment and geography alone thoroughly explain prosperity variations among countries. Acemoglu and Robinson (2012) made the same case for institutions.

However, each of these distinct theories may contain "a grain of truth" about understanding prosperity imbalances between countries (Moran et al., 2007, p. 3). Ideally, prosperity theories should be complementary instead of competing explanations. For example, geography and environmental theories explain how seasonal lands can provide a society and its economy better conditions to prosper (Diamond, 1997); (Sachs, 2001). Institutional theory helps explain how institutions model social prosperity by perpetuating equality loops or by concentrating wealth (Acemoglu & Robinson, 2012; North, 1990). Cultural theory contributes to the understanding of the influence of cultural variables, such as religious beliefs and values, on prosperity (Alesina & Giuliano, 2015; Hofstede, 2001; Landes, 1999; Volonté, 2015). Some scholars, among others La Porta et al. (1999), Treisman (2000), and Michalopoulos and Papaioannou (2017), have therefore taken a systemic approach to prosperity theories.

The relations among environment/geography, culture, institutions, and prosperity are highly complex and involve massive historical dynamics which would normally far exceed the scope of empirical research (Paldam, 2001, p. 384). Nonetheless, La Porta et al.'s (1999) comprehensive study significantly advance research by examining potential determinants of government performance in up to 152 countries. The authors concluded that countries exhibiting inferior government performance are (1) poor, (2) close to the equator, (3) ethnolinguistically heterogeneous, (4) use

French or socialist laws, or (5) have high proportions of Catholics or Muslims (La Porta et al., 1999).

In a similarly ambitious empirical study, Treisman (2000) reached comparable conclusions. Prosperous economies are less corrupt countries with Protestant traditions, histories of British rule, and with prolonged exposure to democracy (short, present-day democracies are not statistically significant) (Treisman, 2000, p. 399).

## References


Acemoglu, D., Johnson, S., & Robinson, J. (2001). The colonial origins of comparative development: An empirical investigation. *American Economic Review, 91*(5), 1369–1401.

Acemoglu, D., Johnson, S., & Robinson, J. (2006). Institutions as a fundamental cause of long-run growth. In P. Aghion & S. N. Durlauf (Eds.), *Handbook of economic growth* (Vol. 1A). Amsterdam: North-Holland.

Acemoglu, D., & Robinson, J. (2012). *Why nations fail. The origins of power, prosperity and poverty*. New York: Crown Business.

Agnew, J. (2010). Deus Vult: The geopolitics of the Catholic Church. *Geopolitics, 15*(1), 39–61.

Alesina, A., Devleeschauwer, A., Easterly, W., Sergio, K., & Wacziarg, R. (2003). Fractionalization. *Journal of Economic Growth, 8*(2), 155–194.

Alesina, A., & Giuliano, P. (2015). Culture and institutions. *Journal of Economic Literature, 53*(4), 898–944.

Anderson, J. (2007). Religion, politics and international relations. The Catholic contribution to democratization's 'third wave': Altruism, hegemony or self-interest? *Cambridge Review of International Affairs, 20*(3), 383–399.

Arango, J. (2000). Explaining migration: A critical view. *International Social Science Journal, 52* (165), 283–296.

Barro, R. J. (1997). *Determinants of economic growth: A cross-country empirical study*. Cambridge, MA: MIT Press.

Barro, R. J., & McCleary, R. M. (2005). Which countries have state religions? *The Quarterly Journal of Economics, 120*(4), 1331–1370.

Becker, S., Pfaff, S., & Rubin, J. (2016). *Causes and consequences of the protestant reformation*. Warwick Economics Research Paper Series.

Becker, S. O., & Woessmann, L. (2009). Was Weber wrong? A human capital theory of Protestant economic history. *Quarterly Journal of Economics, 124*(2), 531–596.

Brown, C., & Lall, U. (2006). Water and economic development: The role of variability and a framework for resilience. *Natural Resources Forum, 30*(4), 306–317.

Cambridge University. (2014). *The Cambridge University dictionary*. Retrieved from: https://dictionary.cambridge.org/

Cantoni, D. (2015). The economic effects of the Protestant reformation: Testing the Weber hypothesis in the German lands. *Journal of the European Economic Association, 13*(4), 561–598.

Castañeda, J. G. (2006). Latin America's left turn. *Foreign Affairs, 85*(3), 28–43. https://doi.org/10.2307/20031965.

Chaves, M., & Cann, D. E. (1992). Regulation, pluralism, and religious market structure: Explaining religion's vitality. *Rationality and Society, 4*(3), 272–290. https://doi.org/10.1177/1043463192004003003.

Delacroix, J., & Nielsen, F. (2001). The beloved myth: Protestantism and the rise of industrial capitalism in nineteenth-century Europe. *Social Forces, 80*(2), 509–553.

Diamond, J. (1997). *Guns, germs, and steel. The fates of human societies*. New York: W.W. Norton & Company.

dos Santos, S. F., & Siqueira Brandi, H. (2014). A canonical correlation analysis of the relationship between sustainability and competitiveness. *Clean Technologies and Environmental Policy, 16* (8), 1735–1746.

Drexler-Dreis, J. (2017). The option for the poor as a decolonial option: Latin American liberation theology in conversation with Teología India and womanist theology. *Political Theology, 18*(3), 269–286.

Droogers, A. (2004). Syncretism, power, play. In A. M. Leopold & J. S. Jensen (Eds.), *Syncretism in religion: A reader*. New York: Routledge.

Engelhardt, T. H. (2007). Why ecumenism fails: Taking theological differences seriously. *Christian Bioethics, 13*(1), 25–51.

Engerman, S., & Sokoloff, K. (2002). *Factor endowments, inequality, and paths of development among new world economies* (NBER Working Paper No. 9259). Retrieved from https://www.nber.org/papers/w9259

Fanfani, A. (1936). *Catholicism, Protestantism, and capitalism*. Norfolk: IHS Press.

Figueroa, H. (2016). *La persistance des idées traditionalistes en Colombie. Religion et politique (1886–1952)*. Paris: L'Harmattan.

Fukuyama, F. (1995). *Trust. The social virtues and the creation of prosperity*. New York: Free Press.

Galeano, E. (1971). *Las venas abiertas de América Latina*. México: siglo xxi editores, s.a. de c.v.

Garcia Portilla, J. (2019). "Ye shall know them by their fruits": Prosperity and institutional religion in Europe and the Americas. *Religions, 10*(6), 362. MDPI AG. https://doi.org/10.3390/rel10060362.

Geertz, C. (1973). *The interpretation of cultures*. New York: Basic Books.

Gill, A. (1998). *Rendering unto Caesar: The Catholic Church and the state in Latin America*. Chicago, IL: Chicago University Press.

Glaeser, E., La Porta, R., Lopez-de-Silanes, F., & Shleifer, A. (2004). Do institutions cause growth? *Journal of Economic Growth, 9*(3), 271–303.

Granato, J., Inglehart, R., & Leblang, D. (1996). The effect of cultural values on economic development: Theory, hypotheses, and some empirical tests. *American Journal of Political Science, 40*(3), 607–631.

Greif, A. (1994). Cultural beliefs and the Organization of Society: A historical and theoretical reflection on collectivist and individualist societies. *Journal of Political Economy, 102*(5), 912–950.

Grier, R. (1997). The effect of religion on economic development: A cross national study of 63 former colonies. *Kyklos, 50*(1), 47–62.

Guiso, L., Sapienza, P., & Zingales, L. (2006). Does culture affect economic outcomes? *Journal of Economic Perspectives, 20*(2), 23–48.

Gutiérrez, G. (1973). *A theology of liberation: History, politics, and salvation*. Maryknoll: Orbis Books.

Helmke, G., & Levitsky, S. (2004). Informal institutions and comparative politics: A research agenda. *Perspectives on Politics, 4*, 725–740.

Herskovits, M. J. (1952). *Les Bases de l'Anthropologie Culturelle*. Payot: Trans. F. Vaudou. Paris.

Herskovits. (1966). *The New World negro: Selected papers in Afroamerican studies*. Bloomington, IN: Indiana University Press.

Hofstede, G. (2001). *Culture's consequences. Comparing values, Behaviours, institutions and organizations across nations*. Thousand Oaks, CA: Sake Publications.

House, R. J., Hanges, P. J., Javidan, M., Dorfman, P. W., & Gupta, V. (Eds.). (2004). *Culture, leadership, and organizations: The GLOBE study of 62 societies*. Thousand Oaks, CA: Sage Publications.

Hsu, A., Alexandre, N., Cohen, S., Jao, P., & Khusainova, E. (2016). *Environmental performance index*. New Haven, CT: Yale University.

Huntington, S. (2004). The Hispanic challenge. *Foreign Policy, 2004*(March/April), 31–45.
Inglehart, R., & Baker, W. (2000). Modernization, cultural change, and the persistence of traditional values. *American Sociological Review, 65*(1), 19–51.
Kasimovskaya, E., & Didenko, M. (2014). International competitiveness and sustainable development: Are they apart, are they together? A quantitative approach. *SBS JABR, 2*, 37–51.
Köhrsen, J. (2017). Evangelikalismus in Lateinamerika. In F. Elwert, M. Radermacher, & J. Schlamelcher (Eds.), *Handbuch Evangelikalismus* (pp. 129–140). Bonn: Bundeszentrale für politische Bildung.
La Porta, R., Lopez-de-Silanes, F., & Shleifer, A. (2008). The economic consequences of legal origins. *Journal of Economic Literature, 46*(2), 285–332.
La Porta, R., Lopez-de-Silanes, F., & Vishny, A. S. (1999). The quality of government. *Journal of Law, Economics and Organization, 15*(1), 222–279.
Lambsdorff, J. G. (2006). Causes and consequences of corruption: What do we know from a cross-section of countries? In S. Rose-Ackerman (Ed.), *International handbook on the economics of corruption* (pp. 3–51). Northampton, MA: Edward Elgar.
Landes, D. (1999). *The wealth and poverty of nations*. New York: W.W. Norton and Company.
Levine, D. (1981). *Religion and politics in Latin America: The Catholic Church in Venezuela & Colombia*. Princeton, NJ: Princeton Legacy Library.
Manow, P. (2004). *The good, the bad, and the ugly: Esping-Andersen's regime typology and the religious roots of the Western welfare state* (MPIfG Working Paper, No. 04/3). Max Planck Institute for the Study of Societies, Cologne. Retrieved from http://www.mpifg.de/pu/workpap/wp04-3/wp04-3.html
Mazar, H. (2008). *An analysis of regulatory frameworks for wireless communications, societal concerns and risk: the case of radio frequency (RF) allocation and licensing*. PhD thesis, Middlesex University.
McCleary, R. M., & Barro, R. J. (2006). Religion and economy. *Journal of Economic Perspectives, 20*(2), 49–72.
McSweeney, B. (2015). Hall, Hofstede, Huntington, Trompenaars, GLOBE: Common foundations, common flaws. In Y. Sanchez & C. Brühwiler (Eds.), *Transculturalism and business in the BRIC states. A handbook*. Dorchester: Gower Applied Business Research.
Merriam-Webster. (n.d.-a). Protestant. In Merriam-Webster.com dictionary. Retrieved March 28, 2021, from https://www.merriam-webster.com/dictionary/protestant
Merriam-Webster. (n.d.-b). Roman Catholic. In Merriam-Webster.com dictionary. Retrieved March 28, 2021, from https://www.merriam-webster.com/dictionary/Roman%20Catholic
Merryman, J., & Pérez, R. (2007). *The civil law tradition: An introduction to the legal Systems of Europe and Latin America* (3rd ed.). Stanford: Stanford University Press.
Merryman, J., & Pérez, R. (2015). *La Tradición Jurídica Romano-Canónica*. Fondo de Cultura Económica: México D.F.
Michalopoulos, S., & Papaioannou, E. (2017). *The long economic and political shadow of history—Volume 3: Europe and the Americas*. London: CEPR Press Centre for Economic Policy Research.
Molano, E. (1983). *La eclesiología del Concilio Vaticano II y el Derecho Canónico*. Pamplona: Universidad de Navarra.
Moran, R., Harris, P., & Moran, S. (2007). Doing business with Latin Americans, doing business with North Americans. In *Managing cultural differences: global leadership strategies for the 21st century*. Elsevier/Butterworth-Heinermann.
Nexon, D. H. (2011). Religion and international relations. No leap of faith required. In J. Snyder (Ed.), *Religion and international relations theory*. New York: Columbia University Press.
North, D. (1990). *Institutions, institutional change and economic performance*. Cambridge: Cambridge University Press.
North, D. (1997). The contribution of the new institutional economics to an understanding of the transition problem. *UNU World Institute for Development Economics Research (WIDER) Lecture, 1*, 1–19.

Olson, M. (1993). Dictatorship, democracy, and development. *American Political Science Review, 87*(3), 567–575.
O'Reilly, J., & Chalmers, M. (2014). *The clergy sex abuse crisis and the legal responses*. New York: Oxford University Press. https://doi.org/10.1093/acprof:oso/9780199937936.001.0001.
Oxford University Press. (2016). *Oxford dictionaries*. Retrieved from http://www.oxforddictionaries.com/
Paldam, M. (2001). Corruption and religion. Adding to the economic model. *Kyklos, 54*(2–3), 383–414.
Papademetriou, D., & Martin, P. (1991). *The unsettled relationship: Labor migration and economic development*. New York: Greenwood Press.
Pew Research Center. (2014). *Religion in Latin America. Widespread Change in a Historically Catholic Region.* Retrieved from https://www.pewforum.org/2014/11/13/religion-in-latin-america/
Prebisch, R. (1950). *The economic development of Latin America and its principal problems*. Lake Success, NY: Economic Commission for Latin America. United Nations. https://repositorio.cepal.org//handle/11362/29973.
Preston, P. (2012). *Development: Theories of development* (Vol. 9). Oxon: Routledge Library Editions.
Ragazzi, M. (2009). Concordats today: From the second Vatican council to John Paul II. *Journal of Markets & Morality, 12*(1), 113–151.
Rose-Ackerman, S. (2006). *International handbook on the economics of corruption*. Northampton, MA: Edward Elgar Publishing.
Sachs, J. (2001). *Tropical underdevelopment* (National Bureau of Economic Research (NBER), Working Paper, 8119), pp. 1–37.
Sachs, J. (2003). *Institutions don't rule: direct effects of geography on per capita income* (Bureau of Economic Research Working Paper, 9490). NBER. pp. 1–13.
Snyder, J. (2011). *Religion and international relations theory*. New York: Columbia University Press.
Staeheli, B. (2003). *Cross-cultural management within Switzerland: An in-depth case study of a Swiss Financial Services Company*. PhD thesis, University of St. Gallen (HSG).
Stiglitz, J. (2002). *Globalization and its discontents*. London: Penguin Books.
Stulz, R. M., & Williamson, R. (2003). Culture, openness, and finance. *Journal of Financial Economics, 70*(3), 313–349.
The Permanent Observer Mission of the Holy See to the United Nations. (2020). Retrieved from https://holyseemission.org/contents/mission/diplomatic-relations-of-the-holy-see.php
Treisman, D. (2000). The causes of corruption: A cross-national study. *Journal of Public Economics, 76*(3), 399–457.
Vallier, I. (1970). *Catholicism, social control, and modernization in Latin America*. Englewood Cliffs, NJ: Prentice-Hall.
Volonté, C. (2015). Culture and corporate governance: The influence of language and religion in Switzerland. *Management International Review, 55*, 77–118.
Wagner, P. L. (1975). The themes of cultural geography rethought. *Yearbook of the Association of Pacific Coast Geographers, 37*, 7–14.
Wallerstein, I. (2006). *World-systems analysis: An introduction*. Durham, NC: Duke University Press.
Weber, M. (1905). *Die protestantische Ethik und der Geist des Kapitalismus*. Zürich: Verlag Wirtschaft und Finanzen.
Werz, N. (2008). Theologie der Befreiung in Lateinamerika. In B. Oberdorfer & P. Waldmann (Eds.), *Die Ambivalenz des Religiösen. Religionen als Friedensstifter und Gewalterzeuger* (pp. 107–131). Rombach: Freiburg et al..

Wilde, M., Geraty, K., Nelson, L., & Bowman, E. (2010). Religious economy or organizational field? Predicting bishops' votes at the second Vatican council. *American Sociological Review, 75*(4), 586–606. https://doi.org/10.1177/0003122410368927.

Wilson, P. (2009). *Europe's tragedy: A history of the thirty years war*. London: Penguin.

Witte, J. (2002). *Law and Protestantism: The legal teachings of the Lutheran reformation*. Cambridge: Cambridge: University Press.

Woodberry, R. (2012). The missionary roots of liberal democracy. *American Political Science Review (APSR), 106*(2), 244–274.

Woodruff, C. (2006). Measuring institutions. In S. Rose-Ackerman (Ed.), *International handbook on the economics of corruption* (pp. 105–124). Cheltenham: Edward Elgar Publishing.

World Bank, International Finance Corporation (IFC), & Oxford University Press. (2004). *Doing business in 2004: Understanding regulation*. Washington DC: World Bank. A copublication of the World Bank, the International Finance Corporation, and Oxford University Press.

World Economic Forum. (2012). *The global competitiveness report 2012–2013*. Geneva: World Economic Forum.

# Part III
# Theoretical Foundations

# Chapter 6
# Corruption and Religion *(A), (B), (1)*

This chapter reviews some prominent empirical studies and possible explanations of the corruption-religion nexus. It concentrates on the analysis of Roman Catholic and Protestant adherents.

## 6.1 Religious Affiliation and Corruption

Numerous empirical (quantitative) studies exist on the relationships between corruption indicators and the proportion of religious adherents. These studies, undertaken at different levels (cross-country, national, subnational), are rigorous and have mostly reached comparable conclusions regardless of their publication dates, methods, and variables:

*Protestantism curbs corruption, in contrast to Roman Catholicism, which tends to increase the perceived corruption*: (Arruñada, 2010; Chase, 2010; Gerring & Thacker, 2004; La Porta et al., 1997, 1999; Lipset & Lenz, 2000; Paldam, 2001; Sandholtz & Koetzle, 2000; Woodberry, 2012). Some of the key findings will be examined.

La Porta et al. (1997) found a significant correlation between corruption and the percentage of adherents to a hierarchical religion (Roman Catholicism, Eastern Orthodox, Islam) in a sample of 33 countries. Hierarchical religions have adverse effects on civic engagement, and therefore on corruption (La Porta et al., 1999); (Lambsdorff, 2006). La Porta et al. (1999) found a robust predictor of transparency (lower corruption) in the percentage of Protestants.

Chase's (2010) study of 180 countries with 11 independent variables corroborated these findings. Thus, a country's dominant religion explains its level of corruption better than GDP and other economic indicators (Chase, 2010). Protestantism tends to reduce the level of perceived corruption within a nation. In contrast, Orthodoxy or Catholicism, when dominant, tend to increase the level of perceived corruption. Treisman (2000) also observed a significant correlation between



J. García Portilla, *"Ye Shall Know Them by Their Fruits"*, Contributions to Economics, https://doi.org/10.1007/978-3-030-78498-0_6

transparency and the percentage of Protestants in a sample of 64 countries. Lipset and Lenz (2000) and Gerring and Thacker (2005) corroborated that result. Paldam (2001) analysed 11 groups of religions, finding lower corruption in countries with a significant proportion of Protestants and tribal religions. Higher corruption appears in countries where Roman Catholicism, Islam, Buddhism, and Hinduism exert considerable influence.

### *6.1.1 Possible Explanations of the Robust Associations between Corruption and Religion*

This phenomenon has attracted broad scholarly attention. Some of the many valid explanations, supported empirically and theoretically, include:

*On the Negative Influence of Roman Catholicism*:

1. Hierarchical religions promote corruption (Lambsdorff, 2006); (La Porta et al., 1997, 1999). This insight further develops arguments first presented by Olson (1993) and Husted (1999). Societies with low accessibility to the higher echelons must accept authoritarian rules and thus also high levels of corruption and inequality (Husted, 1999).
2. Catholic and Muslim countries perform lower in education and learning than Protestant ones (Becker & Woessmann, 2009); (Landes, 1999). Lower education means that public officials are questioned less about their actions (Landes, 1999). The majority of people are thus more prone to manipulation and to accepting hierarchical relations. Therefore, "The maintenance of ignorance" has been one of the most potent institutional strategies of the Catholic Church to influence people's behaviour (Head-König, 2017, pp. 46–47), (see Sect. 18.4). Other denominations and sects also influence people's behaviour by maintaining their ignorance, but these groups do not reach secular levels of legal and political influence on the scale of the Roman Church-State (Fumagalli, 2011; Helmsdorff, 1996; Martin, 1999; Schäfer, 2006).

*On the Positive Influence of Protestantism:*

3. Robust historical and statistical evidence demonstrates that Protestant missionaries profoundly influenced the rise and spread of stable democracy worldwide (Woodberry, 2012).
4. Historically and statistically, Protestantism led to better education and human capital, and thus also to higher economic prosperity and a wide range of innovations (Becker & Woessmann, 2009); (Becker et al., 2016). Such mechanisms empirically support a more comprehensive explanation than traditional Weberian theory and its postulate of a "Protestant work ethics" (Becker et al., 2016); (Woodberry, 2012). For instance, Protestant institutions competing with

state-sponsored religions are more likely to scrutinise abuses by public officials (Svensson, 2005).

**Empirical Expectation**

1. *I expect the overwhelming empirical evidence available to confirm higher corruption rates in historically Roman Catholic countries than in historically Protestant countries (consistent with the title of this book, articulated in Matthew 7: 15–23,* King James Bible, 1769).

## References


Arruñada, B. (2010). Protestants and catholics: Similar work ethic, different social ethic. *The Economic Journal, 120*(547), 890–918.

Becker, S., Pfaff, S., & Rubin, J. (2016). *Causes and Consequences of the Protestant Reformation.* Warwick Economics Research Paper Series.

Becker, S. O., & Woessmann, L. (2009). Was weber wrong? A human capital theory of Protestant economic history. *Quarterly Journal of Economics, 124*(2), 531–596.

Chase, G. (2010). Religion's impact on corruption. *Journal of Business and Economics Perspectives, 5*(1), 102–112.

Fumagalli, O. (2011). Concordats as instruments for implementing freedom of religion. *IUS CANONICUM, 51*(102), 437–446.

Gerring, J., & Thacker, S. C. (2004). Political institutions and corruption: The role of unitarism and parliamentarism. *British Journal of Political Science, 34*(2), 295–330.

Gerring, J., & Thacker, S. (2005). Do neoliberal policies deter political corruption? *International Organization, 59*(1), 233–254.

Head-König, A.-L. (2017). Religion mattered: Religious differences in Switzerland and their impact on demographic behaviour (end of the 18th century to the middle of the 20th century). *Historical Social Research, 42*(2), 23–58.

Helmsdorff, D. (1996). In D. A. Bidegain (Ed.), *Participación política evangélica en Colombia.* Bogotá: Universidad de los Andes. Departamento de Historia. Tesis de Grado.

Husted, B. (1999). Wealth, culture, and corruption. *Journal of International Business Studies, 30*(2), 339–360.

King James Bible. (1769). *The Holy Bible, King James Version.* Cambridge Edition: 1769. Scripture quotations from The Authorized (King James) Version. Rights in the Authorized Version in the United Kingdom are vested in the Crown. Reproduced by permission of the Crown's patentee, Cambridge University Press.

La Porta, R., Lopez-de-Silanes, F., Shleifer, A., & Vishny, R. (1997). Trust in large organisations. *American Economic Review, 137*(2), 333–338.

La Porta, R., Lopez-de-Silanes, F., & Vishny, A. S. (1999). The quality of government. *Journal of Law, Economics and Organization, 15*(1), 222–279.

Lambsdorff, J. G. (2006). Causes and consequences of corruption: What do we know from a cross-section of countries? In S. Rose-Ackerman (Ed.), *International handbook on the economics of corruption* (pp. 3–51). Cheltenham: Edward Elgar.

Landes, D. (1999). *The wealth and poverty of nations.* New York: W.W. Norton and Company.

Lipset, S., & Lenz, G. (2000). Corruption, culture, and markets. In L. E. Huntington (Ed.), *Culture matters: How values shape human Progress* (pp. 112–125). New York, NY: Basic Books.

Martin, D. (1999). The evangelical upsurge and its political implications. In P. Berger (Ed.), *The Desecularization of the world* (pp. 37–49). Washington, DC: Ethics and Public Policy Center and Wm. B. Eerdmans Publishing.
Olson, M. (1993). Dictatorship, democracy, and development. *American Political Science Review, 87*(3), 567–575.
Paldam, M. (2001). Corruption and religion. Adding to the economic model. *Kyklos, 54*(2–3), 383–414.
Sandholtz, W., & Koetzle, W. (2000). Accounting for corruption: Economic structure, democracy, and trade. *International Studies Quarterly, 44*(1), 31–50. https://doi.org/10.1111/0020-8833.00147.
Schäfer, H. (2006). "Die" Pfingstbewegung in Lateinamerika...? Zur Untersuchung des Verhältnisses zwischen religiöser Praxis und gesellschaftlichen Strukturen. *Zeitschrift für Religionswissenschaft, 14*(1), 53–82.
Svensson, J. (2005). Eight questions about corruption. *Journal of Economic Perspectives, 19*(3), 19–42.
Treisman, D. (2000). The causes of corruption: A cross-national study. *Journal of Public Economics, 76*(3), 399–457.
Woodberry, R. (2012). The missionary roots of liberal democracy. *American Political Science Review (APSR), 106*(2), 244–274.

# Chapter 7
# Prosperity and Religion *(A), (B), (1)*

The link between prosperity[1] and religion is uncontestable. In the USA, for instance (the second most competitive country worldwide; World Economic Forum, 2016), religion contributes almost one-third of the national GDP per annum (USD 4.8 trillion). The revenues of US faith-based organisations (USD 378 billion annually) exceed the global annual revenues of Apple and Microsoft combined (Grim & Grim, 2016).

Yet, the relations between prosperity and religion are reciprocal and highly complex (Berger, 1990; McCleary & Barro, 2006). In the first causal arrow, religion is a predictor (independent) variable that affects prosperity. This arrow represents a school of thought (i.e. idealism) that descends from Weber (1905), with the so-called cultural argument that the beliefs of individual Protestants led to higher prosperity. This study argues that the institutional influence of religion has been more decisive than the "cultural path" of this causal relation (see Sects. 5.3.1, 24.1, and Chap. 8). The second causal arrow moves in the opposite direction, with religion as a criterion (dependent) variable (i.e. prosperity affects religion) and stems from Marx (1859 [1913]) (i.e. materialism). Conclusively, both arrows of causality do not compete, but reinforce each other (dialecticism) (Berger, 1990; Guiso et al., 2006; Koch, 2009; McCleary & Barro, 2006) (see Fig. 2.1).

Originally published as "Prosperity and Religion" in: Garcia Portilla, J. (2019). "Ye Shall Know Them by Their Fruits": Prosperity and Institutional Religion in Europe and the Americas. *Religions*, *10*(6), 362. MDPI AG. Retrieved from https://doi.org/10.3390/rel10060362


[1]This section addresses the theoretical background of the relation prosperity–religion. Please refer to Sect. 10.4.3.2 for a discussion on the "Prosperity Gospel" or "Theology of Prosperity" as a typical Pentecostal phenomenon.



J. García Portilla, *"Ye Shall Know Them by Their Fruits"*, Contributions to Economics, https://doi.org/10.1007/978-3-030-78498-0_7

This chapter offers no exhaustive review of the studies published on the prosperity–religion nexus. There are three reasons for limiting the following account to the most significant works. First, the research is too voluminous to be discussed here in full. Second, such a discussion is not the primary purpose of this book. Third, some studies have already performed this task most efficiently. For instance, Becker et al. (2016) have provided the most comprehensive review of studies on the causes and consequences of the Protestant Reformation (compared to business-as-usual Roman Catholicism). The authors cover previous empirical studies, which have used different variables at individual, city, regional, and cross-country levels. The reviewed studies come from the fields of economics, sociology, and political science.

The next sections synthesise the heated debate on prosperity and Christian religion in Europe and the Americas. Section 7.1 analyses religion as a predictor (independent) variable that affects prosperity (first causal arrow), whereas Sect. 7.2 examines the second causal arrow in the opposite direction (i.e. prosperity affects religion).

## 7.1 Religion as a Predictor (Independent) Variable that Affects Prosperity

Key issues in this interaction are how the institution of religion influences the institutions of law and state, and therefore, prosperity (institutional influence of religion) (see Sect. 5.3). On the cultural influence of religion (Weberian), central questions are "how religiosity affects individual characteristics, such as work ethic, honesty and thrift, and thereby influences economic performance" (McCleary & Barro, 2006, p. 49).

### *7.1.1 The Weberian "Cultural" Argument on Christianity and Prosperity* (1)

Max Weber linked religion and economic performance arguing that the Protestant Reformation initiated modern capitalism, with Protestant societies outpacing Catholic ones economically (Weber, 1905). Weber's classic thesis illustrated prosperity differences between diverse religious affiliations using taxable capital available in Baden in 1895. He found that tax returns from financial capital totalled over four millions marks per 1000 Jews; 954,000 marks per 1000 Protestants and 589,000 marks per 1000 Catholics (Weber, 1905, p. 133). Based on this evidence, Weber advanced a Protestant work ethic-based theory of prosperity. Accordingly, Protestant beliefs (e.g. Calvinist, Puritans) would enhance the economy "by fostering traits such as work ethic, honesty (and hence trust), thrift, charity, hospitality to strangers and so on" (McCleary & Barro, 2006, p. 51).

Following Weber (1905), numerous quantitative studies have analysed the empirical relationships between prosperity indicators (mainly GDP) and religious affiliation (mostly the proportion of adherents). Thousands of articles and hundreds of books have discussed (and continue to discuss) Weber's thesis. Some works widely accept his claim as one of the most valid explanations of the rise of Western Civilisation while others criticise particular points (Ferguson, 2011); (Berman, 2003, p. 24); (Becker et al., 2016).

However, empirical research on prosperity determinants typically—and blindly—neglects the influence of religion (Barro & McCleary, 2003, p. 760). Religion as a determinant suffers from similar mainstream disregards in other disciplines such as law (Berman, 2003; Witte, 2002), international relations (Snyder, 2011), or political science (Manow & van Kersbergen, 2009).

### *7.1.2 Some Empirical Studies Refuting Weber's Thesis*

The results and conclusions of several empirical studies associating religion and prosperity vary depending on the type of prosperity proxy variables chosen. Also, the spatial (cross-country, national, or subnational) and temporal configurations of these studies influence the different outcomes.

Acemoglu et al. (2001, 2006) found no effect of religion (adherents) on economic growth in cross-country settings. As shown, concentrating only on religious adherents is problematic (Sect. 5.3.1), yet Delacroix and Nielsen (2001) reported mixed results from comparing different historical periods and proxy variables. Other empirical studies refuting Weber's thesis have been performed at a subnational level. Cantoni (2015), for instance, found no effects of Protestantism on population figures used as proxies of economic growth. He used a dataset comprising 272 cities in the period 1300–1900 in the German Lands of the so-called "Holy" Roman Empire. The main problem of Cantoni's approach lies in accepting city size as a proxy of prosperity. Thus, the city-size argument might lead one to consider Sao Paulo or Mexico DC as far more prosperous than Bern or Brussels today, for instance. Moreover, while Cantoni's finding might be accurate at a subnational level, it cannot account for the historical performance of Germany as a whole compared to other countries with a Catholic tradition (e.g. Portugal or Spain).

### *7.1.3 Most Empirical Studies Confirm Weber's Thesis (Although for Different Reasons)*

Based on their comparative examination and systematic, state-of-the-art synthesis, Becker et al. (2016) concluded that historical Protestantism encouraged a wide range of societal developments. Balancing the empirical evidence, most studies have confirmed a positive impact of Protestantism on prosperity using different variables as well as diverse spatial and temporal configurations. On the whole, most empirical studies examining the consequences of the Reformation associate them with positive developments of governance and the economy (Becker et al., 2016).

Economic prosperity has also been robustly linked with secularisation and declining levels of religiosity (Barro & McCleary, 2003; Inglehart & Baker, 2000). Secularisation precedes economic growth, which means that prosperity did not cause secularisation in the past (Ruck et al., 2018). Historically, Protestantism is a well-established precursor of secularism (Snyder, 2011; Agnew, 2010; Shah & Philpott, 2011; Woodberry, 2012; Berger, 1990; Gregory, 2012; Sect. 8.3.4.4). Therefore, the causal arrows seem to run from historical Protestantism (anti-clericalism) to secularisation, to economic prosperity and security, and to postmaterialist values (Granato et al., 1996; Inglehart & Baker, 2000).

Hence, the effects of Protestantism may not be immediate (i.e. considering the previously explained causal arrows). Capitalism emerged during the three centuries after the Reformation, mainly in the Protestant regions of Europe and the New World, and among Protestant minorities in Catholic countries. In contrast, pre-industrial societies were "zero-sum systems" where little or no economic growth took place (Granato et al., 1996). Consequently, Granato et al. (1996) argued that Protestantism has been decisive as it "undermines a set of religious norms that inhibit economic achievement and are common to most preindustrial societies". Therefore, the authors explain that "Weber is correct in arguing that the rise of Protestantism is a crucial event in the modernization of Europe" (pp. 609–610).

Furthermore, historically Protestant countries still differ considerably in their values and attitudes today compared with Roman Catholic, Orthodox, or Islamic societies. Such enduring effects influence prosperity in the *longue durée,* although few people are still religious in present-day Protestant Europe, for instance (Inglehart & Baker, 2000, p. 49; see also Chap. 10). It is therefore hardly surprising that influential works link empirically good economic outcomes to Protestantism in different sets of countries. However, such studies recognise the effect of historical Protestantism as a pivotal precursor of prosperity pillars rather than as a direct prosperity trigger in a classical Weberian sense. Thus, for instance, the robust empirical associations of Protestantism with prosperity relate to the development of democratic institutions (Woodberry, 2012), the rise of education and printing (Becker & Woessmann, 2009), and the weakening of hierarchical structures (La Porta et al., 1999; Volonté, 2015).

## 7.2 Religion as a Criterion (Dependent) Variable that Is Affected by Prosperity

While previous subsections concentrated on the influence of religion on prosperity, this section analyses the other direction of the arrow (i.e. the influence of prosperity on religion). A crucial question in this interaction is how political institutions and prosperity affect religious participation and beliefs (McCleary & Barro, 2006, p. 49). Hence, theories of secularisation originate from the understanding of this interaction. Two complementary perspectives are identifiable:

1. The supply-side or "top-down" factors of religion. This literature focuses on the strategic role of religious organisations and leaders in the religious markets. Accordingly, competition among providers of religion affects "the nature of the religion product" (e.g. when governments impose state religions and limit entry). This strand descends from Adam Smith (1791) and was developed by Finke and Stark (1992) and Finke and Iannaccone (1993), among others (McCleary & Barro, 2006, p. 50; Norris & Inglehart, 2004, p. 7). This approach has been related to *Rational Choice Theory*, which contends that individuals and organisations act based on the maximisation of utility (i.e. cost–benefit calculations) (Wilde et al., 2010; Young, 1997). Accordingly, the *Religious Competition Theory* argues that religious organisations that believe there is more competition work harder to win and retain members and are usually more versatile and prone to reform than organisations in monopolistic settings (Wilde et al., 2010, p. 589; Finke & Stark, 1992, p. 19). In response to the models of rational choice, the *Neo-Institutional Theory* contends that institutional contexts greatly define actors' choices, decisions, and actions (Immergut, 1998; Ingram & Clay as cited in Wilde et al., 2010, p. 590), (see Sects. 8.2, 8.3.4, 9.1, 10.4.1.2, and 10.4.1.3).
2. The demand-side or "bottom-up" model, which emphasises the mass public preferences alongside industrialisation, "modernisation", and prosperity. In this model, prosperity gradually erodes religious habits, thereby also diminishing the influence of organised religion on politics and governance. This perspective stems from John Wesley (1760), the founder of Methodism; and was further developed by Marx (1859 [1913]), Weber (1905), Hume (1757 [1993]), and Freud (1927), among others. Berger (1990), Norris and Inglehart (2004), among several others, have extended this idea (McCleary & Barro, 2006, p. 50; Norris & Inglehart, 2004, p. 7). Although Weber (1905) dedicates most of his attention to religion as an independent variable, he also recognises that religion can be a dependent variable (Koch, 2009 pp. 12–13).

### *7.2.1 Influence of Prosperity on Religion: The Theory of Existential Security*

Norris and Inglehart (2004) theorised that a sense of existential security (i.e. the feeling that survival and prosperity are secure enough that they can be taken for granted) usually weakens transcendent religion. Accordingly, the theory of existential security contends that secularisation mostly occurs in advanced industrial nations, yet religious values prevail strongly in most developing countries with rapidly growing populations (Norris & Inglehart, 2010, p. 2). The authors explain that religiosity persists, especially among disadvantaged peoples, particularly vulnerable populations in poorer countries that face personal survival threats (Norris & Inglehart, 2010, p. 5). In contrast, with rising levels of existential security (e.g. the emergence of the welfare states and economic prosperity), citizens in nearly all industrial developed nations are more oriented towards secularisation than people in poorer developing countries (Norris & Inglehart, 2010, p. 15).

Furthermore, feelings of vulnerability drive religiosity, even in rich nations, when comparing levels of economic inequality within their societies. For example, religiosity is strongest among the poorest and least secure sectors of US-American society (Norris & Inglehart, 2010, p. 12).

Additionally, Norris and Inglehart (2004) theorise that, currently, "post-Christian forms of spirituality" (e.g. yoga, astrology, or other "New Age" alternative beliefs and practices) are widespread in Western societies. Apparently, these post-Christian beliefs and practices may provide alleviation from the anxiety and stress that the secular world poses in industrial societies (Houtman & Aupers, 2007; Norris & Inglehart, 2010; Pike, 2006; Silver, 2006).

The theory of existential security constitutes a robust and revised version of the secularisation theory with empirical (quantitative) data from the World Values Survey (WVS) of 1981–2001. The WVS project conducted representative national surveys of the basic values and beliefs of the publics in all six continents (in more than 90 independent countries, containing more than 85% of the world's population). Norris and Inglehart (2004) provide significant correlations which consistently link the prevalence of religious practices and values with multiple macro-level, empirical measures of human development, and the social and economic progress of all countries. Moreover, a large body of secondary empirical findings from diverse methods, approaches, and disciplines such as welfare studies, health care, and social psychology, is consistent with the existential security thesis (Norris & Inglehart, 2010, p. 6).

The sermon on "The Use of Money" by John Wesley (1760) constitutes an early empirical example of the theories of secularisation and existential security. Wesley preached, "gain all you can, save all you can, give all you can" but he regretted the fact that, as his congregants became wealthier, they also became less religious (McCleary & Barro, 2006, p. 49–50).

Yet, existential security as a "detrimental" principle of faith seems to have been intuitively recognised, even in more ancient times. The book of Proverbs in the Bible registers the following assertion:

> ...give me neither poverty nor riches; feed me with food convenient for me: lest I be full, and deny thee, and say, Who is the Lord? or lest I be poor, and steal, and take the name of my God in vain (King James Bible, 1769, Proverbs 30: 8-9).

The author of this proverb requests a sober measure of wealth. He recognises that too much prosperity and existential security will lead him to lose his faith in God (i.e. deteriorate his religiosity), but that too little will lead him to sin (i.e. steal).

Similarly, a Protestant stakeholder interviewed in this study referred to the book of Judges in the Bible, which narrates several cycles of struggle and suffering during which the Jews sought the God of Israel (see Sect. 21.7).

> This principle comes down to us historically and repetitively, for example, from the book of Judges [. . .] the more Israel obeyed God's law in the Bible, the better [they] got, whereas whenever they strayed far from God's commandments, they faced the worst crises. [. . .] this pattern is repeated cyclically over and over again in history, leading to social failure and oppression whenever people disobeyed God (Independent Protestant believer).

The previous stakeholder's statement would appear to contradict the theory of existential security at first sight. However, according to the book of Judges (King James Bible, 1769), Israel prospered during numerous generations after obeying God's commandments. Yet, after prospering (i.e. after gaining existential security), the Jews turned away from the God of Israel (i.e. diminished their religiosity). Afterwards, they started worshipping other gods and idols (i.e. post-Judaism), and the entire nation fell into disgrace once more, as a consequence. In the new crises, they repented and restored their obedience to the God of Israel, and subsequently, the Jewish nation achieved prosperity again, only to then take it for granted once more after a few generations and begin a new crisis. This cycle repeats several times; therefore, the narration of the book of Judges relates a cyclical feature that demonstrates consistency with the theory of existential security.

Chapters 18, 19, 20, and 21 (case studies) will show that the theory of existential security is the most prominent principle identified after analysing the qualitative data (case studies). This study applies Critical Discourse Analysis (CDA) as a qualitative method in the case studies (Sect. 17.6). Interestingly, CDA draws from Marxist theory (Hjelm, 2014, p. 856), which this study also links empirically with the theory of existential security.

## 7.3 Summarising the Core Messages of Chapter 7. *Prosperity and Religion*

The relationships of prosperity vis-à-vis religion as a predictor (independent) variable (e.g. Weber) or as a criterion (dependent) variable (e.g. Marx) reinforce each other and produced a vast body of theories and empirical studies. In the first causal arrow, Weber's explanations and findings in *The Protestant Ethic and the Spirit of Capitalism* has attracted much criticism over the last century. The debate remains polarised. Thus, numerous quantitative studies link the relations between Christian religions and prosperity indicators. The corresponding empirical conclusions either support Weber's central thesis (mainly at cross-country levels, e.g. La Porta et al., 1999; Granato et al., 1996) or refute it (mainly selective regional examples or subnational levels; see, for instance, Cantoni, 2015; Delacroix & Nielsen, 2001; Iannaccone, 1998).

In any event, the effects of Christianity on prosperity seem to vary depending on the leading religious denomination influencing a given society. Recent research largely confirms that the Reformation played a vital role in Europe's economic and political trajectory, although for different reasons than those advanced by Weber (Woodberry, 2012; Becker et al., 2016, p. 11). Consequently, a Protestant "work ethic" might oversimplify the intricate process that makes Protestant societies more prosperous than Roman Catholic or Orthodox ones. A particular work ethic is no more than one of many underlying mechanisms and contributing factors.

For instance, education and hierarchy are two decisive prosperity mechanisms related to religious denominations. The historical Protestant focus on education has positively influenced societal and prosperity outcomes (Becker & Woessmann, 2009). Likewise, the hierarchical power relations in Orthodoxy, Islam, or Roman Catholicism have had unfavourable long-term effects on social progress and prosperity (La Porta et al., 1997). Chapters 8, 9, 10, and 11 will elaborate on these issues.

The historical institutional influence of religion has been the crucial factor with regard to prosperity/transparency (more than the current proportion of adherents). Thus, most empirical findings contradict the prevailing Roman Catholic ideology, which has insisted (without, however, providing much empirical evidence) on restoring what it considers a "prosperous and peaceful medieval society" (see, for instance, Ratzinger & Pera, 2006; Restrepo, 1939). The Middle Ages allowed the Roman Church-State to create a theocratical order in which the papacy established a hierarchical society and in which spiritual power prevailed over temporal power. This Roman Catholic ideal meant (and still means) that the ecclesiastical hierarchy determines the legal principles and the basic norms of collective life (Figueroa, 2016, p. 155).

The second causal arrow (religion as a dependent variable vis-à-vis prosperity) resulted in, among others, secularisation theories focusing on either the supply or demand-side of religion. The theory of existential security (Norris & Inglehart, 2004) is an influential model that empirically focuses on the variations of the demand-side and revises the secularisation theory.

While cultural and institutional proxies delineate the quantitative and QCA empirical settings (2/3 of the results of this study), the theory of existential security is particularly relevant in the application of grounded theory in the qualitative part of the research (1/3 of the results). In other words, the empirical focus of the quantitative and QCA parts is the relationship of religion, as a predictor (independent) variable, to prosperity. Yet, after coding and applying grounded theory in the qualitative part, the second arrow of relation (religion as a dependent variable) appeared relevant.

**Empirical Expectation**

2. *I expect the empirical evidence to corroborate a trend towards higher prosperity (competitiveness) in historically Protestant countries and lower competitiveness in historically Catholic countries. This expectation is based on abundant empirical studies linking higher prosperity outcomes with Protestantism at a cross-country level.*

The next chapters further explain the close corruption/prosperity–religion nexus from an institutional-legal and from a theological perspective.

## References

Acemoglu, D., Johnson, S., & Robinson, J. (2001). The colonial origins of comparative development: An empirical investigation. *American Economic Review, 91*(5), 1369–1401.

Acemoglu, D., Johnson, S., & Robinson, J. (2006). Institutions as a fundamental cause of long-run growth. In P. Aghion & S. N. Durlauf (Eds.), *Handbook of economic growth* (Vol. 1A). Amsterdam: North-Holland.

Agnew, J. (2010). Deus Vult: The geopolitics of the Catholic Church. *Geopolitics, 15*(1), 39–61.

Barro, R. J., & McCleary, R. M. (2003). Religion and economic growth across countries. *American Sociological Review, 68*(5), 760–781.

Becker, S., Pfaff, S., & Rubin, J. (2016). *Causes and consequences of the Protestant reformation.* Warwick Economics Research Paper Series.

Becker, S. O., & Woessmann, L. (2009). Was Weber wrong? A human capital theory of Protestant economic history. *Quarterly Journal of Economics, 124*(2), 531–596.

Berger, P. (1990). *The sacred canopy: Elements of a sociological theory of religion.* New York: Doubleday.

Berman, H. (2003). *Law and revolution II: The impact of the Protestant reformations on the Western legal tradition.* Cambridge: Harvard University Press, Belknap Press.

Cantoni, D. (2015). The economic effects of the Protestant reformation: Testing the Weber hypothesis in the German lands. *Journal of the European Economic Association, 13*(4), 561–598.

Delacroix, J., & Nielsen, F. (2001). The beloved myth: Protestantism and the rise of industrial capitalism in nineteenth-century Europe. *Social Forces, 80*(2), 509–553.

Ferguson, N. (2011). *Civilization: The west and the rest.* Allen Lane: Penguin Books.

Figueroa, H. (2016). *La persistance des idées traditionalistes en Colombie. Religion et politique (1886–1952).* Paris: L'Harmattan.

Finke, R., & Iannaccone, L. (1993). Supply-side explanations for religious change. *The Annals of the American Academy of Political and Social Sciences, 527*, 27–39.

Finke, R., & Stark, R. (1992). *The churching of America 1776–1990.* New Brunswick, NJ: Rutgers University Press.

Freud, S. (1927). *The future of an illusion.* New York: Norton.

Garcia Portilla, J. (2019). "Ye shall know them by their fruits": Prosperity and institutional religion in Europe and the Americas. *Religions, 10*(6), 362. MDPI AG. https://doi.org/10.3390/rel10060362.

Granato, J., Inglehart, R., & Leblang, D. (1996). The effect of cultural values on economic development: Theory, hypotheses, and some empirical tests. *American Journal of Political Science, 40*(3), 607–631.

Gregory, B. S. (2012). *The unintended reformation: How a religious revolution secularized society.* Cambridge: Belknap Press of Harvard University Press.

Grim, B., & Grim, M. (2016). The socio-economic contribution of religion to American society: An empirical analysis. *Interdisciplinary Journal of Research on Religion, 12*(3), 1–31.

Guiso, L., Sapienza, P., & Zingales, L. (2006). Does culture affect economic outcomes? *Journal of Economic Perspectives, 20*(2), 23–48.

Hjelm, T. (2014). Religion, discourse and power: A contribution towards a critical sociology of religion. *Critical Sociology, 40*(6), 855–872.

Houtman, D., & Aupers, S. (2007). The spiritual turn and the decline of tradition: The spread of post-Christian spirituality in 14 Western countries, 1981–2000. *Journal for the Scientific Study of Religion, 46*(3), 305–320.

Hume, D. (1757 [1993]). In J. C. A. Gaskin (Ed.), *The natural history of religion*. Oxford: Oxford University Press.

Iannaccone, L. R. (1998). Introduction to the economics of religion. *Journal of Economic Literature, 36*(3), 1465–1496.

Immergut, E. (1998). The theoretical Core of the new institutionalism. *Politics and Society, 26*, 5–35.

Inglehart, R., & Baker, W. (2000). Modernization, cultural change, and the persistence of traditional values. *American Sociological Review, 65*(1), 19–51.

King James Bible. (1769). *The Holy Bible, King James Version.* Cambridge Edition: 1769. Scripture quotations from The Authorized (King James) Version. Rights in the Authorized Version in the United Kingdom are vested in the Crown. Reproduced by permission of the Crown's patentee, Cambridge University Press.

Koch, B. (2009). *The Prosperity Gospel and economic prosperity: race, class, giving, and voting.* Doctoral dissertation. Bloomington: Department of Sociology, University Graduate School, Indiana University.

La Porta, R., Lopez-de-Silanes, F., Shleifer, A., & Vishny, R. (1997). Trust in large organisations. *American Economic Review, 137*(2), 333–338.

La Porta, R., Lopez-de-Silanes, F., & Vishny, A. S. (1999). The quality of government. *Journal of Law, Economics and Organization, 15*(1), 222–279.

Manow, P., & van Kersbergen, K. (2009). Religion and the Western welfare state – The theoretical context. In P. Manow & K. van Kersbergen (Eds.), *Religion, class coalitions and welfare states* (p. 304). New York: Cambridge University Press.

Marx, K. (1859 [1913]). *A contribution to the critique of political economy*. Chicago, IL: Kerr.

McCleary, R. M., & Barro, R. J. (2006). Religion and economy. *Journal of Economic Perspectives, 20*(2), 49–72.

Norris, P., & Inglehart, R. (2004). *Sacred and secular: Religion and politics worldwide*. New York: Cambridge University Press.

Norris, P., & Inglehart, R. (2010). *Are high levels of existential security conducive to secularization? A response to our critics.* Paper for Mid-West Political Science Association annual meeting, Chicago, April 22, 2010.

Pike, S. M. (2006). *New age and neo-pagan religions in America. Columbia contemporary American religion.* New York: Columbia University Press.

Ratzinger, J., & Pera, M. (2006). *Without roots: The west, relativism, Christianity, Islam.* New York: Basic Books.

Restrepo, F. S. (1939). El Corporativismo al alcance de todos. *Revista Javeriana, 52*, 75.

Ruck, D. J., Bentley, R. A., & Lawson, D. J. (2018). Religious change preceded economic change in the 20th century. *Science Advances, 4*(7) [eaar8680]. Inc. https://doi.org/10.1126/sciadv.aar8680.

Shah, T. S., & Philpott, D. (2011). The fall and rise of religion in international relations. History and theory. In J. Snyder (Ed.), *Religion and international relations theory* (pp. 24–59). New York: Columbia University Press.

Silver, D. (2006). Religion without instrumentalization. *Archives Europeennes De Sociologie, 47* (3), 421–434.

Smith, A. (1791). *An inquiry into the nature and causes of the wealth of nations* (6th ed.). London: Strahan.

Snyder, J. (2011). *Religion and international relations theory*. New York: Columbia University Press.

Volonté, C. (2015). Culture and corporate governance: The influence of language and religion in Switzerland. *Management International Review, 55*, 77–118.

Weber, M. (1905). *Die protestantische Ethik und der Geist des Kapitalismus*. Zürich: Verlag Wirtschaft und Finanzen.

Wesley, J. (1760). The use of money, a sermon on Luke. In J. G. Bristol & W. Pine (Eds.), *Sermons on several occasions* (pp. 127–144). Norderstedt: Hansebooks GmbH.

Wilde, M., Geraty, K., Nelson, L., & Bowman, E. (2010). Religious economy or organizational field? Predicting bishops' votes at the second Vatican council. *American Sociological Review, 75*(4), 586–606. https://doi.org/10.1177/0003122410368927.

Witte, J. (2002). *Law and Protestantism: The legal teachings of the Lutheran reformation*. Cambridge: Cambridge University Press.

Woodberry, R. (2012). The missionary roots of liberal democracy. *American Political Science Review (APSR), 106*(2), 244–274.

World Economic Forum. (2016). *The global competitiveness report 2014–2015. Full data edition*. Geneva: The World Economic Forum.

Young, L. A. (1997). *Rational choice theory and religion: Summary and assessment*. New York: Routledge Press.

# Chapter 8
# Institutions, Corruption/Prosperity, and Religion *(A), (B), (D), (1), (3), (6)*

This comprehensive chapter addresses the most crucial aspect of this study: institutions and the institutional influence of religion.

It is divided into four sections. Section 8.1 discusses the importance of institutions concerning transparency/prosperity and the difficulty of differentiating institutions empirically. It also explores other critical issues related to prosperity such as democracy versus hierarchy. Section 8.2 examines the religion-institution nexus and considers the contributions of Roman Catholicism and Protestantism. Section 8.3 analyses the law, the most formal and persistent institution that shapes societies. Referring to the legal traditions in Europe and the Americas, it discusses the pervasive influence of Roman civil and canon law and the role of subsequent Protestant revolutions that sought to counteract that predominance.

## 8.1 Institutions as Triggers of Corruption/Prosperity *(3)*[1]

The quality of institutions has been theoretically and empirically linked to prosperity (and thus also to transparency) outcomes (Acemoglu et al., 2001; Acemoglu & Johnson, 2005; Acemoglu & Robinson, 2012; La Porta et al., 1999; North, 1990; Williamson, 2000). Such studies have credibly associated empirical evidence and theory. Institutions are therefore widely accepted as playing a determinant (causal)

---

[1]Originally published as "Institutions as Triggers of Prosperity" in: Garcia Portilla, J. (2019). "Ye Shall Know Them by Their Fruits": Prosperity and Institutional Religion in Europe and the Americas. *Religions*, *10*(6), 362. MDPI AG. Retrieved from https://doi.org/10.3390/rel10060362



J. García Portilla, *"Ye Shall Know Them by Their Fruits"*, Contributions to Economics, https://doi.org/10.1007/978-3-030-78498-0_8

role in the prosperity of societies even if alternative interpretations may exist (Woodruff, 2006).

However, several problems arise when considering institutions inter alia as triggers of corruption (and prosperity):

1. Scant agreement exists on how to measure formal or informal institutions empirically. Different studies measuring institutions with varied methods measure different things. Sometimes even gauging the outcome in isolation from other factors is challenging (Woodruff, 2006).
2. Endogeneity issues plague the causal approaches of institutions to prosperity, although to a lesser extent the effect of political institutions on corruption. Previous treatments of endogeneity, however, have not been convincing (Kunicová, 2006; Persson & Tabellini, 2003; Woodruff, 2006).
3. It is not entirely clear which institutions are fundamental to prosperity/transparency processes (Woodruff, 2006, p. 106).
4. Formal institutions have little effect on broad prosperity outcomes. However, informal institutions matter and have a more significant effect (Glaeser et al., 2004; Treisman, 2000; Woodruff, 2006).
5. Although quite strong associations often exist, the causal arrow may point in both directions (from corruption to institutional choice and from institutions to corruption) (Rose-Ackerman, 2006, p. xxv).
6. Informal institutions are the most difficult to measure (and change) since they are largely determined by history (Woodruff, 2006, p. 121).

Thus, research on institutions and prosperity/corruption has so far not provided conclusive evidence of causality. The strongest evidence relates to the impact of underlying social structures (informal institutions), which is highly difficult to address, both in prospective and in policy terms (Lambsdorff, 2006; Rose-Ackerman, 2006; Woodruff, 2006).

In practical terms, institutions and transparency/trust may all have coincided with prosperity, as empirical evidence exists for arguing causality in both directions (Armony, 2004; Fukuyama, 1995; Morris, 2003; Uildriks, 2009). Therefore, prosperity, corruption (or its opposite transparency), trust, and institutions are inseparable concepts. One causal cyclical logic that might be expected would be that ethical transparency/trust values promote institutional stability and prosperity (Fukuyama, 1995).

History and culture have shaped current institutional structures (Acemoglu et al., 2001; Acemoglu & Robinson, 2012; Rose-Ackerman, 2006). At the same time, empirical evidence also shows that institutional structures shape cultural values (i.e. trust and civic norms) (Uildriks, 2009, p. 7); (Alesina & Giuliano, 2015). In any event, religion has played a crucial role in corroborating both cultural values and institutions (Arruñada, 2010; Inglehart & Baker, 2000; Manow, 2004; Paldam, 2001; Treisman, 2000).

Acemoglu and Robinson (2012) have explained how inclusive institutions create inclusive markets, incentives, and opportunities for prosperity. Inclusive institutions create positive feedback loops, which prevent an elite's efforts to undermine them.

Throughout its history, Latin America has, however, experienced a negative institutional feedback loop, which has perpetuated corruption, mistrust, and elitist/extractive institutions (Acemoglu & Robinson, 2012; Uildriks, 2009).

If political institutions are key (Acemoglu & Robinson, 2012), who creates them? Lawyers and policy makers have moral and religious backgrounds (i.e. historically, these are predominantly Protestant in North America and Roman Catholic in Latin America). However, Acemoglu and Robinson (2012) neglect the influence of religious values on ruling elites. More importantly, the authors disregard the institutional influence of religion. Instead, they suggest that critical historical junctures (e.g. the death of political leaders, weather conditions) may trigger institutional shifts. However, citing Robert Michels's "iron law of oligarchy", Acemoglu and Robinson (2008, 2012) list countless examples of radical movements and revolutions that simply replaced one tyranny with another without producing positive institutional shifts.

On this evidence, it is therefore essential to recognise *which* revolutions created better institutions. We also need to ask which triggers changed an old regime into a new *status quo*. Thus, countries that had not fully adopted the principles of such revolutions preserved elements of the old regime. These notions are explored below (see especially Sect. 8.3).

### 8.1.1 Institutions, Hierarchy, and Democracy Vis-à-Vis Prosperity/Transparency

This subsection first considers the relation of democracy, hierarchy, and corruption/prosperity and second their significant correlation with religion.

Weak institutions may cause mistrust and thus impair the quality of democratic institutions (Putnam, 1993). At the same time, robust empirical evidence suggests that stable democracies (democracies older than those that have emerged in the last 70 years) reduce corruption in the long term (Treisman, 2000). In other words, weak and recent democracies with little electoral participation and little competition for office tend to have little or no influence on reducing corruption (Rose-Ackerman, 2006); (Lambsdorff, 2006) (Treisman, 2000).

Other studies have also found significant linkages between democracy and transparency (Goldsmith, 1999; Paldam, 2002; Persson & Tabellini, 2003; Sandholtz & Koetzle, 2000). However, they also report the waning significance of democracy when GDP per capita is included in the models. Chapter 3 and Sect. 8.1 have already discussed the highly intertwined relationship between prosperity and transparency and have suggested that both may be part of the prosperity phenomenon.

Making the case for causal relations between corruption, prosperity, and democracy has proven problematic, theoretically and empirically. The strong associations among these factors, along with unclear directions of causality, suggest that they form part of the same, reinforcing feedback loop. Overcoming such unproductive factor segregation, my research model considers transparency, prosperity, and stable democracy as part of the same reinforcing feedback phenomenon (Fig. 2.1 and Sect. 8.2.2.1).

Autocratic rulers (and leaders of highly hierarchical organisations) have incentives to extract the maximum possible revenues to satisfy their self-interest as abundant examples and historical evidence show (Olson, 1993). Hierarchical, centralised bureaucracies corrode interpersonal trust, whereas horizontal, locally led organisations induce interpersonal trust (Putnam, 1993). Historically, the Roman Catholic Church-State has epitomised the hierarchical, centralised institution, whereas decentralisation and local control generally characterise Protestant movements (Inglehart & Baker, 2000, p. 35).

Using different methodologies and datasets, La Porta et al. (1999) and Husted (1999) empirically confirmed that hierarchies contribute to corruption. Adserà et al. (2003) estimated the impact of the level of democracy on corruption in a cross-country study. They highlighted the importance of political instability as encouraging actors to appropriate maximum rents in the short term, leading to increased corruption.

In contrast, stable democratic societies usually reflect greater openness and expanded freedom of choice. More competition for political positions should lead societies to oust poorly performing leaders, at least in theory. Thus, politicians focusing solely on increasing private rents would be voted out of power, and opposition candidates would win elections by promising improvements (Rose-Ackerman, 1978).

However, ample evidence suggests that the Latin American experience is quite the opposite. Notwithstanding advancing democratisation in the last century, the relationships between government stakeholders and civil society have largely remained clientelistic. Moreover, democratisation has generally gone hand in hand with low public trust in state institutions and a generalised "irreverence to the rule of law" by either state actors or civil society (Luzzani, 2002, p. 168). Furthermore, a "democratisation of violence" has also accompanied the rise of democracy in Latin America (Kruijt and Koonings as cited in Uildriks, 2009, p. 2).

In line with Olson (1993), La Porta et al. (1999), and Husted (1999), I argue that one of the critical triggers of corruption (and inequality) in Latin America is the continent's strongly hierarchical (and elitist) societal structure. This structure is part of the legacy of the Roman Catholic Church-State, which has exercised a pervasive influence on formal and informal institutions throughout the region (Levine, 1981).

**Empirical Expectation**

3. *Given that economic prosperity, democracy, and transparency are part of the same phenomenon, I expect these factors to be highly correlated. My quantitative model on corruption* (Sect. 15.3.2) *considers proxy variables for all of these variables.*

## 8.2 Religion and Institutions *(6)*

### *8.2.1 The Roman Catholic Influence on Institutions, Democracy, and Prosperity*

The introductory considerations and the following sections show how the Roman Empire and its inheritor, the Roman Catholic Church-State, have exerted a pervasive historical influence in Europe and the Americas. However, the last five decades have witnessed a reformed discourse in Roman Catholicism following the Second Vatican Council. The following sections explore the relevant background and issues in greater detail.

#### 8.2.1.1 Roman Catholic Political Philosophy

Historically, Roman Catholicism has favoured a monarchical state order as an absolute form of governance ideally suited to governing a large mass of people with a single religion (Cook, 2012, p. 23). This political philosophy descends from Aristotle, who considered the monarchy one of the desirable forms of government, contrary to democracy, one of the worst in his eyes (see his *Politics*). Thomas Aquinas, the single most important philosopher of Catholicism, adopted many Aristotelian political principles and synthesised these with the medieval Catholic ideal of society: "The best regime of a community is government by one person, [. . .] unity is more congruently the effect of one than of many" (Thomas Aquinas, *C. G.* iv. 76, (fn. 4) as cited in Cook, 2012 p. 23).

Therefore, the Roman Church-State and papal authority saw the monarchical constitution as a model for the constitution of the secular state. Such an archaic model of government is still evident in the Vatican's monarchical structure (i.e. Roman Catholic Church-State). Only recently has Catholicism begun to support democracy abroad, strategically and discriminately. Democracy, for Romanism, is a "lesser evil" since monarchical governments are no longer dominant worldwide and also given the threats of secularism and Marxism (Cook, 2012, p. 83); (Anderson, 2007).

#### 8.2.1.2 Change of Discourse Towards Democracy after Vatican II

The Roman Church-State, which avoids democratic forms for internal Church governance, is best suited to either monarchical or a mixed form of secular government. Thus, Romanism rejects democratic constitution and popular sovereignty principles as ideals both for the Church-State and for ecclesiastical states (Rommen, 1945 p. 490); (Cook, 2012, p. 24). As *Civiltà Cattolica*, the Jesuit periodical in Rome, stated in the late 1930s: "Fascism is the regime that corresponds most closely to the concepts of the Church of Rome" (as cited in van Paassen, 1939, p. 465).

However, Vatican II (1962–1965) brought about a myriad of transformations. As Agnew (2010) observed:

> The Second Vatican Council, while it may not have marked a huge disruption in the beliefs and practices of the Church, did involve the adoption of a novel set of more latitudinarian attitudes towards other religions (not least towards other Christians) and the reinvigoration of an epideictic language emphasising reconciliation rather than the previously dominant patristic form accentuating confrontation and judgement (p. 48).

Vatican II affirmed the religious freedom of the Church and cooperation between Church and State as guiding principles (Ragazzi, 2009, p. 118). It ended the requirement of a Latin mass, relaxed confessional obligations and restrictions, and abandoned the Roman Church's claims to power in secular states (Wilde et al., 2010). There is also empirical evidence that "Catholics brought up after Vatican II are indeed more trusting and tolerant" than before (Guiso et al., 2006, p. 33). However, the Roman See has increased its political activity by signing more than 30 concordats with new states after Vatican II (Corral, 2014; Fumagalli, 2011). Therefore, theological change alone falls short of explaining the post-1965 shift of the Roman Church from its traditional hostile stance towards democracy (Anderson, 2007). Anderson (2007) explained this shift in terms of the Church's efforts to maintain its ideological, political, and social hegemony and to preserve its position in ideological, political, religious, and social markets.

Cook (2012) analysed Catholic hegemony after 1965 (Vatican II) in Spain, Croatia, Germany, the USA, Mexico, and the Philippines. He found that hegemony involves maintaining the preeminent place of Roman Catholicism among other religious denominations in pluralistic societies grounded in constitutional democracies. He concluded that depending on the political and religious conditions existing in a particular country, the Roman Church-State either maintains or establishes its hegemony over time (Cook, 2012, p. 345).

Wilde et al. (2010) examined the bishops' openness to reform and ecumenical affairs in their votes (i.e. to vote progressively) while at Vatican II. Using data from more than 100 countries obtained from the Vatican Secret Archive, the authors ran logistic regression analyses and tested the Rational Choice (Religious Competition) and Neo-Institutional theories. Wilde et al. found evidence substantiating both theories. The authors have concluded that bishops from countries that enjoy religious freedom were much more inclined to vote progressively than bishops from countries in which the Roman Catholic Church was the state church (Wilde et al., 2010, p. 599).

In countries where the Roman Catholic Church was the state religion, the probability that a bishop voted progressively at Vatican II decreases drastically, from.95 to.21, as the percentage of Catholic population increases from 75 to 100. However, the effect of the proportion of Catholics varies substantially with different state-church relations. In countries with formal religious freedom, the proportion of Catholics has practically no impact on the way in which bishops typically vote. In turn, in countries where the Roman Church or another religion has been established, bishops display more conservative tendencies as the market share of the Church rises

(Wilde et al., 2010, pp. 593–594). These findings confirm the higher importance of the religious institutional settings vis-à-vis the proportion of adherents and, equally importantly, the decisive influence of religious competition in the configuration of the Vatican II outcomes.

Similarly, Gill (1998) studied the contribution of Roman Catholicism to political change in Latin America. He explained why after Vatican II some Catholic hierarchies supported political reform, while others supported authoritarian regimes or stood aside, in order to preserve the *status quo*. He proposed a market explanation based on quantitative and qualitative data analysis (i.e. cross-country comparisons and twelve case studies). After analysing historical and statistical evidence, Gill concluded that to keep parishioners, Catholic Church leaders defended the interests of the poor and opposed totalitarian governments in countries where evangelical Protestants and spiritist movements had gained ground among poor Catholics. In contrast, bishops maintained strong ties with military rulers in areas where the religious competition was limited. Strong religious competition preceded the Catholic hierarchies move to oppose the military in five of the six antiauthoritarian cases analysed by Gill—Chile, Brazil, El Salvador, Panama, and Nicaragua. However, in five of the proauthoritarian or neutral cases analysed by the author—Bolivia, Argentina, Honduras, Uruguay, and Paraguay—the Catholic Church faced limited competition and did not adopt progressive pastoral policies on a large scale. Indeed, the Catholic hierarchy provided insufficient assistance to pastoral agents in these countries, even though some progressive sectors were being attacked (Gill, 1998, pp. 106, 270).

Gill's results are supported by other studies in cases such as Argentina, where the Catholic Church (as a monopolistic player) was supportive of and cooperative with military dictatorships. In turn, the Chilean Catholic hierarchy responded critically and unsupportively towards the dictatorship in the presence of religious pluralism (i.e. the significant presence of Protestantism) (Waldmann, 2012; Zilla, 2020).

Gill also argues that monopolistic churches are comparable to monopolistic companies because both fail to fulfil their consumers' expectations of both quality and quantity (Gill, p. 85). He illustrates this market strategy in the Roman Church by comparing the number of priests per 10,000 Catholics across countries after Vatican II (in the 1970s). Whereas a typical Latin American country had only around two priests per 10,000 Catholics, Protestant countries such as the USA, Great Britain, Australia, or Sweden had nearly five times the number (around ten priests per 10,000 Catholics). Germany, the birthplace of the Reformation, had almost 46 priests per 10,000 Catholics (Barret cited in Gill, 1998). Gill found then a strong inverse correlation between religious monopoly and Catholic clergy per 10,000 Catholics ($r = -0.75$) (Gill, 1998, pp. 85–87). Accordingly, in the presence of religious competition, more clergy per Catholic population typically means a better provision of religious and social services. Therefore, Woodberry observes:

> …the Catholic Church provided far more education and created more organizational civil society in countries where it competed with CPs [conversionary Protestants] (e.g. the United States, Ireland, and India), than in places it historically could block competition (e.g. Mexico, Spain, and Italy) (Woodberry, 2012, p. 269).

Thus, Roman Catholic hierarchies have often defended the interests of the poor (e.g. promoting democracy) when facing greater competition from Protestantism (Anderson, 2007; Gill, 1998; Woodberry, 2012). Competition compels the Roman Church-State to break traditional alliances with the ruling elites. Protestant missions have often catalysed Roman Catholic mobilisation, thus expanding education and political resources in Latin America (Smith, 1991; Trejo, 2009; Woodberry, 2012). In Mexico, for instance, Woodberry observes:

> in areas with successful Protestant missions, both conservative and liberal bishops expanded education and organized indigenous communities politically; elsewhere they did not. Because the Catholic Church has far more resources and personnel in Mexico than do Protestants, Catholics provided more educational and political resources than Protestants did—but Protestant missions were the catalyst (Trejo, 2009 as cited in Woodberry, 2012, p. 269).

Conversely, in the absence of competition, Catholic hierarchy can easily ignore people's needs and continue its allegiance with abusive political elites (Gill, 1998, 7, 48); (Anderson, 2007, p. 394). Evidently, competition with Protestantism has not been the only factor affecting bishops' decisions to oppose dictatorships, but is, nevertheless, a key component in explaining the variation in institutional responses (Gill, 1998, p. 120).

Nevertheless, a tendency exists to disregard or consider past scholarship as outdated or as non-applicable after the Second Vatican Council. The allegedly altruistic change after millennia of Roman Catholic intransigence has even led the dominant literature to explain modern welfare states as a manifestation of Catholic social doctrine (Boswell, 1993; Esping-Andersen, 1990; Wilensky, 1981). Some authors, however, have found this approach historically inadequate, since it distorts the decisive causes of institutional variance (Manow & van Kersbergen, 2009). In Europe, Manow (2004) notably observes:

> …in some of the allegedly 'Catholic' regimes Christian [Catholic] Democracy never emerged as a political party (Spain, Portugal, France), or early welfare state legislation had an explicitly anti-clerical motivation (Italy, France, Belgium) (Manow, 2004, p. 4).

Political Catholicism has typically led to the formation of Catholic Democratic parties in countries where it has faced competition with Protestant or anti-clerical movements (e.g. Switzerland, Germany, Netherlands, Belgium, Italy) (Ercolessi & Hägg, 2012; Manow, 2004). Similarly, Gill (1998) observes that in Latin America, Catholic Democracy was mostly a lay phenomenon with little to no official endorsement from the Church hierarchy. Although the bishops sometimes openly supported the Christian Democrats' goals, Vatican bans on overt political participation in partisan politics restricted their assistance (p. 206).

Such evidence presented by Manow (2004), Ercolessi and Hägg (2012), and Gill (1998) also supports the Religious Competition and Neo-Institutional theories (Sect. 7.2). Having clarified the influence of Roman Catholic ideology on institutions, below I briefly consider the influence of historical Protestantism on institutions.

### *8.2.2 Protestant Influence on Institutions and Democracy*

Protestantism not only broke the political (as well as institutional and economic) hegemony of the Roman Catholic Church but also interrupted the growing influence of this belief system in Europe. From these processes emerged the modern state and secular institution (which later also influenced democracy, the American Constitution, and the French and Industrial Revolutions) (Becker et al., 2016; Snyder, 2011; Witte, 2002; Woodberry, 2012) (Sect. 8.2.2.1 and Sect. 8.3.4).

Becker et al. (2016) have provided a comprehensive and conclusive synthesis of the literature on the causes and consequences of the Reformation, including its positive and "dark shadow" (negative) effects. The authors conclude that the Protestant Reformation "ended the ancient hegemony of the Catholic Church in Western Europe" (p.1). Also, they observed that the Reformation connects to positive institutional and economic outcomes in a myriad of empirical studies in which Protestantism encourages:

> . . .a host of variables that are important for economic growth, including human capital, governance, entrepreneurship, social ethic, social networks, and missionary work. [. . .] Where the Reformation took hold, it fundamentally altered political, legal, and social institutions. This ultimately resulted in the ascendancy of parliaments, the secularization of law, increased emphasis on education, and the precursors of the welfare state (Becker et al., 2016, p. 21).

Becker et al. (2016) found a mostly "positive picture" of "the effects of the Reformation on education, work ethic, and economic development" (Becker et al., p. 20). However, the authors also found a "dark side" of Protestantism in their review of empirical studies. They traced the negative effect of Protestantism back to Weber (1905), who had already noted sinister consequences of the Reformation, as "an 'iron cage' of secularization, alienating materialism and narrowly instrumental thinking" (Becker et al., 2016, p. 20). Also, Durkheim (1899) found a higher propensity of Protestants to commit *suicide* than Roman Catholics and Jews across regions and countries. Yet, Roman Catholics exhibit a higher tendency to commit *homicides* than Protestants (Durkheim, 1899, pp. 353–354). The higher suicide likelihood of Protestants in Germany and Switzerland has been corroborated empirically by Becker and Woessmann (2015) and Torgler and Schaltegger (2014), respectively.

Furthermore, the Protestant share of the population also correlates with the rise of anti-Semitism and Nazism in Germany during the Weimar Republic. For instance, Protestants were ultimately polarised, especially where they supported the right ends of the political spectrum in Germany, since Catholics were rooted in the political centre with their own party, the *Zentrumspartei* (Spenkuch as cited in Becker et al., 2016, p. 21). However, other authors (Goldhagen, Browning, as cited in Becker et al., 2016) state that German anti-Semitism might be traced back to "Luther's nationalism and obsession with the failed effort to convert the Jews to Protestantism" (p. 20). Yet, these and other similar historical claims that link Luther's ethics and nationalism with Germany being predisposed toward intolerance and authoritarianism "suffer from being over-generalized, poorly construed and rarely tested using systematic evidence" (Becker et al., 2016, pp. 20–21), (see Sect. 8.3.4.1).

#### 8.2.2.1 Protestantism and Democracy

In historical Protestantism, neither a priest, bishop, or pope dictates morality but every Protestant believer does so based on reading and interpreting the Bible. This, in brief, is Luther's democratising "universal priesthood of all believers' principle" (Witte, 2002).

Woodberry's (2012) influential study demonstrated a consistent linkage between Protestantism and democracy. The latter, as other authors have established, is also firmly associated with prosperity (Morton et al., 2005; World Economic Forum, 2016). Woodberry (2012) provided robust historical and statistical evidence that Protestant missionaries profoundly influenced the rise and spread of stable democracy around the world:

1. Historically, Protestants have spread religious liberty, mass education, mass printing, newspapers, voluntary organisations, and colonial reforms, and thus helped to create the conditions for stable democracies.
2. Statistically, "Protestant missions are significantly and robustly associated with higher levels of printing, education, economic development, organizational civil society, protection of private property, and rule of law and with lower levels of corruption" (Woodberry 2004a, 2004c, 2006c, 2011b, 2011c, as cited in Woodberry, 2012, p. 268). The statistical evidence "demonstrates that the historic prevalence of Protestant missionaries explains the variation in democracy better than either the prevalence of the nonreligious or of generic Protestants. Moreover, Protestant missions predict democracy, whereas Catholic missions do not" (Woodberry p. 247).

Consequently, Protestantism is strongly associated with stable, representative democracy in Western Europe. Also, statistically, "the historic prevalence of Protestant missionaries strongly predicts democracy in 142 non-European societies" (Woodberry, 2012, p. 245). Furthermore, Woodberry (2012) found such a consistent association also among European-settler colonies:

> "Protestant-based" United States, Canada, Australia, and New Zealand have been more democratic than "Catholic-based" Argentina, Chile, Uruguay, and Costa Rica. Both sets of countries had similar precolonial conditions (i.e. temperate climates, communal landholding, and small indigenous populations), which weakens theories that climate or pre-Protestant class conditions caused the Protestantism–democracy association (p. 244).

Woodberry's conclusions also weaken theories claiming that secularisation causes democracy (e.g. the USA is far more religious than Uruguay). In this respect, the historical prevalence of Protestant missionaries explains about half the statistical variation in democracy in Latin America, Asia, Africa, and Oceania (Woodberry,

2012, p. 244). The robust controls and consistent analyses performed by Woodberry leave little room for an alternative explanation to Protestantism as a democracy trigger.

On this historical and empirical evidence, Woodberry seriously challenges traditional modernisation theory. For instance, traditionally associated factors of democracy and social developments are often endogenous (and not necessarily direct determinants) (i.e. secular rationality, economic growth, urbanisation, industrialisation, the expansion of the state, and the development of new class structures) (Woodberry, 2012, p. 244). Anderson (2007) reached similar conclusions, in particular that the greater the proportion of the Protestant population, the higher the level of democracy (p. 385).

However, on the "dark side", it is clear that "missionaries committed their own abuses, and some were even racist", or they often ignored abuses given their concentration on conversion as a primary goal (Woodberry, 2012, p. 255). Also, the typical Protestant translation of texts and education in the vernacular, "may have accentuated ethnic heterogeneity and sometimes fostered violence" (Posner, Ranger as cited in Woodberry, 2012, p. 245). However, as Bradbury (2014) concluded, missionaries have been unfairly depicted as colonial forces, imperial agents, annihilators of local societies, and ideologically motivated manipulators of marginalised natives. Although there were a few missionaries to whom those descriptions could be reasonably attributed, such generalisations wilt under the examination of a more rigorous historical inquiry (Bradbury, 2014, p. 427).

Figure 8.1 shows the historical relations between the religious and institutional factors giving rise to prosperity, transparency, and democracy; or instead to hegemonic oppression and corruption.

### *8.2.3 Traditional Institutional Influence of Religion in Latin America*

The Roman Catholic Church-State legitimated Latin American territories as either Spanish or Portuguese colonies from the fifteenth to the early nineteenth century. Equally, Spanish and Portuguese settlement guaranteed a Catholic monopoly from 1500 to the early 1900s, thus securing the Church's hegemony and a feudalist-like economy (Gill, 2013, p. 117). In essence, the conquest was a religious, political, and military endeavour actively supported by the Church. It made Latin America a unique cultural entity in the world, one largely possessing the same language (Spanish or Portuguese) and the same religion (Roman Catholicism) as solid, unifying elements (Navarro, 2016, p. 111).

By the onset of the colonial period, the Iberian Peninsula had established its hegemony in Europe, which enabled it to bring under its rule the richest territories in the Americas (South and Central). The British took what the Spaniards and Portuguese "left over" (North America). North American lands were desert-poor and

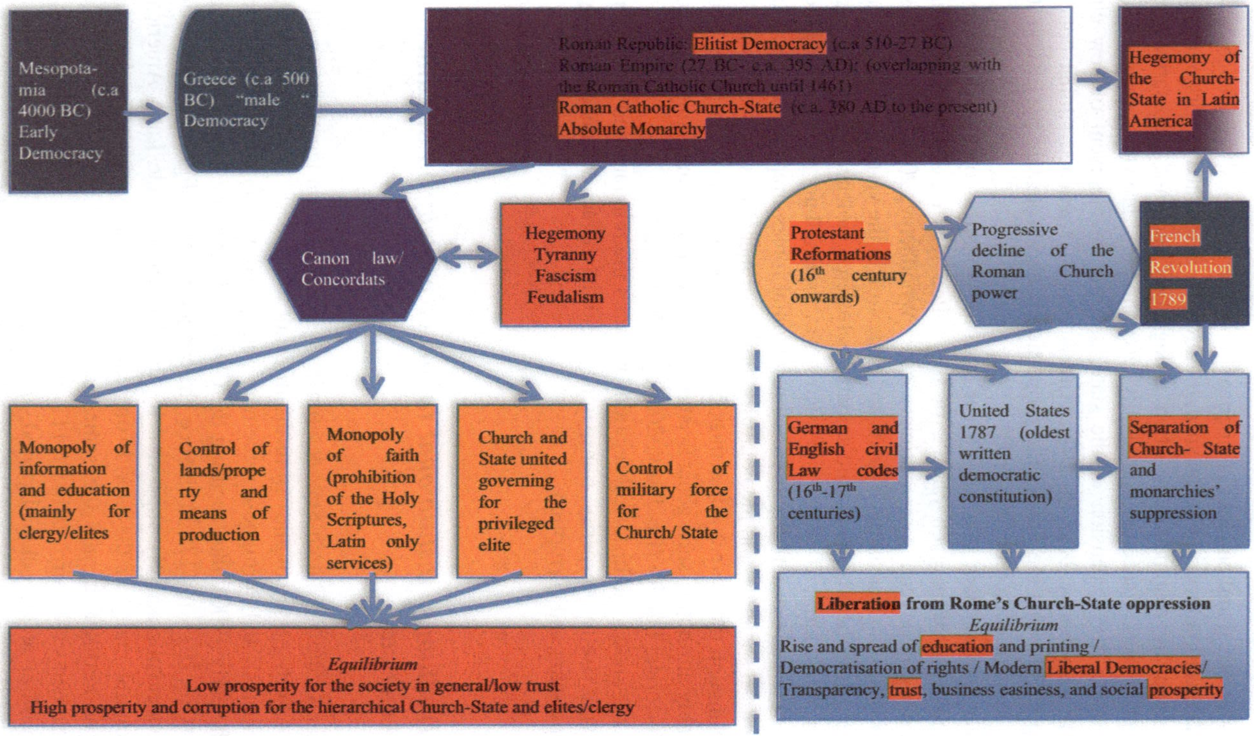


**Fig. 8.1** Factors giving rise to prosperity, transparency, and democracy; or conversely to hegemonic oppression and corruption (Source: Author's collection). Based on this study's theoretical framework (among others: Acemoglu et al., 2011; Berman, 2003; Heussi, 1991; La Porta et al., 1999; Miller, 2012; Snyder, 2011; Woodberry, 2012; Witte, 2002). Note: In this figure, some quantitative variables of interest, QCA conditions, or qualitative codes of this study are highlighted in red. This figure does not include the Orthodox hegemony nor the Marxist Revolution

inhabited by modest aborigines. Importantly, these territories lacked the abundance of gold and jewels found in their South and Central American counterparts (i.e. attested to by the Aztec, Maya and Inca civilisations) (Acemoglu & Robinson, 2012, p. 21).

A positive institutional loop inherited from Great Britain allowed a "reversal of fortune," in which the poorest lands of the Americas (North) became the most powerful country in the world (Acemoglu & Robinson, 2012; Prados de la Escosura, 2004). Acemoglu and Robinson (2012) explain that inclusive institutions permit goods and wealth to be shared more equally. This enabled the British to establish the USA, from the "left-overs" of the Spaniards, and to build the British Empire.

By contrast, the Spaniards took advantage of the indigenous population and built extractive institutions, such as *la mita* ("tax or common service paid by Indians") or *la encomienda* ("enslavement or Spanish labour system"). These were designed to extract wealth from the people and to perpetuate a powerful elite during the colonial period. This situation persisted after the independence of the Latin American states, whose present-day institutions descend from *la mita* or *la encomienda*. Such social inequality has bred corruption, violence, and political instability (ibid).

Even after independence, the Catholic Church-State has been instrumental to securing a population loyal to government, thus perpetuating the *status quo*, i.e. the hegemony of the Roman Church-State. Protestantism was officially banned, including government prohibitions of Bible distributions and Protestant services in Spanish, among others (Gill, 2013, p. 119). In the mid-twentieth century, the Catholic Church continued to secure for itself favourable positions in countries such as Colombia or Argentina (Gill, 1998, 2013; Levine, 1981; Munevar, 2008).

The colonial legacy that Latin American institutions received from religion is characterised by three facts: first, the religious monopoly of the Roman Catholic Church, i.e. the banning of other religious expressions; second, the replacement of indigenous beliefs for Roman Catholicism giving form to syncretic practices persisting to this date; and third, royal patronage (*Patronato Real*), a quasi-perfect fusion of church and state allowing the Spanish King to appoint bishops in the New World, who would also hold government posts, and to preserve the hierarchy Pope-King-Bishop (Navarro, 2016, p. 112).

Since colonisation, the material and symbolic influence of the Roman Catholic Church has reinforced social arrangements in Latin America (Levine, 1981, p. 29). For Levine, the pervasive fusion of Roman Catholicism and politics in Latin America can assume several forms that may include, among others: (1) the content and form of laws; (2) the approved processes for legitimising authority; (3) the essence of accepted sanctions; (4) processes for resolving social conflicts; and (5) educational structures. These and other expressions reflect a conviction that the ideals that inform institutional structures and orient individuals are inextricably linked to those which connect individuals to the spiritual realm (Levine, 1981, p. 20).

Notwithstanding the imposed restrictions, Protestant missionaries slowly introduced Reformed forms of faith until Protestantism could no longer be ignored in the twentieth-century Latin America (Gill, 2013). As Gill observed,

> …Protestant missionaries were able to make their way slowly into various societies and begin converting individuals, including indigenous folk who would then become pastors for these new churches. Once Protestants began indigenizing their churches, it became difficult for governments to prevent their growth. It was one thing to deport foreign missionaries; it was just not possible to deport one's own citizens. Moreover most of these new churches provided valuable social services to communities (e.g. literacy training, food banks for the poor)… (Gill, 2013, p. 119).

Protestant churches also provided the poor with access to medical assistance and other services (Gill, 1998, 2013; Woodberry, 2012). Growing Protestant competition forced many Catholic dignitaries to rethink their strategy with a new "preferential option for the poor" (Gill, 1998, 2013). The Catholic Church promulgated a new social strategy (i.e. *Rerum Novarum* of 1891); Catholic Action; Second Vatican Council of 1965); Medellin Episcopal Conference of 1968). These developments also gave rise to "Liberation Theology" (Büschges, 2018), (see Sect. 10.4.1.4). Regardless of such advances, the Roman Catholic Church still exercises great hegemony in most Latin American countries and traditional intransigent paradigms continue to prevail (Figueroa, 2016; Levine, 1981; Martin, 1999; Munevar, 2008).

The inertia of such institutional legacies and the prevalence of corporatist ideologies (pre-Vatican II) have perpetuated an elitist model of society in Latin America, which continues to be by far the most unequal continent in the world to date (World Bank, 2014).

### 8.2.4 *Summarising the Core Messages of Section 8.2.* **Religion and Institutions**

Regardless of the advances made by Roman Catholicism in the Second Vatican Council (Vatican II: 1962–1965), corporatist ideologies remain prevalent, mostly in Latin America (Figueroa, 2016; Levine, 1981; Martin, 1999; Munevar, 2008). But while Roman Catholic discourse has shifted, the institutional inertia persists and maintains the hierarchical *status quo* and longstanding feudal structures (e.g. through signed concordats).

The Reformation brought forth a wide range of modern institutions. Among these, education and democracy are the most crucial ones for ensuring prosperity/transparency outcomes. Likewise, Protestantism has impacted the secularisation of the state in Protestant countries (and also in Roman Catholics, albeit to a lesser, more indirect extent). Protestantism fosters horizontal power relations and secular-rational attitudes towards authority (Becker et al., 2016; Inglehart & Baker, 2000; Manow & van Kersbergen, 2009; Treisman, 2000; Witte, 2002; Woodberry, 2012). Thus, such egalitarian and secular attitudes are linked to greater transparency and prosperity (Lambsdorff, 2006).

State institutions in Latin America have been closely linked with Roman Catholicism in that they continue feudal-medieval structures. The Protestant Reformation has not been allowed to directly influence institutions in Latin America as it did in

North America or in northern Europe. The following sections expand on these historical relations and concentrate on religion and formal institutions (law) in Europe and the Americas.

*Note*: The *GCI* index includes an institutional indicator. Therefore, no results of institutions are analysed in the empirical setting, in order to exclude endogeneity (i.e. institutions explaining institutions). However, the next section considers the legal tradition, which may serve as an exogenous proxy of the historical institutional influence of religion (or non-religion).

## 8.3 Law, Religion, Revolutions, and State Models *(B), (D), (6)*

### *8.3.1 Legal Traditions in Europe and the Americas*[2]

Countries in Europe and the Americas have either transplanted or developed their legal systems based on some few legal traditions rather than writing new systems of their own (Watson, 1974; La Porta et al., 1998, p. 1115). Thus, the different legal rules, procedures, and institutions at the national and subnational levels share traditional characteristics that allow classification into groups or families. Along these lines, Merryman and Pérez (2007) defined legal tradition as a collection of profoundly ingrained, socially formed views about the essence of law, its place in society and institutions, the proper organisation and function of a legal system, and how the law is or should be made, enforced, interpreted, refined, studied, and taught. The legal tradition is a connection between the legal system and the society of which it is a part (Merryman & Pérez, 2007, p. 2).

Consequently, the most widespread legal traditions worldwide are: first, *Roman civil law,* which includes French and other European and Latin American systems; second, *common law*, which includes most Anglo-Saxon systems; and third, *socialist law,* which comes from former and current socialist countries (including China and Cuba). The historical dominance of Roman law resulted from Roman imperialism and conquest. Likewise, the current dominance of Roman civil law and of the common law traditions in the modern world is a direct product of earlier centuries of European imperialism (Merryman & Pérez, 2007, p. 5) (Fig. 8.2). Additionally, such traditions have also spread across the world through borrowing or imitation (e.g. Japan voluntarily adopted the German legal tradition) (La Porta et al., 1998, p. 1115). Within the first group of legal traditions (Roman civil law), only three

[2]Originally published as "Legal Traditions and Prosperity in Europe and the Americas" in: Garcia Portilla, J. (2019). "Ye Shall Know Them by Their Fruits": Prosperity and Institutional Religion in Europe and the Americas. *Religions*, *10*(6), 362. MDPI AG. Retrieved from https://doi.org/10.3390/rel10060362

significant families currently exist as its heirs: French, German, and Scandinavian (ibid) (Fig. 8.2 and Sect. 8.3.2).

Typically, Southern (Mediterranean) Europe, and Latin America have French law. Northern Europe has mostly German, Scandinavian, or English common law. North America inherited English common law. Post-Soviet states have a socialist legal tradition, but most of them returned to French civil law after the fall of the Berlin Wall (La Porta et al., 2008, p. 289).

Figure 8.2 presents the most important legal traditions in Europe and the Americas from the Middle Ages to the present. From left to right, Roman and canonical legal traditions chronologically progressed through the centuries. They did not abruptly end after the sixteenth to nineteenth centuries, but percolated down after the various revolutions. All legal traditions incorporate Roman law in some form. From bottom to top, a colour gradient represents the closeness to Roman and canon law traditions (ranging to purple). Those legal traditions that are more distant from Roman and canon law (ranging to green) are shown towards the bottom of the table.

Roman and Roman Catholic canon law traditions have defined the institutional *status quo* or the *ancien régime* in Europe and the Americas. Violent national revolutions directed against the existing legal system gradually interrupted this hegemony in favour of more transcendental views of justice (above all in the last five centuries). Successive national revolutions have reformed and renewed the legal

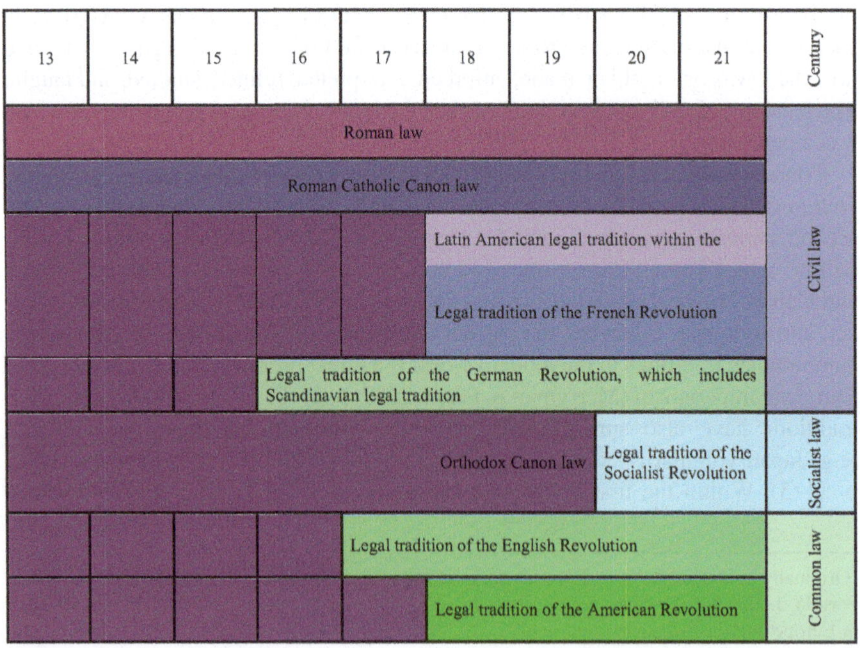


**Fig. 8.2** Legal traditions in Europe and the Americas (Amended from Witte, 2002; Berman, 2003; Merryman & Pérez, 2007; La Porta et al., 2008)

traditions (in some countries more than in others) of the still pervasive and surviving Roman and the Catholic canon law regime. Every country in Europe and the Americas traces its legal system back to a revolution (Berman, 2003, pp. 16–17). The following sections explain each of these traditions chronologically.

### *8.3.2 Legal Traditions and Current Institutional Performance* (3)

The long-term persistence of legal traditions affects institutional performance and therefore also prosperity (Volonté, 2015). Figure 8.3 summarises some performance indicators of otherwise distinct legal traditions. French, German, and Scandinavian legal systems belong to the tradition of Roman Civil law (Merryman & Pérez, 2007). And yet they are all different. Germanic, and in particular the Scandinavian, legal systems descend less from Roman law than the French one (Zweigert and Kotz as cited in La Porta et al., 1998, p. 1119). German and especially Scandinavian legal systems were influenced by the Lutheran Reformation, which, to a certain extent, modified the foundational principles of Roman (and particularly of canon) law.

French civil law comes from the French Revolution, which also intended to transform the influence of Roman and canon law. This transformation, however, was not always possible due to the inertia of the tradition of Roman law for French Revolution jurists. Moreover, the transformation of canon law, for example, was not automatically transplanted to most Latin American countries, which adopted French legal principles after gaining independence (Berman, 2003; Merryman & Pérez, 2007). Several Latin American countries signed concordats with the Roman Church-State after their independence, thus subordinating their civil law to canon law and granting explicit privileges to the Church-State (Salinas, 2013).

As explained in further detail below, countries with French legal origins also have Roman Catholicism as their dominant religion, historically. Likewise, countries with a socialist legal origin are more likely to exhibit a significant historical presence of Orthodox religions. French and socialist legal origins are consistently associated with burdensome regulations and lower incomes. In contrast, countries of English, German, or Scandinavian legal origin have been historically linked to Protestantism, regulate less, and are the most prosperous (La Porta et al., 1999, p. 244; World Bank, International Finance Corporation & Oxford University Press, 2004) (See Fig. 8.3).

The countries that regulate the most (i.e. those of socialist or French legal origins) typically exhibit more corruption, more poverty, greater inefficiency of public institutions, and lower quality of private or public goods. Heavier regulation is associated with inequality, fewer checks and balances, and less enforcement capacity. A large amount of heavy regulation descends from the Roman legal tradition (La Porta et al., 1999; World Bank, International Finance Corporation, & Oxford University Press, 2004).

| | Socialist Soviet law tradition | Roman Civil law tradition | | | Common-law tradition |
|---|---|---|---|---|---|
| | | French-civil-law | German-civil-law | Scandinavian-law | |
| | | | Protestant-influenced legal origins | | |
| **Examples of countries** / **Institutional performance item** | Russia, Ukraine (until the 1990s), Cuba | Most Latin America, parts of Europe, Africa, and Asia | Germany, Austria, Switzerland, Japan | Denmark, Finland, Norway, Sweden | United Kingdom, Ireland, United States, Canada |
| **Quality of law enforcement** | Low | Lowest | Highest | Highest | High |
| **Protection of property rights and propensity to market** | Lowest | Low | High | High | Highest |
| **Government interventionism (intrusive regulation, high tax rates)** | Highest | High | Low | High | Low |
| **Overall government efficiency; political freedom; provision of basic goods** | Lowest (except for education attainment) | Low | High | Highest | High |
| **Corruption** | Highest | High | Low | Lowest | Low |
| **Competitiveness** | Lowest | Low | Highest | Highest | High |

**Fig. 8.3** Comparison of institutional performance between different legal traditions (Amended from Berman, 2003; La Porta et al., 1998, 1999, 2008; Merryman & Pérez, 2007; Transparency International, 2016; World Economic Forum, 2016)

### *8.3.3 The Roman Civil Law Tradition*

The civil law tradition can be traced as far back as the Twelve Tables in ancient Rome (450 B.C). Figures 8.2 and 8.3 show that mostly modern French law and, to a lesser extent, German and Scandinavian law currently represent the tradition of Roman civil law. Today, French civil law is both the most influential and also the most widely distributed system across the world (i.e. it is predominant in Latin America, Southern Europe, and across Asia and Africa). It precedes international law (i.e. the legal developments of the European Union and UN) and even prevails in a few enclaves of the "common law world" (Louisiana, Quebec, and Puerto Rico) (Merryman & Pérez, 2007, pp. 2–3; La Porta et al., 2008, p. 289). La Porta et al. (2008) characterise French civil law as follows:

> [. . .] originates in Roman law, uses statutes and comprehensive codes as a primary means of ordering legal material [. . .]. Dispute resolution tends to be inquisitorial rather than adversarial. Roman law was rediscovered in the Middle Ages in Italy, adopted by the Catholic Church for its purposes, and from there formed the basis of secular laws in many European countries (La Porta et al., 2008, p. 289).

Different historical successive subtraditions constitute modern civil law: (1) Roman civil law (from the Roman Empire); (2) Canon law (from the Roman Catholic Church-State); (3) Commercial law (where pragmatic Italian merchants serve as judges); (4) the influence of revolutions (i.e. German, French, American); and (5) legal science (descending from the various revolutions) (Merryman & Pérez, 2007); (Berman, 2003).

The first three subtraditions (Roman, canon, and commercial law) are the fundamental historical sources of institutions, concepts, and procedures in "civil law countries". In such countries, these three subtraditions embody the essential modern codes (typically: civil, commercial, and penal; civil and criminal procedure) (Merryman & Pérez, 2007, p. 14).

Roman and canon law have the highest historical relevance and are directly related to religion, institutions, and prosperity. Below I explain these two crucial subtraditions.

#### 8.3.3.1 Roman Civil Law

Merryman and Pérez (2007) consider Roman law as being Rome's most significant contribution to Western society. There is no doubt that Roman forms of thought invaded the Western legal system. For the authors, all Western lawyers can be considered Roman lawyers in this respect. Yet, in civil law countries, the prevalence of Roman civil law is much more widespread, prominent, and explicit than in common law countries (Merryman & Pérez, 2007, p. 11).

Roman law was compiled and codified in the sixth century A.D under Justinian in the *Corpus Juris Civilis*. It is the most fundamental part both of the European legal tradition (especially in the Mediterranean Region) and of Latin America's. Today the civil codes of these countries demonstrate the domination of Roman law, as well as its medieval and contemporary revivals (Merryman & Pérez, 2007, pp. 10–11). Weber (1905) also observed that Roman law "has always retained its supremacy in the Catholic countries of Southern Europe", while countries such as England were able to overcome it (p. 37–38).

#### 8.3.3.2 Roman Catholic Jurisprudence (Canon Law) (6)

The pan-European Roman Church-State became the first modern state. It established a body of law that was systematised and compiled in Gratian's *Decretum* (1140), entitled "A Concordance of Discordant Canons" (Berman, 2003, p. 4).

The canonical law of the Roman Catholic Church-State has strongly influenced civil law. For instance, canon law influenced the *jus commune* that the European states received (it was the law generally applicable in Europe). Notably, Roman Catholic canon law includes various forged documents that were regarded as authentic for centuries (Merryman & Pérez, 2007, pp. 11–12). O'Reilly and Chalmers (2014) notably explain that canon law is a legal system that has always

**Table 8.1** Examples of medieval canon laws supported by Catholic Sacraments (Amended from Witte, 2002, pp. 169–170)

| Catholic sacrament | Associated laws |
|---|---|
| Baptism and the Eucharist | Liturgy, religious doctrine, catechesis, and discipline |
| Ordination | Law of the clergy and Church life |
| Marriage | Law of sex, marriage, and family life |
| Extreme unction | Law of wills, inheritance, and trusts |
| Penance | Law of crime, tort, and moral obligation |

governed the Catholic Church and "had once been used to govern nations". However, canon law "is often unfamiliar to those from common law jurisdictions" (p. 316). The authors further observe:

> The Catholic Church has its own code of laws worldwide. Those laws are found in the Code of Canon Law as well as in the particular laws created by internal, local, and national Church legislation. While church entities are bound to follow the laws of the civil jurisdiction, where these exist, all members of the Catholic Church, including laity and clergy, are also bound to follow the laws of the Church, or face internal penalties. [. . .] To understand the Church's process, one must always keep in mind that the institution does not view itself as some sort of religious corporation; its self-understanding and judicial model is akin to being a state. Thus its disciplinary processes are more akin to the law of a government or state rather than a corporate disciplinary model (O'Reilly & Chalmers, 2014, pp. 7–8; 316–317).

Roman Catholic sacraments inspired medieval Catholic canonists and moralists to devise entire legal systems. The sacraments provided the framework for organising some of the legal institutions of the Church and society in the Middle Ages (Table 8.1). However, not all canon law can be subsumed under the sacraments (Witte, 2002, pp. 169–170).

Moreover, the development of natural law is central to Roman Catholic theology. It was influenced in particular by Greek philosophy and Roman law rather than by the Scriptures (Gula, 2002, pp. 120–121; Selling, 2018, p. 9). Importantly, it is through natural law that the Catholic Church-State claims the rightness or wrongness of human conduct. The Catholic Church-State bases such claims on its trust in the human capacity to discern and to choose between right or wrong regardless of religious affiliation (Gula, 2002, pp. 120–121). Natural law is, for Roman Catholicism, a reflection of divine law and immediately accessible to human reason through the traditions of the Church and sacred texts (Berman, 2003, p. 73). The Roman Church-State has resorted to natural law as the foundation of its teachings on sexual behaviour, freedom of religion, justice, fair societies, human life, medical practice, and the connection between societal morals and civil law (Gula, 2002, pp. 120–121).

Contrary to Gula's (2002) idealistic appreciation, the application of natural law and the Code of Canon Law have led, among others, to "the very public failures of the Church to listen to victims and to get rid of abusive priests" (O'Reilly & Chalmers, 2014, p. 397). The authors observe, "the canonical penal process is clunky, vague, and inefficient" (p. 269). Among the several reasons that explain the inadequacy of the Canon Law system of justice, O'Reilly and Chalmers mention:

1. The canon law trial processes are slow, hierarchical, and inquisitional. While traditional criminal procedures in common law countries (e.g. the USA) may take a matter of days, the canonical process can take several years. For instance, a canonical tribunal hears a case then "sends it up to an appeal panel, and Vatican review is likely" (p. 353).
2. "'Due process' is not a standard term with a recognized content in canon law" (Orsy as cited in O'Reilly & Chalmers, 2014, p. 354). Therefore, canonical procedures do not recognise rights such as the presumption of innocence, trial by an independent court, or the right to confront witnesses (p. 354).
3. No separation of powers (i.e. checks and balances) exists in canon law (canon 331). While the Code of Canon Law distinguishes between executive, legislative, and judicial powers, the authority resides internationally in the pope, who is the supreme executive and primary legislator for the Roman Church-State. Locally, the authority resides with the bishop, who is subordinate to the pope (pp. 208–209).
4. Vatican officials and the pope enjoy sovereign immunity as the Vatican is recognised as a sovereign nation. Sovereign immunity defeats any effort of domestic plaintiff lawyers unless they appeal to specific international law instruments (pp. 163–164).
5. No cross-examination exists in canon law, for which only auditors or judges are allowed to ask questions. Also, "only having clerics judging clerics is patently biased because clearly the notion of solidarity among the brotherhood of priests trumped finding a fellow priest guilty" (pp. 264, 268).
6. Secrecy and the avoidance of scandal are mentioned in 24 different canons of the Code (p. 224). The principle of avoiding scandal to the Church explains, among others, the unwillingness of bishops and clerics to interact and cooperate with secular enforcement authorities. Consequently, "turning the accusations over to the civil authorities was never considered a viable option" (p.277). Numerous examples exist in which the Vatican curia encourages bishops not to cooperate with civil investigations over clergy sexual abuse scandals. For instance, "the Vatican blocked the Irish bishops from adopting a policy of 'mandatory reporting' of suspect abusers to the police" (p. 79). Likewise, the Colombian Cardinal Darío Castrillón issued several letters congratulating bishops for not releasing information about the sexual abuse of minors to civil authorities (p. 199).

Therefore, the application of the Code of Canon Law has resulted in a cover-up, whereby the Roman Church-State has left most of the sexual abuse committed by Catholic priests unpunished and uncompensated (Grand Jury of Pennsylvania, 2018). In the USA, O'Reilly and Chalmers (2014) document the quite cumbersome bureaucratic procedure under Catholic Canon Law to suing known or suspected clerics for having committed child abuse:

> Offentimes this process literally took years to complete—particularly if the case was appealed to Rome. [...] When an appeal was filed, it went to one of the Vatican courts. The National Review Board [for the Protection of Children and Young People] reports that

bishops knew that "the Vatican courts tended to err on the side of protecting a priest because of a concern that bishops could seek to use canon law to rid themselves of a priest whom they did not like or with whom they disagreed." [. . .] American Bishops were very concerned that even if there was a "conviction" in an internal diocesan penal trial that the judgment would eventually get overturned by a Vatican appeals court on a technicality. Then the case would either be sent back to be done correctly, or dismissed completely. Bishops had heard of cases that were overturned by Rome on technicalities, with the appeal being sent back with an order to reinstate the priest—even after a criminal conviction in the local civil jurisdiction (O'Reilly & Chalmers, 2014, p. 262).

Furthermore, some priests and bishops who are abusers, have also invoked the "seal of confessional" under the claim of religious freedom "to refuse to report sex abuse and to rebut the prosecutors' demand for disclosures" (O'Reilly & Chalmers, 2014, p. 122). In Pennsylvania (USA), thousands of sexual abuse complaints have been kept in "secret archives" that only the responsible bishop could access under the Code of Canon Law. The FBI analysed Diocesan files and found that the Roman Catholic hierarchy followed the same script-like method to "conceal the truth": (1) uses euphemisms rather than concrete language to describe sexual assaults; (2) does not conduct genuine investigations with properly trained staff; (3) sends priests for "evaluation" at church-run psychiatric treatment centres to create a semblance of integrity; (4) fails to disclose why a priest needs to be removed, or tells his parishioners that he is on "sick leave" or suffering from "nervous exhaustion"; (5) keeps covering the priest's housing and living expenses even if he continues to abuse children; (6) transfers the priest "to a new location where no one will know he is a child abuser"; and finally and most significantly (7) fails to notify the police (Grand Jury of Pennsylvania, 2018, pp. 2–3).

Evidently, the canonical and civil procedures are entirely separate processes that do not naturally interrelate, although there can be some overlaps. However, the Canon Law system has interfered with civil prosecution processes, so that most cases of abusive clergy remain in impunity (Grand Jury of Pennsylvania, 2018). The Canon Law system has proven to use cumbersome, archaic processes with excessive formalities that make "the removal and punishment process exceedingly difficult to manage" (O'Reilly & Chalmers, 2014, p. 253). Even in prosperous countries such as the USA, the canonical penal system is "unwieldy, inefficient, and almost impossible for many dioceses to maintain the personnel and processes as they are required in the Code". O'Reilly and Chalmers appropriately ask the question of where the canonical system can possibly run properly, if not in the USA (p. 401). As the Report of the Grand Jury of Pennsylvania (2011) states:

The canonical process does not make the internal investigations any less biased in favor of protecting the institution, or the people who conduct them any more competent at arriving at the truth, or the victims feel any less re-victimized (supra, 86–87).

O'Reilly and Chalmers (2014) also emphasise the pervasiveness of the clergy's sexual abuse problem, with varied outcomes among virtually all religious organisations, including Protestant faiths. Yet, these denominations do not cover-up their cases with a historical state legal shield such as the Code of Canon Law. Several denominations (e.g. Methodist, Nazarene, Protestant Episcopal Church) have concurred that religious doctrines need not be considered in criminal cases such as clergy abuse. However, denominations such as the Presbyterians claim that the presbytery functions as an ecclesiastical court alternate, which is not analogous to civil law (i.e. a similar claim as in the Catholic Canon Law). Mormons and The Jehovah's Witnesses "are noted for their secrecy and intra-faith methods", which "makes it difficult to accurately assess the scope of sexual abuse" (O'Reilly & Chalmers, 2014, p. 406). In any case, secular authorities investigate and prosecute ordinary citizens, including Protestant ministers, who commit sexual abuse or any other crimes, in regular legal processes.

Finally, in common law countries, (which are also historically Protestant, such as the USA) the conflict between Catholic Canon Law and the law of the state is more visible because the latter has pre-eminence. In turn, that conflict is less visible in most Catholic countries, in which Canon Law has often prevailed over civil norms. Furthermore, legal instruments such as concordats have been typically enforced to accept the force of Canon Law in several Catholic countries.

### *8.3.4 Protestantism, Revolutions, and Law* (6′)

Despite the critical impact of Protestant reformations on the law and on institutions, the influence of religion has been largely neglected or obscured in the mainstream literature[3] (Doe & Sandberg, 2010, p. 9; Berman, 2003, p. 71; Witte, 2002, p. 28; Anderson, 2009, p. 210). The significant contribution that sixteenth-century Lutheran legal theorists made to Western legal thought has been ignored in conventional historical accounts (Berman, 2003, p. 71). As Witte observed, "...some social historians today have dismissed the "Reformation" altogether as a historian's fiction and a historical failure" (pp. 28–29). Thus, a conventional interpretation of the influence of the early Reformers is that:

> ...they inspired no real reformation. Their ideas had little impact on the beliefs and behaviors of common people. Their policies perpetuated elitism and chauvinism more than they cultivated equality and liberty. Their reforms tended to obstruct nascent movements for democracy and market economy and to inspire new excesses in the patriarchies of family, Church, and state. As the editors of the *Handbook of European History 1400–1600* put it, "the Reformation" must now be viewed as an ideological category of "nineteenth century Protestant historical belief," which served more to defend the self-identity of modern mainline Protestants than to define a cardinal turning point in Western history. Recent historiography, the editors continue, has brought "changes of sensibility" that have now "robbed" the term "Reformation" of any utility and veracity (Witte, 2002, p. 29).

[3]It does not refer to the Weberian (cultural) influence of Protestantism on the development of capitalism, about which thousands of articles and hundreds of books have been written (see Sect. 7.1). Rather, it refers particularly to the influence of religion on law and institutions as an established research paradigm. Doe and Sandberg (2010) have observed, regarding the latter, that in Law Schools, the relationship between religion and law has been an overlooked topic of study (p. 9).

However, Witte runs "counter to traditional lines of historical analysis" by demonstrating that the theology and law of the Reformation are "sources of ideas and institutions that were much more than simply the totems of the elite of the bludgeons of the powerful". When viewed through the binocular of law and theology, the author continues, "the Lutheran Reformation is hardly the ideological concept or idle category that some recent historiography suggests" (pp. 29–30).

This section reviews the historical influence of Protestantism, and of the various revolutions that followed in its wake, on the different legal traditions.

#### 8.3.4.1 The Sixteenth-Century German-European Revolution

In 1517, Martin Luther and other Reformers initiated a process that culminated in the abolition of Roman Catholic ecclesiastical jurisdiction in future Protestant countries (i.e. England, Scandinavian countries) (Berman, 2003, p. 6). Luther, a canon law expert, condemned Aquinas's Aristotelian theology and most of the Catholic sacraments due to their lack of biblical foundations (Berman, 2003); (Witte, 2002). Berman portrayed Martin Luther as someone who honestly reflected his preachings and teachings in both his career and life. For the author, the German people of Luther's time considered him a new Elijah, John the Baptist, Daniel, Moses, or other prophet sent by the Lord. For Berman, Luther was the brightest and undoubtedly one of the most influential, innovative, and famous theologians of his day. He was intensely passionate, almost as if he was being spurred on by extraneous forces. Yet, the same passion prompted him to denounce vitriolically those who profoundly disagreed with him. He used scatological words in his condemnations without hesitation. In his later years, he engaged in bigoted verbal attacks on Jews who resisted converting to Christianity, paralleled with assaults on Anabaptists, Turks, papists, and others (Berman, 2003, p. 47).

In Luther's Ninety-five Theses of 1517, and in subsequent debates, he exposed a long list of injustices inherent in canon laws. He also unmasked the "fallacious legal foundation" of papal authority and the "myriad inconsistencies" between the "human laws and traditions" of the Roman Church-State versus the Scriptures (Berman, 2003, p. 74). Luther said that the Roman Church should not be a lawmaking institution and emphasised:

> In the entire canon law of the pope there are not even two lines which could instruct a devout Christian, (. . .) it would be a good thing if canon law were completely blotted out, from the first letter to the last, especially the [papal] decretals. More than enough is written in the Bible about how we should behave in all circumstances. Unless they abolish their laws and ordinances and restore to Christ's churches their liberty and have it taught among them, they are to blame for all the souls that perish under this miserable captivity, and *the papacy is truly the kingdom of Babylon and of the very Antichrist* (LW 44:179, 202–3 as cited in Witte, 2002, p. 55) (author's italics).

Moreover, Luther directly attacked the moral authority of the Roman law (and its lawyers) as part of the same Babylonian system:

> Jurists are bad Christians (WA TR 3, No. 2809b). Every jurist is an enemy of Christ (WA TR 3, Nos. 2837, 3027). I shit on the law of the pope and of the emperor, and on the law of the jurists as well (WA 49:302 as cited in Witte, 2002, p. 2).

Therefore, what began as a reformation of the Church and theology rapidly expanded into a reformation of the law and the state, in Germany and beyond (i.e. in Northern Europe, and later in North America). The key was to deconstruct canon law for the sake of the Gospel and, on this basis, to reconstruct "civil law on the strength of the Gospel" (Witte, 2002, p. 3).

Accordingly, the Lutheran Reformation initially removed medieval Roman and canon laws in the sixteenth-century Germany. Luther considered this process imperative for various reasons: Roman and canon laws fostered papal tyranny and thus enjoyed unbridled powers of legislation, adjudication, and administration. Second, it was abusive and self-serving, and thereby granted the clergy special benefits, privileges, exemptions, and immunities that elevated it above the laity. Third, it served as an instrument of greed and exploitation to support the luxury and bureaucracy of the Roman Church (LW 31:341[4] as cited in Witte, 2002, pp. 55–56). Moreover, since Roman Catholic natural law is founded on the human ability to discern good and evil (Selling, 2018); (Gula, 2002), its refutation by Protestantism also had a biblical foundation:

> The heart is deceitful above all *things*, and desperately wicked: Who can know it? (King James Bible, 1769, Jeremiah 17:9);
>
> Why should ye be stricken any more? ye will revolt more and more: the whole head is sick, and the whole heart faint (King James Bible, 1769, Isaiah 1:5);
>
> For I know that in me (that is, in my flesh,) dwelleth no good thing: for to will is present with me; but *how* to perform that which is good I find not. For the good that I would, I do not: but the evil which I would not, that I do (King James Bible, 1769, Romans 7:18–19).

Given the explicit scriptural claims of the human inability to discern good from evil, Protestant jurists, therefore, considered the Gospel the best source of natural knowledge (Witte, 2002, p. 169). Luther, but most especially his followers, Melanchthon, Eisermann, and Oldendorp considered the Bible the supreme source of law for earthly life. Accordingly, they produced a new jurisprudence, one theologically based on biblical moral principles, upon which they interpreted subordinate species of legal rules (Berman, 2003, p. 8). Consequently, Lutheran jurists laid particular emphasis on the biblical Ten Commandments to ground their jurisprudence, which thus contrasted with the Catholic canonists' focus on the seven sacraments (Berman, 2003); (Witte, 2002) (compare Tables 8.1 and Fig. 8.4).

However, Lutheran jurists also had to adapt traditional canon laws, which subsequently fell under the control of civil authorities (Witte, 2002, pp. 83–84). Therefore, not all Protestant, positive law can be subsumed under the Ten Commandments, but can also have other biblical, as well as Roman or canonical origins (Witte, 2002, p. 170). However, "self-serving papalist accretions" were eradicated,

---

[4]*D. Martin Luthers Werke: Kritische Gesamtausgabe*, 78 vols. (Weimar, 1883–1987).

| **Moral Biblical Law (*King James Bible*, 1769)** | | | | | **Some Lutheran and positive laws under the Ten Commandments*** (Witte, 2002); (Berman, 2003). |
|---|---|---|---|---|---|
| **Great Commandment in the New Testament (NT)** | **Old Testament (OT)** | | **Some curses of disobedience (OT & NT)** | **Some blessings of obedience (OT & NT)** | |
| | **The Great Commandment in OT terms** | **The Ten Commandments (*King James Bible*, 1769, Exodus 20, 1-17)** | | | |
| Matthew 22, 34-40<br><br>**The Great Commandment**<br><br>Master, which is the great commandment in the law?<br><br>Jesus said unto him,<br><br>**Thou shalt love the Lord thy God with all thy heart, and with all thy soul, and with all thy mind.**<br><br>This is the first and great commandment. | Deuteronomy 6, 4-5<br>Hear, O Israel: The Lord our God is one Lord:<br>and **thou shalt love the Lord thy God with all thine heart, and with all thy soul, and with all thy might.** | And God spake all these words, saying, I am the Lord thy God, which have brought thee out of the land of Egypt, out of the house of bondage.<br>**1. Thou shalt have no other gods before me.**<br><br>**2. Thou shalt not make unto thee any graven image,** or any likeness of any thing that is in heaven above, or that is in the earth beneath, or that is in the water under the earth: thou shalt not bow down thyself to them, nor serve them: for I the Lord thy God am a jealous God, visiting the iniquity of the fathers upon the children unto the third and fourth generation of them that hate me; and showing mercy unto thousands of them that love me, and keep my commandments.<br><br>**3. Thou shalt not take the name of the Lord thy God in vain:** for the Lord will not hold him guiltless that taketh his name in vain.<br><br>**4. Remember the sabbath day, to keep it holy.** Six days shalt thou labor, and do all thy work: but the seventh day is the sabbath of the Lord thy God: in it thou shalt not do any work, thou, nor thy son, nor thy daughter, thy manservant, nor thy maidservant, nor thy cattle, nor thy stranger that is within thy gates: for in six days the Lord made heaven and earth, the sea, and all that in them is, and rested the seventh day: wherefore the Lord blessed the sabbath day, and hallowed it. | Deuteronomy 28<br>[Verses 15-68 are dedicated to "*The Consequences of Disobedience*", for example:]<br><br>15: But it shall come to pass, if thou wilt not hearken unto the voice of the Lord thy God, to observe to do all his commandments and his statutes which I command thee this day; that all these curses shall come upon thee, and overtake thee:<br>33: The fruit of thy land, and all thy labors, shall a nation which thou knowest not eat up; *and thou shalt be only oppressed and crushed alway*:"<br><br>Revelation 21,8 But the fearful, and unbelieving, and the abominable, and murderers, and whoremongers, and | Deuteronomy 29, 9<br>Keep therefore the words of this covenant, and do them, that ye may prosper in all that ye do.<br><br>"Deuteronomy 28, 1-2<br>*The Blessings of Obedience*<br><br>And it shall come to pass, if thou shalt hearken diligently unto the voice of the Lord thy God, to observe and to do all his commandments which I command thee this day, that *the Lord thy God will set thee on high above all nations of the earth:*<br>and all these blessings shall come on thee, and overtake thee, if thou shalt hearken unto the voice of the Lord thy God.<br><br>Deuteronomy 30, 16<br>in that I command thee this day to love the Lord thy God, to walk in his ways, and to keep his commandments, and his statutes, and his judgments, that thou mayest live and multiply: and *the Lord thy* | Religious laws of Lutheran communities. Laws governing orthodox doctrine and liturgy, ecclesiastical polity and property, local clergy and Church administrators. |

**Fig. 8.4** Moral biblical law associated with prosperity (when obeyed) or with misfortunes (when disobeyed) and its legal application in Protestant countries (Amended from The Holy Bible (King James Version); Witte, 2002; Berman, 2003)

| **Moral Biblical Law (*King James Bible*, 1769)** | | | | | **Some Lutherian and positive laws under the Ten Commandments*** (Witte, 2002); (Berman, 2003). |
|---|---|---|---|---|---|
| **Great Commandment in the New Testament (NT)** | **Old Testament (OT)**<br>**The Great Commandment in OT terms** | **The Ten Commandments (*King James Bible*, 1769, Exodus 20, 1-17)** | **Some curses of disobedience (OT & NT)** | **Some blessings of obedience (OT & NT)** | |
| | | | sorcerers, and idolaters, and all liars, shall have their part in the lake which burneth with fire and brimstone: which is the second death. | *God shall bless thee in the land whither thou goest to possess it.* | Ibid |
| Matthew 22, 39–40<br><br>And the second is like unto it,<br>**Thou shalt love thy neighbor as thyself.**<br><br>**On these two commandments hang all the law and the prophets.** | Leviticus 19, 17-18 Thou shalt not hate thy brother in thine heart: thou shalt in any wise rebuke thy neighbor, and not suffer sin upon him. Thou shalt not avenge, nor bear any grudge against the children of thy people, but **thou shalt love thy neighbor as thyself:** I am the Lord. | **5. Honor thy father and thy mother:** that thy days may be long upon the land which the Lord thy God giveth thee. | | Revelation 22, 14: Blessed are they that do his commandments, that they may have right to the tree of life, and may enter in through the gates into the city. | Civil law of sex, marriage, and family |
| | | **6. Thou shalt not kill.** | | | Criminal law |
| | | **7.Thou shalt not commit adultery.** | | | Civil law of sex, marriage, and family |
| | | **8.Thou shalt not steal.** | | | Law of property, criminal law |
| | | **9.Thou shalt not bear false witness** against thy neighbor. | | | Law of contract and delict. Law of civil procedure, evidence, and defamation |
| | | **10. Thou shalt not covet** thy neighbor's house, thou shalt not covet thy neighbor's wife, nor his manservant, nor his maidservant, nor his ox, nor his ass, nor any thing that is thy neighbor's. | | | Law of contract and delict.<br>Laws of crimes and civil offences |

* Legislation influencing Protestant countries (e.g. the United States, United Kingdom, Scandinavian countries)

*Note:* Author's italics and emphases

**Fig. 8.4** (Continued)

and canon law in Germany now returned "to its core interpretations and applications of biblical and natural norms" (ibid). In this way, German law was transformed and still largely influences modern Western laws of education, social welfare, and marriage, for instance (Witte, 2002, p. 295). Moreover, "the Ten Commandments provided the Evangelical jurists with a useful framework for organising some of the legal institutions of the state" (Witte, 2002, p. 170) (Fig. 8.4).

Successively, all Europe (and later also other regions) felt the repercussions of the Protestant revolt against the canon-law-based and hierarchical Roman Church-State. The sixteenth-century German Lutheran Revolution of theology, law, and institutions took diverse forms in several European countries. It facilitated the creation of national legal systems that encompassed the complete continuum of jurisdictions (Berman, 2003, p. 8) and generally exalted monarchies over the Roman Church-State (Berman, 2003, pp. 72, 208). In fact, after the Lutheran Reformation,

> the idea of the Pope and Emperor as parallel and universal powers disappears, and the independent jurisdictions of the *sacerdotium* are handed over to the secular authorities' (Skinner, 1978, p. 353).[5]

Consequently, the Lutheran Reformation extended across Europe. Even in the remaining Roman Catholic countries, such as Spain, France, or Austria, royal powers significantly increased over the Roman Church-State within the kingdoms (Berman, 2003, p. 8).

However, as with any revolution, the German Reformation also had a "dark side". Witte notes the acute crisis that reigned in Germany following the rapid deconstruction of law, politics, and society immediately after the Reformation. The bloody peasants' revolt in Germany in 1525, and the widespread confusion over sacraments, preaching, funerals, prayers, holidays, and pastoral duties, exemplifies the chaos at the time. Also, the excesses that occurred at the dawn of the Reformation are well known, as Witte observes:

> They [the Reformers] simply took over hundreds of Church properties, endowments, foundations, charities, almshouses, schools, cathedrals, cemeteries, Church courts, and other properties and institutions that were part of the canon law administration–often ostracizing and occasionally killing former occupants in the process (although Luther repeatedly counselled against violent ejection of monks and nuns, preferring instead to prohibit the enrolment of any new monks. . .) (Witte, 2002, p. 84)

##### 8.3.4.1.1 Lutheran Influence on Scandinavian Countries

The Lutheran Reformation influenced in particular the Scandinavian pattern of church-state relations (Anderson, 2009, p. 211). The Lutheran influence was more intense and took hold faster in Scandinavian countries than in Germany, which remained partly Roman Catholic. The monarchies of Denmark (and countries under its influence, i.e. Norway and Iceland) and Sweden (and thus also Finland) firmly

---

embraced Lutheranism already in the 1520s. These countries also imposed severe criminal penalties on openly non-Lutheran adherents (Berman, 2003, p. 58).

Swedish and Danish monarchs seized the influence and wealth of the Catholic Church-State and assumed the welfare functions previously performed by the Church (e.g. hospital care and relief of the poor) (Anderson, 2009, p. 211). As such, Lutheran state churches "positively contributed to the early introduction of social protection programs and to subsequent welfare state development" (Manow & van Kersbergen, 2009, p. 4).

#### 8.3.4.2 The Seventeenth-Century English-European Revolution

Under the influence of the German sixteenth-century revolution, England also instituted a Protestant state-church to which all citizens had to belong and fell under the authority of the monarch. Later, dissenting Calvinists and other oppressed classes initiated the English or Glorious Revolution (1640–1689), which curbed the influence of the state-church, and established the supremacy of Parliament over the Crown. Subsequently, the English Revolution resulted in a body of legislation based on Calvinist beliefs (Berman, 2003, p. 10). This *"reformation of the Reformation"* fundamentally and lastingly transformed the English legal system, including checks and balances of political power. Likewise, the English Revolution also became a European revolution, succeeding the previous one in Germany (Berman, 2003, p. 201).

Akin to the German Lutheran Reformation, the Ten Commandments are the foundation for a plural system of law in England (Doe & Sandberg, 2010). Notably, the general principle *"Thou shalt love thy neighbour as thyself"* (second part of the Decalogue that Jesus summarised in Matthew 22:37–39, King James Bible, 1769) is a touchstone of civil behaviour (p.163) (See Fig. 8.4).

Likewise, the Protestant Reformation in England and Wales banned the teaching of canon law at universities (Doe & Sandberg, 2010, p. 9). Equally, in the courts of Westminster Hall, invoking canon law was increasingly deplored (Helmoz, 1987); (Pearce, 2010). As Wilcox and Field wrote in their Admonition to Parliament in 1572: "the Canon law is Antichristian and devilishe, and contrarye to the scriptures" (p. 30). However, similarly to Germany, not all canon law was eliminated as an authoritative source. In fact, some ordinances were adapted to ongoing developments in English common law.

The expansion of the British Empire resulted in a wide distribution of common law in the British colonies. This law is therefore still in force in Great Britain, Ireland, the USA, Canada, Australia, and New Zealand (Merryman & Pérez, 2007, p. 4).

#### 8.3.4.3 The Eighteenth-Century United States Revolution

The successive Protestant Reformations brought along progressive legal steps towards democracy and thus increasingly distanced societies from the power of the Roman Church. Each dissenting Protestant revolution built on the developments and achievements of the previous one. The sixteenth-century German-European Reformation had generally increased the royal powers as a means of overthrowing the Roman Church-State. The seventeenth-century English-European Revolution then made further advances by introducing checks and balances for monarchical powers and by limiting the power of the Church-States. Such developments paved the way for the world's first-ever democratic constitution: the eighteenth century American Bill of Rights. In the USA, once again, a dissenting Protestant view based on the previous reformatory advances became dominant and denied the establishment of a State-Church.

Furthermore, the American constitution expanded the democratic rights and liberties of citizens (thus advancing English legislation, which had already guaranteed rights to the aristocracy over the monarchy) (Miller, 2012); (Berman, 2003); (Witte, 2002).

The eighteenth-century French-European revolution also helped to nurture its counterpart in the USA. However, the latter implemented a different system of checks and balances in government powers than those proposed by the French Revolution, for instance (Merryman & Pérez, 2007); (Berman, 2003).

#### 8.3.4.4 The Influence of Protestant Revolutions on Secularism

The Protestant reformations initiated a rapid secularisation process, which decreased the public role of the Roman Church-State and broke down the imperial hierarchy (Philpott, 2001; Snyder, 2011). Moreover, the Protestant reformations and their associated progressive weakening of the Roman Church-State ultimately resulted in the modern sovereign state system in the seventeenth-century (i.e. the Peace of Westphalia in 1648) (Agnew, 2010; Gregory, 2012; Philpott, 2001; Shah & Philpott, 2011; Snyder, 2011).

Much liberal Enlightenment thought was grounded in Protestant secularism (Snyder, 2011, p. 17). Therefore, the laic rejection of Roman Catholicism in revolutionary France resulted from the influence of Protestantism, in particular Calvinism. Most Enlightenment democratic theorists came from a Calvinist background, even if they were not religious (e.g. Locke, Rousseau, Grotius, Franklin, Adams, Henry, Madison, and Hamilton) (Woodberry, 2012, p. 248). Enlightenment theorists secularised ideas previously expressed by Calvinist jurists and theologians (e.g. Nonconformist and Puritan covenants formed the basis of the secular Hobbes's and Locke's social contracts) (Hutson, 1998; Nelson, 2010; Witte, 2007; Lutz, 1980, 1988 as cited in Woodberry, 2012, p. 248).

Furthermore, Locke's principle of equality for all people descends explicitly from Protestant ideals (Waldron; Woodberry and Shah; as cited in Woodberry, 2012, p. 248). Moreover, Protestant dissenters in Protestant liberal democracies spearheaded egalitarian movements such as the abolition of slavery, free trade, and peace (Kaufmann & Pape, 1999; Snyder, 2011; Woodberry, 2012). In this sense, without the Reformation, no liberal peace would exist (Hurd, 2011; Snyder, 2011, p. 17; Gregory, 2012).

Consequently, Protestantism was a vital historical precursor to secularisation (Berger, 1990, p. 113; Gregory, 2012). In its wake, religion has since lost much of its past influence (Norris & Inglehart, 2004) in specific contexts (e.g. Europe, the academia). However, the rest of the world is as religious as ever, and some regions (e.g. the Middle East) are even more religious than before (Berger, 1999).

#### 8.3.4.5 The Eighteenth and Nineteenth-Century French-European Revolution

The successive Protestant reformations inspired or initiated transformations from which arose secular, anti-clerical revolutions, which further decreased the power of the Roman Church-State and expanded civil power. The most notable revolution, the French Revolution, utterly suppressed the monarchy in France and extended to most papal states (e.g. Pope Pius VI was taken prisoner until his eventual death). Some of these states were, however, later restored. The Italian nationalism and anti-clericalism remaining after the French Revolution resulted in the nineteenth-century annexation of Rome and the papal states to the former Italian Kingdom. It was not until 1929 that the current Vatican State was created through the Lateran Treaty with Mussolini's National Fascist Party (Gross, 2004; Hanlon, 2008; Roessler & Miklos, 2003).

Rousseau's *Social Contract* (1762) and the French Revolution (1789) openly identified Roman Catholicism (and Christianity in general) as opposed to any free republic. In such a Manichean conflict between the Church and the Republican state, the Republic ended up radically subordinating the Church. Consequently, the French Republic eliminated the Church's control over education, its ownership of large estates and its right to perform marriage ceremonies (Shah & Philpott, 2011, p. 38).

The new French legal philosophy of rationalism, individualism, utilitarianism, as well as the rejection of orthodox Christian doctrines, were also linked to deism (the belief in a Creator's gift of reason and freewill in exercising that gift (Berman, 2003, p. 10).

French rationalist natural secular jurists considered it possible to abolish the old (i.e. Roman-canonical) legal system altogether and to create an entirely new one. However, the jurists drafting the new system were trained in the old one, of which a significant part was preserved as a result (Merryman & Pérez, 2015).

Eighteenth and nineteenth-century revolutions (i.e. the French and American revolutions, the Italian *Risorgimento* and Latin American independence wars) gave rise to administrative and constitutional law under civil law. Equally important was that the French Revolution also brought forth "secular natural law" (based on deism). Montesquieu and Rousseau promoted the importance of separating government powers (judicial, executive, and legislative), as initiated by the French Revolution. After the nineteenth century, the authority of Roman (and canonical) laws gradually declined. The Revolution meant that nationalist ideologies replaced religious ideologies. Feudal institutions were incompatible with such developments (Merryman & Pérez, 2015).

The French imposed civil codes, abolished guilds and feudal remnants, and undermined aristocratic privileges, thus boosting prosperity in the territories they conquered in Europe (Acemoglu et al., 2011). Consequently, the principal states of Western Europe adopted civil codes, whose archetype is the French Code Napoléon of 1804 (Merryman & Pérez, 2007, p. 10).

An especially explosive revolutionary development occurred in education. French republicans and liberals repeatedly pushed for a state-supervised, compulsory, educational system. In Belgium, the Liberal Party implemented a programme in the 1870s to significantly restrict the role of the Roman Catholic Church in education (Shah & Philpott, 2011, pp. 39–40).

However, even after an age determined by reason and revolution, feudalism survived in Latin America and certain parts of Europe (especially in the South). Feudalism has kept alive the social injustices inherent in its origins. This is understandable because when it came to exporting their methods, the French did not introduce a roadmap for how their model truly worked and left out any guidelines for how it did (Merryman, 1996, p. 116).

For example, the *laïcité* or separation of church and state rooted in the French Revolution was not automatically transplanted to Latin America. In contrast, feudal legal institutions in the British colonies of North America were deprived of their pernicious socio-economic influence already early on (Merryman & Pérez, 2015).

### 8.3.4.6 Maintaining the Roman Catholic *Status Quo* after Independence

#### 8.3.4.6.1 The Adoption of French Civil Law in Latin American Countries

Most Latin American countries bypassed the (Protestant) European revolutionary processes and directly adopted the French Revolution's legal tradition (La Porta et al., 2008; Merryman & Pérez, 2015). Therefore, the French legal tradition profoundly influenced all former Spanish and Portuguese colonies in Latin America. Exceptionally, Cuba adopted a socialist legal tradition later in the 1960s. In turn, some former British colonies in the Caribbean have correspondingly English common law (La Porta et al., 2008).

The influence of the Protestant Reformation on the law and on institutions in Latin America has been minimal or indirect, and has resulted from US-American influence, for instance (i.e. constitutionalism) (Merryman & Pérez, 2015). More importantly, the pervasive influence of the Roman Catholic Church-State meant that Latin American countries adopted the legal tradition of the French Revolution without, however, embracing anti-clerical movements (or with fragile anti-clerical components) (La Porta et al., 2008; Salinas, 2013). Exceptions include Uruguay, Chile, and Cuba, as these countries have had successful anti-clerical or laic movements and because their legal systems have long reflected a clear separation of Church and State. Moreover, these three countries have never signed a concordat with the Roman Church-State (Da Costa, 2009; Ramírez, 2009; Salinas, 2013).

#### 8.3.4.6.2 Concordats with the Roman Catholic Church-State

Concordats are international treaties between the Roman See (the so-called "Holy" See) and the states. In the past, concordats have been criticised as mutual concessions of privileges between Church and State. The three most important and controversial concordats signed by the Catholic Church in the twentieth century were with the Nazi *Reich* in Germany, with Franco in Spain, and with Fascist Italy (Fumagalli, 2011, pp. 438–439).

The term "concordat" refers to the more comprehensive agreements between the states and the Roman See but also identifies a wide variety of instruments (e.g. treaty, convention, accord, protocol, exchange of notes, modus vivendi) (Ragazzi, 2009, 114). A historical treaty-making power allows the Roman Church to sign concordats and ensures its accession to major multilateral treaties (Ryngaert, 2011, 844).

Eleven Latin American countries have in force a concordat with the Roman Catholic Church-State (Argentina, Bolivia, Brazil, Colombia, Ecuador, El Salvador, Haiti, Paraguay, Peru, Dominican Republic, and Venezuela). Such states are called "concordatarian" and the extent to which those agreements grant privileges to the Roman Church varies from country to country (Corral, 2014). The scope of these rights and privileges depends on the negotiating power of the Roman See *vis-à-vis* the contracting state (Ryngaert, 2011, 845). The other Latin American countries maintain fewer diplomatic relations with the Vatican (some less, some more), for instance, through formal agreements or the exchange of letters (Corral, 2014). Concordats may cover diverse affairs, ranging from tax exemptions for the Roman Church to permitting its intervention in military, educational, and real estate issues (Brownlie, 1979; Corral & Petschen, 2004; Figueroa, 2016; Forrest et al., 2006; Levine, 1981).

The template used by the Vatican in most concordats with Latin American countries was introduced by Pope Pio IX (1846–1878) (Salinas, 2013). It accords extraordinarily extensive rights to the Catholic Church-State, for instance, in educational affairs:

> Education in universities, public and private schools and further educational establishments should be under the doctrine of the Catholic Religion. [...] the bishops and other local ordinaries would have the free direction of the theology chairs, of canon law, [and] of all the branches of ecclesiastical teaching. [...] in addition to the influence they will exert through the strength of their ministry over the religious education of youth, they will ensure that in the teaching of any other branch there is nothing contrary to [the Roman Catholic] religion and morality (article 2). Besides, the bishops retain their right of censure over all books and

writings related to dogma and discipline of the Church and public morals (Bolivian concordat model, cited in Salinas, 2013, p. 217).[6]

These concordats are all similar (or in many cases identical) in Latin America. As such, they attest to the Vatican's influence on their wording rather than to the interests of the various diverse states (Salinas, 2013).

As a rule, the concordats ensure religious education in public schools. The conference of bishops, in agreement with the responsible government authorities, approves the curriculum for the teaching of Roman Catholic religion in schools (Schanda, 2004).

The concordats also imply state recognition of the sovereignty of the Roman Catholic Church-State. Consequently, Roman Catholicism is the only religion to possess legal personality under international public law. The other religious denominations are only entitled to have agreements under domestic public law as they have no international legal personality. This privilege of the Roman Catholic Church-State has sometimes been used to the detriment of other religious denominations (Fumagalli, 2011, p. 444).

Therefore, EU institutions, such as the European Court of Human Rights, have indirectly challenged Roman Catholic concordats for introducing legislation not aligned with international standards into domestic law (Fumagalli, 2011, pp. 445–446). In Europe, at least two objections have been levelled at concordats (or treaties and bilateral relations with the Roman Church-State): first, they limit the sovereignty of the state; and second, they promote the denominational inequality due to the privileges of the Roman Catholic Church-State (Cook, 2012; Schanda, 2004).

#### 8.3.4.7 The Twentieth-Century Russian Revolution

In the eleventh and twelfth centuries, Eastern Orthodox Russia opposed the papal Roman Church-State and canon law and established its own hierarchy and canon law. However, Russia maintained its tsarish autocracy and its supreme secular and spiritual authority until 1917. The successive Lutheran, Calvinist, dissenting Protestant and deist revolutions all bypassed Russia. Thus, Russia never experienced an evolutive process from an autocracy to a monarchical high magistracy, to an aristocratic Parliament, and then to a democratic separation of powers. Instead, Russia underwent abrupt transformation through the Bolshevik revolution, inspired in part by the eighteenth-century French Enlightenment, and later proclaimed atheism. Moreover, the Russian Revolution ended up in a totalitarian state that distorted the ideals of social democracy (Berman, 2003, p. 18); (Miller, 2012).

One of the ideal postulates of the atheistic foundations of Soviet law is the "goodness of humankind." This involves the acceptance of an inherent human nature, which is itself capable of establishing a fair and just society (Berman, 2003, p. 18). Such a postulate is opposed to the biblical principle that "nothing

[6]Author's translation of the original Spanish text.

good can be found in humankind," which forms the basis of the Protestant Revolutions (see Sect. 8.3.4 and Fig. 8.4). The atheistic, Soviet legal principle of the "goodness of humankind" resembles Roman Catholic natural law in that it trusts the human capacity to discern good from evil (Selling, 2018, p. 9; Gula, 2002, pp. 120–121). In fact, socialist legal traditions only ever became apparent in countries with an Orthodox or Roman Catholic background but never in countries under Protestant influence. As Andreski (as cited in Grier, 1997) argued, by fostering prosperity, freedom, and equality, Protestantism inhibits the formation of a social environment conducive to the propagation of militant subversion ideologies (p. 49).

Significant differences exist between Soviet, Western European, and American legal systems. Features differentiating Soviet law from other systems include the dictatorship of the Communist Party and the absence of a law higher than that of the state; the repression of basic civil liberties such as the freedom of religion, speech, and press; and the absence of private land ownership (Berman, 2003, p. 19). However, the Russian Revolution's elevation of the parental role of the law, and of the social and economic role of the state, have had repercussions throughout the world (ibid). Interestingly, after the dissolution of the Soviet Union in 1991, most former Soviet countries reinstated the legal tradition of the French Revolution (Merryman & Pérez, 2015); (La Porta et al., 2008).

### *8.3.5 Religion, Law, and State Models*

Significant differences exist between the legal systems (and thus, the state models) of countries in Europe and in the Americas. National legal systems have persisted for decades or even centuries while legal traditions have prevailed for centuries or even millennia. In contrast, political discourses may last for merely a few years or decades. Therefore, the influence of the different legal traditions tends to cluster countries into groups exhibiting affinities between their legal origins and institutional performance. Table 8.2 summarises the various legal revolutions and traditions along with their models of state–church–citizen relations.

The church–state–citizen relationships in Table 8.2 delineate the historical progression from the original medieval model of the *Corpus Christianum*, which was based entirely on Roman and Catholic canon law traditions (Model 1), to modern legal systems.

1. The *Corpus Christianum* is the model of the medieval Pan-European Roman Catholic Church-State. In it, the Roman Church-State is the highest power. As such, it alone may access and interpret the divine and guide its small secular arm: the state. In this conception, both Church and State control and coerce the individual. The individual may access the divine exclusively through the Church and never directly. The entire system of moral and legal codes emanates from the Roman Catholic Church-State in the figure of the pope. Legally speaking, the

**Table 8.2** Moral and religious beliefs and models of state-church-citizen relations in the legal systems in Europe and the Americas (Amended from Witte, 2002; Berman, 2003; Miller, 2012; Cook, 2012; Merryman & Pérez, 2007)

| Legal system | Religious source | Fundamental moral beliefs inspiring law | Main Influencer | Model of Church-State and citizen relations in each legal system[a] |
|---|---|---|---|---|
| **1. Roman and Catholic canon law** (From before Christ and until presently) | Roman Paganism and Roman Catholicism | The sacraments, scholasticism, tradition, selected sacred texts | Thomas Aquinas | 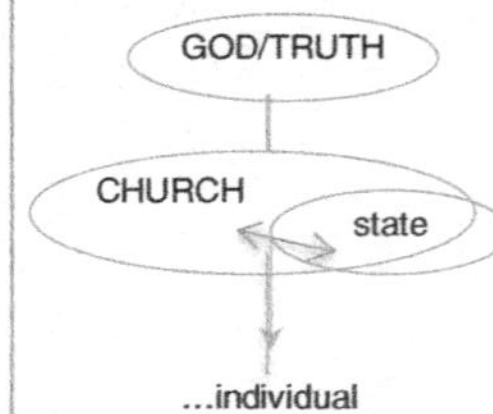 |
| **2. German Revolution** (sixteenth-century onwards) | Lutheranism | At first only the Holy Scriptures (*Sola Scriptura*); conceptualism; later also tradition | Martin Luther | 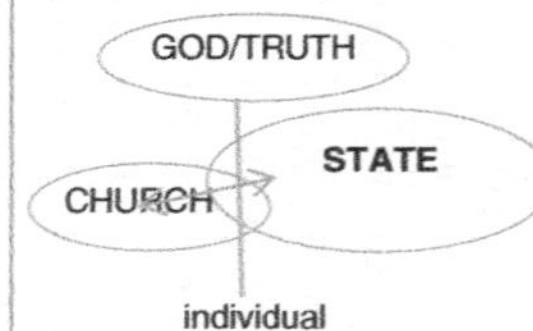 |
| **3. English Revolution** (seventeenth-century onwards) | Anglo-Calvinism Puritanism | The Holy Scriptures (i.e. the Ten Commandments); empiricism; historical tradition | John Calvin | 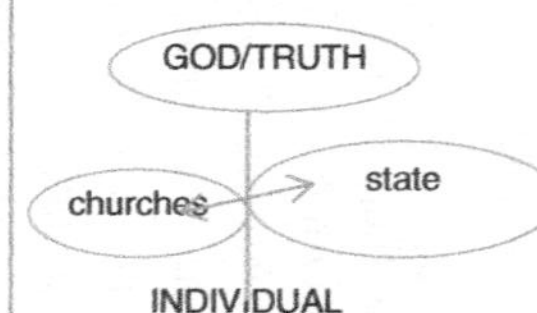 |

| | | | | |
|---|---|---|---|---|
| **4. United States Revolution** (eighteenth-century onwards) | Dissenting Protestantism | The Holy Scriptures; core principles of religious freedom and Church/State separationism (i.e. disestablishment of a national religion, liberty of conscience, free exercise of religion, equality of a plurality of faiths before the law) | Milton; Locke | 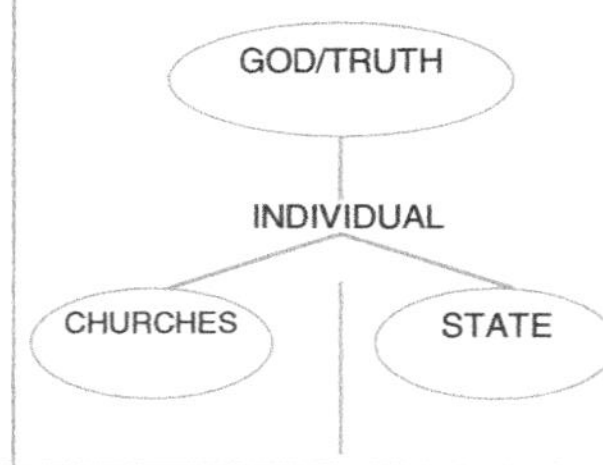 |
| **5. French Revolution** (eighteenth and nineteenth-centuries onwards) | Deism | A Creator's gift of reason and freewill of exercising it. Reason-based natural law and the supremacy of public opinion. Rationalism | Rousseau | 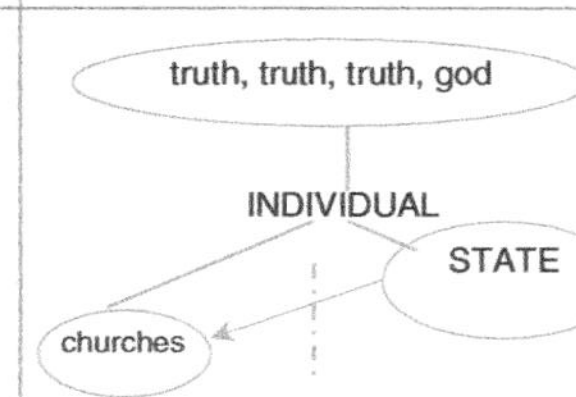 |
| **6. Russian Revolution** (twentieth-century) | Atheism | Soviet Marxist-Leninist atheism advocating for a classless society. Altruistic idealism | Marx; Engels | 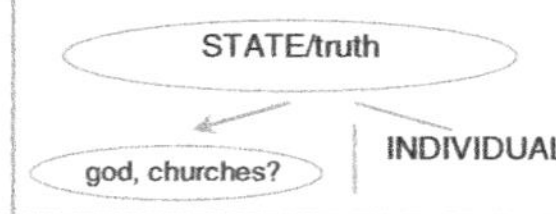 |

[a]The arrows indicate the direction and relations of coercion

model is currently valid for the Roman Church-State; minor changes were made after the Second Vatican Council (Agnew, 2010; Cook, 2012).

2. The second model (German Revolution) enhances the power of the secular authorities (monarchical states), and thereby substantially reduces the influence of the Church. The State provides universal education. The individual has direct access to the Scriptures and enjoys direct communion with God (Becker & Woessmann, 2009; Berman, 2003; Witte, 2002).
3. In the third model (English Revolution), oppressed groups and other dissenting forms of Protestantism (e.g. Calvinism, Puritanism) decreased the power of the state-church and thus of the monarchy. Such a process pushed towards the separation of Church and State and sought to empower the individual, in a large-scale development towards modern democracy based on the advances of the Lutheran Reformation in Germany and northern Europe (Berman, 2003; Doe & Sandberg, 2010).
4. The fourth model (United States Revolution) further progressed the clear separation of Church and State through a Protestant, dissenting process initiated earlier in England (and even before). The resulting democratisation process progressively and continuously further empowered the individual (Berman, 2003; Miller, 2012).
5. The French Revolution (fifth model) almost coincided with that in the USA and both informed each other. However, unlike the previous revolutions, Protestantism played no direct (and merely an indirect) role in France. Liberal anti-clericalism fiercely opposed Roman Catholicism but was also hostile to Protestantism (e.g. ironically, it destroyed bibles just as Roman Catholicism did). Therefore, the French Revolution encouraged individual, relative truths (instead of Catholic dogmas or Protestant, biblical moral foundations) by promoting deism and reason. In this conception, the individual and the democratic state are also strengthened, like in the model of the United States Revolution. Here, however, the state coerces and controls the churches (Berman, 2003; Merryman & Pérez, 2007; Miller, 2012).
6. The sixth model (the Russian Revolution) goes beyond the principles learned of the French Revolution. The state becomes the most powerful entity and hopes to liberate individuals from religious, "opiate-like" beliefs and from economic, class-based exploitation. Consequently, the state significantly coerces religion and enhances both the parental role of the law and the social and economic role of the state (Berman, 2003; Merryman & Pérez, 2007).

### *8.3.6 Summarising the Core Messages of Section 8.3.* Law, Religion, Revolutions, and State Models

Even if most revolutions were defeated, the influence of the various legal traditions has long persisted. For instance, Eastern schism and in particular the German, English, American and French Revolutions ended the monopoly of Roman canon law. The Thirty Year War ended the German Revolution, the English Revolution suffered defeat in the early 1800s, the French Revolution in 1870, and the Russian Revolution in the 1990s (Berman, 2003).

And yet, all these revolutions influenced the different legal traditions. Several elements of those revolutions still coexist in some countries more than others. Roman and canon law percolated into the legal systems of those countries that underwent revolutions to a greater or lesser degree. For instance, the French and German revolutions made the jurists re-adopt and adapt principles of the old regime in order to build on the respective basis (Berman, 2003; Merryman & Pérez, 2007; Witte, 2002). However, Roman and canon law exercised less influence in common law countries (e.g. after the English and United States revolutions) (Berman, 2003; Doe & Sandberg, 2010; Merryman & Pérez, 2007).

The Lutheran German Revolution formed the basis of the various later Protestant, dissenting revolutions, and legal traditions (i.e. British and American). Some of its concepts (e.g. separation of state functions from the church; state-sponsored education) permeate all modern legal systems to this day (Berman, 2003; Witte, 2002). The English Revolution marked a crucial step towards modern democracy and limited the power of the monarchies in Europe. Moreover, the British Empire spread common law throughout its colonies across the world (Berman, 2003; La Porta et al., 2008; Merryman & Pérez, 2007).

The revolution in the USA inspired modern constitutionalism and democratic rights all over the world. The French Revolution also transferred its legal model to its colonies and countries under its influence. For example, the USA exerted constitutional influence on Latin American countries while the French Revolution inspired the independence and the creation of the modern Latin American republics. However, the anti-clericalism of those revolutions was not always assimilated. Instead, along with the French code, Roman and Catholic (i.e. canonical) law has been the predominant legal tradition in most Latin American countries to this day. This attests to the pervasive presence (and power) of Roman Catholicism (i.e. concordats, corporatist states, Catholicism as a state religion) (Barro & McCleary, 2005; Berman, 2003; La Porta et al., 2008; Merryman & Pérez, 2007; Salinas, 2013).

Thus, the basic model of church–state–citizen relations in most Latin American countries more closely resembles the medieval *Corpus Christianum*, i.e. a model based on Roman and Catholic canon law traditions (Model 1). This happened although Latin American countries adopted several elements from the French legal tradition. Examples of corporatist states in which concordats are effective include Colombia, Venezuela, and Honduras.

On the other hand, Chile and Uruguay are liberal democracies with explicit anti-clerical movements that never allowed concordats to be signed with the Roman Church-State. Consequently, their basic model of church–state–citizen relations is closer to that of the French Revolution (Model 5). After its revolution, Cuba adopted the Russian model (Model 6).

In Europe, Switzerland (following the 1848 Constitution) was influenced by dissenting Protestantism and by US federalism and constitutionalism, along with French liberalism (Obinger, 2009). The Swiss Confederation has never signed a concordat with the Roman Church-State, even if agreements exist at the cantonal level.

The anti-clerical, anti-Roman, and anti-canon law sentiments that influenced sixteenth-century Lutheran Germany resembled those of the eighteenth and nineteenth-century post-revolutionary France. In both cases, jurists sought to eliminate the references to Roman and canonical law. Therefore, Germany and France represent the most atypical legal systems in the "civil law world". Their models have assumed intellectual leadership and have been implemented in several other countries (Merryman & Pérez, 2015).

Nonetheless, in both cases, jurists ended up readapting and reincorporating Roman and canon law to suit their new purposes (e.g. the adoption of biblical principles in Lutheranism and of rationalist deism in the French Revolution) (Merryman & Pérez, 2015; Witte, 2002). Consequently, the Roman influence is still highly significant in both cases notwithstanding the substantial legal contributions of the respective revolutions (Merryman & Pérez, 2007, p. 13).

Common law is a different case because British jurists managed to adapt a legal system after the Reformation with precious little influence of Roman and canon law (Doe & Sandberg, 2010). Thus, common law has no hierarchical source of law and is less rigid, less rigorous, and less systematic than civil law. Likewise, common law jurisprudence is less influenced by the rationalist dogmas of the French Revolution (Merryman & Pérez, 2015).

Legal origins associated with Protestant influence (e.g. English common law, German and Scandinavian legal systems) have proven more sustainable. They also exhibit higher institutional performance and prosperity than legal origins associated with a laic rejection of religion (La Porta et al., 2008). Dissenting Protestant religions paved the way for the Enlightenment and for social emancipation (Miller, 2012; Snyder, 2011; Woodberry, 2012).

In contrast, legal origins associated with a laic rejection of religion (e.g. Soviet) have not proven sustainable over time or the elements crucial to their functioning could not be transferred (e.g. French Revolution). For instance, while French legal origins transmitted anti-clerical sentiments to Southern European countries, they were not automatically transferred to most Latin American countries (Merryman & Pérez, 2007). As a result, Southern European countries materialised the sovereignty of their states over the Roman Church-State and thereby attained certain levels of prosperity and institutional performance (higher than in most Latin American countries, but lower than in historically Protestant countries).

For these reasons, Latin American countries with successful anti-clerical movements (e.g. Uruguay, Chile) reached similar prosperity levels as Southern European countries (e.g. Italy, Spain). However, most Latin American countries have been unable to implement anti-clerical laws and to overcome feudal structures, among other reasons, due to concordats and other political and legal commitments towards the Roman Church-State. As a result, their prosperity and institutional performance are lower.

Therefore, when comparing prosperity and institutional performance ("fruits"), it can be argued: 1) the "people's opium" described by Marx in the Russian Revolution applies more to specific types of hierarchical state religions (i.e. Orthodox, Roman Catholicism, Muslim). 2) However, the Marxists' total rejection of any religious expression eventually replaced one type of tyranny (and opium) for another. 3) In contrast, historically dissenting Protestant religions and anti-clerical movements have proven to be the precursors of social emancipation and the "antidote against the opiate" (Berman, 2003; La Porta et al., 2008; Merryman & Pérez, 2007).

The next section explores the relationship between religion, education, and prosperity. Before that, however, I introduce various associated empirical expectations:

**Empirical Expectations**

4. *I expect higher transparency/prosperity levels in countries with Protestant-influenced legal origins (*i.e. *German, English, or Scandinavian) than in non-Protestant countries. The Protestant Reformation introduced the Sola Scriptura principle reflected in Protestant-influenced legal origins.*
5. *I expect lower prosperity/transparency levels in countries that have been influenced by the French legal system, in particular when they have strong clerical ties, and thus have been significantly influenced by Roman and canon law (as in Latin America).*
6. *Given the tradition of controversial and restrictive concordats, I expect a negative influence on transparency and prosperity in the respective concordatarian countries.*
7. *I expect a negative influence on prosperity/transparency in countries rooted in Socialist legal origins, in particular on account of the Soviet legal principle of the "goodness of humankind" (similar to Roman Catholic and Orthodox natural law).*

## References


Acemoglu, D., Cantoni, D., Johnson, S., & Robinson, J. A. (2011). The consequences of radical reform: The French revolution. *The American Economic Review, 101*(7), 3286–3307.

Acemoglu, D., & Johnson, S. (2005). Unbundling institutions. *Journal of Political Economy, 113*(5), 949–995.

Acemoglu, D., Johnson, S., & Robinson, J. (2001). The colonial origins of comparative development: An empirical investigation. *American Economic Review, 91*(5), 1369–1401.

Acemoglu, D., & Robinson, J. A. (2008). Persistence of power, elites, and institutions. *American Economic Review, 98*(1), 267–293.

Acemoglu, D., & Robinson, J. (2012). *Why nations fail. The origins of power, prosperity and poverty*. New York: Crown Business.

Adserà, A., Boix, C., & Payne, M. (2003). Are you being served? Political accountability and quality of government. *The Journal of Law, Economics, and Organization, 19*(2), 445–490.

Agnew, J. (2010). Deus Vult: The geopolitics of the Catholic Church. *Geopolitics, 15*(1), 39–61.

Alesina, A., & Giuliano, P. (2015). Culture and institutions. *Journal of Economic Literature, 53*(4), 898–944.

Anderson, J. (2007). Religion, politics and international relations. The Catholic contribution to democratization's 'third wave': Altruism, hegemony or self-interest? *Cambridge Review of International Affairs, 20*(3), 383–399.

Anderson, K. (2009). The church as nation? The role of religion in the development of the Swedish welfare state. In K. Van Kersbergen & P. Manow (Eds.), *Religion, class coalitions, and welfare states (Cambridge studies in social theory, religion and politics)* (pp. 210–235). Cambridge: Cambridge University Press. https://doi.org/10.1017/CBO9780511626784.009.

Armony, A. (2004). *The dubious link. Civic engagement and democratization*. Stanford: Stanford University Press.

Arruñada, B. (2010). Protestants and catholics: Similar work ethic, different social ethic. *The Economic Journal, 120*(547), 890–918.

Barro, R. J., & McCleary, R. M. (2005). Which countries have state religions? *The Quarterly Journal of Economics, 120*(4), 1331–1370.

Becker, S., Pfaff, S., & Rubin, J. (2016). *Causes and Consequences of the Protestant Reformation*. Warwick Economics Research Paper Series.

Becker, S. O., & Woessmann, L. (2009). Was Weber wrong? A human capital theory of Protestant economic history. *Quarterly Journal of Economics, 124*(2), 531–596.

Becker, S. O., & Woessmann, L. (2015). *Social cohesion, religious beliefs, and the effect of Protestantism on suicide* (CESifo Working Paper No. 5288).

Berger, P. (1990). *The sacred canopy: Elements of a sociological theory of religion*. New York: Doubleday.

Berger, P. (1999). *The Desecularization of the world*. Washington, DC: Ethics and Public Policy Center and Wm. B. Eerdmans Publishing Co.

Berman, H. (2003). *Law and revolution II: The impact of the Protestant reformations on the Western legal tradition*. Cambridge and London: Harvard University Press, Belknap Press.

Boswell, J. (1993). Catholicism, Christian democrats and 'reformed capitalism. In C. Crouch & D. Marquand (Eds.), *Ethics and markets: Cooperation and competition within capitalist economies* (pp. 48–65). Oxford: Blackwell.

Bradbury, S. (2014). Mission, missionaries and development. In M. Clarke (Ed.), *Handbook of research on development and religion* (pp. 413–429). Cheltenham: Edwar Elgar.

Brownlie, I. (1979). *Principles of public international law* (3rd ed.). Oxford: Oxford University Press.

Büschges, C. (2018). 50 years of liberation theology: Introduction. *Iberoamericana, 18*(68), 7–11.

Cook, E. (2012). *Roman Catholic hegemony and religious freedom: A seventh-day Adventist assessment of Dignitatis Humanae*. Texas: Graduate Faculty of Baylor University.

Corral, C. (2014). Los 55 Estados con sus respectivos 220 Acuerdos vigentes con la Santa Sede. (U. C. (UCM), Ed.) *UNISCI Discussion Papers* (34).

Corral, C., & Petschen, S. (2004). *Tratados Internacionales (1996–2003) de la Santa Sede con los Estados. Concordatos Vigentes*. Madrid: Universidad Pontificia Comillas.

Da Costa, N. (2009). La laicidad uruguaya. *Archives De Sciences Sociales Des Religions, 146*, 137–155.

Doe, N., & Sandberg, R. (2010). *Law and religion: New horizons*. Belgium: Leuven Peeters.

Durkheim, E. (1899). *Suicide*. Illinois: Glencoe.

Ercolessi, G., & Hägg, I. (2012). Towards religious neutrality of public institutions in Europe. In F. de Beaufort & P. van Schie (Eds.), *Separation of church and state in Europe. With views on Sweden, Norway, United Kingdom & Ireland, the Netherlands, France, Portugal, Italy and Slovenia*. Brussels: European Liberal Forum.

Esping-Andersen, G. (1990). *The three worlds of welfare capitalism*. Princeton, NJ: Princeton University Press.

Figueroa, H. (2016). *La persistance des idées traditionalistes en Colombie. Religion et politique (1886–1952)*. Paris: L'Harmattan.

Forrest, M., Schnably, S., Wilson, R., Simon, J., & Tushnet, M. (2006). *International human rights and humanitarian law: Treaties, cases, and analysis*. Cambridge: Cambridge University Press.

Fukuyama, F. (1995). *Trust. The social virtues and the creation of prosperity*. New York: Free Press.
Fumagalli, O. (2011). Concordats as instruments for implementing freedom of religion. *IUS CANONICUM, 51*(102), 437–446.
Garcia Portilla, J. (2019). "Ye shall know them by their fruits": Prosperity and institutional religion in Europe and the Americas. *Religions, 10*(6), 362. MDPI AG. https://doi.org/10.3390/rel10060362.
Gill, A. (1998). *Rendering unto Caesar: The Catholic Church and the state in Latin America*. Chicago, IL: Chicago University Press.
Gill, A. (2013). Religious pluralism, political incentives, and the origins of religious liberty. Global challenges. In A. Hertzke (Ed.), *The future of religious freedom* (pp. 107–127). New York: Oxford University Press.
Glaeser, E., La Porta, R., Lopez-de-Silanes, F., & Shleifer, A. (2004). Do institutions cause growth? *Journal of Economic Growth, 9*(3), 271–303.
Goldsmith, A. (1999). Slapping the grasping hand: Correlates of political corruption in emerging markets. *American Journal of Economics and Sociology, 58*(4), 866–883.
Grand Jury of Pennsylvania. (2011). *Report of the Grand Jury*. MISC. NO. 0009901-2008 (Court of Common Pleas, First Judicial District of Pennsylvania, Philadelphia January 21, 2011).
Grand Jury of Pennsylvania. (2018). *40th statewide investigating grand jury REPORT 1 interim—Redacted*. Ebensburg: Grand Jury of Pennsylvania.
Gregory, B. S. (2012). *The unintended reformation: How a religious revolution secularized society*. London: Belknap Press of Harvard University Press.
Grier, R. (1997). The effect of religion on economic development: A cross national study of 63 former colonies. *Kyklos, 50*(1), 47–62.
Gross, H. (2004). *Rome in the age of enlightenment: The post-Tridentine syndrome and the Ancien Régime*. Cambridge: Cambridge University Press.
Guiso, L., Sapienza, P., & Zingales, L. (2006). Does culture affect economic outcomes? *Journal of Economic Perspectives, 20*(2), 23–48.
Gula, R. M. (2002). *Reason informed by faith—Foundations of Catholic morality*. New York: Paulist Press.
Hanlon, G. (2008). *The twilight of a military tradition: Italian aristocrats and European conflicts, 1560–1800*. London: UCL Press Limited.
Helmoz, R. (1987). *Canon law and the law of England*. London: Hambledon Press.
Heussi, K. (1991). *Kompendium der Kirchengeschichte*. Mohr Siebeck.
Hurd, E. S. (2011). Secularism and international relations theory. In J. Snyder (Ed.), *Religion and international relations theory*. New York: Columbia University Press.
Husted, B. (1999). Wealth, culture, and corruption. *Journal of International Business Studies, 30*(2), 339–360.
Hutson, J. H. (1998). *Religion and the founding of the American Republic*. Washington. DC: Library of Congress.
Inglehart, R., & Baker, W. (2000). Modernization, cultural change, and the persistence of traditional values. *American Sociological Review, 65*(1), 19–51.
Kaufmann, C. D., & Pape, R. A. (1999). Explaining costly international moral action: Britain's sixty-year campaign against the Atlantic slave trade. *International Organization, 53*(4), 631–668.
King James Bible. (1769). *The holy bible, king James version*. Cambridge Edition: 1769. Scripture quotations from The Authorized (King James) Version. Rights in the Authorized Version in the United Kingdom are vested in the Crown. Reproduced by permission of the Crown's patentee. Cambridge University Press.
Kunicová, J. (2006). Democratic institutions and corruption: Incentives and constraints in politics. In S. Rose-Ackerman (Ed.), *International handbook on the economics of corruption* (pp. 140–160). Cheltenham: Edward Elgar.

La Porta, R., Lopez-de-Silanes, F., & Shleifer, A. (2008). The economic consequences of legal origins. *Journal of Economic Literature, 46*(2), 285–332.

La Porta, R., Lopez-de-Silanes, F., Shleifer, A., & Vishny, R. (1998). Law and finance. *Journal of Political Economy, 106*(6), 1113–1155.

La Porta, R., Lopez-de-Silanes, F., & Vishny, A. S. (1999). The quality of government. *Journal of Law, Economics and Organization, 15*(1), 222–279.

Lambsdorff, J. G. (2006). Causes and consequences of corruption: What do we know from a cross-section of countries? In S. Rose-Ackerman (Ed.), *International handbook on the economics of corruption* (pp. 3–51). Cheltenham: Edward Elgar.

Levine, D. (1981). *Religion and politics in Latin America: The Catholic Church in Venezuela & Colombia*. Princeton, NJ: Princeton Legacy Library.

Lutz, D. (1980). Covenant to constitution in American political thought. *Publius, 10*, 101–133.

Luzzani, T. (2002). *South America. Global corruption report 2001. Transparency*. Mexico, DF: Instituto Ciudadano de Estudios sobre la Inseguridad (ICESI).

Manow, P. (2004). *The good, the bad, and the ugly: Esping-Andersen's regime typology and the religious roots of the Western welfare state* (MPIfG Working Paper, No. 04/3). Cologne: Max Planck Institute for the Study of Societies. Retrieved from http://www.mpifg.de/pu/workpap/wp04-3/wp04-3.html

Manow, P., & van Kersbergen, K. (2009). Religion and the Western Welfafre state – The theoretical context. In P. Manow & K. van Kersbergen (Eds.), *Religion, class coalitions and welfare states* (p. 304). New York: Cambridge University Press.

Martin, D. (1999). The evangelical upsurge and its political implications. In P. Berger (Ed.), *The Desecularization of the world* (pp. 37–49). Washington, DC: Ethics and Public Policy Center and Wm. B. Eerdmans Publishing.

Merryman, J. (1996). The French Deviation. *American Journal of Comparative Law, 44*(1), 109–119.

Merryman, J., & Pérez, R. (2007). *The civil law tradition: An introduction to the legal Systems of Europe and Latin America* (3rd ed.). Stanford: Stanford University Press.

Merryman, J., & Pérez, P. R. (2015). *La Tradición Jurídica Romano-Canónica*. Fondo de Cultura Económica.

Miller, N. (2012). *The religious roots of the first amendment*. New York: Oxford University Press.

Morris, S. (2003). Corruption and Mexican political culture. *Journal of the Southwest, 45*(4), 671–708.

Morton, H., Siegle, M., & Weinstein, M. (2005). *The democracy advantage. How democracies promote prosperity and peace*. New York: Routledge.

Munevar, J. (2008). Transformación doctrinal y actitudinal de la participación política de las iglesias cristianas evangélicas en Colombia. In Grupo Interdisciplinario de Estudios de Religión, Sociedad y Política, GIERSP (Ed.), *Mirada pluridisciplinar al hecho religioso en Colombia: Avances de investigación* (pp. 375–399). Colombia: Bogotá.

Navarro, J. (2016). Religions and law: Current challenges in Latin America. In S. Ferrari & R. Cristofori (Eds.), *Law and religion, an overview* (pp. 111–127). New York: Routledge.

Nelson, E. (2010). *The Hebrew Republic: Jewish sources and the transformation of European political thought*. Cambridge: Harvard University Press.

Norris, P., & Inglehart, R. (2004). *Sacred and secular: Religion and politics worldwide*. New York: Cambridge University Press.

North, D. (1990). *Institutions, institutional change and economic performance*. Cambridge: Cambridge University Press.

Obinger, H. (2009). Religion and the consolidation of the Swiss welfare state, 1848–1945. In P. Manow & K. van Kersbergen (Eds.), *Religion, class coalitions and welfare states* (pp. 176–209). New York: Cambridge University Press.

Olson, M. (1993). Dictatorship, democracy, and development. *American Political Science Review, 87*(3), 567–575.

O'Reilly, J., & Chalmers, M. (2014). *The clergy sex abuse crisis and the legal responses*. New York: Oxford University Press. https://doi.org/10.1093/acprof:oso/9780199937936.001.0001.

Paldam, M. (2001). Corruption and religion. Adding to the economic model. *Kyklos, 54*(2–3), 383–414.

Paldam, M. (2002). The cross-country pattern of corruption: Economics, culture and the seesaw dynamics. *European Journal of Political Economy, 18*(2), 215–240.

Pearce, A. (2010). England's law of religion–the history of a discipline. In N. Doe & R. Sandberg (Eds.), *Law and religion: New horizons*. Leuven: Uitgeverij Peeters.

Persson, T., & Tabellini, G. (2003). *The economic effects of constitutions: What do the data say?* Cambridge: MIT Press.

Philpott, D. (2001). *Revolutions in sovereignty: How ideas shaped modern international relations*. Princeton, NJ: Princeton University Press.

Prados de la Escosura, L. (2004). When did Latin America fall behind? In *The decline of Latin American economies: Growth, institutions, and crises*. Chicago, IL: University of Chicago Press.

Putnam. (1993). *Making democracy work: Civic traditions in modern Italy*. Princeton, NJ: Princeton University Press.

Ragazzi, M. (2009). Concordats today: From the second Vatican council to John Paul II. *Journal of Markets & Morality, 12*(1), 113–151.

Ramírez, C. J. (2009). Laïcité, liberté de religion et État laïque. Les étapes de la laïcisation cubaine. *Archives de sciences sociales des religions, 54*(146), 157–182.

Roessler, S., & Miklos, R. (2003). *Europe 1715–1919: From enlightenment to world war*. Maryland: Rowman & Littlefield Publishers.

Rommen, H. (1945). *The state in Catholic thought: A treatise in political philosophy*. St. Louis, MO: B. Herder Book.

Rose-Ackerman, S. (1978). *Corruption: A study in political economy*. New York: Academic Press.

Rose-Ackerman, S. (2006). *International handbook on the economics of corruption*. Cheltenham: Edward Elgar Publishing.

Ryngaert, C. (2011). The legal status of the Holy See. *Goettingen Journal of International Law, 3* (3), 829–860.

Salinas, C. (2013). Los concordatos celebrados entre la Santa Sede y los países latinoamericanos durante el siglo xix [the concordats held between the Holy See and Latin American countries in the 19th century]. *Revista de Estudios Histórico-Jurídicos [Sección Historia del Derecho Canónico], 35*, 215–254.

Sandholtz, W., & Koetzle, W. (2000). Accounting for corruption: Economic structure, democracy, and trade. *International Studies Quarterly, 44*(1), 31–50.

Schanda, B. (2004). *Church and State in the New Member States of the European Union*. Fides et Libertas. Retrieved from https://www.irla.org/fides-2004.pdf

Selling, J. A. (2018). Reframing Catholic theological ethics: Summary and application. (A. Abram, Ed.). *Religions, 8*(203), 5–13.

Shah, T. S., & Philpott, D. (2011). The fall and rise of religion in international relations. History and theory. In J. Snyder (Ed.), *Religion and international relations theory* (pp. 24–59). New York: Columbia University Press.

Skinner, Q. (1978). *The foundations of modern political thought, the age of reformation* (Vol. 2). Cambridge: Cambridge University Press.

Smith, C. (1991). *The emergence of liberation theology. Radical religion and social movement theory*. Chicago, IL: University of Chicago Press.

Snyder, J. (2011). *Religion and international relations theory*. New York: Columbia University Press.

Torgler, B., & Schaltegger, C. (2014). Suicide and religion: New evidence on the differences between Protestantism and Catholicism. *Journal for the Scientific Study of Religion, 53*, 316–340.

Transparency International. (2016). *Corruption Perceptions Index 2016*. Retrieved from https://www.transparency.org/news/feature/corruption_perceptions_index_2016

Treisman, D. (2000). The causes of corruption: A cross-national study. *Journal of Public Economics, 76*(3), 399–457.

Trejo, G. (2009). Religious competition and ethnic mobilization in Latin America: Why the Catholic Church promotes indigenous movements in Mexico. *American Political Science Review, 103*(3), 323–342.

Uildriks, N. (2009). *Policing insecurity: Police reform, security, and human rights in Latin America*. Plymouth: Lexington Books.

van Paassen, P. (1939). *Days of our years*. New York: Hillman-Curl.

Volonté, C. (2015). Culture and corporate governance: The influence of language and religion in Switzerland. *Management International Review, 55*, 77–118.

Waldmann, P. (2012). Verbündeter oder Gegner der Herrschenden: Die Rolle der lateinamerikanischen Kirche unter der Militärdiktatur. In B. Oberdorfer & P. Waldmann (Eds.), *Machtfaktor Religion. Formen religiöser Einflussnahme auf Politik und Gesellschaft* (pp. 233–252). Böhlau: Cologne et al..

Watson, A. (1974). *Legal transplants: An approach to comparative law*. Athens: University of Georgia Press.

Weber, M. (1905). *Die protestantische Ethik und der Geist des Kapitalismus*. Zürich: Verlag Wirtschaft und Finanzen.

Wilcox, T., & Field, J. (1572). An admonition to the parliament. In W. H. Frere & C. E. Douglas (Eds.), *Puritan manifestos: A study of the origins of the puritan revolt* (pp. 5–39). London: E.S. Gorham.

Wilde, M., Geraty, K., Nelson, L., & Bowman, E. (2010). Religious economy or organizational Field? Predicting bishops' votes at the second Vatican council. *American Sociological Review, 75*(4), 586–606. https://doi.org/10.1177/0003122410368927.

Wilensky, H. L. (1981). Leftism, Catholicism, and democratic corporatism: The role of political parties in recent welfare state development. In P. Flora & A. J. Heidenheimer (Eds.), *The development of welfare states in Europe and America* (pp. 345–382). New Brunswick: Transaction Books.

Williamson, O. E. (2000). The new institutional economics: Taking stock, looking ahead. *Journal of Economic Literature, 38*(3), 595–613.

Witte, J. (2002). *Law and Protestantism: The legal teachings of the Lutheran reformation*. Cambridge: Cambridge: University Press.

Witte, J. (2007). *The reformation of rights*. Cambridge: Cambridge University Press.

Woodberry, R. (2012). The missionary roots of liberal democracy. *American Political Science Review (APSR), 106*(2), 244–274.

Woodruff, C. (2006). Measuring institutions. In S. Rose-Ackerman (Ed.), *International handbook on the economics of corruption* (pp. 105–124). Cheltenham: Edward Elgar Publishing.

World Bank. (2014). *GNI per capita*. Retrieved from http://data.worldbank.org/indicator/NY.GNP.PCAP.CD?display=map

World Bank, International Finance Corporation (IFC), & Oxford University Press. (2004). *Doing business in 2004: Understanding regulation*. Washington, DC: World Bank. A copublication of the World Bank, the International Finance Corporation, and Oxford University Press.

World Economic Forum. (2016). *The global competitiveness report 2014–2015*. . Full data edition. Geneva: The World Economic Forum.

Zilla, C. (2020). *Evangelicals and politics in Brazil. The relevance of religious change in Latin America*. SWP Research Paper. Stiftung Wissenschaft und Politik. Berlin: German Institute for International and Security Affairs.

# Chapter 9
# Education, Religion, and Corruption/Prosperity *(A), (B), (C), (1), (2)*

This chapter discusses the *longue durée* effect of religion on education and analyses the uneven contributions of Roman Catholicism and Protestantism in this respect.

## 9.1 The Influence of Religion on Education and Human Capital (Prosperity Pillar Mechanism) *(A), (B), (C), (D), (1), (2), (3), (5), (6)*

Historically, acquiring education and accumulating human capital have been persistent human endeavours for centuries. They have also constituted a more primary source of prosperity than economic institutions (Glaeser et al., 2004; Easterlin, 1981; Goldin, 2001; Lindert, 2003; Galor, 2005; Hanushek & Woessmann, 2008; Becker & Woessmann, 2009).

Religious factors have both driven and determined unequal education outcomes in Protestantism and Roman Catholicism. Becker and Woessmann have found a high correlation coefficient (0.78) between Protestantism and literacy across countries. The authors observe that Protestantism resulted in a significant increase in literacy, which contributed to economic development (p. 582). They further explain that religion was vital for economic progress because it inadvertently caused an imbalanced accumulation of human capital. Thus, after centuries, the denominational disparities that arose after the Reformation had an effect on uneven economic results (p. 534). In their empirical study, the authors found that in 1900, all Protestant-majority countries had achieved almost universal literacy, while no Catholic country had done so. Indeed, many of them were well behind. Existing evidence from inside the countries themselves reveals a similar trend (Becker & Woessmann, 2009, p. 544).

Before the Reformation, roughly only 1% of the population (i.e. a small elite) were literate in Germany (Engelsing as cited in Becker & Woessmann, 2009). In the



J. García Portilla, *"Ye Shall Know Them by Their Fruits"*, Contributions to Economics, https://doi.org/10.1007/978-3-030-78498-0_9

passage of time, the Reformation has turned out to be a primary driver of schooling. Thus, even today, Protestants are still more educated (0.8 years more), and more prosperous (5.4% higher income) than Catholics in Germany. Standard regressions confirm these correlations (Becker & Woessmann, 2009, pp. 578). The perpetuation of this educational gap between Protestants and Catholics over time allows the authors to conclude that Luther's educational ideals may have had far-reaching consequences. Protestants in Germany are still better educated, even after more than a century in a public school system that offers fair access to education regardless of religious belief (Becker & Woessmann, 2009, pp. 578–581).

The authors cite several sources showing that similar trends or even wider schooling differences between Protestants and Catholics have existed in other countries such as the USA, Ireland, or Finland. For instance, in Finland in 1880, illiteracy among Catholics was 54.4%, compared with only 1.3% among Lutherans (Markussen as cited in Becker & Woessmann, 2009, p. 544). The following sections explain the differences between Roman Catholic education and Protestant education that can lead to markedly different outcomes.

### *9.1.1 Roman Catholic Education*

Greek philosophy and various other cultural traditions have influenced Roman Catholic theology more strongly than the Holy Scriptures (Selling, 2018, p. 9; Gula, 2002, pp. 120–121; Gruner, 1977, p. 117). For example, Aristotle had a greater influence on Thomas Aquinas' Summa Theologica than the entire Old Testament. Moreover, Catholicism's extended allegorical interpretation of the Scriptures stems from Origen, and ultimately from Plato. The Roman Catholic Church, therefore, places its traditions and hierarchical authority over the Scriptures. This explains the significant disparity between Roman Catholicism and essential biblical foundations (Sect. 10.4.1). Furthermore, the Roman system has long suppressed the Scriptures, thus preventing believers from engaging directly with them. Up until the last century, prohibition or persecution were the norm for those who owned, translated, read, or taught the Scriptures without the sanction of the Church (Cook, 2012; Heussi, 1991).

In turn, the most widespread Roman Catholic teaching practices have been the repetition and memorising of dogmatic texts so as to recite them without much understanding (Plata Quezada, 2008; Heussi, 1991; D'Aubigne, 1862). Therefore, such texts, as well as selected parts of the Gospel, were taught in Latin scholarly language to mostly illiterate peasants even after the Middle Ages in Europe (Androne, 2014; Becker & Woessmann, 2009). Such teaching practices suppressed any critical thinking and demanded absolute obedience to unilateral dogmatic discourses, thus enhancing and perpetuating the hegemony of the Church-State. In fact, "The maintenance of ignorance" has been one of the most effective strategies deployed by the Catholic Church-State to influence people's behaviour (Head-König, 2017, pp. 46–47). Similar practices have been in force until recently, especially in rural areas in some Latin American countries. Similarly, regarding

Catholic education in Latin America, Gill (1998) observes that the Catholic Church allocated the vast majority of educational services to the upper classes. Furthermore, the Roman Church underplayed the link between Bible reading and literacy, fearful that it would cause another Protestant Reformation. Thus, for much of Latin America's existence, the importation of the Bible was prohibited (p. 89).

Moreover, the Roman Church-State has provided far more education in countries where it has had to compete with Protestantism (e.g. USA, India, Ireland) than in countries where it has managed to prevent competition (e.g. Mexico, Spain, Italy). (Woodberry, 2012, p. 269).

#### 9.1.1.1 Jesuitical Education

As with Protestantism, Roman Catholicism cannot be reduced to black and white generalisations. The Catholic Church initiated the Counter-Reformation process in the Council of Trent (1534–1549) and thus contested the advancement of Protestantism. Consequently, the Roman Church-State created new religious orders, among which the Jesuits were the most prominent (Heussi, 1991). Seemingly contradictorily, yet importantly, the Jesuits, despite their loyalty to the pope, were secular before the word was coined (Roy, 2010). One of the novelties introduced by the Jesuits is the focus on analytical skills and higher education through applying the *Ratio Studiorum* (Pavur, 2005). Competing with Protestant education, which enhanced methodical skills by studying the Scriptures (Becker & Woessmann, 2009), the Jesuits' *Ratio Studiorum* advanced Aquinian and Aristotelian teachings. Therefore, Jesuit education had always focused, among others, on the liberal arts, medieval scholasticism, Renaissance humanism, and ethics, thus attaching less importance to any exegetical understanding of the Scriptures (Lukàcs, 1986).

The term *Jesuit* has two definitions: "a member of the Roman Catholic Society of Jesus founded by St. Ignatius Loyola in 1534" and "*one given to intrigue or equivocation*" (Merriam-Webster, n.d.) (author's italics). Similarly, the Oxford Dictionary (2016) defines the term *Jesuitical* as (1) of or regarding the Jesuits; and (2) dissemble, deception, or equivocation in the way identified with the Jesuits (Oxford University Press, 2016). Similar definitions can be found in Spanish (RAE), German (Duden), or other English dictionaries.

In the nineteenth-century Switzerland, "Liberals considered the Jesuit order 'an anathema, as the apotheosis of Catholic obscurantism, intrigue, and subversion'" (Gould, 1999 as cited in Obinger, 2009, p. 181). Therefore, the Swiss "constitution of 1874 banned the pope-loyal Jesuit order..." (Obinger, 2009, p. 181). Beyond Switzerland, Schwarz-Herion (2015) observes the following, regarding the historical influence of the Jesuits:

> the activities of the Jesuits as personal educators of young people from influential families and as confessors at courts (Goerlitz et al. 1982; Fülöp-Miller 1929) gave them the opportunity to manipulate influential persons and potential blackmailing leverage other monarchs and Princes. [...] After some Sovereigns started to get suspicious towards the Jesuits, the Jesuits started to hide behind 1000 masks, pretending to be Brahmans among Brahmans, protestants among protestants, scholars among scholars, etc., always adapting to the circles they were infiltrating (Fülöp-Miller 1929). [...] Since the Jesuits were perceived

as a threat, the Order of the Jesuits got prohibited in 1773 by Pope Clemens XIV due to pressure from several monarchs (Paris and Fülöp-Miller as cited in Schwarz-Herion, 2015, p. 77).[1]

Notwithstanding the bad reputation formerly acquired by the Jesuits, Schwarz-Herion (2015) further observes that their global influence has increased, and the author states her concern in this regard:

> the influence of the Jesuits (SJ) on politics seems to remain unbroken until today. [. . .] Modern Jesuits do not only play an essential role in the Vatican, but are also firmly rooted in international politics: the EU council president Hermann Rompuy said in public: 'We are all Jesuits', pointing out that he was "developing the architecture for the future Europe" (Eppink 2012). [. . .] The political networks of these hierarchically structured religious orders, organized in a military way and boasting with their medieval legacy of the cursaders, might pose a serious obstacle to the Great Transition to sustainable global democracy and thus should not be taken lightly by a vigilant enlightened civil society consisting of many humans who have grown up in modern democratic and laical states (Schwarz-Herion, 2015, p. 112).[2]

In South America, some Jesuit missions have had a lasting, positive impact on modern-day human capital and incomes (10–15% higher compared to the surrounding Roman Catholic population in Southern Paraguay and Northern Argentina) (Valencia, 2017). These missions also advanced education among the Catholic population in different places at a subnational level even if they were largely elitist (Woodberry, 2012) and far less encompassing than the traditional Protestant urge for education (Becker & Woessmann, 2009).

### *9.1.2 Protestant Education*

> Faith rests not on ignorance, but on knowledge.
> (John Calvin, 1559, *Institutio Christianae religionis*)

Historically, and empirically, education is the most crucial feature that Protestantism influenced and through which it promoted economic prosperity. Statistically, the Protestant lead in literacy accounts for nearly all of the Protestant advantage in economic outcomes (Becker & Woessmann, 2009, p. 532).

Several Reformers, including Martin Luther, were university professors and writers who promoted the *Sola Scriptura* principle. For this purpose, Luther and other Reformers translated the Scriptures into vernacular languages and taught illiterate people to read (Becker & Woessmann, 2009; Berman, 2003; Witte, 2002). They believed that proper education enables the individual to distinguish right from wrong, truth from falsehood, and to accurately understand "the essentials of the Christian faith" (Green, 2009; Hillerbrand, 1968, as cited in Androne, 2014, p. 81). This explains the Reformatory emphasis on teaching and studying the Scriptures, and thus on establishing elementary schools for ordinary people (Becker & Woessmann, 2009). As the Bible itself states:

> All Scripture is given by inspiration of God, and is profitable for doctrine, for reproof, for correction, for instruction in righteousness: that the man of God may be perfect, thoroughly furnished unto all good works (King James Bible, 1769, 2 Timothy 3:16).

Similarly, the Scriptures also assert that "Blessed is he that readeth [...]" (King James Bible, 1769, Revelation 1:3). Therefore, the Reformers (as well as other early Christians) focused on developing literacy, to enable the reading and teaching of the Gospel (i.e. exegesis). Over time, this enabled Protestants to further utilise these skills in other, non-religious domains (e.g. trade and commerce). As a result, Protestant societies thrived when people were taught to read the Bible, which provided the intellectual resources required for economic development (Becker & Woessmann, 2009, p. 531).

Furthermore, in Protestant countries, education became accessible to (and often mandatory for) all. It combined the study of the Scriptures (instead of Latin scholastic texts) with vocational training. Consequently, the Lutheran Reformation transformed the elitist monopoly of Roman Church-based education into state-based education (initially, locally and nationally in Germany, and later also in other countries). The Reformers' introduction of a public, "secular" education system with public officials, civic concerns, and laicisation opposed Rome's one-sided, distorted religious and humanistic learning (Witte, 2002, pp. 290–291). With the Reformation, education remained inherently religious, but over time it became progressively secularised by being harnessed to civic purposes and broader political control (Ibid). Consequently, the study of the Gospel has been of fundamental importance in Protestant countries (e.g. at universities such as Harvard, Yale, Cambridge, Oxford, Geneva, and Zürich).

The Protestant nurturing of the educated middle classes was the precursor of the politics of popular accountability in government (Snyder, 2011; Spruyt, 1994). However, while Protestants have perhaps not always provided the majority of resources (e.g. education, book printing), Protestantism has nevertheless compelled governments to establish schools (Woodberry, 2012, p. 246). Likewise, when facing greater competition with Protestantism, Roman Catholic hierarchies have also defended the interests of the poor (e.g. education for non-elites, democracy) (Gill, 1998; Anderson, 2007; Woodberry, 2012).

Historical Protestantism has also favoured mobilisation "from below". It has pursued this goal through the early development of literacy at all social levels, and has thus encouraged wider participation in politics. Conversely, the supra-national influence of Roman Catholicism has favoured mobilisation "from above", leading to a late development of literacy and thus limiting the political participation of the lower social strata (Flora & Heidenheimer, 1981).

In Latin America, in order to spread the Gospel, Protestants also introduced literacy campaigns long before Roman Catholicism (Gill, 1998, p. 89). As the Jesuit Jeffrey Klaiber noted, in Latin America, Protestant missionaries introduced the Bible and have since provided the most readable and best versions of the New Testament in Spanish. Therefore, ironically, Catholic missionaries have had to explain carefully to their Latin American flock that Protestants did not write the Bible and that reading it is not heresy (Klaiber, 1970, p. 99).

#### 9.1.2.1 Summarising the Core Messages of Sect. 9.1.2. *Protestant Education*

Historically (and statistically), one key mechanism driving prosperity/transparency has been the Protestant emphasis on literacy so as to promote reading and understanding the Bible among wider circles (Becker & Woessmann, 2009; Woodberry, 2012). This contrasted starkly with the Roman Catholic practice of reciting parts of the Gospel in Latin scholarly language to mostly illiterate peasants (Androne, 2014; Becker & Woessmann, 2009). The teaching of God's Word in vernacular languages created linguistic and methodical skills (i.e. exegetical understanding) that proved valuable beyond the religious realm (Becker & Woessmann, 2009, p. 542). This practice also led to the accumulation of human capital, and thereby opened and perpetuated an important educational (and hence prosperity) gap between Protestants and Roman Catholics over time.

As part of the Catholic Counter-Reformation, the Jesuits have competed with Protestant education but attaching less importance to the Scriptures in their schooling. Some South American areas influenced by Jesuit missions exhibit 10–15% higher human capital and income than the surrounding Catholic populations. Yet, Jesuit instruction has been largely elitist and far less encompassing than Protestant educational coverage and accomplishment.

## References

Anderson, J. (2007). Religion, politics and international relations. The Catholic contribution to democratization's 'third wave': Altruism, hegemony or self-interest? *Cambridge Review of International Affairs, 20*(3).

Androne, M. (2014). The influence of the protestant reformation on education. *Procedia – Social and Behavioral Sciences, 137*, 80–87.

Becker, S. O., & Woessmann, L. (2009). Was Weber wrong? A human capital theory of protestant economic history. *Quarterly Journal of Economics, 124*(2), 531–596.

Berman, H. (2003). *Law and revolution II: The impact of the protestant reformations on the western legal tradition*. Harvard University Press, Belknap Press.

Cook, E. (2012). *Roman catholic hegemony and religious freedom: A seventh-day adventist assessment of dignitatis humanae*. Graduate Faculty of Baylor University.

D'Aubigne, M. (1862). *Histoire de la Reformation au XVIie siecle*. Librairie de Ch. Meyrueis et Compagnie.

Easterlin, R. (1981). Why isn't the whole world developed? *Journal of Economic History, 41*, 1–19.

Flora, P., & Heidenheimer, A. (1981). Introduction. In P. Flora, & A. Heidenheimer (Eds.), *The development of welfare states in Europe and America*. New Brunswick.

Galor, O. (2005). From stagnation to growth: Unified growth theory. In P. Aghion & S. N. Durlauf (Eds.), *Handbook of economic growth*, Vol. 1A. North-Holland.

Gill, A. (1998). *Rendering unto Caesar: The Catholic Church and the state in Latin America*. Chicago University Press.

Glaeser, E., La Porta, R., Lopez-de-Silanes, F., & Shleifer, A. (2004). Do institutions cause growth? *Journal of Economic Growth, 9*(3), 271–303.

Goldin, C. (2001). The human-capital century and American leadership: Virtues of the past. *Journal of Economic History, 61*, 263–292.

Green, I. (2009). *Humanism and protestantism in early modern english education*. Ashgate.

Gruner, E. (1977). *Die Parteien in der Schweiz. 2. neu bearbeitete und erweiterte Auflage*. A. Francke.

Gula, R. M. (2002). *Reason informed by faith—Foundations of Catholic Morality*. Paulist Press.

Hanushek, E., & Woessmann, L. (2008). The role of cognitive skills in economic development. *Journal of Economic Literature, 46*, 607–668.

Head-König, A.-L. (2017). Religion mattered: Religious differences in Switzerland and their impact on demographic behaviour (End of the 18th century to the Middle of the 20th century). *Historical Social Research, 42*(2), 23–58.

Heussi, K. (1991). *Kompendium der Kirchengeschichte*. Tübingen: Mohr Siebeck.

King James Bible. (1769). *The Holy Bible, King James Version*. Cambridge Edition: 1769. Scripture quotations from The Authorized (King James) Version. Rights in the Authorized Version in the United Kingdom are vested in the Crown. Reproduced by permission of the Crown's patentee, Cambridge University Press.

Klaiber, J. L. (1970). Pentecostal breakthrough. *America, 122*(4), 99–102.

Lindert, P. (2003). Voice and growth: Was Churchill right? *Journal of Economic History, 63*, 315–350.

Lukàcs, L. (1986). *Ratio atque Institutio Studiorum Societatis Iesu* (M. P. Iesu, Ed., Vol. 5). Institutum Historicum Societatis Iesu.

Merriam-Webster. (n.d.). Jesuit. In Merriam-Webster.com dictionary. Retrieved March 28, 2021, from https://www.merriam-webster.com/dictionary/Jesuit

Obinger, H. (2009). Religion and the consolidation of the Swiss Welfare State, 1848-1945. In P. Manow & K. van Kersbergen (Eds.), *Religion, class coalitions and welfare states* (pp. 176–209). Cambridge University Press.

Oxford University Press. (2016). *Oxford Dictionaries*. Retrieved from http://www.oxforddictionaries.com/

Pavur, C. S. (2005). *The ratio studiorum: The official plan for Jesuit education*. The Institute of Jesuit Sources.

Plata Quezada, W. E. (2008). De evangelizador de indios a bastión de criollos. El convento dominicano de Nuestra Señora del Rosario y la sociedad colonial, Santafé de Bogotá, siglos xvi-xviii. In Grupo Interdisciplinario de Estudios de Religión, GIERSP, *Mirada pluridisciplinar al hecho religioso en Colombia: Avances de investigación* (pp. 281–346). Bogotá.

Roy, O. (2010). *Holy ignorance: When religion and culture part ways*. Columbia University Press.

Schwarz-Herion, O. (2015). The role of the different players for the great transition towards the NSP. In O. Schwarz-Herion & A. Omran (Eds.), *Strategies towards the new sustainability paradigm. Managing the great transition to sustainable global democracy*. Springer.

Selling, J. A. (2018). Reframing catholic theological ethics: Summary and application. *Religions, 8* (203), 5–13.

Snyder, J. (2011). *Religion and international relations theory*. Columbia University Press.

Spruyt, H. (1994). *The Sovereign State and its competitors*. Princeton University Press.
Valencia, F. (2017). Missionaries, human capital transmission and economic persistence in South America. In S. Michalopoulos, & E. Papaioannou (Eds.), *The long economic and political shadow of history – Volume 3: Europe and the Americas.* CEPR Press.
Witte, J. (2002). *Law and Protestantism: The legal teachings of the Lutheran Reformation.* Cambridge: University Press.
Woodberry, R. (2012). The missionary roots of liberal democracy. *American Political Science Review (APSR), 106*(2), 244–274.

# Chapter 10
# Culture, Religion, and Corruption/ Prosperity *(A), (B), (C), (1), (2)*

Several empirical studies have considered three proxies of culture: religion (Volonté, 2015; Acemoglu et al., 2001; Paldam, 2001; Granato et al., 1996); language (Volonté, 2015); and ethnic measures (Alesina et al., 2003). However, cultural proxies often overlap with cultural dimensions (Hofstede, 2001) as well as with countries and their institutions (Volonté, 2015). The triad "Protestantism, English, and common law" is a typical example of interrelated overlapping characteristics associated with similar governance regimes (Volonté, 2015) and lower corruption (La Porta et al., 1999). The first three sections below elucidate some of these relationships. The fourth identifies those elements of Roman Catholic and Protestant theologies that may help clarify cultural differences. Section 10.5 explores the concept of syncretism as a process associated with cultural amalgamation, which, in Christianity, has predominantly occurred in Roman Catholicism when blended with ethnoreligious traditions.

## 10.1 Culture and Corruption *(2)*

Cultural determinants may drive corruption and its associated variables (i.e. GDP, institutions, democracy) at the same time (Lambsdorff, 1999, p. 14). Now, however, the causality arrow runs theoretically and empirically from culture to corruption, rather than vice versa (Lambsdorff, 2006, p. 17).

The most important cultural characteristics defining the level of corruption in a country are generalised trust, religion, and acceptance of hierarchy (Lambsdorff, 2006, p. 17). These factors are interrelated (La Porta et al., 1999). Hence, high levels of generalised trust, a large share of Protestants, and low acceptance of hierarchy mean less perceived corruption in a country (Lambsdorff, 2006).

**Supplementary Information** The online version of this chapter (https://doi.org/10.1007/978-3-030-78498-0_10) contains supplementary material, which is available to authorized users.



J. García Portilla, *"Ye Shall Know Them by Their Fruits"*, Contributions to Economics, https://doi.org/10.1007/978-3-030-78498-0_10

Several studies have shown that corruption is more frequent in countries with a high degree of ethnic fragmentation (see, among others, Mauro, 1995; La Porta et al., 1999; Treisman, 2000; Alesina et al., 2003). However, neither Serra (2006) nor Elbahnasawy and Revier (2012) found any significant effect of fractionalisation on corruption. One possible explanation for these dissimilar conclusions might be related to the embedding of all ethnicities in a single indicator of fragmentation across different samples.

My empirical models (Part V) also include linguistically and ethnically aggregated and disaggregated measures as cultural proxies. Thus:

**Empirical Expectation**

8). *I expect no conclusive results for ethnic fractionalisation given the possible overlapping of cultural proxies (*Volonté, 2015*) with other variables and given the varied conclusions of previous empirical results with aggregated measures.*

## 10.2 Culture and Institutions/Prosperity *(2), (3), (5)*

Various cultural aspects have direct empirical relations with institutional/prosperity/transparency outcomes: (1) *trust* (e.g. a higher level of trust implies less litigation). Education also favours trust; (2) *family ties. Familialism* (a significant reliance on family ties) is linked with lower civic sense and less trust. Thus, medieval corporations that were established based on such nuclear families underperformed; (3) *individualism* encourages personal accomplishments and innovation, contrary to collectivism; (4) *generalised morality*, which is limited to small circles in hierarchical societies; and (5) *work attitudes,* in the classical Weberian sense of the Protestant work ethic (Alesina & Giuliano, 2015, pp. 902–910).

## 10.3 Culture and Religion *(B), (C)*

The relationship between culture and religion is complex and subject to ongoing debate. Globalisation has "de-cultured" and "de-territorialised" world religions from their cultural and geographical origins (Roy, 2010). Likewise, secularisation, most of all in Europe or in specific political contexts (e.g. Communism) has partially driven religion out of the cultural sphere (Berger, 1999; Roy, 2010). Conversely, religion may represent most cultural values depending on context (e.g. for Orthodox Jews, Christian Pentecostalists, or Muslim Salafists) or a minor part of such values (e.g. for Jewish atheists, secular Protestants, or Catholic non-believers).

Alesina and Giuliano (2015) leave unmentioned the relation between religion and the cultural traits mentioned above (Sect. 10.2, with the exception of the fifth aspect). However, religion is a decisive institutional and cultural expression, and as such governs social relationships (Volonté, 2015; Stulz & Williamson, 2003; La Porta et al., 1997). Consequently, the cultural and institutional influence of religion underlies the phenomenon that prosperity, transparency, and institutions reinforce each other (Lambsdorff, 2006; Treisman, 2000).

**Trust**

Regarding *trust*, sufficient empirical evidence links values, attitudes, and beliefs (including trust) with religion and prosperity outcomes (Arruñada, 2010; Barro & McCleary, 2003; Guiso et al., 2003; La Porta et al., 1997). Arruñada (2010) compared the values and personal outcomes of Protestants and Catholics in a 32-country sample, based on data form the International Social Survey Programme (ISSP) Survey. The author analysed differences in the theology, church organisation, and social practice of Protestantism and Catholicism. Different indices and indicators of social ethic (e.g. social control, the rule of law, and homogeneous values) and work ethic (e.g. positive working hours) were examined. Some significant findings of Arruñada can be summarised as follows:

- Compared with Roman Catholics, Protestant principles influence individuals to be less attached to close networks of friends and family, possess more homogeneous standards, be more involved in collective social control, and support institutions more (Arruñada, 2010, p. 891).
- Arruñada (2010) and Guiso et al. (2003) found statistical evidence for the fact that Roman Catholics are significantly more tolerant of tax fraud than Protestants. Roman Catholics are statistically less supportive of political and legal institutions and are more willing to cover for their delinquent friends when dealing with the police (Arruñada, 2010, p. 907).
- Protestants hold more homogeneous values than Catholics. Greater homogeneity reduces exchange and transaction costs and promotes impersonal trading and markets (e.g. those in commerce, finance, and industry) (p. 907–908). In turn, Roman Catholicism tends to promote personalised exchange and is less favourable to impersonal commerce (p. 890, 908) (e.g. in medieval times or in most rural areas in Latin America).
- Better-educated Protestants trust churches and religious organisations more, whereas better-educated Catholics trust them less. Thus, the Roman Catholic Church has greater conflict with its educated laity. Education tends to substitute for religion in Roman Catholicism, whereas it complements religion in Protestantism (p. 906).

Similarly, after surveying prominent empirical works linking trust and religion, Volonté (2015) observed:

> Protestants exhibit a higher level of trust in contrast to Catholics, which promotes trade and thereby economic development (La Porta et al., 1997; Glaeser & Glendon, 1998; Guiso et al., 2006). [. . .] Religion and trust are therefore also related to organizational issues. Stulz and Williamson (2003) contend that the Calvinist Reformation promoted decentralization and the creation of multiple churches, and aimed to guard against concentrations of power. In contrast, Roman Catholicism, which is recognized as a religion whose congregations place their trust in people "who know more", has a centralized hierarchical structure with the

Pope as its authoritative head (Levine 1979; La Porta et al., 1999; Stulz & Williamson, 2003, p. 319 as cited in Volonté, 2015, p. 84).

The veneration of the pope as the authoritative head of a hierarchical, centralised structure is the archetypical example of *vertical trust* (Volonté, 2015, p. 84). In turn, Protestants tend to be sceptical of hierarchies. The reformations historically promoted decentralisation (i.e. multiple churches) and democratisation (i.e. priesthood of all believers), and thus protected ordinary people against concentrations of power (*horizontal trust*) (Woodberry, 2012; Witte, 2002; La Porta et al., 1999; Stulz & Williamson, 2003; Levine 1979 as cited in Volonté, 2015, p. 84).

A typical example of horizontal trust refers to common goods (e.g. milk or fruit) left on display for customers to buy using open cash bowls (without supervising cashiers). For Mangalwadi (2011), such traditions exist mostly in historically Protestant countries and derive from applying the moral principles of the Biblical Decalogue. Consequently, regardless of a higher authority (e.g. a priest or a government) overseeing farm produce, God always watches (over) humans (producers and customers). Such a simple principle of accountability has profound reinforcing implications for the value-creating and value-adding chain (Mangalwadi, 2011, pp. 251–254). In non-Protestant societies, following Mangalwadi's example, low trust (or vertical trust) implies hiring an overseeing cashier, adulterated milk, inspectors accepting bribes, and a higher price for a lower quality item. Accordingly, such economies are much less competitive than Protestant economies. But the distinct values persisting through the present owe more to the historical and institutional weight of religion (than to its contemporary influence), even regardless of the secularisation of societies (Inglehart & Baker, 2000). As Glaeser and Glendon (1998) observed, "current social norms may still be the legacy of prior religious beliefs" (p. 431). Likewise, Inglehart and Baker (2000) assert:

> While the majority of individuals have little or no contact with the church today, the impact of living in a society that was historically shaped by once-powerful Catholic or Protestant institutions persists today, shaping everyone—Protestant, Catholic, or other... (p. 36).

**Familialism**

*Familialism* and *low generalised morality* characterise Roman Catholicism as discussed (Sect. 10.4.1) (Esping-Andersen, 1996; Van Kersbergen, 1995; Arruñada, 2010; La Porta et al., 1999). In turn, individualism stems from the French Revolution and secularism was indirectly influenced by the Protestant Revolutions (Sect. 8.3.4.4). Arruñada (2010) found statistically, and consistent with the argument of Putnam (1993) that Catholics give more importance than Protestants to family ties. This more significant role of the family, according to Arruñada, corresponds to Catholics' proclivity for occupational options that promote production within families, which can lead to nepotism and obstruction of institutional functioning (Arruñada, 2010, p. 908).

Investigating these cultural features, various empirical studies (e.g. Granato et al., 1996) have found robust practical interrelations between GDP growth and Protestantism based on cultural measurements (World Values Survey of a 25 cross-country sample). Likewise, Hayward and Kemmelmeier (2011), combining individual and national levels using cross-national panel data, reported that Protestantism persistently fosters capitalism but independently of active religiosity (cultural Protestantism).

Religion has shaped culture to a significant extent in Europe and the Americas (Anderson, 2007; Paldam, 2001; Huntington, 1991). Therefore, my research model places religion inside the "culture box" and maintains that it has manifold relations with variables beyond culture (e.g. institutions; Fig. 2.1). The next sections further analyse the implications of cultural factors, religion, and corruption in Latin America.

## *10.3.1 The Cultural Influence of Religion in Latin America*

### 10.3.1.1 Corruption in Latin America

Some Latin American cultural characteristics prone to corruption are corporatism, authoritarianism, centralism, formalism (double standards), particularism (allegiance within an inner circle), and the dispensing of favours expected of certain roles (Nef, 2001, pp. 159–174). Therefore, corruption and culture are associated in Latin America as an ethical problem arising from society's moral deficiency where traditional values persist (Uildriks, 2009, p. 9).

Hofstede (2001) reached similar conclusions after making a first empirical, quantitative approach to exploring the differences in thinking and social behaviours across 72 countries (using 116,000 questionnaires distributed across IBM, the multinational enterprise). Notwithstanding fierce criticism of the representativeness of the samples and of the categories utilised for analysis, Hofstede's pioneering work provides a numerical glimpse of cultural variables in relation to institutions and prosperity. The author's results were extrapolated, then generalised in six "cultural dimensions" (Hofstede, 2001).

One of the six dimensions used by Hofstede is the "Power Distance Index" (PDI). PDI is the extent to which the least influential individuals in a society expect and accept an unequal distribution of power (Hofstede, 2014). According to the PDI index, most Latin American countries present high scores, contrary to the low PDI scores in North American and North European countries. Table 10.1 summarises the consequences of different PDI scores for political systems, religious life, and organisations, among others (Hofstede, 2001).

As shown, institutionalised religion and the state have established hierarchical power relations in Latin America, thus a high-power distance may be expected on this continent. In contrast, after the Reformation, the institutional disbanding of Roman Catholicism in Northern Europe and the non-institutionalisation of religion in North America led to more social equality.

**Table 10.1** Different Power Distance Index (PDI) and its consequences for social and political systems, religious life, and organisations (adapted from Hofstede, 2001)[a]

| | High PDI scores (Latin American countries) | Low PDI scores (North American and North European countries) |
|---|---|---|
| Type of government | Autocratic or oligarchic | Pluralist governments based on the outcome of majority votes |
| Government stability | Sudden changes (instability) | Stable governments stressing equality |
| Political spectrum | Polarisation between left and right with a weak centre | Political parties tend to occupy the centre |
| Tax system | Tax system protects the wealthy | Tax system aims to redistribute wealth |
| Religion | Success of religions stresses stratification (hierarchical) | Success of religions stresses equality |
| Theories about society | Elitist (Machiavelli, Mosca, Pareto) | Pluralist (More, Marx, Weber) |

[a]Note: PDI provided information for only less than 20 observations for the 65 countries analysed here. Furthermore, PDI overlaps with other proxies of culture and institutions (Volonté, 2015). Therefore, I excluded the PDI index from analysis due to lack of data and risk of endogeneity, and no results were obtained from this variable

#### 10.3.1.2 The Divorce Between Law, Social Norms, and Morals in Latin America

Various factors—corruption, crime, violence, and institutions' loss of prestige—account for the systematic divorce between law, social norms, and morals in most Latin American countries (Mockus et al., 2012).

Table 10.2 shows the respective regulatory systems (divorced in most Latin American countries). The three columns frame the three regulatory systems (law, social norms, and personal morals). The behavioural motivation mechanisms are deployed in the two rows, depending on whether they are positive (incentives above) or associated with negative reasons or punishments (penalties below). Mockus' (2012) conceptual proposal shows that rather than abiding by a single regulatory system, humans are subject to three interacting systems. Such interplay can be harmonic (e.g. in northern Europe) or may generate multiple shocks (as in Latin America) (Mockus et al., 2012, p. 7).

Arruñada (2010) coincides with a similar distinction of these three regulatory systems, which he refers to as "enforcement mechanisms" (parties) (Table 10.2). The author describes that under "third-party" enforcement, specialised authorities such as government rulers, prosecutors, and public forces check community members' behaviour and discipline those who break the laws. In turn, enforcement by a "second party" depends on sanctions and verifications by the party who bears the brunt of the violation's repercussions. Thus, peers in groups are second parties in economic exchanges, and they may also sanction non-compliant partners by various means, such as humiliation, bullying, ostracising, or even deprivation. Finally, through the "first party" enforcement mechanism, human beings sanction

**Table 10.2** Behaviour regulation mechanisms

| *Carrots and sticks* (Mockus et al., 2012): | ±<br>*Laws* | ±±<br>*Social norms* | ±±±<br>*Personal moral standards* |
|---|---|---|---|
| *Enforcement mechanisms* (Arruñada, 2010): | *Third party* | *Second party* | *First party* |
| (+) Incentive (carrots) | Admiration or respect for the law (or recognising the importance of fulfiling it) | Admiration and social recognition (trust—reputation) | Spiritual or self-gratification of conscience (peace of mind) |
| (−) Penalty (sticks) | Fear of legal sanction | Fear of shame or social rejection | Fear of damnation or guilt |

(Adapted from Mockus et al., 2012, p. 7; Arruñada, 2010, p. 892)

themselves with psychological compensations. Accordingly, individuals determine their actions in response to their understanding of a moral code, which also contains many essential economic preferences, such as thriftiness and hard work. In Christianity, concepts such as "salvation" and "everlasting life" fall into this "first party" category of regulatory mechanisms (Arruñada, 2010, p. 892).

For Arruñada, religion directly influences personal moral standards, as well as less clearly influencing social norms and law. For Mockus, law, culture, and morality tend to be congruent in ideal democratic societies. Culture is more demanding than law, and morality is more demanding than culture. The behaviours valid in light of individual morality usually enjoy social approval, although the opposite is not always true. In turn, what is culturally approved is usually legally allowed, although some acceptable legal behaviour is rejected for cultural reasons (Mockus, 2001, p. 3).

In contrast, the divorce from these normative systems occurs in most Latin American countries and applies to corruption and all forms of illegal behaviour (at times even extending to violence). A typical and extreme example is that the right to life is a fundamental right upheld in all Latin American constitutions. However, social organisations (or cultural groups) intent on eradicating the fundamental respect for another person's life have proliferated in Latin America. For such groups, it often becomes even necessary to demonstrate that "you are capable" or "brave enough" to take another person's life so as to gain greater respect or stronger group affiliation. This thinking needs to be understood in terms of the divorce of law and culture. It can, however, also be analysed in terms of a divorce between morality and culture. It is also possible that due to fear, recognition, or shame an individual ends up accepting certain group rules even if these go against one's conscience (e.g. "I prefer not to be considered a 'snitch' even though I know I am doing something with which I morally disagree") (Mockus et al., 2012, p. 6).

In sum, individuals not only respond to the coercive power of the law but, much more stalwartly, they also obey their cultural and moral principles (Mockus et al., 2012, p. 7). Historically, the Roman Catholic Church has influenced the three regulatory systems in Latin America. Thus, a negative influence on the coherence of these systems may be expected when considering Catholic "relativist morals" (Sect. 10.4.1) and restrictive concordats and corporatist legal instruments (Sect. 8.3.4.6).[1] In contrast, the application of the Biblical Decalogue principles in the legal systems of historically Protestant countries (Sect. 8.3.4) introduced coherent moral, social, and legal accountability standards towards God and the neighbour (Fig. 8.4). The previous discussion justifies reviewing the distinct theologies of historical Protestantism and Roman Catholicism as the root-cause of their differences (see below).

## 10.4 Roman Catholic and Protestant Theologies, and Corruption/Prosperity *(1), (3), (6)*

The following sections examine the influence of religion in terms of theological approaches within Roman Catholicism, then explore the same within Protestantism.

### *10.4.1 Roman Catholic Theology and Political Culture*

#### 10.4.1.1 Roman Catholic Theology

Selling (2018) explains Roman Catholic theological ethics in terms of personal intention, that is, good ("virtues") versus evil ("vices"). This Roman Catholic notion derives from its traditional recognition of four "cardinal virtues" established by Greek philosophy and by the three "theological virtues" of Paul's Epistles. Thus, Greek philosophy (especially Aristotelian) once again carries more weight than Scriptural "virtues", of which there are only three (as formulated in the New Testament), (see Sects. 8.2.1.1, 8.3.4.1, 8.3.5, and 9.1.1). Therefore, Roman Catholicism acknowledges as "virtue" the Aristotelian "non-absolute" and "mean" relative point between two extremes (Selling, 2018, p. 9). As such, "good and evil" depend on analysing specific acts, circumstances, and intentions as harmful or beneficial for each person. Accordingly, no "ruling" moral standard would be adequate (not even the Scriptures):

> Even clear commandments, such as "thou shalt not kill" admit of exceptions that have been enshrined in [Catholic] church teaching for centuries (Selling, 2018, p. 8).[2]

Selling (2018) acknowledges that Roman Catholicism "does not subscribe to the vast majority" of the laws of Judaism (p. 10). In other words, Roman Catholicism

[1]Note: I do not define specific variables for this divorce of mechanisms, neither in regression analysis nor in QCA models. However, *legal origin, concordats,* and *population adherents* may serve as proxies, and are therefore included in the empirical setting (Chap. 16 and Part VI).

[2]Joseph Selling is Emeritus Professor of Moral Theology at Catholic University Leuven. He is also the author of the book "Reframing Catholic Theological Ethics" (Oxford University Press, 2016).

does not endorse most Old Testament laws that Jesus and the Apostles, as Jews, followed (Bruce, 2007). Moreover, the moral law that Catholicism explicitly teaches from the Old Testament's Decalogue is elaborated with the help of supplementary meanings through a "natural law reasoning" (Selling, 2018, p. 10). Consequently, the Catholic Decalogue diverges from the original books (King James Bible, 1769, Exodus 20; Deuteronomy 5), which were "written with the finger of God" (King James Bible, 1769, Exodus 31: 18; Deuteronomy 9: 10). The wording of the Ten Commandments, moreover, even varies in Catholic Catechisms of different languages beyond their translation (Fig. 10.1).

| | A | B | C |
|---|---|---|---|
| | **The Ten Commandments (*King James Bible*, 1769, Exodus 20, 1-17)** | **Catholic Catechetical Formula in English** | **Roman Catholic Catechism in Spanish** (author's translation) |
| 1 | And God spake all these words, saying, I am the Lord thy God, which have brought thee out of the land of Egypt, out of the house of bondage.<br><br>**Thou shalt have no other gods before me.** | 1. I am the LORD your God: you shall not have strange Gods before me. | 1. You shall love God above all things.<br>*(Amarás a Dios sobre todas las cosas).* |
| 2 | **Thou shalt not make unto thee any graven image,** or any likeness of any thing that is in heaven above, or that is in the earth beneath, or that is in the water under the earth: thou shalt not bow down thyself to them, nor serve them: for I the Lord thy God am a jealous God, visiting the iniquity of the fathers upon the children unto the third and fourth generation of them that hate me; and showing mercy unto thousands of them that love me, and keep my commandments. | **...?**<br><br>*(Commandment eliminated from the Roman Catholic Catechism)* | **...?**<br><br>*(Commandment eliminated from the Roman Catholic Catechism)* |
| 3 | **Thou shalt not take the name of the Lord thy God in vain:** for the Lord will not hold him guiltless that taketh his name in vain. | 2. You shall not take the name of the LORD your God in vain. | 2. You shall not take God's name in vain.<br>*(No tomarás el nombre de Dios en vano).* |
| 4 | **Remember the sabbath day, to keep it holy.**<br>Six days shalt thou labor, and do all thy work: but the seventh day is the sabbath of the Lord thy God: in it thou shalt not do any work, thou, nor thy son, nor thy daughter, thy manservant, nor thy maidservant, nor thy cattle, nor thy stranger that is within thy gates: for in six days the Lord made heaven and earth, the sea, and all that in them is, and rested the seventh day: wherefore the Lord blessed the sabbath day, and hallowed it. | 3. Remember to keep holy the LORD'S Day. | 3. You shall sanctify the feasts (holidays).<br>*(Santificarás las fiestas).* |
| 5 | **Honor thy father and thy mother:** that thy days may be long upon the land which the Lord thy God giveth thee. | 4. Honor your father and your mother. | 4. Honor your father and your mother.<br>*(Honrarás a tu padre y a tu madre).* |
| 6 | **Thou shalt not kill.** | 5. You shall not kill. | 5. You shall not kill.<br>*(No matarás).* |
| 7 | **Thou shalt not commit adultery.** | 6. You shall not commit adultery. | 6. You shall not commit impure acts.<br>*(No cometerás actos impuros).* |
| 8 | **Thou shalt not steal.** | 7. You shall not steal. | 7. You shall not steal.<br>*(No hurtarás)* |
| 9 | **Thou shalt not bear false witness** against thy neighbor. | 8. You shall not bear false witness against your neighbor. | 8. You shall not say false testimony or lie.<br>*(No dirás falso testimonio ni mentirás).* |
| 10 | **Thou shalt not covet** thy neighbor's house, thou shalt not covet thy neighbor's wife, nor his manservant, nor his maidservant, nor his ox, nor his ass, nor any thing that is thy neighbor's. | 9. You shall not covet your neighbor's wife. | 9. You shall not consent impure thoughts or desires.<br>*(No consentirás pensamientos ni deseos impuros).* |
| -- | -- | 10. You shall not covet your neighbor's goods. | 10. You shall not covet the property of others.<br>*(No codiciarás los bienes ajenos).* |

*Note:* Author's highlighting and emphases

**Fig. 10.1** The Bible's Decalogue compared with the Decalogue of Roman Catechism (English and Spanish) (adapted from A) The Holy Bible. The Authorised (King James) Version. Cambridge Edition: (1769); (B) Catechism of the Catholic Church—The Ten Commandments (Vatican, 2018); (C) Catecismo de la Doctrina Cristiana (Comisión Episcopal de Enseñanza de Madrid, 1962, pp. 6–7)). Note: Author's highlighting and emphases

Figure 10.1 shows the pronounced differences between the Decalogue of the Holy Scriptures (A) and the Roman Catholic Catechism in Spanish (C). The Decalogue of the Roman Catholic Catechism in English (B) stands between the Scriptures and the Spanish Catechism. The Roman Catholic Catechism contains fundamental alterations in the First Table of the Commandments (the first four Commandments relative to loving God; see and compare with Fig. 8.4). The Second Table (concerning loving one's neighbour) remains relatively similar with some minor changes.

While the First Commandment concerns monotheism (A and B), in (C) the wording is completely different, bringing into play other related Biblical ordinance but not the original (Figs. 8.4 and 10.1). Similarly, the Second Commandment of the Decalogue (to make no graven image) is arbitrarily removed from the Roman Catechism (B and C). This makes sense when considering the core practice of venerating images and icons in Roman Catholicism. Such reverence is common to different religious systems (e.g. Babylon, Egypt, Rome); in contrast, however, the Holy Bible condemns it as idolatry (Fig. 8.4).

While the Third Commandment remains relatively similar, the Fourth Commandment varies significantly in A, B, and C. In A, it mentions keeping the Sabbath (Saturday). In B, it refers to the LORD's Day (which is open to interpretation, i.e. Sunday Mass), and in C to "sanctifying the festivals". The three variants differ noticeably, as a result of the interplay between Jewish (Sabbath) and pagan factors (sun worshipping: Sunday) in early Christianity (Bacchiocchi, 1977).

The wording of the other commandments has remained similar, some minor changes aside. Nonetheless, the Roman Catechism contains several articles that further relativise the application of the Commandments, for instance:

Regarding the Ninth Commandment:

> The gravity of a lie is measured against the nature of the truth it deforms, the circumstances, the intentions of the one who lies, and the harm suffered by its victims. If a lie in itself only constitutes a venial sin, it becomes mortal when it does grave injury to the virtues of justice and charity (2484, Catechism of the Catholic Church (Vatican, 2018).

However, the Holy Bible does not mention the existence of "venial sins" such as "soft lies". On the contrary, Jesus said:

> But let your communication be, Yea, yea; Nay, nay: for whatsoever is more than these cometh of evil (King James Bible, 1769, Matthew 5:37).

Here is another example of the relativisation of the Sixth Commandment in the Roman Catechism:

> The prohibition of murder does not abrogate the right to render an unjust aggressor unable to inflict harm. Legitimate defense is a grave duty for whoever is responsible for the lives of others or the common good (2321, Catechism of the Catholic Church (Vatican, 2018).

Here, too, the Scriptures state that Jesus commanded the opposite:

> but I say unto you, *That ye resist not evil*: but whosoever shall smite thee on thy right cheek, turn to him the other also. And if any man will sue thee at the law, and take away thy coat, let him have thy cloak also. And whosoever shall compel thee to go a mile, go with him twain.

> Give to him that asketh thee, and from him that would borrow of thee turn not thou away. Ye have heard that it hath been said, Thou shalt love thy neighbor, and hate thine enemy. But I say unto you, *Love your enemies, bless them that curse you, do good to them that hate you, and pray for them which despitefully use you, and persecute you* (King James Bible, 1769, Matthew 5:39–44; my italics).

Furthermore, meaningful variations on content and wording are also evident in the English and Spanish versions of the Roman Catechism. The Roman Church-State is Catholic. Although this means it is "universal", its Commandments are taught differently in English-speaking (predominantly Protestant) contexts than in Spanish-speaking (predominantly Roman Catholic) ones. Similar differences in wording can also be found in the Catechism's version of the Decalogue in other languages (e.g. compare German with Portuguese or French versions). Since the Catechism eliminated the Second Commandment, the Ninth Commandment was divided in two (thus creating two new Commandments).

##### 10.4.1.1.1 Roman Catholic Theology in Practice

According to Arruñada (2010), Roman Catholicism favours varied moral values, given the content of its moral code and primarily due to its methods of enforcement (p. 895). The double or "diverse moral standards" in Roman Catholicism encourage a "selective charity", thus favouring friends and relatives (*familialism*) over strangers. Regarding enforcement, the "salvation by works" and "purgatory-based" theologies, along with the private confession of sins to a priest, imply heterogeneous subjective moral standards for judging individuals according to the clergy's subjectivity and individual circumstances. In other words, moral norms are adapted according to individual circumstances, and descend from medieval "casuistry" (Arruñada, 2010, p. 895). Moreover, this concurs entirely with the Aristotelian "non-absolute" and "mean" relative point defining "good" or "bad". Therefore, the various predicted statistical results could be expected (see Sect. 10.3).

Another widespread moral tradition refers to the duality between official Catholic discourse and de facto practice. Examples include the constant scandalous abuse of children by priests. For instance, the recent exhaustive Pennsylvania report found that the Roman Catholic hierarchy covered-up for more than 300 priests who had abused over 1000 children in Pennsylvania alone. Although the leaders of the Catholic Church publicly condemn child abuse, in practice the Church hierarchy systematically covers up such scandals (Grand Jury of Pennsylvania, 2018) (see Sect. 8.3.3.2).

#### 10.4.1.2 Roman Catholic Political Culture

Political culture is a system of principles, values, expressive representations, and empirical views that describe the context within which political activity occurs (Verba, 1965, p. 513). *Familialism* and the predominance of the male breadwinner model are two values propagated by Catholic political parties (Esping-Andersen,

1996; Van Kersbergen, 1995). Catholic political culture "[...] is transmitted mainly through nationwide institutions, to the population of a society as a whole—even to those who have little or no contact to religious institutions" (Inglehart & Baker, 2000, p. 36; Emmenegger, 2011, p. 339). Therefore, the social effect of Roman Catholicism does not depend on religiosity (Esping-Andersen, 1996, p. 66; Figueroa, 2016).

Various scholars, including Arruñada (2010), Lambsdorff (2006), and Treisman (2000), have analysed the adverse consequences of *familialism* on corruption. Societies are perceived as less corrupt when impersonal values are more important than particularistic or family values (Lambsdorff, 2006, p. 19). Thus, the adverse impact of Roman Catholicism on corruption stems mainly from the institution. The Roman Church-State transmits values such as the acceptance of hierarchy, *familialism,* double standards, and relativism to the population via education, for instance. Moreover, the pressure to compete with Protestantism has often forced the Catholic Church to strategically adopt more pro-social and more democratic postures in several countries (Gill 1998, 2013; Anderson, 2007; Woodberry, 2012; Wilde et al., 2010) (see Sect. 8.2.1.2). The next two sections briefly consider two current aspects of Roman Catholic theology: ecumenism and liberation theology.

#### 10.4.1.3 Ecumenism: All Roads Lead to Rome

*Ecumenism* and its adjective, *ecumenical,* are defined as "promoting or tending toward worldwide Christian unity or cooperation"; "of, relating to, or representing the whole of a body of churches"; and "worldwide or general in extent, influence, or application" (Merriam-Webster, n.d.). Etymologically, the term derives from Greek *Oikos*, "home". This root is the same for concepts such as *Oikos-logos:* ecology (the study of home) or *Oikos-nomos:* economy (the administration of home). Sixteenth-century late Latin understood "oecumenical or ecumenical" as "belonging to the universal [Catholic] Church". One Roman Catholic deacon and university professor interviewed for this study termed ecumenism as "a process of bringing the separated brethren from the Catholic Church (Protestants, among others) back *'home'*".

However, as Engelhardt (2007) has noted:

> Contemporary Christians are separated by foundationally disparate understandings of Christianity itself. Christians do not share one theology, much less a common understanding of the significance of sin, suffering, disease, and death. These foundational disagreements not only stand as impediments to an intellectually defensible ecumenism, but they also form the underpinnings of major disputes in the culture wars... (p. 25).

Yet, the "ecumenical movement" fosters unity among Christians according to opportune occasions and the needs of the Roman Church-State. These include efforts to eliminate words that complicate mutual relations between denominations and to promote dialogue between competent experts from different churches and communities (Abbott, 1989). According to the Jesuit Walter Abbott, as the challenges of honing ecclesiastical communion are progressively resolved, the Catholic Church expects all Christians to be reunited in a single "Eucharistic" celebration, into a unity which, for him, rests solely within the Roman Church (Abbott, 1989, pp. 347–348).

The Christian desire for unity is indeed founded on the Scriptures (King James Bible, 1769, John 17:11). However, the downscaling to a Christendom centred exclusively on the Roman Catholic Church-State reflects a nostalgia for a monopolistic medieval Church (Agnew, 2010). This notion was expressed by Joseph Ratzinger (the former Pope Benedict XVI) when he referred to the medieval continuum from the Roman Empire to the "Holy" Roman Empire as "European identity" (Ratzinger & Pera, 2006; Agnew, 2010). For Ratzinger, the Christendom *"crisis"* began with what he calls "Germanic Protestantism". Hence, the Protestant Reformation forcefully broke the continuity of the (Catholic) European identity and subordinated the power of the Church to the state, thus creating what he calls "unholy"/Catholic nation-states (Ibid). The Roman Church-State, longing to return to the monopolistic medieval Church, has therefore incessantly sought to bring back "home" the "separated brethren".

The efforts of Roman Catholicism to initiate and maintain such an ecumenical enterprise have been undeniably successful worldwide. The Encyclical *Dignitatis Humanae* has fostered ecumenical relations after Vatican II (Cook, 2012, p. 33). Although Vatican II has promoted reconciliation attitudes towards other religions, it has not "marked a huge disruption in the beliefs and practices of the [Catholic] Church" (Agnew, 2010, p. 48). In turn, historical principles (i.e. *Sola Scriptura*, *Sola Gratia* and *Sola Fide*) that initially gave rise to Protestantism—meaning literally to *Protest* against Rome's tyranny and demagogy—have evidently capitulated today in many Protestant denominations. The following cases exemplify this phenomenon that has facilitated ecumenical relations.

**Lutheranism**

Roman Catholicism and the Lutheran Church have publicly and progressively agreed on several critical issues in numerous documents (i.e. Joint Declarations) with statements such as:

> This Declaration on the Way (In Via) to unity seeks to make more visible the unity we share by gathering together agreements reached on issues of church, ministry, and eucharist. This Declaration, [...] is neither at the beginning nor the end of the journey toward unity (Committee on Ecumenical and Interreligious Affairs, 2015, p. 1).

Particularly remarkable is the Report of the Lutheran-Roman Catholic Commission on Unity—"From Conflict to Communion"—on the occasion of the Lutheran-Catholic Common Commemoration of 500 years of the Reformation in 2017. Through this joint official report, the Lutheran Church has relinquished various fundamental principles that originated five centuries ago with Martin Luther, among others the *Sola Scriptura*. Lutherans now accept statements previously inconceivable such as "The Bishop of Rome by virtue of his office is 'pastor of the whole Church'" (LG 22 as cited in LWF & PCPCU, 2013, p. 69). Likewise, in the Joint Declaration on the Doctrine of Justification (June 1998), Roman Catholic and Lutheran scholars reached a consensus on the question: How is one saved? This formerly dissenting view was crucial to the Protestant Reformation—i.e. salvation by grace alone through faith in Jesus Christ alone (*Sola Gratia* and *Sola Fide*), instead of "salvation by the works" of Catholicism (Cook, 2012, p. 34; Arruñada, 2010). Furthermore, Bergoglio's (aka "Pope Francis") visit to Sweden in 2016, to commemorate the 499th anniversary of the Lutheran Reformation (Sweden, once a strongly Lutheran country and now secularised), was far more than simply a milestone in Catholicism's efforts to regain its "separated brethren".

**Anglicanism**

The Anglican Church's frequent reference to "the middle way between Protestantism and Catholicism" is another important example of the Protestant "homecoming". Anglican theology and practices have moved ever closer to Roman Catholicism (Abram, 2018; Doe, 2010, p. 243; Doe & Sandberg, 2010). In 2011, for instance, the Roman Catholic Church-State received seven Anglican priests and 300 members from six congregations. Several others are rapidly progressing towards full communion with Rome (Cook, 2012, p. 33).

**Pentecostalism**

The ecumenical contacts between the Neo-Pentecostal movement and the charismatic Catholic movement are surprisingly close. In Latin America and beyond, the classical topics of controversial theology between Catholicism and Protestantism, and between liberalism and fundamentalism, are no longer obstacles for theological re-annexation. In fact, confessional boundaries are no longer obeyed (especially in Protestantism) in practising its faith (Schäfer, 1997).

**Mainline Protestantism**

Mainline Protestants and Roman Catholics now share common denominators and jointly oppose secularism. Issues such "as homosexual marriages, abortion, and religion in the public square have proved to be common ground for both groups" (Cook, 2012 p. 34; Miller, 2012, 2017; Colson & Neuhaus, 1995).

Mainline Protestantism (and in general, secular societies) are "amnesiac societies" (Hervieu-Léger, 1993) since "they are less and less capable of maintaining the memory that lies at the heart of their religious existence" (Hervieu-Léger, 1999, p. 80). These features are such neither because societies are increasingly rational nor because they have "found satisfactory alternatives to the traditional forms of religion so crucial in their historical formation" (Hervieu-Léger, 1999, p. 80).

Engelhardt (2007) explains the capitulation of principles in Protestantism as a result of the secularising forces of surrounding societies. For the author, secularisation has debilitated "the historic, zealous commitment of the particular faiths to their particular founding doctrines, thus undermining the theological barriers to intercommunion" (p. 26). Popovich, an Orthodox author, has described this blend of secular thought and religious authority in the following terms:

> Ecumenism is the common name for the pseudo-Christianity of the pseudo-Churches of Western Europe. Within it is the heart of European humanism, with Papism as its head (Popovich, 1994, p. 169).

**Ecumenism and Religious Freedom**

The name "Protestants" derives from the protestation against the papal proposition that its hierarchy and *status quo* should be reestablished in areas where the Edict of Speyer (1526) had already enforced religious freedom. The papacy at the Diet of Speyer II (1529) postulated, among others, the majority rule in matters of faith, the banishment of the Zwinglians, and death-punishment to Anabaptists. The opposition of the reformed princes to the papal proposals was crucial to the success of the Reformation, the liberties of Germany, and the rights of conscience (Wolgast, 1996; Cook, 2012; D'Aubigne, 1862). As Wolgast (1996) noted,

> The protestation received legal status through the appeal that the Protestant princes and imperial cities lodged before two notaries in Speyer on 25 April, 1529. [...] in 1529 the individual conscience was established for the first time as a norm of decisions not to be outvoted in political negotiations. Against the positive law was set the conformity of the evangelical teachings to the scriptures; the legal act of protestation presupposed a religious decision (Wolgast, 1996, 4: p. 104).

Figure 10.2 presents parallels between Roman Catholic concepts of religious freedom at Diet of Speyer II (1529) and *Dignitatis Humanae* of Vatican II (1965), as well as the Protestant definition at the protestation of Speyer.

After analysing several case studies and comparing Catholic concepts of religious freedom of Diet of Speyer II (1529) and *Dignitatis Humanae* of Vatican II (1965) (See Fig. 10.2), Cook concluded:

> … the Catholic Church has not changed its hegemonic nature, only its method of achieving hegemony. Additionally, it strongly suggests that the [Catholic] Church's efforts to arrest and counteract the Protestant Reformation (and any other religion) are far from buried in the past (Cook, 2012, p. 159).

The Protestant definition at the protestation of Speyer concurs with Martin Luther's assertion: "I will preach it, teach it, write it, but I will constrain no man by force, for faith must come freely without compulsion".[3] However, not all strands

| | | | | | | | | |
|---|---|---|---|---|---|---|---|---|
| **Catholic Definition of Religious Freedom** | **Diet of Speyer II, 1529** | Protestants not forced to renounce faith | No propagation of non-Catholic teachings | Catholic juris-dictional authority retained | Celebration of Mass in Lutheran territory | No Catholic allowed to convert | Suspension of force or coercion |
| | ***Dignitatis Humanae*** **of Vatican II (1965)** | Does not deny or endorse religious plurality | Does not authorise erroneous teaching | Catholic juris-dictional authority implicit | *Libertas ecclesiastic a* to fulfill [Catholic] mission | No Catholic conversions allowed | Immunity from coercion as civil right |
| **Protestant Definition of Religious Freedom** | **Protestation of Speyer, 1529** | Liberty to follow one's convictions | Convictions based on God's Word | Majority not to rule over minorities | Each is to respect the other | Rights of all guaranteed by law | No coercion |

**Fig. 10.2** Differences between Protestant and Catholic concepts of religious freedom (adapted from Cook, 2012, pp. 158–159)

[3]Martin Luther, "The First Sermon, March 9, 1522, Incovait Sunday," (as cited in Tappert, 2017, p. 234).

of Protestantism had equally advocated this principle of religious freedom, especially when they acted as state religions and became dominant, magisterial, and conformist. Thus, Protestant dissenters (e.g. Anabaptists) have historically suffered persecution from both Roman Catholic and magisterial Protestant churches (Miller, 2012). As a nineteenth-century Protestant wrote:

> Whenever the church has obtained secular power, she has employed it to punish dissent from her doctrines. Protestant churches that have followed in the steps of Rome by forming alliance with worldly powers have manifested a similar desire to restrict liberty of conscience. An example of this is given in the long-continued persecution of dissenters by the Church of England. During the sixteenth and seventeenth centuries, thousands of nonconformist ministers were forced to flee from their churches, and many, both of pastors and people, were subjected to fine, imprisonment, torture, and martyrdom (White, 1888, p. 443).

Yet, "the dissenting Protestant view of a separated church and state, always a minority position in England and the rest of Europe, and even in early colonial America, became the dominant position in the early [American] republic" (Miller, 2012, p. xviii). Nevertheless, barriers once erected by Protestantism against ecumenism have fallen in light of Roman Catholicism advocating religious freedom for all groups in pluralistic (Protestant) societies (Cook, 2012, p. 50). However, the same religious freedom is denied to "non-Catholics in political communities where Catholics are in the majority" (Pavan, 1989, pp. 4,51). Regarding these variations in the Roman Church's pastoral strategy worldwide, Gill (1998) observes that the Catholic clergy lobby hard for religious freedom where Catholics are a minority and unhindered by existing Church bureaucracies, such as in Russia, certain countries in Asia, and Africa. In contrast, bishops actively advocate for legislation that limits religious freedom in Latin America and Poland, where the Catholic Church is the predominant religious actor. This phenomenon concurs with the assumption of parishioner maximisation, which dictates that if a church is on the defensive, its leaders will try to limit religious liberty. In turn, when a church is increasingly expanding, it will pursue legislation that promotes religious freedom (Gill, 2013, pp. 59, 227).

Similarly, Dowling, referring to such a Machiavelism, observed nearly two centuries ago:

> There is one kind of Romanism to be exhibited in Protestant lands, and another and a widely different in Italy, Spain and other popish lands, where it reigns in its glory (Dowling, 1853, p. 626).

Consequently, it is not surprising that despite ecumenical discussions, tension still exists between Protestants and Catholics (Cook, 2012). On the one side, the Roman Catholic claim to absoluteness has always been regarded as a scandal and an offence (Pauwels, 1963, p. 585). On the other, some small dissenting Protestant denominations (so-called sects) are reluctant to accept Roman Catholic hegemony (see the biblical reasons discussed in Sect. 10.4.2.1) (Miller, 2012, 2017; Cook, 2012; Taggart, 1998). After all, scepticism towards Rome is evident, as:

> Historically, the [Catholic] Church has sought to expand its resources and power in many countries. It has sought to maximize its wealth and resources and to enact laws and policies

> that protect it against competitors such as Protestant Christianity and other faiths (Manuel et al., 2006, p. 4).

Peace among religious denominations is something which is undeniably desirable. However, there is a need for caution when considering that Protestant denominations have mostly relinquished their founding principles, while "Rome never changes" as per the Italian saying. Despite the progress after Vatican II (see Sect. 8.2.1.2), Roman Catholicism has not markedly altered its beliefs and practices (Agnew, 2010, p. 48) or its institutional founding principles (i.e. Canon Law) since medieval times (O'Reilly & Chalmers, 2014). The political repercussions of an ecumenism in "Rome terms" are beyond its theological or religious implications. History warns of the long medieval tyranny of a fused state and Church under the Aristotelian "government by one person" and its relativistic morals, keeping the masses ignorant. Breaking such a *status quo* carried a cost of countless wars and human lives (e.g. the Thirty Years' War that led to Westphalian order) (Snyder, 2011; Agnew, 2010; Cook, 2012; Witte, 2002; Berman, 2003). Evidently, since Vatican II Roman Catholicism has become more tolerant, and thus "Europe has become ever more pluralistic religiously and thus ever less likely to be squeezed back into a singular Catholic mold" (Agnew, 2010, p. 52). Yet, the author warns:

> Surely the trend towards a medieval Church redux is something about which we all should be concerned, not least because states and other agencies will undoubtedly find themselves recruited into one side or another in new "religious wars," both rhetorical and actual (Agnew, 2010, p. 56).

#### 10.4.1.4 Liberation Theology: A Top-Down Movement

Among others, Protestantism, modernity, secular unions, and left-wing political groups increasingly began to threaten the hegemony of the Roman Church-State in Latin America and beyond. These developments made the Roman Church-State realise (at the beginning of the twentieth century) that it had overestimated its strong popular influence. Accordingly, it has endeavoured to build a "New Christendom" in Latin America since the early 1930s (Dussel, 1976; Vekemans 1976 as cited in Smith, 1991). Throughout, the "New Christendom" has served as a strategy to reassure the establishment of Roman Catholicism as the major cultural and institutional influence in modernising Latin America (Smith, 1991). As part of this strategy, the Roman Church-State took the side of "modernity", 'science", and "progress" for the first time in history (Richard 1987 as cited in Smith, 1991).

Accordingly, "Catholic social teachings" and the innovations of Vatican II in the 1960s have concurred with this strategy. Other insurgent developments, including the rise of Marxism, the experience of Camilo Torres, and the Cuban revolution, brought forth a "progressive wing" of Roman Catholicism (Levine, 1981). Catholic theologians, such as Gutiérrez (1973), identified dependency theory, which emerged in the second half of the twentieth century in Latin America (see Sect. 5.4), as key to understanding the region's socio-economic situation (Drexler-Dreis, 2017).

Accordingly, Catholic liberation theologians came to believe that the Latin America's main problem was its dependency on dominant capitalistic oppressors, which would be solved through "liberation" rather than more "development" (Smith, 1991, p. 237). The foundational episode of liberation theology took place during the Second General Conference of the Latin American Episcopal Council (CELAM), held in Medellín, Colombia in 1968. This theology is an "elite-initiated" revitalisation movement aiming to force "redirections in the strategies and resources" within established institutions (Smith, 1991, p. 234).

Gutiérrez is considered the "father of the Liberation Theology". According to Gutiérrez, the aim of liberation theology goes beyond improving living conditions: it consists of a drastic structural shift, a lasting cultural revolution, and a social transformation; an ongoing, never-ending development of a *new man*, a new way to be an individual (Gutiérrez, 1973, p. 880). Gutiérrez tried to reconcile the Marxist ideal of an earthly, egalitarian society through revolution or insurgence with the heavenly salvation of the soul in Christian terms. These two notions are exegetically incompatible when comparing the use of violence as a means to achieve social ends with the application of biblical principles, such as those contained in the Ten Commandments or the Sermon on the Mount (see Sects. 8.3.4 and 10.4.1). Furthermore, a hypothetical communist synthesis has proven not to produce desirable social results (see Sect. 8.3.2; Fig. 8.3 and Table 8.2; Fig. 16.4; Truth Table 11 in Appendix 4.2).

Scheper-Hughes and Scheper (2015) observe that liberation theology was a significant and noticeable social movement in the 1970s and 1980s, which realigned several Catholic clergy members and nuns who had favoured the oppressed during several South American military dictatorships and Central American civil wars. Liberation theologians expanded on their message at the 1968 Medellín Conference of Latin American Bishops, during which the bishops committed to a new social/spiritual compact known as a "preferential option for the poor". This message urged the Latin American Roman Church to break away from its imperialist origins and favouritism for landlords, industrialists, and power elites. However, as the authors stress, liberation theology *never* became the mainstream or hegemonic Catholic theology in Latin America (Scheper-Hughes & Scheper, 2015, pp. 13–14). Regarding its political implications, liberation theology did not draw out what a new society would be like, except for a few examples of socialism. Furthermore, Vatican loyalists have successively replaced progressive bishops in Latin America since the 1990s (Berryman, 2020).

As liberation theology has not been dominant in the Latin American Roman Church, its institutional impact is even less pronounced in the global Catholic Church-State. It is of particular importance that liberation theology has not produced changes in the principles of canon law (although it could have influenced its interpretation) (C. Salinas, personal communication, April 27, 2020; J. Müller, personal communication, March 27, 2020). Gill (1998) notes that the emergence of Catholic scholars proclaiming a new liberation theology shocked the Church's higher echelons (p. 177). Likewise, Scheper-Hughes & Scheper's observation on the pledges of the Catholic hierarchy is subtly different from Gill (1998)'s mixed-methods empirical analysis based on several Latin American cases. For Gill, more than four centuries of monopolistic hegemony of the Catholic Church in Latin America resulted in a lack of commitment to pastoral issues and a profound tendency to appease the political establishment in exchange for patronage and legislative approval for Church teachings. Yet, Catholic hierarchs had to rethink their political and pastoral strategies when religious rivals started gaining dramatic spiritual terrain in the weakest segments of several Latin American countries, starting in the 1930s. Thus, the Catholic hierarchy introduced a pastoral policy of a "preferential option for the poor", during which competition for the souls of the disadvantaged became intense. This new pastoral strategy of the Roman Church clashed with military and authoritarian regimes that followed detrimental policies to the needy. Thus, when facing increasing religious competition, Church hierarchs abandoned their conventional coalition with the political establishment and rejected authoritarianism to sustain a credible commitment to helping the vulnerable. Human rights groups also contributed funds to this opposition, reducing the episcopacy's dependence on the state. However, when there was little competition, bishops tended to disregard the "preferential option for the poor" to retain cordial ties with military rulers and maintain established privileges (Gill, 1998, p.71).

###### 10.4.1.4.1 Marxism and Hegelian Dialectics in Liberation Theology

Catholic-Marxist alliances developed within the liberation theology movement quickly expanded across Latin America and beyond (Levine, 1981). Partly, due to such associations, the recalcitrant ultramontane Catholic wing (Rome, conservative bishops, and right-wing Latin American governments) have opposed liberation theology (Smith, 1991, p. 236).

To a large extent, liberation theology emerges from "Marxism's influence" (Gutiérrez, 1973, p. 9). Fierro (1977) corroborated Gutiérrez's views by arguing that this political theology results from the embodiment of historical materialism and dialectical logic into Western philosophy (Fierro, 1977, p. 2). Such Marxist dialectical materialism derives from Hegelian dialectics and idealism, which are based on the synthesis of opposites or contradictions (thesis–antithesis–synthesis) (Johnson, 2017, p. 157). Unconventionally applying Hegelian logic to understand the emergence of an "elite-initiated" movement like liberation theology might work as follows:

(1) Thesis. *Status quo*. The corporatist, conservative hierarchies of the Roman Church-State join forces with right-wing governments to keep society oppressed (e.g. *Opus Dei*).
(2) Antithesis. Liberation theologists use dependency theories to explain Latin America's problems in terms of external causes (e.g. by blaming industrialised, Protestant countries). The "Option for the poor" is associated with left-wing stakeholders (e.g. some Jesuit priests—consistently loyal to the pope—or Dominicans involved in the insurgency).

(3) Synthesis. The polarisation of society and escalating cycles of armed conflict (wars) are followed by peace negotiations in which the Roman Catholic Church-State serves as a mediator. *Final outcome: Maintenance of the status quo in any case (Roman Church-State hegemony).*

This example applies quite well to countries (e.g. Colombia) whose institutions are characterised by strong corporatist ideologies. In Colombia, the government has traditionally been associated with right-wing conservative forces and intransigent Roman Catholic ideologies (i.e. Vice-President Marta Ramírez and former President Álvaro Uribe among other high-ranking government officers have ties with *Opus Dei*). On the other hand, some Catholic priests were involved in the insurgency, for example, Camilo Torres and Manuel Pérez Martínez (in liberation theology-guerrilla groups like ELN). However, the Roman Catholic Church has also been directly involved as a mediator or conciliator in the Colombian armed conflict (i.e. priests like Dario Echeverri and Gabriel Izquierdo and bishops like Augusto Castro and Nel Beltrán). In the end, the Roman Catholic Church has been directly and indirectly involved on both sides of the conflict. As a result, the *status quo* has been maintained.

This example helps to understand that liberation theology is one strand of Roman Catholicism albeit not the principal one. In Latin America, mostly orthodox old pre-Vatican II views still prevail (Martin, 1999; Figueroa, 2016). Moreover, both wings of Roman Catholicism (right-wing corporatist and left-wing liberation theologians) conform to the Roman Church-State hierarchy (i.e. the papacy). For example, Gutiérrez was invited to the Vatican in 2015, despite Ratzinger's threat to excommunicate him in 1984 (Lamola, 2018).

The dialectic illustrated above suggests that it is doubtful whether liberation theology could lastingly affect Roman Catholic Canon law, for instance. At a practical level, the analyses proposed by liberation theologians (e.g. Gutiérrez, 1973; Boff, 1989) do not apply to everyday Catholic practice. Instead, the primary triggers of Catholic practice are mostly personal and local concerns (Martin, 1999, p. 41).

#### 10.4.1.4.2 Liberation Theology and Protestantism

Religions evolve and, typically, the creation of different denominations is considered to be the product of doctrinal differences (Webster, 2019, p. 1125). Contrasting Scriptural interpretations, diverse paradigms, meanings, and other discrepancies have been the common denominator (Engelhardt, 2007) of Protestant schismogenesis as an ethnographic fact (Webster, 2019, p. 1125). Furthermore, Christian traditions have changed over time and vary among denominations, while the Scriptural texts have remained largely unaffected by time for centuries (i.e. King James or Martin Luther versions). Engelhardt (2007) observed a decisive influence of philosophy and secularism in this respect:

> The mainline Christian churches of the West through importing philosophical rationality into their doing of theology over time transformed their theologies in terms of the demands of the secular culture. After all, if one borrows the logic or rationality of one's theology from philosophy, one will incrementally transform theology into the image and likeness of the surrounding secular culture, since philosophy always carries the mark of a particular age and culture (Engelhardt, 2007, p. 29).

Consequently, liberation theology has influenced Protestant theologians (e.g. Bonino, 1976) and especially some Pentecostal movements (Sepúlveda, 2009). Moreover, the religious experiences of Pentecostals and Catholic Charismatics are very similar (Self, 2009). Figure 10.3 presents the similarities and differences between some features of reading the Bible in historical and present-day currents of Roman Catholicism and Protestantism.

| **Current features of reading the Bible** | **1. Traditional Roman Catholicism (i.e. pre-Vatican II views valid until today)** | **2. Roman Catholic Liberation Theologians (i.e. CEC [Catholic ecclesial communities]). (1960s – today)** | **3. 16th-19th century mainline Protestantism (i.e. Lutheranism, Calvinism), and some current dissenting Protestant "sects".** | **4. Current strand of most contemporary Protestants (e.g. Pentecostals, Neo-Pentecostals)[5]** |
|---|---|---|---|---|
| **Theological understanding** | Excessive sacralisation of some selected parts of the Gospel and complete disregard of others. | No exegesis but "eisegesis" (seeking a theological justification for social struggle). | Theological-scientific rationalist reading of the Scriptures. | Literal, uncritical, and commonly superficial exegesis. |
| **Human capital building** | Ordinary people receive no education to study the Scriptures. | Ordinary people receive little or no education to study the Scriptures. | Ordinary people receive proper education to study the Scriptures (i.e. commonly required for in-depth intertextual exegesis). | Ordinary people receive little or no education to study the Scriptures. |
| **Bearers of the message** | - Only enlightened clergy are able to read the Scriptures.<br>- Common people are prevented direct access to the Scriptures. | Mainly priests and deacons. | "Priesthood of all believers." | Mainly preachers, pastors, apostles. |
| **Social emancipation objective** | Maintainance of the political-religious *status quo* (e.g. Middle Ages) | Social revolution against oppressive political structures (e.g. government, capital) generally maintaining deference for the Roman Catholic hierarchy. | Liberation from the Roman Catholic Church-State and popish tyranny (regarded as "diabolical"). Generally, deference to government institutions. | Mostly apolitical or indifferent |
| **Sources of understanding the Scriptures** | Origenes, Aristotle, Aquinas | Origenes, Aristotle, Aquinas, Marx | *Sola Scriptura* intertextuality (i.e. Luther, Calvin) | Depends on denomination (i.e. some can adopt Origenes' allegorical interpretations in combination with Lutheran principles) |
| **Direction and impact of reading the Bible in the "earthly kingdom."** | No reading. Biblical message exclusively supports established dogmas. | Politicisation of the biblical message (from life to the Bible). | Transformational, cyclical (personal and social). Bidirectional (from the Bible to life and from life to the Bible). | Spiritualisation of the biblical message (from the Bible to life). |

**Fig. 10.3** Ways of reading the Bible in traditional Roman Catholicism, Liberation Theology (post-Vatican II), historical Protestantism, and Pentecostalism (adapted from Sepúlveda, 2009; Becker & Woessmann, 2009; Becker et al., 2016; McCleary, 2013; Witte, 2002; Woodberry, 2012)

The religious currents shown in Fig. 10.3 coexist today. However, each has prevailed more than others in different historical periods. For example, currents 1 and 3 (traditional Roman Catholicism and historical Protestantism) have been antagonists and dominant since the sixteenth century (even earlier in the case of Roman Catholicism). Currents 2 and 4 (Catholic Liberation theologians and Pentecostals) appeared in the second half of the twentieth century and share various features of understanding the Bible.

For many Catholic ecclesial and Pentecostal communities in Latin America, the Bible has long been the first contact with the printed word. Many people have even learned to read with the Bible, which has a deep meaning for those trapped in social and cultural exclusion (Sepúlveda, 2009).

However, vast differences exist when comparing Catholic ecclesial and Pentecostal communities with historical Protestantism (Köhrsen, 2017). First, what Catholic authors call "critical" Bible reading (Gutiérrez, 1973, p. 13) follows the same interpretative principles of traditional Roman Catholicism (i.e. the allegorical interpretation passed on by Origenes, Aristotle, and Thomas Aquinas). Thus, the Old Catholic dogmas are maintained based on superficial reading without either exegesis or proper consideration of intertextual factors.

The so-called critical reading of the Bible, advocated by liberation theologians, favours direct social and political revolution (including insurgence) (Gutiérrez, 1973, p. 69; Levine, 1981, p. 35). Saying that, revolution or insurgence illustrates the rejection of Christian Scriptural principles, such as the "love of one's enemies" proclaimed by Jesus in the Sermon on the Mount (King James Bible, 1769, Matthew 5: 38–48). In turn, the Scriptural principles rejected by liberation theologians formed the basis of Protestant legal revolutions in the past (e.g. German, Scandinavian, American; see Sect. 8.3.4 and Fig. 8.4). Therefore, the principles that Liberation theology seeks to implement in society concur more with the communist law tradition (in societies like Cuba) than with the Protestant revolutions (i.e. common law, German law, Scandinavian law) (see Sect. 8.3.2 and Fig. 8.3 and Table 8.2).

Another critical issue of comparison is the "liberation of what" proposed by the different currents. Liberation theologians advocate freeing societies from "sinful" "oppressive social, economic, and political structures" (Levine, 1981, p. 39). In light of dependency theory, this would mean, among others, liberation from colonial exploitation in Latin America (formerly from the Spanish crown and later from the foreign capital of Protestant countries (e.g. England, USA; see Gutiérrez, 1973; Galeano, 1971). However, dependency analysis disregards the hegemonic relations between the Roman Catholic Church-State and the states, or upholds these, or even praises them as positive (Galeano, 1971, p. 247) (see Sect. 5.4).

On balance, liberation theology is ahistorical (Lamola, 2018). It began as a top-down approach within the Roman Catholic hierarchy rather than a bottom-up initiative from the communities. It applies dependency theory to direct attention away from two millennia of Roman (and Catholic) hegemony towards Iberian imperialism, and especially of Protestant countries (e.g. USA, UK). Moreover, it inspires the use of violence or rebellion as a means of resolving social inequality based on dubious and relativistic moral principles consistent with Number 2321 of the Roman Catholic Catechism of the Catholic Church (Vatican, 2018; see also Sect. 10.4.1).

In contrast, the ideology of historical Protestantism allowed the Reformers to identify the papacy as "the Man of Sin" (see Sect. 10.4.2.1 and 2 Thessalonians, King James Bible, 1769). Such identification was based on in-depth exegesis by historic Protestants, who applied the *Sola Scriptura* principle. Thus, only Jesus sets humankind free from bondage (King James Bible, 1769, John 8: 31–38). Rebellious means against governments should be avoided (King James Bible, 1769, 1 Timothy 2:1–2; 1 Peter 2:17; Romans 13:1). Therefore, the successive Protestant revolutions sought to eliminate the pervasive influence of the Roman Church-State in favour of power independent from Rome (at first by empowering the monarchies and then gradually also citizens; Sect. 8.3.4).

### *10.4.2 Protestant Theology*

When acknowledging the robust systematic evidence on the underlying effect of religion on corruption, authors refer to this as "unfortunate" from a policy perspective (Woodruff, 2006, p. 121) or that it provides "little inspiration to reform" (Lambsdorff, 2006, p. 17). However, when Martin Luther formulated his 95 theses, he was protesting against the rampant corruption and tyranny of the Roman Catholic Church five centuries ago. The resultant movement resumed and advanced the discontent for which the Waldensians, Wycliffe, Tyndale, Hus, and many others had previously been condemned, often sacrificing their lives. The Protestant Reformation sought to return and democratise the original teachings of the Bible, which rested on the *Sola Scriptura* principle, throughout Europe and beyond (Witte, 2002; Doe & Sandberg, 2010; Becker et al., 2016). As shown (Sects. 8.2.2 and 8.3.4), the Protestant reformations had various spillover effects, including the spread of democracy, liberalism, secularisation, and the formation of the modern sovereign state (Woodberry, 2012; Snyder, 2011; Agnew, 2010; Shah & Philpott, 2011; Philpott, 2001; Hurd, 2011; Berger, 1990; Inglehart & Baker, 2000; Treisman, 2000).

*Sola Scriptura* implies that the Bible alone is a sufficient and infallible rule of life. Consequently, Protestants generally place a greater emphasis on one's own relationship with God, while the Roman Catholic Church places a greater emphasis on priestly mediation (Gill, 1998, p. 90). *Sola Scriptura* means that the Holy Scriptures are the only and absolute standardising moral source of Christian principles (historical Protestantism), in contrast to Roman Catholic relativism (see Sect. 10.4.1). Therefore, Arruñada (2010) found that Protestants statistically exhibit a greater social ethos, which leads them to closely scrutinise one another's actions, support legal and political systems, and hold more consistent values (p. 890). Specifically, the *Sola Scriptura* principle enabled historical Protestants to hold more homogenous values, including a universal charity descending from the Gospel (instead of a selective one) (Arruñada, 2010). As Elisha Williams, the eighteenth-century American theologian and founder of Yale University, observed:

> That the sacred scriptures are the alone rule of faith and practice to a Christian, all Protestants are agreed in, and must therefore inviolably maintain, that every Christian has a right of judging for himself what he is to believe and practice in religion according to that rule (Williams, 1998, p. 55).

The very Protestant characteristic of the freedom of conscience initiated several reformations in different countries (Berman, 2003), thus creating a broad range of successive diverse denominations (Sects. 8.3.4, 10.4.1.4.2, 10.4.2, and 10.4.3).

#### 10.4.2.1 Theological Reasons for Traditional Protestant Anti-Clericalism

> My dear brothers never forget, when you hear the progress of the Enlightenment praised, that *the Devil's cleverest ploy is to persuade you that he does not exist.*
> (Charles Baudelaire, 1862, *Le Spleen de Paris*)

Historical Protestants sincerely believed that the Roman Church-State is the "synagogue of Satan"[4] based on an intertextual historicist interpretation of the Bible (see Table 10.3). Some Protestant denominations still adhere to intertextual historicist biblical interpretation and hold the belief that the papacy continues to be "Satan's synagogue" today (see Sect. 10.4.2.2).

Their historicist study of the Book of Revelation provided the Reformers with an influential picture of the history of the Church. This interpretation had consistently allowed Reformers from different epochs and countries to discern "the hidden diabolism of the Roman faith" (Johnstone, 2006, p. 50).

Protestants have long interpreted the Book of Revelation (especially Chap. 13) along with the Book of Daniel in the Old Testament (especially Chaps. 7–8, King James Bible, 1769) (Boxall & Tresley, 2016, p. 4). Such a historicist study has allowed Protestant eschatologists to identify the pope as the Antichrist. This view arises from symbolically associating a persecutory political-religious power (the Roman Church-State) with the beast whom the dragon (Satan) gives his power, seat, and great authority in Revelation 13 (Boxall & Tresley, 2016, p. 4; Johnstone, 2006, p. 55).

---

[4]Derived from the Book of Revelation (King James Bible, 1769). "It expressed the insidious subversion Protestants believed to lie behind Catholic false doctrine and empty piety—a church that appeared Christian was in fact its opposite" (Johnstone, 2006, p. 4).

**Table 10.3** Typical association of the papacy with the "Man of Sin", the Antichrist, beast and harlot according to biblical interpretations of notable Protestant intellectuals (1500–1800)

| Biblical text (King James Bible, 1769) | | |
|---|---|---|
| "Man of Sin" or "Antichrist" (2 Thessalonians 2); or | "Let no man deceive you by any means: for *that day shall not come*, except there come a falling away first, and that *man of sin* be revealed, the son of perdition; who opposeth and exalteth himself above all that is called God, or that is worshipped; so that he as God sitteth in the temple of God, showing himself that he is God" (2 Thessalonians 2: 3-4). | |
| "the beast" (Revelation 13) | "And *the beast* which I saw was like unto a leopard, and his feet were as the feet of a bear, and his mouth as the mouth of a lion: *and the dragon gave him his power, and his seat, and great authority*. And I saw one of his heads as it were wounded to death; and his deadly wound was healed: and all the world wondered after the beast" (Revelation 13: 2-3). | |
| or "The great harlot" (Revelation 17) | "[...] and I saw a woman sit upon a scarlet-colored beast, full of names of blasphemy, having seven heads and ten horns. And the woman was arrayed in purple and scarlet color, and decked with gold and precious stones and pearls, having a golden cup in her hand full of abominations and filthiness of her fornication: and upon her forehead was a name written, MYSTERY, BABYLON THE GREAT, THE MOTHER OF HARLOTS AND ABOMINATIONS OF THE EARTH. And I saw the woman drunken with the blood of the saints, and with the blood of the martyrs of Jesus" (Revelation 17: 3-5). | |
| | "And the woman which thou sawest is that great city, which reigneth over the kings of the earth" (Revelation 17: 18). | |
| Eschatological Interpretation | **Papacy/Roman Catholic Church** | |
| Interpreted by | **Martin Luther (1517 onwards)** | German Reformer and theologian |
| | **Huldrych Zwingli (1519 onwards)** | Swiss Reformer and theologian |
| | **John Calvin (1536 onwards)** | French Reformer and founder of the University of Geneva |
| | **Roger Williams (1644 onwards)** | American promoter of the separation of church and state |
| | **John Wesley (1728 onwards)** | English theologian and co-founder of Methodism |
| | **Isaac Newton** (1733 **onwards)** | English Mathematician, physical scientist, philosopher |
| | **Elisha Williams (1744 onwards)** | American theologian and founder of Yale University |

Note: Author's italics

(Adapted from Boxall & Tresley, 2016; Hoffmann, 2015; Hartman et al., 2002; Stefanovic, 2009; Taggart, 1998; Williams, 1998; Newton, 1733; Luther, 1532)

Table 10.3 shows the examples of prominent Protestant thinkers who shared similar theological conclusions. The interpretation of the popery (Roman Church-State) as the deceiving power from Satan on earth (Babylon-Beast-Harlot) was practically universal among Protestants. This interpretation was prevalent regardless of the historical and political contexts in which Protestants lived until the nineteenth century (Gregg, 1997).

The identification of the Roman Church-State as the Antichrist (or the papacy, in the interpretation of the two beasts in Revelation 13) was widespread among Protestants of different denominations (Table 10.3). The Geneva Bible attests to the interpretation of the Revelation in the early Calvinist tradition and offers a typical example of historicist interpretation. Furthermore, the extensive use of this particular interpretation of the books of Revelation and Daniel (King James Bible, 1769) is evident in Protestant writings, especially until the nineteenth century (Boxall & Tresley, 2016, p. 9).

The first generation of Reformers (and other Protestants) were disillusioned Roman Catholics who converted and admitted "that Catholicism was a very convincing fake" (Johnstone, 2006, p. 41). The Protestant understanding of the diabolical character of Roman Catholicism thus also resulted from the notion that the popery embodies a direct (but hidden) inversion of Christianity (p.41). For example, Roman Catholic worship involves disguising pagan rituals and hence, covering "them with the 'manners' of Christianity" (Calfhill as cited in Johnstone, 2006, p. 48). The veneration of icons explicitly forbidden in the Decalogue (Figs. 8.4 and 10.1) illustrates this point, as it ultimately constitutes idolatry. However, Roman Catholicism still promotes this practice, thus suppressing this Commandment in the Catechism (Fig. 10.1). Johnstone described "Protestant attempts to comprehend the corruption of traditional Catholicism" (p. 27) during the English Reformation in these terms:

> [Protestants] adopted a long-established heretical association of the Pope with Antichrist, and behind Antichrist lay the Devil, the guiding hand of apocalyptic subversion. [...] In effect Catholicism might be a parody, a contradiction of everything sacred to the true faith. But this was hidden behind a pious gloss which had hoodwinked millions into their own eternal destruction. Nor were its victims naive or ignorant; many learned and zealous Christians continued to believe in the veracity of the Roman church (Johnstone, 2006, p. 27).

Furthermore, dissenting and nonconformist Protestants "took reformist arguments a stage further by claiming that de facto Satanism was inherent in *any* national church" and "at the heart of government" (Johnstone, 2006, pp. 254, 188). As an eighteenth-century Protestant wrote:

> There is no reason to consider the antichristian spirit and practices to be confined to that which is now called the Church of Rome. The Protestant churches have much of antichrist in them, and are far from being wholly reformed from [...] corruptions and wickedness (Hopkins, 1972 [1794], p. 328).

The Reformers' belief that Roman Catholicism was the Church of Satan also relied on recognising "the Devil's power to disguise himself within Christian piety" (Johnstone, 2006, p. 41). This is evident in the following Bible verses:

> And the great dragon was cast out, that old serpent, called the Devil, and Satan, which deceiveth the whole world: he was cast out into the earth, and his angels were cast out with him (King James Bible, 1769, Revelation 12: 9);

> And no marvel; for Satan himself is transformed into an angel of light (King James Bible, 1769, 2 Corinthians 11: 14).

The Old Testament Book of Isaiah contains a complementary reference to the intertextual references to the successive kingdoms (beasts) and Satan (Lucifer) in the books of Revelation (NT) and Daniel (OT):

> that thou shalt take up this proverb against the king of Babylon, and say, How hath the oppressor ceased! the golden city ceased! (King James Bible, 1769, Isaiah 14: 4);
>
> How art thou fallen from heaven, O Lucifer, son of the morning! how art thou cut down to the ground, which didst weaken the nations! (King James Bible, 1769, Isaiah 14: 12).

The Prophet Isaiah associates the king of Babylon with an oppressive power and a golden city. Later, Isaiah links this system to Lucifer, who *weakens the nations* (a statement that touches on the core of this study). The Book of Daniel (in parallel to the Book Revelation) (King James Bible, 1769) also interrelates (symbolically as beasts or as a statue) the successive, Satanic powers of Babylon, Medo-Persia, Greece, and finally Rome. Rome inherited parts of the preceding civilisations (e.g. Greek philosophy, Babylonian rituals) (Radmacher et al., 1999; Taggart, 1998). The power of Rome persists to this day through its influence on all legal systems worldwide (Sect. 8.3) and through the Roman Church-State (i.e. the weakening of nations).

For William Tyndale, the papacy had accepted Satan's temptation: "The kingdoms of the earth and the glory of them, which Christ refused" in the desert (Tyndale, The Practice of Prelates, pp. 274–5 as cited in Johnstone, 2006, p. 54). As a result of this arrangement, the papacy shall worship the devil by adopting his role as "Satan's vicar", who corrupts religion. Therefore, the papacy "took up in the like manner all Christendom on high, and brought them from the meekness of the Christ unto the high hill of the pride of Lucifer" (p. 54).

#### 10.4.2.2 Current Protestant Views on the Papacy

The Roman Catholic counter-reformation had attempted to shift attention away from intertextual historicist biblical prophecy since the sixteenth century. Spaniard Jesuits developed a Futurist School (e.g. Francisco de Ribera) and a Preterist School (e.g. Luisz de Alcasar) as alternatives to historicist eschatology. Both schools removed any reference to Rome from prophecy and contradicted the Reformers' linking of the Antichrist with the papacy and with Babylon as the Roman Church-State. The Futurist view stands for a biblical prophecy to be fulfiled in the future, while the Preterists advocate a prophecy already fulfiled in the first century (Johnson, 1981).

Consequently, since the sixteenth century, neither a monolithic nor a unified explanation for biblical prophecy has existed in Roman Catholicism but contrasting opposites (Futurism versus Preterism). However, neither view makes any reference whatsoever to the papacy in biblical prophecy, as opposed to historical

Protestantism. This constitutes a Hegelian dialectical strategy common among Jesuits (similar to the one described in Sect. 10.4.1.4).

Preterist views have gained much scholarly attention even among modern Protestant writers. The suppression of the Papal states in the nineteenth century and Roman Catholicism's loss of power (Sect. 8.3.4.5) have ushered in Preterist views even more vehemently (Johnson, 1981; Taggart, 1998). Thus, the Reformers' *intertextual historicist interpretation* has only few followers today. However, for some remaining Protestant intertextual historicist interpreters, the apparent weakening of Roman Catholicism after the French Revolution (i.e. as a deadly wound) has partially fulfiled the Revelation (Cook, 2012); (Taggart, 1998):

> And I saw one of his heads as it were wounded to death; and his deadly wound was healed: and all the world wondered after the beast (King James Bible, 1769, Revelation 13: 3).

Therefore, even after the successful introduction of the counter-reformation dialectic (Futurism and Preterism), some Protestant denominations still adhere to intertextual historicist interpretation today. Examples of this small group include conservative Lutherans (Wisconsin Evangelical Lutheran Synod, 2018), historical and Restorationist denominations, and the Seventh-day Adventists (SDA) (Taggart, 1998; Bacchiocchi, 2002).

### *10.4.3 Pentecostalism*

The broad diversity of Protestant denominations and sects today makes it difficult to generalise their separate contributions, let alone capture these in a single study. However, distinct Protestant theologies and organisational forms have led to distinct outcomes (Manow, 2004; Woodberry, 2012). For example, while Lutherans pioneered the development of the welfare state, some other currents of Protestantism (e.g. Calvinists, Baptists) slowed this down (Manow, 2004). Another clear example is the asymmetrical emphases on higher education: Calvinists typically make greater educational efforts than other Protestant missionaries, and Pentecostals even less than other Protestant missionaries. Therefore, new forms of Protestantism (i.e. Pentecostalism) placing less emphasis on education are less likely to have a positive social impact than previous Protestant versions (Woodberry, 2012, pp. 251–269).

Pentecostalism has been a singular African variation of Christianity, transmitted via African American culture (MacRobert, cited in Sharpe, 2014, p. 173). Likewise, Pentecostalism partly originated "as one of the ways that Africans responded to the missionary structures and appropriated the message" (Kalu, 2008, p. viii).

Pentecostalism has been the fast-growing and most influential "movement" in recent decades and now includes the majority of Protestants. Figure 10.4 shows the growth trends of Protestantism worldwide.

Africa, Asia, and Latin America have the largest Protestant populations today. However, Protestantism is a relatively young phenomenon in those continents,

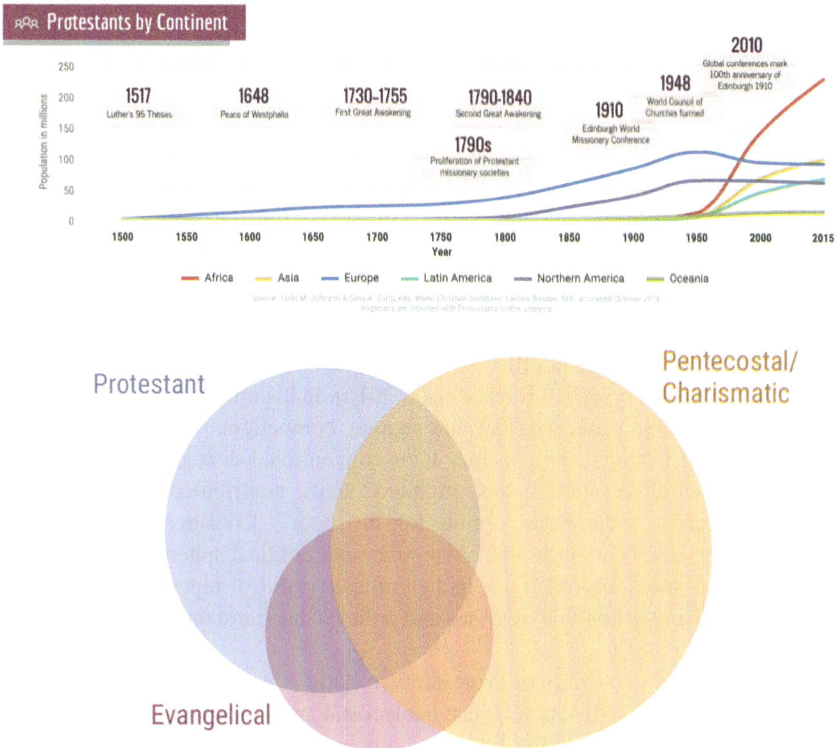


**Fig. 10.4** Protestants by continent and the share of the largest Protestant movements in the world today (Todd & Zurlo, 2016). Used with permission of the authors

where the influence of Pentecostal and Neo-Pentecostal denominations dominates. The Edinburgh World Missionary Conference of 1910 marked a milestone in the spreading of Protestantism through missionary work on those continents (Fig. 10.4) (Todd & Zurlo, 2016).

Today, Pentecostal movements focus their efforts on the eschatological urgency of conversion and invest little in developing human capital (McCleary, 2013; Becker et al., 2016, p. 11). Moreover, Pentecostal theologies are often removed from the historical tradition of the Bible, unlike historical Protestantism. However, Pentecostal movements are extremely varied, making generalisation difficult (Spittler, 2009, p. 66). Nonetheless, the positive social impact of Pentecostalism compared to historical Protestantism is small. For example, Pentecostalism invests little in human development and thus achieves merely low institutional impact (e.g. low development of educational and medical facilities) (McCleary, 2013; Woodberry, 2012; Becker et al., 2016).

#### 10.4.3.1 The Influence of Pentecostalism in Latin America

The increasing number of Protestant denominations from a wide range of currents affects every country differently. Schäfer (2006) devised a comprehensive model and various typologies to classify large Christian groups and their ideologies in Latin America (pp. 58–60). Until 1970, more than 90% of the total population in Latin America were still Roman Catholics. By 2014, this share had decreased to nearly 70% (Protestants: 19%; unaffiliated: 8% in 2014) (Pew Research Center, 2014). Currently, almost one out of five Latin Americans is Protestant (Pew Research Center, 2014, p. 62). As stated, the presence of Protestantism has been crucial in creating competition with the Roman Catholic Church-State and has thus initiated democratic and human capital processes (see Sects. 7.b, 8.2.1.2, and Chap. 9) (Gill, 1998, 2013; Woodberry, 2012; Becker et al., 2016). In his mixed-methods empirical analysis, Gill (1998) observed that the market competition from Protestantism induced Catholic bishops to reconsider their conventional disregard of the needy. The influence of Protestantism has, in many ways, contributed to shaping the Catholic Church's "preferential option for the poor". Considering the Roman Church's strong involvement in the Latin American political sphere, this change in Catholicism's pastoral approach has had significant political repercussions, in particular an increasing aversion to regimes and policies that harm the rights of the poor (p. 80).

However, nearly two-thirds of Protestants in Latin America are now Pentecostal (Pew Research Center, 2014, p. 62). The Pentecostal and Evangelical experience has not been as favourable in Latin America compared to the influence of historical Protestantism after the Reformation (e.g. in Germany, England, and the rest of Northern Europe and North America) (Witte, 2002; Woodberry, 2012; Becker et al., 2016; Berman, 2003; Snyder, 2011; Martin, 1999).

In Latin America, no body of legal norms exists "to promote as the basis for an Evangelical society" (Martin, 1999, p. 41). In contrast with Roman Catholicism, Evangelicals are not very influential politically and "are highly unlikely to acquire serious influence in Latin America" (Martin, 1999, p. 40). Most Evangelical parties could not achieve visible political relevance, although more recently, the civic engagement of Evangelicals has increased in Latin America (Zilla, 2020). Recent examples of heads of state who have either been Evangelicals or supported by Evangelical movements include Jair Bolsonaro in Brazil, Jimmy Morales in Guatemala, and Manuel López Obrador in Mexico (Zilla, 2020).

Yet, Latin American Protestants have no recourse to historical norms that have been worked out over centuries of experience in politics and law and that may thus serve them as guides (unless they consider German, English, Scandinavian, or North American Protestant experiences). Instead, what Protestants have followed in Latin America "are the established practices of corporatism and clientage" (p. 40). As a result, they have often fallen into the same corrupt behaviour as traditional politicians (Helmsdorff, 1996; Schäfer, 2006). Moreover, in Latin America "…the contrast between Evangelicals and Catholics is really not so great" (Martin, 1999,

p. 41). Due to the absence of high-status ecclesiastics and religious intellectuals, who might, moreover, deploy sophisticated norms, Latin American Protestants are "equipped with little more than native good sense and the limited inferences they can draw from the Bible" (Martin, 1999, p. 40).

#### 10.4.3.2 The Prosperity Gospel (PG) as a Mainly Pentecostal Contemporary Phenomenon

While previous sections have analysed the influence of historical Christian denominations on prosperity, this subsection considers a more contemporary phenomenon that is widespread: the Prosperity Gospel (PG).

The Theology of Prosperity or Prosperity Gospel (PG) is a trans-denominational, transnational doctrine, which is closely linked to the Charismatic Movement and Pentecostal Christianity. PG teachings spread the idea that "wealth is a sign of God's blessing and is compensation for prayer and for giving beyond the minimum tithe to one's church, televangelists, or other religious causes" (Koch, 2009, p. 1).

Likewise, Harrison (2005) defines PG as "a relational community of believers, voluntary organisations, fellowships, conferences, and ministries loosely defined by a shared doctrine, a network without definite leader or governing body" (p. 14).[5] Key features of PG are its alignment with growing numbers of churches and megachurches in urban centres and the embracement of mass media and postmodern, consumerist capitalist values. The founding moment of the PG movement has been identified in the "healing revivals" of the post-World War II period in the USA. Subsequently, PG expanded as a doctrine to multiple denominations in different countries, especially in Asia, Africa, and Latin America (Sharpe, 2014; Bowler, 2010, 2013).

##### 10.4.3.2.1 PG Origins: Syncretism with African Rituals and New Thought Movement

**Syncretic Origins of PG in the USA**

PG is a mainly Protestant movement comprising three distinct though intersecting streams: Pentecostalism, New Thought, and African American religion (Bowler, 2010). The following paragraphs describe each of these three streams of the PG amalgamation.

*Strand 1: Pentecostalism and preceding forms of Protestantism.*

PG has been the fastest-growing strand of Pentecostalism since the 1980s. However, it also has deeper roots in the longer history of Protestant promotion of capitalistic ideas stemming from the nineteenth century (e.g. Wesleyan Methodism)

[5]©2005 by M. Harrison. This content is not under a CC-BY licence and has been reproduced with permission. Reproduced with permission of the Licensor through PLSclear.

(Towns, 2008; Sharpe, 2014; Bowler, 2010, 2013). Yet, unlike previous Protestant forms that elevated capitalist accumulation and asceticism (e.g. Calvinism), PG more strongly emphasises the consumption and immodest achievement of economic goods (Lingenthal, 2012, p. 55; Sharpe, 2014, p. 166; Miller, 2007).

*Strand 2: New Thought and white Protestantism.*

PG has also been significantly influenced by a blend of magical-religious rituals of white Protestants (Bowler, 2010, p. 46), which include a miasma of mental magic, bursting with Transcendentalism, Spiritualism, Free Masonry, and New Thought (Bowler, 2010, p. 28). Concurrently, Butler (2009) asserts that PG is a "hybrid" of religious capitalism "that has its roots in 19th century thinkers like E.W. Kenyon and 20th century purveyors like Norman Vincent Peale, and Oral Roberts" (p. 2).

McConnell (1988) also claims that Kenneth Hagin (one of the recognised founding fathers of the PG in the USA) is directly indebted to the ideas of Essek William Kenyon. Likewise, other leading PG preachers and televangelists, such as Kenneth Copeland, Frederick Price, Don Gassett, and others have been linked with Kenyon's teachings. Kenyon is, in turn, closely associated with the nineteenth-century American New Thought movement, which leans heavily on parapsychology (Sharpe, 2014, p. 169). Therefore, McConnell presents PG as a cult-like sect, with deeply non-Christian roots (Sharpe, 2014, pp. 168–169). Equally, Koch (2009) argues that PG proponents "universally admit that the principles they set forth work for Christians and non-Christians alike" (p. 8). For Koch, PG teachings are more closely connected with the secular self-help movement than with those of traditional orthodox Christianity.

The metaphysical New Thought movement emphasises the power of the individual's mind to transform thought and speech into tangible blessings (i.e. wealth, health, happiness). This positive thinking stream found a welcoming environment within mainline Protestantism, thus engendering the recognisable Gospels of wealth (PG) and health (Bowler, 2010, pp. 27, 52).

*Strand 3: African American Protestantism.*

PG also found a comfortable home within black Protestantism (especially in congregations of Methodists and Baptists) in the first half of the twentieth century in the USA. This amalgamation can also be seen as a historical recapitulation of pervasive and persistent Pentecostal and New Thought combinations in African American Protestantism (Bowler, 2010, p. 46).

This time, however, early PG combined with African-derived traditions (e.g. hoodoo, voodoo) that resulted in cross-pollination and black adoption and adaptation of mainly white metaphysical rituals. Black theologies, thus, further spread Spiritualism, focusing on the importance of material blessings (Bowler, 2010, p. 50).

The previous paragraphs have shown the syncretic origins of PG, especially with African American roots and New Thought in the USA. Yet, when PG globalised, the movement continued its syncretism with indigenous traditions of other regions, such as Latin America (Miller, 2007, pp. 24–5). However, it is also important to highlight that Pentecostalism tends to preserve but also demonise the beliefs in indigenous traditions and "spirits" as "the devil's representatives" (Robbins, 2004, pp. 128–9; Sharpe, 2014, p. 173).

#### 10.4.3.2.2 General Criticisms of PG

Nearly all aspects of PG's teachings and practices have been intensely criticised. The most obvious concern that critical social scientists express is that PG preys on the world's most needy people, collecting tithes from the poorest and promising only false hope and exaggerated promises of miraculous healings and unimaginable economic wealth in return (Sharpe, 2014, p. 174). Other criticisms depict PG as an "evangelical-neoliberal machine" (Connolly, 2009), where PG is the spiritual articulation that promotes and reinforces neoliberalism (Wrenn, 2019). This neoliberal portray of PG describes the invisible forces of the market as "evidence" of God's hand (Wrenn, 2019, p. 430). Others describe PG as a US American-led conspiracy to propagate capitalism and consumerism and ruin traditional forms of life in the global South (Robbins, 2004; Coleman, 2002; Kyle, 2006; Sharpe, 2014). However, all these criticisms need to be balanced against the empirical evidence.

The following sections will analyse some of the most contentious issues that increase criticism of PG.

**Corruption**
Leading figures of the PG movement have been repeatedly questioned or charged with financial misconduct and mismanagement. Thus, PG is also known through a series of scandals in different countries, including the USA, Brazil, and other Latin American and African nations (Zilla, 2020, p. 19–20; Lingenthal, 2012, p. 22; Sharpe, 2014, p. 168; Jenkins, 2006, p. 106).

**Political Engagement**
PG, and Pentecostal churches in particular, have been notably linked with having supported right-wing political forces (e.g. Bolsonaro in Brazil, Uribe in Colombia, Trump in the USA) or even oppressive political regimes, such as Pinochet in Chile (Zilla, 2020; Sharpe, 2014; Bastian, 1993; Martin, 1990). However, several empirical studies do not show a necessary association between far-right conservative parties and Pentecostals in different contexts. Instead, the empirical findings point to church adherents tending to vote in parallel with other members of their social classes (Koch, 2009; Sharpe, 2014; Martin, 1990; Robbins, 2004).

#### 10.4.3.2.3 Theological Criticisms of PG

No theological consensus exists regarding the genealogy of PG. However, theologians and other critics, often from within Pentecostalism and other Christian groups, describe PG as an idolatry of money with heretical teachings that deviate from the central sense of the Gospel (i.e. salvation and love) (Harrison, 2005; Sharpe, 2014).

Yet, PG preachers often contend that "Jesus' death and resurrection abolished not only sin and disease but also poverty" (Bowler, 2013, p. 95).

Indeed, several reasons permit critics to consider PG as "a betrayal of the cross". The most obvious question is how Christians can openly pursue economic wealth if the Bible depicts Christ as a "...despised and rejected of men; a man of sorrows, and acquainted with grief..." (King James Bible, 1769, Isaiah 53:3), who announced that "It is easier for a camel to go through the eye of a needle, than for a rich man to enter into the kingdom of God" (King James Bible, 1769, Matthew 19:24).

Yet, PG preachers provide several arguments in defence of wealth, often relying on "proof-texting" biblical passages removed from their textual and historical context (i.e. superficial exegesis) (Barron, 1987; Koch, 2009; Sharpe, 2014). For instance, PG believers often portray Jesus as a rich—rather than an ascetic—figure by using as arguments passages such as the following:

- The visit of the wise men would imply that Jesus attracted prosperity from the day he was born (Dollar, cited in Bowler, 2010, p. 105): "...they saw the young child with Mary his mother, and fell down, and worshipped him: and when they had opened their treasures, they presented unto him gifts; gold, and frankincense, and myrrh" (King James Bible, 1769, Matthew 2:11).
- The dividing of Jesus' garments among the soldiers at his crucifixion could suggest that they were valuable (Dollar, cited in Bowler, 2010, p. 105): "Then the soldiers, when they had crucified Jesus, took his garments, and made four parts, to every soldier a part; and also his coat: now the coat was without seam, woven from the top throughout" (King James Bible, 1769, John 19:23).
- The ability to travel and feed the multitudes on several occasions (e.g. King James Bible, 1769, John 6), and even having Judas as treasurer (e.g. King James Bible, 1769, John 13:29), would attest to Jesus' wealth (Blake, cited in Sharpe, 2014, p. 165; Koch, 2009 p. 1).

PG believers often claim that the traditional austere portrayals of the suffering Christ are incorrect or outdated. However, Christian theologians of differing denominations have criticised PG literalist interpretations as over-simplistic and inadequate readings of the Holy Scriptures (Sharpe, 2014, p. 168), or as "twisting Bible verses out of context to suit their own self-help philosophy" (Horton, 2009, p. 4). A lack of a deep exegesis often excludes or minimises the importance of other conflicting passages for the PG beliefs that clearly indicate Christ's ascetic life, inter alia:

> And Jesus said unto him, Foxes have holes, and birds of the air *have* nests; but the Son of man hath not where to lay *his* head (King James Bible, 1769, Luke 9:58; original emphases);
>
> Is not this the carpenter, the son of Mary...? (King James Bible, 1769, Mark 6:3);
>
> Jesus answered, My kingdom is not of this world... (King James Bible, 1769, John 18:36).

As critic theologians have observed,

> "There is much in the Bible that connects the right relation with God to prosperity" (Cobb, 2009). "Yet there is little equivocation in its [the Bible's] core message that the good life is not one dened by material acquisition and ostentatious consumption but by purposeful acts motivated by generosity and concern for others" (Dillon, 2009).

In this sense, one of the most contentious theological issues that raise controversy is related to the tithes and offerings that the faithful contribute to their congregations:

**Tithes**

Tithing is a practice that involves giving at least 10% of one's gross income to the believer's Church, or related charities. The promise is that believers will get a hundredfold return from unexpected sources (Butler, 2009; Sharpe, 2014). Thus, the faithful see a cost-effective investment in tithing (Zilla, 2020, p. 18).

PG believers base tithing in a myriad of biblical passages that certainly support giving in diverse contexts. However, the practice has been associated with PG preachers' misuse and corruption scandals (Sharpe, 2014). In the USA, PG churches, such as Creflo Dollar's World Changers, for instance, even verify that members have paid their full tithes by asking them to submit tax records and keep detailed financial reports (Bowler, 2010, p. 115). In Brazil, surveys show that 52% of PG adherents (Evangelicals) tithe to their congregations vis-à-vis 34% of Catholics that contribute in some way to their Church (Corrêa, 2013). However, the Roman Catholic Church still receives subsidies or financial benefits from the Brazilian state ("institutional tithes") although the Brazilian Constitution explicitly forbids public institutions to subsidise any church or religion (Art. 19) and enshrines religious freedom and equality principles (Zilla, 2020, p. 21).

Nevertheless, tithing is not new or exclusive of the PG movement, but this principle has been applied in diverse ways, in virtually all Judeo-Christian traditions, since ancient times (e.g. Plumptre, 1818). Surprisingly, the systematic study of tithing has received little scholarly attention. According to Murray (2011), a detailed historical review of the tithing system is entirely absent, as well as analysis of the recurrent criticisms about exploiting tithing practices, and a critical engagement to understand the biblical and theological principles that comprise tithing (p. 5).

The role of giving and tithing in the Scriptures is too voluminous to be considered in its full extent in this study. However, Budiselić (2015) has advanced in the systematic understanding of biblical and theological foundations of the tithing system. PG and other Christians claim a biblical obligation to tithe to their churches/pastors. Budiselić's contribution is crucial in order to understand and criticise such an assertion and practice. He examines Old Testament examples and all the references to tithing in the New Testament to present arguments for and against claims that Christians should tithe.

Budiselić concludes that Christians have a responsibility to give (e.g. to support those in need and to proclaim the Gospel). However, church tithing can in no way be considered a literal commandment for Christians today. Yet, it was a commandment with specific content and form for the Jews. For instance, the Israelites contributed up to 20% of their goods or more in support of the Levites and the temple, for helping the poor and foreigners, and for the festivals. Nonetheless, the New Testament raises the standard of voluntary giving with abundant principles that include offering to up to 100% of one's capital, with rewarding promises (Budiselić, 2015, p. 44). The following biblical passages illustrate this principle:

> Then Peter began to say unto him, Lo, we have left all, and have followed thee. And Jesus answered and said, Verily I say unto you, There is no man that hath left house, or brethren, or sisters, or father, or mother, or wife, or children, or lands, for my sake, and the gospel's, but he shall receive a hundredfold now in this time, houses, and brethren, and sisters, and mothers, and children, and lands, with persecutions; and in the world to come eternal life (King James Bible, 1769, Mark 10:28–30).
>
> give, and it shall be given unto you; good measure, pressed down, and shaken together, and running over, shall men give into your bosom. For with the same measure that ye mete withal it shall be measured to you again (King James Bible, 1769, Luke 6:38).
>
> Sell that ye have, and give alms; provide yourselves bags which wax not old, a treasure in the heavens that faileth not, where no thief approacheth, neither moth corrupteth (King James Bible, 1769, Luke 12:33).
>
> I have showed you all things, how that so laboring ye ought to support the weak, and to remember the words of the Lord Jesus, how he said, It is more blessed to give than to receive (King James Bible, 1769, Acts 20:35).

Consequently, Christians are encouraged in the Scriptures to give to the weak, to all in need, *and* to support the proclamation of the Gospel. However, following Budiselić's reasoning, PG believers would tithe to their churches/pastors based on two faulty assumptions: 1) Christians *must not* give at least 10% of the income to their church/pastor (but they should instead give as much as they can to voluntarily support those in need and to proclaim the Gospel); 2) not all Jews were giving 10% (and their contributions were not only addressed to the priesthood) (Budiselić, p. 44). Certainly, the New Testament does encourage giving to support the preachers, but it does not require a defined percentage:

> Even so hath the Lord ordained that they which preach the gospel should live of the gospel (King James Bible, 1769, 1 Corinthians 9:14).
>
> …for the laborer is worthy of his hire (King James Bible, 1769, Luke 10:7).

Accordingly, tithing/offering to one's church/pastor is just one of the ways of practising giving. However, the Scriptures do not exhort giving in order to make a single church/pastor millionaire. Furthermore, church tithing cannot be considered as an imperative way of giving because, among others, the conditions defined in the Old Testament are not entirely applicable today (e.g. the Levites and the temple are physically absent[6]) (Budiselić, 2015). Therefore, the imperative urge of PG and other preachers' requesting tithes seems biblically inconsistent in light of these considerations, and has led in many cases to its misuse and corruption. Equally inconsistent would be the subsidies or "institutional tithes" some governments pay to the official established churches as they are not "voluntary" contributions anymore; rather, they act like taxes (sometimes paid by believers and non-believers alike).

[6]Yet, the New Testament refers to the temple as a type of the coming Messiah (Jesus Christ): "Jesus answered and said unto them, Destroy this temple, and in three days I will raise it up. Then said the Jews, Forty and six years was this temple in building, and wilt thou rear it up in three days? But he spake of the temple of his body. When therefore he was risen from the dead, his disciples remembered that he had said this unto them; and they believed the Scripture, and the word which Jesus had said" (King James Bible, 1769, John 2:19–22).

#### 10.4.3.2.4 Is PG a Poor people's Movement? Empirical Results from Studies

There is anything but consensus regarding PG and class. Scholars of religion often consider PG a typical "poor people's movement" that offers the needy the "opiate" of upward mobility (Bowler, 2010, 2013; Koch, 2009; Cox, 2001; Gifford, 1990; Hollinger, 1991). However, studies show that the PG movement attracts converts from all social classes, including well-educated, middle-class Latin Americans and Africans (Miller, 2007, p. 21; Sharpe, 2014, p. 173).

Others contend that the PG justifies the affluence of those who have been upwardly mobile by arguing that this is spiritually deserved and derived (Koch, 2009; Gifford, 1990; Bruce, 1990). However, a theological test of PG's supernatural claims does not exist nor does it appear feasible. Furthermore, measuring the income levels of PG believers has proven challenging, and few studies are available (mostly performed in the USA). Among other challenges, PG constituents often resist to disclose members' income, church budgets, and pastors' salaries (Bowler, 2010, 2013).

Nonetheless, Koch studied PG in the USA by analysing more than a thousand telephone surveys. He determined that income does not affect adherence to PG. However, "blacks, the 'born-again' or 'evangelical', and those who are less educated are more likely to seek out Prosperity messages" (Koch, 2009, p. v). Surprisingly, PG adherence does not affect the believers' generosity to religious and non-religious causes. The author concludes that members of PG are not over-represented among those with higher or lower incomes. Instead, PG adherents are "between blessings", which neither allows for the inference of the evident success nor the sheer failure of the overt PG claims (Koch, 2009, p.81). Comparably, Bowler's (2010) study indicates that American PG adherents enjoyed a comfortable lifestyle (p. 229).

Finally, PG critics document several cases of economic exploitation and disappointed hopes. However, studies also confirm that large numbers of PG converts have decisively improved their lives by joining the movement (e.g. by learning financial management and entrepreneurship) (Robbins, 2004, p. 136; Sharpe, 2014, p. 176; Miller, 2007, p. 176). Therefore, empirical studies on PG and class render mixed evidence.

#### 10.4.3.2.5 Summarising the Core Messages of Sect. 10.4.3.2 The Prosperity Gospel (PG)

The world-expanding PG contemporary movement that claims believers will prosper by tithing and declaring affirmations has syncretic roots in Pentecostalism, New Thought, and African American religion. Critics have disproven virtually all PG's teachings and practices, and raised criticisms on the corruption of ministers, exploitation of the poor, support of far-right parties, and controversial theological claims. This section balances and analyses such criticisms, finding mixed evidence for those claims:

- Corruption scandals related to PG mismanagement have occurred in virtually all countries where the movement has reached (Sharpe, 2014).
- No necessary association exists between PG and far-right political parties, although notable examples exist.
- Although PG approaches the Scriptures literalistically, it does not apply an interlinear exegesis. A lack of interlinear exegesis renders out-of-context interpretations of the Bible.
- Tithing is an ancient biblical practice that the PG movement has misconstrued to make it imperative. According to the Bible, Christians should give as much as they can to support the needy and to proclaim the Gospel, but not to maintain the wealth of a preacher or a church.
- Critics often depict PG as a movement of unscrupulous preachers who economically exploit the poor. The empirical evidence shows that PG is composed mainly of middle classes and blacks, but faithful from all social classes belong to PG. Likewise, although PG cases of exploitation exist, studies also document positive experiences of PG conversions.

**Empirical Expectations**

9). *I expect prosperity/transparency levels to be directly (positively) related to the proportion of Protestants and inversely (negatively) related to the proportion of Roman Catholics. This expectation is valid for the cross-country sample of Europe and the Americas, as confirmed by empirical studies (*e.g. La Porta et al., 1997*;* Chase, 2010*).*

10). *However, I do not expect a significant positive influence of the Protestant population on prosperity/transparency in Latin America. Firstly, Protestantism in Latin America has been relatively recent compared to its five-hundred-year history of asserting the Reformation in Europe. In Latin America, Protestantism is a recent phenomenon. It dates back no more than fifty years, and its proportion has not surpassed 20 per cent (*Todd & Zurlo, 2016*). Secondly, most of the Protestant growth in Latin America comes from Pentecostal currents, whose positive impact has been far weaker than historical Protestant denominations (*McCleary, 2013*;* Woodberry, 2012*;* Becker et al., 2016*).*

## 10.5 Syncretism

The concept of syncretism is related to the concept of culture and thus, has no-agreed upon definition. The inconsistent etymology and complex history of the term make it problematic to define (Leopold & Jensen, 2004, p. 14). According to Droogers (2004), determining what syncretism is constitutes a difficult challenge as several definitional debates exist around the term. Controversies abound over the phenomenon's commonality and intricacy, which stems from a refusal to consider the phenomenon's normalcy—i.e. that all religions are syncretic configurations (p. 376).

Pakkanen (1996) even claims that syncretism is an impractical "theoretical invention" as it refers to explaining "syncretism with syncretism" (Pakkanen, 1996, pp. 86–87). Yet, for Stewart and Shaw (1994), syncretism "refers to the synthesis of different religious forms. It is a contentious and contested term which has undergone many historical transformations in meaning. Some see it as a disparaging, ethnocentric label for religious traditions..." (p. i).[7] Leopold and Jensen (2004) explain that the traditional definition of syncretism wrongly assumes that culture, religion, and ethnicity are, in essence, pure (p. 2). However, most syncretistic formations are "unconscious" as a natural result of social interactions, while others are consequences of cultural domination (Leopold & Jensen, 2004, p. 4).

Kraemer (1962) argued that non-Christian religions are intrinsically syncretistic and thus, syncretism is predominantly non-Christian. For the author, syncretism is also inevitable in Christianity, but it has occurred here as an illegitimate fusion rather than doing so innately. Therefore, the principal criticism against syncretism as a concept is that it implies pejorative references to non-Christian religions. Likewise, the term has historically been tied to Christian theological disagreements (Leopold & Jensen, 2004, p. 8).

### 10.5.1 Syncretism and Christianity

The Gospels and the Book of the Acts of the Apostles (King James Bible, 1769) relate that the first Christians were almost entirely converted Jews. Kippenberg (2004) observes that Jews refused pagan rituals, considering them idolatry (p. 35). Judaism has been naturally anti-syncretic as the Scriptures forbid mingling with foreign religious elements (Fig. 8.4). The New Testament relates, however, that the Gospel was also spread to the Gentiles soon afterwards. Examples of this are the conversion and baptism of Cornelius, the Italian centurion (Acts 10); the Ethiopian Eunuch (Acts 8); and the mission of the Apostle Paul to the heathens in Greece and Asia. Consequently, Rudolph (2004) notes that the mission and propagation of a faith inevitably leads to syncretism (for the author, this is exemplified by Paul's preaching to the Greeks in Acts 17) (p. 71). Likewise, the Book of Acts of the Apostles records that tension occurred among "Christian Jews" and "Christian Gentiles" on issues such as circumcision (e.g. Acts 11). Therefore, for Kippenberg (2004), Christianity has been a syncretistic religion, especially in its early days (p. 29). However, the syncretic process of Christianity skyrocketed when it became the official religion of the Roman Empire.

[7]©1994 by Stewart & Shaw. Reproduced with permission of the Licensor through PLSclear.

Benavides (2004) observes that under Constantine, the Christian divinity began functioning as a traditional Roman god of victory—i.e. a divinity whose adoration was ritualised before the war and praised after victory (Wardman as cited in Benavides, 2004, p. 202). Although there was a contradictory bond between the Christian divinity and the *Sol Invictus*, the new divinity already incorporated some of the revered attributes by Heliogabalus and the Emessan priests when the Roman state adopted Christianity as the official religion (Benavides, 2004, p. 202). Consequently, the Roman (Catholic) Christianity adopted pantheistic components coming, among others, from the Roman Empire and Greece. Leopold & Jensen contend that as a result of its long mission history, the Roman Church-State has established a more comprehensive frame for integrating new or external components into Catholic doctrine and policy (p. 18). Therefore, according to the authors, for Jesuits, Franciscans, and Dominicans, among other Catholic orders, syncretism has been a way of broadening their mission in different parts of the world, including the east and Latin America (p. 16). Hence, among others, the effects of Catholic mission have produced amalgams between indigenous gods and Catholic saints, for instance (p.18).

However, the Protestant Reformation has been a typical anti-syncretistic movement (Spica, 2018; Leopold & Jensen, 2004). Spica observes: "The Reformers criticized the fact that the Christian message had been lost from its original purity, and this was the reason for reforming the church" (p. 241). The "original purity" refers to the *Sola Scriptura* principle defended by the Reformers (see Sect. 10.4.1.3). Therefore, the failed ecumenical attempts of Erasmus and Calixt in the sixteenth century are partly explained, in that they saw logical evidence of the truth within Christianity's in pagan writings, particularly in Aristotelian philosophy (Engel, 1976 as cited in Leopold & Jensen, 2004, p. 15). However, the initial anti-syncretistic attitude of Protestantism partly succumbed with the advent of Pentecostalism (see following subsection and Sect. 10.4.3).

#### 10.5.1.1 Syncretism and Christianity in Latin America

In Latin America, another "syncretism with syncretism" instance has occurred in Pakkanen (1996)'s terms. In this process, Catholics of the Roman rite blend popular Catholic religiosity (e.g. idols, images, incense, shamans, nomenclature) with pre-Columbian ethnoreligious traditions. Johnson and Zurlo (2016) have defined these typical Latin American believers as "*Christopagans*". As Spica observes:

> Even when we say that Latin America is mostly Christian or Catholic, the notions of this Christianity or Catholicity are very different from typical European Catholicity. Here, popular Catholicity assumes the diverse beliefs and practices of African and native peoples, modifying and adapting the original beliefs of European Catholicism to the ways of life, challenges and worldviews of the Latin American people. [...] This differentiated religiosity, though, still calls itself Catholic despite evidence of mergers with prehispanic religiosity. [...] In addition to Catholicity, we are now seeing many neo-Pentecostal religions emerging in Latin America. Although they often try to deny syncretism and defend a certain purity of faith, they are extremely syncretic, especially in ritual matters. This is clear, for example, in

> their use of popular music in worship, in their dances of praise and in their way of understanding Christian belief (Spica, 2018, pp. 236–237).

Benavides (2004) documents the syncretic processes that occurred during the expansion of Roman Catholicism among Andean, Aztec, and Mayan populations. Herskovits (1966) also noted that native and African gods are identified with saints of the Catholic Church in the New World. However, according to the author, African cultural remembrances (such as shouting and mourning) are more moderate and religious relations are more discreet in Protestant regions than in Catholic areas (Herskovits as cited in Apter, 2004. p. 165). Nevertheless, most of the current Protestant denominations worldwide have a strong Pentecostal influence, which highly syncretises African and native rituals (see Sect. 10.4.3). Furthermore, the Pentecostal influence has also been pervasive in Roman Catholicism. As an interviewee noted in this research:

> It's very difficult to distinguish among Catholic Charismatics, Renewed Pentecostals, and Neo-Pentecostals as their rituals are almost the same. You have to get deep background information to distinguish them. Hermeneutically, it's difficult to differentiate them; all of them clap hands and rite and preach the same, but they want to be differentiated: Catholics as Catholics and Pentecostals as Pentecostals, as such, as they don't congregate together (Ecumenical academic theologian).

However, the process of syncretism with indigenous or African rituals varies within different Latin American countries and subregions, depending on the historical presence of these ethnicities. The following cases, coupled with primary information from this study (interviews), show this pattern.

##### 10.5.1.1.1 Colombia

Uribe (2003) refers to Colombia as a territory that has been full of magic and witchcraft for centuries. The arrival of the Spaniards, with the rigid bastion of Catholicism, not only provoked a displacement of the indigenous people but an uprooting of the black slaves from their places of origin. This uprooting was the first cause of the magical-religious conformation in Colombia. The colonial society gradually became a space in which African fetishisms, indigenous gods, and the exaggerated belief in saints and miraculous medals found their convergence point in relationships of domination. The social organisation was mediated by race, where the Catholic Spaniards occupied the hegemonic tip of the pyramid, and the Blacks and Indians were at the base. Thus, the beliefs and traditions of the Indians and Blacks were presented as barbaric and diabolic in the face of Catholic superiority. However, these traditions continued to be practised, mingled with Catholicism, and survived the Colony and the Enlightenment, remaining intact when Protestantism emerged in Colombia. The association of indigenous and black beliefs with the demonic was prolonged and intensified with the advent of the Evangelicals and Pentecostals,[8] thus creating a new syncretic platform (Lozano, 2009).

A Colombian Roman Catholic Theologian partly coincides with Lozano's account:

> When the Spaniards arrived, they came to catechise instead to evangelise. They [natives] were taught to cross themselves, to recite the creed and some prayers by memory. And then it was assumed that "Christians", sons of God were made, and then they proceeded to baptise them. But there was never an Evangelisation process; the term Jesus or the Word never came; the Word was not taught directly, and this is another reason why the Bible is almost not read. . .(Roman Catholic Theologian).

A Colombian Protestant interviewee in this study also concurs with the assertion about syncretism in Protestantism:

> The problem is that there is a syncretism between Protestant Christianity and necromancy. [. . .] Many of the rites of this African culture and ceremonies have been passed on to the Protestant Church. The clapping and the dancing in the churches have its roots in Africa where people worship in that manner. Claps, drums, and dance. You can see it in the Protestant world, and it is even being practised today in the United States. "I clap and dance because I feel good," they say. I call them Epicurean Christians (Independent, free Protestant believer–academic).

#### 10.5.1.1.2 Cuba

In Cuba, the syncretic connection is even more evident (see Sect. 20.3). The massive influx of African slaves as cheap labour to cultivate sugar since colonial times contributed to the emergence of spiritism, voodooism, and syncretised forms with Roman Catholicism (e.g. Santería) (Contreras, 2013, p. 177; Ramírez, 2009, p. 167; Sánchez, 1992, pp. 90–91). In practice, an amalgamation of rituals is evident. A priest of the Afro-Cuban religion (a spiritistic religion) expressed the singular importance of Roman Catholicism in their rituals:

> We have respect and veneration for the Catholic Church as a mother and centre. Our saints [icons] must receive light in Catholic rituals, for example with holy water. It is an essential requirement for our ordination as Babalawo or "Santo" [a spiritistic saint] to be baptised in the Catholic Church. The Catholic Church knows and is aware of this requirement for sanctification, but never acknowledges this publicly. [. . .] Francis [pope Jorge Bergoglio] met with Yoruba and Protestants when he came to Cuba. He is simple, but he has a higher rank than any country or president, as Rome is the centre of the world (Cuban Babalawo priest).

---

[8]For Robbins (2004), the process of demonisation in Pentecostalism transforms ancestral spirits into agents of the Devil, prompting people to dedicate their energies to combatting it. This practice serves to further establish the Devil's presence and its significance in post-conversion life (pp. 128–9).

Complementing the words of the Babalawo priest, a Cuban Roman Catholic Theologian explains the relationship of Afro-Cuban rituals with Roman Catholicism:

> The Afro-Cuban religion did not have its own rite, so they adopted the Roman Catholic rituals. The Roman Catholic Church did not commit to this, but as for the priests, it is a convenient way to fill the Church with adherents. The Priests are happy with that, although they know they are making a theological mistake. This means that the Roman Catholic Church has accepted syncretism for convenience (Cuban Roman Catholic Theologian).

A representative of the Cuban National Council of Churches partly confirmed the claim of the previous two interviewees: "...one can count more Roman Catholics as many Babalawos are baptised as Roman Catholics".

#### 10.5.1.1.3 Uruguay

In Uruguay, at least two aspects mediate the relative low prominence of syncretism compared with the previous cases: the low Afro-descendant and indigenous populations, and the high secularisation of the society (see Chap. 19). Here, the interviewees have only referred to the introduced Brazilian influence of syncretic rituals:

> In Uruguay, syncretic rituals come by transfer from Brazil, especially Umbanda and spiritist rites. But they come by contact with Brazil since the Afro-descendant presence in Uruguay is low (Uruguayan Roman Catholic Priest).

An ecumenical academic theologian shares a similar perception:

> Here the cult of Yemanjá has increased a lot. That is santería, and it comes from people of African ancestry from Brazil. We have the Candomblé, music with which black slaves were pressured in Montevideo; that music has been declared cultural heritage of humanity and is what identifies Uruguay. However, as an Uruguayan, I do not feel identified with the Candomblé. It's because of the cultural difference we have. [...] And I do not know what the Catholic Church thinks. I haven't heard any comments in favour or against it.

### *10.5.2 Summarising the Core Messages of Sect. 10.5 Syncretism*

Syncretism as a concept suffers from many problems with its definition, which is historically linked to theological disagreements in Christianity. While syncretism has been a natural process in all religions, Jews and historical Protestants have tended to be more anti-syncretic given their Scriptural base of beliefs. In turn, the importance of traditions, in Roman Catholicism for instance, has led to include more non-orthodox rituals in its practice. In Pentecostalism, the syncretic practices are apparent, partly due to its marked African influence. In Latin America, "syncretism with syncretism" has occurred with the expansion of Roman Catholicism and contemporary Protestantism (mostly Pentecostalism) and blend with indigenous and African practices. Latin American syncretism with indigenous or African rituals varies depending on the presence of these ethnicities. Therefore, the empirical (quantitative and QCA) part of this study includes measurements of ethnicities as cultural proxies of syncretism.

Finally, the syncretic process in Latin America has blended religions, music, languages, and cuisine, among other cultural expressions (Wilson, 2004).

## References


Abbott, W. M. (1989). *The documents of Vatican II*. Crossroad Publishing.

Abram, A. (2018). Editorial. Introduction to the special issue of religions—"The future of Catholic theological ethics". *Religions*, 1–4.

Acemoglu, D., Johnson, S., & Robinson, J. (2001). The colonial origins of comparative development: An empirical investigation. *American Economic Review, 91*(5), 1369–1401.

Agnew, J. (2010). Deus Vult: The geopolitics of the Catholic Church. *Geopolitics, 15*(1), 39–61.

Alesina, A., Devleeschauwer, A., Easterly, W., Sergio, K., & Wacziarg, R. (2003). Fractionalization. *Journal of Economic Growth, 8*(2), 155–194.

Alesina, A., & Giuliano, P. (2015). Culture and institutions. *Journal of Economic Literature, 53*(4), 898–944.

Anderson, J. (2007). Religion, politics and international relations. The Catholic contribution to democratization's 'third wave': Altruism, hegemony or self-interest? *Cambridge Review of International Affairs, 20*(3).

Apter, A. (2004). Herskovits's heritage: Rethinking syncretism in the African diaspora. In A. M. Leopold & J. S. Jensen (Eds.), *Syncretism in religion: A Reader*. New York: Routledge.

Arruñada, B. (2010). Protestants and catholics: Similar work ethic, different social ethic. *The Economic Journal, 120*(547), 890–918.

Bacchiocchi, S. (1977). *From Sabbath to Sunday. A historical investigation of the rise of sunday observance in early Christianity*. The Pontifical Gregorian University Press.

Bacchiocchi, S. (2002). Islam and the Papacy in Prophecy. *Biblical perspectives, 86*. Endtime Issues, Berrien Springs, Michigan.

Barro, R. J., & McCleary, R. M. (2003). Religion and economic growth across countries. *American Sociological Review, 68*(5), 760–781.

Barron, B. (1987). *The health and wealth gospel*. InterVarsity Press.

Bastian, J. (1993). The metamorphosis of Latin American Protestant groups: A sociohistorical perspective. *Latin American Research Review, 28*(2), 33–61.

Becker, S., Pfaff, S., & Rubin, J. (2016). *Causes and consequences of the protestant reformation*. Warwick Economics Research Paper Series.

Becker, S. O., & Woessmann, L. (2009). Was Weber wrong? A human capital theory of protestant economic history. *Quarterly Journal of Economics, 124*(2), 531–596.

Benavides, G. (2004). Syncretism and legitimacy in Latin American religion. In A. M. Leopold & J. S. Jensen (Eds.), *Syncretism in religion: A reader*. Routledge.

Berger, P. (1990). *The Sacred Canopy: Elements of a sociological theory of religion*. Doubleday.

Berger, P. (1999). *The desecularization of the world*. Ethics and Public Policy Center and Wm. B. Eerdmans.

Berman, H. (2003). *Law and revolution II: The impact of the protestant reformations on the western legal tradition*. Harvard University Press, Belknap Press.

Berryman, P. (2020). Liberation theology. In D. T. Orique, S. Fitzpatrick-Behrens, & V. Garrard (Eds.), *The Oxford handbook of Latin American Christianity*. https://doi.org/10.1093/oxfordhb/9780199860357.013.14
Boff, L. (1989). The originality of the liberation theology. In E. B. Maduro (Ed.), *The future of liberation theology: Essays in honour of Gustavo Gutierrez*. Orbis.
Bonino, J. M. (1976). *Christians and Marxists: The mutual challenge to revolution*. William B. Eerdmans.
Bowler, C. (2010). *Blessed: A history of the American prosperity gospel*. Doctoral dissertation. Graduate Program in Religion in the Graduate School of Duke University.
Bowler, K. (2013). *Blessed: A history of the American prosperity gospel*. Oxford University Press.
Boxall, I., & Tresley, R. M. (2016). *The book of revelation and its interpreters. Short studies and an annotated bibliography*. Rowman & Littlefield.
Bruce, F. F. (2007). *Außerbiblische Zeugnisse über Jesus und das frühe Christentum*. Brunnen.
Bruce, S. (1990). *Pray TV: Televangelism in America*. Routledge.
Budiselić, E. (2015). The role and place of tithing in the context of Christian giving – Part 2. *Evangelical Journal of Theology, IX, 1*, 31–58.
Butler, A. (2009). *Christianity and the crash – The immanent frame*. Social Science Research Council. Retrieved from https://tif.ssrc.org/2009/12/23/christianity-and-the-crash/
Chase, G. (2010). Religion's impact on corruption. *Journal of Business and Economics Perspectives, 5*(1), 102–112.
Cobb, J. (2009). *Christianity and the crash – The immanent frame*. Social Science Research Council. Retrieved from https://tif.ssrc.org/2009/12/23/christianity-and-the-crash/
Coleman, S. (2002). The faith movement: A global religious culture? *Culture and Religion: An Interdisciplinary Journal, 3*(1), 3–19.
Colson, C., & Neuhaus, R. J. (1995). *Evangelicals and catholics toward a common mission together*. Word Publishing.
Comisión Episcopal de Enseñanza de Madrid. (1962). *Catecismo de la Doctrina Cristiana* (S. C. Madrid, Ed.). Luis Vives.
Committee on Ecumenical and Interreligious Affairs. (2015). *Declaration on the Way Church, Ministry, and Eucharist.* (E. L. Bishops., Ed.). Augsburg Fortress.
Connolly, W. (2009). *Christianity and the crash – The immanent frame*. Social Science Research Council. Retrieved from https://tif.ssrc.org/2009/12/23/christianity-and-the-crash/
Contreras, D. (2013). Iglesia Católica y estado en la República de Cuba: pasado y presente de sus relaciones Catholic Church and State in Cuba: past and present relationships. *América Latina Hoy, 63*, 177–195.
Cook, E. (2012). *Roman catholic hegemony and religious freedom: A seventh-day adventist assessment of dignitatis humanae*. Graduate Faculty of Baylor University.
Corrêa, P. (2013). Honrar a Dios... con tarjeta de crédito o efectivo. El auge evangélico en Brasil [Honouring God... by credit card or cash. The Evangelical boom in Brazil]. *Nueva Sociedad* (248), 134–143. Retrieved from http://nuso.org/media/articles/downloads/3997_1.pdf
Cox, H. (2001). *Fire from heaven: The rise of pentecostal spirituality and the reshaping of religion in the 21st century*. Da Capo Press.
D'Aubigne, M. (1862). *Histoire de la Reformation au XVIie siecle*. Librairie de Ch. Meyrueis et Compagnie.
Dillon, M. (2009). *Christianity and the crash – The immanent frame*. Social Science Research Council. Retrieved from https://tif.ssrc.org/2009/12/23/christianity-and-the-crash/
Doe, N. (2010). The concept of Christian Law–A case study: Concepts of 'A Church' in a comparative and ecumenical context. In N. Doe & R. Sandberg (Eds.), *Law and religion: New horizons*. Uitgeverij Peeters.
Doe, N., & Sandberg, R. (2010). *Law and religion: New horizons*. Leuven Peeters.
Dowling, J. (1853). *The history of Romanism: From the earliest corruptions of Christianity to the present time*. E. Walker.

Drexler-Dreis, J. (2017). The option for the poor as a decolonial option: Latin American Liberation Theology in Conversation with Teología India and Womanist Theology. *Political Theology, 18*(3), 269–286.
Droogers, A. (2004). Syncretism, power, play. In A. M. Leopold & J. S. Jensen (Eds.), *Syncretism in religion: A reader.* Routledge.
Dussel, E. D. (1976). *History and the theology of liberation: A Latin American perspective.* Orbis Books.
Elbahnasawy, N. G., & Revier, C. F. (2012). The determinants of corruption: Cross-country-panel-data analysis. *The Developing Economies, 50*(4), 311–333.
Emmenegger, P. (2011). Job security regulations in Western democracies: A fuzzy set analysis. *European Journal of Political Research, 50*(3), 336–364.
Engelhardt, T. H. (2007). Why ecumenism fails: Taking theological differences seriously. *Christian Bioethics, 13*(1), 25–51.
Esping-Andersen, G. (1996). Welfare states withoout work: The impasse of labour shedding and familialism in Continental European social policy. In *Welfare states in transition: National adaptations in global economies.* Sage.
Fierro, A. (1977). *The militant gospel: An analysis of contemporary political theologies.* SCM.
Figueroa, H. (2016). *La persistance des idées traditionalistes en Colombie. Religion et politique (1886-1952).* L'Harmattan.
Galeano, E. (1971). *Las venas abiertas de América Latina.* siglo xxi editores, s.a. de c.v.
Gifford, P. (1990). Prosperity: A new and foreign element in African Christianity. *Religion, 20*, 373–388.
Gill, A. (1998). *Rendering unto Caesar: The Catholic Church and the state in Latin America.* Chicago: Chicago University Press.
Gill, A. (2013). Religious pluralism, political incentives, and the origins of religious liberty. Global challenges. In A. Hertzke (Ed.), *The future of religious freedom* (pp. 107–127). Oxford University Press.
Glaeser, L., & Glendon, S. (1998). Incentives, predestination and free will. *Economic Inquiry, 36*(3), 429–443.
Granato, J., Inglehart, R., & Leblang, D. (1996). The effect of cultural values on economic development: Theory, hypotheses, and some empirical tests. *American Journal of Political Science, 40*(3), 607–631.
Grand Jury of Pennsylvania. (2018). *40th Statewide Investigating Grand Jury REPORT 1 Interim—Redacted.* Grand Jury of Pennsylvania.
Gregg, S. (1997). *Revelation: Four views. A parallel commentary.* Nelson.
Guiso, L., Sapienza, P., & Zingales, L. (2003). People's opium? Religion and economic attitudes. *Journal of Monetary Economics, 50*(2), 225–282.
Guiso, L., Sapienza, P., & Zingales, L. (2006). Does culture affect economic outcomes? *Journal of Economic Perspectives, 20*(2), 23–48.
Gutiérrez, G. (1973). *A theology of liberation: History, politics, and salvation.* Orbis Books.
Harrison, M. (2005). *Righteous riches: The word of faith movement in contemporary African American Religion.* Oxford University Press.
Hartman, S. S., Böcher, O., Benrath, G. A., Seebaß, G., & et al. (2002). Antichrist. In *Theologische Realenzyklopädie.*
Hayward, R. D., & Kemmelmeier, M. (2011). Weber revisited: A cross-national analysis of religiosity, religious culture, and economic attitudes. *Journal of Cross-Cultural Psychology, 42*(8), 1406–1420.
Helmsdorff, D. (1996). *Participación política evangélica en Colombia* (D. A. Bidegain, Ed.). Universidad de los Andes. Departamento de Historia. Tesis de Grado.
Herskovits. (1966). *The new world negro: Selected papers in Afroamerican studies.* Indiana University Press.
Hervieu-Léger, D. (1993). *La religion pour mémoire.* Cerf.

Hervieu-Léger, D. (1999). Religion as collective memory. In P. Berger (Ed.), *The desecularization of the world* (p. 79). Ethics and Public Policy Center and Wm. B. Eerdmans.
Hoffmann, B. (2015). *Die Konstruktion religiöser Freiheit in den Vereinigten Staaten* (Vol. Master of Law UZH Frühjahrssemester 2015) (P. D. M.A., Ed.). Universität Zürich Rechtswissenschaftliche Fakultät.
Hofstede, G. (2001). *Culture's consequences. Comparing values, behaviours, institutions and organizations across nations*. Sake.
Hofstede, G. (2014). *The Hofstede Centre Website.* Retrieved from http://geert-hofstede.com/dimensions.html
Hollinger, D. (1991). Enjoying God forever: An historical/sociological profile of the health and wealth gospel in the U.S.A. In P. Gee & J. Fulton (Eds.), *Religion and power, decline and growth: Sociological analyses of religion in Britain, Poland, and the Americas* (pp. 53–66). British Sociological Association Sociology of Religion Study Group.
Hopkins, S. (1972 [1913]). *A Treatise on the millennium.* Religion in America, series II. Arno Press.
Horton, M. (2009). *Christianity and the crash – The immanent frame.* Social Science Research Council. Retrieved from https://tif.ssrc.org/2009/12/23/christianity-and-the-crash/
Huntington, S. (1991). *The third wave: Democratization in the late twentieth century.* University of Oklahoma Press.
Hurd, E. S. (2011). Secularism and international relations theory. In J. Snyder (Ed.), *Religion and international relations theory.* Columbia University Press.
Inglehart, R., & Baker, W. (2000). Modernization, cultural change, and the persistence of traditional values. *American Sociological Review, 65*(1), 19–51.
Jenkins, P. (2006). *The new faces of Christianity: Believing the Bible in the Global South.* Oxford University Press.
Johnson, A. F. (1981). Revelation. In F. E. (Ed.), *The expositor's Bible commentary. Vol 12: Hebrews through Revelation* (p. 409). Zondervan Publishing House.
Johnson, R. B. (2017). Dialectical pluralism: A metaparadigm whose time has come. *Journal of Mixed Methods Research, 11*(2), 156–173.
Johnson, T. M., & Zurlo, G. A. (2016). *World Christian database.* Retrieved from: Center for the Study of Global Christianity at Gordon-Conwell Theological Seminary website: www.globalchristianity.org
Johnstone, N. (2006). The synagogue of Satan: Anti-Catholicism, false doctrine and the construction of contrariety. In N. Johnstone (Ed.), *The devil and demonism in early modern England.* Cambridge University Press.
Kalu, O. (2008). *African Pentecostalism: An introduction.* Oxford University Press.
King James Bible. (1769). *The Holy Bible, King James Version.* Cambridge Edition: 1769. Scripture quotations from The Authorized (King James) Version. Rights in the Authorized Version in the United Kingdom are vested in the Crown. Reproduced by permission of the Crown's patentee, Cambridge University Press.
Kippenberg, H. G. (2004). In praise of syncretism: The beginnings of Christianity conceived in the light of a diagnosis of modern culture. In A. M. Leopold & J. S. Jensen (Eds.), *Syncretism in religion: A reader.* Routledge.
Koch, B. (2009). *The prosperity Gospel and economic prosperity: Race, class, giving, and voting.* Doctoral dissertation. University Graduate School, Department of Sociology, Indiana University. Bloomington.
Köhrsen, J. (2017). Evangelikalismus in Lateinamerika. In F. Elwert, M. Radermacher, & J. Schlamelcher (Eds.), *Handbuch Evangelikalismus* (pp. 129–140). transcript Verlag.
Kraemer, H. (1962). Synkretismus. In *Die Religion in Geschichte und Gegenwart. Handworterbuch fur Theologie und Religionswissenschaft.* Dritte Auflage, Band 6, 563–568. Tubingen.
Kyle, R. (2006). *Evangelicism: An Americanized Christianity.* Transaction Publishers.
Lambsdorff, J. G. (1999). Corruption in empirical research—A review. In *9th International Anti-Corruption Conference, Durban, South Africa 10–15 December, 1999* (pp. 1–18). Durban.

Lambsdorff, J. G. (2006). Causes and consequences of corruption: What do we know from a cross-section of countries? In S. Rose-Ackerman (Ed.), *International handbook on the economics of corruption* (pp. 3–51). Edward Elgar.

Lamola, M. J. (2018). Marx, the Praxis of liberation theology, and the bane of religious epistemology. *Religions, 9*(74), 1–14.

La Porta, R., Lopez-de-Silanes, F., & Vishny, A. S. (1999). The quality of government. *Journal of Law, Economics and Organization, 15*(1), 222–279.

La Porta, R., Lopez-de-Silanes, F., Shleifer, A., & Vishny, R. (1997). Trust in large organisations. *American Economic Review, 137*(2), 333–338.

Leopold, A. M., & Jensen, J. S. (2004). *Syncretism in religion: A reader*. Routledge.

Levine, D. H. (1979). Religion and politics, politics and religion: an introduction. *Journal of Inter-American Studies and World Affairs, 21*(1), 5–29.

Levine, D. (1981). *Religion and politics in Latin America: The catholic church in Venezuela & Colombia.* Princeton Legacy Library.

Lingenthal, L. (2012). *Pentecostalism in Brazil: Churches, businesses, and political parties.* Kas International Reports.

Lozano, L. C. (2009). ¿Guerra espiritual evangélica o brujería indígena? Prácticas mágico-religiosas de los excombatientes paramilitares en contextos de guerra en Córdoba (Colombia). *Universitas humanística Universidad de Los Andes, 68*, 69–95.

Luther, M. (1532). *Ein tröstliche predigt von der zukunfft Christi und den vorgehenden zeichen des Jüngsten tags.* Wittenberg.

Mangalwadi, V. (2011). *The book that made your world. How the Bible created the soul of Western civilization*. Thomas Nelson.

Manow, P. (2004). *The good, the bad, and the ugly: Esping-Andersen's regime typology and the religious roots of the Western welfare state*. MPIfG Working Paper, No. 04/3, Max Planck Institute for the Study of Societies, Cologne. Retrieved from http://www.mpifg.de/pu/workpap/wp04-3/wp04-3.html

Manuel, P. C., Reardon, L. C., & Wilcox, C. (2006). *The catholic church and the nation-state: Comparative perspectives*. Georgetown University Press.

Martin, D. (1990). *Tongues of fire*. Oxford: Blackwell.

Martin, D. (1999). The evangelical upsurge and its political implications. In P. Berger (Ed.), *The desecularization of the world* (pp. 37–49). Ethics and Public Policy Center and Wm. B. Eerdmans.

Mauro, P. (1995). Corruption and growth. *Quarterly Journal of Economics, 110*(3), 681–712.

McCleary, R. M. (2013). *Protestantism and human capital in Guatemala and the Republic of Korea*. Asian Development Bank.

McConnell, D. (1988). *A different gospel: Biblical and historical insights into the word of faith movement*. Hendrickson Publishers.

Merriam-Webster. (n.d.). Ecumenical. In Merriam-Webster.com dictionary. Retrieved March 28, 2021, from https://www.merriam-webster.com/dictionary/ecumenical

Miller, D. (2007). *Global pentecostalism: The new face of Christian social engagement*. University of California Press.

Miller, N. (2012). *The religious roots of the first amendment*. Oxford University Press.

Miller, N. P. (2017). *500 years of protest and liberty: From Martin Luther to modern civil rights*. Pacific Press Publishing Association.

Mockus, A. (2001). *Cultura ciudadana, programa contra la violencia en Santa Fe de Bogotá, Colombia, 1995-1997*. Banco Interamericano de Desarrollo.

Mockus, A., Murraín, H., & Villa, M. (2012). *Antípodas de la violencia: Desafíos de cultura ciudadana para la crisis de (in)seguridad en América Latina*. Banco Interamericano de Desarrollo.

Murray, S. (2011). *Beyond tithing*. Wipf & Stock.

Nef, J. (2001). Government corruption in Latin America. In O. D. Gerald & E. Caiden (Eds.), *Where corruption lives* (pp. 159–174). Kumarian Press.

Newton, S. I. (1733). *Observations upon the prophecies of Daniel, and the apocalypse of St. John.*

O'Reilly, J., & Chalmers, M. (2014). The clergy sex abuse crisis and the legal responses. Oxford University Press. https://doi.org/10.1093/acprof:oso/9780199937936.001.0001

Pakkanen, P. (1996). *Interpreting early hellenistic religion: A study based on the mystery cult of Demeter and the Cult of Isis.* Papers and Monographs of the Finnish Institute at Athens 3. D. Layias and E. Souvatzidakis.

Paldam, M. (2001). Corruption and religion. Adding to the economic model. *Kyklos, 54*(2–3), 383–414.

Pauwels, C. F. (1963). Ecumenical theology and conversions. In A. D. Lee (Ed.), *Vatican II: The theological dimension.* The Thomist Press.

Pavan, P. (1989). Declaration on religious freedom. In H. Vorgrimler (Ed.), *Commentary on the documents of Vatican II.* Crossroads Publishing.

Pew Research Center. (2014). *Religion in Latin America. Widespread change in a historically catholic region.* Retrieved from https://www.pewforum.org/2014/11/13/religion-in-latin-america/

Philpott, D. (2001). *Revolutions in sovereignty: How ideas shaped modern international relations.* Princeton University Press.

Plumptre, J. (1818). *Three discourses on tithes: No. I. On trust in God. No. II. On the origin of tithes, and tithes under the law. No. III. On tithes under the Gospel.* Printed by J. Hodson, The Making of the Modern World. https://link.gale.com/apps/doc/U0103407763/MOME?u=gallen&sid=MOME&xid=8c349501

Popovich, J. (1994). *Orthodox faith and life in Christ* (A. Gerostergios, Trans.). Institute for Byzantine and Modern Greek Studies.

Putnam. (1993). *Making democracy work: Civic traditions in modern Italy.* Princeton University Press.

Radmacher, E., Allen, R., & House, H. (1999). *Nelson's new illustrated Bible commentary.* Thomas Nelson.

Ramírez, C. J. (2009). Laïcité, liberté de religion et État laïque. Les étapes de la laïcisation cubaine. *Archives de sciences sociales des religions, 54*(146), 157–182.

Ratzinger, J., & Pera, M. (2006). *Without roots: The West, Relativism, Christianity, Islam.* Basic Books.

Robbins, J. (2004). The globalization of Pentecostal and charismatic Christianity. *Annual Review of Anthropology, 33*, 117–143.

Roy, O. (2010). *Holy ignorance: When religion and culture part ways.* Columbia University Press.

Rudolph, K. (2004). Syncretism: From theological invective to a concept in the study of religion. In A. M. Leopold & J. S. Jensen (Eds.), *Syncretism in religion: A reader.* New York: Routledge.

Sánchez, Y. (1992). *Religiosidad cotidiana en la narrativa reciente hispanocaribeña* (Vol. 3). (S. S. Hispánicos, A. L. Pozuelo, & Y. Sánchez, Eds.) Hispanica Helvetica.

Schäfer, H. (1997). Oh Lord of heaven, give us power on earth! Fundamentalism and charisma: The reconquest of the field of action in Latin America. *Mesoamerica, 18*(33), 125–146.

Schäfer, H. (2006). "Die" Pfingstbewegung in Lateinamerika...? Zur Untersuchung des Verhältnisses zwischen religiöser Praxis und gesellschaftlichen Strukturen. *Zeitschrift für Religionswissenschaft*, 53–82.

Scheper-Hughes, N., & Scheper, J. (2015). The final conversion of Pope Francis. *Berkeley Review of Latin American Studies*, 13–67.

Self, C. E. (2009). Formación de conciencia, conversión y convergencia: Reflexiones acerca de las comunidades eclesiales de base y el emergente movimiento pentecostal en América Latina. In M. Bergunder (Ed.), *Movimiento pentecostal y comunidades de base en América Latina* (pp. 84–103). Universidad de Heidelberg.

Selling, J. A. (2016). *Reframing catholic theological ethics* (1st ed.). Oxford University Press.

Selling, J. A. (2018). Reframing catholic theological ethics: Summary and spplication. (A. Abram, Ed.). *Religions, 8*(203), 5–13.

Sepúlveda, J. (2009). Movimiento pentecostal y Teología de la Liberación: Dos manifestaciones de la Obra del Espíritu Santo para la renovación de la Iglesia. In M. Bergunder (Ed.), *Movimiento pentecostal y comunidades de base en América Latina* (pp. 104–117). Universidad de Heidelberg.

Serra, D. (2006). Empirical determinants of corruption: A sensitivity analysis. *Public Choice, 126* (1-2), 225–256.

Shah, T. S. & Philpott, D., (2011). The fall and rise of religion in international relations. History and theory. In J. Snyder (Ed.), *Religion and international relations theory* (pp. 24–59). Columbia University Press.

Sharpe, M. (2014). Name it and claim it: Prosperity Gospel and the global Pentecostal reformation. In M. Clarke (Ed.), *Handbook of research on development and religion* (pp. 164–179). Edwar Elgar.

Smith, C. (1991). *The emergence of liberation theology. Radical religion and social movement theory*. University of Chicago Press.

Snyder, J. (2011). *Religion and international relations theory*. Columbia University Press.

Spica, M. A. (2018). Pluralism with syncretism: A perspective from Latin American religious Diversity. *Open Theology, 4*, 236–245. https://doi.org/10.1515/opth-2018-0017.

Spittler, R. P. (2009). ¿Los pentecostales y carismáticos son fundamentalistas? Una visión general acerca del uso americano de estas categorías. En: Movimiento pentecostal y comunidades de base en América Latina La recepción de conceptos teológicos de liberación a través de la teología pentecostal. In M. Bergunder (Ed.), *Movimiento pentecostal y comunidades de base en América Latina* (pp. 51–69). Universidad de Heidelberg.

Stefanovic, R. (2009). *The revelation of Jesus Christ, commentary on the book of revelation*. Andrews University Press.

Stewart, C., & Shaw, R. (1994). *Syncretism/anti-syncretism: The politics of religious synthesis*. European Association of Social Anthropologists. Routledge.

Stulz, R. M., & Williamson, R. (2003). Culture, openness, and finance. *Journal of Financial Economics, 70*(3), 313–349.

Taggart, W. C. (1998). *The three parts of Babylon: Teaching a historicist interpretation of the Leopardlike, Lamblike and Scarlet Beasts (Rev 13 and 16:19 as Reflected in Rev 17) Based upon the Douglas Waterhouse Construct* (Vol. Dissertations. Paper 723) (U. A. Information, Ed.). Andrews University Press.

Tappert, T. G. (2017). *Selected writings of Martin Luther 1520-1523* (Vol. 2). Fortress Press.

The Lutheran World Federation (LWF) & The Pontifical Council for Promoting Christian Unity (PCPCU). (2013). *From Conflict to Communion. Lutheran-Catholic Common Commemoration of the Reformation in 2017. Report of the Lutheran-Roman Catholic Commission on Unity*. Evangelische Verlagsanstalt GmbH.

Todd, M., & Zurlo, G. (2016). *World Christian database*. Brill. Retrieved from www.globalchristianity.org

Towns, J. (2008). The origin of prosperity gospel: Part II: perfectionism, *Talking Pentecostalism*. Retrieved from http://talkingpentecostalism.blogspot.com.au/2008/04/origin-of-prosperity-doctrine-in.html

Treisman, D. (2000). The causes of corruption: A cross-national study. *Journal of Public Economics, 76*(3), 399–457.

Uildriks, N. (2009). *Policing insecurity: police reform, security, and human rights in Latin America*. Lexington Books.

Uribe, C. A. (2003). Magia, brujería y violencia en Colombia. *Revista de estudios Sociales, 15*, 59–73.

Van Kersbergen, K. (1995). *Social capitalism: A study of Christian democracy and the welfare state*. Routledge.

Vatican. (2018). *Catechism of the Catholic Church. Catechism of the Catholic Church - Part Three: Life In Christ, Section Two: The Ten Commandments*. Retrieved from http://www.vatican.va/archive/ccc_css/archive/catechism/command.htm

Verba, S. (1965). Comparative political culture. In L. W. Pye & S. Verba (Eds.), *Political culture and political development*. Princeton University Press.

Volonté, C. (2015). Culture and corporate governance: The influence of language and religion in Switzerland. *Management International Review, 55*, 77–118.

Webster, J. (2019). Denominations as (theological) institutions: An afterword. *Anthropological Quarterly, 92*(4), 1123–1134.

White, E. (1888). *The great controversy between Christ and Satan during the Christian dispensation*. Pacific Press.

Wilde, M., Geraty, K., Nelson, L., & Bowman, E. (2010). Religious economy or organizational field? Predicting Bishops' votes at the second Vatican council. *American Sociological Review, 75*(4), 586–606. https://doi.org/10.1177/0003122410368927.

Williams, E. (1998). The essential rights and liberties of protestants. In E. Sandoz (Ed.), *Political Sermons of the American founding era* (pp. 1730–1805). Liberty Fund.

Wilson, C. G. (2004). The Caribbean: marvelous Cradle-Hammock and painful Cornucopia. In A. M. Leopold & J. S. Jensen (Eds.), *Syncretism in religion: A reader*. Routledge.

Wisconsin Evangelical Lutheran Synod. (2018). *Doctrinal statements: Antichrist*. Retrieved from https://wels.net/about-wels/what-we-believe/doctrinal-statements/antichrist/

Witte, J. (2002). *Law and protestantism: The legal teachings of the Lutheran reformation*. Cambridge: University Press.

Wolgast, E. (1996). Speyer, protestation of. In H. J. Hillerbrand (Ed.), *The Oxford encyclopedia of the reformation* (Vol. 4). Oxford University Press. trans.

Woodberry, R. (2012). The missionary roots of liberal democracy. *American Political Science Review (APSR), 106*(2), 244–274.

Woodruff, C. (2006). Measuring institutions. In S. Rose-Ackerman (Ed.), *International handbook on the economics of corruption* (pp. 105–124). Edward Elgar.

Wrenn, M. (2019). Consecrating capitalism: The United States prosperity gospel and neoliberalism. *Journal of Economic Issues/Association for Evolutionary Economics, 53*(2), 425–432. https://doi.org/10.1080/00213624.2019.1594528.

Zilla, C. (2020). *Evangelicals and politics in Brazil. The relevance of religious change in Latin America. SWP Research Paper. Stiftung Wissenschaft und Politik*. German Institute for International and Security Affairs.

# Chapter 11
# Language and Religion

*In the beginning was the Word, and the Word was with God, and the Word was God. The same was in the beginning with God. All things were made by him; and without him was not any thing made that was made (King James Bible, 1769, John, 1:1–3).*

The importance of studying language in order to understand social phenomena is not new. The last decades have witnessed a growing academic interest in the study of language and of discourse analysis in the social sciences (Heracleous, 2006). Consequently, "...language (and language use) is increasingly being understood as the most important phenomenon, accessible for empirical investigation, in social and organizational research" (Alvesson & Karreman, 2000, p. 1126).

In this sense, studying language in practice has played an important role since ancient times. The biblical citation at the beginning of this section, first written thousands of years ago, directly links language to the Creation and the divine. This notion is currently recognised in systemic approaches to language, where "language is action" and "creates realities" (Foucault, 1972; Echavarria, 2006, pp. 34–36).

Austin (1962) also challenged the traditional notion of "to say something is just to state something" and instead posited that "to say something...is to do something" (p. 12). Likewise, "language is not a medium for representing the world, but for intervening in it" (Argyris et al. as cited in Romme, 2003, p. 563). These notions have led to recognising the prominent role of language as a means of shaping institutions and society. Furthermore, ample theoretical and empirical evidence points to language as a suitable proxy for culture (Stulz & Williamson, 2003; Grinblatt & Keloharju, 2001; Ronen & Shenkar, 1985; Hofstede, 1980 as cited in Volonté, 2015, p. 83). Language, religion, and legal origins are all highly correlated and associated with particular institutional performances (Chakrabarti et al., 2008; Volonté, 2015; Mazar, 2008).



J. García Portilla, *"Ye Shall Know Them by Their Fruits"*, Contributions to Economics, https://doi.org/10.1007/978-3-030-78498-0_11

## 11.1 The Role of the Bible in Shaping Language and Societies

The Bible has been translated into numerous vernacular languages:

### *11.1.1 German*

Several studies have discussed the profound influence of the Reformation on the spread and standardisation of the German language through Luther's translation of the Bible (Volz & Greenslide, 1963; Besch, 1999; Greenslade, 1963). It was mainly through the vernacular translation of the Bible that people learned to read and that human capital was enhanced. This process has resulted in higher literacy rates among Protestants to this day (Becker & Woessmann, 2009). Consequently, the language of Luther's translation became more than part of German national heritage, first for Protestants, and later penetrating every German-speaking home (Ritter, 1963).

### *11.1.2 English*

Similarly to German, the English language had almost no prestige before the Protestant Reformation. Later, different dialects and different Bible translations challenging the unity of the English kingdom motivated King James to commission a scholarly and reputable translation of the Scriptures. The Authorised (King James) Version (KJV) has served ever since as a unifier and dominant cultural conditioner in English-speaking thought, language, and literature (Lewis, 1969; McGrath, 2001; Daniell, 2003).

### *11.1.3 Other Native Languages*

Bible translations have helped to keep alive native languages otherwise threatened with extinction across the world (Moor & Voinov, 2015).

### *11.1.4 Latin, Roman Empire, and Roman Catholicism*

The Roman Empire spread Latin. Celtic speakers, for example, adopted the Latin imperial language and thus gave birth to French (Moor & Voinov, 2015). Moreover,

Latin never died but evolved into Roman languages descending from Vulgar Latin (e.g. Spanish, French, Italian, Portuguese, Rumanian, Catalan, Romansh) (Wright, 1988). Furthermore, the Roman Church-State inherited Latin as its official language. However, the Vulgate Latin translation of the Bible only became official for Roman Catholicism at the Council of Trent (1545–1563), which was prompted by the Protestant Reformation. The Latin translation was intended only for the clergy and theologians (Lampe, 1969).

Consequently, the Roman Church-State condemned—and sought to impede—any effort to bring the Holy Scriptures within reach of common people, in order to prevent what happened in Germany and England. The fate suffered by those Reformers who translated the Bible into Spanish (Reina and Valera) was a common one: They were persecuted and exiled from Spain (Hauben, 1967).

To uphold the Catholic Church-State, the governments of several Latin American countries banned Protestant services and the printing of the Bible in Spanish until the last century (Gill, 1998). Thus, the influence of the Bible on Latin languages has been limited. Figure 10.1 illustrates one example: The content of the Roman Catholic Catechism Decalogue in "Catholic" languages (e.g. Spanish and Portuguese) differs from that in "Protestant" languages (e.g. English and German). In "Protestant languages" the Ten Commandments in the Catholic Catechism resemble more the Bible's wording (King James Bible, 1769, Exodus 20, 1–17) than in "Catholic languages" (Sect. 10.4.1.1).

**Empirical Expectation**

11). *I expect German and English-speaking countries to be more competitive/transparent than those speaking Roman languages. German and English are associated with the Reformation, whereas Roman languages are associated with the status quo of the Roman Empire,* i.e. *Roman Church-State.*

## References


Alvesson, M., & Karreman, D. (2000). Varieties of discourse: On the study of organizations through discourse analysis. *Human Relations, 53*(9), 1125–1149.

Austin, J. (1962). *How to do things with words*. Harvard University Press.

Becker, S., & Woessmann, L. (2009). Was Weber wrong? A human capital theory of protestant economic history. *Quarterly Journal of Economics, 124*(2), 531–596.

Besch, W. (1999). *Die Rolle Luthers in der deutschen Sprachgeschichte*. Universitätsverlag C. Winter.

Chakrabarti, R., Gupta-Mukherjee, S., & Jayaraman, N. (2008). Mars–Venus marriages: Culture and cross-border M&A. *Journal of International Business Studies, 40*(2), 216–236.

Daniell, D. (2003). *The Bible in English*. Yale University Press.

Echavarria, R. (2006). *Ontología del lenguaje*. Comunicaciones Noreste Ltda.

Foucault, M. (1972). *The archaeology of knowledge*. Routledge.

Gill, A. (1998). *Rendering unto Caesar: the Catholic Church and the state in Latin America*. Chicago University Press.
Greenslade, S. (1963). *The Cambridge history of the Bible: The West from the reformation to the present day*. Cambridge University Press.
Grinblatt, M., & Keloharju, M. (2001). How distance, language and culture influence stockholdings and trades. *Journal of Finance, 56*(3), 1053–1073.
Hauben, P. (1967). *Three Spanish Heretics and the reformation*. Librairie Droz.
Heracleous, L. (2006). *Discourse, interpretation, organization*. Cambridge University Press.
King James Bible. (1769). *The Holy Bible, King James Version*. Cambridge Edition: 1769. Scripture quotations from The Authorized (King James) Version. Rights in the Authorized Version in the United Kingdom are vested in the Crown. Reproduced by permission of the Crown's patentee, Cambridge University Press.
Lampe, G. (1969). *The Cambridge history of the Bible* (Vol. 2). Cambridge University Press.
Lewis, C. (1969). The literary impact of the authorised version. In W. Hooper (Ed.), *Selected literary essays*. Cambridge University Press.
Mazar, H. (2008). *An analysis of regulatory frameworks for wireless communications, societal concerns and risk: the case of radio frequency (RF) allocation and licensing*. PhD thesis, Middlesex University.
McGrath, A. (2001). *In the beginning: The story of the King James Bible and how it changed a nation, a language, and a culture*. Hodder & Stoughton.
Moor, M., & Voinov, V. (2015). *Language vitality through Bible translation* (Berkeley insights in linguistics and semiotics) (Vol. 9, 5th ed.). Peter Lang Inc., International Academic.
Ritter, G. (1963). *Luther: His life and work*. Harper and Row Publishers.
Romme, A. (2003). Difference: Organization design. *Organization Science, 14*(5), 558–573.
Ronen, S., & Shenkar, O. (1985). Clustering countries on attitudinal dimensions: A review and synthesis. *Academy of Management Review, 10*(3), 435–454.
Stulz, R. M., & Williamson, R. (2003). Culture, openness, and finance. *Journal of Financial Economics, 70*(3), 313–349.
Volonté, C. (2015). Culture and corporate governance: The influence of language and religion in Switzerland. *Management International Review, 55*, 77–118.
Volz, H., & Greenslide, S. e. (1963). *The Cambridge history of the Bible* (Vol. 3). Cambridge University Press.
Wright, R. (1988). Did Latin die? *Omnibus* (15), 27–29.

# Chapter 12
# Environment/Geography and Prosperity/Transparency *(E), (4), (7)*

This section analyses the prosperity-environment/geography nexus and the corruption-environment/geography nexus. It concludes the theoretical review of this study.

## 12.1 Prosperity and Environment/Geography *(4), (7)*

A direct empirical relationship exists between the environment/geography and the prosperity of nations (Diamond, 1997; Sachs, 2001). Diamond (1997) found that several environmental factors enabled European states to prosper and conquer other continents. Such aspects include the availability of docile animals for domestication, access to a storable vegetal protein, or a favourable climate and environment (Diamond, 1997). Similarly, Sachs (2001) observes:

> Perhaps the strongest empirical relationship in the wealth and poverty of nations is the one between ecological zones and per capita income. Economies in tropical ecozones are nearly everywhere poor, while those in temperate ecozones are generally rich. And when temperate economies are not rich there is tipically a straightforward explanation, such as decades under communism or extreme geographical isolation (Sachs, 2001, p. 1).[1]

After controlling for the quality of institutions, Sachs (2003) empirically explains cross-country patterns of national income. The author claims that geography and environment affect per capita income even more directly than institutions. He found "a systematic gradation of average per capita income, with high latitudes both North and South showing higher per capita income than low, tropical latitudes" (Sachs, 2001, p. 4). Furthermore, Sachs (2003) observes that empirical studies:





J. García Portilla, *"Ye Shall Know Them by Their Fruits"*, Contributions to Economics, https://doi.org/10.1007/978-3-030-78498-0_12

> have demonstrated that levels of per capita income, economic growth, and other economic and demographic dimensions are strongly correlated with geographical and ecological variables such as climate zone, disease ecology, and distance from the coast (Gallup et al., 1998; Mellinger et al., 2000; Gallup & Sachs, 2001; Sachs & Malaney, 2002, as cited in Sachs, 2003, pp. 1–2).[2]

Latitude "impacts economic activity through insolation, precipitation, and other climatic factors" (Sachs, 2001, p. 4). Consequently, countries located in the inter-tropical or equatorial zone tend to be poorer than those located in temperate zones. Sachs argued that lower agricultural yields and greater mortality due to tropical diseases, for example, explain lower prosperity levels near the equator. For instance, lower food productivity in the equatorial zone is well documented due to factors such as: (1) the fragility and poverty of the inter-tropical soils, which lose their fertility rapidly; (2) a high prevalence of parasites and pests associated with the high biodiversity of the equatorial zone; (3) high costs on net photosynthesis due to high respiration and metabolic processes; and (4) enormous fluctuations in water availability (Gallup & Sachs, 2001; Sachs, 2003; Garcia, 2003, 2012).

Therefore, Brown and Lall (2006) explained 60% of per capita GDP variance across countries in terms of rainfall statistics and a binary variable accounting for war. Their analysis of global datasets shows a statistically significant relationship between greater rainfall variability and lower GDP per capita. The authors demonstrated that climate variability, notably rainfall variability, is a significant determinant of economic growth. The amount and variability of rainfall were significant factors in the prosperity "of early agricultural economies and contributed to the differences in the wealth of nations since the early 19th century" (Brown & Lall, 2006, p. 315). Furthermore, the authors claim that climate variability impacts can often be mitigated.

The relationship between latitude and savings provides another example of this association between environment/geography and prosperity. Ecosystem dynamics in the equatorial zone include high biodiversity and rapid nutrient cycling due to high temperatures, with low nutrient accumulation in soil (e.g. the Amazon forest). In contrast, seasonal dynamics and lower temperatures in temperate zones account for slow nutrient cycling and biomass accumulation. Temperate seasonal ecosystems, therefore, tend to accumulate more biomass in less biodiversity. Examples of this phenomenon include big sequoias in forests, the proliferation of large algae in the oceans, and big fat mammals. In comparison, equatorial ecosystems are highly biodiverse, but their individuals are much smaller than their temperate counterparts. Temperature and speed differences in nutrient cycles greatly determine the ethology of organisms. For example, temperate species must "save" fat and energy for winter (in order to prevent death). In contrast, equatorial species tend to consume the available resources immediately due to high competition (MacArthur, 1972; Garcia, 2003).

---

A similar dynamics may have encouraged human beings in temperate zones to store goods (e.g. grains, cheese, jam) for winter, and later to accumulate and reinvest the excess capital. In contrast, the permanent availability of natural resources (in the absence of seasons) means that humans in the equatorial zone tend to consume rather than store and invest.

This example might lead one to the assumption that the temperate countries located in the tropics of Cancer and Capricorn and beyond would exhibit better prosperity indicators on the whole. Thus, countries in the northern and southern hemispheres should be all prosperous and less corrupt than those on the equator. However, Russia and other former Soviet Union countries, located in the northern hemisphere, would be exceptions to this rule. Acemoglu and Robinson (2012) criticise the environment/geography approach to prosperity for its narrow scope. While explaining the prosperity differences between continents broadly, geographical determinism cannot account for variations *within* continents themselves (Acemoglu & Robinson, 2012).

Yet, in the Americas, this assumption would suffice to understand the prosperity of the USA and Canada and, to a lesser extent, of Brazil, Chile, Uruguay, and Argentina—in contrast with the poorer countries located on the equator (e.g. Venezuela). However, environmental and geographical determinism theory would not explain why South American countries (beyond the equator—e.g. Argentina) have lower prosperity and higher corruption rates or inequality than those of North America. Thus, although important, geography and the environment are merely two pieces of a giant puzzle. This is exactly where institutions (including religion) and other historical factors contribute to formulating feasible explanations (see Sect. 8.2.3).

## 12.2 Corruption and Environment/Geography *(4), (7)*

The trajectories by which geographical and environmental factors might affect corruption are mainly indirect and occur via economic development (Treisman, 2000, p. 430). In this respect, an abundance of natural resources (i.e. fuels and minerals) tends to generate conditions for rent-seeking and corruption (Leite & Weidemann, 1999; Ades & Di Tella, 1999). Specifically, an abundance of oil is found to increase the level of corruption in a country (Montinola and Jackman as cited in Lambsdorff, 2006, pp. 21–22). Venezuela, Nigeria, or Arab countries are examples of countries located on the equator characterised by an abundance of natural resources and by high levels of corruption.

Moreover, more natural resources (e.g. fuel) do not necessarily mean better environment quality (e.g. climate). Environment quality indicators are what Brown and Lall (2006), Sachs (2001), Diamond (1997), and others have associated with prosperity, and thus with transparency (Treisman, 2000). The *Environmental Performance Index (EPI)* aggregates some of those indicators besides others (see Sect. 5.6).

**Empirical Expectation**

12). *I expect a robust positive relationship between the EPI and prosperity/ transparency. However, I do not expect the EPI to explain the entire variability of GCI/CPI.*

This chapter closes the theoretical description of the most prominent corruption/ prosperity determinants referred to in Fig. 2.1. The next chapters explain the research paradigms, design, and methodology of this study.

## References


Acemoglu, D., & Robinson, J. (2012). *Why nations fail. The origins of power, prosperity and poverty*. Crown Business.

Ades, A., & Di Tella, R. (1999). Rents, competition, and corruption. *American Economic Review, 89*, 982–994.

Brown, C., & Lall, U. (2006). Water and economic development: The role of variability and a framework for resilience. *Natural Resources Forum, 30*, 306–317.

Diamond, J. (1997). *Guns, germs, and steel. The fates of human societies*. W. W. Norton.

Gallup, J. L., Sachs, J. D., & Mellinger, A. D. (1998) *Geography and economic development*. In Annual World Bank Conference on Development Economics (April), The World Bank.

Gallup, J. L., & Sachs, J. D. (2001). The economic burden of malaria. *The Supplement to The American Journal of Tropical Medicine & Hygiene, 64*(1,2).

Garcia, J. (2003). Carbon fixation in soils and climate change in peatlands and high mountain "paramo" ecosystems. Original in Spanish: *Análisis del potencial de emisión de dióxido de carbono del páramo de Chingaza y lineamientos para su conservación en el contexto del Mecanismo de Desarrollo Limpio*. (Trabajo de Grado Carrera de Ecología. Facultad de Estudios Ambientales y Rurales. Universidad Javeriana.

Garcia, J. (2012). Climate change in mountain ecosystems. An Andean perspective at IPROMO 2012. *Mountain Research Initiative Newsletter, 7*, 48–49.

Lambsdorff, J. G. (2006). Causes and consequences of corruption: What do we know from a cross-section of countries? In S. Rose-Ackerman (Ed.), *International handbook on the economics of corruption* (pp. 3–51). Edward Elgar.

Leite, C., & Weidemann, J. (1999). *Does mother nature corrupt? Natural resources, corruption, and economic growth*. International Monetary Fund Working Paper, 99/85.

MacArthur, R. (1972). *Patterns in the distribution of species*. Princeton University Press.

Mellinger, A. D., Sachs, J. D., & Gallup, J. L. (2000). Climate, coastal proximity, and development. In G. L. Clark, M. P. Feldman, & M. S. Gertler (Eds.), *Oxford handbook of economic geography*. Oxford University Press.

Sachs, J. (2001). *Tropical underdevelopment*. National Bureau of Economic Research., Working Paper, 8119, NBER, 1–37.

Sachs, J. (2003). *Institutions don't rule: direct effects of geography on per capita income*. Bureau of Economic Research Working Paper, 9490 (NBER), 1–13.

Treisman, D. (2000). The causes of corruption: A cross-national study. *Journal of Public Economics, 76*(3), 399–457.

# Part IV
# Research Paradigms, Methodology, and Research Design

This part provides a general methodological overview of the study. However, specific protocols for each research component are included at the beginning of each chapter. Before describing the various methods, what follows introduces the paradigms underpinning this study.

# Chapter 13
# Applied Research Paradigms

The paradigms and biases underlying this study reflect its dialectical pluralism (DP) (mixed methods research) and a complex thinking perspective.

## 13.1 Research Paradigms

### *13.1.1 Research Paradigm 1 (Dialectical Pluralism)*

Dialectical Pluralism (DP) is a broad paradigm with manifold benefits for developing the meta-paradigm required in this research. The DP is an approach to research and policy that considers multiple paradigms carefully, thoroughly, and respectfully (Johnson, 2017). The basic idea behind the meta-paradigmatic perspective of this study is.

> to empathetically and thoughtfully work with more than one paradigm (or perspective or theory) to produce a new, more complex 'whole.' The whole might be mostly divergent, mostly convergent, or, most often, a combination of divergent and convergent perspectives, practices, values, and assumptions (J. C. Greene as cited in Johnson, 2017, p. 159).

This mixed methods study applies DP as its primary paradigm. Hence, it investigates the possible influence of religion on prosperity from multiple paradigmatic, theoretical, and methodological perspectives.

Chapter 5 reveals that the main weakness of mainstream theories attempting to explain prosperity is that they tend to reject approaches from other disciplines. However, each of the explanatory theories employed in this study to understand prosperity imbalances between the investigated countries may contain a grain of truth (Moran et al., 2007, p. 3). Therefore, gaining a comprehensive and systemic understanding of the situation is vital and requires the explanatory theories of prosperity to be synthesised in a general model.



J. García Portilla, *"Ye Shall Know Them by Their Fruits"*, Contributions to Economics, https://doi.org/10.1007/978-3-030-78498-0_13

The traditional approach of mutual rejection of separate disciplines demonstrates the need for a transdisciplinary paradigm to the causes of the historical prosperity imbalance in Europe and the Americas. A model encompassing different theories in a holistic and transdisciplinary manner is necessary in order to understand the whole picture. Likewise, this also allows the inclusion of more variables that potentially influence prosperity. In fact, "the most productive conceptual frameworks are often those that integrate different approaches, lines of investigation, or theories that no one had previously connected" (Maxwell, 2013, p. 35).

Consequently, DP is an ideal paradigm for the aims and concerns of this study. This approach not only respects "different perspectives, but it is also designed to strategically enable adherents to carefully consider differences *and* possible 'syntheses' of their knowledge, abilities, and values". This kind of synthesis is dynamic (Johnson, 2017, p. 161).

### *13.1.2 Research Paradigm 2 (Complex Thinking)*

This study adopts the paradigm of complexity, since this opposes, yet contains mechanicist and systemic paradigms (Morin, 2001). Historically, the complex thinking paradigm emerged as an evolutive result of systemic thinking, which arose from mechanicism (Zuñiga & Tarride, 2010). These three approaches are reviewed separately below in light of this study.

**Mechanicist Paradigm**
One of the principles characterising the mechanicist paradigm is the concept of linear causality. This principle is a standard paradigm, which also guides traditional positivist science, including economics. Many prosperity theories (especially within the neoclassical economic approach) fall into this traditional paradigm (Chap. 5).

**Systemic Paradigm**
The systemic paradigm rejects the dominant reductionism of the mechanisist paradigm. It focuses on the interrelations between a system's constituents and those between that system and its environment. It favours a holistic view and thus maintains the principle of generality that also characterises the mechanicist paradigm. However, it also recognises the systems' particularities (Zuñiga & Tarride, 2010, pp. 1115–1116).

Theories revised in this study such as environment/geography (Sachs, 2003; Diamond, 1997) or institutions (Acemoglu & Robinson, 2012) (Chap. 4) have incorporated elements of the systemic paradigm. By including historical components and following unconventional approaches, these theories lay the foundations for systemic explanations of the origins of prosperity. However, by denying other disciplines' approaches, they remain "trapped" in the mechanicist paradigm, thus accepting monocausal, linear explanations.

**Complexity Paradigm**
The complexity paradigm overcomes the adoption of either the mechanicist or the systemic approach in favour of a dialogic, complementary perspective (Zuñiga & Tarride, 2010). Accordingly, this study applies a linear, mechanicist approach (e.g. regressions) combined with systemic models (see QCA and CDA). Yet, the various theories (Chap. 5) are revised and the results analysed from a dialogic perspective. Likewise, complex logic leads the synthesis, analysis, and conclusions which are drawn. Therefore, this research rejects neither the mechanicist nor the systemic paradigm. On the contrary, it brings these paradigms into dialogue under the "complexity paradigm".

Below I briefly describe the researcher's scientific and personal paradigm biases.

## 13.2 Paradigm Biases

### *13.2.1 Scientific*

In order of importance, according to the Philosophy of Social Sciences Inventory (PSSI) scoring test, the scientific paradigms guiding this study are: Mixed research methods: 6.0; Idealism: 5.3; Quantitative research methods: 4.5; Nomothetic methods: 4.5; Rationalism: 4.0; Empiricism: 4.0; Fallibilism: 3.6; Ethical realism: 3.5; Qualitative research methods: 3.5; Humanism: 3.5; Ontological relativism: 3.5.

#### 13.2.1.1 Biases

Several types of bias can threaten the validity of any meta-study (e.g. language, location, time, outcome, funding) (Hussain et al., 2019). Publication bias can be a salient issue that occurs when the researcher is favourably oriented towards studies with statistically significant results, while rejecting those that are contrary to expectations. Publication bias could also lead to an overestimation of effects in meta-analysis. Likewise, confirmatory bias "is the tendency to emphasize and believe experiences which support one's views and to ignore or discredit those which do not" (Mahoney, 1977, p. 161). To counter these threats and limitations, this study applied some of the strategies recommended by Brown et al. (2017) and Hussain et al. (2019):

- A systematic review of empirical studies in journals of multiple electronic databases (Hussain et al., 2019).
- Triangulation for crosschecking information through multiple sources and procedures (see Sect. 17.6.3.3).
- Peer review processes as a source through which quality checks can be improved (Brown et al., 2017). This research was submitted to peer reviewers and critical friends (see Appendix 5).

- Publication in Open Access Journals. Online, "open access journals improve the readability and reduce publication bias" (Hussain et al., 2019, p. 59; Brown et al., 2017). Some sections of this study were published in an open access peer-reviewed journal (Published: 1 June 2019; Garcia Portilla, 2019).
- Sharing the data and making it publically available would reduce the probability of publication bias (Brown et al., 2017; Hussain et al., 2019). Some sections and appendices of this study have been publically available on the website of the open access peer-reviewed journal since June 2019 (Garcia Portilla, 2019).
- Multi-lingual analysis (Spanish, English, French, and German) of the literature and primary data (i.e. interviews) instead of ignoring studies that are not published in the researcher's mother tongue (Egger et al., 1997; Hussain et al., 2019).

### *13.2.2 Personal*

Maxwell's textbook "Qualitative Research Design" states:

> Traditionally, what you bring to the research from your own background and identity has been treated as "bias," something whose influence needs to be *eliminated* from the design, rather than a valuable component of it. This has been true to some extent even in qualitative research, despite the fact that qualitative researchers have long recognized that in this field, the researcher *is* the instrument of the research. In opposition to the traditional view, . . .[s] eparating your research from other aspects of your life cuts you off from a major source of insights, hypotheses, and validity checks (Maxwell, 2013, pp. 37–38).

Therefore, the explicit incorporation of the researcher's personal identity and experience has gained extensive theoretical and philosophical support (e.g. Berg & Smith, 1988; Denzin & Lincoln, 2000; Jansen & Peshkin, 1992 as cited in Maxwell, 2013, p. 38). In fact,

> . . .the most admirable scholars within the scholarly community . . . do not split their work from their lives. They seem to take both too seriously to allow such dissociation, and they want to use each for the enrichment of the other (Wright Mills as cited in Maxwell, 2013, p. 38).

Studies identifying their author's personal positions are praised, among others, as follows: "Seen as virtuous, subjectivity is something to capitalize on rather than to exorcise" (Glesne & Peshkin as cited in Maxwell, 2013, p. 38). Or "mine your experience, there is potential gold there!" (Strauss as cited in Maxwell, 2013, p. 38). Maxwell (2013) therefore proposes a particular technique for incorporating the researcher's subjectivity and experience in a study: "researcher identity memo". This acknowledges the researcher's personal perspective and stance. Taking Maxwell's cue, I have included a positionality memo in Appendix 5 to ensure that my perspective does not unduly influence the analysis and coding, in particular in the qualitative part. Among others, Appendix 5 includes the strategies for objective data treatment, and amplifies the following personal information about the researcher:

#### 13.2.2.1 Personal Experiences from Each Belief System

**Roman Catholicism**
- I grew up in a Roman Catholic family in Colombia (a strongly Roman Catholic country);
- I was educated for 12 years in Roman Catholic schools and received Catholic religious instruction;
- I studied for five years at a Pontifical Jesuit university.

**Atheism (after being a firm Catholic believer)**
- I spent ten years living as a self-confessed atheist who embraced atheistic values;
- I socialised in and applied the paradigm of scientific materialism (positivism).

**Dissenting Protestantism (after being a convinced atheist)**
- I spent 12 years living as converted, free Christian and I have studied the Bible on my own;
- I have lived and studied in the United Kingdom and Switzerland (two historically Protestant countries) (Inglehart & Baker, 2000).

#### 13.2.2.2 Strategies for Objective Data Treatment

The following strategies were employed to ensure objective data treatment: (1) Two independent quantitative researchers were engaged to select the variables using solely quantitative criteria (e.g. cross-validation) in regressions and QCA. (2) Two independent qualitative researchers were engaged to impartially validate the qualitative coding (a total of four independent researchers) (see Appendix 5). (3) The selected variables (chosen from a pool of more than 70 indicators) were associated with qualitative codes to prioritise them from a mixed methods perspective. (4) The quantitative and qualitative (QCA) databases and the twelve codes applied comparatively to the four case studies' qualitative data are available for inspection (see Supplementary Materials). However, the names and original interviews conducted as part of this study will not be made publicly available to protect the interviewees' identities.

## References

Acemoglu, D., & Robinson, J. (2012). *Why nations fail. The origins of power, prosperity and poverty*. Crown Business.
Berg, D. N., & Smith, K. K. (1988). *The self in social inquiry: Researching methods*. Sage.
Brown, A. W., Mehta, T. S., & Allison, D. B. (2017). Publication bias in science: What is it, why is it problematic, and how can it be addressed? In K. Jamieson, D. Kahan, & D. Scheufele (Eds.),

*The Oxford handbook of the science of science communication* (pp. 93–101). Oxford University Press.

Denzin, N. K., & Lincoln, Y. S. (2000). Introduction: The discipline and practice of qualitative research. In N. K. Denzin & Y. S. Lincoln (Eds.), *Handbook of qualitative research* (2nd ed., pp. 1–28). Sage.

Diamond, J. (1997). *Guns, germs, and steel. The fates of human societies*. W.W. Norton.

Egger, M., Zellweger-Zähner, T., Schneider, M., Junker, C., Lengeler, C., & Antes, G. (1997). Language bias in randomised controlled trials published in English and German. *Lancet, 350* (9074), 326–329. https://doi.org/10.1016/S0140-6736(97)02419-7.

Garcia Portilla, J. (2019). "Ye shall know them by their fruits": Prosperity and institutional religion in Europe and the Americas. *Religions, 10*(6), 362. https://doi.org/10.3390/rel10060362.

Hussain, R., Hassali, M. H., Patel, M., & Babar, Z. (2019). Publication bias. In *Encyclopedia of pharmacy practice and clinical pharmacy*. Elsevier. https://doi.org/10.1016/B978-0-12-812735-3.00610-5

Inglehart, R., & Baker, W. (2000). Modernization, cultural change, and the persistence of traditional values. *American Sociological Review, 65*(1), 19–51.

Johnson, R. B. (2017). Dialectical pluralism: A metaparadigm whose time has come. *Journal of Mixed Methods Research, 11*(2), 156–173.

Mahoney, M. J. (1977). Publication prejudices: An experimental study of confirmatory bias in the peer review system. *Cognitive Therapy and Research, 1*(2), 161–175.

Maxwell, J. (2013). *Qualitative research design. An interactive approach* (3rd ed.). Sage.

Moran, R., Harris, P., & Moran, S. (2007). *Doing business with Latin Americans, doing business with North Americans. Managing cultural differences: Global leadership strategies for the 21st century*. Elsevier/Butterworth-Heinemann.

Morin, E. (2001). *El Método I: La Naturaleza de la Naturaleza*. Cátedra.

Sachs, J. (2003). *Institutions don't rule: Direct effects of geography on per capita income*. Bureau of Economic Research Working Paper, *9490* (NBER), 1–13.

Zuñiga, M., & Tarride, M. I. (2010). Requirements of complexity for complex organizational conceptions. (U. d. Industrial Engineering Department, Ed.). *Kybernetes, 39*(7), 1112–1127.

# Chapter 14
# Methodology

This study applies a "mixed methods approach to grounded theory" (MM-GT) and combines qualitative and quantitative elements in several phases of the research process (i.e. data collection, analysis, inference). Such an approach serves to achieve "broad purposes of breadth and depth of understanding and corroboration" (Johnson, Onwuegbuzie, & Turner as cited in Schoonenboom & Johnson, 2017, p. 108).

Equally, MM-GT works well for research questions focusing on *why* and *how* the investigated phenomena function (including their qualitative and quantitative aspects). Consequently, MM-GT is appropriate here, since it concerns "meanings and processes or explanatory relationships" (and thus also causation) (Johnson et al., 2010, p. 72).

Mixed methods, such as those applied here, have proven useful for studying religious and secular milieus. One of their main advantages is that they ensure an increased validity of descriptions and explanations (Stolz, 2017).

This study is driven by an *equal-status mixed methods research* approach (Johnson, 2016). Thus, qualitative and quantitative components have equal value and weight. Figure 14.1 presents the research design:

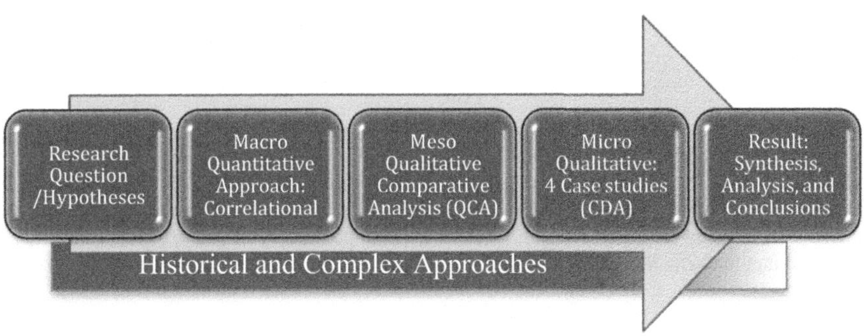


**Fig. 14.1** Research design (Source: Author's)



J. García Portilla, *"Ye Shall Know Them by Their Fruits"*, Contributions to Economics, https://doi.org/10.1007/978-3-030-78498-0_14

This flowchart also shows the integrated sequential methods used in this research: each method informs the application of the other methods.

As will be explained, different research components, each corresponding to different yet complementary epistemological approaches, provide complementary results at different levels of analysis. In other words:

- The "macro" approach is that quantitative component that exhibits general trends for countries and variables at a continental scale with minimum inferencing of causal relations. *Correlations* are used to test whether variables are related at a cross-country level (i.e. whether a population's religious affiliation is linked to corruption).
- QCA is the "meso" approach used to analyse both quantitative and qualitative data, and thus enabling inferences about causality. QCA clusters countries into groups of affinity and is used here to trace causal mechanisms (i.e. whether the adoption of Protestantism as a state religion is a necessary and sufficient condition for high levels of prosperity and transparency). QCA also allows briefly explaining each country situation in the dataset (around 60 countries). QCA analysis includes four case studies (the same cases are analysed in the "micro approach"—i.e. the next method).
- The most detailed approach ("micro") used in this study corresponds to the qualitative case studies on four selected countries for the purpose of specific analysis aimed at substantiating causal explanations. *Case studies* facilitate understanding differences and similarities, as well as causal mechanisms, from a qualitative perspective. This book includes four case studies on countries with (1) diverse geographical backgrounds, (2) different composition and dominance of Christian denominations, and (3) legal systems rooted in different origins.

In sum, the regression analysis of this study quantitatively explores the relations among factors/variables. QCA adds causality considerations and bridges quantitative relations and qualitative analysis. The four case studies are purely qualitative.

## References

Johnson, R. B. (2016). *Mixed methods research design and analysis with validity: A primer. Version 4.2.* Department of Professional Studies. University of South Alabama.

Johnson, R. B. (2017). Dialectical pluralism: A metaparadigm whose time has come. *Journal of Mixed Methods Research, 11*(2), 156–173.

Johnson, R., McGowan, M., & Turner, L. (2010). Grounded theory in practice: Is it inherently a mixed method? *The Research in the Schools. Mid-South Educational Research Association, 17* (2), 65–78.

Stolz, J. (2017). Milieus and mixed methods describing and explaining religion and secularity in Switzerland. *Kölner Zeitschrift für Soziologie und Sozialpsychologie (Suppl 2),* 2(69), 361–386.

# Part V
# Empirical Results (Macro & Meso Components)

Part V consists of two main chapters: [1]

1. The quantitative part of this study (Chap. 15) corresponds to regression analysis, where the relationship between variables is used to test some prominent prosperity/corruption theories. This part does not seek to prove causation, but instead empirically explores whether a population's religious affiliation is related to competitiveness/transparency. Its empirical investigation also extends to studying the traditional paradigm of some common determinants of corruption that are related to *religious adherents*. Among others, the corruption model applied here tests the interrelations between *GDP*, *political liberties* (democracy proxy), and *language* and *ethnic fractionalisation*.
2. The second part (Chap. 16) advances the understanding of corruption and competitiveness with a more complex causal approach (QCA). Compared to the regression analysis, this approach expands on three aspects: first, qualitative proxy conditions for the institutional influence of religion (i.e. concordats); second, split measures of language and ethnic variables (instead of packed indices of fractionalised measurements); and third, the analysis of four short cases.

*Recapitulation of Hypotheses and Empirical Expectations*

Chapters 15 and 16 will empirically test the hypotheses and expectations advanced in Parts I and III. To facilitate the analysis, the hypotheses and empirical expectations are briefly restated here.

*Hypotheses*

Hypothesis 1: Roman Catholicism has negatively impacted prosperity (competitiveness and transparency) in Europe and the Americas.

---

[1] *Note:* In the following sections, italics are used to identify variables or parameters.

Hypothesis 2: The Protestant Reformation has positively impacted prosperity (competitiveness and transparency) in Europe and the Americas.

Hypothesis 3: Environmental performance positively impacts prosperity in Europe and the Americas (i.e. moderating or moderated by the impact of religion).

*Empirical Expectations*

1. I expect the overwhelming empirical evidence available to confirm higher corruption rates in historically Roman Catholic countries than in historically Protestant countries (consistent with the title of this book articulated in Matthew 7: 15–23, *King James Bible*, 1769).
2. I expect the empirical evidence to corroborate a trend towards higher prosperity (competitiveness) in historically Protestant countries and lower competitiveness in historically Catholic countries. This expectation is based on abundant empirical studies linking higher prosperity outcomes with Protestantism at a cross-country level.
3. Given that economic prosperity, democracy, and transparency are part of the same phenomenon, I expect these factors to be highly correlated. My quantitative model on corruption (Sect. 15.3.4) considers proxy variables for all of these variables.
4. I expect higher transparency/prosperity levels in countries with Protestant-influenced legal origins (i.e. German, English, or Scandinavian) than in non-Protestant countries. The Protestant Reformation introduced the *Sola Scriptura* principle reflected in Protestant-influenced legal origins.
5. I expect lower prosperity/transparency levels in countries that have been influenced by the French legal system, in particular when they have strong clerical ties, and thus have been markedly influenced by Roman and canon law (as in Latin America).
6. Given the tradition of controversial and restrictive concordats, I expect a negative influence on transparency and prosperity in the respective concordatarian countries.
7. I expect a negative influence on prosperity/transparency in countries rooted in Socialist legal origins, in particular on account of the Soviet legal principle of the "goodness of humankind" (similar to Roman Catholic and Orthodox natural law).
8. I expect no conclusive results for ethnic fractionalisation given the possible overlapping of cultural proxies (Volonté, 2015) with other variables and given the varied conclusions of previous empirical results with aggregated measures.
9. I expect prosperity/transparency levels to be directly (positively) related to the proportion of Protestants and inversely (negatively) related to the proportion of Roman Catholics. This expectation is valid for the cross-country sample of Europe and the Americas, as confirmed by empirical studies (e.g. Chase, 2010; La Porta et al., 1997).
10. However, I do not expect a significant positive influence of the Protestant population on prosperity/transparency in Latin America. Firstly, Protestantism

in Latin America has been relatively recent compared to its five-hundred-year history of asserting the Reformation in Europe. In Latin America, Protestantism is a recent phenomenon. It dates back no more than 50 years, and its proportion has not surpassed 20% (Todd & Zurlo, 2016). Secondly, most of the Protestant growth in Latin America comes from Pentecostal currents, whose positive impact has been far weaker than historical Protestant denominations (Becker et al., 2016; McCleary, 2013; Woodberry, 2012).

11. I expect German and English-speaking countries to be more competitive/transparent than those speaking Roman languages. German and English are associated with the Reformation, whereas Roman languages are associated with the *status quo* of the Roman Empire, i.e. Roman Church-State.
12. I expect a robust positive relationship between the EPI and prosperity/transparency. However, I do not expect the EPI to explain the entire variability of GCI/CPI.

## References

Becker, S., Pfaff, S., & Rubin, J. (2016). *Causes and consequences of the protestant reformation.* Warwick Economics Research Paper Series.

Chase, G. (2010). Religion's impact on corruption. *Journal of Business and Economics Perspectives, 5*(1), 102–112.

King James Bible. (1769). *The Holy Bible, King James Version.* Cambridge Edition: 1769. Scripture quotations from The Authorized (King James) Version. Rights in the Authorized Version in the United Kingdom are vested in the Crown. Reproduced by permission of the Crown's patentee, Cambridge University Press.

La Porta, R., Lopez-de-Silanes, F., Shleifer, A., & Vishny, R. (1997). Trust in large organisations. *American Economic Review, 137*(2), 333–338.

McCleary, R. M. (2013). *Protestantism and Human Capital in Guatemala and the Republic of Korea.* Asian Development Bank.

Todd, M., & Zurlo, G. (2016). *World Christian database.* (Leiden/Boston: Brill, Ed.) Retrieved from www.globalchristianity.org

Volonté, C. (2015). Culture and corporate governance: The influence of language and religion in Switzerland. *Management International Review, 55*, 77–118.

Woodberry, R. (2012). The missionary roots of liberal democracy. *American Political Science Review (APSR), 106*(2), 244–274.

# Chapter 15
# Component 1 (Macro): Quantitative (Regression) Analysis

Several analyses were conducted to reach different explanatory models and thereby to determine the most critical variables in the datasets. This quantitative part is correlational, not experimental (causal). Therefore, the importance of a variable is based on its explanatory power, not on causal relations.

The *competitiveness GCI* index contains numerous sub-indices, which are aggregated into 12 different categories (World Economic Forum, 2016). Among the sub-indices, GCI comprises *corruption (CPI)* (or its opposite, *transparency perception*), as well as some of its determinants. However, the interactions between the variables of interest and *corruption*, on the one hand, and between the variables of interest and *competitiveness*, on the other, were analysed and modelled separately.[1]

This chapter has three sections. The first overviews the process of modelling competitiveness (GCI) and corruption (CPI). The second corresponds to the methodological protocols and limitations. The third presents the empirical results of the regression analysis for GCI and CPI.

Originally published as "Materials and Methods" in: Garcia Portilla, J. (2019). "Ye Shall Know Them by Their Fruits": Prosperity and Institutional Religion in Europe and the Americas. *Religions*, *10*(6), 362. MDPI AG. Retrieved from https://doi.org/10.3390/rel10060362


**Supplementary Information** The online version of this chapter (https://doi.org/10.1007/978-3-030-78498-0_15) contains supplementary material, which is available to authorized users.

[1]Please refer to Appendices 1–2 and Supplementary Materials for a detailed description of the variables and their interactions in the general research model. Also included in these appendices is a summary of the theories, indicators, and sources utilised in the models.



J. García Portilla, *"Ye Shall Know Them by Their Fruits"*, Contributions to Economics, https://doi.org/10.1007/978-3-030-78498-0_15

## 15.1 Modelling Competitiveness and Corruption

### *15.1.1 Modelling Competitiveness (GCI) (Stages 1 and 2)*

I modelled several variables associated with theories of prosperity (see Chap. 5 and Appendices 1–2, and Supplementary Materials) as possible exogenous determinants of competitiveness in most countries worldwide. For example, the *Environment Performance Index (EPI)* is linked to geographical and environmental determinants, while *religion* (adherents) is related to cultural and Weberian theory. *State religion* and *legal origins* are proxies of the institutional influence of religion. I tested the possible different contributions of those variables to explain the variation in *competitiveness (GCI).*

The next generation of models focused on countries in Europe and the Americas, i.e. those two continents under study here. Finally, the subsequent generation of models isolated the influence of variables such as *state religion* and *share of population adherents* on different religious affiliations. Such isolation ought to benefit the model fitness as these variables are related (Barro & McCleary, 2005) and might overfit the model.

### *15.1.2 Modelling Corruption (CPI Stage 3)*

Analysing *corruption* as a criterion variable (stage 3) associates several common predictor variables frequently used in the literature to explain corruption: *GDP* per capita, *religion, or political liberties* (Rose-Ackerman, 2006) (see Part III, Chap. 6, and Appendix 2). The modelling of *corruption* focused on Europe and the Americas. However, unlike the modelling of *competitiveness*, it bypassed the first generation of models (worldwide).

## 15.2 Methods of Regression Analysis

### *15.2.1 Methodological Limitations*

#### 15.2.1.1 Latest Available Data Measured at Different Time Periods

To draw the most accurate picture of existing reality, this study is based on the latest data available for all the investigated variables (most data come from 2016 reports). However, 2016 data were not available for all variables (care was taken to ensure that data were not older than 20 years). Saying this, slightly older data would not amount to a significant limitation. The prosperity performance of most Western countries exhibits comparatively long-term persistence (of a century or more) and thus indicates historical inertia (Michalopoulos & Papaioannou, 2017; Acemoglu & Robinson, 2012; Acemoglu & Robinson, 2008). The same applies to some environmental variables such as geography, latitude (Diamond, 1997), or state religion (Barro & McCleary, 2005).

#### 15.2.1.2 Regression Analysis Is Not a Causal Approach

A significant correlation does not always indicate causation (Arruñada, 2010, p. 908). Moreover, causal approaches to the present dataset and research design (i.e. based on the latest available data) might not be desirable for two reasons: First, this would lead to endogeneity problems. Testing plain variables as evident in the model would render regression results inconsistent due to the likely presence of endogeneity (i.e. because of simultaneous causality). Reverse causality is a widespread issue in regression models. Likewise, testing variable causality blindly (i.e. merely statistically, without any historical or theoretical consideration) would not be appropriate either. Thus, the historical approach to the variables under investigation is explained and addressed in detail (Figs. 1.1 and 8.1; Chaps. 6–12). Second, adopting a causal approach would require Instrumental Variable (IV) estimation, a complex experimental design, and a definition of independent, dependent, and control variables. It would also need instrumental variables, which might not exist in reality (or might be highly challenging to identify and define). While a time series approach would partially resolve the issues arising from a causal quantitative approach, it is not addressed in this study (see below). However, one other method in this research (QCA) uses a causality approach.

#### 15.2.1.3 This Regression Analysis Excludes a Time Series Approach

A time series would be an ideal approach to test whether variables are related over short or rather over long periods. This approach would allow identifying whether relationship patterns between variables exist over time. Conceptually, it would make sense to relate performance in a period t with explanatory factors measured in period $t$-1. One example would be if increasing or decreasing religiosity or the influence of a Christian denomination coincided with a prosperity variable (i.e. whether changes in a population's religious affiliation relate to changes in corruption).

The relationship between prosperity and religion in Protestant versus Catholic societies could be tested in time and space. Regarding time, for example, countries that were Roman Catholic before the Protestant Reformation (e.g. England, Germany or Switzerland) were pre-industrial (mainly primary sector economies) in the Middle Ages. In geographical space, for instance, countries currently under pervasive Roman Catholic influence (e.g. Spain or Latin America) tend to exhibit lower performance than Protestant ones.

Analysing Christian religion reveals that the Reformation initiated gradual changes, including its slow institutionalisation and influence on democracy, literacy, and the state (Becker et al., 2016; Woodberry, 2012; Witte, 2002). Consequently, a time series approach ought to cover longer periods (at least several centuries) based on the assumption that the prosperity of most Western countries maintains almost the same relative position over long-term time periods (a century or more) (Michalopoulos & Papaioannou, 2017; Acemoglu & Robinson, 2008).

A time series approach might also alleviate endogeneity issues, as current performance cannot (directly) influence past conditions. Still, relevant reverse causality might exist via indirect correlation. Nevertheless, a time series approach also has the disadvantage that the same available data does not exist for all variables. Some variables are measured yearly, some every 5 years, and some every 50 years (most have only been measured during the last 50 years or less). For some essential variables, no information and proxies exist, thus making it necessary to create new databases to cover particular periods (e.g. Pre-Reformation and Reformation). Undoubtedly, the time series approach is promising, yet requires considerable time and resources (which, however, exceed the scope of the present book). Notwithstanding this reservation, future research might consider applying this approach.

The current approach uses "legal origin" (La Porta et al., 1999) and "state religion" (Barro & McCleary, 2005) to capture some variable relationships over long periods. Barro and McCleary (2005) proved that a growing fraction of adherents to a country's main religion increases the probability of a "state religion". This gradual process means that few Western countries changed their status of having a "state religion" in the twentieth century.

### *15.2.2 Data and Empirical Strategy*

**Population**

The countries studied here were selected based on data availability (the same consideration applies to QCA, see Chap. 16). Data stem from constructed and from secondary (existing) data available in public databases. Further, the data consist of censuses of currently available indicators for the following cross-country analyses:

*Stage 1. Worldwide* (107 countries): The database comprises data series available on competitiveness, corruption, social inequality, as well as other social, environmental, and economic indicators. It also includes indicators of denominational tradition and religious background for most of the surveyed countries.

*Stages 2 and 3. Europe and the Americas* (66 countries—competitiveness; 61 countries—corruption): Cases with straightforward data access for most variables in Europe and the Americas.[2] Unlike in other regions, Christianity has been the

[2]Due to data availability issues, some countries were excluded (e.g. most of the small island states in the Caribbean). However, most countries in Europe and the Americas provide rich data. See Supplementary Materials for detailed information on countries, sources and main variables.

dominant religion for at least the past two centuries in Europe and the Americas. The populations of these continents currently adhere largely to Roman Catholic, Orthodox, or Protestant churches of various denominations (Johnson & Zurlo, 2016).

### *15.2.3 Protocol*

I followed an 11-step protocol (summarised below):

**Stage 1: Competitiveness in the World**

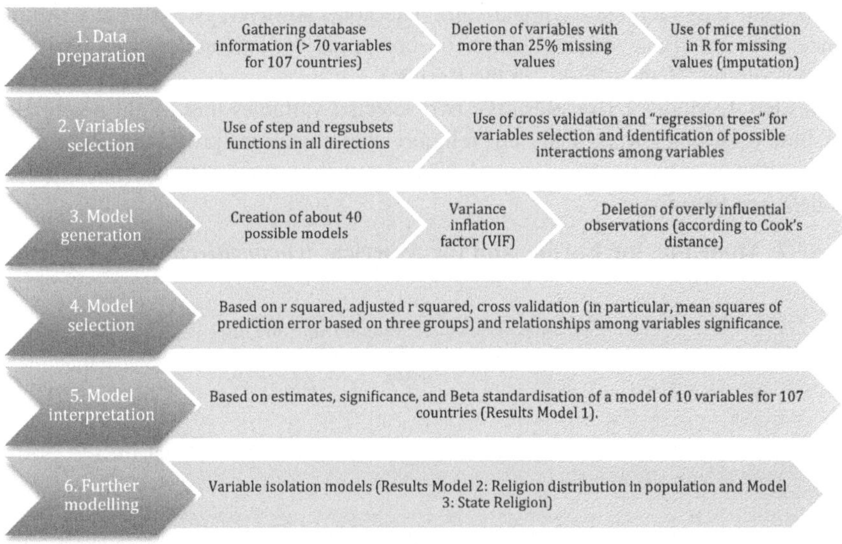


Step 1 aimed to include as many countries as possible in the database. However, not all the variables had the same data available for all the observations. Variables such as the *GLOBE* cultural index (House et al., 2004) were excluded from the analysis as the corresponding data were only available for a sample of three dozen countries. If less than 25% of values were still missing in the remaining dataset, they were imputed using Multivariate Imputation by Chained Equations in R (mice).

Step 2 involved using automated functions to help select from a high number of variables (see diagram above) from different theoretical backgrounds (see Appendix 1). Although the results of one automated model search may be arbitrary, about 40 of these models were created using different approaches to eliminate path-dependence and bias.

Step 3 concentrated on meeting linear regression assumptions in all the models. Assumptions were tested in a continuous process whenever a new model was created. Among other assumptions, I tested for multicollinearity by checking the

Variance Inflation Factor (VIF) and the correlation value. VIF results refused multicollinearity and, along with low correlation value, suggest that these variables are orthogonal. Likewise, all significant correlations among the predictor and criterion variables were controlled for.

Step 4 involved using cross-validation based on the prediction quality of shuffled groups of observations. Those model and variables exhibiting the best prediction ability were selected. "Step" is an automatic method based on the R function step (), which is also used to perform variable selection. These methods are useful when the number of explanatory variables is large, and when fitting all possible models proves unfeasible (University of Columbia, 2017).

Step 5 used Beta standardisation, which is necessary for comparing influence among variables. This indicates the significance of each variable in the context of others (and thus facilitates comparison). The goal, however, is not to test significance. Nor can Beta standardisation be computed for interaction variables (see second column "Standardised" in the Results).

In Step 4, Model 1 (see Results), two selected variables that might potentially outshine each other were analysed: religious denomination (proportion in population) and state religion. Consequently, I isolated these variables and ran separate models (see Step 6).

**Stage 2: Modelling for Europe and the Americas (*competitiveness*).**

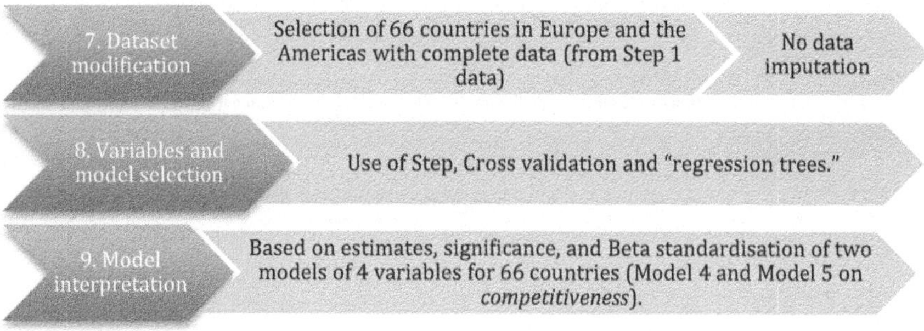


Europe and the Americas exhibited higher data quality and availability. Consequently, there was no need to impute data as in the world models (Stage 1: Models 1, 2, and 3). Therefore, stable regional models with higher reliability (i.e. avoiding data imputation and thus reducing bias) were created (Stage 2: Models 4 and 5).

Step 7. Due to data availability issues, some countries were excluded (e.g. most of the small island states in the Caribbean). Step 8 was similar to steps 2, 3, and 4, while step 9 was similar to step 5.

**Stage 3: Modelling for Europe and the Americas (*corruption*).**

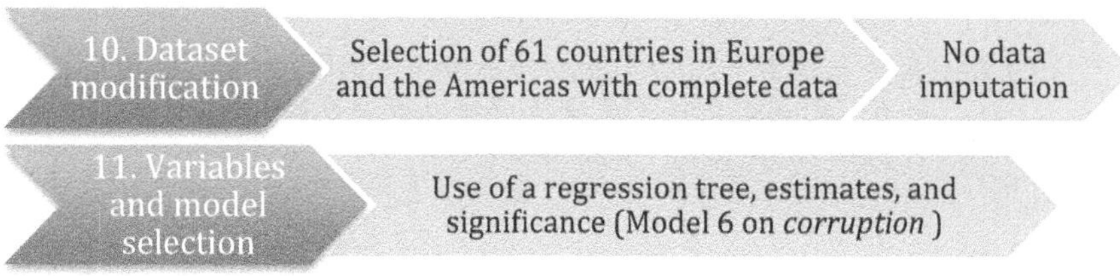


*The competitiveness index (GCI) includes corruption* (or its opposite, *transparency*) perception (*CPI*). However, to analyse whether transparency has the same direction as competitiveness, I ran a model that considers corruption as a criterion variable applicable to both Europe and the Americas.

Step 10. The corruption index (*CPI*) lacks data in several observations; therefore, fewer countries were selected from the dataset than in stage 2 (Step 7: Competitiveness).

Step 11. Regression trees are used for classification purposes or to predict outcomes when the response variable is numerical or continuous as in this situation (Morgan, 2014).

## 15.3 Empirical Results of Regression Analysis[3]

Appendices 1–2 provide a detailed description of the variables, theories, categories, and sources used here, as well as of the interactions between the variables in the general research model. Presented below are the results for competitiveness (Models 1–5 and conclusions) and for corruption (Model 6 and conclusions).

### *15.3.1 Competitiveness*

#### 15.3.1.1 Stage 1: Competitiveness in the World

The analysis of competitiveness as a criterion variable associates different predictor variables usually corresponding to theories of prosperity. Model 1 was chosen from more than 30 other models as it has the highest cross-validations and satisfactorily explains GCI variability.

[3]Some parts of this section were originally published as "Empirical Results (Correlational Analysis)" in: Garcia Portilla, J. (2019). "Ye Shall Know Them by Their Fruits": Prosperity and Institutional Religion in Europe and the Americas. *Religions*, *10*(6), 362. MDPI AG. Retrieved from https://doi.org/10.3390/rel10060362

#### 15.3.1.1.1 Model 1

$$
\begin{aligned}
GCI_i = \beta_0 + \beta_1 \mathrm{EPI}_i + \beta_2 Mulatto_i + \beta_3 Asian_i + \beta_4 \mathrm{Protestant\_St.Rel}_i \\
+ \beta_5 \mathrm{Catholic\_pop}_i + \beta_6 Orthodox\_pop_i + \beta_7 \mathrm{Protestant\_pop}_i \\
+ \beta_8 \mathrm{Muslim\_pop}_i + \beta_9 \mathrm{German\_LO}_i + \varepsilon i
\end{aligned}
$$

*Positive Correlations*

The most significant variable is the *Environment Performance Index (EPI)*, which is highly positively correlated with competitiveness *GCI* (0.72). If *EPI* was removed from the model, *R*-squared would drop by 17%. However, the same model without *EPI* exhibits similar results to Model 1 (Table 15.1) for the remaining variables. Here, an increase of *EPI* by one point is associated with a *GCI* growth of 0.026 points. *EPI* occupies larger units (mean value 70) than *GCI* (mean value 4) (The scale is standardised, meaning that these values refer to the non-standardised ranges; see Appendix 1 and Supplementary Materials).

A second important variable positively related to *competitiveness (GCI)* is the German legal origin: "*GERMAN (LO)*". Such countries have on average a higher *GCI* by 0.229.

Third, if Protestantism was the state religion "*PROTESTANT (S.R)*" (e.g. UK, Sweden, Denmark), then the overall effect would be positive on *GCI*. Establishing Protestantism as a state religion leads to a GCI increase of 0.223, which is far greater (almost double) than for a highly Protestant population. This confirms the higher

**Table 15.1** Model 1. Competitiveness in the world

| Coefficients: | Estimate | Standardised | Std. error | *t* value | Pr(>\|*t*\|) | |
|---|---|---|---|---|---|---|
| (Intercept) | 2.74106 | 0 | 0.274644 | 9.98 | $2.25 \times 10^{-16}$ | *** |
| EPI | 0.026048 | 0.586 | 0.002671 | 9.752 | $6.86 \times 10^{-16}$ | *** |
| Mulatto (ethn) | −0.443397 | −0.117 | 0.172934 | −2.564 | 0.011951 | * |
| Asian (ethn) | −1.880652 | −0.194 | 0.434192 | −4.331 | $3.74 \times 10^{-5}$ | *** |
| PROTESTANT (S. R) | 0.577261 | 0.223 | 0.168104 | 3.434 | 0.00089 | *** |
| Catholics (%) | −0.574504 | −0.273 | 0.220611 | −2.604 | 0.010722 | * |
| Orthodox (%) | −0.78216 | −0.27 | 0.23189 | −3.373 | 0.001085 | ** |
| Protestants (%) | −0.541959 | −0.146 | 0.310636 | −1.745 | 0.084344 | . |
| Muslims (%) | −0.472164 | −0.203 | 0.234843 | −2.011 | 0.047269 | * |
| GERMAN (L.O.) | 0.942412 | 0.229 | 0.1817 | 5.187 | $1.25 \times 10^{-6}$ | *** |
| – | | | | | | |

Signif. codes: 0 '***' 0.001 '**' **0.01 '*' 0.05 '.' 0.1 ''** 1. Residual standard error: 0.2961 on 97 degrees of freedom. Multiple *R*-squared: 0.8355, Adjusted *R*-squared: 0.8142. *F*-statistic: 39.35 on 12 and 93 DF, *p*-value: $<2.2 \times 10^{-16}$

Source: Author's collection

importance of the institutional influence of religion compared with that of the proportion of adherents (in line with Sect. 7.1.)[4]

*Negative Correlations*

All variables related to *religion distribution in a population—Catholics (%), Orthodox (%), Protestants (%), Muslims (%))*—are negatively correlated with *GCI* although these correlations are only marginally significant. Nonetheless, the *Orthodox population* causes the most substantial negative effect. An increase by one percentage point of the *Orthodox population* leads to a decrease of 0.0078 units in GCI. The same goes for changes in the *Roman Catholic population*, where an increase in one percentage point of their population would mean a *GCI* decrease by 0.0057. Likewise, if the share of the *Protestant population* increased by one percentage point, *GCI* would decrease by 0.0054 units. Finally, if the share of the *Muslim population* increased by one percentage point, *GCI* would decrease by 0.0047 units.

On the other hand, *Mulatto* and *Asian ethnical* values both have a negative effect. A growth of one percentage point in the mulatto/Asian population means a 0.00117/ 0.00194 decrease in *GCI,* respectively.

**Models Analysing Major Religious Population Groups or State Religions Separately**

Model 1 (Table 15.1) has shown a differential influence of the *religion distribution in a population* and of *state religion* on *GCI*. Models 2 (Table 15.2) and 3 (Table 15.3) were run to separate any potential differential influence. Separate analysis of the two variables eliminates the possibility that a religious population distribution and a state religion would "overfit" the model.

#### 15.3.1.1.2 Model 2 with Population Percentage

Model 2 shows the relation between the *percentage of religious adherents* and *competitiveness* while excluding *state religion* variables.

$$\begin{aligned} GCI_i = {} & \beta_0 + \beta_1 \mathrm{EPI}_i + \beta_2 \mathrm{Caucasian}_i + \beta_3 Mulatto_i + \beta_4 Asian_i + \beta_5 Dogmas_i \\ & + \beta_6 Socialist_i + \beta_7 \mathrm{German}_i + \beta_8 \mathrm{Catholic\_pop}_i + \beta_9 \mathrm{Muslim\_pop}_i \\ & + \beta_{10} Orthodox\_pop_i + \varepsilon i \end{aligned}$$

Model 2 (Table 15.2) confirms the findings of Model 1 (Table 15.1) in the same order:

[4]Exceptionally, while "*Agnostic*" and "*Independent*" variables of religion distribution in a population positively affected GCI, they were not significant enough to be included in the model.

**Table 15.2** Model 2: Competitiveness in the world including the percentage of *religious adherents* and excluding *State religion* variables

| Coefficients: | Estimate | Standardised | Std. error | *t* value | Pr(>\|*t*\|) | |
|---|---|---|---|---|---|---|
| (Intercept) | 2.68713 | 0 | 0.411929 | 6.523 | $3.22 \times 10^{-9}$ | *** |
| EPI | 0.031948 | 0.718076 | 0.003588 | 8.904 | $3.35 \times 10^{-14}$ | *** |
| Caucasian (ethn) | 0.3062 | 0.182286 | 0.137576 | 2.226 | $2.84 \times 10^{-2}$ | * |
| Mulatto (ethn) | −0.49164 | −0.129827 | 0.212469 | −2.314 | 0.022804 | * |
| Asian (ethn) | −2.262534 | −0.233818 | 0.607969 | −3.721 | 0.000334 | *** |
| Dogmas | −0.06555 | −0.161069 | 0.033539 | −1.954 | $5.36 \times 10^{-2}$ | . |
| SOCIALIST (L.O.) | −0.223811 | −0.125531 | 0.111884 | −2 | 0.048283 | * |
| GERMAN (L.O.) | 0.608521 | 0.147437 | 0.221393 | 2.749 | 0.007151 | ** |
| Catholics (%) | −0.435477 | −0.217661 | 0.131934 | −3.301 | 0.001355 | ** |
| Muslims (%) | −0.349915 | −0.155187 | 0.191688 | −1.825 | 0.071044 | . |
| Orthodox (%) | −0.742669 | −0.235604 | 0.192192 | −3.864 | 0.000203 | *** |
| – | | | | | | |

Signif. codes: 0 '***' 0.001 '**' **0.01 '*' 0.05 '.' 0.1** ' ' 1. Residual standard error: 0.3554 on 96 degrees of freedom. Multiple $R$-squared: 0.7559, Adjusted $R$-squared: 0.7304. $F$-statistic: 29.72 on 10 and 96 DF, $p$-value: $<2.2 \times 10^{-16}$

Source: Author's collection

1. *EPI* is the most significant variable.
2. Increasing *Orthodox, Catholic,* and *Muslim* populations negatively influence *GCI.* However, the *Protestant population* and *other Christian adherents* are not significant in Model 2.
3. Model 2 confirms the direction and influence of most other variables in Model 1. However, in Model 2, *Caucasian* ethnic values positively influence GCI. Likewise, *Dogmas* and *Socialist* legal origin negatively impact GCI.

#### 15.3.1.1.3 Model 3 (Including State Religion)

Model 3 (Table 15.3) excludes the *percentage of religion adherents* variables. *State religion* variables alone explain most of the variability otherwise explained by religious population.

$$GCI_i = \beta_0 + \beta_1 \mathrm{EPI}_i + \beta_2 \mathrm{Caucasian}_i + \beta_3 Mulatto_i + \beta_4 Asian_i + \beta_5 \mathrm{Catholic}_i \\ + \beta_6 \mathrm{Protestant}_i + \beta_7 Socialist_i + \beta_8 \mathrm{German}_i + \varepsilon i$$

The results of Model 3 (Table 15.3) ratify those of the previous models. The most significant positive influence on *GCI* comes from *EPI, Protestant state religion, Caucasian ethnicity,* and *German legal origin.* In contrast, *Asian* and *Mulatto ethnicities, Roman Catholic state religion,* and *Socialist legal origin* would negatively affect *GCI.*

**Table 15.3** Model 3: Competitiveness in the world including *state religion* and excluding the percentage of *religion adherents*

| Coefficients: | Estimate | Standardised | Std. error | $t$ value | Pr(>\|t\|) | |
|---|---|---|---|---|---|---|
| (Intercept) | 1.94889 | 0 | 0.205025 | 9.506 | $1.57 \times 10^{-15}$ | *** |
| EPI | 0.032097 | 0.721417 | 0.003403 | 9.433 | $2.25 \times 10^{-15}$ | *** |
| Caucasian (ethn) | 0.233095 | 0.138765 | 0.137925 | 1.69 | $9.42 \times 10^{-2}$ | . |
| Mulatto (ethn) | −0.432751 | −0.114276 | 0.197873 | −2.187 | 0.03115 | * |
| Asian (ethn) | −1.41671 | −0.146408 | 0.503625 | −2.813 | 0.00594 | ** |
| CATHOLIC (S.R) | −0.245126 | −0.156268 | 0.091698 | −2.673 | $8.82 \times 10^{-3}$ | ** |
| PROTESTANT (S. R) | 0.307335 | 0.118639 | 0.147376 | 2.085 | 0.03966 | * |
| SOCIALIST (L.O.) | −0.232813 | −0.130581 | 0.113454 | −2.052 | 0.04286 | * |
| GERMAN (L.O.) | 0.60705 | 0.147081 | 0.231532 | 2.622 | 0.01015 | * |
| – | | | | | | |

Signif. codes: 0 '***' 0.001 '**' **0.01 '*' 0.05 '.' 0.1** '' 1. Residual standard error: 0.3552 on 98 degrees of freedom. Multiple $R$-squared: 0.7536, Adjusted $R$-squared: 0.7307. $F$-statistic: 32.96 on 9 and 97 DF, $p$-value: $<2.2 \times 10^{-16}$

Source: Author's collection

#### 15.3.1.2 Stage 2: Modelling Competitiveness (Europe and the Americas)

The following models were produced explicitly for Europe and the Americas, excluding the noise existing in the world database. Likewise, Models 4 and 5 serve to compare whether the same variables chosen in the previous "world" models are still significant in Europe and the Americas.

##### 15.3.1.2.1 Model 4: Results of Cross-Validation

$$GCI_i = \beta_0 + \beta_1 Hostilities_i + \beta_2 \text{German\_lan}_i + \beta_3 \text{Catholic\_pop}_i + \beta_4 \text{Orthodox\_pop}_i + \beta_5 \text{EPI}_i + \varepsilon i$$

This result shows the high robustness of this model (Table 15.4), in that it explains almost 66% of *GCI* variability with four significant variables at a 99% confidence level:

1. *EPI* is the most important variable because it accounts for most of the *GCI* variability. The increase in *EPI* by one percentage point is related to a "GCI" growth of approximately 0.038 percentage points.
2. The second most important variable is the *Orthodox population*, which exerts the most substantial negative effect in the model. If the *Orthodox population* increased by one percentage point, *GCI* would decrease by approximately 0.010 percentage points.

**Table 15.4** Model 4: Competitiveness in Europe and the Americas (cross-validation method)

| Coefficients: | Estimate | Standardised | Std. error | *t* value | Pr(>\|*t*\|) | |
|---|---|---|---|---|---|---|
| (Intercept) | 1.583 | 0 | 0.48642 | 3.254 | 0.00188 | ** |
| Hostilities | 0.07461 | 0.18955 | 0.03368 | 2.215 | 0.03063 | * |
| German (lang) | 0.82223 | 0.24086 | 0.26625 | 3.088 | 0.00307 | ** |
| Catholics (%) | −0.49853 | −0.29507 | 0.15608 | −3.194 | 0.00225 | ** |
| Orthodox (%) | −1.04274 | −0.44616 | 0.21537 | −4.842 | $9.66 \times 10^{-6}$ | *** |
| EPI | 0.03829 | 0.52268 | 0.00596 | 6.424 | $2.53 \times 10^{-8}$ | *** |
| – | | | | | | |

Signif. codes: 0 '***' 0.001 '**' **0.01 '*' 0.05 '.' 0.1 '** ' 1. Residual standard error: 0.3771 on 59 degrees of freedom. Multiple $R$-squared: 0.6556, Adjusted $R$-squared: 0.6264. $F$-statistic: 22.46 on 5 and 59 DF, $p$-value: $1.54 \times 10^{-12}$
Source: Author's collection

3. Similarly, the effect of the *Roman Catholic population* also negatively influences competitiveness. If the *Roman Catholic population* increased by one percentage point, *GCI* would drop by approximately 0.005 percentage points. This finding, along with the previous one (2), is consistent with La Porta et al.'s (1999) conclusions about the negative influence of hierarchical religions on prosperity.
4. Finally, the proportion of the *German-speaking population* positively affects *GCI*. An increase of 1 percentage point in *the German-speaking population* would mean a *GCI* increase by approximately 0.008 percentage points. This finding would confirm a positive relationship (as outlined in Sect. 11.1).

#### 15.3.1.2.2 Model 5: Results with Step

$$GCI_i = \beta_0 + \beta_1 Hostilities_i + \beta_2 \text{GERMAN\_LEGAL}_i + \beta_3 \text{Catholic\_pop}_i + \beta_4 \text{Orthodox\_pop}_i + \beta_5 \text{EPI}_i + \varepsilon i$$

"Step" is a fundamentally different method, yet mostly exhibits the same results (Table 15.5) as those of cross-validation (Table 15.4). Step analysis further confirms the choice of the right variables (based on reality, not on random data effects). Here, the only difference is that Step analysis chose *GERMAN (legal origin)* instead of *German language* (percentage of German-speaking population) with 99% confidence. The chapters that discuss the theoretical framework and conclusions further discuss these variables and findings.

*GERMAN (legal origin)* is a binomial variable, meaning that if a country is of *German legal origin*, then its *GCI* is 0.759 higher. If it is not of *German legal origin*, then the variable does not affect *GCI*. Only these two extremes exist.

On the other hand, the variable *Social Hostilities due to religion* also appears in Models 4 (Table 15.4) and 5 (Table 15.5). It exhibits the lowest value of standardised

**Table 15.5** Model 5: Competitiveness in Europe and the Americas (Step method)

| Coefficients: | Estimate | Standardised | Std. error | $t$ value | Pr(>\|$t$\|) | |
|---|---|---|---|---|---|---|
| (Intercept) | 1.606434 | 0 | 0.479997 | 3.347 | 0.00143 | ** |
| Hostilities | 0.075303 | 0.191317 | 0.033201 | 2.268 | 0.027 | * |
| GERMAN (L.O.) | 0.759773 | 0.260367 | 0.224315 | 3.387 | 0.00126 | ** |
| Catholic_pop | −0.499403 | −0.295584 | 0.153919 | −3.245 | 0.00194 | ** |
| Orthodox_pop | −1.04258 | −0.446087 | 0.212236 | −4.912 | $7.49 \times 10^{-6}$ | *** |
| EPI | 0.037974 | 0.518342 | 0.005882 | 6.456 | $2.24 \times 10^{-8}$ | *** |
| – | | | | | | |

Signif. codes: 0 '***' 0.001 '**' **0.01 '*' 0.05 '.' 0.1** ' ' 1. Residual standard error: 0.3719 on 59 degrees of freedom. Multiple $R$-squared: 0.6651, Adjusted $R$-squared: 0.6367. $F$-statistic: 23.43 on 5 and 59 DF, $p$-value: $6.91 \times 10^{-13}$

Source: Author's collection

beta and also low values. More importantly, this variable appeared only at 90% confidence value (all other results had a 99% confidence value). Therefore, this variable is not sufficiently significant.

Finally, standard deviation confirmed the results of both cross-validation (Table 15.4) and Step (Table 15.5) and found the same, most robust coefficients. Consequently, only four variables in the models had statistical significance.

#### 15.3.1.3 Conclusions for Competitiveness

##### 15.3.1.3.1 Conclusions for Competitiveness in the World (All Models)

*The consistent results of the five previous models are:*

1. A positive influence of *EPI* on *GCI*;
2. A positive influence of a *German legal origin* (or *German language*) on *GCI*;
3. A negative influence of an *Orthodox population* on *GCI*;
4. A negative influence of a *Roman Catholic population* (or *Roman Catholic State Religion*) on *GCI*.

These results are valid for the world—Models 1 (Table 15.1), 2 (Table 15.2), and 3 (Table 15.3)—, as well as for Europe and the Americas—Models 4 (Table 15.4) and 5 (Table 15.5)—.

*Partially conclusive findings:*

Ethnic influence appeared with some degree of importance in the world models but disappeared in Europe and the Americas.

*Socialist legal origin* negatively influenced GCI—Models 2 (Table 15.2), and 3 (Table 15.3)—.

The influence of the share of *Protestants in the population* is not conclusive. In Model 1 (Table 15.1), *Protestants* negatively affected *GCI*, after *Orthodox* and *Roman Catholics*. However, in Model 2 (Table 15.2), which analyses religious population, the influence of *Protestants* disappeared.

Neither *Protestant population* (1) nor *Protestant State Religion* (2) are significant variables for competitiveness in Europe and the Americas—Models 4 (Table 15.4) and 5 (Table 15.5)—. Hypothetical reasons for such findings include, respectively, (1) the high influence of Pentecostalism in the Protestant population today might neutralise the possible positive effect of historical Protestantism. Pentecostalism impacts little on human capital and institutions (Becker et al., 2016; McCleary, 2013; Woodberry, 2012) and has often fallen into established practices "of corporatism and clientage" (Martin, 1999, p. 40; Schäfer, 1997) (Sect. 10.4.3). (2) While Switzerland and the USA are the most competitive (*GCI*) countries, they do not have Protestantism as their state religion, despite being historically Protestant (Barro & McCleary, 2005; Inglehart & Baker, 2000).

Nonetheless, *Protestant State Religion* exhibited a positive significance on Model 3 (State Religion). This suggests that *Protestant State Religion* is more important for *GCI* than the proportion of *Protestants in the population*. The effect of *Protestant State Religion* on higher *GCI* might also be related to its influence in diminishing the institutional power of the Roman Church (Sect. 8.3.4). The latter conclusions both confirm Fanfani's claim as early as 1936 (as cited in Grier, 1997) that the separation of state and church is the critical prosperity trigger. Such a separation occurred mainly in Protestant countries for anti-clerical reasons. Fanfani argued that religion per se harms prosperity unless it leads to the separation of ecclesiastical and political/ economic powers in a country (as historical Protestantism did).

###### 15.3.1.3.2 Conclusions for Competitiveness in Europe and the Americas

In Europe and the Americas, Models 4 and 5 discover a combination of variables that largely explains *GCI* variability in the following order of importance:

**Environmental Performance Index (EPI)**
I found a high correlation of EPI with competitiveness *(GCI)*, as suggested by the environment-and-geography theory of prosperity (Diamond, 1997; Sachs, 2001; Brown & Lall, 2006). This index has by far the highest positive influence on *GCI* of all the variables considered and explains most of the *GCI* diversity. Higher *EPI* strongly implies higher *GCI.*

**Legal Origin**
As predicted in the variables description sections (Chap. 3–12), I found a highly positive relation of *German legal origin* and *German language* with *GCI.* The influence of the Reformation on the German legal system has been widely discussed (Witte, 2002; Berman, 2003) (Sect. 8.3.4). Likewise, several studies (Besch, 1999; Greenslade, 1963) have discussed the influence of the Reformation on the dissemination and standardisation of the German language (Sect. 11.1).

## 15.3.2 Corruption

### 15.3.2.1 Proxy Predictor Variables for the Regression Model of Corruption

The quantitative model used here tested some proxy variables of selected main determinants of corruption (Rose-Ackerman, 2006; Alesina et al., 2003). Such predictor variables are:

1. Proxies of economic prosperity: the *log GDP* per capita (*GDPPC*) and the *Index of Economic Freedom* (*IEF*);
2. Proxies of democracy: the *Political Rights and Civil Liberties Index* (*PRCL*) and the *Political Stability Index* (*STABIL*).
3. Proxies of culture: the *percentage of Roman Catholics* (*CATH*), and *Protestants* (*PROT*) in the population. This also includes *ethnic, linguistic, and religious fractionalisation* measures (*ETHF*, *LING* and *RELF*, respectively).

For each variable, the latest available data were used (one observation per country). Please refer to Annex 1 for details on the variables and sources.[5]

$$CPI_i = \beta_0 + \beta_1 GDPPC_i + \beta_2 IEF_i + \beta_3 PRCL_i + \beta_4 STABIL_i + \beta_5 PROT_i \\ + \beta_6 CATH_i + \beta_7 ETHF_i + \beta_8 LINGF_i + \beta_9 RELF_i + \varepsilon i$$

### 15.3.2.2 Regression Results for Corruption in Europe and the Americas

Data analysis includes a regression tree (see Fig. 15.1). The *Political Rights and Civil Liberties Index (PRCL)* is the most critical factor in determining the *Corruption Perception Index (CPI)*. Lower corruption levels ($CPI = 81.5$) are evident in countries with a (*PRCL*) $\geq 44$ and that also have a higher log GDP per capita ($GDPPC > 10.6$). Such results are entirely consistent with the respective theoretical predictions (Sects. 3.1, 3.3 and 8.1 indicate that these variables are part of the same phenomenon). In line with theory (Sect. 6.1), transparency increases even more if the country in question also has a high proportion of *Protestants* ($PROT > 0.24$) in its population ($CPI = 84.75$).

This regression tree confirms that *PRCL*; *GDPPC*, and *PROT* are all positively related to transparency (or vice versa, negatively related to corruption). *GDPPC* and

[5]*Note:* I have previously explained the essential theoretical variables and clarified that prosperity, democracy, and transparency are all part of the same outcome in terms of my research aims. Therefore, the variables researched in this regression model do not show causal effects. Finding causality between corruption and GDP, PRCL, IEF, or STABIL is problematic due to endogeneity issues (Lambsdorff, 2006) (i.e. in reality, they might all form part of the same phenomenon or syndrome and all belong to the GCI index) (World Economic Forum, 2016). Further, correlations only exhibit relations but no causalities (Sect. 15.2.1).

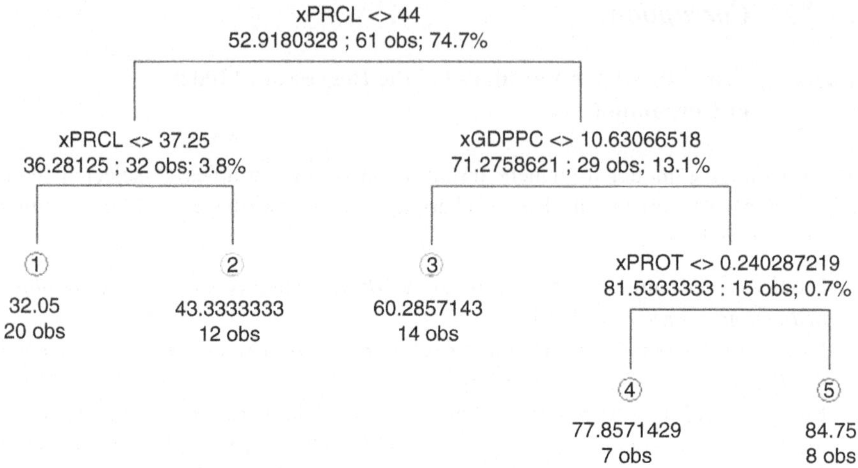


**Fig. 15.1** Regression tree, with the mean value of *CPI*, the number of observations, and percentage deviance. The minimum number of observations per node for a split to be attempted is set to 15. Any split not decreasing the overall lack of fit by a factor of 0.005 is not attempted. (Source: Author's collection)

*PROT* do not seem to play an essential role in countries with low PRCL (democracy). This result is also in line with theory. For instance, Treisman (2000) found that only stable democracy (before 1950) reduces corruption. Most of the Protestant upsurge in the developing world has stemmed from Pentecostalism after 1950 (Johnson & Zurlo, 2016), which only marginally impacts human capital and institutions (Becker et al., 2016; McCleary, 2013; Woodberry, 2012).

The estimates in Table 15.6 corroborate the relation between lower *corruption* (or higher transparency) and a high proportion of Protestants in the population. Similarly, other predictor variables, above all *GDPPC*, *PRCL*, *LING* correlate with lower corruption levels (i.e. higher *CPI*). The negative impact of the share of Catholics in the population is less visible, with a lower coefficient in magnitude. These results are entirely compatible with theory, in particular with Treisman (2000).

As indicated by the positive coefficients for *LING*, linguistic fractionalisation tends to imply lower corruption. This trend is illustrated by countries (e.g. Luxembourg, Canada, or Switzerland) facing low corruption and featuring in the top ten countries of the present sample regarding language fractionalisation. Conversely, a higher level of ethnic fractionalisation (*ETHF*) tends to be associated with higher levels of corruption, as established by other empirical studies (Sect. 10.1). This observation confirms that linguistic heterogeneity does not necessarily coincide with ethnic heterogeneity. For instance, most Latin American countries are relatively homogenous concerning language but less so regarding "ethnicity" or "race".

**Table 15.6** Model 6: Corruption in Europe and the Americas

| Coefficients: | Estimate | Std. error | *t* value | Pr(>\|*t*\|) | |
|---|---|---|---|---|---|
| (Intercept) | −95.7267 | 22.615 | −4.233 | 0.0000962 | *** |
| GDPPC | 10.5639 | 2.1555 | 4.901 | 0.0000101 | *** |
| IEF | 0.2921 | 0.1499 | 1.949 | 0.05686 | . |
| PRCL | 0.546 | 0.1721 | 3.173 | 0.00256 | ** |
| STABIL | 4.0372 | 2.7122 | 1.489 | 0.14276 | |
| PROT | 17.9297 | 6.2714 | 2.859 | 0.00614 | ** |
| CATH | −2.242 | 4.2163 | −0.532 | 0.59721 | |
| ETHF | −10.4336 | 6.4496 | −1.618 | 0.11189 | |
| LING | 13.9763 | 6.6231 | 2.11 | 0.03976 | * |
| RELF | −1.1927 | 5.9927 | −0.199 | 0.84303 | |
| – | | | | | |

Signif. codes: 0 '***' 0.001 '**' **0.01** **'*'** **0.05** **'.'** **0.1** **' '** 1 Residual standard error: 7.503 on 51 degrees of freedom. Multiple *R*-squared: 0.8848, Adjusted *R*-squared: 0.8645. *F*-statistic: 43.54 on 9 and 51 DF, *p*-value: $<2.2 \times 10^{-16}$
Source: Author's collection

The regressions do not display any significant relation between religion fractionalisation *RELF* and corruption. Consequently, low corruption is present in both multicultural, free societies with high measured religious fractionalisation (e.g. USA, United Kingdom, Canada), and countries with low religious fractionalisation (e.g. Luxembourg or Belgium). A "packed" index of fractionalisation measures works like a "black box" as analysing interactions between the components (i.e. each language or ethnicity) is impossible.

#### 15.3.2.3 Conclusions for Corruption in Europe and the Americas

Generally speaking, the conclusions reached here about the selected variables resemble those of previous research (Treisman, 2000; Paldam, 2001; Arruñada, 2010; Chase, 2010; and to a less extent La Porta et al., 1999). Results were validated using different databases and methods.

##### 15.3.2.3.1 Proportion of Protestants

The findings confirm my hypothesis that corruption levels are directly (i.e. negatively) related to the proportion of Protestants in countries in Europe and the Americas. Thus, the share of the Protestant population might play an essential role in reducing corruption. This result is consistent throughout the regressions and the regression tree and confirms previous empirical studies (e.g. La Porta et al., 1997; Treisman, 2000; and Chase, 2010). The influence of Protestantism is further explored using the QCA method, which enables one to consider other variables also playing an essential role besides population share.

#### 15.3.2.3.2 Proportion of Roman Catholics

Much of the previous empirical literature report that Roman Catholicism, Orthodox, and Islam religions correlate negatively with transparency (high corruption or low *CPI*) (Paldam, 2001; La Porta et al., 1997; Chase, 2010). However, the negative relation between *Roman Catholics adherents* in the population and corruption (*CPI)* is not conclusive in my results. While *Roman Catholics adherents* are present with a negative yet not particularly significant coefficient in the regression model, they are absent in the regression tree. Treisman (2000) reported comparable results when including proxy measurements for democracy and economic development in the model similar to mine. Those factors are, as discussed, interrelated rather than competing explanations.

As stated in the theoretical part (Sects. 3.3 and 8.1), prosperity, democracy, and transparency might all be part of the same phenomenon. When regressing all those variables together, the model might dull the influence of other variables (e.g. *Proportion of Roman Catholics*). QCA further analyses this issue along with different variables.

#### 15.3.2.3.3 Fractionalisation Measurements

No clear pattern exists in ethnic, linguistic, or religious fractionalisation. Only linguistic fractionalisation is significant in the regression analysis, but no fractionalisation measurement appears in the regression tree analysis. Fractionalisation indices express "how diverse" countries are regarding language, religion, and ethnicities. Further, the indices aggregate and "pack" such diversity into one figure (Alesina et al., 2003). Consequently, fractionalisation measurements prevent analysing the interactions of each specific religion, language, or ethnicity units using criterion (prosperity) variables. Such aggregation constitutes the main limitation of fractionalisation measurements. Therefore, the QCA section uses a disaggregated value to reflect the shares of the main ethnicities and languages spoken in a given country or region (Central Intelligence Agency of the United States [CIA], 2016).

#### 15.3.2.3.4 Political Rights and Civil Liberties

As observed in the regression tree analysis, the political rights and civil liberties (*PRCL*) variable is the most significant factor relative to *CPI*. This finding was expected, on account of its theoretical relation with Protestantism (Sect. 8.2.2). Woodberry (2012) and Becker et al. (2016) have provided ample empirical and historical evidence for the essential role of Protestantism (i.e. Protestant missionaries) in the rise and spread of stable democracies around the world.

15.3.2.3.5 Gross Domestic Product (GDP) Per Capita

As explained, *GDP* per head was expected to be a significant predictor variable and is negatively related to corruption in the tree regression method.

### *15.3.3 General Conclusion: Models of Religious Population (Competitiveness and Corruption)*

Generally, the models presented here suggest that Orthodox and Roman Catholic populations correlate negatively with competitiveness in Europe and the Americas. However, their role in corruption appears less evident in the corruption model. In contrast, a Protestant population might play an essential role in reducing corruption. Nevertheless, the role of the Protestant population in competitiveness is less clear. The next component (QCA) expands on the understanding of these variables along with other proxies.

## References


Acemoglu, D., & Robinson, J. A. (2008). Persistence of power, elites, and institutions. *American Economic Review, 98*(1), 267–293.

Acemoglu, D., & Robinson, J. (2012). *Why nations fail. The origins of power, prosperity and poverty*. Crown Business.

Alesina, A., Devleeschauwer, A., Easterly, W., Sergio, K., & Wacziarg, R. (2003). Fractionalization. *Journal of Economic Growth, 8*(2), 155–194.

Arruñada, B. (2010). Protestants and catholics: Similar work ethic, Different social ethic. *The Economic Journal, 120*(547), 890–918.

Barro, R. J., & McCleary, R. M. (2005). Which countries have state religions? *The Quarterly Journal of Economics, 120*(4), 1331–1370.

Becker, S., Pfaff, S., & Rubin, J. (2016). *Causes and consequences of the protestant reformation*. Warwick Economics Research Paper Series.

Berman, H. (2003). *Law and revolution II: The impact of the protestant reformations on the western legal tradition*. Harvard University Press, Belknap Press.

Besch, W. (1999). *Die Rolle Luthers in der deutschen Sprachgeschichte*. Universitätsverlag C. Winter.

Brown, C., & Lall, U. (2006). Water and economic development: The role of variability and a framework for resilience. *Natural Resources Forum, 30*(4), 306–317.

Central Intelligence Agency (CIA). (2016). *Religions*. In the world fact book. Retrieved from https://www.cia.gov/library/publications/resources/the-world-factbook/index.html

Chase, G. (2010). Religion's impact on corruption. *Journal of Business and Economics Perspectives, 5*(1), 102–112.

Diamond, J. (1997). *Guns, germs, and steel. The fates of human societies*. W.W. Norton.

Fanfani, A. (1936). *Catholicism, protestantism, and capitalism*. IHS Press.

Garcia Portilla, J. (2019). "Ye shall know them by their fruits": Prosperity and institutional religion in Europe and the Americas. *Religions, 10*(6), 362. MDPI AG. Retrieved from https://doi.org/10.3390/rel10060362

Greenslade, S. (1963). *The Cambridge history of the Bible: The west from the reformation to the present day*. Cambridge University Press.
Grier, R. (1997). The effect of religion on economic development: A cross national study of 63 former colonies. *Kyklos, 50*(1), 47–62.
House, R. J., Hanges, P. J., Javidan, M., Dorfman, P. W., & Gupta, V. (Eds.). (2004). *Culture, leadership, and organizations: The GLOBE study of 62 societies*. Sage.
Inglehart, R., & Baker, W. (2000). Modernization, cultural change, and the persistence of traditional values. *American Sociological Review, 65*(1), 19–51.
Johnson, T. M., & Zurlo, G. A. (2016). *World Christian database*. Retrieved from: Center for the Study of Global Christianity at Gordon-Conwell Theological Seminary website: www.globalchristianity.org
La Porta, R., Lopez-de-Silanes, F., Shleifer, A., & Vishny, R. (1997). Trust in large organisations. *American Economic Review, 137*(2), 333–338.
La Porta, R., Lopez-de-Silanes, F., & Vishny, A. S. (1999). The quality of government. *Journal of Law, Economics and Organization, 15*(1), 222–279.
Lambsdorff, J. G. (2006). Causes and consequences of corruption: What do we know from a cross-section of countries? In S. Rose-Ackerman (Ed.), *International handbook on the economics of corruption* (pp. 3–51). Edward Elgar.
Martin, D. (1999). The evangelical upsurge and its political implications. In P. Berger (Eds.), *The desecularization of the world* (pp. 37–49). Ethics and Public Policy Center and Wm. B. Eerdmans.
McCleary, R. M. (2013). *Protestantism and Human Capital in Guatemala and the Republic of Korea*. Asian Development Bank.
Michalopoulos, S., & Papaioannou, E. (2017). *The long economic and political shadow of history—Volume 3: Europe and the Americas*. CEPR Press Centre for Economic Policy Research.
Morgan, J. (2014). *Classification and regression tree analysis*. Department of Health Policy and Management, Boston University School of Public Health.
Paldam, M. (2001). Corruption and religion. Adding to the economic model. *Kyklos, 54*(2-3), 383–414.
Rose-Ackerman, S. (2006). *International handbook on the economics of corruption*. Edward Elgar.
Sachs, J. (2001). *Tropical underdevelopment*. National Bureau of Economic Research. Working Paper, 8119 (NBER), 1–37.
Schäfer, H. (1997). Oh Lord of heaven, give us power on earth! Fundamentalism and charisma: The reconquest of the field of action in Latin America. *Mesoamerica, 18*(33), 125–146.
Treisman, D. (2000). The causes of corruption: A cross-national study. *Journal of Public Economics, 76*(3), 399–457.
University of Columbia. (2017). *Variable selection*. Department of Statistics. Retrieved from http://www.stat.columbia.edu/~martin/W2024/R10.pdf
Witte, J. (2002). *Law and protestantism: The legal teachings of the Lutheran reformation*. Cambridge: Cambridge: University Press.
Woodberry, R. (2012). The missionary roots of liberal democracy. *American Political Science Review (APSR), 106*(2), 244–274.
World Economic Forum. (2016). *The global competitiveness report 2014–2015* (Full Data Edition). Geneva: The World Economic Forum.

# Chapter 16
# Component 2 (Meso): Qualitative Comparative Analysis (QCA)

This chapter comprises three sections. The first explains the QCA research model logic after a brief introduction. The second introduces the QCA methodology. The third presents the QCA results for competitiveness and corruption and focuses on the four case studies discussed here.

**QCA: A Brief Introduction**

QCA is a causal approach situated between qualitative and quantitative methods (Giugni & Yamasaki, 2009; Ragin, 1987; Rihoux, 2003). QCA is appropriate for studies involving small (5–55) observations or samples (Rihoux & Ragin, 2009). However, studies with a large number of samples also exist (Schneider & Wagemann, 2012).

Unlike regression analyses, QCA is *not* a statistical technique that focuses on the likelihood of the relations among variables. Instead, it is a method based on Boolean logic, rooted in set theory, and founded on the notions of sufficiency, the necessity of conditions, and conjunctural causation (Bara, 2014, p. 707; Ragin, 2000). The *necessary* conditions for an outcome are more the exception than the rule in the social sciences. Therefore, alternative combinations of conditions, which are jointly *sufficient* to explain the outcome, can be more significant (Ragin, 2000).

QCA assumes combinatorial and multiple causalities. It means that in QCA an outcome results from factors that react simultaneously with other conditions through several possible paths (Giugni & Yamasaki, 2009; Ragin, 1987). As Giugni and Yamasaki (2009) observe, QCA implies that causality is multiple and that various "pathways" lead to a specific outcome. Thus, a phenomenon must not necessarily require one single cause (or set of causes). Furthermore, causality is conjunctural, which means that conditions interact "in concert" or "chemically" with each other. Consequently, causality is combinatory rather than additive (Mill; Becker as cited in Giugni & Yamasaki, 2009, p. 471).

---

**Supplementary Information** The online version of this chapter (https://doi.org/10.1007/978-3-030-78498-0_16) contains supplementary material, which is available to authorized users.



J. García Portilla, *"Ye Shall Know Them by Their Fruits"*, Contributions to Economics, https://doi.org/10.1007/978-3-030-78498-0_16

Therefore, QCA enables distinguishing paths to success from paths to failure, which do not necessarily mirror each other (Schneider & Wagemann, 2012, p. 8). Likewise, QCA allows identifying configurations of factors (conditions—in this case, theories explaining prosperity differences—see Chap. 5) leading to an outcome (e.g. *transparency* and *competitiveness*).

Furthermore, QCA bases its logic on set memberships. Whether a country experiences high levels of corruption, for instance, can be expressed as a question of set membership: Is country X a member of those states that remain transparent/competitive or not? QCA clusters countries into affinity groups and enables nested case studies to be conducted. It also allows the explanation of actual circumstances in the investigated countries. QCA facilitates understanding differences and similarities, as well as causal mechanisms, through within-case and inter-case comparisons (Ragin, 2003).

Moreover, this study applies the fuzzy-set variant of QCA (fsQCA), which allows cases to have varying degrees of set membership (Schneider & Wagemann, 2012, p. 13). It means that fsQCA capture empirically "different shades of grey" instead of "dividing the world into black and non-black" to inform the analysis and interpretation of results (Schneider & Wagemann, 2012, p. 13). A case does not always have to be a complete member (or a complete non-member) of a group; it may be also a partial member of a set. The membership scores may drop at any point between the two extremes (i.e. between the 0-full non-membership value and the 1-full membership value) (Schneider & Wagemann, 2012, pp. 13–14).

In sum, QCA helps to find explanations for outcomes based on associations of necessity and sufficiency. It therefore allows comparing and analysing different indicators associated with theories of prosperity and their causal effect on the outcome.

I apply QCA to examine which combinations of conditions (for example, of different variables linked to prosperity theories) associate regularly with transparency/competitiveness or, on the contrary, with corruption. The analysis covers 65 countries in Europe and the Americas (see Appendices 3–5 and Supplementary Materials).

## 16.1 QCA Research Model

Appendix 3 contains a detailed model and definitions of the conditions, outcome, sources, and qualitative anchors. Below, I merely briefly explain the underlying rationale. I followed a mixed methods research approach (quantitative and qualitative) and I based the variables selection on the primary prosperity determinants identified quantitatively by theories from different fields (Fig. 16.1).

The database with prosperity variables in different countries constitutes the outcome (*Competitiveness: GCI and Corruption: CPI*). On the other hand, the data of the various theories of prosperity (*Environment Performance (EPI), Religion population, State Religion Legal Origin, Institutions, Ethnicities*) constitute the

| | Category (prosperity theory associated) | Subcategory / (Results group) | Main Theoretical discussion related to outcome | | |
|---|---|---|---|---|---|
| Conditions | Religion | Christian denomination (proportion in population) / (1) | From Weber (1905) to Becker et al. (2016) | The three following works analyse all the categories:<br><br>1. La Porta, et al. (1999); 2. Acemoglu & Robinson, (2012); 3. Michalopoulos & Papaioannou, (2017):<br><br>However, they consider institutions and outcomes mainly from an economic perspective (i.e. excluding Concordats with the Vatican as institutions).<br><br>Likewise, these three works analyse culture in its narrow form of religious determinism on culture (adherents). | * Religion and Institutions overlap at this point |
| | Institutions | Agreements with the Vatican / (all 5) | Witte (2002); Miller (2012); Cook (2012) | | |
| | | State religion / (2) | (Barro and McCleary, 2005) | | |
| | | Legal origin / (3) | (La Porta et al., 1999); (Merryman & Pérez, 2007) | | |
| | Environment and geography / (all 5) | | (Diamond, 1997); (Sachs, 2001; 2003) | | |
| | Cultural determinants (other than religion) | Main Languages fractionalisation / (4) | (Hofstede, 2001); (Alesina et al., 2003) | | |
| | | Main Ethnical fractionalisation / (5) | (Alesina et al., 2003) | | |
| Outcome | Competitiveness / (all 5) | | (Grim, Clark , & Snyder , 2014) | | |
| | Corruption / (all 5) | | (Rose-Ackerman, 2006); (Chase, 2010) | | |

**Fig. 16.1** Categories of conditions and outcome and principal theoretical works (Source: Author's figure)

causal conditions (for the conditions and outcomes of this study, see Fig. 16.1 or Appendix 3).

Extensive empirical research supports the entire set of theories interrelated here (see Part III; Fig. 16.1, Appendix 3). Further, the whole set of theories robustly explains the prosperity differences in the examined countries. Indicators were chosen to consider the theoretical discussions related in Part III and Fig. 16.1. These were derived from a diverse range of publicly available sources. The latest available data for the indicators provided a picture of present-day reality (2016 reports; this is analogous to the quantitative part, i.e. Chap. 15). However, not all the variables were available in 2016 (none, however, was older than 20 years). Appendix

3 contains the databases and sources used, as well as a more detailed explanation of each indicator.

The different years of publication of the original data sources are not a significant problem here. I have previously discussed the issue of long-term persistence (centuries) of countries' relative prosperity performance as well as religious and environment variables (Chap. 8 and Sect. 15.2.1.1). Besides providing theoretical support, the previous quantitative component of this research (regressions) used cross-validation, trees, and an automated method of variables selection (Chap. 15). This confirmed the crucial variables, thus making data selection more objective.

Below, I explain how outcomes and causal conditions were calibrated.

## 16.2 Qualitative Comparative Analysis Methodology

Qualitative Comparative Analysis (QCA) is used to analyse both quantitative and qualitative data, thus enabling causal inferences. The QCA methodology allows for up to seven variables to be tested for their impact on an outcome variable. A truth table is built from qualitative, quantitative, or both kinds of data to show all possible configurations of those variables. The truth table is then analysed algebraically (rather than statistically) to generate one or more statements identifying various conjunctions of sufficient conditions for the outcome to have occurred (Bazeley, 2012, p. 823).

### *16.2.1 Calibration of Outcome and Causal Conditions*

*Outcome requiring explanation:* The corruption and competitiveness of different countries (see Chaps. 3–4).

*Relevant causal conditions:* Theories discussed in the theoretical framework (see Chaps. 5–12; Appendix 3 discusses calibration in detail).

The calibration process followed the strategy described by Schneider and Wagemann (2012). The authors advise that empirical evidence and theoretical information must be used to calibrate fuzzy-set membership scores. Also, the calibration process may be guided by established social science information, obvious evidence, and the researchers' data. Likewise, quantitative data parameters and statistical distributions can be helpful in terms of calibration (p. 41).

Accordingly, the following aspects informed the calibration of the fuzzy-set membership scores: relevant theoretical and social scientific knowledge, and obvious facts (see Parts II and III); empirical evidence and the researcher's data collection (see Appendices 1–2 and Supplementary Materials); statistical distributions and parameters of quantitative data (see Chap. 15). However, the quantitative scales and statistical parameters (Appendices 1–2 and Chap. 15) were *not* automatically transformed to calibrate the fuzzy-sets by default. Schneider and Wagemann

(2012) highly discourage such an automatic transformation because it fails to achieve the criterion of using calibration parameters that are independent of the data. Therefore, this is unlikely to result in set membership scores that correctly represent the significance of the concept being captured (Schneider & Wagemann, 2012, pp. 41).

First, all relevant conditions were divided into five groups (1) predominant religion (population), (2) state religion, (3) legal origin, (4) languages, and (5) ethnicities. Conditions were combined according to their theoretical relevance. Subsequently, data were calibrated with two goals in mind: to reflect reality as much as possible while striking a balance (i.e. excluding two cases where the condition is met out of 50).

Conditions were calibrated using the "direct method", i.e. focusing on qualitative anchors (Ragin, 2000). Anchors were chosen to reflect reality based on the distribution of each condition in the data. At the same time, to understand the effects and interaction of each condition, they required sufficient presence. Many possible anchor configurations were tested to find the optimal solution for each condition. Appendix 3 includes all the conditions and qualitative anchors, as well as a description of indicators.

#### 16.2.1.1 EPI and Concordats Present in All Groups (Along with the Outcome)

The only subcategories exhibiting merely one indicator were the *Environment Performance Index (EPI)* and *Concordats* (Agreements with the Vatican). This made including these subcategories in all the result groups feasible.

*Concordats* are a new qualitative indicator, established here based on Corral and Petschen (2004). This indicator accounts for the international agreements signed by countries with the Roman Catholic Church.

The Roman Catholic Church-State is the inheritor of the Roman Empire and its imperial territoriality (Hofstede, 2001). Therefore, Romanism is the only religious system that, at one and the same time, is a state exercising political (and not only symbolic) functions in today's geopolitical order (Agnew, 2010). Therefore, "Agreements with the Vatican: *Concordats*" is an essential proxy of the legal, institutional, and political closeness of a state with the Roman See (see Appendix 3 for details on the calibration and thresholds of the other indicators).

### *16.2.2 Truth Tables*

After calibration, truth tables were created for each of the five condition groups to measure both competitiveness and corruption. Each of the groups contains one truth table for a positive outcome and another for a negation of the outcome (i.e. its opposite). Accordingly, 20 truth tables were created in total (see Appendix 4).

Inclusion cut-off (incl.cut) was between 0.85 and 0.9 in all cases. Venn diagrams were created to facilitate orientation in truth tables. Sufficiency and necessity analysis was conducted. As the last step, all truth tables and analyses were interpreted both column-wise and row-wise.

Truth tables involve mixed-origin data analyses (quantitative, i.e. *EPI, CPI*; qualitative, i.e. *Concordats*). Conclusions were drawn only from configurations displaying high consistency and high coverage scores.

Consistency thresholds (incl.) were defined by a gap between truth table rows with higher and lower consistency scores (see Schneider & Wagemann, 2012, p. 128). Generally, scores below 0.75 should be avoided. Analysis strictly disregarded consistency scores lower than 0.9, thus producing even more reliable results.

## *16.2.3 Venn Diagrams*

Venn diagrams visualise truth tables to facilitate analysis and the presentation of results. However, truth tables contain more detailed information, for instance, which countries belong to each combination of conditions and measures of belonging (e.g. PRI and incl; see Appendix 4 for conventions and actual truth tables. Section 16.3 presents Venn diagrams for competitiveness. For reasons of space, please refer to Appendix 5 for the Venn diagrams of *corruption*).

### 16.2.3.1 Colours in Venn Diagrams

Green = outcome 1 in the truth table. Green sections indicate that an outcome exists for a specific condition.

Orange = outcome 0 in the truth table. Orange sections indicate that no outcome exists. In other words, such a combination does not lead to the outcome (e.g. low corruption).

White = logical remainder in the truth table (empty row). White sections indicate that logical remainders exist (no cases exist for this combination of conditions).

### 16.2.3.2 Background Colours in Venn Diagrams

Background colours in Venn diagrams denote what happens if no condition is present. Attention to green is called for as this means that if no condition is present, then the outcome is high (it suffices to have one such case to cause a change in colours in Venn diagrams, but not in interpretation). A white background means that no cases exist where no condition is present. An orange background means that when no condition is present, the outcome is not present, and at least one case exists to support this. A blue background indicates a logical contradiction between cases, thus probably indicating a problem.

## 16.3 Analysis of QCA Results

Five different models and their opposites were tested. Together, they addressed the most significant variables identified in the literature review (Chaps. 3–12) and in the quantitative section of this study (regressions) (Chap. 15). Furthermore, the indicators identified in the literature review were included, yet not considered in the quantitative section (i.e. *Concordats*, due to their qualitative origin).

Given that QCA seeks to establish causal conditions, the present models identify pathways to *competitiveness* and *transparency* and their opposite (i.e. *low competitiveness* and *corruption*). No necessary conditions were found and merely a few conditions with sufficient coverage. The truth tables cluster the countries as close to reality as possible. The analyses are based on coverage (cov.r ~0.5) and consistency (incl. = or >0.9) (For a guide to interpretation and to the conventions used in the truth tables, see Appendix 4. See Appendices 4–5 for truth tables, Venn diagrams, and QCA minimisation using the enhanced Quine–McCluskey algorithm). The Venn diagrams below summarise the most important findings for *competitiveness* for all the groups of conditions. The Venn diagrams for *corruption* can be consulted in Appendix 5.

### *16.3.1 Competitiveness*

#### 16.3.1.1 Predominant Religion (Proportion of Adherents) and Competitiveness

**For high *competitiveness*, high *EPI* suffices if *Concordats* with the Vatican are low and if the *Roman Catholic* and *Orthodox* population is low** (Fig. 16.2).

Sufficiency analysis determined with enough coverage (Cov.r) that low *Concordats*, low *Roman Catholic*, and low *Orthodox* religions in the population are sufficient for high competitiveness. Therefore, high competitiveness always occurs if these conditions are met (but this may also happen in other cases).

***Note:*** *Agnostic and atheistic categories are not sufficiently present to affect the model as results remain unchanged. Consequently, to simplify the model, these categories were removed.*

<table>
<tr><td>Positive outcome</td><td>Negative outcome</td></tr>
<tr><td>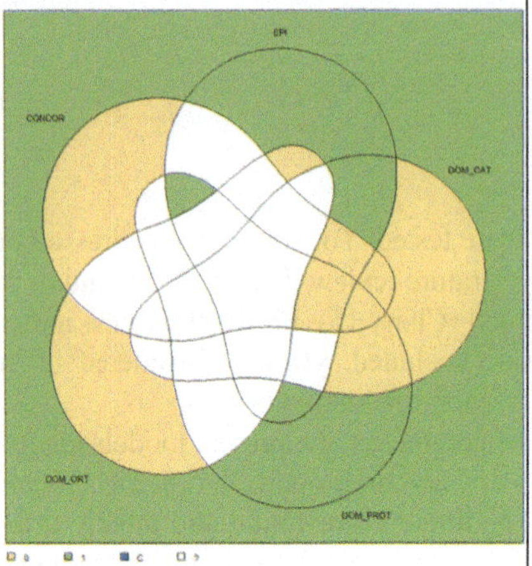
</td><td>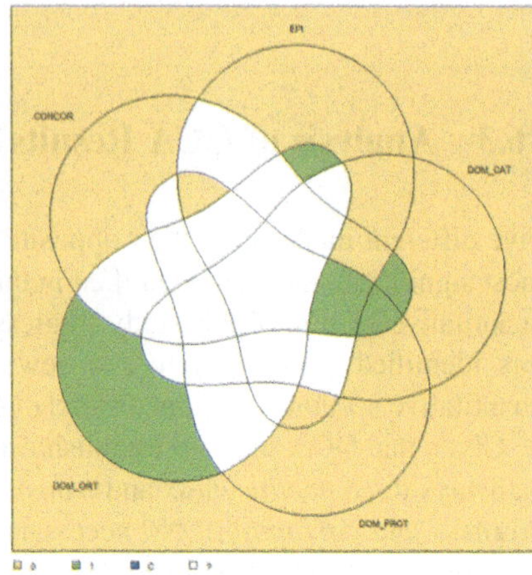
</td></tr>
<tr><td>EPI and Protestant religion in the population positively impact competitiveness.</td><td>A combination of Concordats and Roman Catholic religion in the population decreases competitiveness. Orthodox religion in the population also has a weak adverse effect.</td></tr>
</table>

**Fig. 16.2** Venn diagrams with positive and negative outcomes for *Competitiveness* with *Predominant Religion adherence* in Europe and the Americas (Source: Author's figure)

#### 16.3.1.2 State Religion and Competitiveness

No *State Religion* positively affects *competitiveness*. Having *Concordats* with the Vatican negatively influences competitiveness (Fig. 16.3).

The truth table "State Religion and Competitiveness" (Truth Table 7 in Appendix 4.2) shows a cluster of Latin American countries with perfect coverage and consistency for the negative outcome. Such Latin American cluster presents substantial evidence for the negative outcome of competitiveness with high *Concordats*, low *EPI*, and the presence of *Catholic State religion*.

Regression model 1 ("Competitiveness in the world," Sect. 15.3.1.1) shows a positive effect of Protestant state religion, which disappeared in the models of Europe and the Americas. Cluster 11 in Truth Table 5 (Appendix 4.2) displays those countries that produce the positive outcome with Protestant state religion (DNK, FIN, GBR, ISL, NOR, SWE). Section 8.3.4 has shown that these countries established their state religions under the influence of the Protestant sixteenth-century revolution in Germany. The USA went one step further and removed state religion.

*Note*: Albania, the only *Muslim state* country in the dataset, also presents perfect coverage and consistency for the negative outcome of "State Religion and

| Positive outcome | Negative outcome |
|---|---|
| 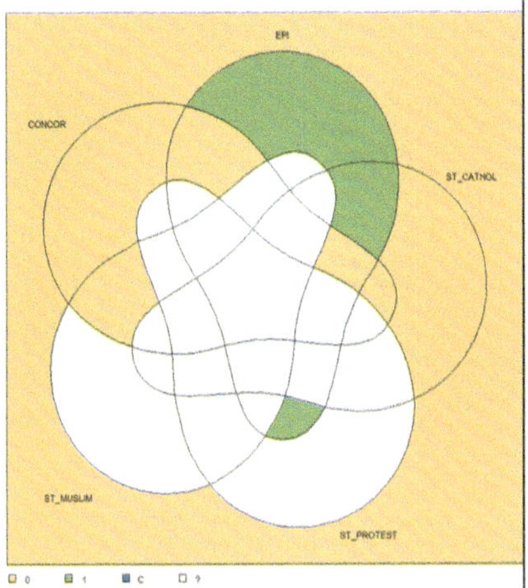  | 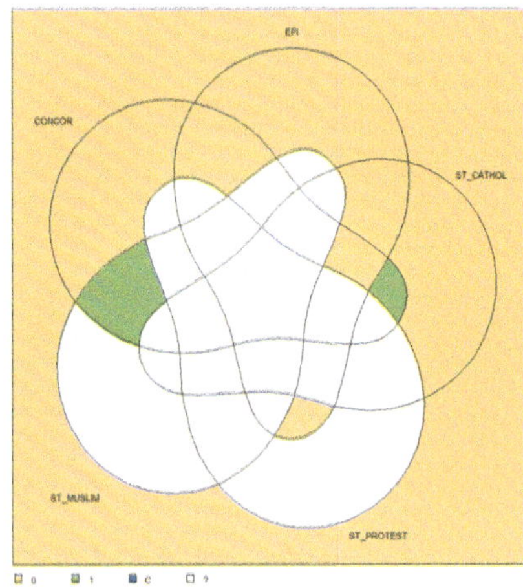  |
| A strong positive influence of *EPI* is clearly visible. Both *Protestant* and *Catholic State religions* have a neutral effect in this analysis. Not enough *Muslim State* countries exist in the dataset to judge the effect of Islam. | *Concordats* negatively influence competitiveness. |

**Fig. 16.3** Venn diagrams with positive and negative outcomes for *Competitiveness* with *State Religion* in Europe and the Americas (Source: Author's figure)

Competitiveness" (Truth Table 7 in Appendix 4.2). However, Albania is not that interesting, because it is only one country, which is not enough to draw any definitive conclusions. Probably, if more *Muslim States* were included in the dataset, such analysis would be useful. In contrast, Latin American countries provide robust evidence since ten of them are present in the outcome.

#### 16.3.1.3 Legal Origin and Competitiveness

The most important factor for high competitiveness is EPI. Additionally, factors like German, English, and Scandinavian legal origin help to increase competitiveness.

The positive outcome for *Legal Origin* and *Competitiveness* in the Fig. 16.4 (see also Truth Table 9 in Appendix 4.2) shows that countries having high competitiveness are those influenced by the Protestant Reformation (Barro & McCleary, 2005; Johnson & Zurlo, 2016; Woodberry, 2012; Obinger, 2009).

However, two countries are the exception to the previous rule in the present clusters (Truth Table 9 in Appendix 4.2). The first is Ireland, a country with *Catholic State Religion* (Barro & McCleary, 2005; Barrett et al. 2001). The second is Austria, a historically Catholic country (Inglehart & Baker, 2000, p. 36), whose population has mostly been Roman Catholic (Johnson & Zurlo, 2016). Moreover, Ireland and

| Positive outcome | Negative outcome |
|---|---|
| 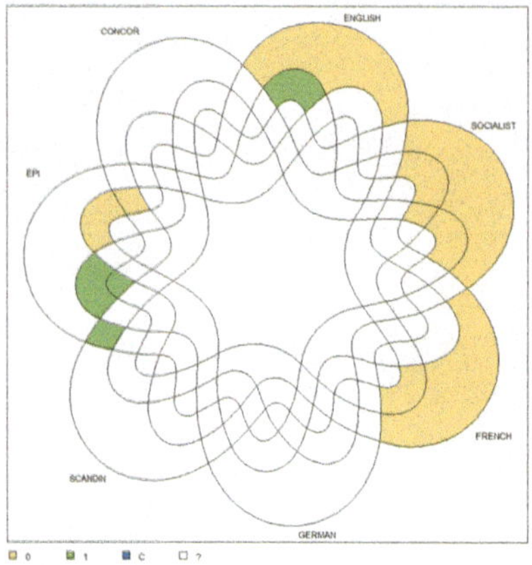 | 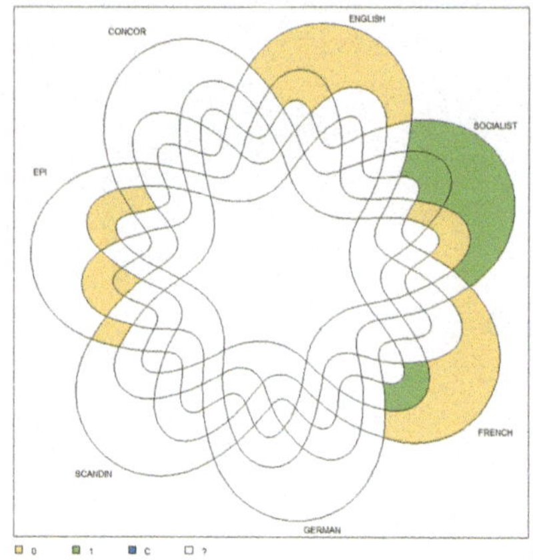 |
| Countries with *German legal origin* (both with or without concordats) are highly competitive. *English legal origin* also helps to increase competitiveness but only in combination with high *EPI*. *English and Scandinavian legal origins* also enhance competitiveness (but it is not possible to determine their relationship to *EPI* and concordats due to lack of diversity). | A large number of cases (12) support the claim that a combination of French legal origin, Concordats, and low EPI, is associated with low competitiveness.<br>This trend is robust and demonstrated mainly by countries from Latin America. Also, countries with a socialist legal origin tend to have low competitiveness if they have low *EPI*.<br>No group with high *EPI* exhibits low competitiveness. Conditions leading to low competitiveness are the same as those leading to high corruption (Appendices 4–5). |

**Fig. 16.4** Venn diagrams with positive and negative outcomes for *Competitiveness* with *Legal Origin* in Europe and the Americas (Source: Author's figure)

Austria are the only outliers in the group of traditional Roman Catholic countries, which typically have *French Legal Origin* (La Porta et al., 1999). Ireland adopted *English Legal Origin* (common law). Similarly, *German Legal Origin* profoundly influenced Austrian jurisprudence (ibid).

Regression analysis also confirmed that German Legal Origin has a consistently positive influence on competitiveness (Sects. 15.3.1.1.3 and 15.3.1.2.2). The theoretical framework corroborates this result (Sect. 8.3.4.1) (Witte, 2002; Berman, 2003). Further, *German Legal Origin* leads to high competitiveness despite the presence of high *Concordats*. This applies to Austria and Germany, where Adolf Hitler signed the *Reichskonkordat* with the Roman See in 1933 (valid to date). In sum, competitiveness seems to follow the same pattern as corruption with regard to *Legal Origin* (Appendix 5).

#### 16.3.1.4 Languages and Competitiveness

The analysis of languages and competitiveness delivered no important results. However, it confirmed the result of the previous analyses, for which the combination of low *EPI*, *high Concordats*, and *Roman languages* is associated with low competitiveness (Fig. 16.5).

| Positive outcome: | Negative outcome: |
|---|---|
| 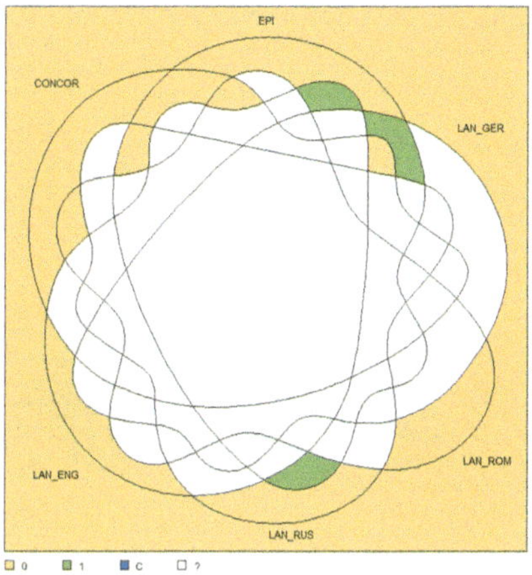  | 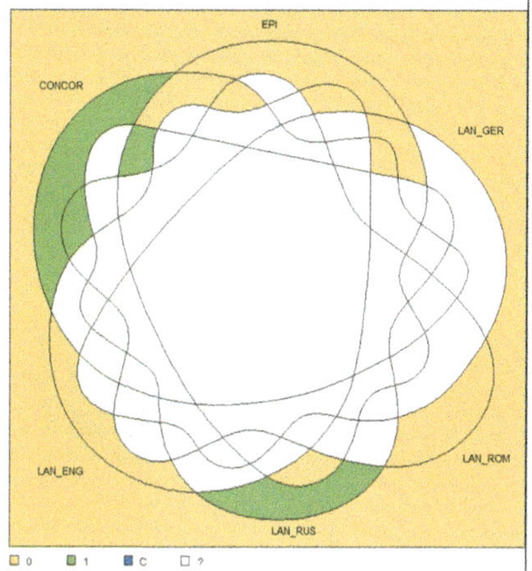  |
| QCA did not identify enough groups to conclusively establish a positive outcome. However, *EPI* is again crucial for high competitiveness. Likewise, all countries with high *competitiveness* have low *Concordats,* excepting Germany and Austria. | Truth Table 15 (Appendix 4) shows a cluster of 11 South American countries having low competitiveness. These countries have low *EPI*, high *Concordats* and speak *Roman languages*. Hence, a combination of these conditions leads to low competitiveness, but none of these conditions alone does.<br>It seems that the Russian language is not an essential condition for low or high competitiveness. The Russian language is present in the cases of Ukraine and Moldavia (low EPI) and Lithuania (high EPI). |

**Fig. 16.5** Venn diagrams with positive and negative outcomes for *Competitiveness* with *Languages* in Europe and the Americas (Source: Author's figure)

In this group, coverage is not high enough to formally establish sufficient conditions. Clusters created by languages are not as accurate as the groups differentiated in the previous three analyses.

#### 16.3.1.5 Ethnicities and Competitiveness

Sufficiency analysis suggests that if a country has high *EPI* and both high and low *white ethnicities*, and if all other conditions are low (*Concordats, Latino, Mestizo,* and *other non-white ethnicities*), then it always exhibits high *competitiveness* (Fig. 16.6).

Many combinations of conditions in this group (Ethnicities and Competitiveness) have low PRI. The evidence supporting these findings is not robust (Truth Tables 17 and 19 in Appendix 4.2).

Table 16.1 summarises the QCA results for *corruption*. Venn diagram analyses of corruption often resemble those of *competitiveness* (Appendix 5).

| Positive outcome | Negative outcome |
|---|---|
| 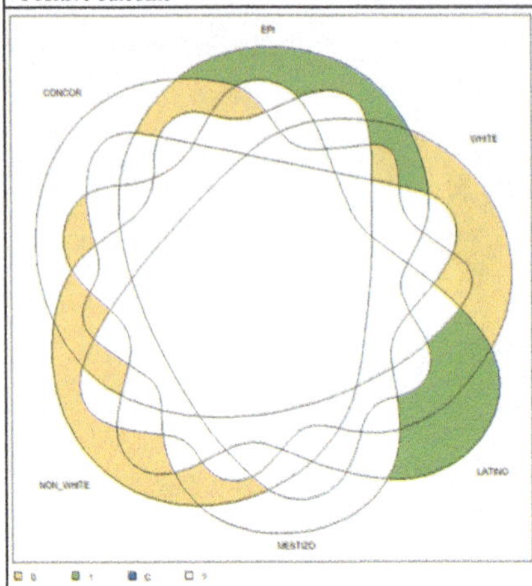 | 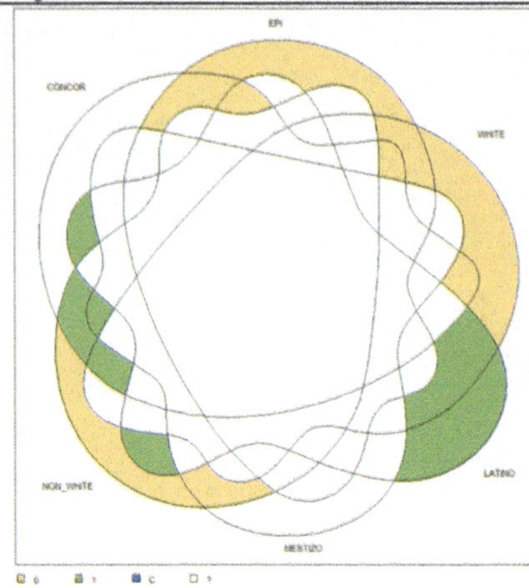 |
| Many (18) countries have *white ethnicity*, high *EPI* conditions and have high *competitiveness*. It seems that the combination of *white*, high *EPI* and high *Concordats* does not lead to high *competitiveness*, while *white*, high *EPI* and low *Concordats* does. | To attain a negative outcome (low *competitiveness*), a country should have high *Concordats*, low *EPI*, predominantly no *white ethnicities*, but predominantly other *non-white ethnicities* (Truth Table 19 in Appendix 4). |

**Fig. 16.6** Venn diagrams with positive and negative outcomes for *Competitiveness* with *Ethnicities* in Europe and the Americas (Source: Author's figure)

## *16.3.2 QCA Results for Outcome Corruption*

The results in Table 16.1 are generally in line with the different theories explaining corruption/prosperity (Chaps. 5–6). Thus, factors associated with Protestantism as a rule denote paths to low *corruption* (or high transparency), such as Protestant adherents, Protestant State religion, German and English legal origin, and the German and English language. In contrast, factors associated with Roman Catholicism (or also Eastern Orthodoxy) involve paths to high *corruption*, such as Catholic adherents and Catholic State Religion, French legal origin, or Roman/Russian languages.

The various truth tables (Appendix 4) show that countries with similar conditions often belong to the same clusters. All these results substantiate Volonté's (2015) finding, namely the overlapping of different cultural and institutional factors towards the outcome. Thus, countries with similar conditions often appear in the same groups. Clusters and group selections have therefore proven to work well. While each path and condition could be analysed in-depth further to establish an even broader theoretical understanding of the results, I analyse only four cases in detail. These cases are the same case studies further considered in more detail in Part VI.

**Table 16.1** Main QCA results for the five groups of conditions

| | Group (condition) | Positive outcome | Negative outcome |
|---|---|---|---|
| 1 | Predominant religion in population (proportion of adherents) | High *EPI* and *Protestant religion adherence* are associated with lower *corruption*, especially if both are present | *Concordats* in combination with *Roman Catholic religion adherence* increase corruption. *Orthodox religion* has a similar negative effect |
| 2 | State Religion | *EPI* and *Protestant State religion* again have a positive effect, i.e. decrease corruption. The difference is that *Concordats* might also have a positive effect only in the absence of *State Religion* | Groups of countries with high *corruption* indicate the substantial adverse effect of *Concordats* in combination with *Roman Catholic State religion. Concordats* combined with *Roman Catholic or Muslim state religion* have a negative effect, i.e. increase corruption |
| 3 | Legal Origin | *German* and *English legal origin* help reduce corruption, while *French* and *Socialist legal origins* and *Concordats* tend to increase corruption.<br>All countries belonging to groups with *Scandinavian, German,* and *English legal origins* have low *corruption* (and always high *EPI*). Countries with *Socialist legal origin* in combination with *Concordats* and high *EPI* tend to have low corruption | Most countries with high corruption are of *French legal origin* and have high *Concordats.* This trend is robust (mainly caused by 13 Latin American countries).<br>No group with high *EPI* has high corruption. Also, countries with *Socialist legal origin* combined with low *EPI* tend to have higher *corruption.*<br>The adverse effect of French and Socialist legal origins and Concordats disappears if a country has high EPI |
| 4 | Languages | Every country with low corruption has high *EPI.* The *German language* always leads to low corruption. Some *German*-speaking countries have high *concordats.* No country belonging to a group of *Roman language* has low corruption | All countries belonging to groups with high *corruption* have low *EPI* (except for some Russian- speaking countries). In general, the *Russian language* tends to lead to higher *corruption. German* and *English*-speaking countries, in general, do not have high *corruption.* High *EPI*, low *Roman*, low *English* and low *Russian* language is a sufficient condition for low *corruption* (in this combination, *corruption* is undoubtedly low, although low *corruption* may be achieved in other ways) |
| 5 | Ethnicities | High *EPI* and high *white* ethnicities in combination with both high and low Concordats leads to | Countries with high *corruption* almost never have predominantly *white* ethnicities, are often |

(continued)

**Table 16.1** (continued)

| | Group (condition) | Positive outcome | Negative outcome |
|---|---|---|---|
| | | low corruption. A sufficient path to low corruption is high *EPI*, high *white*, low *Latino*, low *mestizo*, and low other *non-white* ethnicities. Low *corruption* may happen in other ways, but always occurs in this configuration | *non-white*, and always have low *EPI*. All predominantly *mestizo* countries have high corruption. The effect of other conditions is not evident |

Source: Author's figure. See Appendix 4.3 for truth tables and Appendix 5 for Venn diagrams of corruption

## 16.3.3 *QCA Cases*

This subsection analyses four qualitative cases (Switzerland, Uruguay, Cuba, and Colombia) from a QCA perspective (Please refer to Chap. 17 for further information on the criteria for case selection and more detailed case analyses).

Regarding configurations that indicate enough coverage, high consistency, and an actual outcome, only Colombia and Switzerland (the two extreme cases) exhibited several consistent results. The other two cases (Cuba and Uruguay) only revealed one or two consistent outcomes (see below). The respective outcomes for Colombia and Switzerland are summarised in tabular form below. The extreme cases have either positive outcomes without negative ones (Switzerland) or negative outcomes without positive ones (Colombia) for both *competitiveness* and *corruption*.

### 16.3.3.1 Switzerland

Figure 16.7 summarises the solutions for competitiveness, Fig. 16.8 those for corruption.

#### 16.3.3.1.1 Competitiveness

The combination of the following factors explains (highly consistently) Switzerland's high *Competitiveness* (Fig. 16.7):

1. High Environment Performance (*EPI*);
2. Absence of *State Religion*;
3. Absence of a *Concordat* between the Swiss Confederation and the Vatican/ Roman Catholic Church-State;
4. High relative adherence to *Protestant religion*;
5. *German legal origin*;
6. High proportion of *German-speaking population* (Swiss);
7. High proportion of *white ethnicity*.

| Switzerland | Conditions for Competitiveness | Solution | Cluster | Consistency (incl. = or > 0.9). |
|---|---|---|---|---|
| Positive outcome (high competitiveness) | | **The positive outcome for competitiveness is associated with the following factor combination:** | | |
| | (1) Christian denomination (share of population) | High EPI and adherence to the Protestant religion | CAN,DNK,FIN,GBR,CHE,ISL,NLD,NOR,SWE | 0.975 |
| | (2) State religion | No *State Religion*, low *Concordats*, high EPI | BEL,BGR,CAN,CZE,EST,GRC,CHE,NLD,ROU,RUS,USA | 0.89 |
| | (3) Legal origin | German legal origin, low *Concordats*, high EPI | CHE* | 1 |
| | (4) Main linguistic fractionalisation | Mainly German (Swiss) | CHE* | 0.99 |
| | (5) Main ethnic fractionalisation | White ethnicity, high EPI, low *Concordats* | BEL,BGR,CAN,CZE,EST,FIN,GBR,GRC,CHE,IRL,ISL,LUX,NLD,NOR,ROU,RUS,SWE,USA | 0.94 |
| Negative outcome (low competitiveness) | | **The negative outcome for competitiveness is associated with the following factor combination:** | | |
| | None | NA | NA | NA |

**Fig. 16.7** Conditions, solutions, and clusters for competitiveness (Switzerland) (Source: Author's figure)

Regarding *legal origin* and *languages* (groups 3 and 4), Switzerland stands alone in its corresponding clusters. In group 3, this is probably because the other two countries belonging to *German legal origin* (Germany and Austria) have high *Concordats*. In group 4, Switzerland probably stands alone due to its multi-lingual background (French, Italian, Romansh, and predominant (Swiss) *German*). The other German-speaking countries exhibit no such condition.

#### 16.3.3.1.2 Corruption

Unlike the competitiveness analysis, not all group solutions are consistent for Switzerland with regard to corruption: *State religion* (2) and *ethnicities* (5) are not consistent. However, the following conditions may be said to encourage low *corruption* (high transparency) in the case of Switzerland (Fig. 16.8):

1. High Environment Performance (*EPI*);
2. Absence of a *Concordat* between the Swiss Confederation and the Vatican State;
3. High relative adherence to the *Protestant* religion;
4. *German legal origin*; and.
5. High proportion of *German-speaking* population (Swiss).

| Switzerland | Conditions for Corruption | Solution | Cluster | Consistency (incl. = or > 0.9). |
|---|---|---|---|---|
| Positive outcome (low corruption) | | **The positive outcome for corruption (high transparency) is associated with the following factor combination:** | | |
| | (1) Christian denomination (proportion in population) | High EPI, low *Concordats*, adherence to Protestant religion | CAN,DNK,FIN, GBR,CHE,ISL,NLD,NOR,SWE | 0.96 |
| | (2) State religion | - | - | - |
| | (3) Legal origin | German legal origin, High EPI, low *Concordats* | CHE* | 1 |
| | (4) Main linguistic fractionalisation | Mainly German (Swiss), High EPI, low *Concordats* | CHE* | 1 |
| | (5) Main ethnic fractionalisation | - | - | - |
| Negative outcome (high corruption) | | **The negative outcome for corruption (low transparency) is associated with the following factor combination:** | | |
| | None | NA | NA | NA |

**Fig. 16.8** Conditions, solutions, and clusters for corruption (Switzerland) (Source: Author's figure)

Analysing corruption calls for the same considerations as when analysing competitiveness. The outcome is the same: Switzerland appears on its own in the clusters of groups 3 and 4 (legal origin and languages).

In Switzerland, most conservative Catholics escaped modernisation and centralism by relocating to the mountains, while Liberals and Protestants mostly remained in flat areas that became industrialised (Obinger, 2009). The federal government has been mainly liberal (anti-clerical) and close to Protestantism (ibid). Likewise, the Protestant population was in the majority until the 1970s (Federal Statistical Office, 2017). Currently, the Protestant cantons are the most competitive, while the mountainous Roman Catholic cantons are the least competitive in the Swiss Confederation (UBS Switzerland AG, 2016).

#### 16.3.3.2 Uruguay

In the case of Uruguay, consistency and coverage are generally not high enough to draw significant conclusions.

##### 16.3.3.2.1 Competitiveness

Regarding the positive outcome—*competitiveness* related to *predominant religion*—Uruguay clustered uniquely with Chile (incl. 0.88) in an outcome where one of the most critical factors determining high competitiveness is EPI (Truth Table 1 in Appendix 4.2).

Uruguay exhibits the highest levels of social progress in Latin America (Sect. 4.2) as well as high safety (UNODC, 2013). Along with Chile, it is the only country in Latin America with low perceptions of corruption (Transparency International, 2016). Likewise, Chile and Uruguay are liberal democracies with explicit anti-clerical movements that never allowed concordats to be signed with the Roman Church-State.

Further, Uruguay is by far Latin America's most secular country with the lowest religiosity and lowest proportion of Roman Catholics on the continent (Pew Research Center, 2014, p. 46; Gallup, 2010). The Roman Catholic Church-State did not significantly establish itself in Uruguay, unlike in most Latin American countries. After gaining independence in 1828, Uruguay continued a secular direction with the recognition of civil unions in 1837. In 1917, the Uruguayan constitution completely separated church and state. Religious instruction was banned from public schools and divorce became legalised. Consequently, Uruguayan governments have since progressively reduced the influence of the Roman Catholic Church-State without, however, repressing religion as in Communist systems (Barber, 2012). Thus, for instance, the early and effective separation of church and state meant that the State gained complete control over its education system already in 1877. This is unusual in Latin America (Da Costa, 2009).

##### 16.3.3.2.2 Corruption

Like Cuba, the only condition with an incl. near 0.9 is the positive outcome for *corruption* related to *predominant religion* in the population (incl. 0.831) (Truth Table 21 in Appendix 4.2). In this group, Uruguay clustered with Chile and Cuba. This cluster shows three countries with an unusual performance outside the entire group of Latin American countries. First, they exhibit the relative lowest corruption in the region. Second, Chile and Uruguay separated church and state in their constitutions unusually early in Latin America (1925 and 1918, respectively); Cuba did so in the wake of the Communist revolution (1959). Thirdly, none of these countries has signed a Concordat with the Roman Catholic Church-State. Some other Latin American countries such as Brazil also separated church and state relatively early, but signed international agreements with the Roman See. Fourthly, they exhibit favourable environmental performance (EPI). Geographically, Argentina should also appear in this cluster for geographical and environmental reasons. This, however, is not the case. Argentina has a Concordat with the Vatican/Roman Catholic Church-State, and its constitution still privileges the Roman Catholic Church.

### 16.3.3.3 Cuba

#### 16.3.3.3.1 Competitiveness

(Cuba has no data on competitiveness)

#### 16.3.3.3.2 Corruption

In the case of Cuba, coverage and consistency are generally not high enough to draw significant conclusions from the analysis. However, two important findings are:

1. Cuba appears, with high consistency (0.907), in the cluster MDA, MKD, UKR, BIH, CUB for the negative outcome of corruption associated with *legal origin* (Truth Table 31 in Appendix 4.2). All the countries in this cluster have a *socialist legal origin* and are located mostly in Europe, except for Cuba.
2. The sole other consistent condition with an incl. near 0.9 is the positive outcome of *corruption* for *predominant religion* in the population (incl. 0.831) (Truth Table 21 in Appendix 4.2). In this group, Cuba clustered with Chile and Uruguay, those countries with the lowest perceived corruption in Latin America (Transparency International, 2016).

Cuba ranks in the middle of world distribution on the transparency index (Transparency International, 2016). Compared to the cases studied (Europe and the Americas), the countries clustering with Cuba exhibit moderate to high corruption due to their *Socialist Legal Origin*. However, compared to the rest of Latin American countries, the cluster including Cuba shows moderate to low corruption (i.e. not as high as countries such as Venezuela, Colombia, or Paraguay). In other words, separating the Catholic Church from the state had a positive influence (all three countries in this cluster—Cuba, Chile, and Uruguay—have vigorously implemented this separation). Nonetheless, adopting a socialist legal origin negatively impacts transparency (as the cluster of socialist countries, including Cuba, shows). Moreover, Cuba does not exhibit as much transparency as either Chile or Uruguay. The remaining clusters to which Cuba belongs do not exhibit high enough consistency (Appendix 13.2).

### 16.3.3.4 Colombia

The analysis of Colombia is diametrically opposed to that of Switzerland.

Figure 16.9 summarises the solutions for competitiveness, Fig. 16.10 those for corruption.

#### 16.3.3.4.1 Competitiveness

The analysis of competitiveness and corruption in the case of Colombia reveals similar conclusions.

Note that Paraguay is the only country, alongside Colombia, that clusters for low competitiveness (Fig. 16.9) and high corruption (Fig. 16.10). Therefore, the QCA analysis for Paraguay may be expected to resemble Colombia with regard to competitiveness and corruption.

#### 16.3.3.4.2 Corruption

The combination of the following factors explains highly consistently the prevalence of low competitiveness and high corruption in Colombia *(as well as in Paraguay)*:

1. Low Environment Performance (*EPI*);
2. Concordat with the Vatican;
3. Roman Catholicism as state religion;
4. High adherence to Roman Catholicism;
5. French legal origin,

| **Colombia** | **Conditions for Competitiveness** | **Solution** | **Cluster** | **Consistency (incl. = or > 0.9).** |
|---|---|---|---|---|
| Positive outcome (high competitiveness) | None | **The positive outcome for competitiveness is associated with the following factor combination:** NA | NA | NA |
| Negative outcome (low competitiveness) | | **The negative outcome for competitiveness is associated with the following factor combination:** | | |
| | (1) Christian denomination (proportion in population) | Concordats and Roman Catholic religion | ARG,COL,ECU,MEX,PER,PRY,VEN | 0.931 |
| | (2) State religion | High concordats, low EPI, Catholic State religion | ARG,BOL,BRA,COL,DOM,GTM,PER,PRY,SLV,VEN | 1 |
| | (3) Legal origin | French legal origin, Concordats, low EPI | DOM,MEX,SLV,GTM,BRA,COL,ECU,PER,ARG,BOL,PRY,VEN | 1 |
| | (4) Main linguistic fractionalisation | Low EPI, high Concordats, Roman languages | BOL,BRA,COL,DOM,ECU,GTM,MEX,PER,PRY,SLV,VEN | 1 |
| | (5) Main ethnic fractionalisation | Low EPI, non-white population, high concordats | COL,ECU,MEX,PRY,SLV | 1 |

**Fig. 16.9** Conditions, solutions, and clusters for competitiveness (Colombia) (Source: Author's figure)

6. Roman language (Spanish); and.
7. High proportion of other non-white population.

Colombia is well-known in Latin America for its dominant Roman Catholic Church and widespread religiosity (Levine, 1981, pp. 7–8) and is considered "the most clerical Roman Catholic society of the continent" (Munevar, 2008, p. 389). However, it follows Mexico on the blacklist of the top 50 countries where persecution of Christians is most severe in the world. Colombia and Mexico are the only two countries in the Western hemisphere on that list, along with countries in the Middle East and Africa (Open Doors, 2015). Colombia also exhibits very high homicide and corruption rates compared to the rest of the world (UNODC, 2013; Transparency International, 2016).

In conclusion, a "Catholic and conservative hegemony" has existed in Colombia until 1991, when the Constitution of Rights was promulgated and religious pluralism became legally recognised (Figueroa, 2008, pp. 256–270). However, as a result of centuries of hegemony, the Roman Catholic Church-State still enjoys ample privileges with the Colombian state (Munevar, 2008; Figueroa, 2016).

| Colombia | Conditions for Corruption | Solution | Clusters | Number of cases | Consistency (incl. = or > 0.9). |
|---|---|---|---|---|---|
| Positive outcome (transparency/low corruption) | None | **The positive outcome for *corruption (high transparency)* is associated with the following factor combination:** NA | NA | NA | NA |
| Negative outcome (high corruption) | | **The negative outcome for corruption (low transparency) is associated with the following factor combination:** | | | |
| | (1) Christian denomination (proportion in population) | Concordats and Roman Catholic religion. | ARG,COL,ECU, MEX,PER,PRY,VEN | 7 | 0.933 |
| | (2) State religion | High concordats, low EPI, Catholic State religion | ARG,BOL,BRA,COL,DOM,GTM,HTI,PER,PRY,SLV, VEN | 11 | 1 |
| | (3) Legal origin | French legal origin, Concordats, low EPI | DOM,MEX,SLV, GTM,HTI,BRA,COL,ECU,PER,ARG,BOL,PRY,VEN | 13 | 1 |
| | (4) Main linguistic fractionalisation | Low EPI, high Concordats, Roman languages | BOL,BRA,COL,DOM,ECU,GTM,HTI,MEX,PER,PRY,SLV,VEN | 12 | 1 |
| | (5) Main ethnic fractionalisation | Low EPI, non-white population, high Concordats | COL,ECU,MEX,PRY,SLV | 5 | 1 |

**Fig. 16.10** Conditions, solutions, and clusters for corruption (Colombia) (Source: Author's figure)

# References


Acemoglu, D., & Robinson, J. (2012). *Why nations fail. The origins of power, prosperity and poverty*. Crown Business.

Agnew, J. (2010). Deus Vult: The geopolitics of the Catholic Church. *Geopolitics, 15*(1), 39–61.

Alesina, A., Devleeschauwer, A., Easterly, W., Sergio, K., & Wacziarg, R. (2003). Fractionalization. *Journal of Economic Growth, 8*(2), 155–194.

Bara, C. (2014). Incentives and opportunities: A complexity-oriented explanation of violent ethnic conflict. *Journal of Peace Research, 51*(6), 696–710.

Barber, N. (2012). *Uruguay: A secular outpost legalizes abortion*. Retrieved from http://www.huffingtonpost.com/nigel-barber/uruguay-a-secular-utopia_b_1917005.html

Barrett, D. B., Kurian, G. T., & Johnson, T. M. (2001). *World Christian encyclopedia* (2nd ed.). Oxford University Press.

Barro, R. J., & McCleary, R. M. (2005). Which countries have state religions? *The Quarterly Journal of Economics, 120*(4), 1331–1370.

Bazeley, P. (2012). Integrative analysis strategies for mixed data sources. *American Behavioral Scientist, 56*(6), 814–828.

Becker, S., Pfaff, S., & Rubin, J. (2016). *Causes and consequences of the protestant reformation*. Warwick Economics Research Paper Series.

Berman, H. (2003). *Law and revolution II: The impact of the protestant reformations on the Western Legal tradition*. Harvard University Press, Belknap Press.

Chase, G. (2010). Religion's impact on corruption. *Journal of Business and Economics Perspectives, 5*(1), 102–112.

Cook, E. (2012). *Roman Catholic hegemony and religious freedom: A seventh-day adventist assessment of dignitatis humanae*. Graduate Faculty of Baylor University.

Corral, C., & Petschen, S. (2004). *Tratados Internacionales (1996-2003) de la Santa Sede con los Estados. Concordatos Vigentes*. Universidad Pontificia Comillas.

Da Costa, N. (2009). La laicidad uruguaya. *Archives de sciences sociales des religions* (146), 137–155.

Diamond, J. (1997). *Guns, germs, and steel. The fates of human societies*. W.W. Norton.

Federal Statistical Office. (2017). *Language, religion and culture survey*. Retrieved from https://www.bfs.admin.ch/bfs/en/home/statistics/population/surveys/esrk.html

Figueroa, H. (2008). Balance historiográfico sobre el protestantismo en Colombia. 1940-2007. In GIERSP, *Mirada pluridisciplinar al hecho religioso en Colombia: Avances de investigación*. Grupo Interdisciplinario de Estudios de Religión, Sociedad y Política, GIERSP.

Figueroa, H. (2016). *La persistance des idées traditionalistes en Colombie. Religion et politique (1886-1952)*. L'Harmattan.

Gallup. (2010). *Religiosity highest in world's poorest nations*. Retrieved from http://www.gallup.com/poll/142727/religiosity-highest-world-poorest-nations.aspx

Giugni, M., & Yamasaki, S. (2009). The policy impact of social movements: A replication through qualitative comparative analysis. *Mobilization, 14*(4), 467–484.

Grim, B. J., Clark, G., & Snyder, R. E. (2014). Is religious freedom good for business?: A conceptual and empirical analysis. *Interdisciplinary Journal of Research on Religion, 10*(4), 1–19.

Hofstede, G. (2001). *Culture's consequences. Comparing values, behaviours, institutions and organizations across nations*. Thousand Oaks: Sake.

Inglehart, R., & Baker, W. (2000). Modernization, cultural change, and the persistence of traditional values. *American Sociological Review, 65*(1), 19–51.

Johnson, T. M., & Zurlo, G. A. (2016). *World Christian Database*. Retrieved 04 2016, from Center for the Study of Global Christianity at Gordon-Conwell Theological Seminary. www.globalchristianity.org

La Porta, R., Lopez-De-Silanes, F., Shleifer, A., & Vishny, R. (1999). The quality of government. *Journal of Law, Economics and Organization, 15*(1), 222–279.

Levine, D. (1981). *Religion and politics in Latin America: The Catholic Church in Venezuela & Colombia.* Princeton Legacy Library.

Merryman, J., & Pérez Perdomo, R. (2007). *The civil law tradition: An introduction to the legal systems of Europe and Latin America* (3rd ed.). Stanford University Press.

Michalopoulos, S., & Papaioannou, E. (2017). *The long economic and political shadow of history—Volume 3: Europe and the Americas.* CEPR Press Centre for Economic Policy Research.

Miller, N. (2012). *The religious roots of the first amendment.* Oxford University Press.

Munevar, J. (2008). Transformación doctrinal y actitudinal de la participación política de las iglesias cristianas evangélicas en Colombia. In GIERSP., *Mirada pluridisciplinar al hecho religioso en Colombia: Avances de investigación.* Bogotá, Colombia: Grupo Interdisciplinario de Estudios de Religión, Sociedad y Política.

Obinger, H. (2009). Religion and the consolidation of the Swiss Welfare State, 1848-1945. In P. Manow & K. van Kersbergen (Eds.), *Religion, class coalitions and welfare states* (pp. 176–209). Cambridge University Press.

Open Doors. (2015). *World Watch List (WWL).* The 50 countries where persecution of Christians is most extreme. Retrieved from https://www.opendoorsusa.org/wp-content/uploads/2019/01/WWL2019_FullBooklet.pdf

Pew Research Center. (2014). *Religion in Latin America. Widespread change in a historically Catholic Region.* Retrieved from: https://www.pewforum.org/2014/11/13/religion-in-latin-america/

Ragin, C. (1987). *The comparative method.* University of California Press.

Ragin, C. C. (2000). *Fuzzy-set social science.* University of Chicago Press.

Ragin, C. (2003). *Making comparative analysis count.* COMPASSS Working Paper 2003-10.

Rihoux, B. (2003). Bridging the gap between the qualitative and quantitative worlds? A retrospective and prospective view on qualitative comparative analysis. *Field Methods, 15*, 351–365.

Rihoux, B., & Ragin, C. C. (2009). *Configurational comparative methods: Qualitative comparative analysis (QCA) and related techniques* (Vol. 1–51). Sage. https://doi.org/10.4135/9781452226569.

Rose-Ackerman, S. (2006). *International handbook on the economics of corruption.* Edward Elgar.

Sachs, J. (2001). *Tropical underdevelopment.* National Bureau of Economic Research, Working Paper, 8119 (NBER), 1–37.

Sachs, J. (2003). *Institutions don't rule: Direct effects of geography on per capita income.* Bureau of Economic Research Working Paper, 9490 (NBER), 1–13.

Schneider, C., & Wagemann, C. (2012). *Set-theoretic methods for the social sciences.* Cambridge University Press.

Transparency International. (2016). Retrieved from Corruption perception index http://www.transparency.org/cpi2013/results

UBS Switzerland AG. (2016). *L'indicateur de compétitivité des cantons 2016.* UBS Switzerland AG Chief Investment Office WM Case postale, CH-8098 Zurich.

UNODC. (2013). *The Global Study on Homicide. Research and Trend Analysis Branch (RAB), Division of Policy Analysis and Public Affairs (DPA).* (D. o. under the supervision of Jean-Luc Lemahieu, Ed.)

Volonté, C. (2015). Culture and corporate governance: The influence of language and religion in Switzerland. *Management International Review, 55*, 77–118.

Weber, M. (1905). *Die protestantische Ethik und der Geist des Kapitalismus.* Verlag Wirtschaft und Finanzen.

Witte, J. (2002). *Law and Protestantism: The legal teachings of the Lutheran Reformation.* University Press.

Woodberry, R. (2012). The missionary roots of liberal democracy. *American Political Science Review (APSR), 106*(2), 244–274.

# Part VI
# Component 3 (Micro): Case Studies

**Switzerland, Uruguay, Cuba, and Colombia**

This component analyses four case studies against the background of a literature review and applying Critical Discourse Analysis (CDA). The case study approach is holistic and seeks to understand generalisable processes and patterns to construct an example of Grounded Theory (GT). In the present study, this approach combines *within-case* and *cross-case* causal inferences (comparative cases and QCA) in order to elucidate the causal mechanisms giving rise to empirical regularities (Goertz, 2017). To offer the broadest possible comparability, multiple case studies were conducted rather than a single in-depth case study.

This part contains six chapters. While the following chapter describes the selection criteria and methods, the four subsequent chapters develop the four case studies. The closing chapter compares and contrasts the four cases.

Reference

Goertz, G. (2017). *Multimethod research, causal mechanisms, and case studies: An integrated approach*. Princeton University Press.

# Chapter 17
# Case Selection Criteria, Methods, and Data Treatment

Nested cases (at the opposite ends of a negative-to-positive scale) were selected from the quantitative database (Appendices 1–4 and Supplementary Materials) for more in-depth empirical (i.e. within-case) analysis. Four countries were compared: Switzerland, Uruguay, Cuba, and Colombia. These cases are also linked to the correlated variables in the quantitative model and to the sufficient conditions in the QCA.

Cases were selected based on the "extreme case method". This consists of a selection of cases exemplifying extreme or unusual values of one of the variables of analysis. This approach is appropriate for exploratory research (Gerring & Seawright, 2008). The QCA cases (Sect. 16.3.3) already mentioned some of the variables that characterise these countries as extreme. Section 17.5 further illustrates and compares some of the variables considered. The cases also analyse within-country variations by region (whenever possible) (i.e. more Catholic versus more Protestant areas in Switzerland, Uruguay, Colombia). Such analysis may also be a source of inferential leverage. This approach combines *within-case* and *cross-case* causal inferences to elucidate the causal mechanisms giving rise to empirical regularities (Goertz, 2017). To offer the broadest possible comparability, multiple case studies were conducted rather than a single in-depth case study.

## 17.1 Extreme Positive Case (Worldwide): Switzerland

Switzerland has the highest competitiveness score in the world (World Economic Forum, 2016), one of the lowest homicide rates (0.6 (UNODC, 2013)), and one of the lowest corruption indices in the world (85 (Transparency International, 2016)). The country also enjoys widely acclaimed political, economic, and social stability.

**Supplementary Information** The online version of this chapter (https://doi.org/10.1007/978-3-030-78498-0_17) contains supplementary material, which is available to authorized users.



J. García Portilla, *"Ye Shall Know Them by Their Fruits"*, Contributions to Economics, https://doi.org/10.1007/978-3-030-78498-0_17

Its population and cantonal (i.e. federated) system exhibit a mixed distribution of Roman Catholics and Protestants, making it an ideal case to analyse and compare the historical influences of these denominations. Furthermore, the author developed this research in Switzerland, which facilitated accessing and gathering primary and secondary information.

## 17.2 Extreme Positive Case (Latin America): Uruguay

Uruguay has the highest social progress score in Latin America (Porter et al., 2015). Besides Chile, it is also one of the most transparent countries in Latin America (Transparency International, 2016) and one of the continent's most secular countries (Pew Research Center, 2014). These facts make Uruguay a worthwhile case for examining whether the factors that made Uruguay less religious have also made the country less corrupt and more equal. Consequently, this case provides vital information for understanding the interrelations between the variables under study.

## 17.3 Cuba: *A sui generis Case* (Communist Proxy)

Cuba is the only Communist country in the Americas. Communism and secularism are still in force in a country of contrasts: Cuba has one of the lowest homicide rates in the Americas (4.2 (UNODC, 2013)) but also one of the continent's lowest social progress indexes (Porter et al., 2015).

The Cuban government actively suppressed religion for decades. However, since the fall of the Soviet Union, the government has increased religious liberty by opening up political space for religious belief and practice. This opening has resulted in a dramatic flourishing of religious life in recent years (Goldenziel, 2009). Further, Cuba might also serve as a proxy of former socialist countries that have tried to eradicate the influence of religion on the state through adopting Marxist ideology. Cuba currently faces corruption levels comparable to former Soviet countries (Transparency International, 2016).

## 17.4 Extreme Negative Case: Colombia

Colombia is a proxy country in Latin America. It is characterised by pervasive Roman Catholicism (i.e. with a valid Concordat, and one of the highest proportion of adults raised as Roman Catholics worldwide (Pew Research Center, 2014)). Other dominant features include high levels of corruption (Transparency International, 2016), and one of the world's lowest equality (World Bank, 2016) and safety rankings (World Economic Forum, 2017). Moreover, the author's first-hand experience of working in government, civil society, and international agencies in his native country provided direct insight (along with his extensive network).

## 17.5 Summary of Case Selection Criteria

Each of the selected countries serves as a proxy of a larger group of countries (Latin American Strong Catholic, Secular, Communism, Protestant or mixed Old World.). Comparing Switzerland and Latin American countries illuminates how religion and prosperity indicators evolve differently within diverse political systems and against the background of different historical roots.

Nested (extreme) cases were chosen for more in-depth empirical, quantitative and QCA analysis (see Supplementary Materials). Table 17.1 summarises the four cases.

## 17.6 Methods and Data Treatment

The qualitative approach adopted here concentrated on which patterns in particular (Silverman, 2005, p. 9) might trigger the observed effects, and hence complemented the analysis of empirical correlations and QCA. The aim was to gain a greater understanding of the research problem (Zikmund, 2003, p. 111), hence complementing the statistical and QCA analyses of the previous chapters, even if this approach implies that matters are "subjective in nature" (Zikmund, 2003, p. 132).

### *17.6.1 Qualitative Method: Critical Discourse Analysis (CDA) and Religion*

Discourse analysis is central to this study, mainly because discourse, knowledge, and power are closely related (Burr, 2003, p. 67; Carabine, 2001, pp. 267–268). One especially fruitful type of discourse analysis was established by the French philosopher Michel Foucault. He suggested examining the interconnections between discourse, knowledge, and power based on his key concept of "genealogy". This, as we will see, is related to institutions and prosperity.

Foucault (1972) developed an elaborate conceptual framework for discourse analysis and proposed a rigorous methodological system to underpin such analysis. However, he did not provide a "how to guide" to genealogy. Hence, methodologies and applications vary (Carabine, 2001).

Importantly, CDA cannot be applied mechanically (Hjelm, 2014). Nor does any universal CDA methodology exist (Fairclough, 2010, p. 6). On the contrary, every

**Table 17.1** A qualitative comparison of the four case studies

| Item/Country | Colombia | Cuba | Uruguay | Switzerland |
|---|---|---|---|---|
| Social Progress Index | Medium | Low | High | High |
| Equality | Low | High | High | High |
| Crime and homicide rate | High | Low | Low | Low |
| Freedom of conscience and religious freedom | Recent (1991). However, the hegemonic power of the Church remains in place | Recent (1992) | Old. 1837; 1918 total separation of church and state | Old. 1798; the 1848 Constitution guaranteed freedom of religion, even if church and state were not completely separate |
| Influence of the Roman Catholic Church on state affairs | High | Low | Low | Low |
| Religiosity | High | Medium-high (mostly Catholic and Afro-Cuban) | Low | Low |
| Competitiveness | Medium | Low | Medium | High |
| Education levels | Low | Medium | High | High |
| Influence of the Roman Catholic Church on education | High | Low | Low | Low |
| Corruption | High | High | Low | Low |
| Historical influence of the Protestant Reformation | Low | Low | Low | High |
| Percentage of Roman Catholics | High | Medium | Low (below 50%) | Low (below 50%) |
| Concordats with the Roman See | Yes | No | No | No, but some cantons have agreements. Switzerland has a unique dual legal system for the Church |
| Christian persecution | High | Medium | Low | Low |
| Syncretism of spiritism rituals with Roman Catholic traditions | High | High | Low | Low |

(continued)

**Table 17.1** (continued)

| Item/Country | Colombia | Cuba | Uruguay | Switzerland |
|---|---|---|---|---|
| Incidence of liberation theology (LT) | Medium | Low (Cuban revolution influenced LT) | Low | Low |

(Source: Author's figure. Based on Beltrán & Quiroga, 2017; Beltrán, 2008; Blanco, 2008; Figueroa, 2016; Gill 1998, 2013; Koonings and Kruijt 2004; Crahan, 1979, 2017; Levine, 1981; Munevar, 2008; Obinger, 2009; Open Doors, 2015; Pew Research Center, 2014; Transparency International, 2016; World Economic Forum, 2016)

analytical approach to discourse requires specific design (Hjelm, 2014, p. 860). Oswick (2012) shares similar views and sees CDA as the only discursive method for considering ideology and power. CDA bridges cultural and linguistic studies in a critical approach. Thus, it enables researchers to adequately examine the role of religion in creating, transforming, reproducing, and sustaining inequalities (Hjelm, 2014, pp. 855–58).

Equally importantly, CDA is ethically committed to exposing the processes through which discourses disseminate social structures that perpetuate hegemony (i.e. maintain and assert the interests of dominant groups or classes) (Fairclough and Wodak 1997; Wodak as cited in Heracleous, 2006, p. 4) and suppress alternative constructions (Hjelm, 2014, p. 860).

CDA is one of the most used methodologies for analysing language and texts in a wide range of fields, including management and organisation studies (The Editors, 2010, p. 1192). However, studies employing CDA are scarce in the sociology of religion, and the valuable research potential of CDA has been underused as a result (Hjelm, 2014; Moberg, 2013). Therefore, Hjelm (2014) has strongly encouraged sociologists of religion to apply CDA, due to the obvious lack of critical approaches to religion that take inequality and hegemony seriously (p. 857).

### *17.6.2 Critical Discourse Analysis Protocol*

Fairclough (1992), Fairclough (2010), and Gee (2011) have developed stringent guidelines for applying Critical Discourse Analysis (CDA). According to Fairclough (2010) selecting a CDA methodology involves developing a theoretical framework relevant to a specific research project than choosing from an existing repertoire of methods (Fairclough, 2010, p. 225).

What makes CDA unique is its division of analysis into three, cross-fertilising aspects: (1) Textual analysis, (2) Analysis of discourse practice, and (3) Analysis of social practice (including the relationship to existing hegemonies) (Hjelm, 2014, p. 861; Fairclough, 1992, p. 73). These categories are of central interest for this study as they help produce a comprehensive understanding of the impact of religion on the three levels of analysis:

*The first level of analysis (textual)* involves closely studying a range of texts such as political constitutions or Christian documents including The Holy Bible. Especially the Scriptures are central to analysing Christianity, as the text has remained largely unaffected by time for centuries (i.e. King James or Martin Luther versions). In contrast, Christian traditions have changed over time and vary among denominations.

*The second level (analysis of discourse practice)* considers the paradigms and public discourse of Protestants, Roman Catholic Church-State leaders, and government and civil society stakeholders.

*The third level (analysis of social practice)* explores the coherence between formal and de facto discourses, including the "commonsensical" language of social practices. Typically, producing documents for their own sake neither relates to nor explains social practice. Nevertheless, it is possible to analyse their coherence and influence in institutions. Comparing lived reality beyond formal discourses allows identifying patterns of social acceptance related to corruption and prosperity.

### 17.6.3 Data Treatment

Sixty semi-structured interviews were conducted and analysed using memos and open coding. Protestant and Roman Catholic Church-State leaders, government, academics, and civil society stakeholders were interviewed in a snowball system between 2015 and 2017. Interviews were conducted in English, German, and French, in the German and French-speaking regions of Switzerland. Interviews in Latin America were conducted in Spanish and English (i.e. English speakers in the Colombian Caribbean). All interviews were translated into English before coding. For reasons of scope, not all the data or stakeholders interviewed appear in the main body of this book. Table 17.2 shows the total number of interviews conducted in each country.

Interviewees were mostly religious leaders or educated and informed stakeholders. Many stakeholders interviewed were also university professors or academic researchers. Protestants, Catholics, or non-religious interviewees were also asked about their different ideologies.

**Table 17.2** Interviews conducted in this research

| Country | Colombia | Cuba | Uruguay | Switzerland | Total interviews |
|---|---|---|---|---|---|
| Number of interviews | 16 | 15 | 12 | 17 | 60 |

(Source: Author's figure)

#### 17.6.3.1 Protecting Interviewee Identity

Before interviewing, stakeholders agreed to release their data on condition of anonymity. Consequently, the discussion offered in this book and the corresponding public datasets only contain stakeholders' general institutional affiliations for comparison/triangulation purposes (e.g. government officer, university expert-lawyer, Catholic priest, Protestant preacher). Other sensitive data possibly enabling identification were omitted.

#### 17.6.3.2 Coding

Two qualitative researchers independently coded the data to align code application and code definitions (a total of three independent researchers). Moreover, the author took position in a separate memorandum (Appendix 5).

#### 17.6.3.3 Triangulation

Triangulation is essential for crosschecking information through multiple procedures and sources. It produces either corroboration or convergence in the case of agreement or divergence in the case of disagreement.

The notion of identifiable Roman Catholic or Protestant traditions requires gathering theoretical and historical data as well as qualitative data from interviewees. Although interviewees shared their perceptions of religious traditions, these perceptions do not provide robust evidence of historical linkages or ramifications. Present-day interviewees can only share their impressions of what their country has inherited from its religious background.

Therefore, findings were triangulated using a triple strategy: (1) Diverse stakeholder perspectives were included in each code (e.g. interviews with a government officer, a Catholic priest, a Protestant pastor); (2) public documents or discourses; and (3) other materials (e.g. historical, theoretical, textbooks).

The next four chapters provide background information on the religion–prosperity–institution nexuses for each of the four cases. Each case study includes charts that compare the different stakeholder principles identified in terms of (1) Prosperity, (2) Corruption, or (3) Church-State relations. Each chart is followed by a three-level CDA analysis.

Case details vary depending on historical importance, the information relevant for comparison, and scope. More information is deliberately provided for Switzerland, since this is the only European country compared and contrasted with the three selected Latin American countries. Such detailed background information and three empirical analyses concern prosperity, corruption, and church-state relations. Consequently, the case of Switzerland also draws more detailed conclusions from its three empirical analyses. By comparison, each Latin American case contains briefer background information and merely one empirical analysis (Uruguay: prosperity; Cuba: corruption; Colombia: prosperity). The respective conclusions are synthesised in Chap. 22.

Each case begins by characterising the background information and the main features of the prosperity–corruption–religion nexus. This is followed by empirical analysis.

## References


Beltrán, W. M. (2008). Aproximación histórico-interpretativa al proceso de diversificación religiosa en Colombia. In S. y. Grupo Interdisciplinario de Estudios de Religión, *Mirada pluridisciplinar al hecho religioso en Colombia: Avances de investigación*. Universidad de San Buenaventura.

Beltrán, W. M., & Quiroga, J. D. (2017). Pentecostalismo y política electoral en Colombia (1991-2014). *Colombia Internacional, 91*, 187–212.

Blanco, M. Ó. (2008). La Nación católica durante la Regeneración (1886-1900): perspectivas historiográficas. *Anuario Historia Regional y de las Fronteras, 13*(1), 157–180.

Burr, V. (2003). *Social constructionism* (2nd ed.). Routledge.

Carabine, J. (2001). Unmarried motherhood 1830-1990: A genealogical analysis. In S. T. M. Wetherell (Ed.), Discourse as data – A guide for analysis. Sage.

Crahan, M. E. (1979). Salvation through Christ or Marx: Religion in revolutionary Cuba. Special Issue:The Church and Politics in Latin America. *Journal of Interamerican Studies and World Affairs, 21*(1), 156–184.

Crahan, M. E. (2017). Cuba: Religion and civil society. *Social research, 84*(2), 383–405.

Fairclough, N. (1992). *Discourse and social change*. Polity Press.

Fairclough, N. (2010). *Critical discourse analysis: The critical study of language* (2nd ed.). Pearson Education.

Fairclough, N., & Wodak, R. (1997). Critical discourse analysis. In T. A. van Dijk (Ed.), *Discourse as social interaction: Discourse studies: A multidisciplinary introduction* (Vol. 2, pp. 258–284). Sage.

Figueroa, H. (2016). *La persistance des idées traditionalistes en Colombie. Religion et politique (1886-1952)*. L'Harmattan.

Foucault, M. (1972). *The archaeology of knowledge*. Routledge.

Gee, J. (2011). *How to do discourse analysis*. Routledge.

Gerring, J., & Seawright, J. (2008). Case selection techniques in case study research: A menu of qualitative and quantitative. *Political Research Quarterly, 61*(2), 294.

Gill, A. (1998). *Rendering unto Caesar: The Catholic Church and the state in Latin America*. Chicago University Press.

Gill, A. (2013). Religious pluralism, political incentives, and the origins of religious liberty. Global challenges. In A. Hertzke (Ed.), *The future of religious freedom* (pp. 107–127). Oxford University Press.

Goertz, G. (2017). *Multimethod research, causal mechanisms, and case studies: An integrated approach*. Princeton University Press.

Goldenziel, J. (2009). Sanctioning faith: Religion, state, and U.S.-Cuban relations. *Journal of Law & Politics, 25*(179), 179–210.

Heracleous, L. (2006). *Discourse, interpretation, organization*. Cambridge University Press.

Hjelm, T. (2014). Religion, discourse and power: A contribution towards a critical sociology of religion. *Critical Sociology, 40*(6), 855–872.

Koonings, K., & Kruijt, D. (2004). *Armed actors: Organised violence and state failure in Latin America*. Zed Press.

Levine, D. (1981). *Religion and politics in Latin America: The Catholic Church in Venezuela & Colombia*. Princeton Legacy Library.
Moberg, M. (2013). First-, second-, and third-level discourse analytic approaches in the study of religion: Moving from meta-theoretical reflection to implementation in practice. *Religion, 43*(1), 1–22.
Munevar, J. (2008). Transformación doctrinal y actitudinal de la participación política de las iglesias cristianas evangélicas en Colombia. In Grupo Interdisciplinario de Estudios de Religión, Sociedad y Política, GIERSP, *Mirada pluridisciplinar al hecho religioso en Colombia: Avances de investigación* (pp. 375–399). Bogotá, Colombia.
Obinger, H. (2009). Religion and the consolidation of the Swiss Welfare State, 1848-1945. In P. Manow & K. van Kersbergen (Eds.), *Religion, class coalitions and welfare states* (pp. 176–209). Cambridge University Press.
Open Doors. (2015). *World Watch List (WWL)*. The 50 countries where persecution of Christians is most extreme. Retrieved from https://www.opendoorsusa.org/wp-content/uploads/2019/01/WWL2019_FullBooklet.pdf
Oswick, C. (2012). Discourse analysis and discursive research. In G. S. (Ed.), *The practice of qualitative organizational research: Core methods and current challenges*. Sage.
Pew Research Center. (2014). *Religion in Latin America. Widespread Change in a Historically Catholic Region*. Retrieved from https://www.pewforum.org/2014/11/13/religion-in-latin-america/
Porter, M., Stern, S., & Green, M. (2015). *Social Progress Index 2015*. Retrieved from https://www.socialprogress.org/?tab=2&code=NOR
Silverman, D. (2005). *Doing qualitative research* (2nd ed.). Sage.
The Editors. (2010). Critical discourse analysis (CDA) in context: Alternative perspectives on the analysis of discourse. *Journal of Management Studies, 47*(6), 1192–1193. https://doi.org/10.1111/j.1467-6486.2010.00942.x.
Transparency International. (2016). *Corruption perceptions index 2016*. Retrieved from https://www.transparency.org/news/feature/corruption_perceptions_index_2016
UNODC. (2013). *Global study on homicide 2013: Trends, contexts, data*. Retrieved from https://www.unodc.org/documents/data-and-analysis/statistics/GSH2013/2014_GLOBAL_HOMICIDE_BOOK_web.pdf
World Bank. (2016). *GNI* per capita. Retrieved from http://data.worldbank.org/indicator/NY.GNP.PCAP.CD?display=map
World Economic Forum. (2016). *The global competitiveness report 2014–2015* (Full Data Edition). The World Economic Forum.
World Economic Forum. (2017). *The travel & tourism competitiveness report*. World Economic Forum.
Zikmund, W. (2003). *Business Research Methods* (7th ed.). Thomson South-Western.

# Chapter 18
# a) Switzerland: Extreme Positive Case Study (Worldwide)

> *"In the name of God Almighty" (Preamble to the Federal Constitution of the Swiss Confederation, 2018)*
> *"Protestants value rationality and hard work, and see wealth as a reward from God, an ethos which helped lay the foundations of modern Swiss prosperity". [...]*
>
> *"Due to the influx of Italian, Spanish, and Portuguese workers, Catholics have outnumbered Protestants in Switzerland since the 1970s" (Swiss Federal Department of Foreign Affairs—FDFA Presence Switzerland, 2018).*

These passages from official Swiss government sources reflect the obvious historical importance of Christian religion in institutional affairs in Switzerland. This case study seeks to briefly describe the possible impacts of the two major historical religions (Protestants and Catholics) on Switzerland's institutions, and thus on the country's prosperity.

Switzerland is the world's oldest democratic nation-state, the oldest federal state in Europe and the world's most competitive country (World Economic Forum, 2016, 2017). By international standards, its institutional structure is exceptionally well-organised. Such outstanding characteristics are worthy of admiration considering the challenges facing an ethnically, linguistically, socioeconomically, and religiously diverse society. Moreover, such social divisions do not necessarily all cluster territorially (Gruner as cited in Obinger, 2009, p. 180). The following sections consider the roots of prosperity and Christian religion in Switzerland.

---

**Supplementary Information** The online version of this chapter (https://doi.org/10.1007/978-3-030-78498-0_18) contains supplementary material, which is available to authorized users.



J. García Portilla, *"Ye Shall Know Them by Their Fruits"*, Contributions to Economics, https://doi.org/10.1007/978-3-030-78498-0_18

## 18.1 Religious Roots of Swiss Prosperity

Obinger's (2009) detailed historical study concludes "that religion is indeed important for explaining the developmental trajectory of the Swiss welfare state ..." (p. 177). It also extends significantly beyond Weber's (1905) understanding of Protestant rationality and hard work suggested by the FDFA (2018) (see citation at the beginning of this chapter). For Obinger (2009), religion has impacted Swiss social policy in complex and indirect ways. He identifies at least two channels of influence: first, the country's heterogeneous religious make-up, and thus its denominational divide, which has profoundly impacted state and institution building in Swiss society. Secondly, Switzerland's party system reflects the impact of religion on public policy in the "complexion of the federal government" (Obinger, 2009, p. 177). Both channels concern the strong religious tensions that dominated the modern Swiss state and nation-building from the outset. In this light, the next sections analyse some historical institutional changes and several variations concerning the country's religious distribution.

## 18.2 Roman Catholics and Protestants in Switzerland

While Switzerland has traditionally been religiously diverse, Reformed Protestantism has predominated since the Protestant Reformation (Baumann & Stolz, 2009). However, since the 1970s Roman Catholicism has been the predominant religious denomination (see initial FDFA citation). Figure 18.1 maps Switzerland's denominations nearly two centuries after the beginning of the Protestant Reformation (sixteenth century).

The dark grey areas represent those regions where Roman Catholicism persisted after the Protestant Reformation. Notably, they correspond mainly to the central cantons of Lucerne and its environs, Fribourg, north-western Bern (present-day Jura), and the southern cantons of Valais and Ticino. The bright grey areas represent the Reformed cantons. These are Zürich, Bern, and Basel (i.e. today's German-speaking region), and Lausanne and Geneva in the French-speaking part. The striped and mid-grey areas represent mixed regions, some more Roman Catholic, others more Protestant. Today's cantons of St. Gallen and Grisons were fairly diverse.

This religious landscape was the result of successive wars between Roman Catholics and Protestants during the sixteenth and seventeenth centuries. Until the nineteenth century, religion meant state religion. Changing denomination or marrying across denominational boundaries involved losing one's citizenship and led to banishment. Therefore, Protestants and Catholics lived as "clearly defined political entities" (Head-König, 2017, p. 24). Moreover, such traditional denominational divides have determined the major trends and cultural characteristics of Switzerland's cantons to this day (Baumann & Stolz, 2009, p. 49).

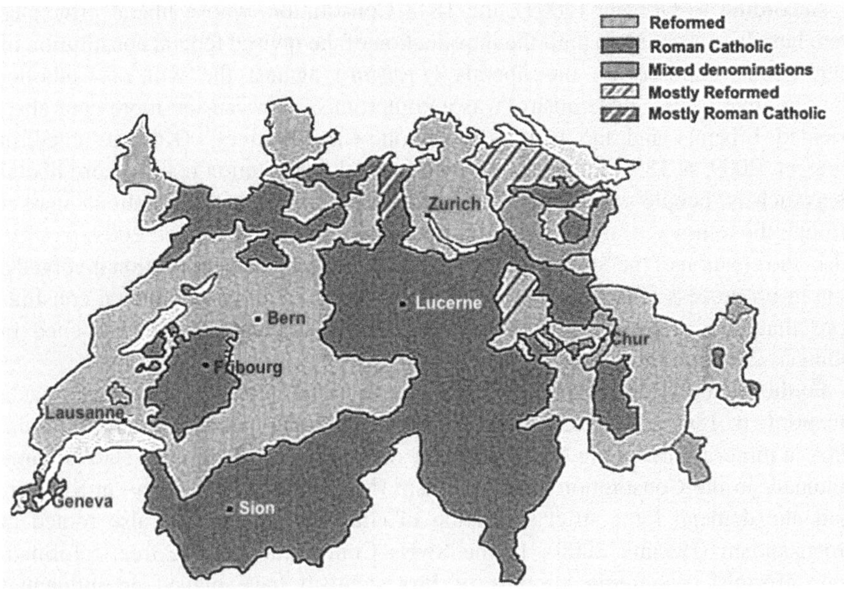


**Fig. 18.1** Denominations in Switzerland (1700) (adapted from Montandon, Gilbert, & Altermatt 1991 as cited in Baumann & Stolz, 2009, p. 100); used with permission. Author's translation of the French original

## 18.3 Federalism and Liberalism

In political terms, Catholic-Conservatives have traditionally been federalist. This antecedent originated in the same founding document of the Confederacy, the Federal Charter of 1291 between the communes of Uri, Schwyz, and Unterwalden (Catholic cantons until today) (Comité pour une Nouvelle Histoire de la Suisse, 2006). Liberals have been anti-clerical and centralist-oriented, and sided with the Protestant endeavour to overthrow the ancient order from the 1830s onward (Gould as cited in Obinger, 2009, p. 180). Liberal ideology inherently involved an attack on the Roman Catholic Church-State and its preponderant role in education and other areas of society (p. 180).

In 1848, the Swiss Federal State resulted from a late religious war (Gruner, 1977; Obinger, 2009, p. 180). Protestants emerged victorious from this denominational inter-cantonal civil war (*Sonderbund*), which meant that Protestants and non-denominational liberals were largely responsible for writing the Federal Constitution of 1848 (Obinger, 2009). Moreover, they have also dominated federal power until recently. By contrast, Roman Catholics have mostly been a political minority (not numerically) (Campiche & De Rham, 1977, p. 86; Girod, 1977). Social Democrats and Christian (Catholics) Democrats together held the government majority from 1959 to 2004. However, the existence of a significant and robust Catholic Democracy is barely evident (Linder as cited in Haenni, 2009).

According to Obinger (2009), the 1848 Constitution, whose liberal principles were largely preserved up until the introduction of the revised federal constitution of 1999), was imposed by the liberals (*Freisinn*) against the will of Catholic-Conservative forces. Federalism "was a compromise between the more centralist-oriented Liberals and the federalist Catholic-Conservatives" (Kölz as cited in Obinger, 2009, p. 180). Consequently, the Federal Constitution realises core liberal ideas such as "people's sovereignty, secularism, and the creation of a national market through the removal of trade barriers between the cantons" (Obinger, 2009, p. 180). Also, the creation of the Swiss Federal Constitution and state organisation involved a bottom-up process influenced chiefly by and borrowing from the "liberal constitutions that emerged at the cantonal level from 1830 onward" (Kölz as cited in Obinger, 2009, p. 180).

Furthermore, the Swiss Federal Constitution used United States federalism as a blueprint (p. 180). This circumstance is linked to American Protestantism. In the USA, a minority dissenting Protestant view of a separated church and state became dominant in the Constitution and federalism (Miller, 2012). Similarly, in Switzerland, the demand for a strict separation of church and state was also rooted in Protestantism (Haenni, 2009). In the Swiss Confederation, "the free, reformed, nonconformist, dissenting currents of Protestantism have played an influential role" in the country's institutions (Manow, 2004, p. 5; Manow & van Kersbergen, 2009).

Swiss liberalism for its part forced the transition from a loose confederation to a federal state and also sought to impose various ideas of the French Revolution (Rosenberg as cited in Haenni, 2009). However, liberal religious ideals (mainly Protestant) have also shaped the freedoms consecrated in the Swiss Federal Constitution. The Constitutional preamble invoking God (cited above) indicates an obviously religious influence rather than a secular (*laïque*) one (Zeugin, 2006, p. 14).

## 18.4 Economic Backwardness of the Roman Catholic Periphery

Following the 1848 Constitution, Swiss Roman Catholics perceived the liberal centralist government as a threat to traditional Catholic norms and way of life. Federalism provided local autonomy and an institutional shelter, and thus enabled preserving the privileges and influence of the Roman Church-State in Catholic regions. As a result, Catholics concentrated in rural areas where they maintained their traditions, created a Catholic counterculture at the cantonal level against modernisation, industrialisation, government centralisation, and secularisation. They mostly remained firmly attached to the ancient order and opposed developments in science and technology (Obinger, 2009, p. 190). Moreover, the Catholic periphery "reinforced antimodernist and anti-centralist attitudes" due to its economic backwardness and dependency on the more industrialised liberal centres (Altermatt as cited in Obinger, 2009, p. 190).

### *18.4.1 Education in Roman Catholic Cantons*

Under the Federal Constitution of 1848, the cantons enjoyed almost exclusive jurisdiction in education and welfare, among other matters. Catholics exploited such local policies of autonomy to protect the strong influence of the Roman Catholic Church-State on education and marital affairs (Obinger, 2009, pp. 190–191).

Stadler (as cited in Head-König, 2017) mentions the difference between a conservative and a more liberal-radical Catholicism in what he calls "Catholic dualism". Conservative Catholicism was prevalent in rural regions where the first sector (agriculture and livestock) was predominant (most Catholic cantons such as Valais, Ticino, Jura, and Schwyz). In contrast, liberal Catholicism emerged "in regions whose population tended to emancipate itself partially from the stronghold of the Church" (p. 28; e.g. in Lucerne, where counter-Reformation Jesuits had influenced the educational system).

Concerning the principal type of Catholicism in most Catholic cantons (conservative), Head-König (2017) refers to the socio-economic power of the Roman Church-State:

> . . . rural Catholic societies were governed by and virtually saturated with religious precepts. The Church not only controlled church attendance, the observation of the numerous religious holidays, the obligation to participate in religious processions (Joris 1973, 94) and to receive Holy Communion at Easter, but also instructed adults not only on their moral shortcomings and sexual disorders, but also in respect of evening gatherings and evening schools (p. 45).

Head-König further dedicates a section of her discussion to "The Maintenance of Ignorance". This term describes the strategies for keeping people ignorant as one of the most potent tools used by the Catholic Church-State to influence social behaviour. Such strategies were widely deployed in Catholic enclaves, at least until during the interwar period, and included: limiting contact with the outside world, both physically and intellectually; limiting access to information and to authorised literature; influencing the education system; overseeing emigration (Head-König, 2017, pp. 46–47).

## 18.5 Cultural Struggle (*Kulturkampf*)

The cultural struggle between Catholic-conservative and liberal anti-clerical forces erupted in Europe with the declaration of papal infallibility in 1870 and with the First Vatican Council of 1871. The Council opposed the separation of church and state, secularisation, and scientific progress (Linder, 2005, p. 37; Haenni, 2009, p. 38; Obinger, 2009, p. 181). At the time, the total revision of the 1874 Federal Constitution constituted a response to the strictures of the Vatican Council. It included denominational exemptions, which were directed particularly against the authoritarianism of the Roman Catholic Church. Among others, *Kulturkampf* measures sought to control Catholic religious education, Church appointments and properties. Consequently, the Catholic Church no longer enjoyed undisputed influence, not even in Catholic cantons (Head-König, 2017, p. 27). According to Gérard Pfulg, a Catholic author, amidst the *Kulturkampf*, Catholics were presented as civilisation enemies; they were reproached for their blind attachment to the Roman See, and their Swiss patriotism was, therefore doubted (Pfulg as cited in Schmid, 1981, p. 70).

The *Kulturkampf* was strongly felt in the Bernese Jura and in the region of Geneva (Hafner as cited in Schmid, 1981, p. 70). At the federal level, a critical example of the *Kulturkampf* was the banning of the—consistently loyal to the pope—Jesuit order in article 51 of the 1874 Constitution:

> The order of the Jesuits and its affiliated societies shall not be accepted in any part of Switzerland. Their members are prohibited from exercising any office in the Church or at schools.[1]

Historically, the Jesuit order has been associated with the Counter-Reformation and political intrigues (O'Malley, 1993). Several European and other countries (including Catholic Spain and Portugal) forced them into exile. Even Pope Clement XIV suppressed the Jesuit order from the Roman Catholic Church just before the French Revolution. However, the Jesuits managed to gradually re-establish themselves in the Church and in those countries from which they had been expelled. Switzerland lifted their ban in 1973 via a national referendum (Gilles-Attinger, 2002).

## 18.6 Diplomatic Relations Between the Swiss Confederation and the Roman See

The Protestant Reformation had a lasting influence on Swiss politics, at home and abroad. Therefore, Swiss diplomatic relations with the Roman See have been fraught by tensions since the Protestant Reformation (Python, 1994, p. 478). The Swiss Federal Council ordered the papal nuncio in Lucerne to leave Switzerland in the *Kulturkampf* in 1873. A nuncio returned to Bern 50 years later. However, the Swiss Confederation remained without a diplomatic mission in the Vatican (Roman See) until 1991, when a non-resident special envoy was appointed. Then, since 2004, the Swiss government promoted this special envoy to a non-resident Ambassador to the

[1]Author's translation of the German original: "*Der Orden der Jesuiten und die ihm affiliierten (angeschlossenen) Gesellschaften dürfen in keinem Teile der Schweiz Aufnahme finden, und es ist ihren Gliedern jede Wirksamkeit in Kirche und Schule untersagt*" *(Schweiz – Bundesverfassung 1874).*

Vatican (Roman See) (currently the Ambassador of Switzerland in Ljubljana, Slovenia) (Amrein, 2012; FDFA, 2018).

### *18.6.1 Cantonal Concordats*

As the diplomatic relations between the Swiss Confederation and the Roman See were consistently fragile, the possibility of a Concordat at the federal level would have been inconceivable. However, valid agreements with the Roman Catholic Church-State exist at the cantonal level, especially on administrative matters concerning dioceses, bishops, and parishes. The following cantons and municipalities have such agreements: *Cantons*: Aargau (1828); Bern (1828, 1864); Fribourg (1924); St. Gallen (1845); Lucerne (1926); Thurgau (1828); Ticino (1884); Municipalities: Chur (1870); Basel (1884, 1968, 1978) (Corral & Petschen, 2004); (Corral, 2014).

### *18.6.2 Pontifical Swiss Guard*

The pontifical Swiss Guard has existed since the Protestant Reformation (1506). It participated in military combats during the Italian wars and was briefly disbanded during the French Revolution. The current 100–110 "Defenders of the [Catholic] Church freedom" (according to their papal title of 1512) must be Swiss Catholic soldiers. Some even descend from Guard families (Python, 1994).

## 18.7 Current Confessional Ties in the Swiss Population

In Swiss politics, religion still plays a role at the institutional level. Examples include (1) the involvement of ecclesiastical institutions in education and social aspects, (2) the consultation of constitutional articles to the Churches before voting, (3) the military chaplaincy in the army (Campiche & De Rham, 1977, p. 85).

Regarding population distribution, the distribution of Roman Catholics and Protestants in the Swiss Confederation has long persisted. The mainly Protestant enclaves of 1700 (Fig. 18.1) have largely remained Protestant as Fig. 18.2 shows. The same generally applies to Roman Catholic enclaves.

Nevertheless, analysing data trends during the twentieth century reveals drastic changes in population distribution. Table 18.1 shows demographic changes in the last two centuries for both Roman Catholics and Protestants. A sustained decrease in the Protestant population, a sustained increase of Roman Catholics, and particularly an increase of "other" (religions and non-religions) are evident.

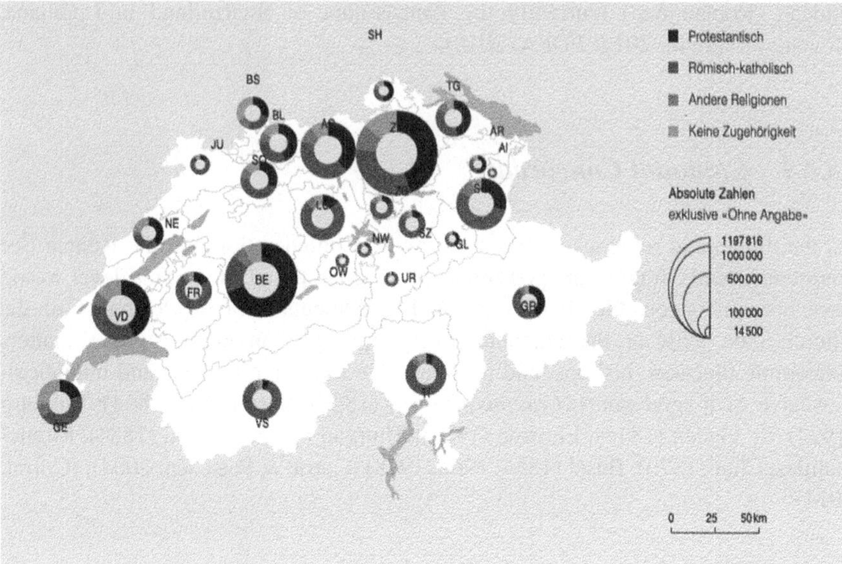


**Fig. 18.2** Denominations by Cantons (2000) (Stapferhaus Lenzburg 2006 as cited in Baumann & Stolz, 2007, p. 44). © 2007 transcript Verlag, Bielefeld. This work is licensed under a Creative Commons Attribution-NonCommercial-NoDerivatives 3.0 License (Author's translation of this figure's legend: *Protestantisch* = Protestants; *Römisch-katolisch* = Roman Catholics; *Andere Religionen* = Other religions; *Keine Zugehörigkeit* = No affiliation; *Absolute Zahlen* = Absolute numbers; *exklusive «Ohne Angabe»* = excluding "not specified")

**Table 18.1** Changes in the demographic distribution of Protestants and Roman Catholics in Switzerland in the last two centuries (adapted from Head-König, 2017; FDFA, 2018; Federal Statistical Office, 2017)

| Percentage of (%) | 1837 | 1900 | 1960 | 2017 |
|---|---|---|---|---|
| Protestants | 59.4 | 57.8 | 52.7 | 24.9 |
| Roman Catholics | 40.5 | 41.6 | 45.9 | 37.3 |
| Other | 0.1 | 0.6 | 1.4 | 37.8 |

Although the majority of the Swiss population officially belonged to the two main churches (Catholic or Protestant) until 1960, early signs of secularisation had already manifested in 1900 in larger Swiss towns. Besides, secularisation affected both Catholics (in Basel, around only one third were practising members of the faith) and Protestants (in Zürich, only one in ten attended church on Sundays) (Head-König, 2017).

Subsequently, after the 1970s, not only did Roman Catholics outstrip Protestants in numbers, but the most important historical change in the last half-century was the profound "de-Christianisation" of Swiss society. Characteristic of this shift is a profound decrease in the proportion of both Catholics and Protestants in relation to the total number of inhabitants. This transformation was countered by an essential increase in secular groups (agnosticism and atheism), non-membership, as well as by

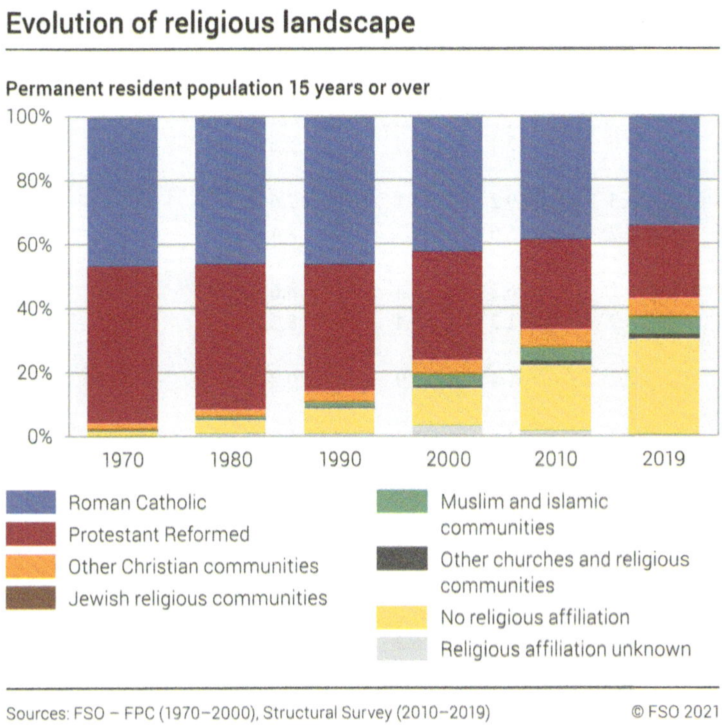


**Fig. 18.3** Evolution of religious landscape in Switzerland (1970–2000) (Federal Statistical Office, 2020)

other religious groups (see Fig. 18.3, and Tables 18.1 and 18.2). This pattern is observable both in Switzerland and across other Western European countries (Berger, 1999; Todd & Zurlo, 2016).

Roman Catholics are currently in the majority in most of the cantons and cities, as well as in the entire Swiss Confederation. To compare the urban-rural divide in Switzerland, Table 18.2 presents the proportion of religious adherents in some of the main Swiss cities and cantons in 2018.

However, the current proportions of religious adherents alone do not speak of the religiosity of the population, and even less, of the social effects of religion (Hayward & Kemmelmeier, 2011; Esping-Andersen, 1996; Barro & McCleary, 2003; McCleary & Barro, 2006), (see Sect. 5.3). In turn, "current social norms" are the "legacy of prior religious beliefs" (Glaeser & Glendon, 1998, p. 431) and owe more to the historical and institutional weight of religion than to its contemporary influence (Inglehart & Baker, 2000; Norris & Inglehart, 2004; Arruñada, 2010; Chaves & Cann, 1992; Wilde et al., 2010). Therefore, regardless of the higher proportion of Roman Catholics or the secularisation of the society, the Swiss institutional structure still responds to a traditional Protestant and liberal influence (Obinger, 2009; Inglehart & Baker, 2000; Python, 1994,; Campiche & De Rham, 1977). Moreover, Protestant churches have traditionally been entangled with the political structure of

**Table 18.2** Proportions of religious adherents in different Swiss cantons and cities in 2018 (adapted from Federal Statistical Office, 2020)

| Cantons and cities | Protestants | Catholics | Other Christians | Other religious communities (e.g. Muslims, Jews) | No religion |
|---|---|---|---|---|---|
| Bern (canton) | 49.0 | 15.4 | 6.4 | 5.6 | 22.3 |
| Bern (city) | 33.5 | 19.2 | 5.1 | 7.6 | 33.5 |
| Zurich (canton) | 27.2 | 25.6 | 6.3 | 8.4 | 31.2 |
| Zurich (city) | 19.1 | 26.5 | 5.4 | 8.6 | 39.0 |
| Geneva (canton) | 8.9 | 32.2 | 5.4 | 8.2 | 42.7 |
| Geneva (city) | 7.2 | 31.4 | 5.9 | 9.2 | 43.5 |
| Basel (canton) | 29.3 | 24.9 | 5.3 | 6.9 | 32.2 |
| Basel (city) | 14.4 | 15.5 | 5.8 | 11.6 | 51.4 |
| Vaud (canton) | 22.3 | 28.7 | 6.1 | 6.6 | 34.4 |
| Lausanne (city) | 12.7 | 29.1 | 6.5 | 10.1 | 39.6 |
| St Gallen (canton) | 20.4 | 42.4 | 6.2 | 8.7 | 20.9 |
| St Gallen (city) | 18.7 | 34.0 | 8.3 | 10.2 | 27.0 |
| Lucerne (canton) | 9.9 | 59.2 | 4.5 | 5.8 | 19.6 |
| Lucerne (city) | 10.9 | 48.3 | 5.4 | 6.7 | 27.6 |
| Ticino (canton) | 3.9 | 63.5 | 5.2 | 3.0 | 22.8 |
| Lugano (city) | 3.2 | 59.1 | 6.6 | 4.5 | 24.9 |
| Total in Switzerland | 23.0 | 35.0 | 6.0 | 7.0 | 28.0 |

the cantons, as they are, in fact, "canton churches" (Gould, 1999 and Cattacin et al., 2003 as cited in Obinger, 2009, p. 180).

## 18.8 Competitiveness of the Swiss Cantons and Religion

High competitiveness in Switzerland might be associated with the federal model of government. Among other aspects, Swiss federalism is empirically related to sustainable growth, business development, efficient government, and increasing social capital. The federal system also encourages the cantons to compete over tax rates and other business conditions (Feld et al., 2017).

The USA, which also has a federal government, is the second most competitive country in the world (World Economic Forum, 2016). However, such an argument cannot be generalised. Sudan, Iraq, India, and Mexico, among others, also have federal-type governments and are not as competitive as the USA or Switzerland. Likewise, federalism (although important) alone does not explain the significant differences in competitiveness between Swiss cantons.

The previous maps (Figs. 18.1 and 18.2) show the predominant Protestant or Roman Catholic historical enclaves that have existed in the Swiss Confederation over the last few centuries until the present (2000). Compared in terms of current competitiveness among Swiss cantons, Protestant Cantons are as a rule most competitive, Roman Catholic ones least competitive.

Swiss competitiveness concentrates in the northern, central, and western regions. The southern and eastern territories are the least competitive (see Fig. 18.4). According to UBS Switzerland AG (2016), mountainous topography limits the competitiveness of the large low-competitive southern cantons (Valais, Ticino, Grisons) and other small mountainous cantons. Nonetheless, when compared internationally, even the least competitive cantons in Switzerland, achieve higher values in innovation per capita than France, Italy, or Austria. Exceptionally, Uri, the least innovative canton in Switzerland with the highest proportion of Roman Catholics, attains similar innovation values per capita than Italy (UBS Switzerland AG, 2016; Federal Office of Statistics, 2017).

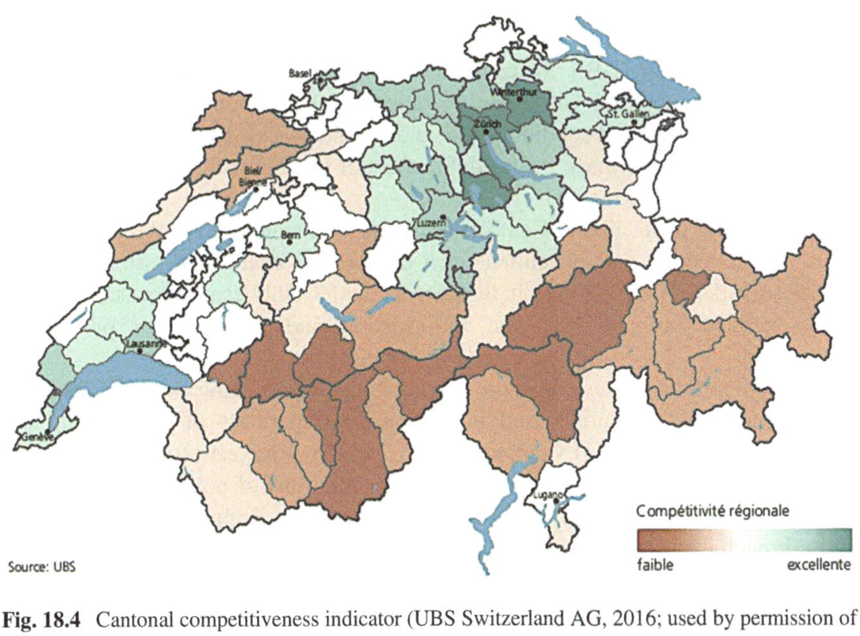


**Fig. 18.4** Cantonal competitiveness indicator (UBS Switzerland AG, 2016; used by permission of the authors)

The dark green areas show the most competitive regions (Fig. 18.4). They correspond to Protestant cantons (e.g. Zürich, Geneva, Lausanne, Basel, Bern) or mixed ones (e.g. Thurgau and St. Gallen). Decreasing to bright green, competitiveness drops to the dark red territories, the least competitive ones. These are Roman Catholic cantons (e.g. Valais, Jura, and Ticino) or mixed ones (e.g. Grisons). Exceptions are Lucerne and Zug, which, although predominantly Roman Catholic, are also highly competitive.

This review suggests that various factors in combination explain the roots of competitiveness in Switzerland. Two factors seem crucial for competitiveness. First, environment and geography: Generally, a canton located in the mountains has more difficulties in developing infrastructure and services than cantons in flat areas.

The second reason adds an important aspect to the first. Before the Protestant Reformation (sixteenth century), even flat areas, where competitiveness is concentrated today (e.g. Zürich), had a mainly rural economy with no tendency towards economic expansion. However, subsequent industrialisation increased literacy and human capital, two of the principal contributions of the Protestant Reformation (Cantoni, 2015; Becker et al., 2016; Becker & Woessmann, 2009; Comité pour une Nouvelle Histoire de la Suisse, 2006).

Moreover, both Protestantism and Roman Catholicism persisted in Switzerland after the Protestant Reformation (Figs. 18.1 and 18.2). Although the number of adherents is not as significant as six decades ago, the longstanding consequences of liberal and conservative ideologies are still evident in institutions. Conservative Catholicism retreated to the mountains, thus preserving the privileges of the Church-State and serving "The Maintenance of Ignorance" (Head-König, 2017). Consequently, mountainous Catholic Cantons such as Uri, Jura, Valais, and Appenzell Innerrhoden have, even to date, the lowest human capital (i.e. education) in the Swiss Confederation (UBS Switzerland AG, 2016, p. 13). Still, most of these cantons are even more innovative per inhabitant than surrounding Catholic countries with diverse geographical conditions (flat and mountainous). The influence of liberal federal institutions may have nuanced the effect of low human capital, thus making Catholic cantons more innovative.

On the other hand, liberal Catholicism mainly remained in the flat regions and cities (e.g. Lucerne) and benefitted from educational centres, infrastructure, and services (Clark & Kaiser, 2003). In this respect, both Catholic and Protestant regions in Switzerland profited from the Reformation and its influence on federal institutions.

More importantly, the long-term effect of the Reformation is still evident in Switzerland today, culturally and institutionally (regardless of the current low religiosity). Volonté (2015)'s empirical study of 753 firm-years found that Protestants and Swiss-Germans tend to prevent concentrations of power (i.e. two-tiered board structures in corporate management). Conversely, Roman Catholics and the Swiss-French tend to tolerate strong leadership and hierarchical structures (i.e. single-tier boards) in Switzerland.

The following subsections (18.9–18.11) synthesise and analyse the empirical information collected for Switzerland in terms of CDA (Critical Discourse Analysis).

## 18.9 Empirical Analysis and CDA for Switzerland (1. Prosperity)

### *18.9.1 Textual Analysis (Theological)*

The Christian (i.e. biblical) principle of prosperity is associated with obeying the Commandments (set of moral laws). A fairly harmonious discourse exists among Protestant stakeholders regarding this principle. This might be due to conformity to the original *Sola Scriptura* principle of the Protestant Reformation.

Among the below stakeholders (Table 18.3), the Protestant Free Pastor (g) refers to the Old Testament and to more recent examples of disobedience wreaking havoc on civilisations, whereas obedience to the biblical principles ensured prosperity. Similarly, the Independent Protestant Believer (n) links Swiss precision and perfection with the New Testament principle of achieving perfection for a perfect God, rather than for imperfect humans. On the other hand, Roman Catholic stakeholders prefer a somewhat more secular (non-theological) approach to prosperity in Switzerland. None of the Catholic interviews referred to a biblical principle. The Catholic Church-Government Stakeholder intermediary (q) is skeptical about a possible religious (or biblical) relationship between prosperity and industrialisation. Nonetheless, (q) mentions “Catholic piety” and “Sacramental theology” as possible explanations of the rural trend in Catholic cantons and cites other material reasons. Protestantism has heavily criticised sacramental theology for lacking an entirely biblical basis (Witte, 2002).

### *18.9.2 Analysis of Discourse Practice (Theoretical Triangulation)*

Like Fukuyama (1995), the Free Church Pastor (f) links Swiss people’s trustworthiness with high productivity and quality, and with a possible religious (Protestant) influence *à la* Weber. The Protestant Free Pastor (g) mentions that the elite controls education in hierarchical (e.g. Roman Catholic or Orthodox) societies. This argument is in line with Head-König’s (2017, p. 45) analysis of Swiss Catholic cantons (Sect. 18.4.) Likewise, the Free Protestant Believer (n) establishes an explicit theoretical relation with Fukuyama (1995). Lastly, for the non-practising Catholic Academic (l) “Protestant chauvinism [. . .] perverts Max Weber’s original line of reasoning”, which is frequently used to explain the prosperity of nations. After

**Table 18.3** Principles of prosperity according to stakeholders interviewed in Switzerland (Source: Author's figure)

| Prosperity | |
|---|---|
| Stakeholder | Fundamental principles identified (interviews) |
| The Holy Bible | "Keep therefore the words of this covenant, and do them, that ye may *prosper* in all that ye do" (King James Bible, 1769, Deuteronomy 29:9). |
| f) Protestant Free Church Pastor 1 | "The Swiss mentality is to stick to what is right. We stick to what we say [... and this] lead us to *trust* in ourselves. Then we are proud of [...] the high quality of what we produce".<br>"[...] Protestants are hard-working. [...] Catholic Cantons tend to be agricultural and livestock-oriented partly because they are in mountainous areas where it is not easy to develop economically". |
| g) Protestant Free Church Pastor 2. | "There is absolutely a relationship between occultism and development. The more a culture is involved in occultism, the faster it is destroyed. [...] That was the 'cyclical' history of the Jews [book of Judges]. [...] [C]ivilisations that live with [according to] the Bible all manage very well. They have prospered successfully such as the USA and Germany with Protestantism. Using the Bible, they have become world powers. [...] [T]he economies of Catholic countries are less well developed because the Catholic elites manipulate the power to keep people low and poor in general (e.g. education). They do not want people to know too much. Protestantism strengthens education and culture attains high moral standards. European countries and cultures like Spain, Italy, and Poland [mainly Catholics] or Romania or Greece [mainly Orthodox] are influenced by *corrupt* ethical codes. The Catholic elite keeps people poor and dominated by mystics and superstition". |
| l) Non-practising (Catholic) (Academic) | "The [Protestant] Reformation is a major reason for development. At the bottom of everything lies Protestant chauvinism, which perverts Max Weber's original line of reasoning. To some extent, religion is not constant. Sometimes religiosity strengthens and weakens in a cyclical development and runs in parallel cycles to the economy". |
| m) Independent, Catholic believer (Employee) | "Catholics tend to be more conservative here in Switzerland. [...] In Schwyz [...], where Catholics are a majority, people tend to be more helpful than in the large cities of other Cantons. [...] [P]erhaps [...] the conservative mindset has kept them [Catholics] in a medieval economy". |
| n) Independent, free Protestant believer (Academic) | "Francis Fukuyama says that trust, culture, and religion can explain development. In Switzerland, 85% of industrialisation occurred in Protestant Cantons. [...] Huguenots [...] established the high-precision industry like watchmaking. The perfection evident in this work comes from the idea of doing any work for God's glory and not for men's glory; as we must be perfect as God is perfect [Matthew 5,48]". |
| q) Catholic Church-State-Government intermediary | "I am not so sure if the religious history of this country can really explain this [Swiss prosperity]. [...] There might be a relation [between denomination] and industrialisation. There must be a connection. But the influence might come from both directions. [...] [I]n Zürich, it was more interesting for the government [...] and also for the people to become Protestants than [...] in Central Switzerland, because of the *liberties; the distance they could maintain from being ruled by the hierarchical [Catholic] Church. They could have more freedom*. [...] I do not think that Catholics are less intelligent or less likely to work than others. It is more about interaction. Catholic piety, which relates everything in everyday life to faith, asserts that it is easier to live on a farm than in a city. It is less rational and more about nature, and perhaps also about establishing greater affinity with sacramental theology". |

harshly criticising Weber's theory of the Protestant work ethic, stakeholder (l) refers implicitly to the theory of existential security (Norris & Inglehart, 2004). The latter explains why society becomes more secularised when enough freedom and security exist. Stakeholder (l) was most critical of a possible relationship between religion and prosperity.

### *18.9.3 Analysis of Social Practice*

The Roman Catholic Believer (m) positively associates a more conservative Catholic mindset with examples of helpfulness. However, stakeholder (m) links a conservative mentality with a "medieval economy", and thus partly explains the fact that most Catholic cantons are not as industrialised as Protestant ones. Catholic Church-Government intermediary Stakeholder (q) partly agrees with the relationship established between a conservative mentality and a medieval economy, when referring to "a less rational ... Catholic piety". Various authors, for instance, Obinger (2009) and Head-König (2017) have provided evidence that the connection between Catholicism and a medieval economy extends beyond an intuitive link (see also Sects. 18.3–18.4). Likewise, the Protestant Free Pastor (f) states that most Catholic cantons are located in the mountains, which also partly explains why they are less competitive. This view concurs with a recent analysis of cantonal competitiveness (UBS Switzerland AG, 2016). As such, this evidence shows that the combination of at least two factors—geography AND religion, instead of one OR the other—greatly determines cantonal competitiveness.

#### **18.9.3.1 Law and Institutions**

The Catholic Church-Government intermediary Stakeholder (q) recognises a mutual relationship between denomination and industrialisation. Stakeholder (q) also provides relevant examples, including the causes of the Reformation in Zürich and in Basel and the desire to free oneself "*from the control of the hierarchical [Catholic] Church*".

## 18.10 Empirical Analysis and CDA for Switzerland (2. Corruption)

### *18.10.1 Textual Analysis (Theological)*

The Scriptures explicitly encourage believers to refrain from accepting bribes (Table 18.4). In addition, the three last Commandments of the Decalogue (*8. Thou shalt not steal; 9. Thou shalt not bear false witness against thy neighbor; and 10.*

**Table 18.4** Principles of corruption according to stakeholders interviewed in Switzerland (Source: Author's figure)

| Corruption Stakeholder | Fundamental principles identified (interviews) |
|---|---|
| The Holy Bible | "Keep thee far from a false matter; and the innocent and righteous slay thou not: for I will not justify the wicked. And thou shalt take no gift: for the gift blindeth the wise, and perverteth the words of the righteous" (King James Bible, 1769, Exodus 23: 7–8). |
| a) Roman Catholic Priest 1. | "We are a small country with a very dense population. Very developed civil societies work through associations. [...] That system works well in civil society to organise citizens as well as in politics. [...] That keeps everyone accountable to others [...]...the State was against Catholicism because the Church was not democratic. [...] *In the 19th century, we [Swiss] created a Church law that is parallel to the canonical law of the Catholic Church.* This happened only within Catholicism because it was not acting according to legal principles. For this reason, the Church, along with the state, had to create a law according to democratic principles. This means that we now have a dual legal structure that is unique in the world. [...] [Now] lay members who are in associations, according to democratic law, manage the Church's finances. The money does not land in the hands of bishops but in those of lay people and Church associations, which are responsible for financial affairs. [...] This is the case in Switzerland, not because of Liberation Theology, but because *the State forced the Church to be more democratic* in order to be accepted as a public juridical body. [...] Rome was not very happy with the case of Switzerland". |
| e) Roman Catholic Theologian | "I think it is true that there is a much stricter discourse on responsibility and honesty [in a Reformed context]. [...] I believe that in Switzerland, which is very Reformed [Protestant], there is a dual discourse. [...] Corruption [in Switzerland] is lived in another way. [...] many things do not meet the eye and are not spoken about". |
| h) Protestant Pastor (Reformed Evangelical) | "In the Protestant tradition, it's very important that your life and principles are the same [coherent]. In Catholic traditions [there] are double standards: You have principles for monks, and for the poor, and [for] lay people. In Catholicism, you have the doctrine on one side and reality on another. These things [doctrine and reality] are always different, and the difference is accepted in Catholicism. [...] In the Protestant tradition, you have lower standards, but you are expected to meet them. Not, though, in Roman Catholicism [where matters are the other way around]". [...] "Rabbinic Judaism has similarities with Protestantism [as] for both; the Scriptures come first and occupy a central role. [...] When Jesus, a Jew, spoke about the truth to Pilate, a Roman, Pilate asked Jesus, what is truth? [John 18, 37–38]. This shows how incompatible Roman philosophy can be with Jewish culture..." |
| l) Non-practising Catholic (Academic) | "I don't know why Catholics should be corrupt or shouldn't. I'm Catholic, but I'm not especially associated with it. I'm Catholic... [because] family enforces this when you grow up. This is also true in other countries. ... *As a Swiss Catholic, I have more in common with a Nordic Protestant than with an Italian Catholic.* [...] The Church is there, but might not be the cause of corruption". |
| m) Independent, Catholic believer (Employee) | "Here in Switzerland, direct democracy and our type of government [Federal] might mean more accountability and less corruption. It's always better to share decisions with a lot of people rather than to concentrate them [decisions] on a few [people]. Perhaps, in a monarchy or a Republic, power is concentrated, which increases the risk of a totalitarian regime and corruption". |

(continued)

**Table 18.4** (continued)

| Corruption | |
|---|---|
| Stakeholder | Fundamental principles identified (interviews) |
| n) Independent free Protestant believer (Academic) | "For us in the German-Swiss tradition truth and facts are perhaps more important than relations, and it seems that in Latin contexts it is the other way around. The Bible is our source of truth [Protestants]. Latin contexts are influenced by Roman and Greek philosophy, where truth is relative. [. . .] The indulgences were just the tip of the iceberg of corruption in the Catholic Church. They allowed one to do as one pleased. If you repent, for instance, contribute either money or say some Hail Mary prayers, you are completely absolved by a priest. You could have even killed or abused people. [. . .] That [corruption] is what Luther also fought in the Reformation as the Bible clearly states that only God can forgive sins. [. . .] Pope Francis still offers indulgences to his followers on Twitter". |
| q) Catholic Church-Swiss Government intermediary | "I think the whole system of Switzerland is such that everything next to your town has a strong impact. Every unit has its own police, its own prison, etc. [. . .] Social control is quite efficient because we have no big cities. [. . .] We shouldn't forget that our banks have money that shouldn't have been there, so we are not 100% clean. It was not illegal, but it was not very moral either. [. . .] The state does not allow church taxes to flow directly into our hierarchical structure, but to those who organise themselves to collect this source of income. This idea also exists in the United States, where there is no taxation without representation, and it is applied to the Church as well. This is a unique case in the world. [. . .] The bishop formally proposes a priest, but if the local Catholics do not elect him, he will receive no pay. This is quite a special tradition. It goes back to medieval times in Switzerland, and was strengthened by the Reformation. This led to the elimination of hierarchical thinking. And then the state organised church life to a certain degree". |

*Thou shalt not covet (. . .) any thing that is thy neighbor's*) should provide the conscious Christian believer to abstain from corrupt activities.

Similar to the above prosperity analysis for Switzerland (Sect. 18.9), Protestant stakeholders refer to guiding biblical principles. Stakeholder (n) (i.e. Independent Free Protestant Believer) asserts that the Bible is the source of truth. This recalls the *Sola Scriptura* principle of Protestantism and contrasts with the relative truth characteristic of the Greco-Roman background. The Protestant Reformed Evangelical Pastor (h) also reflects on the discussion of "truth" by drawing attention to the biblical dialogue between Jesus, a Jew, and Pilate, a Roman. For stakeholder (h), both Protestantism and Rabbinic Judaism consider the Scriptures the source of truth, which is incompatible with relativistic Roman philosophy. Therefore, in line with the previous prosperity analysis, Roman Catholic stakeholders do not refer to a consolidated Scriptural basis, but instead to a variegated one, specifically associating corruption with secular issues. Such variegated associations of Roman Catholic stakeholders concur more with the Aristotelian "non-absolute" and "mean" relative points that Selling (2018) considers typical of Roman Catholic ethics.

### *18.10.2 Analysis of Discourse Practice (Theoretical Triangulation)*

For the Roman Catholic Priest (a), Switzerland is a small country where citizens can organise themselves in associations in which they can participate and are accountable for their actions. These characteristics, among others, distinguish Switzerland (i.e. make the country more competitive and less corrupt) from other countries, according to a Catholic priest (a). This argument concurs with Ostrom (2015), who explains the mechanisms underlying participatory institutions (e.g. Swiss alpine pastures management).

### *18.10.3 Analysis of Social Practice*

The Roman Catholic Theologian (e) believes that corruption is concealed in Switzerland. He mentions the dual Protestant discourse in this respect, but admits that Protestantism has stricter honesty and responsibility principles. The Protestant Reformed Evangelical Pastor (h) makes a similar observation on double standards, which he identifies in Roman Catholicism, where doctrine and lived reality are opposed or different, while in Protestantism lower standards are expected to be fulfiled.

On the other hand, the Non-practising Catholic Academic (l) identifies with *Nordic Protestants* rather than with *Italian Catholics.* This exemplifies McSweeney's (2015) argument about the impossibility of Roman Catholicism constituting a self-contained cultural unit. Furthermore, in Switzerland, as in other Protestant countries, the Reformation secularised both the state and local Roman Catholicism (Becker et al., 2016; Manow & van Kersbergen, 2009; Inglehart & Baker, 2000). Thus, the self-identification of a Catholic stakeholder (l) with a Nordic Protestant is somewhat foreseeable.

Stakeholder (n) (i.e. Independent Free Protestant Believer) mentions a duality of truth relations in the German-Swiss cultural context as opposed to a Latin context. This view is linked to the concepts developed by Hall (1990) (low-context for German-Swiss and high-context for Latin societies). Stakeholder (n) also refers to the roots of corruption in Roman Catholic doctrines. These include the concept of indulgences used by Jorge Bergoglio, also known as "Pope Francis", to promote events like the Catholic World Youth Day in 2013 (Kington, 2013).

#### 18.10.3.1 Law and Institutions

Among the interviewed stakeholders, the Catholic priest (a) mentions that the Swiss government forced the Roman Catholic Church-State to adopt democratic practices on Swiss territory from the nineteenth century. He further asserts that the Swiss managed to create a parallel church law to Catholic canon law. This argument concurs with the legal principles and Protestant revolutions explained in Sect. 8. 3.4. Here, the Catholic Church-Government Stakeholder (q) explains that the current Swiss mechanisms of participation and transparency in the fiscal management and elections of priests and bishops in the Swiss Catholic Church are unique worldwide. The Catholic Stakeholder (q) links this to the Protestant Reformation. Such notions complement Obinger's (2009) and Python's (1994) observations on the profound influence of the Protestant Reformation on Swiss politics and institutions (Sects. 18.2–18.6).

Similarly, the Independent Catholic Believer (m) relates two essential factors to the prevalence of high transparency in Switzerland: federalism and direct democracy. Both factors have positively affected transparency (and prosperity) (Obinger, 2009) (Sect. 18.3). Democracy is also related to Protestantism (Woodberry, 2012). Conversely, the Roman Catholic Church-State has a monarchic structure, which historically has opposed democratic systems (Cook, 2012).

The Catholic Church-Government intermediary (Stakeholder q) points to the efficiency of social control in small Swiss towns (in line with the Roman Catholic priest (a). Also, similarly to the Roman Catholic Theologian (e), Stakeholder (q) challenges the reputation of Swiss transparency with specific examples such as the morality of the banks.

## 18.11 Empirical Analysis and CDA for Switzerland (3. Church-State Relations)

### *18.11.1 Textual Analysis (Theological)*

The New Testament clearly distinguishes between earthly (government) and spiritual (heavenly) powers, which are and should maintain separated (Table 18.5). According to the biblical principle of the separation of powers, the Protestant Free Church Pastor 1 (f) asserts that the attitude of the Swiss federal government is secular. Similarly, the Ecumenical Pastor (i) explains that the non-hierarchical organisation of the federal government and the Protestant Church even influence Roman Catholicism in Switzerland.

**Table 18.5** Principles of church-state relations according to stakeholders interviewed in Switzerland (Source: Author's figure)

| | Church-State relations |
|---|---|
| Stakeholder | Fundamental principles identified (interviews) |
| The Holy Bible | "Jesus answered, My kingdom is not of this world: [. . .]" (King James Bible, 1769, John 18: 36). "[. . .] Render therefore unto Caesar the things which are Caesar's; and unto God the things that are God's" (King James Bible, 1769, Matthew 22: 21). |
| a) Roman Catholic Priest 1. | "Catholic Churches within Switzerland are not organised on a national level but on the cantonal level, as all Catholic affairs are organised this way. There are, however, organisations that coordinate the different Catholic parishes". |
| b) Roman Catholic Priest 2. (Ecclesiastical office of the Catholic Church) | "Switzerland and the Holy See do have a bilateral agenda, but compared to a regular sovereign nation, this cannot be considered a priority. [. . .]<br>The Holy See's main interests would not go beyond keeping channels of communication open and cultivating good relations with the [Swiss] Confederation. [. . .]<br>The specific character of Swiss democracy leaves little room for development [of a new agreement with the Holy See (i.e. Concordat)]. Only some kind of state crisis at the cantonal level might provoke discussion and perhaps facilitate negotiating some international agreement.<br>The principal work of the Nunciature in Bern has to do with the Catholic Church in Switzerland. The Holy See is unique among embassies because it represents a unique entity among sovereign entities in our world". |
| f) Protestant Free Church Pastor 1 | "The general attitude of the [Swiss Federal] government is secular. The relation between the state and the churches is getting weaker and weaker, except for the Roman Catholic Church. Catholic [political] parties are strong and the embassy of the Vatican in Bern has a far greater influence than the Protestant churches, which have no embassy. Also, the Protestant population is decreasing, and Protestant leaders have, in general, inferior feelings of themselves and admire the Catholic Church very much". |
| h) Protestant Pastor (Reformed Evangelical) | "Until 1970, living together without being legally married (cohabitation) was forbidden in Switzerland. Uri was the last canton to accept cohabitation. In the past, only the first son could inherit the parents' land in Switzerland, perhaps also due to the biblical tradition". |
| i) Ecumenical Pastor | "The Swiss Protestant Church is in many ways like the Swiss federal government. For example, there is not a single head but a multi-party system. Here in Switzerland, even the Catholic Church is different because this is not a hierarchical society. But Catholics are subject to the Vatican anyway. This is why there is a branch of Catholics (*Christkatholisch*) that doesn't accept the Pope's authority. Protestants and Catholics are not united here just because Protestants refuse to accept the Pope's authority in Switzerland". |
| k) Academic expert-lawyer | "Religious law has strongly influenced the Swiss legal system for many centuries. [. . .] The influence of the Church was mostly dominant until the mid eighteenth century. . . [until] a significant change occurred in 1798 with the French Revolution. However, its influence [i.e. the French Revolution's] did not last because the Helvetic Republic ended already in 1803. [. . .] There is a large gap between Protestant and Catholic cantons, most of which have their own tradition of how religion influenced their laws. [. . .] Religion has distinctively influenced inheritance law, Protestant marriage, natural law, canon law, and others depending on denomination, area, period, and fields. [. . .] |

(continued)

**Table 18.5** (continued)

| | Church-State relations |
|---|---|
| Stakeholder | Fundamental principles identified (interviews) |
| | Between 1840 and 1880, the Catholic and Protestant traditions even strengthened their differences due to the *Kulturkampf.* [...] The influence of the Catholic Church was strictly reduced at the federal level after the establishment of the Swiss Confederation in 1848. However, several Catholic cantons continued to uphold canonical ideals, and the clergy was actively involved in political processes. [...] Also, people's religious beliefs strongly influenced the political process of creating law via direct democracy. A certain impact is still evident today". |
| l) Non-practising Catholic (Academic) | "There are several cases of [state–church] separations and mixtures. [...] Nordic countries have high levels of trust in the state, which largely explains why no conflict between church and state occurs. The contrary happens in France, where the Church convinces people not to trust the state and vice versa. In Switzerland, Protestants have maintained that the Catholic Church is evil and creates distrust". |
| m) Independent, Catholic believer (Employee) | "In Switzerland, if you are Catholic, you have to pay much higher taxes than if you belong to the Reformed Protestant Church. If you are an atheist or belong to a Protestant Free Church, you do not even have to pay any Church taxes. I think Catholic taxes are a lot higher because it [Catholicism] is like a 'mafia Church.' Indeed, Catholics have huge cathedrals, frescoes, and lots of gold icons and that, of course, costs much more to buy and maintain than having a simple wooden cross in a Protestant Church.<br>In Valais, if you want to build a house, you have to sign up to the municipality (*Gemeinde*) and then you have to go to the Catholic Priest who has the final say [...] (if you have given enough money to the Church or have attended Sunday mass often enough). In Italy, mafia members confess their sins in church and information is exchanged in the confession box". |
| n) Independent free Protestant believer (Academic) | "The Roman Catholic Church was very corrupt at that time [Reformation time], and Reformers wanted to reform the Church, but not to separate it from the state. But they [the Reformers] and Luther realised that this [reforming the Church from within] was impossible. Therefore, Zwingli advocated the separation of church and state, but that was much later. [...]<br>The separation between church and state has never been complete here. Now, for example, we have taxes [for Catholics and Reformed Protestants]. And we have the issue of empty Protestant Church buildings being managed by the government". |
| p) Swiss Federal Government officer | "According to international diplomatic law, nothing regulates the relations between the Holy See and the Swiss Confederation, except for the Vienna Convention.<br>The main interest of the Swiss Confederation and the Holy See is to have diplomatic relations, as is normally the case with sovereign states. Second, to regulate bilateral issues, such as the Swiss pontifical guard at the Holy See. There are also other issues, like the status of bishops in Switzerland.<br>There are no plans for the Swiss Confederation and the Holy See to sign a new agreement [i.e. Concordat]. Switzerland used to have diplomatic relations but did not appoint an ambassador to the Holy See. [...] And then, until 2004, we started having an ambassador to the Holy See, but this official did not reside in Rome. [...] The present Ambassador of Switzerland to the Holy See resides in |

(continued)

**Table 18.5** (continued)

| | Church-State relations |
|---|---|
| Stakeholder | Fundamental principles identified (interviews) |
| | Slovenia. He also accredited as the ambassador to another country. Other than Italy, Switzerland has the largest colony in the Vatican". |
| q) Catholic Church-Swiss Government intermediary | "Legally and officially, there is a clear separation between the state and the churches. Their relations are governed by the cantons [... and] are very important for the financing and self-organisation of the churches. There are twenty-six different [church taxes] systems. Even though they have some similarities, especially in the German-speaking cantons, the French- and Italian-speaking parts of Switzerland have very different systems. [...] Geneva and Neuchatel work mainly under a French system. They receive no state funds and have no church taxes. They [...] live especially on the contributions of [...] their congregations.<br>[...] The bishop does not need to call the President of Switzerland to tell him what to do [...]. The distance here is quite large and both sides respect it. [...] In some cases, Church representatives offer their congregation voting advice. Normally, this concerns religious aspects that are fundamental to life, like abortion, suicide, etc. [...] I think Switzerland has a culture that is strongly influenced by the Christian tradition, but nowadays secularisation and the separation of church and state are plainly evident, [...]The [Christian] tendency still exists, but it is less notorious [...] in the context of our direct democracy.<br>[...] there was a time when Protestants strongly dominated the Swiss government [...]. The Swiss constitution of 1848 (and beyond) is a liberal construct. [...] even within the Catholic Church, there were strong rivalries between liberal and conservative Catholics as was the case in Ticino and Lucerne. [...] Internally, the situation in the Catholic Church became more difficult after the first Vatican Council in 1870, where the bishops defined the infallibility of the pope. This led to polarisation. [...] We said that we would not accept this new dogma about the infallibility of the pope. Thus we separated... [*Katholisch / Christkatholisch*]. Ultramontane thought [beyond the Alps heading to Rome] [...] was difficult for the young Swiss State. [...] A Church-State had existed for a long time. [...] [*Christkatholisch*] reached some agreements with the liberal Protestants over political questions. [...] though they were quite a small group, they were influential. [...] Their philosophy is, "We do not want to have the pope, and we have no celibacy among our priests; they can marry" [...]<br>I would mention three important causes for the emergence of this special [democratic] legal system for the Catholic Church in Switzerland. *The first is the [cooperative] corporations*. [...] For example, if you go to [...] the Alps, you will see that cattle farmers organise themselves in [cooperative] corporations [...]. *The second cause is the Reformation*, which strongly promoted participation among its followers in taking church decisions. This practice goes quite well together with democratic feelings in Switzerland. *The third influence stems from the time when the Reformed [and] Catholic denominations in Switzerland opposed each other.* [...] [for example] in Cantons St. Gallen and Grisons. [...] For decisions concerning religious affairs, Parliament was divided Protestant deputies [...] decided on proceedings relevant to Protestants, while Catholic members of Parliament decided Catholic issues. In St. Gallen, this is called '*Katholischer Konfessionsteil*' [Catholic section of the Canton St. Gallen]. Or in Grisons, *Corpus Catolico* [body |

(continued)

**Table 18.5** (continued)

| | Church-State relations |
|---|---|
| Stakeholder | Fundamental principles identified (interviews) |
| | of Catholics], and [on another group] the body of Protestants. They agreed to have peace because [. . .] they would decide in favour of their church[es] [. . . instead of interfering] with the other denomination.<br>You cannot understand the relation between church and state in Switzerland without understanding the political system. This is the most important aspect to understand. [. . .] Direct democracy has a very high influence on this system, and this does not exist in other countries. The pronounced form of federalism, which enables every town to set its taxes, makes this organisation unique". |
| s) Swiss Diplomatic Officer (non-official communication) | "No plans for possible future bilateral agreements with the Holy See, at the federal or cantonal level, have been announced. [Education, Lands and Properties, Religious Freedom, and Ecumenism issues] are discussed and treated bilaterally [with the Holy See] in a similar way as with every other state: diplomatic dialogue and channels (ambassador to the Holy See, with the State Secretariat, or other authorities and services; nuncio or his deputy, with the DFA or other authorities and services), or at the political level on the occasion of bilateral visits, or between experts/persons or services in charge of specific issues". |

### *18.11.2 Analysis of Discourse Practice (Theoretical Triangulation)*

The Catholic Church-Swiss Government intermediary (q) describes the Reformation and the liberal influence on the separation of church and state in terms of the democratic scheme of the Swiss Catholic Church, which is unique worldwide. Such historical analyses concur with Obinger's (2009) review, while the Protestant influence on the separation of church and state is consistent with Miller's (2012) framework.

### *18.11.3 Analysis of Social Practice*

#### 18.11.3.1 Law and Institutions

Although the Swiss federal state is laic, church and state have never been totally separate in Switzerland. Moreover, the influence of religion on institutions is evident at the following levels:

*a) Supranational:* The Roman Catholic Church-State has gained ever greater political influence through its embassy in Bern (Nunciature) that no other church has. At the same time, the federal government increasingly acknowledges the state sovereignty and legitimacy of the Roman Catholic Church-State (e.g. by strengthening diplomatic channels and by appointing an ambassador to the Holy See). (Stakeholders: Roman Catholic Priest 2 (b); Protestant Free Church Pastor 1 (f); Swiss Federal Government Officer (p); s) Swiss Diplomatic Officer). These findings substantiate Obinger (2009) and Python (1994).

*b) National:* The Independent, Catholic Believer (m, employee) and the Independent Free Protestant Believer (n, academic) both mention church taxes and cathedral administration as two examples of a non-complete separation of church and state. The Academic Expert-Lawyer (k) outlines a possible way of religious influence taking effect, namely by people's beliefs directly influencing laws and policies through direct democracy. Both Stakeholder (k) and the Catholic Church-Swiss Government intermediary (q) acknowledge that the former Protestant and liberal influence diminished the power of the Catholic Church-State at the federal level; this is in line with Obinger (2009).

*c) Cantonal/regional/local:* The Catholic Church-Swiss Government intermediary (q) explains pronounced differences between German-speaking, French and Italian-speaking, and mixed-denomination cantons. The Academic Expert-Lawyer (k) explains that the clergy has long been very present in the political process in several Catholic cantons. Moreover, the Catholic Church (Roman See) has signed Concordats with several cantons (Corral & Petschen, 2004). The Independent, Catholic Believer (m, employee) provides an example of Church interference in state affairs in the Catholic canton of Valais.

## 18.12 Conclusions

### *18.12.1 General*

The strong religious tensions between Protestants and Catholics have shaped the Swiss model of government and the country's institutions. While Catholics have defended a federalist, decentralised approach to escape modernisation, Protestants and liberals successfully pushed for a predominantly liberal, anti-clerical constitution and for a federal state. As Obinger (2009) observed:

> The retreat of Catholics form the federal arena in the wake of the events of the 1840s was a strategic response to the secular Federal Constitution imposed by the Liberals. A federal polity strongly based on the idea of local autonomy and the associated devolution of power provided the institutional shelter that allowed Catholics to maintain their traditions, to preserve the influence of the Roman Church in Catholic areas, and to create a Catholic counterculture at the cantonal level. More specifically, Catholics considered the cantons as bulwarks against modernization and its concomitants such as big government, bureaucratization, and secularization. Because they were mostly concentrated in rural areas and showed strong leanings to the ancient order with its enshrined privileges of the Roman Church, Catholics opposed industrialization and were highly sceptical of new developments in science and technology. [. . .] Catholics therefore sought to gain political control at the cantonal level in order to protect the Catholic subsociety from the intrusion by the Liberals who then controlled the federal arena. Because the cantons enjoyed almost exclusive jurisdiction in affairs such as education and welfare under the Federal Constitution of 1848, Catholics exploited local policy autonomy to protect the strong influence of the Roman Catholic Church on education and marital affairs, at least until the constitutional revision in 1874 (pp. 190–191).

Later, following the *Kulturkampf*, the Catholic Church-State could no longer exercise its previously undisputed influence, not even in Catholic cantons.

As a result, the Swiss Confederation has had weak diplomatic relations with the Roman See. The absence of a Concordat at the federal level and the absence of a Swiss resident ambassador in the Vatican still suggest that diplomatic relations continue to be weak. However, Concordats with some Cantons exist. Moreover, from 2004, the federal government has appointed a non-resident ambassador to the Vatican, thus creating closer ties with the Roman Catholic Church-State. On the other hand, although Catholic and Protestant enclaves persisted for a long time, the Protestant share of the total population has decreased by more than half since the nineteenth century. The greatest decline has occurred over the last 60 years, during which other religious denominations and non-religions have sharply increased. Today, Swiss society is highly secularised.

### *18.12.2 Competitiveness and Transparency*

As a general rule, Protestant cantons are more competitive than the mountainous Roman Catholic cantons. However, even these "low" competitive cantons score higher on innovation/inhabitant values than the traditionally Catholic neighbouring countries (e.g. Austria, Italy, or France).

The historical retreat to the mountains and the anti-modernising reaction against the majoritarian liberal-Protestant federal government might partially explain the lower competitiveness of most Roman Catholic cantons. Nevertheless, the liberal-Protestant federal government seems to have influenced institutions in Catholic cantons by decreasing the pervasive power of the Roman Church-State and by forcing the hierarchical non-democratic Church to democratise. Switzerland's unique democratising of Catholicism may well be related to the principles of accountability and transparency. Besides, such an influence may also partially explain the relatively higher score on the innovation-per-habitant parameter attained by "low-competitive mountain Catholic cantons" compared to Italy, Austria, or France.

### *18.12.3 Prosperity (Competitiveness and Transparency) and Biblical Moral Principles*

Analysing the primary information shows that most Protestant stakeholders consistently mention biblical concepts as the moral foundation of prosperity. The original Protestant principle of the *Sola Scriptura* might lie at the heart of such consistency.

In contrast, Roman Catholic stakeholders do not consistently refer to the Scriptures as a moral foundation. Instead, they tend to refer to diverse theories and philosophical influences from secular sources. This would seem to corroborate

McSweeney's (2015) argument that several kinds of Roman Catholicism might exist as philosophical currents and cultural backgrounds.

Accepting biblical principles as the truth might create a uniform moral standard for enhancing trust, as argued by Stakeholder (f) in the prosperity analysis. On the contrary, in the absence of a moral standard, corrupt ethical codes (see Stakeholder (g)) might lead to a vast range of "negative" socially accepted norms, low productivity (Mockus et al., 2012), and low "spontaneous sociability" (low trust) (Fukuyama, 1995). Furthermore, individuals not only respond to the coercive power of the law, but obey their own moral principles (Mockus et al., 2012, p. 7). This might explain, perhaps even crucially, why the Protestant Reformation—based on the *Sola Scriptura* principle—contributed, among other factors, to creating trust in Swiss society.

### *18.12.4 Recommendations for Future Research*

This case study has identified two promising fields on which little or no systematic research exists and that would help better understand religion and prosperity in Switzerland: a) the influence of religion on law and institutions at the cantonal level; and b) the relevance and impact of the Concordats signed between several Swiss cantons and the Roman Catholic Church-State.

## References

Amrein, M. (2012). *Letzte Etappe einer langen Normalisierung: Die Frage einer Schweizer Botschaft beim Heiligen Stuhl steht wieder zur Debatte*. Neue Zürcher Zeitung, p. 13.

Arruñada, B. (2010). Protestants and catholics: Similar work ethic, Different social ethic. *The Economic Journal, 120*(547), 890–918.

Barro, R. J., & McCleary, R. M. (2003). Religion and economic growth across countries. *American Sociological Review, 68*(5), 760–781.

Baumann, M., & Stolz, J. (2007). Eine Schweiz – viele Religionen Risiken und Chancen des Zusammenlebens. transcript Verlag, Bielefeld.

Baumann, M., & Stolz, J. (2009). *La nouvelle Suisse religieuse. Risques et chances de sa diversité*. Genève: Labor et fides.

Becker, S. O., & Woessmann, L. (2009). Was weber wrong? A human capital theory of protestant economic history. *Quarterly Journal of Economics, 124*(2), 531–596.

Becker, S., Pfaff, S., & Rubin, J. (2016). *Causes and consequences of the protestant reformation*. Warwick Economics Research Paper Series.

Berger, P. (1999). *The desecularization of the world*. Washington, DC: Ethics and Public Policy Center and Wm. B. Eerdmans Publishing Co.

Campiche, R., & De Rham, G. (1977). Hypothèses sur religion et politique en Suisse. *Revue Suisse de Sociologie, 3*, 83–89.

Cantoni, D. (2015). The economic effects of the protestant reformation: Testing the weber hypothesis in the German lands. *Journal of the European Economic Association, 13*(4), 561–598.

Chaves, M., & Cann, D. E. (1992). Regulation, pluralism, and religious market structure: Explaining religion's vitality. *Rationality and Society, 4*(3), 272–290. https://doi.org/10.1177/1043463192004003003.

Clark, C., & Kaiser, W. (2003). *Culture wars: Secular-catholic conflict in nineteenth-century Europe*. Cambridge: Cambridge University Press.

Comité pour une Nouvelle Histoire de la Suisse. (2006). *Geschichte der Schweiz und der Schweizer*. Schwabe.

Cook, E. (2012). *Roman catholic hegemony and religious freedom: A seventh-day adventist assessment of dignitatis humanae*. Waco, TX: Graduate Faculty of Baylor University.

Corral, C. (2014). *Los 55 Estados con sus respectivos 220 Acuerdos vigentes con la Santa Sede*. (U.C. (UCM), Ed.) *UNISCI Discussion Papers* (34).

Corral, C., & Petschen, S. (2004). *Tratados Internacionales (1996–2003) de la Santa Sede con los Estados. Concordatos Vigentes*. Madrid: Universidad Pontificia Comillas.

Esping-Andersen, G. (1996). Welfare states withoout work: The impasse of labour shedding and familialism in Continental European social policy. In *Welfare states in transition: National adaptations in global economies*. London: Sage.

Federal Department of Foreign Affairs (FDFA). (2018). *Presence Switzerland*. Retrieved from: https://www.eda.admin.ch/eda/en/home/fdfa/organisation-fdfa/general-secretariat/presence-switzerland.html

Federal Statistical Office. (2017). *Language, religion and culture survey*. Retrieved from: https://www.bfs.admin.ch/bfs/en/home/statistics/population/surveys/esrk.html

Federal Statistical Office. (2020). *Evolution of religious landscape. Permanent resident population 15 years or over*. Retrieved from: https://www.bfs.admin.ch/content/bfs/en/home/statistics/population/languagesreligions/religions.assetdetail.11527930.html

Feld, L., Schaltegger, C., Burret, H., & Schmid, L. (2017). *Föderalismus und Wettbewerbsfähigkeit in der Schweiz*. Zürich: NZZ Libro Zürich.

Fukuyama, F. (1995). *Trust. The social virtues and the creation of prosperity*. New York: Free Press.

Gilles-Attinger. (2002). *Dictionnaire Historique de la Suisse (DHS)*. Hauterive: Sàrl - Marnière.

Girod, R. (1977). Clivages confessionnels et gouvernement de tous les parties. *Revue Suisse de Sociologie, 3*, 93–104.

Glaeser, L., & Glendon, S. (1998). Incentives, predestination and free will. *Economic Inquiry, 36* (3), 429–443.

Gruner, E. (1977). *Die Parteien in der Schweiz. 2. neu bearbeitete und erweiterte Auflage*. Bern: A. Francke.

Haenni, A. M. (2009). *Religiöse Einflüsse auf die Alters- und Hinterlassenenversicherung der Schweiz – Die Rolle der Schweizerischen Konservativen Volkspartei im Entstehungsprozess der AHV von 1918 bis 1948*. Bern: Institut für Politikwissenschaft Universität Bern HS.

Hall, E. (1990). *Understanding Cultural Differences*. Yarmouth, Maine: Intercultural Press.

Hayward, R. D., & Kemmelmeier, M. (2011). Weber revisited: a cross-national analysis of religiosity, religious culture, and economic attitudes. *Journal of Cross-Cultural Psychology, 42*(8), 1406–1420.

Head-König, A.-L. (2017). Religion mattered: Religious differences in switzerland and their impact on demographic behaviour (End of the 18th century to the middle of the 20th century). *Historical Social Research, 42*(2), 23–58.

Inglehart, R., & Baker, W. (2000). Modernization, cultural change, and the persistence of traditional values. *American Sociological Review, 65*(1), 19–51.

King James Bible. (1769). *The Holy Bible, King James Version*. Cambridge Edition: 1769. Scripture quotations from The Authorized (King James) Version. Rights in the Authorized Version in the United Kingdom are vested in the Crown. Reproduced by permission of the Crown's patentee, Cambridge University Press.

Kington, T. (2013). *Vatican offers 'time off purgatory' to followers of Pope Francis tweets.* Retrieved from: https://www.theguardian.com/world/2013/jul/16/vatican-indulgences-pope-francis-tweets

Linder, W. (2005). *Schweizerische Demokratie: Institutionen, Prozesse, Perspektiven* (ISBN 978-3-258-06842-8 ed.). Bern: Haupt.

Manow, P. (2004). The good, the bad, and the ugly: Esping-Andersen's regime typology and the religious roots of the Western welfare state, MPIfG Working Paper, No. 04/3, Max Planck Institute for the Study of Societies, Cologne. Retrieved from: http://www.mpifg.de/pu/workpap/wp04-3/wp04-3.html

Manow, P., & van Kersbergen, K. (2009). Religion and the Western Welfafre State - The theoretical context. In P. Manow & K. van Kersbergen (Eds.), *Religion, class coalitions and welfare states* (p. 304). New York: Cambridge University Press.

McCleary, R. M., & Barro, R. J. (2006). Religion and economy. *Journal of Economic Perspectives, 20*(2), 49–72.

McSweeney, B. (2015). Hall, Hofstede, Huntington, Trompenaars, GLOBE: Common foundations, common flaws. In Y. Sanchez & C. Brühwiler (Eds.), *Transculturalism and Business in the BRIC States. A handbook.* Dorchester: Gower Applied Business Research.

Miller, N. (2012). *The religious roots of the first amendment.* New York: Oxford University Press.

Mockus, A., Murraín, H., & Villa, M. (2012). *Antípodas de la violencia: Desafíos de cultura ciudadana para la crisis de (in)seguridad en América Latina.* Washington, DC: Banco Interamericano de Desarrollo.

Norris, P., & Inglehart, R. (2004). *Sacred and secular: Religion and politics worldwide.* New York: Cambridge University Press.

O'Malley, J. (1993). *The first jesuits.* Cambridge, MAs: Harvard University Press.

Obinger, H. (2009). Religion and the consolidation of the Swiss Welfare State, 1848-1945. In P. Manow & K. van Kersbergen (Eds.), *Religion, class coalitions and welfare states* (pp. 176–209). New York: Cambridge University Press.

Ostrom, E. (2015). *Govenring the commons. The evolution of institutions for collective action. Political economy of institutions and decisions.* Cambridge: Cambridge University Press.

Python, F. (1994). La Suisse, les Catholiques et le Saint-Siège aux XIXe et XIe Siècles. *Revue d'Allemagne et des pays de langue allemande, 26*(3), 465–478.

Schmid, C. (1981). *Conflict and consensus in Switzerland.* Berkeley: University of California Press.

Selling, J. A. (2018). Reframing catholic theological ethics: Summary and application (A. Abram, Ed.). *Religions, 8*(203), 5–13.

Switzerland Government. (2018). *Constitution fédérale de la Confédération suisse.* Retrieved from https://www.admin.ch/opc/fr/classified-compilation/19995395/index.html

Todd, M., & Zurlo, G. (2016). *World Christian database.* (Leiden/Boston: Brill, Ed.) Retrieved from www.globalchristianity.org

UBS Switzerland AG. (2016). *L'indicateur de compétitivité des cantons 2016.* Zurich: UBS Switzerland AG.

Volonté, C. (2015). Culture and corporate governance: The influence of language and religion in Switzerland. *Management International Review, 55*, 77–118.

Weber, M. (1905). *Die protestantische Ethik und der Geist des Kapitalismus.* Zürich: Verlag Wirtschaft und Finanzen.

Wilde, M., Geraty, K., Nelson, L., & Bowman, E. (2010). Religious economy or organizational field? Predicting bishops' votes at the second vatican council. *American Sociological Review, 75* (4), 586–606. https://doi.org/10.1177/0003122410368927.

Witte, J. (2002). *Law and protestantism: The legal teachings of the lutheran reformation.* Cambridge: Cambridge: University Press.

Woodberry, R. (2012). The missionary roots of liberal democracy. *American Political Science Review (APSR), 106*(2), 244–274.

World Economic Forum. (2016). *The global competitiveness report 2014–2015. Full Data Edition.* Geneva: The World Economic Forum.

World Economic Forum. (2017). *The travel & tourism competitiveness report*. Geneva: World Economic Forum.

Zeugin, M. G. (2006). *Politik und Religion in der Schweiz. Wie weit beeinflussen kirchliche Organisationen die schweizerische Politik?* Referent: Prof. Dr. Hans Peter Faganini Korreferent: Prof. Dr. James W. Davis Verfasser. St. Gallen, Switzerland: University of St. Gallen Graduate School of Business, Economics, Law and Social Sciences.

# Chapter 19
# b) Uruguay: Extreme Positive Case Study (Latin America)

*All religious cults are free in Uruguay. The State does not endorse any religion (Article 5 of the 1967 Constitution).*

Uruguay is one of the highest-scoring Latin American countries in social indicators such as transparency (Transparency International, 2016), political rights and civil liberties (Freedom House, 2016), and social progress (Porter et al., 2015). Accordingly, it has been closer to Western European countries rather than other Latin American countries with regard to institutional performance, collective vision, and demographic composition (Roniger, 2016, p. 416; Transparency International, 2016; Porter et al., 2015). It has been the exception compared to the rest of Latin America due to its stable democratic institutions, great political stability, and prosperity (Klaiber, 1997). Therefore, Uruguay has been praised as "*the Switzerland of Latin America*" (Fitzgibbon, 1956; Roniger, 2016, p. 416).

Uruguay has enjoyed a positive reputation and good performance for most of its life as an independent nation. However, the sixteenth-century Spanish colonisers considered this small country a "land without any profit", due to its lack of precious metals and modest indigenous civilisations (Corbo, 2011, p. 284; Da Costa, 2009, p. 140). Consequently, the Spaniards' colonial extractive institutions (e.g. the feudal structures of the Roman Catholic Church-State) never became deeply rooted in Uruguay, unlike in the rest of the continent (Fitzgibbon, 1956; Klaiber, 1997; Da Costa, 2009; Corbo, 2011). This coincides with what Acemoglu and Robinson (2012) have called a "reversal of fortune", where the weakness of extractive institutions has decisively "flipped the coin".

As a result, the Roman Catholic Church-State never gained the social importance in Uruguay than it has had in the rest of Latin America. This facilitated various liberal social measures in Uruguay, largely due to the absence of an institutional apparatus and power quotas considered fundamental and asserted by the Roman Church-State in other parts of the world (Da Costa, 2009, p. 140; Corbo, 2011,

**Supplementary Information** The online version of this chapter (https://doi.org/10.1007/978-3-030-78498-0_19) contains supplementary material, which is available to authorized users.



J. García Portilla, *"Ye Shall Know Them by Their Fruits"*, Contributions to Economics, https://doi.org/10.1007/978-3-030-78498-0_19

p. 285). The following sections briefly explain the progressive secularisation (anti-clerical) that led to the liberal institutions of the Uruguayan (welfare) state.

## 19.1 Religion and Secularisation in Uruguay

Secularisation and religiosity levels in Uruguay are closer to Western European levels than to Latin American averages. Among Latin American countries, Uruguay has by far the lowest proportion of Roman Catholics (42%), yet the highest proportion of religiously unaffiliated adults (37%) (Pew Research Center, 2014). Such high levels of secularisation (and low relative Catholicism) are understandable when considering the historical laicising process that began in the nineteenth-century Uruguay (Caetano & Geymonat, 1997; Guigou, 2005; Da Costa, 2003 as cited in Da Costa, 2016, p. 229).

The idea of medieval "Christendom" inherited from Hispanic times became obsolete and residual in Uruguay already during the nineteenth century (which is early compared to the rest of Latin America). Roman Catholicism represented a religious and political culture that legitimised social and racial asymmetries. Therefore, the country's intellectual and political leadership agreed that totalising religion (the *Old Regime*) needed to be overcome. Consequently, "critical" religious and philosophical thinking succeeded—but did not entirely oust—the Old Regime (Hernández, 2017, p. 111).

In this way, Uruguay closely followed the *laïcité* model of the French Revolution without ever completely replicating it (i.e. including pluralist connotations). This process resulted in the widespread secularisation of institutional fields, displaced religion to the domestic sphere, and guaranteed the freedom of consciousness and religion (Roniger, 2016, p. 414).

Like Switzerland, the Uruguayan understanding of *laïcité* also implied a mode of collective life legitimated by state neutrality and popular sovereignty (Blancarte, 2006; Da Costa 2011 as cited in Roniger, 2016, p. 415). Table 19.1 summarises the historical process towards secularisation in Uruguay.

A central and early innovation involved placing public education in Uruguay under civic control and the total absence of any religious content in school curricula since the nineteenth century (Asiaín, 2010). This process was related to persistent human capital building and prosperity (Becker & Woessmann, 2009).

Roman Catholicism interpreted the 1917 Constitution as a severe blow to its intentions. It became aware of the definitive loss of the old and longed-for medieval "Christendom" and of the irreversible reality of living in a pluralistic and secular society. This led to the Church retreating from public life and gradually reduced its sociocultural influence (Corbo, 2011, p. 303).

**Table 19.1** Historical steps of the secularisation process in Uruguay adapted from (Da Costa, 2009, pp. 138–140; Caetano and Geymonat as cited in Roniger, 2016, p. 414)

| Year | Steps towards secularisation in Uruguay |
|---|---|
| 1837 | The state recognises civil marriage |
| 1861 | Secularisation of public cemeteries (previously ran by the Roman Church-State) |
| 1863 | The Bishop of Montevideo was banished |
| 1877 | Education Act enacted, removing religion from the educational system |
| 1879 | Civil Registration Act enacted, passing registration from the Roman Church to the state |
| 1885 | Convents Act enacted, annulling the legal status of all convents |
| 1906 | Crucifixes removed from all public hospitals |
| 1907 | Divorce Act enacted.<br>Religious references deleted from the oath taken by members of Parliament. |
| 1917 | Constitutional reform establishes the legal and actual separation of church and state |
| 1919 | Renaming of holidays and towns (now given secular names) |

## 19.2 Role of Protestantism in Secularisation (Nineteenth Century)

The modernisation of the Uruguayan state and society involved the promotion of several core values, including religious pluralisation, freedom of worship, and the desacralisation of political and civic activities. The legitimisation of the role of religion in modern society became the subject of an intense polemic between Catholics, Protestants, and liberals in Uruguay (Hernández, 2017, p. 143).

Anti-clericalism became the link between Protestants, liberals, and Freemasons in their fight against Roman Catholicism as the common enemy. The objectives of this alliance were fourfold: (1) absolute separation of church and state; (2) elimination of all religious education from state schools; (3) creation of a secular registry of births; (4) reduction of religious holidays to no more than four dates according to the French model (the other holidays were suppressed as they were considered harmful to trade and commerce) (Hernández, 2017, pp. 128–129; Da Costa, 2009, pp. 138–140).

Protestantism opposed the corporate conception of traditional Roman Catholic society (corporatism). Consequently, Protestantism emerged as a religious alternative upholding the values of freedom, republicanism, and democracy. Its principal interest was to achieve specific changes in social organisation in line with the Anglo-American model (Amestoy, 1994, p. 617; Hernández, 2017, p. 116). Particularly significant was the missionary activity of Methodism within Protestantism. Methodism portrayed and compared itself with Roman Catholicism in the terms expressed in Table 19.2.

Thus, Protestantism became coupled with the anti-clerical secularist programme of liberalism. The dilemma of Protestantism as an ally of liberalism was, however, dealing with the most radical liberal postures that considered religion (in general) opposed to social progress. In this respect, Protestantism maintained a critical attitude towards ideological radicalism within liberalism. This manifested itself later in the inclusion of the freedom of religion and consciousness in the constitution,

**Table 19.2** Self-portraits of Protestantism (Methodism) compared to Roman Catholicism in the nineteenth-century Uruguay (adapted from Mann as cited in Hernández, 2017, p. 116)

| Methodism | Roman catholicism |
|---|---|
| "Religion of common sense", "of the right reason" | "adverse to common sense, opposed to reason" |
| "of the civilisation" | "hindrances to civilisation" |
| "of freedom" | "enemies of freedom" |
| "of the moral purity" | "crude, petty, and degrading materialism" |
| "a spiritual religion" | "vain pomp" and the "empty appearance" |
| "the religion of the Bible" | "persecutors of the Bible" |

as opposed to the French model of *laïcité* (which radically subordinated any religious expression) (Hernández, 2017, p. 143; Roniger, 2016, p. 414).

## 19.3 The Role of Roman Catholicism

In the particular dispute that Roman Catholicism maintained with Protestantism, the Roman Church-State resorted to political power. Roman Catholicism claimed that it was the duty of the state to safeguard national religion against Protestantism and liberalism. Therefore, according to the prevailing Roman Catholic opinion, religious freedom was to be rejected. The Roman Church-State demanded eradicating biblical and apologetic literature of Protestant origin, which in extreme cases resulted in the burning of bibles (Hernández, 2017, pp. 127, 136, 144). However, the government did not impede dissenting proselytism and refrained from intervening in the ensuing anti-clerical demonstrations. Therefore, the state was no longer the "extended hand" of the Church (Hernández, 2017, pp. 144–145).

The Roman Church-State made numerous attempts to reverse secularisation. These, however, did not succeed in Uruguay (unlike in Argentina) due to the Church-State receiving little support in Uruguay. The measures included: (1) creation of a national clergy to promote the introduction of "regular corporations" and the development of Catholic associationism; (2) establishing a press and media loyal to the Church (i.e. opposed to the liberal press); (3) rural missions; (4) Catholic congresses and a Catholic club; and above all (5) the foundation of educational institutions to counteract secularism and anti-clericalism in education (Corbo, 2011).

## 19.4 Present-Day State-Church Relations

More recent controversies have revolved around the question of whether the Uruguayan Republic is regressing in its secular traditions. Examples of ample discussion have been the state-funded installation of a cross on a public road to celebrate the papal visit (1987), erecting a statue of John Paul II (2005), and other Roman Catholic icons in public spaces (Da Costa, 2009, p. 142).

## 19.5 Empirical Analysis and CDA (Prosperity)

### *19.5.1 Textual Analysis (Theological)*

None of the stakeholders interviewed referred directly to a Christian (i.e. biblical) principle of prosperity being connected to obedience to the Commandments (Moral Law). However, Protestant stakeholders provided the closest direct references to biblical concepts (Table 19.3).

The Protestant Free Pastor 1 (f) refers to spiritual prosperity (in the heavenly kingdom; John 14: 3, King James Bible, 1769) rather than to physical prosperity in this world. Similarly, the Independent Free Protestant Believer (n) mentions that after becoming prosperous ('too well'), they forget about God, which implicitly refers to the Old Testament proverb:

> ... feed me with food convenient for me: lest I be full, and deny thee, and say, Who is the Lord? ... (King James Bible, 1769, Proverbs 30:8–9).

The other stakeholders prefer a more secular (non-theological) approach to prosperity in Uruguay. None referred directly to a biblical principle. This contrasts with the other three cases (Switzerland, Colombia, Cuba), but can be expected considering Uruguay's high secularisation.

### *19.5.2 Analysis of Discourse Practice (Theoretical Triangulation)*

The Ecumenical Academic Theologian (i) links trustworthiness, the respect for the law, and prosperity (housing), similarly to Fukuyama (1995). When the Independent Free Protestant Believer (n) mentions that after becoming prosperous ('too well'), they forget God, he is also referring implicitly to the theory of existential security (Norris & Inglehart, 2004). This theory explains why societies become more secularised when enough freedom and security exist, but become more religious in times of crisis (see Sect. 7.2.1).

For the Independent Free Protestant Believer, causality tends to run from prosperity to secularism. This view, however, denies the historic "reverse of fortune" resulting from progressive secularisation and subsequent human capital building in Uruguay.

### *19.5.3 Analysis of Social Practice*

Three stakeholders provide largely similar general descriptions of the different colonies (towns with different religious backgrounds). Despite some minor

**Table 19.3** Principles of prosperity according to stakeholders interviewed in Uruguay (Source: Author's figure)

| Prosperity | |
|---|---|
| Stakeholder | Fundamental principles identified (interviews) |
| The Holy Bible | "Keep therefore the words of this covenant, and do them, that ye may *prosper* in all that ye do" (King James Bible, 1769, Deuteronomy 29:9). |
| e) Roman Catholic theologian | "I believe that the prosperity situation of Uruguay throughout history does not provide a single answer. On the one hand, it is a small country, and it is much easier to have an overview and know what is happening throughout the country. It is a country that has a tiny population, compared to other countries in Latin America, which also allows the implementation of social policies. [. . .]" |
| f) Protestant Free Church Pastor 1. | "In this Church, there are no promises of healing, nor prosperity. In this respect, the soul and its orientation towards what is to come are clearly important. From those promises, one can draw peace and strength, but there is no promise that you will get better from your illness or prosperity. This is a distinctly Christian church, but in following Jesus. Jesus established a basis, and we want to prepare for what is to come on that basis. Not for this world, since this world passes away. But there is a future promise that Jesus will come to seek his people [John 14: 3]". |
| i) Ecumenical academic theologian. | "The Swiss [from Nueva Helvecia] are still more closed; the Waldensians are more open, more progressive. But the working system is the same, i.e. through associations, cooperatives, etc. A characteristic of this area is that you will not find settlements (invasions). If land belongs to someone, nobody builds on that land; it's empty. If you go to La Paz, you will see a plot of land in the corner next to the school and the Plaza. Doroteo García donated that land to a Mr. Malcolm (an Englishman) who had a field close to the little town and that helped him when he came to mark the town, etc. Later, Mr. García, in gratitude, gave him that land, but he never drew up the documents and for that reason, this land has remained unbuilt to this day. No one has built on that land. The same thing is happening here. You will find only a few humble or derelict houses because, in general, the level of housing in this area is good. You will find low-income families, but with good housing. There are no settlements like those in Montevideo and other cities.<br>Here, the Spanish colony was very methodical in its production; but they were not progressive and were absorbed by these colonies (Waldensians) that were always more hardworking and open to progress". |
| j) Ecumenical Pastor | "Here in Colonia and in Uruguay, in general, many people prospered thanks to the Swiss; even the government copied things from them. We [Swiss colony] are an example in the country. The cheese we make, the cheese colony, was born here. There are cheese factories in the rest of the country. And they have learned the Swiss technique from here.<br>We know how to save when there is plenty because that is what our grandparents taught us and when there is not, the Swiss have a reservation. Here you take good care of that. 'Machete' is our |

(continued)

**Table 19.3** (continued)

| Prosperity | |
|---|---|
| Stakeholder | Fundamental principles identified (interviews) |
| | expression for being stingy. To be 'Swiss' is to be a collaborator. The immigrants came with nothing except tools. But they were hungry. We even inherited the need to care; we save because it is very difficult to have nothing and go hungry.<br>The Waldensians came to colonise four years before the Swiss colony (1858). Our immigrants [Swiss] began arriving in 1861 or 1862, and the Swiss colony [Nueva Helvecia] prospered a lot. They [the Waldenses] did not prosper quite as well, because religion somehow blocked them. This [Nueva Helvecia] was an open colony; maybe we lost the language of being open, but the Swiss still keep some of the traditions, for instance, dance, food, orchestras, etc., even 150 years later [. . .]". |
| n) Independent, free Protestant believer (Entrepreneur) | "Recently, Uruguay was said to be one of the least religious countries in Latin America. I suppose that is because we are doing 'too well', and therefore forget to look up (towards God). Uruguay has a very 'light' religiosity, nothing deep, in general". |
| p) Government officer | "To this day, Colonia is very prosperous. During the major crisis of 2002, Rosario [Catholic] closed five of its factories, and there was a massive loss of jobs because it was purely manufacturing. In contrast, Valdense [Protestant Waldensians] and Nueva Helvecia [Swiss mixed], who worked more and lived more than their land yielded did not have that problem, because they had a diversified economy.<br>All immigrants have strongly influenced this area. Although they [immigrants] all have something in common, they are also very different. The Waldensian is a little more closed than the Swiss (Nueva Helvecia). Rosario's inhabitant is carnivalesque. We have a saying: 'The Waldensian does not drink mate herb, because he cannot waste time; he has many tasks to do; the one in Nueva Helvecia drinks mate herb, but in his house; and the one in Rosario drinks in the shade of the parsley, because they never cut the parsley.' The Waldensians dedicate themselves first to their daily chores and religion; the Swiss (Nueva Helvecia) retire to the privacy of their house while the Rosarians live the 'crazy life'". |

differences, they generally identify Waldensians and Swiss colony inhabitants as "hard workers" and "prosperous", whereas Rosarians (Catholics) are seen as "not progressive" and "carnivalesque". These perceptions point to a Weberian Protestant work ethic in the Colonia province, in line with the global trend discussed in this study (Table 19.4).

**Table 19.4** Perceptions of three stakeholders on the prosperity and performance of towns with different religious and cultural backgrounds in Uruguay (Source: Author's figure)

| Province/town | i) Ecumenical academic theologian, | j) Ecumenical Pastor | p) Government officer |
|---|---|---|---|
| Rosario (Roman Catholic town) | Methodical, yet not progressive. | | • "Carnivalesque" (drinks mate in the shade of the parsley, which he never cuts).<br>• During the major crisis of 2002, Rosario closed five of its factories, resulting in many redundancies. |
| Valdense (Waldensians Protestant colony) | More open, more hard-working, more progressive (than Swiss colonists and Rosarians). | The Waldensians did not prosper in the same way (as the Swiss colonists), because religion somehow blocked them. | • Hard workers (do not drink mate herb, because they are busy)<br>• Slightly more reserved than the Swiss<br>• Prosperous, diversified economy (not affected by the 2002 crisis). |
| Nueva Helvecia (Swiss colony, mixed religious) | More reserved (than the Waldensians and Rosarians) | Swiss colony (Nueva Helvecia) prospered a lot. | • Hard workers (drink mate herb, but in the privacy of their home)<br>• Prosperous, diversified economy, (not affected by the 2002 crisis). |

## References


Acemoglu, D., & Robinson, J. (2012). *Why nations fail. The origins of power, prosperity and poverty*. New York: Crown Business.

Amestoy, N. R. (1994). *Las mentalidades protestantes en AA.VV., Historia General de la Iglesia en América Latina*. Tomo IX. Salamanca: CEHILA/Sígueme.

Asiaín, P. C. (2010). Religión en la Educación Pública. Deberes del Estado uruguayo a la luz del Derecho Humanitario Internacional. *Revista de Derecho de la Universidad de Montevideo, 9* (17), 65–88.

Becker, S. O., & Woessmann, L. (2009). Was weber wrong? A human capital theory of protestant economic history. *Quarterly Journal of Economics, 124*(2), 531–596. https://doi.org/10.1162/qjec.2009.124.2.531.

Blancarte, R. (2006). La laicidad: la construcción de un concepto de validez universal. In N. Da Costa (Ed.), *Laicidad en América Latina y Europa* (pp. 31–36). Montevideo: CLAEH.

Caetano, G., & Geymonat, R. (1997). *La secularización uruguaya (1859–1919): Catolicismo y privatización de lo religioso*. Montevideo: Taurus-Obsur.

Corbo, T. S. (2011). La Iglesia y el proceso de secularización en el Uruguay Moderno (1859-1919). *Hispania Sacra, LXIII, 127*, 283–303.

Da Costa, N. (2009). La laicidad uruguaya. *Archives de sciences sociales des religions, 146*, 137–155.

Da Costa, N. (2016). Religión en prisión. Cambios en el laico Uruguay. Religion in prison, changes in the very secular Uruguay. *Sociedad y Religion, XXVI*(46), 224–238.

Fitzgibbon, R. (1956). *Uruguay. Portrait of a democracy. An informal survey of the Switzerland of Latin America*. London: George Allen and Unwin.

Freedom House. (2016). *Freedom in the world 2016. Anxious dictators, wavering democracies: Global freedom under pressure*. Washington, DC: Freedom House.

Fukuyama, F. (1995). *Trust. The social virtues and the creation of prosperity*. New York: Free Press.

Guigou, N. (2005). *La Nación Laica. Religión civil y mito-praxis en el Uruguay*. Montevideo: La Gotera.

Hernández, M. S. (2017). Catolicismo y Protestantismo en los inicios del Uruguay moderno (1876-1880). *Boletín del Instituto de Historia Argentina y Americana "Dr. Emilio Ravignani", 3*(46), 110–146.

*King James Bible*. (1769). *The Holy Bible, King James Version*. Cambridge Edition: 1769. Scripture quotations from The Authorized (King James) Version. Rights in the Authorized Version in the United Kingdom are vested in the Crown. Reproduced by permission of the Crown's patentee, Cambridge University Press.

Klaiber, J. L. (1997). *Iglesia, dictaduras y democracia en América Latina*. Lima: Pontificia Universidad Católica del Perú, Fondo Editorial.

Norris, P., & Inglehart, R. (2004). *Sacred and secular: Religion and politics worldwide*. New York: Cambridge University Press.

Pew Research Center. (2014). *Religion in Latin America. Widespread change in a historically catholic region*. Retrieved from https://www.pewforum.org/2014/11/13/religion-in-latin-america/

Porter, M., Stern, S., & Green, M. (2015). *Social progress index 2015*. Retrieved from https://www.socialprogress.org/?tab=2&code=NOR

Roniger, L. (2016). How a shattered civil religion is rebuilt through contestation: Uruguay and the legacy of authoritarianism/Reconstruir una religión civil a través de la confrontación: Uruguay y el legado del autoritarismo. *Revista de Ciencia Política, 36*(2), 411–432.

Transparency International. (2016). *Corruption perceptions index 2016*. Retrieved from: https://www.transparency.org/news/feature/corruption_perceptions_index_2016

# Chapter 20
# c) Cuba: A *Sui Generis* Case Study (Communist Proxy)

> *It is illegal and punishable to oppose faith or religious belief to the Revolution, to education or to the fulfilment of the duties of working, to defend the country with arms, to revere its symbols and the other duties established by the Constitution (Article 54: (3) Political Constitution of 1976 of the Republic of Cuba, valid until 1992).*
> *The State recognises, respects, and guarantees religious freedom. In the Republic of Cuba, religious institutions are separate from the State. Different beliefs and religions enjoy equal consideration (Article 8: Political Constitution of 1992 of the Republic of Cuba, valid to this day).*

Since the socialist revolution, Cuba has exhibited one of the highest social indicator scores in Latin America (e.g. health, literacy, and personal safety) (Feinberg, & Piccone, 2014; Gold, 2015; United Nations Development Programme—UNDP, 2016; Vekemans & Segundo, 1963, p. 83). However, its communist regime has made Cuba the third most hostile country to economic and political freedom worldwide (after North Korea and Venezuela) (Miller & Kim, 2017; Freedom House, 2016). On balance, however, the Cuban social progress index is one of the lowest in Latin America (Porter et al., 2015).

The religious overview is as contradictory as Cuba's social indicators. Historically, direct political influence and formal participation in religion have been low compared to most Latin American countries, even from before the Cuban Revolution. However, widespread religiosity and syncretism strongly permeate religious and secular belief systems in Cuba. Consequently, the institutional influence of religion has been relatively weak compared to the pervasive cultural influence of religion in Cuba (Crahan, 2017, pp. 386, 388; Crahan, 1979, p. 159).

The overall indifference to institutionalised religion in Cuba stems from anti-colonial/anti-imperial sentiments. The Roman Catholic Church-State has been perceived as tied to colonial Spain. Protestant churches have in turn been linked to US

---

**Supplementary Information** The online version of this chapter (https://doi.org/10.1007/978-3-030-78498-0_20) contains supplementary material, which is available to authorized users.



J. García Portilla, *"Ye Shall Know Them by Their Fruits"*, Contributions to Economics, https://doi.org/10.1007/978-3-030-78498-0_20

interests. For instance, the Roman Catholic hierarchy strongly opposed Cuba's independence from Spain, and the US government recommended that US churches ought to use humanitarian aid to promote democracy in Cuba (Crahan, 1979, p. 159; Goldenziel, 2009, p. 206; Ramírez, 2009, p. 169).

The Cuban Revolution impacted the institutional strength of religion (i.e. by abolishing Church privileges, reducing formal membership, and spreading secular education). However, the level of belief among the Cuban population maintained remarkably stable from the 1950s to the present (ca. 75 to 85%) (Crahan, 2017, p. 390).

## 20.1 Colonial Times Until the First Half of the Twentieth Century

As in the rest of Latin America, Spanish colonisation introduced Roman Catholicism in Cuba. Consequently, the Catholic Church has always had a strong presence in Cuba, and has formed a complex relationship with the political establishment (Contreras, 2013, p. 177; Ramírez, 2009, p. 167).

Independence from Spain (1898) and relations with the USA led to an influx of Protestant missionaries. As a result, several Protestant denominations have been installed in Cuba since the late nineteenth-century, including Methodist, Baptist, Lutheran, Adventist, Presbyterian, and Quaker (Contreras, 2013, p. 178; Ramírez, 2009, p. 171).

Before the Revolution, the Roman Church-State did not have a strong influence in Cuba, unlike in most Latin American countries (Goldenziel, 2009, p. 182; Crahan, 2017, pp. 386, 388; Crahan, 1979, p. 159; Ramírez, 2009, p. 171). Nevertheless, the Roman Church-State privileged *de facto* or *de jure* relations with the government, thus enforcing the hegemonic power exerted by Rome until the Cuban Revolution. For instance, the state obliged Protestant churches to register officially, while the Roman Church-State was exempt from such an obligation (Ramírez, 2009, p. 171). Such privileges promoted elitism and created a highly non-egalitarian pre-revolutionary society (like in most Latin American countries) (Crahan, 1979, p. 170).

## 20.2 The Revolution: 1960s to the Present

Among other factors, the relative weakness of the Roman Church-State in Cuba provided opportunities for liberals, US Protestants, and communists, and ultimately led to the Revolution. Naturally, Protestants were more progressive and less counter-revolutionary than Roman Catholics (Crahan, 1979, pp. 159, 170, 172).

When the revolutionary regime adopted Marxism and forged ties with the Soviet Bloc, it adopted an atheistic constitution and became hostile to any form of religion.

The law on education gave the state the exclusive right to build schools and provide education. Private schools became state property. This severely affected religious and, above all, Roman Catholic schools, which had outnumbered other types of schools before the Revolution (Contreras, 2013, p. 179; Crahan, 1979, p. 179).

The general reaction of Cuban society to the adoption of Marxism in the 1960s was negative, due to the religious implications. Accordingly, the hostilities to religion led to exiling Roman Catholic priests and Protestant pastors. Properties were seized and dozens of clerics and laypersons were tortured (Crahan, 1979, p. 174; Ramírez, 2009, p. 173).

In the 1970s and 80s, the Cuban Revolution stimulated other social movements in Latin America, including Liberation Theology within Roman Catholicism and later also in Protestantism (Berges & Cárdenas, 1993; Ramírez, 2009). Fidel Castro, Cuba's communist leader for almost five decades, publicly expressed a positive view of religion for the first time in 1985. Castro admitted that religion could also have the potential to alter reality, revolutionise a nation, end oppression, and restore justice (Castro & Betto, 2006, p. 5).

The collapse of the Soviet Union in the early 1990s resulted in a severe economic crisis in Cuba, (known as the "special period") (Goldenziel, 2009, p. 202). This, in turn, led to a revival of religious activity, which was closely linked to the unfolding socioeconomic crisis during the 1990s (Ramírez, 2009, p. 174). This fairly typical phenomenon corroborates the theory of existential security (Norris & Inglehart, 2004). Accordingly, Afro-Cuban and Pentecostal religions have witnessed rapid growth, like other faiths in Cuba (Goldenziel, 2009, p. 202).

The Cuban regime responded to the crisis by implementing a new constitution (1992), which included religious freedom and the substitution of an atheist state with a secular one (Goldenziel, 2009; Contreras, 2013). Granting greater religious freedom was part of a strategic political ploy to strengthen the socialist regime (Goldenziel, 2009).

Three aspects are worth mentioning in this respect:

1. The collapse of the Soviet Union and the crucial role of the Roman Church-State at the time. The Cuban regime realised the value of an important political trade-off: counting on Rome as an ally (not as an enemy) to maintain dictatorship. Thus, greater religious freedom allowed the regime to cultivate relations with the Catholic hierarchy (Goldenziel, 2009; Crahan, 2017; Contreras, 2013);
2. Religious freedom helped the regime to legitimise itself in a religious society (whose religiosity underwent a revival after the 1990s crisis) (Goldenziel, 2009);
3. Constitutional religious liberty permitted the Cuban regime to circumvent US trade regulations, thus enabling economic aid to flow into Cuba via religious groups. Furthermore, the Cuban establishment took various measures to avoid US-like Protestant opposition by co-opting and regulating the Council of Churches through a clientelistic-corporatist scheme. This mechanism allows Council members to benefit from increased political power while limiting their autonomy to censure the government (Goldenziel, 2009).

After Cuba opened itself in 1991, Afro-Cuban organisations also came into the corporatist fold (Goldenziel, 2009, p. 201).

Finally, the break between the Roman Church-State and the Cuban government after the Revolution demonstrated Rome's ability to survive and adapt to unfavourable conditions (Contreras, 2013, p. 177). The Cuban revolution showed the Roman Church-State that it could include Marxist elements in its dialectic and thus support left-wing dictators to gain political revenue. Consequently, despite initial resistance to liberation theology, the Roman Church-State hierarchy accepted this to a certain extent, as an element integral to upholding its hegemony (see Sect. 10.4.1.4.1).

Although the Catholic Church-State still does not achieve the same power in Cuba as in other Latin American countries, it still has the necessary elements to achieve this goal. It relies on a centuries-long legacy and on a well-consolidated hierarchical structure, from the Vatican down to Cuban priests and believers (Contreras, 2013, p. 193). Indeed, the Roman Catholic Church has the richest and most ancient, extensive, and organised presence of any religion, both in Cuba and worldwide (Goldenziel, 2009, p. 195).

In turn, the Protestant experience in Cuba largely confirms the findings of various scholars (e.g. Helmsdorff, 1996; Schäfer, 2006; and Martin, 1999) for other Latin American countries: The Council of Churches (which represents most Protestant denominations) has adopted the same established practices of corporatism and clientage (Goldenziel, 2009).

## 20.3 Religion Adherents and Prominent Syncretism in Cuba

Protestants have amounted 3 to 6 percent of the Cuban population according to different estimates (Goldenziel, 2009, p. 206; Crahan, 2017, p. 397). About 70% of Cubans claim to practice spiritism. Also, roughly two-thirds of Cubans have traditionally identified as Roman Catholics, thus indicating the high degree of syncretism in the country (Crahan, 2017, p. 384; Hearn, 2008, p. 17; see also Sect. 10.5.1.1.2).

## 20.4 Empirical Analysis and CDA for Cuba (Corruption)

### *20.4.1 Textual Analysis (Theological)*

None of the interviewed stakeholders refers directly to a Christian (i.e. biblical) principle of corruption potentially linked to the moral law. However, the Protestant Methodist Pastor (h) mentioned the role of the Protestant (Methodist) Church in

**Table 20.1** Principles of corruption according to stakeholders interviewed in Cuba (Source: Author's figure)

| Corruption | |
|---|---|
| Stakeholder | Fundamental principles identified (interviews) |
| The Holy Bible | "Keep thee far from a false matter; and the innocent and righteous slay thou not: for I will not justify the wicked. And thou shalt take no gift: for the gift blindeth the wise, and perverteth the words of the righteous" (*King James Bible*, 1769, Exodus 23:7–8). |
| b) Roman Catholic Priest 2. | "Corruption comes from below, from people with limitations. Cuban people survive from the 'black bag' [black market and rubbish]. And there is a struggle to see whom to damage, [which is] typical of the black market that is unscrupulous. And that struggle will end when people have the opportunity to meet their needs in another [legal] way". |
| e) Roman Catholic Theologian | "As people live badly, they cheat on the state. And the Church [Catholic] says this is not a sin. Why so? Because it's *Fair Compensation*, a Catholic doctrine. The state has taken the properties of the people; it is fair that people seek their compensation. In this sense, it's okay to cheat on the state or to steal like Robin Hood. In 1961, the relations between church and state were impossible. The Church was the largest landowner in Cuba and then the US. The Church supported the revolution and thought its lands would be protected. That was not the case.<br>Now, the closeness between the pope and state are necessary because it suits the state and it is convenient for the Church. The Church wants to receive privileges and status, and the state wants to show piousness and social sensitivity. It is like a 'Mafia kiss' ('*un beso de mafiosas*')". |
| f) Protestant Pastor 1 (Pentecostal) | "Christians [Protestants] also do unlawful things but to a lesser extent than the rest. Christians [Protestants], in general, do not party; do not drink alcohol; are not adulterers. They do not commit idolatry. We are committed to God and keep a high [moral] standard here in Cuba.<br>[But] in Cuba, you live outside the law. Cubans think with their bellies. The US has the Cuban Adjustment Act (dry and wet feet). I hope that in heaven there will be a Cuban Adjustment Act, too (laughs)". |
| g) Protestant Pastor 2 (Adventist) | "There is a culture of 'to solve' in Cuba: in society, in general in the population. The concept of "theft" has been distorted and softened by 'to solve'". |
| h) Protestant Pastor 3 (Methodist) | "[...] Nowadays, what is said is not done. No one abides by the laws.<br>The difference between before the revolution and now is that now corruption is widespread and before it was not.<br>If we go out walking in the street, I can give you 10,000 examples of corruption. For example, in that little corner, in that cafe, most of their products are not legal. They are not selling what they have to sell, and so on.<br>Or, for example, if we go to a flea market selling agricultural products, they do not measure a fair weight. They are trying to deceive people and are burdening the system. They are evading |

(continued)

**Table 20.1** (continued)

| Corruption | |
|---|---|
| Stakeholder | Fundamental principles identified (interviews) |
| | taxes, and so on.<br>If we go to a government institution or we go to a ticket agency there will be "no tickets". But if you pay a bribe of $20 or $10, regardless of the destination, you can get a ticket. This has become a culture, a culture of corruption.<br>I am an evangelical [Methodist], and we evangelicals are very concerned about these issues. For us, in our Church, when we do an event and have to buy food, we think twice, because it is a matter of conscience and we know where the products come from". |
| k) Non-Christian (atheist, agnostic) (Academic) | "You have to pay more [a bribe] for a government certification with good spelling. Otherwise, they will give you with bad spelling, sometimes on purpose. [Also] Many Cubans watch television through an illegal package. Cubans normally are seeking to break the law and do what they want.<br>Corruption was minimal after the revolution, and now it has increased. Buying a car was a reward only for good workers". |
| m) Employee, Independent citizen | "Unnecessary bureaucracy and corruption is eating away Cuba". |
| n) Tourism professional | Here it is common to evade the law and to pay bribes to get things done. Otherwise, you could wait all your life without anything happening.<br>Here we have a saying: 'The government pretends to pay me, and I pretend to work' (*El gobierno hace como que me paga y yo hago como que trabajo*). |
| p) Government official | "In Cuba, we now have 'indirect democracy,' which means that you vote for representatives who vote for governors. Here, Cubans say that 'Fidel gives everything' [to the people] and the state is infallible, like God.' *However, the 'new man' whom Che Guevara dreamt of has become the corrupt Cuban and a hooker* (Jinetera). Today there are very low moral standards here. Immorality is rife, *Jineteras*. Rampant state corruption and everywhere else. Unnecessary bureaucracy. But before the Revolution, there was much more corruption, aristocracy and Catholicism.<br>To whom shall the needy look? Shall they look to the government or the church? They are both immoral, and if we focus on them, we will become more immoral. We can be better and lower corruption only by looking at God's perfection." |

Note: No quantitative data on competiveness is available for Cuba and little qualitative data resulted from coding prosperity.

preventing cheating from spreading in Cuban society. This is indirectly in line with Exodus 23 (*King James Bible*, 1769) (Table 20.1).

The Roman Catholic Theologian (e) mentions the Roman Catholic doctrine of *Fair Compensation*, which "justifies" stealing or cheating in certain situations (like

Robin Hood). This doctrine is opposed to Exodus 23 (*King James Bible*, 1769) (Table 20.1). Likewise, the "necessary Mafia kiss" between church and state is against another biblical principle: "Render therefore unto Caesar the things which are Caesar's; and unto God the things that are God's" (*King James Bible*, 1769, Matthew 22:21).

### 20.4.2 Analysis of Discourse Practice (Theoretical Triangulation)

The atheist, socialist legal principle of the "goodness of humankind" (Berman 2003, p. 18) resembles Roman Catholic natural law, in that it trusts the human capacity to discern good from evil (Selling, 2018, p. 9; Gula, 2002, pp. 120–21). Arruñada (2010) explains that Roman Catholicism enhances corruption due to the relativistic contents of its moral code and its dubious enforcement mechanisms (p. 895). These statements are valid in Cuban society, as exemplified above in various ways: (1) by the practice of *Fair Compensation* (see Roman Catholic Theologian (e)); (2) by the Protestant Methodist Pastor's comments on cheating and stealing (h); (3) by the common Cuban proverb "The government pretends to pay me, and I pretend to work" (Tourism professional (n)); and (4) by the non-Christian atheist's example of cheating to pay a bribe (k).

### 20.4.3 Analysis of Social Practice: Law and Institutions

The Tourism professional (n) highlights the evasion of laws and payment of bribes as the natural way of life in Cuba. Likewise, the non-Christian atheist (k) refers to similar examples of breaking the law. Such examples are consistent with the systematic separation of law, culture, and morals common in most Latin American countries (Mockus et al., 2012; see also Sect. 10.3.1.2).

The Government Official (p) argues in a similar direction and indirectly challenges the socialist legal tradition (Sect. 8.3.4.7). His criticism refers to what Marxist theory calls the ideal "new man". In practice, however, this has produced a corrupt Cuban and the hooker (*Jinetera*). Stakeholder (p) expands this perspective, observing that low moral standards pervade the government and the Church. What remains is the need to consider God's perfection the sole point of reference.

## References


Arruñada, B. (2010). Protestants and catholics: Similar work ethic, Different social ethic. *The Economic Journal, 120*(547), 890–918.

Berges, J., & Cárdenas, R. (1993). El pastorado protestante y la Nueva Teología Cubana. In J. Berges & R. Cárdenas (Eds.), *La religión. Estudio de especialistas cubanos sobre la temática religiosa*. La Habana: Política.

Berman, H. (2003). *Law and revolution II: The impact of the protestant reformations on the western legal tradition*. Cambridge, London: Harvard University Press, Belknap Press.

Castro, F., & Betto, F. (2006). *Fidel and religion: Fidel Castro in conversations with Frei Betto on Marxism and Liberation Theology* (2nd edn, M. Todd, Trans.). Melbourne: Oceana Press (Original work published 1985).

Contreras, D. (2013). Iglesia Católica y estado en la República de Cuba: Pasado y presente de sus relaciones Catholic Church and State in Cuba: Past and present relationships. *América Latina Hoy, 63*, 177–195.

Crahan, M. E. (1979). Salvation through Christ or Marx: Religion in revolutionary cuba. Special issue: The church and politics in Latin America. *Journal of Interamerican Studies and World Affairs, 21*(1), 156–184.

Crahan, M. E. (2017). Cuba: Religion and civil society. *Social Research, 84*(2), 383–405.

Feinberg, R. E., & Piccone, T. (2014). *Cuba's economic change in comparative perspective*. Latin American Initiative at Brookings; Center for the Study of the Cuban Economy (CEEC), University of Havana; and Center for Research on the International Economy (CIEI), 129. Retrieved from https://www.brookings.edu/wp-content/uploads/2016/06/Cubas-Economic-Change-English-web-1.pdf

Freedom House. (2016). *Freedom in the world 2016. Anxious dictators, wavering democracies: Global freedom under pressure*. Washington, DC: Freedom House.

Gold, M. (2015). *People and state in socialist Cuba. Ideas and practices of revolution*. New York: Palgrave Macmillan.

Goldenziel, J. (2009). Sanctioning faith: Religion, state, and U.S.-Cuban relations. *Journal of Law and Politics, 25*(179), 179–210.

Gula, R. M. (2002). *Reason informed by faith—foundations of catholic morality*. Paulist Press.

Hearn, A. H. (2008). *CUBA religion, social capital, and development*. Durham and London: Duke University Press.

Helmsdorff, D. (1996). *Participación política evangélica en Colombia*. (D. A. Bidegain, Ed.) Bogotá: Universidad de los Andes. Departamento de Historia. Tesis de Grado.

*King James Bible*. (1769). *The Holy Bible, King James Version*. Cambridge Edition: 1769. Scripture quotations from The Authorized (King James) Version. Rights in the Authorized Version in the United Kingdom are vested in the Crown. Reproduced by permission of the Crown's patentee, Cambridge University Press.

Martin, D. (1999). The evangelical upsurge and its political implications. In P. Berger (Ed.), *The desecularization of the world* (pp. 37–49). Washington, DC: Ethics and Public Policy Center and Wm. B. Eerdmans Publishing Co.

Miller, T., & Kim, A. B. (2017). *Index of economic freedom*. Washington, DC: The Heritage Foundation. Retrieved from http://www.heritage.org/index

Mockus, A., Murraín, H., & Villa, M. (2012). *Antípodas de la violencia: Desafíos de cultura ciudadana para la crisis de (in)seguridad en América Latina*. Washington, DC: Banco Interamericano de Desarrollo.

Norris, P., & Inglehart, R. (2004). *Sacred and secular: Religion and politics worldwide*. New York: Cambridge University Press.

Porter, M., Stern, S., & Green, M. (2015). *Social progress index 2015*. Retrieved from https://www.socialprogress.org/?tab=2&code=NOR

Ramírez, C. J. (2009). Laïcité, liberté de religion et État laïque. Les étapes de la laïcisation cubaine. *Archives de Sciences Sociales des Religions, 54*(146), 157–182.

Schäfer, H. (2006). »Die« Pfingstbewegung in Lateinamerika…? Zur Untersuchung des Verhältnisses zwischen religiöser Praxis und gesellschaftlichen Strukturen. *Zeitschrift für Religionswissenschaft*, pp 53–82.

Selling, J. A. (2018). Reframing catholic theological ethics: Summary and application (A. Abram, Ed.). *Religions, 8*(203), 5–13.

United Nations Development Programme—UNDP. (2016). *Human Development Index (HDI)*. Retrieved from http://hdr.undp.org/en/content/human-development-index-hdi

Vekemans, R., & Segundo, J. L. (1963). Essay of a socio-economic typology of the Latin American countries. En E. de Vries, J. Medina, & B. Higgins (Eds.), *Social aspects of economic development in Latin America* (Conference: Expert Working Group on Social Aspects of Economic Development in Latin America., Vol. 1). UNESCO. Retrieved from https://unesdoc.unesco.org/ark:/48223/pf0000054509.locale=es

# Chapter 21
# d) Colombia: Extreme Negative Case Study

> *The Catholic, Apostolic and Roman religion is that of the Nation; the public powers will protect it and make it respected as an essential element of the social order (Article 38, Political Constitution of Colombia of 1886, valid until 1991).*
> *Public education shall be organised and directed under the Catholic Religion [. . .] (Article 41, Constitution of Colombia of 1886, valid until 1991).*
> *The State is not atheist, agnostic, or indifferent to the religious feelings of Colombians (Article 2, Law 133 of 1994, currently valid).*

For most of Colombia's history, most "Colombians have been in absolute poverty and plagued by violence and insecurity" (Robinson, 2016, pp. 10, 11). Indeed, serious security risks (violence and terrorism) mean that Colombia ranks bottom of the 136 countries rated for tourists and businesses. In the 2017 Travel & Tourism Competitiveness Report, Colombia scored 2.6 on a scale of the most dangerous countries worldwide (min 2.59; max 6.65; median 5.60) (World Economic Forum, 2017). Colombian levels of corruption are also very high (Transparency International, 2016), and Colombia is one of the most inequitable countries in the world (World Bank, 2016).

Robinson (2016) convincingly argues that the causes lie in the country's historical extractive political institutions (low quality of democracy and weak state). However, he disregards the crucial and profound institutional influence of Roman Catholicism on moulding Colombian political institutions.

The vital role of Roman Catholicism in establishing the social, political, institutional, and religious *status quo* in Colombia is plainly evident and well-documented (Figueroa, 2016; Levine, 1981; Blanco, 2008; Munevar, 2008; Beltrán, 2008). The largely successful project pursued by the Roman Church-State in Colombia (so-called *Christilandia* according to the Jesuit Felix Restrepo) consists of three

**Supplementary Information** The online version of this chapter (https://doi.org/10.1007/978-3-030-78498-0_21) contains supplementary material, which is available to authorized users.



J. García Portilla, *"Ye Shall Know Them by Their Fruits"*, Contributions to Economics, https://doi.org/10.1007/978-3-030-78498-0_21

pillars: (1) political (a confessional state); (2) economic (a corporatist state); and (3) cultural (a Catholic and conservative "Hispanicism") (Figueroa, 2016).

Roman Catholicism deployed Hispanicism (characterised by its triad of language, religion, and race) as its best cultural weapon. Hispanicism shielded the interests of the Roman Church-State against the threats of Bolshevik-Socialist atheism, French liberal anti-clericalism, and triumphant Anglo-Saxon Protestant modernity. Likewise, its feudal-medieval corporatism enabled the Roman Church-State to respond to both modern "right-wing" capitalism/neoliberalism and "left-wing", socialist threats. The whole package needed to be tied politically and legally to a confessional state and constitution legitimised by a Concordat (Figueroa, 2016; Levine, 1981).

Despite the mild erosion of the hegemony of Roman Catholicism in recent decades, the coherence of the Roman Church-State project is still pervasive in Colombia (Figueroa, 2016); (Beltrán, 2008). The *Christilandia* project of Colombian society has been a product of the country's most conservative and intolerant wing of Roman Catholicism. Such conservative views have been dominant in Colombia, regardless of the existence of less intransigent sectors, which have traditionally been weaker (Figueroa, 2016; Levine, 1981; Munevar, 2008; Beltrán, 2008). Consequently, Colombian Romanism (Catholicism) has forcefully advocated such a theocratic, hierarchical, organic, and corporate society (Figueroa, 2016).

## 21.1 Brief Historical Background

Contrary to popular belief in Colombia, the Roman Catholic Church-State is *not* a Colombian institution. It has, however, been very present since independence from Spain and even before. Colombia was a strategic ecclesiastical, political, and economic centre for Spain and the Roman Church-State in the colonial period.

After independence, Simon Bolivar petitioned the Roman Church-State (so-called "Holy" See or Roman See) to sign a Concordat with Colombia (New Granada). This move allowed legitimising the newly independent state and to continue the "*patronato*" without the Spanish Crown. Consequently, the Roman Church-State recognised Colombia as the first independent Latin American Nation in 1835 (Salinas, 2013).

Politically, several historical periods alternated between anti-clerical liberals and conservative Catholic "hegemonies" (as well as federalists and centralists), leading to traumatic civil wars. The liberal principles of the French Revolution had a decisive influence, especially in the first five Colombian constitutions until 1886 (Uribe, 1985). The extent of this liberal influence, which can be traced back to John Locke, led former president Lopez Michelsen to affirm that Colombian institutions descend from "Calvinism" (Lopez Michelsen, 1966). Far from that, Protestant and liberal ideals and influence were severely and systematically avoided in the following centuries in Colombia. Moreover, the Calvinist influence on liberalism occurred only indirectly via the French Revolution (Sect. 8.3.4.4).

## 21.2 The Progressive and Short-Lasting Liberal Constitution of 1863 (Rionegro)

Ironically, Colombia became the first Latin American country to decree the separation of church and state in 1863. The Rionegro Constitution of Colombia (1863) was an anti-clerical effort promulgated under the auspices of the Liberals in power. It was a very progressive and pioneering Constitution that provided full freedom of religion and other individual liberties. However, it only lasted 23 years. No other religion rivalled the primacy of Roman Catholicism in Colombia, where the state was weak and poor. After a Conservative revolt that resulted in a civil war of marked religious character, Colombia discarded the liberal Constitution of Rionegro and undid much of the Liberal effort to lessen the power of the Roman Catholic Church. It then promulgated its most conservative, intransigent, and long-lasting Constitution in 1886. The 1886 Constitution declared Roman Catholicism to be the religion of the nation, and public authorities were empowered to enforce respect for it. The constitutional provisions of 1886 led Colombia to sign a concordat that reiterated the establishment of Catholicism as the state religion (Delpar, 1980). Thus, Colombia did not formally separate church and state until its current Constitution (1991).

## 21.3 The Constitution of 1886 (Valid Until 1991) and the Concordat

The Conservative victory in the nineteenth-century civil wars ensured the substantial removal of liberal principles from the Constitution of 1886. The Roman See imposed the conditions on the state to grant constitutional privileges to the rights of the Roman Catholic Church. These rights were ratified in the Concordat of 1887. Thus, Colombia retained its well-rooted colonial institutions, a powerful Roman Church-State, a unified social and economic elite, and a strong central state (Levine, 1981; Figueroa, 2016).

The Concordat of 1887 was progressively modified, favouring the Roman See, until 1973. Since the Middle Ages, no other country has enforced such a complete integration of church and state (ideal medieval Christendom), as reflected in Colombia's Concordat (Salinas, 2013; Levine, 1981; Figueroa, 2016). Several articles of the 1886 Constitution were identical to those of the Concordat. Among others, under the Colombian Concordat, the following legal instruments were enforced. For instance, Article 3 accepts the force of canon law: "Canon Law is independent of civil law and is not part of it, but the authorities of the Republic will respect it" (Concordat 73, Art. 3). Consequently, civil courts cannot judge the Church hierarchy, only the Roman See can.

In the Colombian Concordat, the Roman Church-State is defined as an "essential element of the social order" (Art. 1). Consequently, the Roman Church-State has played a major role in various areas of society:

1. Public and private education at all levels, which had to be maintained “in conformity with the dogmas of the Catholic religion” (Art. 12) (religious instruction was mandatory);
2. More than 63% of Colombia’s territory are “mission territories”, in which the Church exercised broad civil powers (Art. 31) (Levine, 1981; de Roux, 2001);
3. The armies of the republic enjoy exemptions known as “military privileges”, which are determined by the pope in a separate decree (Art. 20);
4. Registering births and marriages (Art. 17–19), and the management of death, including cemeteries (Art. 30). Parish records had preference over civil records.

Moreover, the Colombian government is obliged to pay the Roman Church-State an annual fee (Art. 22, 25), in addition to granting tax exemptions for Roman Church-State properties (Art. 6). Regarding education, the Concordat enforces further contentious measures: The government is obliged to prevent “the propagation of ideas contrary to the respect and veneration of the Church and Catholic dogma” in *literary and scientific subjects and, in general, in all branches of instruction*. Diocesan ordinaries, personally or by delegates, should inspect and revise the texts of religion and morals. In the universities, the archbishop of Bogotá identified those books that would serve as texts for religion and morality. Also, to ensure the uniform teaching of these subjects, the archbishop, together with the other prelates, would choose the texts at public schools (Art. 13).

Levine (1981) notes that it is hard to envisage a more powerful tool of ostracisation, or a more revealing indication of the convergence of religious and civil forces, than these structures (p.71). Neothomism inspired such conservative arrangements by opposing social change based on the belief of an indisputable “Roman Catholic truth” (Figueroa, 2016, p. 298). Thus, Colombia’s large Roman Catholic population is a natural result of such an intransigent institutional regime rather than of the free choice of believers. Colombia has the highest proportion of adults raised as Roman Catholics in the world (92%), after Paraguay (94%) (Pew Research Center, 2014, p. 12) (Colombia and Paraguay share the same clusters for low competitiveness and high corruption in QCA; Sect. 16.3.3.4).

During the conservative regime, the presence of liberals, and even more of Protestants, was strictly limited. Liberals and Protestants, as opponents of the regime, were stigmatised as heretical and dangerous groups (Beltrán, 2008). The president was empowered to take away their civil rights, imprison them, and condemn them to exile (Figueroa, 2016, p. 58). Such a tyrannical social order led to radicalisation and bloody conflicts, for instance, between liberals and conservatives (e.g. *La Violencia*) (Levine, 1981; Figueroa, 2016).

## 21.4 The Corporatist State

In the Middle Ages, the corporations enjoyed enormous privileges. Political power and social organisation depended entirely on them. The authority of the Roman Church-State was beyond question. All social expressions formed part of a unique organism described by Thomas Aquinas as "harmonious". The Protestant Reformation, and thus the rise of nation-states, as well as the French Revolution, led to a crisis of the corporatist model. This also explains the attacks of the Roman Church-State on modernity and democracy in Colombia (especially before Vatican II, but also afterwards) (Figueroa, 2016; Levine, 1981).

In Colombia, corporatism has maintained a medieval oligarchic society by the corporations relentlessly defending their interests to the detriment of public welfare. The state continues to approve laws and policies for the benefit of corporate associates. As a result, this hierarchical inequality has produced endemic violence across the country, which increased significantly during the same years in which corporatist proposals were implemented (Figueroa, 2016, pp. 15, 19; Levine, 1981). Moreover, corporatism, violence, and deadly conflicts have exacerbated in the country's most conservative departments (e.g. Antioquia, Norte de Santander, Nariño) (Figueroa, 2016).

## 21.5 Partial End of a Totalitarian Roman Catholic Hegemony

The 1990s began with a new constitution. This was the result of a student movement and of a peace agreement that the liberal government signed with a liberal-intellectual guerrilla (M-19) (Buenahora, 1992). The new Constitution of 1991 included (although only to a modest extent) the views of ethnic minorities, Protestant Christians, and other social groups. Accordingly, the new Constitution questioned the pervasive presence of Roman Catholicism and removed its privileged status as a "state religion", at least formally. Moreover, the new constitution opened up the path for religious pluralism (Munevar, 2008; Beltrán & Quiroga, 2017).

The participation of Protestants in drafting the Constitution of 1991, in the Religious Freedom Law (Law 133 of 1994), and in the Convention of Internal Public Law (Decree 354 of 1998), has helped dismantle the denominationally Catholic character of the Colombian State (Beltrán & Quiroga, 2017, p. 205). Thus, one of the fruits of the 1991 Constitution is the decline in poverty over the last decade, and an unusual series of clashes and crises for the elites (Robinson, 2016, p. 75). However, Protestant intervention in politics failed to abolish the Concordat altogether (Beltrán & Quiroga, 2017, p. 206). The Concordat of 1973 had to be renegotiated with the Roman See and was reduced to six articles (7, 8, 12, 14, 19, and 20) out of the 33 articles in the original text (Garzón, 2011). As the Attorney General formally put matters in 1993:

> … the Concordat does not recognise several *jus cogens* rules of international human rights law, namely: religious freedom; equal rights in marriage, during it and in case of dissolution of the bond; the freedom of teaching; respect for the autonomy, rights, and freedoms of indigenous people; and the right to education (Procuraduría General de la Nación, 1993).

In spite of these reforms, the Colombian government is still required to pay a perpetual fee to the Roman See. Religious instruction in public schools according to the Roman Church Magisterium for Catholics also remains firmly in place.

In practice, the Roman Church-State still has considerable privileges, despite being compelled to participate in a meanwhile competitive religious market. Roman Catholicism enjoys the prerogatives arising from more than four centuries of monopoly: First, a privileged relationship with the Colombian State, as guaranteed by the Concordat, which remains in force with modifications despite the 1991 Constitution. Second, clear educational privileges based on the Concordat and its past institutionalisation. Third, an enormous amount of property and cultural wealth, as evident in a solid corporate organisation and extensive infrastructure. And lastly, access to domains otherwise reserved for powerful institutions, such as the mass media (Beltrán, 2008, p. 189).

Thus, the centuries-long Catholic monopoly and hegemony have lastingly impacted Colombian culture, as is visible today. The traditions, styles of action, practices, procedures, and axes of conflict are well established everywhere in Colombia and are often characteristic of feudal-medieval times (Levine, 1981, p. 58; Blanco, 2008; Munevar, 2008). Moreover, the influence of the Roman Church-State is still closely bound up with politics in Colombia. The ideological function of the Roman Church (with a less direct link to religious beliefs) still plays a vital role as a cultural point of reference underpinning the Colombian ethos (Figueroa, 2016; Munevar, 2008; Beltrán, 2008). Moreover, even after religious freedom was guaranteed in the 1991 Constitution, 79% of the population remains Roman Catholic (Pew Research Center, 2014).

## 21.6 Protestantism in Colombia

As Roman Catholicism was closely linked with conservatism, Protestantism was naturally allied to liberalism and anti-clericalism. Accordingly, Protestantism gained ground mainly during liberal periods. Protestants were, however, discriminated and excluded from wider society as "second-class citizens" (Beltrán, 2008). The situation has improved since the Second Vatican Council (1962–1965), and especially the Pentecostal movement has flourished since the 1960s (Beltrán, 2008). However, Pentecostal and Neopentecostal movements have played only a marginal role in Colombian public life (Munevar, 2008, p. 389). Moreover, whenever Protestants participate in politics, they often fall into the same corrupt behaviour as traditional politicians; the longstanding practices are too well established (Helmsdorff, 1996).

## 21.7 Empirical Analysis and CDA for Colombia (Prosperity)

### *21.7.1 Textual Analysis (Theological)*

The Christian (i.e. biblical) principle of prosperity is closely linked to obedience to the Commandments (Moral Law). A quite harmonious discourse exists among the different Protestant stakeholders regarding this principle. Thus, for instance, the Protestant Free Pastor 1 (f) refers to San Andres and Providence Island as a prosperous place before the arrival of "Catholics from mainland Colombia" destroyed the local system of values. Similarly, the Protestant Free Pastor 2 (g) refers to the importance of biblical values: They create trust in society. The Independent Protestant believer (n) cites examples from the Old Testament, for instance, Israel prospered whenever it obeyed God, but struggled and suffered whenever disobedience prevailed (Table 21.1).

In contrast, Roman Catholic stakeholders prefer a somewhat more secular (non-theological) approach to the prosperity issue in Colombia. None refers to a biblical principle. Roman Catholic Priest 1 (a) mentions the change of discourse, towards progress, after the Second Vatican Council (1965). Roman Catholic Priest 3 (c) mentions that "development" resulted from liberalisation after the introduction of the 1991 Constitution (as corroborated in previous sections). This discourse is expected and in line with the previous sections. It also coincides with the views of similar stakeholders (i.e. Catholics) in the case study of Switzerland.

### *21.7.2 Analysis of Discourse Practice (Theoretical Triangulation)*

The Free Church Pastor (f) and the Government Official (p) link trustworthiness, values, and prosperity, similarly to Fukuyama (1995). Stakeholder (n) cites the example of Israel as a society that was (cyclically) obedient to God whenever in crisis. Yet no sooner did Israel prosper, disobedience soared—until the next crisis. This principle refers implicitly to the theory of existential security (Norris & Inglehart, 2004), which explains why societies become more secularised whenever freedom and security exist in sufficient measure, but become religious in times of crisis (Sect. 7.2.1).

### *21.7.3 Analysis of Social Practice: Law and Institutions*

The Roman Catholic Priest 3 (c) argues that the liberalisation of education (i.e. emancipation from Roman Catholicism) after the introduction of the 1991 Constitution has caused corruption and crime. He advocates a conservative approach, one in line with *old-regime* Roman Church discourse (pre-Vatican II).

**Table 21.1** Principles of prosperity according to stakeholders interviewed in Colombia (Source: Author's figure)

| Prosperity | |
|---|---|
| Stakeholder | Fundamental principles identified (interviews) |
| The Holy Bible | "Keep therefore the words of this covenant, and do them, that ye may *prosper* in all that ye do" (*King James Bible*, 1769, Deuteronomy 29:9). |
| a) Roman Catholic Priest 1. | "The enemies of the Catholic Church were Communism, liberalism, and the Secret Societies (Freemasonry). In 1965, the Second Vatican Council ruled that the Church could not oppose progress, liberalism, and modern civilisation". |
| c) Roman Catholic Priest 3. | "After 1991, Colombia opened up to free markets, imports and exports, which generated development, but also sparked much corruption. Corruption and crime are linked to the issue of relaxation and liberality in education". |
| f) Protestant Free Church Pastor 1. | "...Protestantism remained here, and over the years the values of our society were marked by that essence. San Andres was a prosperous territory. They could also sleep with their doors and windows open at night and hang their clothes outside [...] to dry. You did not have to worry about [...people] stealing anything from you. They would have farms far away from their homes and no one would steal. People would end up in trouble just for stealing a coconut. When someone was killed on this island, it was an island-wide crisis. It shocked everybody that blood was shed. It was a major episode. All the church bells would ring because there was a murder. That was a society that Colombia came to found here. It was a society that was built by Protestantism and its values, but was eventually [...] destroyed by a new value system led by Catholicism [and] implanted by continental Colombia". |
| g) Protestant Free Church Pastor 1. | "You could say that while society is based on biblical principles and values, the lives of others will be more respected and more valuable. But as society moves away from God, there is more crime and less development". |
| i) Ecumenical academic theologian. | "Garcia Márquez tries to explain why we [Colombians] are the way we are. He says that we are a cultural blend of the types of Spaniards who arrived, the indigenous people we were ancestrally, and mixed with Africans. This makes us a paradoxical country, a country full of cultural contradictions. Colombia is a society of narcos. [...] Congress and the presidential campaigns have been ruled by drug money. We want to excuse and cover things up, but the structure of Colombian society [...is] the result of a culture of drug trafficking". |
| n) Independent, free Protestant believer (Academic) | "Whenever the law of God and moral standard as found in the Bible declines, the economy goes down, morality goes down, the crime rate goes up, and the result is a degenerated society. The closer you live in harmony with biblical principles, the more harmoniously you will live. [...] This principle comes down to us historically and repetitively, for example, from the book of Judges [...] the more Israel obeyed God's law in the Bible, the better [they] got, whereas whenever they strayed far from God's commandments, they faced the worst crises. [...] this pattern is repeated cyclically over and over again in history, leading to social failure and oppression whenever |

(continued)

**Table 21.1** (continued)

| Prosperity | |
|---|---|
| Stakeholder | Fundamental principles identified (interviews) |
| | people disobeyed God. In the same sense, you can explain society today. For example, how do you explain that humans suffer famines and animals have enough to eat and are fit in Africa? Voodoo and spiritist practices [that humans do and animals do not do] can give you the answer". |
| p) Government official | "Some of the factors that may affect our productivity are that we have a low level of trust in our public institutions since their accountability and transparency are dubious. Likewise, many government employees are not doing their duties. Instead, they are checking personal e-mails, Facebook, etc. [. . .] The sense of public property here is not that they belong to everyone but that they belong to no one and that we have to take advantage of them". |
| s) Colombian Embassy Official | "[. . .] there is no legal framework for cooperation between Colombia and the Holy See. Caritas Internationalis develops its work through the National Secretariat of Social Pastoral (Cáritas Colombiana). This includes rural development, helping the population (the victims of the conflict), prevention and attention to emergencies, promotion of human rights, gender equality, peacebuilding and social inclusion. The payment of the Concordat fee (per the Concordat of 1887) by the Government of Colombia to the Catholic Church is still in force. The Ministry of Foreign Affairs processes this payment, but the resources to make it effective are consolidated by the Ministry of Finance and Public Credit within the annual national budget. |

# References


Beltrán, W. M. (2008). Aproximación histórico-interpretativa al proceso de diversificación religiosa en Colombia. In S. y. Grupo Interdisciplinario de Estudios de Religión, *Mirada pluridisciplinar al hecho religioso en Colombia: Avances de investigación*. Bogotá, DC: Universidad de San Buenaventura.

Beltrán, W. M., & Quiroga, J. D. (2017). Pentecostalismo y política electoral en Colombia (1991-2014). *Colombia Internacional, 91*, 187–212.

Blanco, M. Ó. (2008). La Nación católica durante la Regeneración (1886-1900): perspectivas historiográficas. *Anuario Historia Regional y de las Fronteras, 13*(1), 157–180.

Buenahora, J. (1992). *El proceso constituyente: de la propuesta estudiantil a la quiebra del bipartidismo*. Bogotá: Editorial Tercer Mundo.

de Roux, R. (2001). Les étapes de la laïcalisation en Colombie. In J.-P. B. (dir.), *La modernité religieuse en perspective comparée* (p. 101). Paris: Karthala.

Delpar, H. (1980). Colombian liberalism and the roman catholic church, 1863-1886. *Journal of Church and State, 22*(2), 271–294.

Figueroa, H. (2016). *La persistance des idées traditionalistes en Colombie. Religion et politique (1886–1952)*. Paris: L'Harmattan.

Garzón, B. J. A. (2011). *El Concordato desde una perspectiva Histórico Política de los dos partidos tradicionales en Colombia* (Trabajo de Grado Carrera de Ciencia Política. Director Augusto Ramírez Ocampo. ed.). Bogotá, DC: Pontificia Universidad Javeriana Facultad de Ciencias Políticas y Relaciones Internacionales.

Helmsdorff, D. (1996). *Participación política evangélica en Colombia.* (D. A. Bidegain, Ed.) Bogotá: Universidad de los Andes. Departamento de Historia. Tesis de Grado.

*King James Bible.* (1769). *The Holy Bible, King James Version.* Cambridge Edition: 1769. Scripture quotations from The Authorized (King James) Version. Rights in the Authorized Version in the United Kingdom are vested in the Crown. Reproduced by permission of the Crown's patentee, Cambridge University Press.

Levine, D. (1981). *Religion and politics in Latin America: The Catholic Church in Venezuela & Colombia.* Princeton Legacy Library.

Lopez Michelsen, A. (1966). *La estirpe Calvinista de nuestras instituciones políticas.* Bogotá: Antares - Tercer Mundo.

Munevar, J. (2008). Transformación doctrinal y actitudinal de la participación política de las iglesias cristianas evangélicas en Colombia. In Grupo Interdisciplinario de Estudios de Religión, Sociedad y Política, GIERSP, *Mirada pluridisciplinar al hecho religioso en Colombia: Avances de investigación* (pp. 375–399). Bogotá, Colombia.

Norris, P., & Inglehart, R. (2004). *Sacred and secular: Religion and politics worldwide.* New York: Cambridge University Press.

Pew Research Center. (2014). *Religion in Latin America. Widespread change in a historically catholic region.* Retrieved from https://www.pewforum.org/2014/11/13/religion-in-latin-america/

Procuraduría General de la Nación. (1993). *Conceptos del Procurador General de la Nacion en los Procesos D-018, D-116 Y D-136.* Bogota.

Robinson, J. A. (2016). La miseria en Colombia (The Misery in Colombia). *Revista Desarrollo y Sociedad, 76*, 9–88. https://doi.org/10.13043/dys.76.1.

Salinas, A. C. (2013). Los concordatos celebrados entre la Santa Sede y los países latinoamericanos durante el siglo xix [The Concordats held between the Holy See and Latin American Countries in the 19th Century]. *Revista de Estudios Histórico-Jurídicos [Sección Historia del Derecho Canónico], 35*, 215–254.

Transparency International. (2016). *Corruption perceptions index 2016.* Retrieved from https://www.transparency.org/news/feature/corruption_perceptions_index_2016

Uribe, V. D. (1985). *Las constituciones de Colombia* (2a amp y aum ed.). Madrid: Cultura Hispánica.

World Bank. (2016). *GNI per capita.* Retrieved from http://data.worldbank.org/indicator/NY.GNP.PCAP.CD?display=map

World Economic Forum. (2017). *The travel and tourism competitiveness report.* Geneva: World Economic Forum.

# Chapter 22
# Summary Overview of the Four Case Studies

Historically, Switzerland's population and cantonal system have been characterised by mixed denominational distribution (Roman Catholics and Protestants). Even if the two main denominations have not always coexisted harmoniously, and despite internal differences, Switzerland is nowadays the most competitive (prosperous) country worldwide with well-recognised political, economic, and social stability. The Swiss case (Chap. 18) explored the nexuses of prosperity and of a religiously mixed society in which the Protestant Reformation played a prominent historical role in shaping federal institutions. Following the 1848 anti-clerical Constitution, many Conservative Catholics remained in mountainous and rural areas, in an attempt to maintain the old order, including the pervasive influence of the Catholic Church-State on education (also, to ensure the "maintenance of ignorance") (Obinger, 2009; Head-König, 2017). In turn, liberals and Protestants mostly remained in flat areas that were subsequently industrialised. Currently, the historical Protestant cantons tend to be the most competitive, and the mountainous Roman Catholic cantons the least competitive, in the Swiss Confederation (UBS Switzerland AG, 2016) (see Figs. 18.2 and 18.4). Historically mixed confessional cantons (e.g. Thurgau and St. Gallen) perform in the middle of the cantonal ranking of competitiveness (11th and 13th, respectively, out of 26 cantons) (UBS Switzerland AG, 2016) (see Figs. 18.1, 18.2, and 18.4). As the case study has suggested, Protestantism in Switzerland may have also contributed to prosperity via democratisation, state secularism and the creation of trust and moral standards. Yet, the influence of Protestantism owes more to its accumulated historical impact on institutions than to the proportion of current followers. Institutionally, "Protestant churches were traditionally 'canton churches' and thus strongly enmeshed with every canton's political structure" (Gould 1999 and Cattacin et al. 2003 as cited in Obinger, 2009, p. 180). In turn, the proportion of Protestants has been outnumbered by Roman Catholics since the 1970s in Switzerland, and Catholics are in the majority in most Swiss cities and cantons nowadays (FDFA, 2018; Federal Statistical Office, 2020) (see Tables 18.1 and 18.2).



J. García Portilla, *"Ye Shall Know Them by Their Fruits"*, Contributions to Economics, https://doi.org/10.1007/978-3-030-78498-0_22

In Uruguay, as well as in Switzerland, Protestantism has played a crucial role along with liberalism in introducing anti-clericalism (and religious freedom) in its constitution and therefore also in its institutions. Protestantism, then, has played a decisive role in shaping the trajectory of democracy, human capital, ethics, transparency, secularisation, and social progress.

The anti-clerical elements of the Revolution helped Cuba succeed in various indicators (e.g. education quality and coverage, equality, health). The Cuban regime seized, dismantled, and limited the institutional influence of Roman Catholicism on these areas of public life. However, a strong cultural influence of a highly syncretised Roman Catholicism persists in Cuba even if its institutional influence has been curbed. Also, the Communist regime, by adopting Marxism, "threw the baby out with the bathwater" through persecuting all types of religion, including Protestant liberals. Finally, the Cuban regime conveniently turned to Rome to legitimise itself after the collapse of the Soviet Union and to silence Protestantism with a corporatist strategy. The socialist legal tradition had an effect opposite to its claims (e.g. lack of freedom, corruption), even if its anti-clerical element was an advantage. Comparing the Cuban experience to other Latin American countries with leftist dictatorships (e.g. Venezuela) helps understand their failure to achieve the Cuban indicators (e.g. education). Evidently, there is much stronger polarisation and a younger, leftist government in Venezuela, but even there, the Catholic "Church has long had a bias in the use of its resources towards the middle and upper classes" (Smilde, 2018, p. 1; Levine, 1981). The crucial factor in this regard is whether or not the power and influence of the Roman Church-State are reduced.

In Colombia, liberal attempts failed repeatedly and resulted in violent conflicts in which the Roman Catholic Church-State closed ranks with conservatives and imposed a corporatist medieval-like state. A "Catholic and conservative hegemony" has existed in Colombia until 1991 (Figueroa, 2008). In the 1991 Constitution, Protestantism allied itself with liberal forces. This alliance made it possible to finally introduce religious freedom, among others, by removing most of the contentious articles from the Concordat (nevertheless, the Concordat remains valid, as does institutional corporatism).

Subnationally, the four cases studied here confirm the trend of Protestant versus Roman Catholic influence although under the national umbrella (e.g. Catholic areas in Switzerland are far more prosperous than liberal regions in Colombia). Swiss Protestant cantons are generally more prosperous than Roman Catholic ones. More conservative regions in Colombia tend to experience more violence and conflict than liberal ones. Uruguayan towns (e.g. in Colonia) tend to be perceived as more prosperous when under Protestant influence.

Although several theories were useful in the analysis of interviews, a common, salient notion in all four case studies was the theory of existential security (Norris & Inglehart, 2004, 2010) (see Sect. 7.2). After coding in relation to prosperity, the theory of existential security was sufficiently exemplified: in Switzerland, the non-practising Catholic stakeholder (l) claimed that religiosity runs in parallel cycles to the economy. In Uruguay, the Independent Free Protestant Believer (n) mentioned that after becoming prosperous ('too well'), they forget God. In Cuba, the revival of religious activity was closely linked to the severe socioeconomic crisis after the collapse of the Soviet Union in the 1990s (Ramírez, 2009; Goldenziel, 2009). In Colombia, the Independent Protestant believer (n) mentions the book of Judges (*King James Bible*, 1769), in which Israel prospered after obeying God, but struggled and suffered after disobedience prevailed.

Finally, the textual analyses (theological) in the four cases revealed that Protestant stakeholders provided the closest direct references to biblical concepts as the moral foundation of prosperity. In contrast, Roman Catholic stakeholders do not consistently refer to the Scriptures as a moral foundation. Instead, they tend to refer to diverse theories and philosophical influences from secular sources. This finding, consistent in diverse geographical settings, corroborates Arruñada's (2010) explanation that Protestants possess more homogeneous moral standards compared to the varied moral values in Roman Catholicism (Sects. 10.3; 10.4.1.1.1). Likewise, this outcome supports McSweeney's (2015) argument that several kinds of Roman Catholicism might exist as philosophical currents and cultural backgrounds.

## References


Arruñada, B. (2010). Protestants and catholics: Similar work ethic, different social ethic. *The Economic Journal, 120*(547), 890–918.

Federal Department of Foreign Affairs (FDFA). (2018). *Presence Switzerland.* Retrieved from https://www.eda.admin.ch/eda/en/home/fdfa/organisation-fdfa/general-secretariat/presence-switzerland.html

Federal Statistical Office. (2020). *Evolution of religious landscape. Permanent resident population 15 years or over.* Retrieved from https://www.bfs.admin.ch/content/bfs/en/home/statistics/population/languagesreligions/religions.assetdetail.11527930.html

Figueroa, H. (2008). Balance historiográfico sobre el protestantismo en Colombia. 1940-2007. In GIERSP, *Mirada pluridisciplinar al hecho religioso en Colombia: Avances de investigación.* Bogotá, Colombia: Grupo Interdisciplinario de Estudios de Religión, Sociedad y Política, GIERSP.

Goldenziel, J. (2009). Sanctioning faith: Religion, state, and U.S.-Cuban relations. *Journal of Law and Politics, 25*(179), 179–210.

Head-König, A.-L. (2017). Religion mattered: Religious differences in Switzerland and their impact on demographic behaviour (End of the 18th century to the middle of the 20th century). *Historical Social Research, 42*(2), 23–58.

*King James Bible.* (1769). *The Holy Bible, King James Version.* Cambridge Edition: 1769. Scripture quotations from The Authorized (King James) Version. Rights in the Authorized Version in the United Kingdom are vested in the Crown. Reproduced by permission of the Crown's patentee, Cambridge University Press.

Levine, D. (1981). *Religion and politics in Latin America: The Catholic Church in Venezuela & Colombia.* Princeton Legacy Library.

McSweeney, B. (2015). Hall, Hofstede, Huntington, Trompenaars, GLOBE: Common foundations, common flaws. In Y. Sanchez & C. Brühwiler (Eds.), *Transculturalism and business in the BRIC states. A handbook.* Gower Applied Business Research.

Norris, P., & Inglehart, R. (2004). *Sacred and secular: Religion and politics worldwide.* New York: Cambridge University Press.

Norris, P., & Inglehart, R. (2010). *Are high levels of existential security conducive to secularization? A response to our critics*. Paper for Mid-West Political Science Association annual meeting, Chicago, April 22, 2010.
Obinger, H. (2009). Religion and the consolidation of the Swiss Welfare State, 1848-1945. In P. Manow & K. van Kersbergen (Eds.), *Religion, class coalitions and Welfare States* (pp. 176–209). New York: Cambridge University Press.
Ramírez, C. J. (2009). Laïcité, liberté de religion et État laïque. Les étapes de la laïcisation cubaine. *Archives de sciences sociales des religions, 54*(146), 157–182.
Smilde, D. (2018). The Catholic Church and the Venezuela Crisis, 20 years on. In *Berkley Forum: Venezuela and the Role of Religious Institutions during State Crises*. Berkley Center for Religion, Peace & World Affairs. Retrieved from https://berkleycenter.georgetown.edu/responses/the-catholic-church-and-the-venezuela-crisis-20-years-on
UBS Switzerland AG. (2016). *L'indicateur de compétitivité des cantons 2016*. Zurich: UBS Switzerland AG.

# Part VII
# Discussion and Conclusions

# Chapter 23
# Integrative Conclusions

Overall, the results of this study are remarkably consistent across methods and models. Its main findings may be summarised as follows:

(a) *Competitiveness:*
The combination of the following factors induces competitiveness in Europe and the Americas: (1) high Environment Performance (EPI); (2) German legal origin; (3) the absence of a French legal origin and of a Concordat with the Roman See; (4) the absence of a socialist legal origin; (5) low proportion of Roman Catholicism or Orthodoxy.

(b) *Corruption:*
The combination of the following factors causes high corruption in Europe and the Americas: (1) low Environment Performance (EPI); (2) Roman Catholicism as a state religion; (3) low adherence to Protestantism; (4) a Concordat with the Roman See; and (5) French legal origin.

Likewise, and consistent with the corresponding theory, the quantitative model on corruption (Sect. 15.3.2) corroborates a high correlation of prosperity, democracy, transparency, and Protestantism. The model thus fulfils empirical expectation 3.[1]

The consistency of the theoretical framework (Part III) with the findings across methods (quantitative, QCA, case studies) confirms my hypotheses (Sect. 2.3 and empirical expectations 1 and 2). The following sections expand the conclusions per condition and empirical expectation.

---

Integrative conclusions are also called "meta-inferences" (Johnson, 2016). "A *meta-inference* can be defined as a conclusion generated through an integration of the inferences that have been obtained from the results of the qualitative and quantitative strands of a mixed methods study" (Teddlie and Tashakkori as cited in Stolz, 2017).

---

[1]Please refer to Part V for a recapitulation of hypotheses and empirical expectations in this study.



J. García Portilla, *"Ye Shall Know Them by Their Fruits"*, Contributions to Economics, https://doi.org/10.1007/978-3-030-78498-0_23

## 23.1 Environment Performance Index (EPI)

The EPI is the most critical variable for explaining prosperity (GCI and CPI) differences. It correlates strongly with prosperity in the quantitative models, while QCA substantiated a direct and robust causal relation. In the quantitative part, the EPI helped to increase model fitness, while in QCA, it was that condition that was closest to being necessary. Removing EPI from the quantitative and QCA analyses considerably reduces the explanatory power of the respective models (e.g. Model 1, see Sect. 15.3.1.1.1). However, if EPI is removed, the remaining variables (or conditions) continue to be significant or still maintain their presence, thus yielding similar results (although with less fitness in the regression models, for instance). Thus, EPI explains most of the prosperity variability, whereas the other significant variables also play a vital role in modulating the outcome.

EPI robustness, as causal for prosperity, provides rich evidence in support of the "environment and prosperity theory" (Sachs, 2001; Diamond, 1997). Thus, my results confirm the inferences anticipated in the literature review, thus also fulfiling empirical expectation 12. Moreover, the case study on Switzerland found a particular relation between environmental factors (geography or topography) and competitiveness. Swiss cantons located in mountainous regions tend to exhibit lower competitiveness than non-mountainous ones. Flat topography may facilitate access and trade, for instance. Still, this alone does not explain why some Swiss mountainous cantons are more innovative per inhabitant than other, neighbouring countries (e.g. Austria or Italy).

## 23.2 Legal Traditions

The second variable most consistently related to prosperity (GCI and CPI) is *legal origin*. This is true of the corresponding quantitative models and also explains the QCA outcome of *legal origin*. German legal origin has a consistently positive effect (correlations and QCA), while QCA also identifies Scandinavian legal origin as positive in terms of *competitiveness* and *transparency*. The Protestant Reformation heavily influenced German and Scandinavian legal systems (Witte, 2002; Snyder, 2011; Berman, 2003; Sect. 8.3.4).

In contrast, *Socialist* and *French* legal origins negatively influence GCI and transparency (as confirmed by QCA and partly by correlations). Both legal origins have diminished the influence of the Church on state affairs. However, their impact as legal systems as a whole is detrimental to competitiveness and transparency compared to "Protestant" legal origins (*German and Scandinavian*). English legal origin appears to have neither a robustly positive nor a negative influence on prosperity. However, some scholars (La Porta et al., 2008) have reported a strong positive influence of English, German, and Scandinavian legal origins on institutions.

### 23.2.1 Legal Traditions, Religion, and Prosperity

My empirical results show a strong relationship between prosperity indicators (competitiveness and transparency) and various other indicators (legal origin, religious institutions, and denomination). Theoretically, my results are in line with the findings of La Porta et al. (1999, 2008) on legal origins; with Acemoglu and Johnson (2005) and Acemoglu and Robinson (2008, 2012) on institutions; and with Witte (2002) and Berman (2003) on the influence of religious denominations on law and institutions.

The underlying logic is that the *Sola Scriptura* principle of the Protestant Reformation influenced German, English, and Scandinavian legal origins (Witte, 2002; Doe & Sandberg, 2010; Manow & van Kersbergen, 2009). On the other hand, French legal origin stems from the French Revolution, which had strong secularising effects in Europe, but whose influence was not entirely "exported" overseas (e.g. to Spanish and Portuguese colonies in Latin America). Socialist legal origin originates in the Bolshevik Revolution and contains atheist elements (Miller 2012; Berman 2003). While all of these modern legal origins replaced medieval canon law, each borrowed certain of its elements to a different extent. Canon law owed more to Greek philosophy than to the Scriptures (Selling, 2018; Gula, 2002). However, canon law is still valid today, above all in the Roman Catholic Church-State, and especially in (but not limited to) countries under its direct influence.

The incorporation of several principles originating directly in the Holy Scriptures via the Protestant Reformation was one of the main triggers of change in medieval legislation codes (i.e. medieval canon law)—and thus in the institutions of Protestant countries (Witte, 2002).

The Protestant Reformation demanded that papacy's far-reaching powers in medieval canon law be refuted. However, canon law could not be ousted entirely anywhere. Thus, certain aspects have been preserved (through indirect influence), although to a lower degree, even in Protestant countries such as the USA. In Lutheran territories, for instance, canon law was tested against the Holy Scriptures, and only those aspects that passed exacting scrutiny were upheld (Helmholz, 1992).

In theory, common law is one of the legal traditions exerting the least influence on Roman and canon law. This study, however, has shown that Scandinavian and especially German law (which in theory belong to Roman Civil Law) yield better results than common law countries. Protestant anti-clericalism has permeated both common law and German-Scandinavian legislations. The present QCA results help explain the different prosperity outcomes in terms of the greater heterogeneity of English common law countries, along with various other conditions: *1) EPI:* English common law countries are located in distant geographies (and have dissimilar EPI rankings) from the British Isles and North America (high) to the Caribbean (low). In contrast, Scandinavian and German law countries are more EPI homogeneous (high) and share similar geographical/environmental conditions in northern Europe. *2) State religion:* Common law countries have Protestant (e.g. UK), no (e.g. US), or even Catholic (e.g. Ireland) state religion. In turn, Scandinavian and German law countries have either Protestant or no state religion (i.e. absent Catholic state religion). *3) Ethnicities:* Common law countries exhibit higher ethnical heterogeneity, ranging from mostly white (e.g. the British Isles and North America) to mostly black (e.g. Jamaica) ethnicities. In contrast, Scandinavian and German law countries are more homogeneous (i.e. mostly white ethnicities). The different ethnicities and their associated cultural attributes (e.g. informal institutions) may interfere in the implementation of formal codes (law) (Lambsdorff, 2006; Alesina et al., 2003; Alesina & Giuliano, 2015; Volonté, 2015) and in the syncretisation of religion (see the Cuban case).

The legal code of the French Revolution exhibits another pattern: It yields good results only if anti-clericalism is present. Countries with strong anticlerical movements such as France, Italy, Uruguay, or Chile provide better results than countries with a strong influence of the Roman Church-State on their legal and institutional systems (e.g. most Latin American countries).

One of the crucial elements determining prosperity differences in countries of French legal origin is the level of anti-clericalism adopted in legislation. Uruguay adopted the French legal code and boldly incorporated the secular-democratic principles descending from the French Revolution in its constitution and other institutions (e.g. education). Consequently, Uruguay is one of the highest-scoring Latin American countries in social indicators such as transparency (Transparency International, 2016), political rights, and civil liberties (Freedom House, 2016), and has achieved the highest social progress in Latin America (Porter et al., 2015), due partly to the persistence of such institutional arrangements.

In contrast, while Colombia also adopted the legal code of the French Revolution, until 1991 it completely neglected the anticlerical principles of this code by signing a Concordat and by implementing a series of denominational constitutions. Consequently, medieval extractive institutions have persisted, making Colombia one of the most inequitable and dangerous countries in the world to date.

Cuba, by comparison, adopted the socialist legal tradition. Moreover, the Cuban Revolution in the 1960s led to strong anti-clericalism (and atheism). Accordingly, Cuba has achieved higher than average levels of equality, literacy, and public health compared to other Latin American countries. While corruption is moderate, low social progress and highly restricted liberties (Porter et al., 2015) tip the balance towards an overall negative outcome.

The German legal tradition widely influenced Switzerland, although the Napoleonic code took root in some cantons (La Porta et al., 2008). The Swiss Constitution (1848) is profoundly anticlerical, but not atheist (e.g. its preamble invokes God). Its liberal-Protestant principles, combined with the country's federalist structure, make Switzerland the most competitive country worldwide. Thus, the results for *legal origin* entirely fulfil empirical expectations 4, 5, 6, and 7.

## 23.3 State Religion

Quantitative analysis partly revealed that establishing Protestantism as a state religion has an almost twofold effect on competitiveness compared to a high Protestant population. This confirms the higher importance of religious institutions compared to the proportion of adherents. Also, the higher importance of state Protestantism over a Protestant population seems in line with the historical claim that no single Protestant-Catholic conflict resulted in a Protestant victory without state or external support (te Brake as cited in Nexon, 2011, p. 152). Historically, political leaders (including the pope) have more strongly influenced the institutionalisation of religion than theologians. Current adherence rates reflect such institutionalisation in many countries (Barro & McCleary, 2005).

Nonetheless, QCA has shown that establishing any state religion, including Protestantism, is detrimental to prosperity (*GCI* and *transparency*) in most cases. This seemingly contradictory result may explain the positive effects of separating church and state (secularisation) as an advance of Protestant state religion (e.g. Switzerland, USA; see Sect. 15.3.1.3). However, secularisation *per se* (e.g. French or socialist revolution) may not always lead to positive outcomes. This becomes clear when state religion results are analysed along with the results of the last condition (*legal origin*).

Together, both conclusions (about legal origin and state religion) corroborate empirical expectation 4. The reason is that legal origins commonly associated with Protestantism are positive for prosperity. *English legal origin* is the exception as its outcome seems to be neutral (considering the nuances previously discussed). On the other hand, French legal origin (typically associated with Roman Catholicism) negatively influences prosperity and transparency.

## 23.4 Religious Affiliation in the Population

Religious adherence (by denomination) is mostly negatively correlated with GCI or is insignificant in quantitative models. Especially consistent, however, are the negative correlations of Orthodox and Roman Catholic adherents with GCI. Protestant adherence is not conclusively correlated with GCI and exhibits a positive influence on transparency (for models, see Sect. 15.3). QCA also produces mixed results. Changes in magnitude, from one to two digits, in the Protestant population do not significantly change corruption levels, as shown by the two clusters of Latin American countries (for Truth Tables, see Appendix 4).

Therefore, the influence of a Protestant population is not one of the essential conditions (compared to state religion or legal origin, for instance). However, Barro and McCleary (2005) have stressed the importance of the proportion of religious adherents as directly triggering a state religion (whose effect on prosperity almost doubles that of the population). Consequently, although the direct influence of a

Protestant population is not conclusive, it helps to build institutions that partially remove old hegemonic structures (e.g. feudal-hierarchical elitists from the medieval papalist monarchical order). This conclusion concurs with Woodberry (2012), who demonstrated the importance of the Protestant population in initiating democratic processes worldwide (except for Pentecostalism).

Also, the Swiss case study shows how liberals and Protestants closed ranks in the federal government to democratise the Catholic Church in Switzerland. Saying that, in Latin America, the Protestant population is not necessarily less corrupt than the Catholic one (Helmsdorff, 1996; Schäfer, 2006; Martin, 1999). This may be directly related to Woodberry's findings, given that most Protestant growth in Latin America, Asia, and Africa generally comes from Pentecostalism. This, however, does not exert a positive social influence, unlike historical forms of Protestantism (Woodberry, 2012).

Another potential effect is that historically Protestant countries may become more emancipated than "new-world Protestant" ones profoundly influenced by Pentecostalism. Therefore, a Protestant population may be relevant when it can bring about institutional changes capable of decreasing the detrimental influence of institutional Roman Catholicism. While Protestant adherents might prove less important than deinstitutionalising the public sphere of the Roman Church, they may be needed to drive forward the latter process.

Denominational ties (proportion of adherents) are important modulators, but not as decisive as the legal (institutional) ties associated with religion. For example, Ireland and Austria are predominantly Roman Catholic countries; and yet, their competitiveness is higher than predominantly Roman Catholic Spain or Portugal (dominated by French law). Ireland shares common law (and the English language) with the United Kingdom, while Austria shares the German legal tradition (and the German language) with Germany. However, neither Catholic Ireland is as prosperous as Protestant Great Britain, nor is Catholic Austria as prosperous as mostly Protestant Germany.[2]

These findings on religious adherents partly fulfil empirical expectation 9, as population mostly influences prosperity only indirectly. Direct influence is rather weak. However, these results do fulfil empirical expectation 10. The different Latin American clusters that formed due to slightly different proportions of Protestants do not exhibit significant differences in corruption outcomes (Appendix 4).

[2]Subnationally, highly productive Catholic regions in Germany also exist (e.g. Bavaria today), evidently under the effect of a historically mostly Protestant and liberal influenced Federal Government. Hughes (1935) empirically identified a pattern of industrialisation of Catholic regions in Germany, during which Catholic farmers were dragged away from their land to work in surrounding industries established by Protestant capitalists. The author further concludes that (1) the advancement of modern industry in Germany's Catholic regions was a kind of non-Catholic invasion; (2) Catholics, as a whole, held inferior positions in their workplaces; and (3) the industrial invasion impacted Catholic areas unevenly. (pp. 287; 290). Each region has different industrialisation triggers (e.g. the availability of raw materials, or the "push" of companies such as Audi or Siemens, which fled the communist expropriation in East Germany) (Hughes 1935; Schaal & Wehling, 2020).

## 23.5 Concordats

The findings on concordats were highly consistent and confirmed a negative causal relation between *Concordats* with the Roman Catholic Church-State and prosperity (*GCI* and *Transparency*). This variable has proven decisive in case analysis, along with EPI, legal origin, and state religion. Therefore, empirical expectation 6 was fulfiled. Countries with valid concordats have implemented domestic legislation subject to canon and Roman law.

Concordats in Latin America have lawfully perpetuated hierarchical power relations, control over education, and other Church privileges. Thus, education, family, and social values are permeated by a relativistic Roman Catholic theology based on Aquinas and Aristotle. In practice, this means that central Roman Catholic values such as *familialism,* double standards, elitism, and a relativistic ethic pervade the institutions and culture of countries under Catholic influence. As shown, the obvious result is low prosperity (i.e. high corruption and low competitiveness).

Countries with Concordats and German legal origin—Germany and Austria—are the exceptions to the previous rule. The longstanding influence of anti-clericalism on law and institutions (Sect. 8.3.4) and on language (Sect. 11.1) ever since the sixteenth-century German Protestant Revolution has remained pervasive to this day. On the positive side, the persistence of anticlericalism may counteract some detrimental aspects of the Concordats in both countries.

Countries with a German legal origin (Germany, Austria, Switzerland) also have comparable geographical and environmental conditions. They are also highly competitive. Predominantly Roman Catholic Austria is the least prosperous of the three. Protestant Germany is more prosperous than Austria but less prosperous than Switzerland. Germany has a valid Concordat that Hitler signed with the Roman Church-State, Austria also has a Concordat, yet Switzerland has none. Evidence shows that Switzerland is the most prosperous of these three countries (see Sect. 16.3.1, Fig. 16.3; Supplementary Materials; and Truth Tables 9 and 11 in Appendix 4.3.3). Likewise, another contributing factor that is a common denominator in the two most competitive countries (Switzerland and the USA) is that their (federal) constitutions are explicitly anticlerical (and neither have Concordats). Concordats are proxies of state-church relations and thus, of the institutional influence of religion on society. Therefore, the absence of concordats may well indicate a certain degree of laicism in government affairs such as education, military, or real estate (see Sects. 8.3.4.6.2 and 16.2.1). However, having a Concordat does not constitute a monocausal explanation of lack of prosperity, as this research has emphasised in multiple combinations of triggers.

## 23.6 Languages

Quantitative model 4 (Sect. 15.3.1.2.1) shows that the German language positively correlates with *competitiveness*. The German language is also positively associated with transparency (QCA, Table 16.1; Appendices 4.3.4 and 5.4). I discussed the role of the Bible translations in standardising languages (German) and in unifying kingdoms (Great Britain), thus contributing to spreading cultural values conducive to enhancing competitiveness and transparency (Sect. 11.1).

Conversely, *Roman languages* (combined with *high Concordats* and low *EPI*) are associated with low competitiveness in QCA (Sect. 16.3.1.4). The Colombian case has shown how the Roman Church-State used Hispanicism as a powerful tool to isolate countries from the anticlericalist dynamics of Anglo-Saxon Protestantism,[3] French liberalism, and Soviet communism (Figueroa, 2007).

In Colombia, conservative traditionalists identified Hispanicism as a cultural weapon for maintaining corporatist ideals, a medieval-type hierarchical society, and for upholding the principles of seigneurial and counter-reformist Spain (Figueroa, 2016, p. 21). The Hispanicist triad illustrated by Figueroa (2016)—language, religion, and race—grew stronger with the rise of institutional (legal-political confessionalism) and economic corporatism, both part of a concerted corporate strategy to maintain hegemony. Consequently, such features are part of the same phenomenon. Rather than competing explanations, they are intervening ones. Therefore, empirical expectation 11 was fulfiled.

## 23.7 Ethnicities

*Caucasian* ethnic values exhibited a positive influence in QCA and in two quantitative models (Sect. 15.3.1). For Huntington, being "overwhelmingly white, British and Protestant" (Huntington, 2004, p. 31) is fundamental to US prosperity. Although the author has received fierce criticism for stating racist, stereotyping generalisations (McSweeney, 2015), the empirical results of this study suggest that Huntington's assertion may not be misguided (see Sect. 15.3.1 and Truth Tables 17 and 19 in Appendix 4.2). However, the QCA clusters reveal that *ethnicities* are not a critical condition (unlike legal origin or state religion). As shown, *ethnicities* are the least important condition in plausible groups and empirical evidence for QCA.

Moreover, the quantitative model of corruption (Sect. 15.3.2) has indicated that the measure of "ethnic fractionalisation" produced no obvious conclusion, thus

[3]Hispanicism has been effective at preventing the success of anticlerical movements. Yet, it has been counteracted to a certain degree by other political or legal influences—for instance, US-American constitutionalism, which has succeeded throughout Europe and the Americas (Merryman & Pérez, 2015) (see Sect. 8.3.4.6.1). Likewise, Hispanicism does not prevent Colombia being the closest political ally of the USA in Latin America (Brock, 2011).

corroborating empirical expectation 8. Nonetheless, ethnicity results for Latin America might approximate the level of religious syncretism. Countries with a larger African or indigenous population (or both) exhibit higher levels of syncretism, for instance, spiritistic rituals and Roman Catholicism or Protestantism (see the Cuban and Colombian cases) (Contreras, 2013, p. 177; Ramírez, 2009, p. 167; Sánchez, 1992, pp. 90–91). Accordingly, multicultural countries such as Cuba, Brazil, Jamaica, Bolivia, or Colombia can be expected to display higher religious syncretism than more homogenous ones like Uruguay or Argentina. This issue needs to be further explored, theoretically and empirically.

## References


Acemoglu, D., & Johnson, S. (2005). Unbundling institutions. *Journal of Political Economy, 113* (5), 949–995.

Acemoglu, D., & Robinson, J. A. (2008). Persistence of power, elites, and institutions. *American Economic Review, 98*(1), 267–293.

Acemoglu, D., & Robinson, J. (2012). *Why Nations Fail. The origins of power, prosperity and poverty*. New York: Crown Business.

Alesina, A., & Giuliano, P. (2015). Culture and Institutions. *Journal of Economic Literature, 53*(4), 898–944.

Alesina, A., Devleeschauwer, A., Easterly, W., Sergio, K., & Wacziarg, R. (2003). Fractionalization. *Journal of Economic Growth, 8*(2), 155–194.

Barro, R. J., & McCleary, R. M. (2005). Which countries have state religions? *The Quarterly Journal of Economics, 120*(4), 1331–1370.

Berman, H. (2003). *Law and revolution II: The impact of the protestant reformations on the western legal tradition*. Cambridge, London: Harvard University Press, Belknap Press.

Brock, L. (2011). Von der "nationalen Sicherheit" zum "demokratischen Frieden" und witer voran? In: Burchardt; Öhlschläger; Wehr, *Lateinamerika: Ein (un)sicherer Kontinent*. Baden: Nomos.

Contreras, D. (2013). Iglesia Católica y estado en la República de Cuba: pasado y presente de sus relaciones Catholic Church and State in Cuba: past and present relationships. *América Latina Hoy, 63*, 177–195.

Diamond, J. (1997). *Guns, germs, and steel. The fates of human societies*. New York: W.W. Norton & Company.

Doe, N., & Sandberg, R. (2010). *Law and religion: New horizons*. Leuven Peeters.

Figueroa, H. (2007). El imperio espiritual español: Lengua, raza y religión (1930–1942). *Anuario Colombiano de Historia Social y de la Cultura, 34*, 165–206.

Figueroa, H. (2016). *La persistance des idées traditionalistes en Colombie. Religion et politique (1886–1952)*. Paris: L'Harmattan.

Freedom House. (2016). *Freedom in the world 2016. Anxious dictators, wavering democracies: Global freedom under pressure*. Washington, DC: Freedom House.

Gula, R. M. (2002). *Reason informed by faith—foundations of Catholic Morality*. Paulist Press.

Helmholz, R. H. (1992). In R. H. Helmholz (Ed.), *Canon law in protestant lands* (Vol. 11, 1st ed.). Berlin: Duncker & Humblot.

Helmsdorff, D. (1996). *Participación política evangélica en Colombia*. (D. A. Bidegain, Ed.) Bogotá: Universidad de los Andes. Departamento de Historia. Tesis de Grado.

Hughes, E. C. (1935). The industrial revolution and the catholic movement in Germany. *Social Forces, 14*(2), 286–292. https://doi.org/10.2307/2571262.

Huntington, S. (2004). The hispanic challenge. *Foreign Policy. March/April 2004*, 31–45.

Johnson, R. B. (2016). *Mixed methods research design and analysis with validity: A primer. Version 4.2*. South Alabama: Department of Professional Studies. University of South Alabama, Mobile, AL.

La Porta, R., Lopez-de-Silanes, F., & Vishny, A. S. (1999). The quality of government. *Journal of Law, Economics and Organization, 15*(1), 222–279.

La Porta, R., Lopez-de-Silanes, F., & Shleifer, A. (2008). The economic consequences of legal origins. *Journal of Economic Literature, 46*(2), 285–332.

Lambsdorff, J. G. (2006). Causes and consequences of corruption: What do we know from a cross-section of countries? In S. Rose-Ackerman (Ed.), *International handbook on the economics of corruption* (pp. 3–51). Cheltenham and Northampton, MA: Edward Elgar.

Manow, P., & van Kersbergen, K. (2009). Religion and the Western Welfare State - The theoretical context. In P. Manow & K. van Kersbergen (Eds.), *Religion, class coalitions and welfare states* (p. 304). New York: Cambridge University Press.

Martin, D. (1999). The evangelical upsurge and its political implications. In P. Berger (Ed.), *The Desecularization of the World* (pp. 37–49). Washington, DC: Ethics and Public Policy Center and Wm. B. Eerdmans Publishing Co.

McSweeney, B. (2015). Hall, Hofstede, Huntington, Trompenaars, GLOBE: Common foundations, common flaws. In Y. Sanchez & C. Brühwiler (Eds.), *Transculturalism and Business in the BRIC States. A handbook*. Dorchester: Gower Applied Business Research.

Merryman, J., & Pérez, P. R. (2015). *La Tradición Jurídica Romano-Canónica*. Fondo de Cultura Económica: México D.F..

Miller, N. (2012). *The Religious roots of the first amendment*. New York: Oxford University Press.

Nexon, D. H. (2011). Religion and international relations. No leap of faith required. In J. Snyder (Ed.), *Religion and international relations theory*. New York: Columbia University Press.

Porter, M., Stern, S., & Green, M. (2015). *Social progress index 2015*. Retrieved from: https://www.socialprogress.org/?tab=2&code=NOR

Ramírez, C. J. (2009). Laïcité, liberté de religion et État laïque. Les étapes de la laïcisation cubaine. *Archives de sciences sociales des religions, 54*(146), 157–182.

Sachs, J. (2001). Tropical underdevelopment. *National Bureau of Economic Research. Working Paper, 8119* (NBER), 1–37

Sánchez, Y. (1992). *Religiosidad cotidiana en la narrativa reciente hispanocaribeña* (Vol. 3). (S. S. Hispánicos, A. L. Pozuelo, & Y. Sánchez, Eds.) Lausanne: Hispanica Helvetica.

Schaal, D. & Wehling, W. (2020). *Die industrielle Entwicklung in Sachsen Chronologie*. Kulturstiftung des Freistaates Sachsen Koordinierungsstelle Sächsische Industriekultur. Retrieved from https://www.industriekultur-in-sachsen.de/fileadmin/user_upload/IK-Chronologie.pdf

Schäfer, H. (2006). »Die« Pfingstbewegung in Lateinamerika…? Zur Untersuchung des Verhältnisses zwischen religiöser Praxis und gesellschaftlichen Strukturen. *Zeitschrift für Religionswissenschaft*, 53–82.

Selling, J. A. (2018). Reframing catholic theological ethics: Summary and application. (A. Abram, Ed.). *Religions, 8*(203), 5–13.

Snyder, J. (2011). *Religion and international relations theory*. New York: Columbia University Press.

Stolz, J. (2017). Milieus and mixed methods describing and explaining religion and secularity in Switzerland. *Kölner Zeitschrift für Soziologie und Sozialpsychologie (Suppl 2), 2*(69), 361–386.

Transparency International. (2016). *Corruption perceptions index 2016*. Retrieved from: https://www.transparency.org/news/feature/corruption_perceptions_index_2016

Volonté, C. (2015). Culture and corporate governance: The influence of language and religion in Switzerland. *Management International Review, 55*, 77–118.

Witte, J. (2002). *Law and protestantism: The legal teachings of the Lutheran Reformation*. Cambridge: Cambridge University Press.

Woodberry, R. (2012). The missionary roots of liberal democracy. *American Political Science Review (APSR), 106*(2), 244–274.

# Chapter 24
# Other Considerations

## 24.1 The Institutional and Cultural (Adherents) Influence of Religion[1]

Institutional factors related to religion exert a stronger structural and long-term influence on prosperity (competitiveness and corruption) than the cultural influence of religion (adherents). Several pieces of evidence corroborate this conclusion: (1) the abundant historical, theological, and theoretical information; (2) the empirical results on *State religion, Concordats,* and *Legal origin*; (3) the analysis of specific cases.

Models 1 and 3 (Sect. 15.3.1) confirmed empirically that the influence of Protestant state religion almost twice exceeds that of adherents, for instance. Further, seriously considering the role of the Roman Catholic Church as a state actor has profound implications. The importance of Roman Catholicism is based more on its institutional and political ideology, rather than on its belief system (although religious belief is also necessary for maintaining political ideology and the *status quo*). However, empirical works considering religion and prosperity variables have mostly concentrated solely on the influence of religious adherents. This has resulted in a minimisation paradigm that disregards the institutional influence of religion. Therefore, the relationships between prosperity and religion have tended to be trivialised or misunderstood when analysing religion as a background prosperity factor.

Incorporating the institutional influence of religion allows understanding, for example, why Switzerland has lower levels of corruption (and higher prosperity)

---

[1]Some parts of this chapter were originally published as "General Conclusions" in: Garcia Portilla, J. (2019). "Ye Shall Know Them by Their Fruits": Prosperity and Institutional Religion in Europe and the Americas. *Religions*, *10*(6), 362. MDPI AG. Retrieved from https://doi.org/10.3390/rel10060362





J. García Portilla, *"Ye Shall Know Them by Their Fruits"*, Contributions to Economics, https://doi.org/10.1007/978-3-030-78498-0_24

when the majority of its population is currently Roman Catholic (i.e. given its 1848 anticlerical, liberal, and Protestant-friendly federal constitution). Uruguay is a similar case to some extent. The majority of Uruguay's population is Roman Catholic (although Uruguay is the most secular country in Latin America) (Pew Research Center, 2014) and one of the least corrupt (and with the highest social progress) in the region. Uruguay's constitution is markedly anticlerical.

The opposite case is Colombia, where the still valid and modified Concordat (1887), pre-1991 constitution, and other arrangements represent a classical Catholic Christendom prototype of a full state-church fusion (Levine, 1981, p. 71). These arrangements have meant that the high proportion of Roman Catholics in Colombia resulted naturally from such restrictive conservative policies and legal instruments. In Switzerland, Protestant-liberals won the *Sonderbund* war, thus paving the way for the 1848 anticlerical constitution. In Colombia, the opposite happened: Conservative-Catholics won the war that led to the 1886 Constitution. In 1991, the new constitution included some liberal elements after a peace process with liberal guerrillas.

A key to understanding the pervasively negative influence of Roman Catholicism on state relations/performance is hierarchy. Hierarchy in church and state is opposed to democracy and transparency, thus promoting power abuse from the higher echelons down.

Thus, the historical institutional influence of Roman Catholicism or Protestantism affects corruption/prosperity rates more directly than the current proportion of believers (Inglehart & Baker, 2000). Nonetheless, institutional religion and the proportion of believers are well connected empirically (Barro & McCleary, 2005). The cases of Switzerland, Colombia, and Uruguay show that the current population adherents result visibly from the historical institutional influence of religion.

## 24.2 Models

The models developed and applied in this study allow analysing determining factors layer by layer. For example, geography and environment are the first determinants. However, variation within zones may be mediated (or moduled) not only by environment, latitude, topography, and climate but also by institutional background, as best represented by legal traditions. Moreover, legal traditions have a direct historical relationship with the successive legal revolutions against the *status quo* (Roman and canon law part of Roman Catholicism or Orthodoxism). The crucial role of Protestantism (and anticlericalism) in such legal revolutions paved the path for modernity and democratic institutions.

This fresh perspective enables us to understand why countries in similar geographic and environment settings exhibit marked differences. For instance, Argentina, Chile, and Uruguay share similar environmental and geographical conditions, and yet Argentina is less prosperous (i.e. more corrupt) than Chile and Uruguay. The reason being that Argentina is far more clerical than the other countries (i.e. Argentina has a Concordat) (see Truth Tables 1 and 3 in Appendix 4.3.1). The same consideration of multiple causalities, given in Sect. 23.5, applies here. The Argentinian Concordat indicates direct interference of the Roman Catholic Church-State in the secular affairs of Argentina, and the presence of a more clerical society than in Uruguay and Chile.[2]

## 24.3 Returning to the General Research Interest: *"Ye Shall Know Them By Their Fruits" (The Social Experiments)*

### *24.3.1 The Roman* and *Catholic* Ancien Régime

Roman Catholicism has had more than enough time to enforce its Aquinian-Aristotelian social experiment through applying the corresponding theological concepts to politics, law, and social organisation. Romanism has deployed its *ancien régime* for over a millennium, from the European Middle Ages to the present (especially in several Latin American countries).

The Roman *and* Catholic experiment shows that applying Aquinian-Aristotelian principles creates undesirable prosperity scenarios in wider society (while maximising the power and prosperity of the Church). These principles contrast sharply with what Roman Catholicism claims would make a society prosperous and harmonious (Ratzinger & Pera, 2006; Restrepo, 1939). This, as shown, is a medieval society of greatest benefit of the Catholic Church.

It remains debatable (as during the Reformation) the "natural law" that the Roman Church-State bases on the human capacity discerning between right or wrong. The Roman Church-State has adopted natural law as the foundation for its teachings on sexual behaviour, freedom of religion, justice, fair societies, human life, medical practice, and the connection between societal morals and civil law (Gula, 2002, pp. 120–121). In practice, the application of Roman Catholic "natural law" has often produced the opposite to its intended principles: centuries-long hegemony and—to this day—corruption and low competitiveness. In the end, the legitimacy of the Roman Catholic Church-State has not been reliant on the capacity of its "truth" to persuade, but on its legal right as the bearer of authority to subordinate and command (Sanks, 1974, pp. 11–13).

Thousands of years of hegemony characterise the Roman Catholic Church as a global political-religious institution. The associated corruption in all the countries under its influence may well be related to the corrupt fruits for which "we shall know

[2]For instance, Gill (1998) explained that Chile and Argentina are the two Latin American cases that more appropriately resemble a scientifically controlled experiment, since they share many constant variables (within acceptable limits). The Chilean episcopate became an ardent opponent of the Pinochet dictatorship, even at the cost of the extreme repression of its clergy. On the contrary, the Argentine bishops are recognised not only for ignoring the military's violations but also for engaging effectively in public administration (Gill, 1998, p. 121).

them" in the parable of Jesus (*King James Bible*, 1769, Matthew 7:15–23). Among others, these fruits have also been the abuse scandals, maintenance of ignorance, and persecution of God's Word, in the name of Jesus Christ.

### 24.3.2 Protestant Reformation

The application of Protestant (i.e. biblical) principles (Fig. 8.4) on law instead of relativism has produced an ethical code that enhances trust, transparency, and prosperity (see Sects. 8.3, 9.1.2, 10.3, 15.3, 16.3.1, Fig. 8.3, Appendix 4.3; and Supplementary Materials). The influence of biblical principles in the legislation of Protestant countries also concurs with the following verse of the Scriptures:

> And what nation is there so great, that hath statutes and judgments so righteous as all this law, which I set before you this day? (*King James Bible*, 1769, Deuteronomy 4: 8).

Prosperity and educational differences between Protestants (higher) and Roman Catholics (lower) are still evident in Germany and Switzerland. Such differences are even higher comparing national levels (cross-country). Scandinavian countries are all prosperous and have embraced Lutheranism even more strongly than Germany to the point of making it their state religion (see Sect. 8.3.4.1 and Chap. 9).

However, the present and future do not seem encouraging as the world progressively returns to Rome. On the one hand, many historical strands of Protestantism that previously resisted the Catholic hegemony have now relinquished their founding principles and accept ecumenism in "Rome terms". On the other, the Pentecostalist trend within Protestantism has weakened the latter's historical socio-political impact (Sect. 10.4.1.3).

### 24.3.3 The French Revolution

An experiment similar to (and deriving from) the various Protestant revolutions was the French Revolution. This, too, diminished the hegemonic power of the Church and its associated aristocratic-oligarchic-elitist privileges. Such privileges were curbed in France and Belgium, for instance. Nevertheless, this trend continued in Spain and Portugal, although in weaker form, and has been almost inexistent in most of Latin America (Sects. 8.3.4.5, 8.3.4.6, 8.3.5).

### 24.3.4 Communism

Nor have the social experiments of communism (e.g. seizing the liberties and property of ordinary people in the Soviet Union and Cuba) produced ideal results either. In contrast, the social experiment of the Protestant revolutions (or of the French Revolution) initiated positive social developments in the long term (e.g. seizing the privileges and properties of the Roman Church-State, not of those of common people). Unlike the *ancien régime*, all the other social experiments have invested more in human capital building through making education public and state-controlled. On balance, the Protestant Reformation has produced the highest prosperity for society as a whole.

## 24.4 Suggestions for Future Research

The results of this study open up various avenues for future research. The QCA evidence generated here allows further analysis of every country in Europe and the Americas. Future research might also continue to apply the vast amount of information collected and already codified in this study.

Further research on the institutional influence of religion could complement the present analysis through (quantitative) time series and (qualitative) cases studies (e.g. Venezuela and the USA). Other indicators of potential value for further qualitative and quantitative analyses might include the number of years since officialising relations with the Roman See per country, the number of dioceses, diocesan priests, persons per diocesan priests, the total number of priests, and the total number of persons per priest/per year/per country.

## References

Barro, R. J., & McCleary, R. M. (2005). Which countries have state religions? *The Quarterly Journal of Economics, 120*(4), 1331–1370. https://doi.org/10.1162/003355305775097515.

Garcia Portilla, J. (2019). "Ye shall know them by their fruits": Prosperity and institutional religion in Europe and the Americas. *Religions, 10*(6), 362. MDPI AG. doi:https://doi.org/10.3390/rel10060362.

Gill, A. (1998). *Rendering unto Caesar: the Catholic Church and the state in Latin America.* Chicago: Chicago University Press.

Gula, R. M. (2002). *Reason informed by faith—Foundations of catholic morality.* Paulist Press.

Inglehart, R., & Baker, W. (2000). Modernization, cultural change, and the persistence of traditional values. *American Sociological Review, 65*(1), 19–51.

*King James Bible.* (1769). *The Holy Bible, King James Version.* Cambridge Edition: 1769. Scripture quotations from The Authorized (King James) Version. Rights in the Authorized Version in the United Kingdom are vested in the Crown. Reproduced by permission of the Crown's patentee, Cambridge University Press.

Levine, D. (1981). *Religion and politics in Latin America: The Catholic Church in Venezuela & Colombia.* Princeton Legacy Library.

Pew Research Center. (2014). *Religion in Latin America. widespread change in a historically catholic region.* Retrieved from: https://www.pewforum.org/2014/11/13/religion-in-latin-america/

Ratzinger, J., & Pera, M. (2006). *Without roots: The west, relativism, Christianity, Islam.* New York: Basic Books.

Restrepo, F. S. (1939). El Corporativismo al alcance de todos. *Revista Javeriana, 52*, 75.

Sanks, T. H. (1974). *Authority in the Church: A study in changing paradigms.* Missoula, MT: Scholar's Press.

# Chapter 25
# Concluding Remarks

The cross-method results of this study show that prosperity and transparency respond mainly to three reinforcing (rather than competing) explanatory mechanisms. They are, in order of importance: (1) Environment, geography, topography, latitude; (2) Religion (considering its institutional influence, legal origin, proportion of adherents, syncretism) and; (3) Other non-religious political factors such as communism.

More specifically, a combination of factors causing corruption and low competitiveness in countries in Europe and the Americas includes: (1) low Environmental Performance (EPI); (2) Roman Catholicism as a State Religion; (3) high adherence to Orthodoxy or Roman Catholicism; (4) Concordat with the Vatican; and (5) French (clerical) or socialist legal origin.

Consequently, the influence of the Protestant Reformation in Northern Europe, and later, its extended effect in North America, have produced a loop of trust, transparency, and prosperity. In contrast, the hegemony of the Roman Catholic Church-State has not yet been broken in most Latin American countries. The results are high corruption and low prosperity.

Methodologically, Woodberry's conclusion to his in-depth study of the explanatory influence of Protestantism on democracy also applies here:

> Although any piece of this evidence can be critiqued, the cumulative evidence makes finding a consistent alternative explanation extremely difficult. If alternative explanations are not consistent between contexts and methods, it is not clear why we should prefer them over an explanation that works consistently across such a wide variety of contexts and methods (Woodberry, 2012, p. 268).

I wish to end this book with some thought-provoking lines from the Old Testament:

> Blessed is the nation whose God is the Lord; *and* the people *whom* he hath chosen for his own inheritance (*King James Bible*, 1769, Psalms 33:12; original emphases).

The previous verse shall in no way be understood as otherness or exclusion, since the Scriptures also state:



J. García Portilla, *"Ye Shall Know Them by Their Fruits"*, Contributions to Economics, https://doi.org/10.1007/978-3-030-78498-0_25

> Thus saith the Lord, [. . .] For I know their works and their thoughts: it shall come, that I will gather all nations and tongues; and they shall come, and see my glory (*King James Bible*, 1769, Isaiah 66: 1, 18).

> For thus saith the Lord of hosts; Yet once, it is a little while, and I will shake the heavens, and the earth, and the sea, and the dry *land*; and I will shake all nations, and the Desire of all nations shall come: and I will fill this house with glory, saith the Lord of hosts (*King James Bible*, 1769, Haggai 2: 6–7).

> And it shall be to me a name of joy, a praise and an honor before all the nations of the earth, which shall hear all the good that I do unto them: and they shall fear and tremble for all the goodness and for all the prosperity that I procure unto it (*King James Bible*, 1769, Jeremiah 33: 9).

## References

*King James Bible*. (1769). *The Holy Bible, King James Version*. Cambridge Edition: 1769. Scripture quotations from The Authorized (King James) Version. Rights in the Authorized Version in the United Kingdom are vested in the Crown. Reproduced by permission of the Crown's patentee, Cambridge University Press.

Woodberry, R. (2012). The missionary roots of liberal democracy. *American Political Science Review (APSR), 106*(2), 244–274.

# Appendices

## I. Appendices to Component 1 (Macro) (Quantitative Analysis—Correlations, Chap. 15)



J. García Portilla, *"Ye Shall Know Them by Their Fruits"*, Contributions to Economics, https://doi.org/10.1007/978-3-030-78498-0

## *1. QUAN Appendix A. Competiveness Variables (Models 1–5; Chap. 15, Sect. 15.3.1)*

Note: This appendix does not include the entire set of variables (>70) analysed at the beginning but the selected ones after the data treatment in steps 1 and 2 (as well as the subcategories that were significant statistically).

| Type of variable | Category (prosperity theory associated) | Sub-category | Variable | Code | Source | Original value rank | Description |
|---|---|---|---|---|---|---|---|
| **Predictor variables of interest** | Religion | Religious denomination (proportion in population) | Roman Catholic | Catholics (%) | (Johnson & Zurlo 2016) | % 0-100 | Percentage of population in each country belonging to different religious affiliations. |
| | | | Protestant | Protestants (%) | | % 0-100 | |
| | | | Muslim | Muslims (%) | | % 0-100 | |
| | | | Orthodox | Orthodox (%) | | % 0-100 | |
| | | | Christianity: Other (% Adherents) | Other Christians | (Teorell, *et al.* 2017) | % 0-100 | |
| | | Societal religious norms | Global Restrictions on religion (GRI) | Restrictions | (Pew Global Religious Diversity 2014) | 0-10 | The GRI is a fine-grained index calculated by combining 20 elements on a 0—10 scale (zero indicates very low government constraints on religion, and 10 means very high restrictions) (Pew Research Center, 2014). |
| | | | Social Hostilities (due to religion) | Hostilities | | 0-10 | The Social Hostilities Index (SHI) measures acts of religious intolerance perpetrated by private individuals, organisations, and groups in society. It involves violent struggle or terrorism motivated by religion, gang or sectarian activity, persecution for religious purposes, and other forms of religious coercion or assault (Pew Research Center, 2014). |

| Type of variable | Category (prosperity theory associated) | Sub-category | Variable | Code | Source | Original value rank | Description |
|---|---|---|---|---|---|---|---|
| **Predictor variables of interest** | | | Interference of Religious Dogmas | Dogmas | (Teorell, *et al.* 2017) | 1, - 10 | To what extent are religious dogmas allowed to influence the civil order and state institutions? (1–10).<br><br>1. It is a theocratic state. Religious dogmas determine the legal order and governmental institutions.<br>4. Secular and religious norms clash with the state's basic constitution or create a mixed structure.<br>7. The government is primarily secular. Yet, religious dogmas have a significant impact on the justice system and governmental institutions.<br>10. It is a secular state (Bertelsmann Stiftung as cited in Teorell, et al. 2017 p. 114) |
| | | | Freedom of Religion in Constitution | Constitution | | 1,2,96 | Does the constitution guarantee religious liberty?<br>1. Yes<br>2. No<br>96. Other<br>(Elkins et al. as cited in Teorell, et al. 2017 p. 122) |
| | | | Conflict intensity | Conflict | | 1, - 10 | How serious are social, ethnic and religious conflicts? 1-10.<br>1. There are no violent incidents based on social, ethnic or religious differences.<br>4. There are only a few violent incidents. Radical political actors have limited success in mobilising along existing cleavages. Society and the political elite, however, are divided along social, ethnic or religious lines.<br>7. There are violent incidents. Mobilized groups and protest movements dominate politics. Society and the political elite are deeply split into social classes, ethnic or religious communities.<br>10. There is civil war or a widespread violent conflict based on social, ethnic or religious differences. Bertelsmann Stiftung http://www.bti-project.org/index/<br>(Bertelsmann Stiftung, 2016, cited in Teorell, et al. 2017 p. 107) |

| Type of variable | Category (prosperity theory associated) | Sub-category | Variable | Code | Source | Original value rank | Description |
|---|---|---|---|---|---|---|---|
| **Predictor variables of interest** | Institutions | State religion | Muslim | MUSLIM (S.R) | (Barro, R. J. and McCleary, R. M. 2005) | 0,1 | The most significant type of state monopoly in history has been the state's monopoly on religion. The selection of a state religion is a political process involving relations between the religious actor and the state (Barro & McCleary, 2005, p. 1332). The main feature of a state religion is its official promotion of the religion's monopoly status, partly through entry restrictions and partly through incentives (Smith as cited in Barro & McCleary 2005, p. 1331). The authors categorise official state religion as an all-or-nothing choice. The data is taken for the year 2000. This variable can also be part of the societal religious norms subcategory and along with Christian denomination, being part of the predictor variable of interest. However, for practical reasons, this variable appears only here in category "institutions". |
| | | | Catholic | CATHOLIC (S.R) | | 0,1 | |
| | | | Protestant | PROTESTANT (S.R) | | 0,1 | |
| | | Legal origin | English Common Law | ENGLISH (L.O.) | (La Porta, *et al.* 1999) | 0,1 | It identifies "the legal origin of the Company Law or Commercial Code of each country. There are five possible origins: (1) English Common Law; (2) French Commercial Code; (3) German Commercial Code; (4) Scandinavian Commercial Code; and (5) Socialist/Communist laws" (© 2002 by Rafael La Porta, Florencio López-de-Silanes, Cristian Pop-Eleches and Andrei Shleifer, p. 31). These legal traditions originated respectively in England, France, Germany, Scandinavia, and the Soviet Union and were later distributed worldwide through voluntary adoption, imitation, colonisation, and conquest (La Porta et al. 1998, 1999) |
| | | | French Commercial Code | FRENCH (L.O.) | | 0,1 | |
| | | | Socialist/Communist Laws | SOCIALIST (L.O.) | | 0,1 | |
| | | | German Commercial Code | GERMAN (L.O.) | | 0,1 | |
| | | | Scandinavian Commercial Code | SCANDINAVIAN (L.O.) | | 0,1 | |
| | Environment and geography | | Latitude (average) | Latitude | (Teorell, *et al.* 2017) | 0-1 | "The absolute value of the latitude of the capital city, divided by 90 (to take values between 0 and 1)" (Teorell, *et al.* 2017, p. 446) |

| Type of variable | Category (prosperity theory associated) | Sub-category | Variable | Code | Source | Original value rank | Description |
|---|---|---|---|---|---|---|---|
| Other Predictor variables | | | Environment Performance Index | EPI | (Hsu, *et al.* 2016) | 0-100 | The Environmental Performance Index (EPI) rates countries based on their performance on high-priority environmental aspects in two components: ecosystems conservation and human health. The EPI then rates national results in nine areas with over 20 indicators under these two components (Hsu, et al. 2016) |
| | Cultural determinants (other than religion) | Main Languages fractionalisation | English | English (lang) | (CIA 2016) | % 0-100 | The share of main native speakers in the population |
| | | | French | French (lang) | | % 0-100 | |
| | | | Spanish | Spanish (lang) | | % 0-100 | |
| | | | Russian | Russian (lang) | | % 0-100 | |
| | | | German | German (lang) | | % 0-100 | |
| | | | Portuguese | Portug. (lang) | | % 0-100 | |
| | | | Italian | Italian (lang) | | % 0-100 | |
| Other Predictor variables | | Main Ethnical fractionalisation | Caucasian | Caucasian (ethn) | | % 0-100 | The proportion of ethnicities in population |
| | | | Latino | Latino (ethn) | | % 0-100 | |
| | | | African | African (ethn) | | % 0-100 | |
| | | | Amerindian | Amerind. (ethn) | | % 0-100 | |
| | | | Mestizo | Mestizo (ethn) | | % 0-100 | |
| | | | Mulatto | Mulatto (ethn) | | % 0-100 | |
| | | | Asian | Asian (ethn) | | % 0-100 | |

| Type of variable | Category (prosperity theory associated) | Sub-category | Variable | Code | Source | Original value rank | Description |
|---|---|---|---|---|---|---|---|
| **Criterion Variable** | Prosperity | | Global Competitivene ss Index (GCI) | Competitiveness | (World Economic Forum 2016) | (1–7) | "Competitiveness is defined as the set of institutions, policies and factors that determine a country's level of productivity. The level of productivity, in turn, sets the level of prosperity that can be reached by an economy". The Global Competitiveness Index (GCI) is a comprehensive framework that measures the microeconomic and macroeconomic foundations of national competitiveness, grouped into 12 categories. The twelve categories that comprise this index are institutions, technological readiness, innovation, higher education and training, health and primary education, business sophistication, infrastructure, macroeconomic environment, labour market efficiency, market size, financial market development, and goods market efficiency (World Economic Forum 2016). |

## 2. QUAN Appendix B. Corruption Variables (Model 6; Sect. 15. 3.2)

| Type of variable | Category (corruption theory associated) | Subcategory | Variable | Code | Source | Original value rank | Description |
|---|---|---|---|---|---|---|---|
| Predictor variables of interest | Religion | Christian denomination (proportion in population) | Roman Catholic | CATH | (Johnson & Zurlo, 2016) | % 0-100 | Percentage of population in each country belonging to different religious affiliations. |
| | | | Protestant | PROT | | % 0-100 | |
| | | Main Religion fractionalisation | | RELF | Alesina *et al.* (2003) | 0-1 | "Average value of five different indices of ethnolinguistic fractionalisation. Its value ranges from 0 to 1. The five component indices are: (1) index of ethnolinguistic fractionalisation in 1960, which measures the probability that two randomly selected people from a given country will not belong to the same ethnolinguistic group (the index is based on the number and size of population groups as distinguished by their ethnic and linguistic status); (2) probability of two randomly selected individuals speaking different languages; (3) probability of two randomly selected individuals do not speak the same language; (4) per cent of the population not speaking the official language; and (5) per cent of the population not speaking the most widely used language. Original Sources: Easterly and Levine, 1997. The sources of the components of the average index are (1) Atlas Narodov Mira, 1964; (2)Muller, 1964; (3) Roberts, 1962; (4) and (5) Gunnemark, 1991" (as cited in Alesina et al., 2003, p.192). |
| Other Predictor variables | Cultural determinants (other than religion) | Main Languages fractionalisation | | LINGF | | | |
| | | Main Ethnical fractionalisation | | ETHF | | | |
| | Economic determinants | Gross domestic product (GDP) per capita | | GDPPC | (World Bank 2016) | US$ | GDP per capita, PPP (current international $) |

| Type of variable | Category (corruption theory associated) | Subcategory | Variable | Code | Source | Original value rank | Description |
|---|---|---|---|---|---|---|---|
| Other Predictor variables | | Index of Economic Freedom | | IEF | (The Heritage Foundation 2017) | 0-100 | "The Index of Economic Freedom takes a comprehensive view of economic freedom. Some of the aspects of economic freedom that are evaluated are concerned with a country's interactions with the rest of the world. The 12 aspects of economic freedom measured in the Index may be grouped into four broad categories:<br>• The rule of law (property rights, judicial effectiveness, and government integrity);<br>• Government size (tax burden, government spending, and fiscal health);<br>• Regulatory efficiency (business freedom, labour freedom, and monetary freedom); and<br>• Market openness (trade freedom, investment freedom, and financial freedom)" Terry Miller and Anthony B. Kim, 2017 Index of Economic Freedom (Washington: The Heritage Foundation, 2017), http://www.heritage.org/index |
| | Political determinants | Political rights and civil liberties | | PRCL | (Freedom House 2016) | 0-100 | "Index of political rights. Higher ratings indicate countries that come closer "to the ideals suggested by the checklist questions of: (1) free and fair elections; (2) those elected rule; (3) there are competitive parties or other competitive political groupings; (4) the opposition has an important role and power; and (5) the entities have self-determination or an extremely high degree of autonomy" (Freedom House, 2016). |
| | | Political stability | | STABIL | (Kaufman *et al.* 2010) | -2.5-2.5 | "Political Stability and Absence of Violence/Terrorism measures perceptions of the likelihood of political instability and/or politically-motivated violence, including terrorism. Estimate gives the country's score on the aggregate indicator, in units of a standard normal distribution, i.e. ranging from approximately -2.5 to 2.5" (Kaufmann, Kraay, & Mastruzzi, 2010) https://datacatalog.worldbank.org/political-stability-and-absence-violenceterrorism-estimate |
| Criterion Variable | Corruption Perception Index (CPI) | | | CORRUPTION | (Transparency International 2016) | 0-100 | The Corruption Perceptions Index developed by Transparency International (2016), is a composite index drawing on corruption indices of 11 independent institutions (including, among others, the World Economic Forum, the European Intelligence Unit, and the World Bank). The index summarises perceptions of business people and country experts around the world, both residents and expatriates. The CPI values range from 0 to 100. Lower values indicate a higher degree of corruption (i.e. a lower degree of transparency). |

## II. Appendices to Component 2 (Meso) (Qualitative Comparative Analysis—QCA, Chap. 16)

## *3. QCA Appendix A. Calibration Thresholds and Description of Conditions and Outcome According to Indicators, Categories, and Sources of Origin*

| Type of variable | Category (prosperity theory associated) | Subcategory | Indicator | Code | Source | Original value rank | Qualitative Anchors 0 | 0.33 | 0.66 | 1 | Description |
|---|---|---|---|---|---|---|---|---|---|---|---|
| Conditions | Religion | Christian denomination (proportion in population) | Roman Catholic | DOM_CAT | (Johnson & Zurlo, 2016) | % 0-100 | <=0.2 | 0.5 | 0.8 | >0.8 | Percentage of population in each country belonging to different religious affiliations. |
| | | | Protestant | DOM_PROT | | % 0-100 | <=0.01 | 0.1 | 0.5 | >0.5 | |
| | | | Orthodox | DOM_ORT | | % 0-100 | <=0.03 | 0.4 | 0.8 | >0.8 | |
| | | | Muslim | DOM_MUSL | | % 0-100 | <=0.03 | 0.47 | >0.47 | NA | |
| | | | Atheists & Agnostics | DOM_AG_AT | | % 0-100 | <=0.03 | 0.33 | 0.5 | >0.5 | |
| | Institutions | Agreements with the Vatican | Concordats | CONCOR | (Corral and Petschen, 2004) | (1–4) | 0 | NA | 3 | 4 | The condition "Concordats" was created adopting the information about the status of the countries' agreements with the Vatican contained in (Corral & Petschen, 2004):<br><br>1. Null or apparent low influence of Vatican/Roman Catholic Church in State affairs.<br>2. Some diplomatic relations with the Vatican/Roman Catholic Church might be present. |

| Type of variable | Category (prosperity theory associated) | Subcategory | Indicator | Code | Source | Original value rank | Qualitative Anchors 0 | 0.33 | 0.66 | 1 | Description |
|---|---|---|---|---|---|---|---|---|---|---|---|
| | | | | | | | | | | | 3. Agreements and interference of the Vatican/Roman Catholic Church in State affairs (Education, Military, Lands, Ecclesiastical) 4. Currently valid Concordat with the Vatican/The Roman Catholic Church. Vatican/The Roman Catholic Church is in most cases, the official Religion of the State. |
| | | State religion | Roman Catholic | ST_CATHOL | (Barro, R. J. and McCleary, R. M. 2005) | 0,1 | 0 | NA | NA | 1 | The most significant type of state monopoly in history has been the state's monopoly on religion. The selection of a state religion is a political process involving relations between the religious actor and the state (Barro & McCleary, 2005, p. 1332). The main feature of a state religion is its official promotion of the religion's monopoly status, partly through entry restrictions and partly through incentives (Smith as cited in Barro & McCleary 2005, p. 1331). The authors categorise official state religion as an all-or-nothing choice. The data is taken for the year 2000. This variable can also be part of the societal religious norms subcategory and along with Christian denomination, being part of the predictor variable of interest. However, for practical reasons, this variable appears only here in category "institutions". |
| | | | Protestant | ST_PROTEST | | 0,1 | 0 | NA | NA | 1 | |
| | | | Muslim | ST_MUSLIM | | 0,1 | 0 | NA | NA | 1 | |
| | | Legal origin | English Common Law | ENGLISH | (La Porta, *et al.* 1999) | 0,1 | 0 | NA | NA | 1 | It identifies "the legal origin of the Company Law or Commercial Code of each country. There are five possible origins: (1) English Common Law; (2) French Commercial Code; (3) German Commercial Code; (4) Scandinavian Commercial Code; and (5) Socialist/Communist |
| | | | German Commercial Code | GERMAN | | 0,1 | 0 | NA | NA | 1 | |

| Type of variable | Category (prosperity theory associated) | Subcategory | Indicator | Code | Source | Original value rank | Qualitative Anchors 0 | 0.33 | 0.66 | 1 | Description |
|---|---|---|---|---|---|---|---|---|---|---|---|
| | | | Scandinavian Commercial Code | SCANDINAVIAN | | 0,1 | 0 | NA | NA | 1 | laws" (© 2002 by Rafael La Porta, Florencio López-de-Silanes, Cristian Pop-Eleches and Andrei Shleifer, p. 31). These legal traditions originated respectively in England, France, Germany, Scandinavia, and the Soviet Union and were later distributed worldwide through voluntary adoption, imitation, colonisation, and conquest (La Porta et al. 1998, 1999) |
| | | | French Commercial Code | FRENCH | | 0,1 | 0 | NA | NA | 1 | |
| | | | Socialist/Communist Laws | SOCIALIST | | 0,1 | 0 | NA | NA | 1 | |
| | Environment and geography | | Environment Performance Index | EPI | (Hsu, *et al.* 2016) | 0-100 | <=65 | 80 | 88 | >88 | The Environmental Performance Index (EPI) rates countries based on their performance on high-priority environmental aspects in two components: ecosystems conservation and human health. The EPI then rates national results in nine areas with over 20 indicators under these two components (Hsu, et al. 2016) |
| | Cultural determinants (other than religion) | Main Languages fractionalisation | English | LAN_ENG | (CIA 2016) | % 0-100 | <=0.02 | 0.2 | 0.8 | >0.8 | Share of main native speakers in population |
| | | | German | LAN_GER | | % 0-100 | <=0.02 | NA | 0.8 | >0.8 | |
| | | | Russian | LAN_RUS | | % 0-100 | <=0.01 | 0.1 | 0.5 | >0.5 | |
| | | | Romance languages | LAN_ROM | | % 0-100 | <=0.02 | 0.4 | 0.9 | >0.9 | |
| | | Main Ethnical | Caucasian | WHITE | | % 0-100 | 0 | 0.3 | 0.8 | >0.8 | Proportion of ethnicities in population |

| Type of variable | Category (prosperity theory associated) | Subcategory | Indicator | Code | Source | Original value rank | Qualitative Anchors | | | | Description |
|---|---|---|---|---|---|---|---|---|---|---|---|
| | | | | | | | 0 | 0.33 | 0.66 | 1 | |
| | | fractionalisation | Latino | LATINO | | % 0-100 | 0 | 0.4 | 0.8 | >0.8 | |
| | | | African | AFRICAN | | % 0-100 | <=0.04 | 0.4 | 0.9 | >0.9 | |
| | | | Amerindian | AMERIDIAN | | % 0-100 | <=0.04 | 0.4 | >0.4 | NA | |
| | | | Mestizo | MESTIZO | | % 0-100 | <=0.04 | 0.4 | 0.8 | >0.8 | |
| | | | Mulatto | MULATTO | | % 0-100 | <=0.04 | 0.4 | >0.4 | NA | |
| | | | Other non-white | NON_WHITE | | % 0-100 | <=0.04 | 0.4 | 0.8 | >0.8 | |
| Outcome | Prosperity | | Global Competitiveness Index (GCI) | Competitiveness | (World Economic Forum 2016) | (1–7) | <=3.7 | 4.5 | 5.2 | >5.2 | The Global Competitiveness Index (GCI), a comprehensive framework that measures the microeconomic and macroeconomic foundations of national competitiveness, grouped into 12 categories (World Economic Forum 2016).<br><br>The twelve categories that comprise this index are Institutions, technological readiness, innovation, higher education and training, health and primary education, business sophistication, infrastructure, macroeconomic environment, labour market efficiency, market size, financial market development, and goods market efficiency.<br>(World Economic Forum 2016). |

| Type of variable | Category (prosperity theory associated) | Subcategory | Indicator | Code | Source | Original value rank | Qualitative Anchors | | | | Description |
|---|---|---|---|---|---|---|---|---|---|---|---|
| | | | | | | | 0 | 0.33 | 0.66 | 1 | |
| | Corruption Perception Index (CPI) | | | CORRUPTION | (Transparency International 2016) | 0-100 | <=30 | 45 | 70 | >70 | Transparency International develops the Corruption Perceptions Index (2016). It is a composite index drawing on corruption indices of 11 independent institutions (including, among others, the World Economic Forum, the European Intelligence Unit, and the World Bank). The index summarises perceptions of business people and country experts around the world, both residents and expatriates. The CPI values range from 0 to 100. Lower values indicate a higher degree of corruption (i.e. a lower degree of transparency). |

# *4. QCA Appendix B. Truth Tables and "QCA Minimisation Using the Enhanced Quine–McCluskey Algorithm"*

## 4.1 Interpretation Guide

### 4.1.1 Truth Tables

In the truth tables, especially the rows exhibiting outcome=1 (entire rows in yellow) merit attention. These are the rows where the outcome is present. The combination of ones and zeros for each row refers to the combination of conditions leading to the outcome.

Exceptionally, I have also highlighted in yellow two clusters (but not the entire row) and their incl proximate to 0.9 (sufficiency inclusion). Such clusters are of interest for the analysis of QCA cases (Cuba and Uruguay; see Chap. 16 in main text and truth Tables 1 and 21 in Appendix 4.2).

**Conventions:**

OUT: outcome value

n: number of cases in configuration (with the same combination of conditions)

incl: sufficiency inclusion score

PRI: Proportional Reduction in Inconsistency

Both incl and PRI are parameters of fit. If we wish to draw any conclusion from the rows, "incl" ought to be at least close to 0.9 or higher (better). The higher the number of cases, the better.

### 4.1.2 Sufficient Conditions in the Tables "QCA Minimisation Using the Enhanced Quine–McCluskey Algorithm":

Two parameters of fit inform the interpretation of QCA results: the consistency and the coverage scores. The consistency score indicates the degree to which the empirical data is entirely in line with a result, or how much deviation is evident. If the findings pass a plausible consistency threshold, they can be considered significant (scores below 0.80 should be avoided). The coverage score provides information on the share of cases that explain results, which is how comprehensive or trivial the findings are. Both scores run between 0 (worst) and 1 (perfect) and are provided for each path as well as the entire solution (Schneider & Wagemann, 2012, p. 128; Fiedler, Graevingholt, & Mross, 2018, p. 11).

The Quine–McCluskey algorithm is used to simplify Boolean algebra expressions based on finding all prime implicants. The rules of Boolean algebra help to minimise logical expression (Schneider & Wagemann, 2012, p. 115). While similar to Karnaugh mapping, it is better suited to computer algorithms. It also allows testing whether minimisation of Boolean functions has been reached.

**Conventions:**

CAPITAL LETTERS: the presence of the condition (e.g. 1 for high COMPETITIVENESS).

Lowercase letters: negation or absence of the condition (e.g. 1 for not high competitiveness = usually low competitiveness).

For example, "EPI*LATINO" means high EPI index and high Latino population, while "epi*latino" means something like low EPI index and low Latino population.

: Each line is one possible way of attaining the outcome (e.g. low corruption, high competitiveness).

incl.: (consistency=inclusion). This is the inclusion score for sufficiency relations (should be at least 0.9).

cov.r: Coverage. If it is lower than 0.5, the results do not have enough power.

* Means that these conditions must be all present (logical AND). The logical operator AND describes the necessity of each condition combined with another condition for an outcome of interest to be in place.

+ Means that at least one of the conditions must be present—alternative ways for an outcome (logical OR). The logical operator OR denotes that it is sufficient for any condition (or combination) separated by OR to be present for the outcome of interest to be also present.

Applied to sets of elements, AND (*) yields the intersection of sets while OR (+) results in their union (Fiedler, Graevingholt, & Mross, 2018).

## 4.2 Truth Tables and "QCA Minimisation Using the Enhanced Quine–McCluskey Algorithm" for Outcome Competitiveness

### 4.2.1 Predominant Religion (Proportion of Adherents) and Competitiveness

*A. Positive Outcome*

*1. Truth Table*

| | CONCOR | EPI | DOM_CAT | DOM_PROT | DOM_ORT | OUT | n | incl | PRI | cases |
|---|---|---|---|---|---|---|---|---|---|---|
| 1 | 0 | 0 | 0 | 0 | 0 | 1 | 1 | 0.951 | 0.835 | BIH |
| 2 | 0 | 0 | 0 | 0 | 1 | 0 | 5 | 0.717 | 0 | MDA,MKD,MNE,SRB,UKR |
| 3 | 0 | 0 | 0 | 1 | 0 | 1 | 2 | 0.912 | 0.769 | JAM,TTO |
| 5 | 0 | 0 | 1 | 0 | 0 | 0 | 2 | 0.882 | 0.676 | CHL,URY |
| 7 | 0 | 0 | 1 | 1 | 0 | 0 | 3 | 0.847 | 0.59 | HND,NIC,PAN |
| 9 | 0 | 1 | 0 | 0 | 0 | 1 | 1 | 0.996 | 0.987 | CZE |
| 10 | 0 | 1 | 0 | 0 | 1 | 0 | 4 | 0.833 | 0.244 | BGR,GRC,ROU,RUS |
| 11 | 0 | 1 | 0 | 1 | 0 | 1 | 11 | 0.975 | 0.958 | CAN,DNK,EST,FIN,GBR,CHE,ISL,NLD, NOR,SWE,USA |
| 13 | 0 | 1 | 1 | 0 | 0 | 1 | 3 | 0.933 | 0.827 | BEL,IRL,LUX |
| 17 | 1 | 0 | 0 | 0 | 0 | 0 | 1 | 0.898 | 0.642 | ALB |
| 21 | 1 | 0 | 1 | 0 | 0 | 0 | 7 | 0.649 | 0.164 | ARG,COL,ECU,MEX,PER,PRY,VEN |
| 23 | 1 | 0 | 1 | 1 | 0 | 0 | 5 | 0.65 | 0.199 | BOL,BRA,DOM,GTM,SLV |
| 27 | 1 | 1 | 0 | 1 | 0 | 1 | 2 | 0.907 | 0.795 | DEU,LVA |
| 29 | 1 | 1 | 1 | 0 | 0 | 0 | 11 | 0.773 | 0.519 | AUT,ESP,FRA,HRV,ITA,LTU,MLT,POL, PRT,SVK,SVN |
| 31 | 1 | 1 | 1 | 1 | 0 | 0 | 2 | 0.773 | 0.375 | CRI,HUN |

*2. QCA Minimisation Using the Enhanced Quine–McCluskey Algorithm*

n OUT = 1/0/C: 20/40/0

Total: 60

| | incl | PRI | cov.r | cov.u |
|---|---|---|---|---|
| 1 concor*dom_cat*dom_ort | 0.904 | 0.841 | 0.539 | 0.033 |
| 2 concor*EPI*dom_prot*dom_ort | 0.948 | 0.851 | 0.393 | 0.081 |
| 3 EPI*dom_cat*DOM_PROT*dom_ort | 0.957 | 0.932 | 0.473 | 0.031 |

*B. Negative Outcome*

*3. Truth Table*

| | CONCOR | EPI | DOM_CAT | DOM_PROT | DOM_ORT | OUT | n | incl | PRI | cases |
|---|---|---|---|---|---|---|---|---|---|---|
| 1 | 0 | 0 | 0 | 0 | 0 | 0 | 1 | 0.75 | 0.165 | BIH |
| 2 | 0 | 0 | 0 | 0 | 1 | 1 | 5 | 1 | 1 | MDA,MKD,MNE,SRB,UKR |
| 3 | 0 | 0 | 0 | 1 | 0 | 0 | 2 | 0.705 | 0.231 | JAM,TTO |
| 5 | 0 | 0 | 1 | 0 | 0 | 0 | 2 | 0.753 | 0.324 | CHL,URY |
| 7 | 0 | 0 | 1 | 1 | 0 | 0 | 3 | 0.78 | 0.41 | HND,NIC,PAN |
| 9 | 0 | 1 | 0 | 0 | 0 | 0 | 1 | 0.698 | 0.013 | CZE |
| 10 | 0 | 1 | 0 | 0 | 1 | 1 | 4 | 0.946 | 0.756 | BGR,GRC,ROU,RUS |
| 11 | 0 | 1 | 0 | 1 | 0 | 0 | 11 | 0.41 | 0.002 | CAN,DNK,EST,FIN,GBR,CHE,ISL,NLD, NOR,SWE,USA |
| 13 | 0 | 1 | 1 | 0 | 0 | 0 | 3 | 0.679 | 0.173 | BEL,IRL,LUX |
| 17 | 1 | 0 | 0 | 0 | 0 | 0 | 1 | 0.817 | 0.358 | ALB |
| 21 | 1 | 0 | 1 | 0 | 0 | 1 | 7 | 0.931 | 0.836 | ARG,COL,ECU,MEX,PER,PRY,VEN |
| 23 | 1 | 0 | 1 | 1 | 0 | 1 | 5 | 0.913 | 0.801 | BOL,BRA,DOM,GTM,SLV |
| 27 | 1 | 1 | 0 | 1 | 0 | 0 | 2 | 0.637 | 0.205 | DEU,LVA |
| 29 | 1 | 1 | 1 | 0 | 0 | 0 | 11 | 0.704 | 0.374 | AUT,ESP,FRA,HRV,ITA,LTU,MLT,POL, PRT,SVK,SVN |
| 31 | 1 | 1 | 1 | 1 | 0 | 1 | 2 | 0.864 | 0.625 | CRI,HUN |

*4. QCA Minimisation Using the Enhanced Quine-McCluskey Algorithm*

| n | OUT = 1/0/C: 23/37/0 | | | | |
|---|---|---|---|---|---|
| | Total: 60 | | | | |
| | | incl | PRI | cov.r | cov.u |
| 1 | concor*dom_cat*dom_prot*DOM_ORT | 0.886 | 0.733 | 0.275 | 0.239 |
| 2 | CONCOR*DOM_CAT*DOM_PROT*dom_ort | 0.889 | 0.769 | 0.284 | 0.023 |
| 3 | CONCOR*epi*DOM_CAT*dom_ort | 0.941 | 0.882 | 0.383 | 0.122 |
| | M1 | 0.902 | 0.809 | 0.657 | |

## 4.2.2 State Religion and Competitiveness

### *A. Positive Outcome*

### *5. Truth Table*

| | CONCOR | EPI | ST_ CATHOL | ST_ PROTEST | ST_ MUSLIM | OUT | n | incl | PRI | cases |
|---|---|---|---|---|---|---|---|---|---|---|
| 1 | 0 | 0 | 0 | 0 | 0 | 0 | 10 | 0.668 | 0.291 | BIH,JAM,MDA,MKD,MNE,NIC,SRB,TTO,UKR,URY |
| 5 | 0 | 0 | 1 | 0 | 0 | 0 | 3 | 0.787 | 0.476 | HND,CHL,PAN |
| 9 | 0 | 1 | 0 | 0 | 0 | 1 | 11 | 0.889 | 0.772 | BEL,BGR,CAN,CZE,EST,GRC,CHE,NLD,ROU,RUS,USA |
| 11 | 0 | 1 | 0 | 1 | 0 | 1 | 6 | 0.936 | 0.932 | DNK,FIN,GBR,ISL,NOR,SWE |
| 13 | 0 | 1 | 1 | 0 | 0 | 1 | 2 | 0.874 | 0.594 | IRL,LUX |
| 17 | 1 | 0 | 0 | 0 | 0 | 0 | 2 | 0.795 | 0.496 | ECU,MEX |
| 18 | 1 | 0 | 0 | 0 | 1 | 0 | 1 | 0.5 | 0 | ALB |
| 21 | 1 | 0 | 1 | 0 | 0 | 0 | 10 | 0.456 | 0 | ARG,BOL,BRA,COL,DOM,GTM,PER,PRY,SLV,VEN |
| 25 | 1 | 1 | 0 | 0 | 0 | 0 | 7 | 0.812 | 0.699 | AUT,DEU,FRA,HUN,LVA,POL,SVK |
| 29 | 1 | 1 | 1 | 0 | 0 | 0 | 8 | 0.677 | 0.3 | CRI,ESP,HRV,ITA,LTU,MLT,PRT,SVN |

### *6. QCA Minimisation Using the Enhanced Quine–McCluskey Algorithm*

| *n* | OUT = 1/0/C: 19/41/0 | | | | |
|---|---|---|---|---|---|
| | Total: 60 | | | | |
| | | incl | PRI | cov.r | cov.u |
| 1 | concor*EPI*st_cathol*st_muslim | 0.903 | 0.845 | 0.494 | 0.155 |
| 2 | concor*EPI*st_protest*st_muslim | 0.884 | 0.733 | 0.483 | 0.144 |
| | M1 | 0.896 | 0.812 | 0.638 | |

### *B. Negative Outcome*

### *7. Truth Table*

| | CONCOR | EPI | ST_ CATHOL | ST_ PROTEST | ST_ MUSLIM | OUT | n | incl | PRI | cases |
|---|---|---|---|---|---|---|---|---|---|---|
| 1 | 0 | 0 | 0 | 0 | 0 | 0 | 10 | 0.811 | 0.596 | BIH,JAM,MDA,MKD,MNE,NIC,SRB,TTO,UKR,URY |
| 5 | 0 | 0 | 1 | 0 | 0 | 0 | 3 | 0.803 | 0.515 | HND,CHL,PAN |
| 9 | 0 | 1 | 0 | 0 | 0 | 0 | 11 | 0.597 | 0.171 | BEL,BGR,CAN,CZE,EST,GRC,CHE,NLD,ROU,RUS,USA |
| 11 | 0 | 1 | 0 | 1 | 0 | 0 | 6 | 0.064 | 0 | DNK,FIN,GBR,ISL,NOR,SWE |
| 13 | 0 | 1 | 1 | 0 | 0 | 0 | 2 | 0.815 | 0.406 | IRL,LUX |
| 17 | 1 | 0 | 0 | 0 | 0 | 0 | 2 | 0.798 | 0.504 | ECU,MEX |
| 18 | 1 | 0 | 0 | 0 | 1 | 1 | 1 | 1 | 1 | ALB |
| 21 | 1 | 0 | 1 | 0 | 0 | 1 | 10 | 1 | 1 | ARG,BOL,BRA,COL,DOM,GTM,PER,PRY,SLV,VEN |
| 25 | 1 | 1 | 0 | 0 | 0 | 0 | 7 | 0.564 | 0.301 | AUT,DEU,FRA,HUN,LVA,POL,SVK |
| 29 | 1 | 1 | 1 | 0 | 0 | 0 | 8 | 0.789 | 0.543 | CRI,ESP,HRV,ITA,LTU,MLT,PRT,SVN |

*8. QCA Minimisation Using the Enhanced Quine–McCluskey Algorithm*

| *n* | OUT = 1/0/C: 11/49/0 | | | | |
|---|---|---|---|---|---|
| | Total: 60 | | | | |
| | | incl | PRI | cov.r | cov.u |
| 1 | CONCOR*epi*st_cathol*st_protest*ST_MUSLIM | 1 | 1 | 0.024 | 0.024 |
| 2 | CONCOR*epi*ST_CATHOL*st_protest*st_muslim | 1 | 1 | 0.287 | 0.287 |
| | M1 | 1 | 1 | 0.311 | |

## 4.2.3 Legal Origin and Competitiveness

*A. Positive Outcome*

*9. Truth Table*

| | CONCOR | ENGLISH | SOCIALIST | FRENCH | GERMAN | SCANDIN | EPI | OUT | n | incl | PRI | cases |
|---|---|---|---|---|---|---|---|---|---|---|---|---|
| 4 | 0 | 0 | 0 | 0 | 0 | 1 | 1 | 1 | 5 | 0.927 | 0.921 | DNK,FIN,NOR,SWE,ISL |
| 6 | 0 | 0 | 0 | 0 | 1 | 0 | 1 | 1 | 1 | 1 | 1 | CHE |
| 9 | 0 | 0 | 0 | 1 | 0 | 0 | 0 | 0 | 5 | 0.727 | 0.439 | HND,NIC,PAN,URY,CHL |
| 10 | 0 | 0 | 0 | 1 | 0 | 0 | 1 | 0 | 4 | 0.864 | 0.701 | BEL,GRC,NLD,LUX |
| 17 | 0 | 0 | 1 | 0 | 0 | 0 | 0 | 0 | 4 | 0.712 | 0 | MDA,MKD,UKR,BIH |
| 18 | 0 | 0 | 1 | 0 | 0 | 0 | 1 | 0 | 5 | 0.844 | 0.48 | BGR,CZE,EST,RUS,ROU |
| 33 | 0 | 1 | 0 | 0 | 0 | 0 | 0 | 0 | 2 | 0.748 | 0.6 | JAM,TTO |
| 34 | 0 | 1 | 0 | 0 | 0 | 0 | 1 | 1 | 4 | 1 | 1 | IRL,GBR,CAN,USA |
| 70 | 1 | 0 | 0 | 0 | 1 | 0 | 1 | 1 | 2 | 1 | 1 | AUT,DEU |
| 73 | 1 | 0 | 0 | 1 | 0 | 0 | 0 | 0 | 12 | 0.421 | 0 | DOM,MEX,SLV,GTM,BRA,COL,ECU,PER,ARG,BOL,PRY,VEN |
| 74 | 1 | 0 | 0 | 1 | 0 | 0 | 1 | 0 | 6 | 0.729 | 0.41 | FRA,ITA,PRT,ESP,MLT,CRI |
| 81 | 1 | 0 | 1 | 0 | 0 | 0 | 0 | 0 | 1 | 0.863 | 0 | ALB |
| 82 | 1 | 0 | 1 | 0 | 0 | 0 | 1 | 0 | 7 | 0.667 | 0.279 | HRV,HUN,LVA,LTU,POL,SVK,SVN |

*10. QCA Minimisation Using the Enhanced Quine–McCluskey Algorithm*

| *n* | OUT = 1/0/C: 12/46/0 | | | | |
|---|---|---|---|---|---|
| | Total: 58 | | | | |
| | | incl | PRI | cov.r | cov.u |
| 1 | english*socialist*french*GERMAN*scandin*EPI | 1 | 1 | 0.063 | 0.063 |
| 2 | concor*english*socialist*french*german*SCANDIN*EPI | 0.927 | 0.921 | 0.137 | 0.137 |
| 3 | concor*ENGLISH*socialist*french*german*scandin*EPI | 1 | 1 | 0.105 | 0.105 |
| | M1 | 0.966 | 0.96 | 0.305 | |

## *B. Negative Outcome*

### *11. Truth Table*

| | CONCOR | ENGLISH | SOCIALIST | FRENCH | GERMAN | SCANDIN | EPI | OUT | n | incl | PRI | cases |
|---|---|---|---|---|---|---|---|---|---|---|---|---|
| 4 | 0 | 0 | 0 | 0 | 0 | 1 | 1 | 0 | 5 | 0.073 | 0 | DNK,FIN,NOR,SWE,ISL |
| 6 | 0 | 0 | 0 | 0 | 1 | 0 | 1 | 0 | 1 | 0 | 0 | CHE |
| 9 | 0 | 0 | 0 | 1 | 0 | 0 | 0 | 0 | 5 | 0.741 | 0.468 | HND,NIC,PAN,URY,CHL |
| 10 | 0 | 0 | 0 | 1 | 0 | 0 | 1 | 0 | 4 | 0.681 | 0.299 | BEL,GRC,NLD,LUX |
| 17 | 0 | 0 | 1 | 0 | 0 | 0 | 0 | 1 | 4 | 0.946 | 0.811 | MDA,MKD,UKR,BIH |
| 18 | 0 | 0 | 1 | 0 | 0 | 0 | 1 | 0 | 5 | 0.805 | 0.35 | BGR,CZE,EST,RUS,ROU |
| 33 | 0 | 1 | 0 | 0 | 0 | 0 | 0 | 0 | 2 | 0.622 | 0.4 | JAM,TTO |
| 34 | 0 | 1 | 0 | 0 | 0 | 0 | 1 | 0 | 4 | 0.303 | 0 | IRL,GBR,CAN,USA |
| 70 | 1 | 0 | 0 | 0 | 1 | 0 | 1 | 0 | 2 | 0 | 0 | AUT,DEU |
| 73 | 1 | 0 | 0 | 1 | 0 | 0 | 0 | 1 | 12 | 1 | 1 | DOM,MEX,SLV,GTM,BRA,COL,ECU,PER,ARG,BOL,PRY,VEN |
| 74 | 1 | 0 | 0 | 1 | 0 | 0 | 1 | 0 | 6 | 0.734 | 0.42 | FRA,ITA,PRT,ESP,MLT,CRI |
| 81 | 1 | 0 | 1 | 0 | 0 | 0 | 0 | 1 | 1 | 1 | 1 | ALB |
| 82 | 1 | 0 | 1 | 0 | 0 | 0 | 1 | 0 | 7 | 0.871 | 0.721 | HRV,HUN,LVA,LTU,POL,SVK,SVN |

### *12. QCA Minimisation Using the Enhanced Quine–McCluskey Algorithm*

| *n* | OUT = 1/0/C: 17/41/0 | | | | |
|---|---|---|---|---|---|
| | Total: 58 | | | | |
| | | incl | PRI | cov.r | cov.u |
| 1 | english*SOCIALIST*french*german*scandin*epi | 0.953 | 0.842 | 0.255 | 0.255 |
| 2 | CONCOR*english*socialist*FRENCH*german*scandin*epi | 1 | 1 | 0.326 | 0.326 |
| | M1 | 0.979 | 0.953 | 0.581 | |

### 4.2.4 Languages and Competitiveness

#### *A. Positive Outcome*

#### *13. Truth Table*

| | CONCOR | EPI | LAN_ GER | LAN_ ROM | LAN_ RUS | LAN_ ENG | OUT | n | incl | PRI | cases |
|---|---|---|---|---|---|---|---|---|---|---|---|
| 1 | 0 | 0 | 0 | 0 | 0 | 0 | 0 | 5 | 0.784 | 0.523 | BIH,MKD,MNE,SRB,TTO |
| 2 | 0 | 0 | 0 | 0 | 0 | 1 | 0 | 1 | 0.874 | 0.799 | JAM |
| 3 | 0 | 0 | 0 | 0 | 1 | 0 | 0 | 2 | 0.748 | 0 | MDA,UKR |
| 5 | 0 | 0 | 0 | 1 | 0 | 0 | 0 | 5 | 0.748 | 0.554 | HND,CHL,NIC,PAN,URY |
| 17 | 0 | 1 | 0 | 0 | 0 | 0 | 0 | 12 | 0.898 | 0.818 | BEL,BGR,CZE,DNK,FIN,GRC,ISL, LUX,NLD,NOR,ROU,SWE |
| 18 | 0 | 1 | 0 | 0 | 0 | 1 | 1 | 4 | 1 | 1 | CAN,GBR,IRL,USA |
| 19 | 0 | 1 | 0 | 0 | 1 | 0 | 1 | 2 | 0.997 | 0.985 | EST,RUS |
| 25 | 0 | 1 | 1 | 0 | 0 | 0 | 1 | 1 | 0.99 | 0.985 | CHE |
| 33 | 1 | 0 | 0 | 0 | 0 | 0 | 0 | 2 | 0.774 | 0 | ALB,ARG |
| 37 | 1 | 0 | 0 | 1 | 0 | 0 | 0 | 11 | 0.389 | 0 | BOL,BRA,COL,DOM,ECU,GTM,M EX,PER,PRY,SLV,VEN |
| 49 | 1 | 1 | 0 | 0 | 0 | 0 | 0 | 7 | 0.816 | 0.489 | HRV,ITA,LTU,MLT,POL,SVK,SV N |
| 51 | 1 | 1 | 0 | 0 | 1 | 0 | 0 | 1 | 0.75 | 0 | LVA |
| 53 | 1 | 1 | 0 | 1 | 0 | 0 | 0 | 4 | 0.699 | 0.33 | CRI,ESP,FRA,PRT |
| 57 | 1 | 1 | 1 | 0 | 0 | 0 | 0 | 3 | 0.833 | 0.8 | AUT,DEU,HUN |

#### *14. QCA Minimisation Using the Enhanced Quine–McCluskey Algorithm*

| *n* | OUT = 1/0/C: 7/53/0 | | | | |
|---|---|---|---|---|---|
| | Total: 60 | | | | |
| | | incl | PRI | cov.r | cov.u |
| 1 | concor*EPI*lan_ger*lan_rom*lan_rus*LAN_ENG | 1 | 1 | 0.123 | 0.103 |
| 2 | concor*EPI*lan_ger*lan_rom*LAN_RUS*lan_eng | 0.997 | 0.985 | 0.092 | 0.082 |
| 3 | concor*EPI*LAN_GER*lan_rom*lan_rus*lan_eng | 0.99 | 0.985 | 0.031 | 0.01 |
| | M1 | 0.997 | 0.994 | 0.216 | |

#### *B. Negative Outcome*

#### *15. Truth Table*

| | CONCOR | EPI | LAN_ GER | LAN_ ROM | LAN_ RUS | LAN_ ENG | OUT | n | incl | PRI | cases |
|---|---|---|---|---|---|---|---|---|---|---|---|
| 1 | 0 | 0 | 0 | 0 | 0 | 0 | 0 | 5 | 0.735 | 0.413 | BIH,MKD,MNE,SRB,TTO |
| 2 | 0 | 0 | 0 | 0 | 0 | 1 | 0 | 1 | 0.498 | 0.201 | JAM |
| 3 | 0 | 0 | 0 | 0 | 1 | 0 | 1 | 2 | 1 | 1 | MDA,UKR |
| 5 | 0 | 0 | 0 | 1 | 0 | 0 | 0 | 5 | 0.646 | 0.372 | HND,CHL,NIC,PAN,URY |
| 17 | 0 | 1 | 0 | 0 | 0 | 0 | 0 | 12 | 0.521 | 0.146 | BEL,BGR,CZE,DNK,FIN,GRC,ISL,LUX,NLD,N OR,ROU,SWE |
| 18 | 0 | 1 | 0 | 0 | 0 | 1 | 0 | 4 | 0.336 | 0 | CAN,GBR,IRL,USA |
| 19 | 0 | 1 | 0 | 0 | 1 | 0 | 0 | 2 | 0.785 | 0.015 | EST,RUS |
| 25 | 0 | 1 | 1 | 0 | 0 | 0 | 0 | 1 | 0.34 | 0.015 | CHE |
| 33 | 1 | 0 | 0 | 0 | 0 | 0 | 1 | 2 | 1 | 1 | ALB,ARG |
| 37 | 1 | 0 | 0 | 1 | 0 | 0 | 1 | 11 | 1 | 1 | BOL,BRA,COL,DOM,ECU,GTM,MEX,PER,PR Y,SLV,VEN |
| 49 | 1 | 1 | 0 | 0 | 0 | 0 | 0 | 7 | 0.824 | 0.511 | HRV,ITA,LTU,MLT,POL,SVK,SVN |
| 51 | 1 | 1 | 0 | 0 | 1 | 0 | 1 | 1 | 1 | 1 | LVA |
| 53 | 1 | 1 | 0 | 1 | 0 | 0 | 0 | 4 | 0.802 | 0.559 | CRI,ESP,FRA,PRT |
| 57 | 1 | 1 | 1 | 0 | 0 | 0 | 0 | 3 | 0.333 | 0.2 | AUT,DEU,HUN |

### *16. QCA Minimisation Using the Enhanced Quine–McCluskey Algorithm*

| *n* | OUT = 1/0/C: 16/44/0 | | | | |
|---|---|---|---|---|---|
| | Total: 60 | | | | |
| | | incl | PRI | cov.r | cov.u |
| 1 | CONCOR*epi*lan_ger*lan_rus*lan_eng | 1 | 1 | 0.407 | 0.371 |
| 2 | concor*epi*lan_ger*lan_rom*LAN_RUS*lan_eng | 1 | 1 | 0.096 | 0.06 |
| 3 | CONCOR*EPI*lan_ger*lan_rom*LAN_RUS*lan_eng | 1 | 1 | 0.047 | 0.011 |
| | M1 | 1 | 1 | 0.478 | |

## 4.2.5 Ethnicities and Competitiveness

### *A. Positive Outcome*

### *17. Truth Table*

| | CONCOR | EPI | WHITE | LATINO | MESTIZO | NON_ WHITE | OUT | n | incl | PRI | cases |
|---|---|---|---|---|---|---|---|---|---|---|---|
| 2 | 0 | 0 | 0 | 0 | 0 | 1 | 0 | 2 | 0.823 | 0.382 | JAM,TTO |
| 4 | 0 | 0 | 0 | 0 | 1 | 1 | 0 | 3 | 0.76 | 0.381 | CHL,NIC,PAN |
| 5 | 0 | 0 | 0 | 1 | 0 | 0 | 1 | 1 | 0.868 | 0 | UKR |
| 6 | 0 | 0 | 0 | 1 | 0 | 1 | 0 | 1 | 0.8 | 0 | BIH |
| 9 | 0 | 0 | 1 | 0 | 0 | 0 | 0 | 5 | 0.834 | 0.602 | HND,MDA,MKD,SRB,URY |
| 13 | 0 | 0 | 1 | 1 | 0 | 0 | 1 | 1 | 0.917 | 0.5 | MNE |
| 17 | 0 | 1 | 0 | 0 | 0 | 0 | 1 | 1 | 1 | 1 | DNK |
| 25 | 0 | 1 | 1 | 0 | 0 | 0 | 1 | 18 | 0.938 | 0.891 | BEL,BGR,CAN,CZE,EST,FIN,GBR,GRC,CHE,IRL,ISL,LUX,NLD,NOR,ROU,RUS,SWE,USA |
| 34 | 1 | 0 | 0 | 0 | 0 | 1 | 0 | 3 | 0.578 | 0 | BOL,DOM,PER |
| 36 | 1 | 0 | 0 | 0 | 1 | 1 | 0 | 5 | 0.417 | 0 | COL,ECU,MEX,PRY,SLV |
| 37 | 1 | 0 | 0 | 1 | 0 | 0 | 0 | 1 | 0.333 | 0 | VEN |
| 41 | 1 | 0 | 1 | 0 | 0 | 0 | 0 | 2 | 0.813 | 0.389 | ALB,ARG |
| 42 | 1 | 0 | 1 | 0 | 0 | 1 | 0 | 2 | 0.714 | 0.2 | BRA,GTM |
| 49 | 1 | 1 | 0 | 0 | 0 | 0 | 0 | 4 | 0.784 | 0.565 | FRA,ITA,MLT,PRT |
| 53 | 1 | 1 | 0 | 1 | 0 | 0 | 0 | 1 | 0.596 | 0.323 | ESP |
| 57 | 1 | 1 | 1 | 0 | 0 | 0 | 0 | 10 | 0.731 | 0.459 | AUT,CRI,DEU,HRV,HUN,LTU,LVA,POL,SVK,SVN |

### *18. QCA Minimisation Using the Enhanced Quine–McCluskey Algorithm*

| n | OUT = 1/0/C: 21/39/0 | | | | |
|---|---|---|---|---|---|
| | Total: 60 | | | | |
| | | incl | PRI | cov.r | cov.u |
| 1 | concor*epi*LATINO*mestizo*non_white | 0.863 | 0.327 | 0.133 | 0.021 |
| 2 | concor*EPI*latino*mestizo*non_white | 0.944 | 0.904 | 0.546 | 0.433 |
| | M1 | 0.913 | 0.851 | 0.566 | |

## *B. Negative Outcome*

### *19. Truth Table*

| | CONCOR | EPI | WHITE | LATINO | MESTIZO | NON_ WHITE | OUT | n | incl | PRI | cases |
|---|---|---|---|---|---|---|---|---|---|---|---|
| 2 | 0 | 0 | 0 | 0 | 0 | 1 | 0 | 2 | 0.891 | 0.618 | JAM,TTO |
| 4 | 0 | 0 | 0 | 0 | 1 | 1 | 0 | 3 | 0.85 | 0.613 | CHL,NIC,PAN |
| 5 | 0 | 0 | 0 | 1 | 0 | 0 | 1 | 1 | 1 | 1 | UKR |
| 6 | 0 | 0 | 0 | 1 | 0 | 1 | 1 | 1 | 1 | 1 | BIH |
| 9 | 0 | 0 | 1 | 0 | 0 | 0 | 0 | 5 | 0.749 | 0.398 | HND,MDA,MKD,SRB,URY |
| 13 | 0 | 0 | 1 | 1 | 0 | 0 | 1 | 1 | 0.917 | 0.5 | MNE |
| 17 | 0 | 1 | 0 | 0 | 0 | 0 | 0 | 1 | 0.623 | 0 | DNK |
| 25 | 0 | 1 | 1 | 0 | 0 | 0 | 0 | 18 | 0.493 | 0.107 | BEL,BGR,CAN,CZE,EST,FIN,GBR,GRC,CHE,IRL,ISL,LUX,NLD,NOR,ROU,RUS,SWE,USA |
| 34 | 1 | 0 | 0 | 0 | 0 | 1 | 1 | 3 | 1 | 1 | BOL,DOM,PER |
| 36 | 1 | 0 | 0 | 0 | 1 | 1 | 1 | 5 | 1 | 1 | COL,ECU,MEX,PRY,SLV |
| 37 | 1 | 0 | 0 | 1 | 0 | 0 | 1 | 1 | 1 | 1 | VEN |
| 41 | 1 | 0 | 1 | 0 | 0 | 0 | 0 | 2 | 0.881 | 0.611 | ALB,ARG |
| 42 | 1 | 0 | 1 | 0 | 0 | 1 | 1 | 2 | 0.929 | 0.8 | BRA,GTM |
| 49 | 1 | 1 | 0 | 0 | 0 | 0 | 0 | 4 | 0.648 | 0.291 | FRA,ITA,MLT,PRT |
| 53 | 1 | 1 | 0 | 1 | 0 | 0 | 0 | 1 | 0.602 | 0.333 | ESP |
| 57 | 1 | 1 | 1 | 0 | 0 | 0 | 0 | 10 | 0.772 | 0.541 | AUT,CRI,DEU,HRV,HUN,LTU,LVA,POL,SVK,SVN |

### *20. QCA Minimisation Using the Enhanced Quine–McCluskey Algorithm*

| *n* | OUT = 1/0/C: 14/46/0 | | | | |
|---|---|---|---|---|---|
| | Total: 60 | | | | |
| | | incl | PRI | cov.r | cov.u |
| 1 | concor*epi*LATINO*mestizo*non_white | 0.934 | 0.673 | 0.167 | 0.059 |
| 2 | CONCOR*epi*latino*mestizo*NON_WHITE | 0.945 | 0.877 | 0.203 | 0.047 |
| 3 | concor*epi*white*LATINO*mestizo | 1 | 1 | 0.119 | 0.011 |
| 4 | CONCOR*epi*white*latino*NON_WHITE | 1 | 1 | 0.225 | 0.082 |
| 5 | epi*white*LATINO*mestizo*non_white | 1 | 1 | 0.119 | 0.012 |
| | M1 | 0.951 | 0.895 | 0.463 | |

## 4.3 Truth Tables and "QCA Minimisation Using the Enhanced Quine–McCluskey Algorithm" for Outcome *Corruption*

### 4.3.1 Predominant Religion (Proportion of Adherents) and Corruption

*A. Positive Outcome*

*21. Truth Table*

| | CONCOR | EPI | DOM_CAT | DOM_PROT | DOM_ORT | OUT | n | incl | PRI | cases |
|---|---|---|---|---|---|---|---|---|---|---|
| 1 | 0 | 0 | 0 | 0 | 0 | 0 | 1 | 0.865 | 0.675 | BIH |
| 2 | 0 | 0 | 0 | 0 | 1 | 0 | 5 | 0.574 | 0 | MDA,MKD,MNE,SRB,UKR |
| 3 | 0 | 0 | 0 | 1 | 0 | 0 | 4 | 0.798 | 0.6 | GUY,JAM,SUR,TTO |
| 5 | 0 | 0 | 1 | 0 | 0 | 0 | 3 | 0.831 | 0.674 | CUB,CHL,URY |
| 7 | 0 | 0 | 1 | 1 | 0 | 0 | 3 | 0.721 | 0.463 | HND,NIC,PAN |
| 9 | 0 | 1 | 0 | 0 | 0 | 1 | 1 | 0.911 | 0.769 | CZE |
| 10 | 0 | 1 | 0 | 0 | 1 | 0 | 5 | 0.65 | 0.122 | BGR,BLR,GRC,ROU,RUS |
| 11 | 0 | 1 | 0 | 1 | 0 | 1 | 11 | 0.958 | 0.934 | CAN,DNK,EST,FIN,GBR,CHE,ISL,NLD,NOR,SWE,USA |
| 13 | 0 | 1 | 1 | 0 | 0 | 0 | 3 | 0.879 | 0.733 | BEL,IRL,LUX |
| 17 | 1 | 0 | 0 | 0 | 0 | 0 | 1 | 0.83 | 0.496 | ALB |
| 21 | 1 | 0 | 1 | 0 | 0 | 0 | 7 | 0.598 | 0.142 | ARG,COL,ECU,MEX,PER,PRY,VEN |
| 23 | 1 | 0 | 1 | 1 | 0 | 0 | 6 | 0.561 | 0.154 | BOL,BRA,DOM,GTM,HTI,SLV |
| 27 | 1 | 1 | 0 | 1 | 0 | 1 | 2 | 1 | 1 | DEU,LVA |
| 29 | 1 | 1 | 1 | 0 | 0 | 0 | 11 | 0.849 | 0.677 | AUT,ESP,FRA,HRV,ITA,LTU,MLT,POL,PRT,SVK,SVN |
| 31 | 1 | 1 | 1 | 1 | 0 | 0 | 2 | 0.818 | 0.496 | CRI,HUN |

*22. QCA Minimisation Using the Enhanced Quine–McCluskey Algorithm*

| *n* | OUT = 1/0/C: 14/51/0 | | | | |
|---|---|---|---|---|---|
| | Total: 65 | | | | |
| | | incl | PRI | cov.r | cov.u |
| 1 | concor*EPI*dom_cat*dom_ort | 0.943 | 0.907 | 0.487 | 0.049 |
| 2 | EPI*dom_cat*DOM_PROT*dom_ort | 0.962 | 0.941 | 0.475 | 0.038 |
| | M1 | 0.947 | 0.917 | 0.525 | |

## *B. Negative Outcome*

### *23. Truth Table*

| | CONCOR | EPI | DOM_CAT | DOM_PROT | DOM_ORT | OUT | n | incl | PRI | cases |
|---|---|---|---|---|---|---|---|---|---|---|
| 1 | 0 | 0 | 0 | 0 | 0 | 0 | 1 | 0.718 | 0.325 | BIH |
| 2 | 0 | 0 | 0 | 0 | 1 | 1 | 5 | 1 | 1 | MDA,MKD,MNE,SRB,UKR |
| 3 | 0 | 0 | 0 | 1 | 0 | 0 | 4 | 0.698 | 0.4 | GUY,JAM,SUR,TTO |
| 5 | 0 | 0 | 1 | 0 | 0 | 0 | 3 | 0.65 | 0.326 | CUB,CHL,URY |
| 7 | 0 | 0 | 1 | 1 | 0 | 0 | 3 | 0.76 | 0.537 | HND,NIC,PAN |
| 9 | 0 | 1 | 0 | 0 | 0 | 0 | 1 | 0.704 | 0.231 | CZE |
| 10 | 0 | 1 | 0 | 0 | 1 | 1 | 5 | 0.952 | 0.878 | BGR,BLR,GRC,ROU,RUS |
| 11 | 0 | 1 | 0 | 1 | 0 | 0 | 11 | 0.417 | 0.066 | CAN,DNK,EST,FIN,GBR,CHE,ISL,NLD,NOR,SWE,USA |
| 13 | 0 | 1 | 1 | 0 | 0 | 0 | 3 | 0.668 | 0.267 | BEL,IRL,LUX |
| 17 | 1 | 0 | 0 | 0 | 0 | 0 | 1 | 0.833 | 0.504 | ALB |
| 21 | 1 | 0 | 1 | 0 | 0 | 1 | 7 | 0.933 | 0.858 | ARG,COL,ECU,MEX,PER,PRY,VEN |
| 23 | 1 | 0 | 1 | 1 | 0 | 1 | 6 | 0.92 | 0.846 | BOL,BRA,DOM,GTM,HTI,SLV |
| 27 | 1 | 1 | 0 | 1 | 0 | 0 | 2 | 0.64 | 0 | DEU,LVA |
| 29 | 1 | 1 | 1 | 0 | 0 | 0 | 11 | 0.632 | 0.213 | AUT,ESP,FRA,HRV,ITA,LTU,MLT,POL,PRT,SVK,SVN |
| 31 | 1 | 1 | 1 | 1 | 0 | 0 | 2 | 0.821 | 0.504 | CRI,HUN |

### *24. QCA Minimisation Using the Enhanced Quine–McCluskey Algorithm*

| *n* | OUT = 1/0/C: 23/42/0 | | | | |
|---|---|---|---|---|---|
| | Total: 65 | | | | |
| | | incl | PRI | cov.r | cov.u |
| 1 | concor*dom_cat*dom_prot*DOM_ORT | 0.893 | 0.802 | 0.275 | 0.253 |
| 2 | CONCOR*epi*DOM_CAT*dom_ort | 0.944 | 0.899 | 0.375 | 0.353 |
| | M1 | 0.92 | 0.857 | 0.628 | |

## 4.3.2 State Religion and Corruption

### *A. Positive Outcome*

### *25. Truth Table*

| | CONCOR | EPI | ST_ CATHOL | ST_ PROTEST | ST_ MUSLIM | OUT | n | incl | PRI | cases |
|---|---|---|---|---|---|---|---|---|---|---|
| 1 | 0 | 0 | 0 | 0 | 0 | 0 | 12 | 0.568 | 0.279 | BIH,GUY,JAM,MDA,MKD,MNE,NIC,SRB,SUR,TTO,UKR,URY |
| 5 | 0 | 0 | 1 | 0 | 0 | 0 | 4 | 0.695 | 0.43 | CUB,HND,CHL,PAN |
| 9 | 0 | 1 | 0 | 0 | 0 | 0 | 12 | 0.781 | 0.606 | BEL,BGR,BLR,CAN,CZE,EST,GRC,CHE,NLD,ROU,RUS,USA |
| 11 | 0 | 1 | 0 | 1 | 0 | 1 | 6 | 1 | 1 | DNK,FIN,GBR,ISL,NOR,SWE |
| 13 | 0 | 1 | 1 | 0 | 0 | 0 | 2 | 0.824 | 0.571 | IRL,LUX |
| 17 | 1 | 0 | 0 | 0 | 0 | 0 | 2 | 0.705 | 0.407 | ECU,MEX |
| 18 | 1 | 0 | 0 | 0 | 1 | 0 | 1 | 0.5 | 0 | ALB |
| 21 | 1 | 0 | 1 | 0 | 0 | 0 | 11 | 0.408 | 0 | ARG,BOL,BRA,COL,DOM,GTM,HTI,PER,PRY,SLV,VEN |
| 25 | 1 | 1 | 0 | 0 | 0 | 1 | 7 | 0.938 | 0.898 | AUT,DEU,FRA,HUN,LVA,POL,SVK |
| 29 | 1 | 1 | 1 | 0 | 0 | 0 | 8 | 0.82 | 0.605 | CRI,ESP,HRV,ITA,LTU,MLT,PRT,SVN |

### *26. QCA Minimisation Using the Enhanced Quine–McCluskey Algorithm*

| *n* | OUT = 1/0/C: 13/52/0 | | | | |
|---|---|---|---|---|---|
| | Total: 65 | | | | |
| | | incl | PRI | cov.r | cov.u |
| 1 | concor*EPI*st_cathol*ST_PROTEST*st_muslim | 1 | 1 | 0.153 | 0.153 |
| 2 | CONCOR*EPI*st_cathol*st_protest*st_muslim | 0.938 | 0.898 | 0.142 | 0.142 |
| | M1 | 0.969 | 0.961 | 0.295 | |

### *B. Negative Outcome*

### *27. Truth Table*

| | CONCOR | EPI | ST_ CATHOL | ST_ PROTEST | ST_ MUSLIM | OUT | n | incl | PRI | cases |
|---|---|---|---|---|---|---|---|---|---|---|
| 1 | 0 | 0 | 0 | 0 | 0 | 0 | 12 | 0.809 | 0.682 | BIH,GUY,JAM,MDA,MKD,MNE,NIC,SRB,SUR,TTO,UKR,URY |
| 5 | 0 | 0 | 1 | 0 | 0 | 0 | 4 | 0.767 | 0.564 | CUB,HND,CHL,PAN |
| 9 | 0 | 1 | 0 | 0 | 0 | 0 | 12 | 0.637 | 0.349 | BEL,BGR,BLR,CAN,CZE,EST,GRC,CHE,NLD,ROU,RUS,USA |
| 11 | 0 | 1 | 0 | 1 | 0 | 0 | 6 | 0 | 0 | DNK,FIN,GBR,ISL,NOR,SWE |
| 13 | 0 | 1 | 1 | 0 | 0 | 0 | 2 | 0.766 | 0.429 | IRL,LUX |
| 17 | 1 | 0 | 0 | 0 | 0 | 0 | 2 | 0.798 | 0.593 | ECU,MEX |
| 18 | 1 | 0 | 0 | 0 | 1 | 1 | 1 | 1 | 1 | ALB |
| 21 | 1 | 0 | 1 | 0 | 0 | 1 | 11 | 1 | 1 | ARG,BOL,BRA,COL,DOM,GTM,HTI,PER,PRY,SLV,VEN |
| 25 | 1 | 1 | 0 | 0 | 0 | 0 | 7 | 0.447 | 0.102 | AUT,DEU,FRA,HUN,LVA,POL,SVK |
| 29 | 1 | 1 | 1 | 0 | 0 | 0 | 8 | 0.65 | 0.234 | CRI,ESP,HRV,ITA,LTU,MLT,PRT,SVN |

### *28. QCA Minimisation Using the Enhanced Quine–McCluskey Algorithm*

| *n* | OUT = 1/0/C: 12/53/0 | | | | |
|---|---|---|---|---|---|
| | Total: 65 | | | | |
| | | incl | PRI | cov.r | cov.u |
| 1 | CONCOR*epi*st_cathol*st_protest*ST_MUSLIM | 1 | 1 | 0.022 | 0.022 |
| 2 | CONCOR*epi*ST_CATHOL*st_protest*st_muslim | 1 | 1 | 0.298 | 0.298 |
| | M1 | 1 | 1 | 0.32 | |

## 4.3.3 Legal Origin and Corruption

### *A. Positive Outcome*

Conditions for low corruption

### *29. Truth Table*

| | CONCOR | ENGLISH | SOCIALIST | FRENCH | GERMAN | SCANDIN | EPI | OUT | n | incl | PRI | cases |
|---|---|---|---|---|---|---|---|---|---|---|---|---|
| 4 | 0 | 0 | 0 | 0 | 0 | 1 | 1 | 1 | 5 | 1 | 1 | DNK,FIN,NOR,SWE,ISL |
| 6 | 0 | 0 | 0 | 0 | 1 | 0 | 1 | 1 | 1 | 1 | 1 | CHE |
| 9 | 0 | 0 | 0 | 1 | 0 | 0 | 0 | 0 | 6 | 0.592 | 0.369 | HND,NIC,PAN,URY,CHL,SUR |
| 10 | 0 | 0 | 0 | 1 | 0 | 0 | 1 | 0 | 4 | 0.783 | 0.583 | BEL,GRC,NLD,LUX |
| 17 | 0 | 0 | 1 | 0 | 0 | 0 | 0 | 0 | 5 | 0.614 | 0.105 | MDA,MKD,UKR,BIH,CUB |
| 18 | 0 | 0 | 1 | 0 | 0 | 0 | 1 | 0 | 6 | 0.697 | 0.293 | BLR,BGR,CZE,EST,RUS,ROU |
| 33 | 0 | 1 | 0 | 0 | 0 | 0 | 0 | 0 | 3 | 0.697 | 0.571 | JAM,TTO,GUY |
| 34 | 0 | 1 | 0 | 0 | 0 | 0 | 1 | 1 | 4 | 1 | 1 | IRL,GBR,CAN,USA |
| 70 | 1 | 0 | 0 | 0 | 1 | 0 | 1 | 1 | 2 | 1 | 1 | AUT,DEU |
| 73 | 1 | 0 | 0 | 1 | 0 | 0 | 0 | 0 | 13 | 0.344 | 0 | DOM,MEX,SLV,GTM,HTI,BRA,COL,ECU,PER,ARG,BOL,PRY,VEN |
| 74 | 1 | 0 | 0 | 1 | 0 | 0 | 1 | 0 | 6 | 0.767 | 0.49 | FRA,ITA,PRT,ESP,MLT,CRI |
| 81 | 1 | 0 | 1 | 0 | 0 | 0 | 0 | 0 | 1 | 0.878 | 0 | ALB |
| 82 | 1 | 0 | 1 | 0 | 0 | 0 | 1 | 1 | 7 | 1 | 1 | HRV,HUN,LVA,LTU,POL,SVK,SVN |

### *30. QCA Minimisation Using the Enhanced Quine–McCluskey Algorithm*

| *n* | OUT = 1/0/C: 19/44/0 | | | | |
|---|---|---|---|---|---|
| | Total: 63 | | | | |
| | | incl | PRI | cov.r | cov.u |
| 1 | english*socialist*french*GERMAN*scandin*EPI | 1 | 1 | 0.058 | 0.058 |
| 2 | concor*english*socialist*french*german*SCANDIN*EPI | 1 | 1 | 0.136 | 0.136 |
| 3 | concor*ENGLISH*socialist*french*german*scandin*EPI | 1 | 1 | 0.106 | 0.106 |
| 4 | CONCOR*english*SOCIALIST*french*german*scandin*EPI | 1 | 1 | 0.145 | 0.145 |
| | M1 | 1 | 1 | 0.446 | |

## *B. Negative Outcome*

Conditions for high corruption

### *31. Truth Table*

| | CONCOR | ENGLISH | SOCIALIST | FRENCH | GERMAN | SCANDIN | EPI | OUT | n | incl | PRI | cases |
|---|---|---|---|---|---|---|---|---|---|---|---|---|
| 4 | 0 | 0 | 0 | 0 | 0 | 1 | 1 | 0 | 5 | 0 | 0 | DNK,FIN,NOR,SWE,ISL |
| 6 | 0 | 0 | 0 | 0 | 1 | 0 | 1 | 0 | 1 | 0 | 0 | CHE |
| 9 | 0 | 0 | 0 | 1 | 0 | 0 | 0 | 0 | 6 | 0.76 | 0.629 | HND,NIC,PAN,URY,CHL,SUR |
| 10 | 0 | 0 | 0 | 1 | 0 | 0 | 1 | 0 | 4 | 0.696 | 0.417 | BEL,GRC,NLD,LUX |
| 17 | 0 | 0 | 1 | 0 | 0 | 0 | 0 | 1 | 5 | 0.907 | 0.784 | MDA,MKD,UKR,BIH,CUB |
| 18 | 0 | 0 | 1 | 0 | 0 | 0 | 1 | 0 | 6 | 0.83 | 0.604 | BLR,BGR,CZE,EST,RUS,ROU |
| 33 | 0 | 1 | 0 | 0 | 0 | 0 | 0 | 0 | 3 | 0.596 | 0.429 | JAM,TTO,GUY |
| 34 | 0 | 1 | 0 | 0 | 0 | 0 | 1 | 0 | 4 | 0.273 | 0 | IRL,GBR,CAN,USA |
| 70 | 1 | 0 | 0 | 0 | 1 | 0 | 1 | 0 | 2 | 0 | 0 | AUT,DEU |
| 73 | 1 | 0 | 0 | 1 | 0 | 0 | 0 | 1 | 13 | 1 | 1 | DOM,MEX,SLV,GTM,HTI,BRA,COL,ECU,PER,ARG,BOL,PRY,VEN |
| 74 | 1 | 0 | 0 | 1 | 0 | 0 | 1 | 0 | 6 | 0.698 | 0.337 | FRA,ITA,PRT,ESP,MLT,CRI |
| 81 | 1 | 0 | 1 | 0 | 0 | 0 | 0 | 1 | 1 | 1 | 1 | ALB |
| 82 | 1 | 0 | 1 | 0 | 0 | 0 | 1 | 0 | 7 | 0.547 | 0 | HRV,HUN,LVA,LTU,POL,SVK,SVN |

### *32. QCA Minimisation Using the Enhanced Quine–McCluskey Algorithm*

| *n* | OUT = 1/0/C: 19/44/0 | | | | |
|---|---|---|---|---|---|
| | Total: 63 | | | | |
| | | incl | PRI | cov.r | cov.u |
| 1 | english*SOCIALIST*french*german*scandin*epi | 0.918 | 0.805 | 0.258 | 0.258 |
| 2 | CONCOR*english*socialist*FRENCH*german*scandin*epi | 1 | 1 | 0.334 | 0.334 |
| | M1 | 0.963 | 0.932 | 0.592 | |

## 4.3.4 Languages and Corruption

### *A. Positive Outcome*

### *33. Truth Table*

| | CONCOR | EPI | LAN_GER | LAN_ENG | LAN_ROM | LAN_RUS | OUT | n | incl | PRI | cases |
|---|---|---|---|---|---|---|---|---|---|---|---|
| 1 | 0 | 0 | 0 | 0 | 0 | 0 | 0 | 6 | 0.717 | 0.471 | BIH,MKD,MNE,SRB,SUR,TTO |
| 2 | 0 | 0 | 0 | 0 | 0 | 1 | 0 | 2 | 0.443 | 0 | MDA,UKR |
| 3 | 0 | 0 | 0 | 0 | 1 | 0 | 0 | 6 | 0.657 | 0.515 | CUB,HND,CHL,NIC,PAN,URY |
| 5 | 0 | 0 | 0 | 1 | 0 | 0 | 0 | 2 | 0.798 | 0.713 | GUY,JAM |
| 17 | 0 | 1 | 0 | 0 | 0 | 0 | 1 | 12 | 0.903 | 0.845 | BEL,BGR,CZE,DNK,FIN,GRC,ISL,LUX,NLD,NOR,ROU,SWE |
| 18 | 0 | 1 | 0 | 0 | 0 | 1 | 0 | 3 | 0.547 | 0.162 | BLR,EST,RUS |
| 21 | 0 | 1 | 0 | 1 | 0 | 0 | 1 | 4 | 1 | 1 | CAN,GBR,IRL,USA |
| 25 | 0 | 1 | 1 | 0 | 0 | 0 | 1 | 1 | 1 | 1 | CHE |
| 33 | 1 | 0 | 0 | 0 | 0 | 0 | 0 | 2 | 0.782 | 0 | ALB,ARG |
| 35 | 1 | 0 | 0 | 0 | 1 | 0 | 0 | 12 | 0.307 | 0 | BOL,BRA,COL,DOM,ECU,GTM,HTI,MEX,PER,PRY,SLV,VEN |
| 49 | 1 | 1 | 0 | 0 | 0 | 0 | 1 | 7 | 0.955 | 0.872 | HRV,ITA,LTU,MLT,POL,SVK,SVN |
| 50 | 1 | 1 | 0 | 0 | 0 | 1 | 1 | 1 | 1 | 1 | LVA |
| 51 | 1 | 1 | 0 | 0 | 1 | 0 | 0 | 4 | 0.749 | 0.435 | CRI,ESP,FRA,PRT |
| 57 | 1 | 1 | 1 | 0 | 0 | 0 | 1 | 3 | 1 | 1 | AUT,DEU,HUN |

### *34. QCA Minimisation Using the Enhanced Quine–McCluskey Algorithm*

| *n* | OUT = 1/0/C: 28/37/0 | | | | |
|---|---|---|---|---|---|
| | Total: 65 | | | | |
| | | incl | PRI | cov.r | cov.u |
| 1 | EPI*lan_eng*lan_rom*lan_rus | 0.914 | 0.868 | 0.61 | 0.056 |
| 2 | CONCOR*EPI*lan_ger*lan_eng*lan_rom | 0.957 | 0.886 | 0.209 | 0.009 |
| 3 | concor*EPI*lan_ger*lan_rom*lan_rus | 0.913 | 0.861 | 0.496 | 0.056 |
| | M1 | 0.922 | 0.881 | 0.675 | |

### *B. Negative Outcome*

### *35. Truth Table*

| | CONCOR | EPI | LAN_GER | LAN_ENG | LAN_ROM | LAN_RUS | OUT | n | incl | PRI | cases |
|---|---|---|---|---|---|---|---|---|---|---|---|
| 1 | 0 | 0 | 0 | 0 | 0 | 0 | 0 | 6 | 0.721 | 0.478 | BIH,MKD,MNE,SRB,SUR,TTO |
| 2 | 0 | 0 | 0 | 0 | 0 | 1 | 1 | 2 | 1 | 1 | MDA,UKR |
| 3 | 0 | 0 | 0 | 0 | 1 | 0 | 0 | 6 | 0.634 | 0.482 | CUB,HND,CHL,NIC,PAN,URY |
| 5 | 0 | 0 | 0 | 1 | 0 | 0 | 0 | 2 | 0.497 | 0.287 | GUY,JAM |
| 17 | 0 | 1 | 0 | 0 | 0 | 0 | 0 | 12 | 0.471 | 0.155 | BEL,BGR,CZE,DNK,FIN,GRC,ISL,LUX,NLD,NOR,ROU,SWE |
| 18 | 0 | 1 | 0 | 0 | 0 | 1 | 1 | 3 | 0.912 | 0.838 | BLR,EST,RUS |
| 21 | 0 | 1 | 0 | 1 | 0 | 0 | 0 | 4 | 0.308 | 0 | CAN,GBR,IRL,USA |
| 25 | 0 | 1 | 1 | 0 | 0 | 0 | 0 | 1 | 0.34 | 0 | CHE |
| 33 | 1 | 0 | 0 | 0 | 0 | 0 | 1 | 2 | 1 | 1 | ALB,ARG |
| 35 | 1 | 0 | 0 | 0 | 1 | 0 | 1 | 12 | 1 | 1 | BOL,BRA,COL,DOM,ECU,GTM,HTI,MEX,PER,PRY,SLV,VEN |
| 49 | 1 | 1 | 0 | 0 | 0 | 0 | 0 | 7 | 0.693 | 0.128 | HRV,ITA,LTU,MLT,POL,SVK,SVN |
| 50 | 1 | 1 | 0 | 0 | 0 | 1 | 0 | 1 | 0.758 | 0 | LVA |
| 51 | 1 | 1 | 0 | 0 | 1 | 0 | 0 | 4 | 0.755 | 0.449 | CRI,ESP,FRA,PRT |
| 57 | 1 | 1 | 1 | 0 | 0 | 0 | 0 | 3 | 0.172 | 0 | AUT,DEU,HUN |

*36. QCA Minimisation Using the Enhanced Quine–McCluskey Algorithm*

| *n* | OUT = 1/0/C: 19/46/0 | | | | |
|---|---|---|---|---|---|
| | Total: 65 | | | | |
| | | incl | PRI | cov.r | cov.u |
| 1 | CONCOR*epi*lan_ger*lan_eng*lan_rus | 1 | 1 | 0.409 | 0.376 |
| 2 | concor*lan_ger*lan_eng*lan_rom*LAN_RUS | 0.869 | 0.804 | 0.143 | 0.11 |
| | M1 | 0.96 | 0.935 | 0.519 | |

## 4.3.5 Ethnicities and Corruption

*A. Positive Outcome*

*37. Truth Table*

| | CONCOR | EPI | WHITE | LATINO | MESTIZO | NON_WHITE | OUT | n | incl | PRI | cases |
|---|---|---|---|---|---|---|---|---|---|---|---|
| 2 | 0 | 0 | 0 | 0 | 0 | 1 | 0 | 4 | 0.643 | 0.194 | GUY,JAM,SUR,TTO |
| 4 | 0 | 0 | 0 | 0 | 1 | 1 | 0 | 3 | 0.636 | 0.158 | CHL,NIC,PAN |
| 5 | 0 | 0 | 0 | 1 | 0 | 0 | 0 | 1 | 0.496 | 0 | UKR |
| 6 | 0 | 0 | 0 | 1 | 0 | 1 | 0 | 1 | 0.6 | 0 | BIH |
| 9 | 0 | 0 | 1 | 0 | 0 | 0 | 0 | 6 | 0.766 | 0.594 | CUB,HND,MDA,MKD,SRB,URY |
| 13 | 0 | 0 | 1 | 1 | 0 | 0 | 0 | 1 | 0.769 | 0.25 | MNE |
| 17 | 0 | 1 | 0 | 0 | 0 | 0 | 0 | 1 | 0.824 | 0.626 | DNK |
| 25 | 0 | 1 | 1 | 0 | 0 | 0 | 1 | 19 | 0.852 | 0.783 | BEL,BGR,BLR,CAN,CZE,EST,FIN, GBR,GRC,CHE,IRL,ISL,LUX,NLD, NOR,ROU,RUS,SWE,USA |
| 34 | 1 | 0 | 0 | 0 | 0 | 1 | 0 | 4 | 0.396 | 0 | BOL,DOM,HTI,PER |
| 36 | 1 | 0 | 0 | 0 | 1 | 1 | 0 | 5 | 0.417 | 0 | COL,ECU,MEX,PRY,SLV |
| 37 | 1 | 0 | 0 | 1 | 0 | 0 | 0 | 1 | 0.333 | 0 | VEN |
| 41 | 1 | 0 | 1 | 0 | 0 | 0 | 0 | 2 | 0.764 | 0.335 | ALB,ARG |
| 42 | 1 | 0 | 1 | 0 | 0 | 1 | 0 | 2 | 0.643 | 0.167 | BRA,GTM |
| 49 | 1 | 1 | 0 | 0 | 0 | 0 | 0 | 4 | 0.784 | 0.561 | FRA,ITA,MLT,PRT |
| 53 | 1 | 1 | 0 | 1 | 0 | 0 | 0 | 1 | 0.596 | 0.323 | ESP |
| 57 | 1 | 1 | 1 | 0 | 0 | 0 | 1 | 10 | 0.923 | 0.855 | AUT,CRI,DEU,HRV,HUN,LTU,LVA ,POL,SVK,SVN |

*38. QCA Minimisation Using the Enhanced Quine–McCluskey Algorithm*

| *n* | OUT = 1/0/C: 29/36/0 | | | | |
|---|---|---|---|---|---|
| | Total: 65 | | | | |
| | | incl | PRI | cov.r | cov.u |
| 1 | EPI*WHITE*latino*mestizo*non_white | 0.874 | 0.818 | 0.598 | – |
| | M1 | 0.874 | 0.818 | 0.598 | |

## *B. Negative Outcome*

## *39. Truth Table*

| | CONCOR | EPI | WHITE | LATINO | MESTIZO | NON_ WHITE | OUT | n | incl | PRI | cases |
|---|---|---|---|---|---|---|---|---|---|---|---|
| 2 | 0 | 0 | 0 | 0 | 0 | 1 | 1 | 4 | 0.914 | 0.806 | GUY,JAM,SUR,TTO |
| 4 | 0 | 0 | 0 | 0 | 1 | 1 | 1 | 3 | 0.929 | 0.837 | CHL,NIC,PAN |
| 5 | 0 | 0 | 0 | 1 | 0 | 0 | 1 | 1 | 1 | 1 | UKR |
| 6 | 0 | 0 | 0 | 1 | 0 | 1 | 1 | 1 | 1 | 1 | BIH |
| 9 | 0 | 0 | 1 | 0 | 0 | 0 | 0 | 6 | 0.657 | 0.405 | CUB,HND,MDA,MKD,SRB,URY |
| 13 | 0 | 0 | 1 | 1 | 0 | 0 | 1 | 1 | 0.923 | 0.75 | MNE |
| 17 | 0 | 1 | 0 | 0 | 0 | 0 | 0 | 1 | 0.706 | 0.374 | DNK |
| 25 | 0 | 1 | 1 | 0 | 0 | 0 | 0 | 19 | 0.465 | 0.216 | BEL,BGR,BLR,CAN,CZE,EST,FIN, GBR,GRC,CHE,IRL,ISL,LUX,NLD, NOR,ROU,RUS,SWE,USA |
| 34 | 1 | 0 | 0 | 0 | 0 | 1 | 1 | 4 | 1 | 1 | BOL,DOM,HTI,PER |
| 36 | 1 | 0 | 0 | 0 | 1 | 1 | 1 | 5 | 1 | 1 | COL,ECU,MEX,PRY,SLV |
| 37 | 1 | 0 | 0 | 1 | 0 | 0 | 1 | 1 | 1 | 1 | VEN |
| 41 | 1 | 0 | 1 | 0 | 0 | 0 | 0 | 2 | 0.881 | 0.665 | ALB,ARG |
| 42 | 1 | 0 | 1 | 0 | 0 | 1 | 1 | 2 | 0.929 | 0.833 | BRA,GTM |
| 49 | 1 | 1 | 0 | 0 | 0 | 0 | 0 | 4 | 0.65 | 0.289 | FRA,ITA,MLT,PRT |
| 53 | 1 | 1 | 0 | 1 | 0 | 0 | 0 | 1 | 0.602 | 0.333 | ESP |
| 57 | 1 | 1 | 1 | 0 | 0 | 0 | 0 | 10 | 0.548 | 0.145 | AUT,CRI,DEU,HRV,HUN,LTU,LVA ,POL,SVK,SVN |

## *40. QCA Minimisation Using the Enhanced Quine–McCluskey Algorithm*

| *n* | OUT = 1/0/C: 22/43/0 | | | | | | |
|---|---|---|---|---|---|---|---|
| | Total: 65 | | | | | | |
| | | incl | PRI | cov.r | cov.u | (M1) | (M2) |
| 1 | epi*white*latino*NON_WHITE | 0.931 | 0.887 | 0.443 | 0.111 | 0.244 | 0.111 |
| 2 | concor*epi*LATINO*mestizo*non_white | 0.938 | 0.835 | 0.165 | 0.066 | 0.066 | 0.066 |
| 3 | CONCOR*epi*latino*mestizo*NON_WHITE | 0.953 | 0.918 | 0.22 | 0.044 | 0.044 | 0.044 |
| 4 | epi*white*LATINO*mestizo*non_white | 1 | 1 | 0.11 | 0.011 | 0.011 | 0.011 |
| 5 | concor*epi*white*LATINO*mestizo | 1 | 1 | 0.11 | 0 | 0.011 | |
| 6 | concor*epi*white*mestizo*NON_WHITE | 0.918 | 0.823 | 0.244 | 0 | | 0.011 |
| | M1 | 0.921 | 0.863 | 0.639 | | | |
| | M2 | 0.921 | 0.863 | 0.639 | | | |

# *5. QCA Appendix C. QCA Venn Diagrams of Outcome* Corruption

## 5.1 Predominant Religion (Proportion of Adherents) and Corruption

<table>
<tr><th>Positive outcome</th><th>Negative outcome</th></tr>
<tr><td>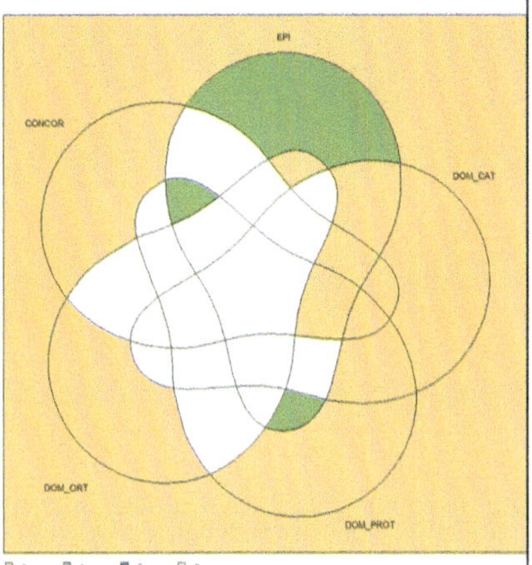
</td><td>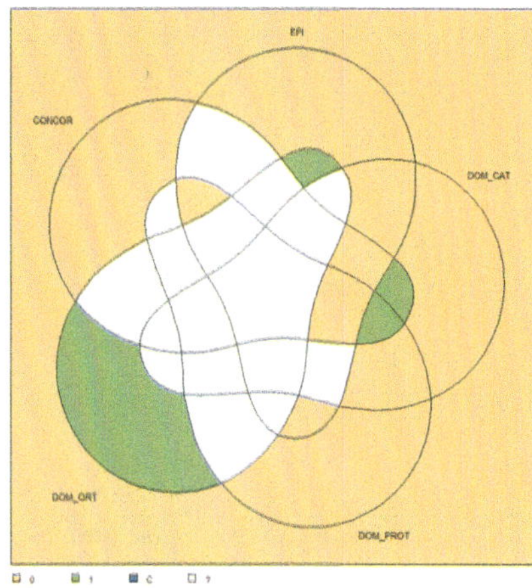
</td></tr>
<tr><td>High EPI and Protestant religion adherence are associated with lower corruption, especially if both are present.</td><td>Concordats in combination with Roman Catholic religion adherence increase corruption. Orthodox religion has a similar negative effect.</td></tr>
</table>

**Fig. A.1** Venn diagrams with positive and negative outcomes for *Corruption* with *Predominant Religion adherence* in Europe and the Americas (Source: Author's figure).

## 5.2 State Religion and Corruption

<table>
<tr><th>Positive outcome</th><th>Negative outcome</th></tr>
<tr><td>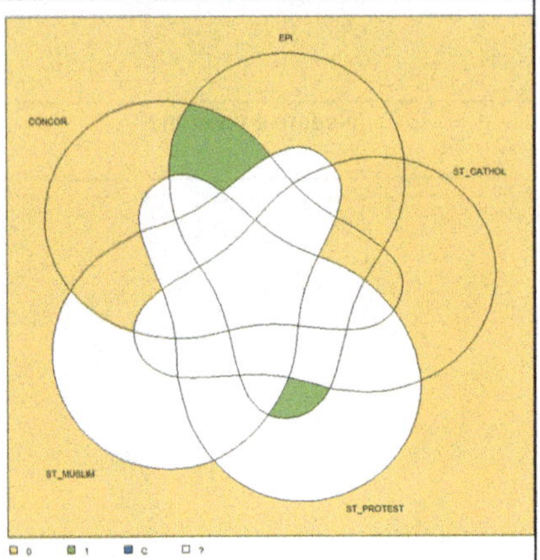
</td><td>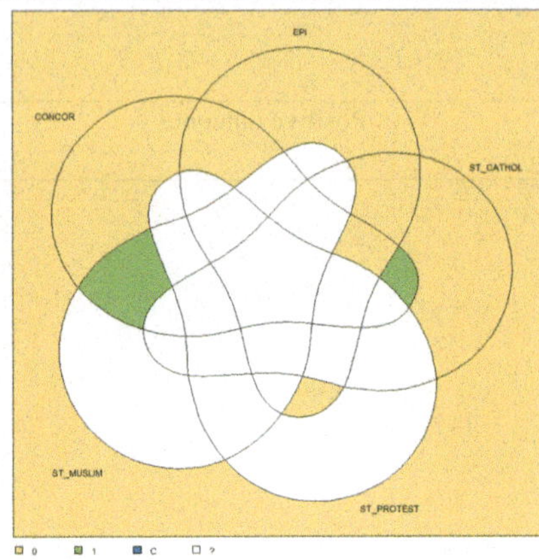
</td></tr>
<tr><td>EPI and Protestant State religion again have a positive effect, i.e. decrease corruption. The difference is that Concordats might also have a positive effect only in the absence of State Religion.</td><td>Groups of countries with high corruption indicate the substantial adverse effect of Concordats in combination with Roman Catholic State religion. Concordats combined with Roman Catholic or Muslim state religion have a negative effect, i.e. increase corruption.</td></tr>
</table>

**Fig. A.2** Venn diagrams with positive and negative outcomes for *Corruption* with *State Religion* in Europe and the Americas (Source: Author's figure)

## 5.3 Legal Origin and Corruption

*German* and *English legal origin* help reduce corruption, while *French* and *Socialist legal origins* and *Concordats* tend to increase corruption.

| Positive outcome | Negative outcome |
|---|---|
| 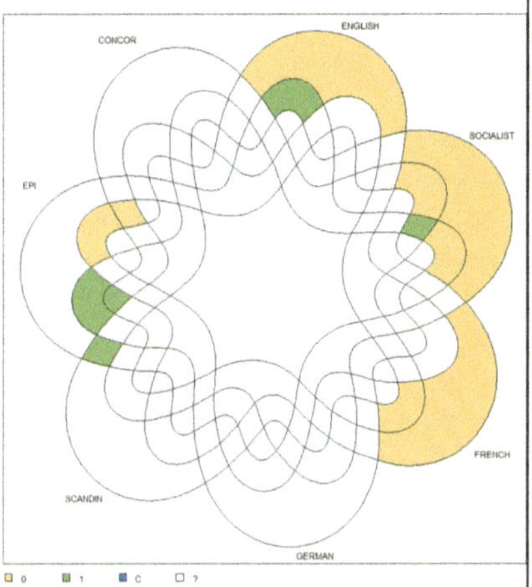 | 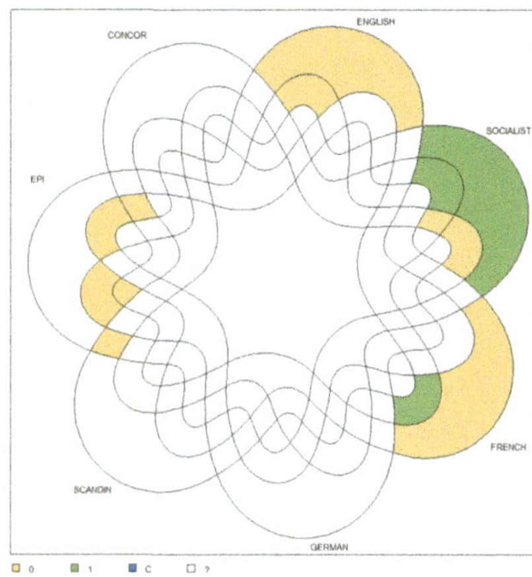 |
| All countries belonging to groups with *Scandinavian, German* and *English legal origins* have low *corruption* (and always high *EPI*). Countries with *Socialist legal origin* in combination with *Concordats* and high *EPI* tend to have low corruption. | Most countries with high corruption are of *French legal origin* and have high *Concordats*. This trend is robust (mainly caused by 13 Latin American countries).<br><br>No group with high *EPI* has high corruption. Also, countries with *Socialist legal origin* combined with low *EPI* tend to have higher *corruption*. |

**Fig. A.3** Venn diagrams with positive and negative outcomes for *Corruption* with *Legal Origin* in Europe and the Americas (Source: Author's figure)

The adverse effect of French and Socialist legal origins and Concordats disappears if a country has high EPI.

## 5.4 Languages and Corruption

| Positive outcome | Negative outcome |
|---|---|
| 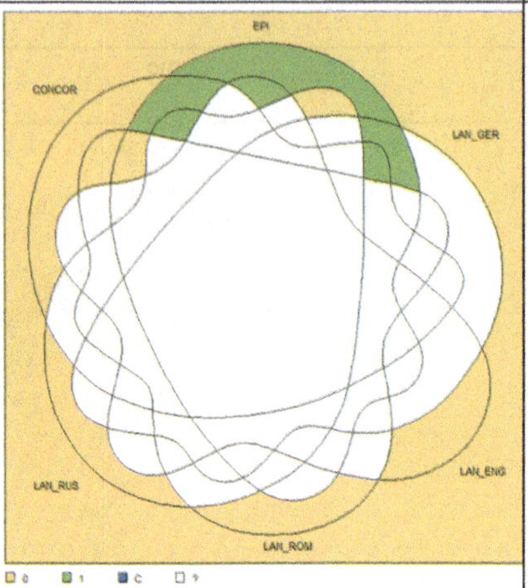  | 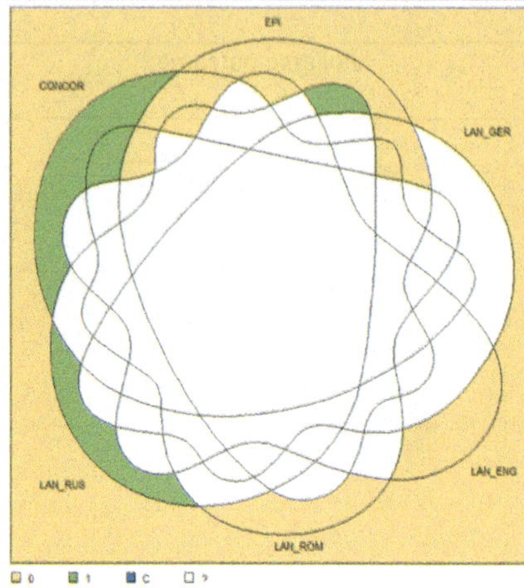  |
| Every country with low corruption has high *EPI*. The *German language* always leads to low corruption. Some of the *German*-speaking countries have high *concordats*. No country belonging to a group of *Roman language* has low corruption. Also, *Russian*-speaking countries, except for Lithuania, do have high corruption. | All countries belonging to groups with high *corruption* have low *EPI* (except for some Russian speaking countries). In general, the *Russian language* tends to lead to higher *corruption*. *German* and *English*-speaking countries, in general, do not have high *corruption*. High *EPI*, low *Roman*, low *English* and low *Russian* languages is a sufficient condition for low *corruption* (in this combination, *corruption* is undoubtedly low, although low *corruption* may be achieved in other ways). |

**Fig. A.4** Venn diagrams with positive and negative outcomes for *Corruption* with *Languages* in Europe and the Americas (Source: Author's figure)

The analysis of *languages* and *corruption* confirmed the results of the previous analysis: (1) a robust influence of *EPI* and *German language* on low *corruption* and (2) *Russian* and *Roman languages* are connected with higher *corruption*. Enough coverage also exists for a sufficient condition for low *corruption: high EPI, low Roman, low English* and *low Russian languages.*

## 5.5 Ethnicities and Corruption

| Positive outcome | Negative outcome |
|---|---|
| 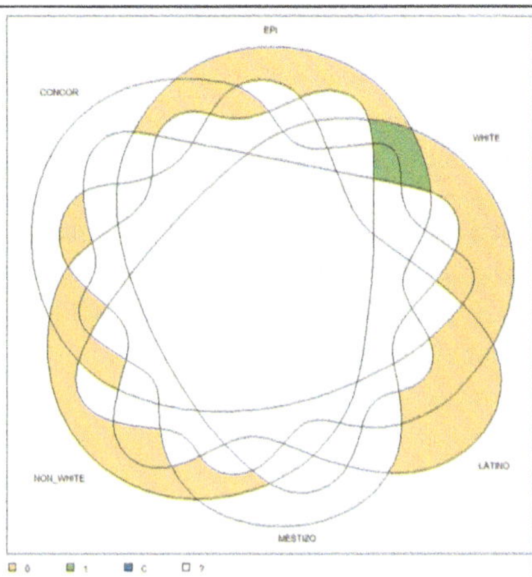 | 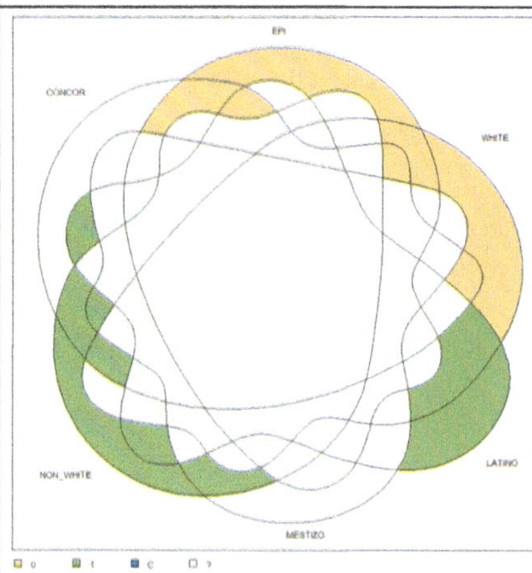 |
| High *EPI* and high *white* ethnicities in combination with both high and low Concordats leads to low corruption. A sufficient path to low corruption is high *EPI*, high *white*, low *Latino*, low *mestizo*, and low other *non-white* ethnicities. Low *corruption* may happen in other ways, but always occurs in this configuration. | Countries with high *corruption* almost never have predominantly *white* ethnicities, are often *non-white,* and always have low *EPI*. All predominantly *mestizo* countries have high corruption. The effect of other conditions is not evident. |

**Fig. A.5** Venn diagrams with positive and negative outcomes for *Corruption* with *Ethnicities* in Europe and the Americas (Source: Author's figure)

In the truth tables (Appendix 13.2), we can check the belonging of countries to different groups. Countries with similar conditions are often in the same groups, therefore, clusters and group selections have proven to work well.

## III. Researcher Identity Memo

*How my personal experience has shaped my research interests*

I have divided this memo into five parts (A, B, C, D, E) and thirteen stages to explain how each has influenced my beliefs and assumptions in relation to this study.

### *A. The Dark Ages*

Like 92% of Colombian adults, I was raised as a Roman Catholic without ever questioning why I was (or should be) Catholic. Interestingly, Colombia has the second highest proportion of adults raised as Roman Catholics worldwide while it is also one of the most unequal, corrupt, and violent countries.

#### 1. Childhood

I was born to middle-class parents in a very conservative town in Colombia. I was educated at a regional (and privileged) high school owned and administered exclusively by the Roman Catholic Church to this day (like most important educational centres in Colombia, where access to education is limited to the few).

In Colombia, people remember my hometown (Pasto) for opposing independence in favour of the Spanish Catholic monarchy. Such submissive subservience of the population to the Roman Catholic Church remains to some extent until today.

I had not met a single non-Roman Catholic until I was 15 years old. At school and at home, I learned that people who were not Catholics were "sons of the devil" and were dangerous.

I received a repressive education, especially at school. The guiding principle was that "it is forbidden to think beyond what is established". We were forced to attend mass at school and religious instruction was compulsory.

Nevertheless, the society in which I grew up accepts a set of values where "evil is good, and the one who cheats is a hero". Great respect and admiration existed for well-known gangsters, drug dealers and "cool criminals" among my classmates and neighbours.

Aside from this, I had some friends who practised "white magic rituals" with the saints worshipped in the Roman Catholic Church. I soon became involved in sorcery, as we believed these practices were "sacred". A few weeks later, one of my "magic friends" committed suicide with his girlfriend (and their baby). My life became miserable in every respect. It was determined by suffering, fear, superstition, ignorance, want, and disgrace.

Moreover, I was nearly kidnapped twice. The robbers threatened to kill me just to steal my watch or phone. I struggled a lot with evil people, bullying, ignorance, and criminality. There was so much about this repressive society that I simply failed to understand.

## *B. The Enlightenment*

### 2. Adolescence

Philosophers such as Nietzsche or Marx were unknown in my entire elementary and high school education. I was fortunate to meet a "crazy outsider", who introduced me to these philosophers, whose ideas opened up a completely new world to me at that time. I understood that like all those people who believe or follow a religion I had been deliberately manipulated with a "people's opium". As a result, I ended up declaring myself a complete materialist and atheist. I became a truth-seeker and embraced science and reason in search of a more coherent and rational framework of values.

This quest for knowledge freed me from most of my superstitions. I understood that the power of the mind could create all kinds of enchantments. There was no longer any such thing as witchcraft in my life, but only positive and negative energy. I became an advocate of scientific positivism. I began searching for explanations through science, which led me to move to Bogota (the capital) to pursue a scientific career in the natural sciences. My life started to change for the better. I had found the path to a better life. I firmly believed that nothing in my life would stop me from embracing my chosen materialistic and rationalistic perspective.

Bogota is an enormous city where people tend to be better educated and where services are better than in the rest of the country. I also realised that people were less fervent Catholics than in my hometown. In fact, not everybody was Catholic in Bogota's cosmopolitan environment. I discovered that not everybody admired Pablo Escobar and other criminals as heroes. Quite the opposite in fact. I also had to adapt my values to a more balanced and secular society where I had begun finding more like-minded people.

### 3. My Father's Crisis

I received news about my father, who had forged a successful career for himself as a singer after abandoning us. He had fallen into a profound depression and eventually ended up using all kinds of drugs. His state deteriorated drastically and he lost everything he had. He was admitted twice to rehabilitation clinics. After recovering, his situation grew even worse, until he ended up a homeless and begging for money in the streets. His addiction was extreme and lasted about a decade.

I was ashamed of my father and did not want to hear anything about him. At the same time, I was establishing my career and professional network. One day, my father was approached in the street by a Christian group (Protestant) and told him about Jesus. Miraculously, in only one day, he was completely and forever healed. This was unbelievable for all his relatives and friends as no doctor had managed to help him.

Soon, he joined a Christian (Protestant) Church and became a singer there. His life was wholly renewed, and he became a new and very faithful man. He looked for my mother and me to ask for forgiveness. My mother had forgiven him, but did not want to hear about him anymore. I was more hard-hearted and did not forgive him; I said that for me, he had already died years ago. I also mentioned that it was good that he had recovered from his addiction, but between being a drug addict and a fundamentalist Christian, his was the "least worse" option. This deeply saddened my father. He started to cry and prayed fervently and earnestly for my mother and me for about one year.

### 4. My Crisis

After haughtily rejecting my father, many strange things started to happen in my life during that year. One of the most important was that despite a successful career start and an extensive network I was—incredibly but true—unable to find a proper job. I started to feel what scarcity means. Nobody wanted to hire me, regardless of my impressive CV and professional network.

As a result, for nearly 2 years I subsisted on borrowing money from banks, friends, relatives, neighbours, etc. Having to pay off debts often made me feel desperate. I owed money to everyone I knew.

## *C. The Reformation*

### 5. The Paradigm Change

After nearly a decade of atheism, I met someone who suggested a business opportunity: selling quality environmental American products through a well-recognised, multi-level transnational corporation (Amway). The idea of selling sounded disgusting to me, but I did not have other income option, so I accepted the offer.

The company is very successful worldwide. It is based firmly on Calvinist values, which the company disseminates through its training programmes and literature. One of the principles they taught me was that for a business to be successful, it was essential to donate at least 10% of net profits to a charity or a philanthropic project. This made no sense to me at all, and I thought the idea was fundamentalist. I said I would be happy to give when I became a millionaire.

However, book after book written by successful entrepreneurs confirmed that giving came first and the quintessential prerequisite for success. This fundamental stance was even confirmed by an unlikely source: a highly respected professor from

MIT. I was impressed and convinced, and decided to start donating 50% of the net profits of my sales (although I was still paying off my debts).

Impressively, from the very first time I gave, I experienced a new and pleasant feeling, which encouraged me to keep on giving for the sole pleasure of doing it. Inexplicably, that month I started selling much more and began receiving vast amounts of money from different sources. By the end of the month, I had paid off all my debts.

## 6. An Experiment to Prove God's Existence

One of my clients was a devout Protestant Christian, and she was always speaking about Jesus. I listened, since I did not want to disappoint her, but still thought Evangelicals were crazy fundamentalists.

She challenged my atheism and asked me to do a rational experiment to prove the existence of God. The experiment involved kneeling down alone in my room and asking God whether he existed; he should give me a proof of his existence in a defined period of time. If nothing happened (as one could expect), I would continue my life as usual, but if I had an affirmative reply, I had to recognise his existence.

I accepted the challenge, and I did the experiment. I gave God one month to demonstrate his existence. After feeling ridiculous, after all I was talking to walls, I forgot about the experiment, and my life continued.

During that month, my profits soared. My cash flow increased substantially, and my debts decreased. Unexpectedly, I was offered my dream job (the salary was three times higher than my expectations!). Unbelievably, after much financial hardship, I bought my own flat. I was so impressed with how giving had worked and had solved my financial crisis!

Another client that month also happened to be a Protestant Christian and talked to me about God. I was not paying attention until she mentioned that the Bible states that we can prove the existence of God. She did not have to say so, as she was unaware of everything that was happening to me!

I asked where the Bible said so, as I had never adequately read its teaching. She replied that in Malachi 3:10 (*King James Bible*, 1769), the Lord says:

> Bring ye all the tithes into the storehouse, that there may be meat in mine house, and prove me now herewith, saith the LORD of hosts, if I will not open you the windows of heaven, and pour you out a blessing, that there shall not be room enough to receive it.

I could not believe these events had all happened in the same month in which I had asked for proof, and I had actually forgotten about it. I quickly went to search for a Bible, and when I found the corresponding passage, I was extremely impressed. It described what was what actually happening to me. I had been living a life of scarcity for nearly two years, not to mention the past hardships, and now I was receiving money and things to an extent I had never considered possible.

I knelt impressed and asked God to forgive my scepticism. All these changes had happened precisely in the same month that I asked God for proof of his existence! It was improbable that this change of fortune had happened by chance. These events would definitely impress any rational mind, like all of God's gifts!

I began reading the Bible and found that this book was alive, unlike any other book I had read. Everything I was reading in the Bible started to happen in my own life. My eyes were opened and I started to understand how life and the world work. I also gained insight into many mysteries that I would otherwise never have understood.

## 7. Reconciliation: Meeting My Father Again

Following the principles of the Bible improved my life more than I could ever have imagined. I started experiencing unlikely miracles every single day of my life.

One of the biblical principles that I repeatedly encountered was: *"Honour thy father and thy mother: that thy days may be long upon the land which the LORD thy God giveth thee"* (*King James Bible*, 1769, Exodus 20:12).

So I was amazed by the biblical promise of living longer if honouring one's parents. Realising how mercilessly I had behaved towards my father, I decided to travel to my hometown. I convinced my mother to come and visit my father to forgive him.

My suggestion pleased her very much, as she saw a renewed and faithful son. And so we went to my father's place! He was expecting us, came towards us, embraced us and cried. Our reunion was unbelievable!

My father exclaimed: "Glory to the Lord Jesus as He has listened to my prayers and crying and made the miracle I requested, that you two, come to my house and search me to forgive me".

## 8. Box of Blessings Unlocked

Ever since I started believing in God and following the biblical principles, all my dreams became true one after the other. It was like unlocking a large container of gifts and blessings that I had desired all my life!

Among many other miracles, I won two of the most prestigious scholarships to study in the United Kingdom and Switzerland, the countries of my dreams.

Then I understood how real Psalm 37:4 is: *"Delight thyself also in the LORD: and he shall give thee the desires of thine heart"* (*King James Bible*, 1769). I was also growing in understanding and wisdom.

*My studies in England*

In England, I had the opportunity to visit Lewes, a small town near London full of history. I attended a fair that reenacted how British people used to live in the Middle Ages. To my surprise, I felt like home there. It was pretty similar to how my parents and grandparents used to live in my Colombian hometown.

I immediately wondered how Colombia and England could feel that similar if they were so different geographically and culturally? I assumed that perhaps the only difference was time. I asked one of the experts at the fair how people in England had experienced the change from medieval times to a heavily industrialised country?

Her answer kindled my curiosity even more: "England was a country of peasants without education. It was not until the Reformers came and taught peasants to read the Bible and write that they eventually became entrepreneurs. Roman Catholic peasants remained uneducated". Her comment was a revelation.

When I was studying my Bachelor's degree in ecology in Bogota (1999–2004), I had observed the existence of several developmental patterns that were associated with climatic and environmental conditions. However, I also noticed a missing factor that would help better explain the differences between countries. In England, I began finding various clues to this missing element.

## *D. My Personal Experience and My Doctoral Research*

Afterwards, it occurred to me that countries with a Roman Catholic tradition struggled with similar problems: corruption, insecurity, inequality, poor education, or violence (e.g. Latin America, as well as Italy, Spain, and Portugal in Europe). In contrast, those with a Protestant background exhibited the lowest indicators of these variables and were industrialised, developed countries (e.g. United Kingdom, Switzerland, Germany, USA, etc.).

I realised that the Roman Catholic traditions are more important for the Church than what the Bible says, and in fact that many traditions directly contradict it! This insight prompted me to explore the history of "the Reformers": Martin Luther in Germany, John Calvin and Huldrych Zwingli in Switzerland, William Tyndale and John Wycliffe in England were among other courageous men who had dared to question the authority of the papacy.

I started feeling that the history of Western civilisation during the last two thousand years had happened in my own life: a period of obscurantism marked by a strong influence of the Roman Catholic Church; a period of atheist enlightenment; and a period of Protestant Reformation (except that the last two were in inverse order). I started reading any literature on the topic. The more I discovered, the more passionate I became.

I also started speaking to different academics and experts. Despite the scientific literature available on the topic, to my surprise, most scholars did not take this subject very seriously. At an academic conference, one simply said that developed countries were just "lucky". Another even called Max Weber a "pseudo-theorist". However, a recognised economist told me that economic theories do not work, but that "Weberian Protestant Ethics" were an important field in which to do research.

After this, while working in a UN development agency, I told myself that if I ever had the opportunity to do a PhD, I would be eager to develop this research idea (the influence of religion on countries' prosperity) further.

All these successive events made change my career focus completely. I now feel I have found what indeed makes sense in my life.

## 9. Advantages of My Personal Experience for My Doctoral Research

After travelling to more than four dozen countries around the world, learning four different languages, and discovering how significant religious values are, I bring various attributes to academic research:

- a transdisciplinary and multi-lingual perspective;
- a passion to discover the roots of human freedom;
- devoting several years before starting my PhD to seeking different sources;
- first-hand experience of my research topic through living around one-third of my life in each of the systems investigated (Roman Catholic, atheist, dissenting Protestant).

My personal life means that I am very well aware of the advantages and disadvantages of these three systems, based on living in different countries and on practical experience. My scientific research complements my experience, while my study informs both theory and practice.

## 10. Disadvantages of My Personal Experience for My Doctoral Research

A significant disadvantage of this study is that it will create much controversy and encounter fierce criticism. The Protestant Reformers and scholars like Weber also faced similar challenges in their times. Controversy is needed to bring about changes.

I am aware that the results of this study will be very uncomfortable for many and will prompt harsh criticism. They might make more enemies than friends as they are "politically incorrect" by today's standards. I am, however, confident that this is the only way to change the paradigm of ignorance in which our society is caught up.

One apparent disadvantage of this study is that its author lacks a scientific background in sociology or economics. Nevertheless, my studies in environmental and political sciences provide me with a broader perspective. After all, many good signs of progress in science come from scholars working in different fields, most likely because they bring fresh approaches and biases to the debate.

## 11. Audience

The transdisciplinary nature of this research makes it interesting for social and natural scientists alike. Equally, it will speak to Roman Catholics, Protestants, atheists, and all other readers seeking to understand the roots of Western civilisation and its development.

## 12. Biases

The following personal experiences from each belief system influence my biases:

*Roman Catholicism:*

- I grew up in a Roman Catholic family in Colombia, a strongly Roman Catholic country;
- I was educated for 12 years in Roman Catholic schools and received Catholic religious instruction;
- I studied for 5 years at a Pontifical Jesuit university.

*Atheism (after being a firm Catholic believer):*

- I spent ten years living as a self-confessed atheist who embraced atheistic values;
- I was socialised in and applied the paradigm of scientific materialism (positivism).

*Dissenting Protestantism (after being a convinced atheist):*

- I spent 12 years living as converted free Christian and I have studied the Bible on my own;
- I have lived and studied in the United Kingdom and Switzerland (two historically Protestant countries) (Inglehart & Baker, 2000).

## 13. Strategies for Objective Data Treatment:

I employed the following strategies to ensure objective data treatment: (1) Two independent quantitative researchers were engaged to select the variables solely using quantitative criteria (e.g. cross-validation) in regressions and QCA. (2) Two independent qualitative researchers were engaged to impartially validate the qualitative coding (a total of four independent researchers). (3) The selected variables (chosen from a pool of more than 70 indicators) were associated with qualitative codes to prioritise them from a mixed methods perspective. (4) The quantitative and qualitative (QCA) databases and the twelve codes applied comparatively to the four case studies' qualitative data are available for inspection (see Supplementary Materials). However, the names and original interviews conducted as part of this study will not be made publicly available to protect the interviewees' identity.

# *E. Supplement: What Happened to My Father and My Faith*

My father began encouraging me to find a place to congregate with other believers in Jesus. I disliked the idea, as I never wanted to become what I have always criticised as an atheist: a fundamentalist who faints and jumps in ugly, dark, and smelly churches on Sundays.

So we decided to pray together with my father, and I asked God that he might show me the truth. I was tired of hearing every single religion declaring that it alone possessed the truth. My father said he would not rest until he saw me in a congregation.

A few days after praying with my father, I received a good job offer in a distant city. The place was a bit unfriendly, as I had no friends or relatives there. The food also complicated matters, because as a vegetarian, I had never seen so many people eat such vast amounts of meat three times a day. There were almost no options for me.

One day at lunchtime in that strange city, I felt alone and realised I had no money, not even to buy food. So I started complaining to God about why I was experiencing scarcity if I was sharing my money giving to the poor. Immediately, walking down the street, I found a banknote, which allowed me to buy a meal. I knelt down and gave thanks to God for such a miracle.

However, I continued complaining about the fact that there was nothing vegetarian to eat! I walked two more blocks with no orientation and found an incredible vegan restaurant that served delicious food.

The people were friendly and told me I could eat there, even if I had no money. They were definitely different from the rest of the world for their gentleness, wisdom, knowledge, and kindness, among other values. I was delighted and began eating there every day.

One day, a kind person came and sat beside me to share the table and asked me where I was attending church. I replied that I was not going to any church. She was surprised; she told me that the restaurant was run by a Christian group that she belonged to and that I was very welcome to join.

When I asked her more questions about their philosophy, she explained that in the Bible, the ideal diet recommended by God was vegan, which was why the restaurant was vegan. She also told me that this Christian group existed all over the world as a result of the Protestant Reformation and based on its faith on the Lutheran principle of "*Sola Scriptura*", which I had begun looking for after finding out about Martin Luther.

I was so impressed that I asked if I could visit her Church next Sunday, but she replied that this was impossible: "*On Sundays, we work. It's the first day of the week, we congregate on the true day of the Lord, the Sabbath*".

For in Exodus 20:9-11, the Lord says:

> Six days shalt thou labour, and do all thy work: But the seventh day is the sabbath of the Lord thy God: in it thou shalt not do any work, thou, nor thy son, nor thy daughter, thy manservant, nor thy maidservant, nor thy cattle, nor thy stranger that is within thy gates: For in six days the Lord made heaven and earth, the sea, and all that in them is, and rested the seventh day: wherefore the Lord blessed the sabbath day and hallowed it (*King James Bible*, 1769).

I was even more impressed after this. The following Saturday, I went to that place, which was just beautiful, quiet, and harmonious. The atmosphere was most congenial and the people amazing. I decided that this is the place where I wanted to be! I immediately called my father and told him that I had found the right place for me to congregate: the Seventh-day Adventist Church.

My father was so happy and exclaimed:

*Hallelujah, praise The Lord, He has answered our prayers, now I am in peace for my son is in your ways.*

Only 3 days later, my father died of fulminant pancreatitis. He passed away peacefully, and I understood that he had achieved his purpose in his life, among others, to accompany me until I found the right way.

My story illustrates that if you persist in finding answers, the truth or whatever purpose, you will have it. As Jesus says in Matthew 7:7–8: "*Ask, and it shall be given you; seek, and ye shall find; knock, and it shall be opened unto you: For every one that asketh receiveth; and he that seeketh findeth, and to him that knocketh it shall be opened*" (*King James Bible*, 1769). This is precisely what I have experienced.

We must work on our dreams, and finally, we will attract what we long for. My personal experience leads me to conclude that we can achieve many goals, dreams, and purposes in our life by struggling on our own. That, I am convinced, is the longest and hardest way. However, if we have God with us, by our side, this is the most efficient and shortest way to a fulfilling life.

As it is written: "*And ye shall know the truth, and the truth shall make you free*" (John 8:32). Jesus is "*the way, the truth, and the life*" (*King James Bible*, 1769, John 14:6).

And my desire for you is: "Therefore God give thee of the dew of heaven, and the fatness of the earth, and plenty of corn and wine" Amen (*King James Bible*, 1769, Genesis 27: 28).

# Index





J. García Portilla, *"Ye Shall Know Them by Their Fruits"*, Contributions to Economics, https://doi.org/10.1007/978-3-030-78498-0

The manufacturer's authorised representative in the EU is Springer Nature Customer Service Centre GmbH, Europaplatz 3, 69115 Heidelberg, Germany. If you have any concerns regarding our products, please contact ProductSafety@springernature.com

Printed and bound by CPI Group (UK) Ltd, Croydon, CR0 4YY
30/09/2026
02225291-0014